Foundations of American Criminal
Due Process at Trial

The Trial of Paul before Felix by William Hogarth (1747–1751).
Credit: Public domain, via Wikimedia Commons.

Foundations of American Criminal Due Process at Trial

FRANCIS R. HERRMANN

Professor of Law Emeritus, Boston College Law School, USA

BROWNLOW M. SPEER

Former Chief Appellate Attorney, Committee for Public Counsel Services, USA

OXFORD
UNIVERSITY PRESS

OXFORD
UNIVERSITY PRESS

Oxford University Press is a department of the University of Oxford.
It furthers the University's objective of excellence in research, scholarship,
and education by publishing worldwide. Oxford is a registered trade mark of
Oxford University Press in the UK and in certain other countries.

Published in the United States of America by Oxford University Press
198 Madison Avenue, New York, NY 10016, United States of America.

Library of Congress Cataloging-in-Publication Data
Names: Herrmann, Francis R., author. | Speer, Brownlow M., author.
Title: Foundations of American criminal due process at trial /
Francis R. Herrmann, Brownlow M. Speer.
Description: New York : Oxford University Press, 2025. |
Includes bibliographical references and index.
Identifiers: LCCN 2024039822 | ISBN 9780199812110 (hardback) |
ISBN 9780190466169 (epub) | ISBN 9780199969449 (updf) |
ISBN 9780199364770 (online)
Subjects: LCSH: Due process of law—United States. | Criminal
procedure—United States. | Criminal justice, Administration of—United States. |
Trial practice—United States.
Classification: LCC KF4765 .H47 2025 | DDC 345.73/075—dc23/eng/20240828
LC record available at https://lccn.loc.gov/2024039822

DOI: 10.1093/9780199364770.001.0001

Printed by Marquis Book Printing, Canada

Note to Readers
This publication is designed to provide accurate and authoritative information in regard to the
subject matter covered. It is based upon sources believed to be accurate and reliable and is intended
to be current as of the time it was written. It is sold with the understanding that the publisher is not
engaged in rendering legal, accounting, or other professional services. If legal advice or other expert
assistance is required, the services of a competent professional person should be sought. Also, to
confirm that the information has not been affected or changed by recent developments, traditional
legal research techniques should be used, including checking primary sources where appropriate.

*(Based on the Declaration of Principles jointly adopted by a Committee of the
American Bar Association and a Committee of Publishers and Associations.)*

You may order this or any other Oxford University Press publication
by visiting the Oxford University Press website at www.oup.com.

MIX
Paper | Supporting
responsible forestry
FSC
www.fsc.org
FSC® C103567

To Doris
To the memory of Eugene and Irene

Contents

Figures

Acknowledgments

Brownlow Speer delighted in the study of legal history, as well as in the practice of criminal law. His knowledge of and enthusiasm for both was matchless. Sadly, during the course of our collaborative efforts in researching and writing this text, Brownlow passed away from a sudden illness. The remaining author has carried on as best he could, spirited by the memory of his friend. The book would not have been at all possible without Brownlow and without the unflagging encouragement of many friends of both authors at the Massachusetts Committee for Public Counsel Services, Boston College Law School, the Jesuit Community at Boston College, and many companions who will be thanked personally.

We wish particularly to give great thanks to colleagues who have very generously taken the time to read and critique earlier versions of this text. From deep wells of historical knowledge, they have offered their valuable insights, additions, corrections, and encouragement. To Mary Sarah Bilder, Founders Professor of Law at College Law School; to George Fisher, Judge John Crown Professor of Law at Stanford Law School; to Richard Helmholz, Ruth Wyatt Rosenson Distinguished Service Professor Emeritus of Law at the University of Chicago School of Law; and to David Seipp, Professor of Law and Law Alumni Scholar at the Boston University School of Law, we express our deepest gratitude. Any mistakes are entirely those of the authors.

List of General Abbreviations

AJLH	American Journal of Legal History
Am L Rev	American Law Review
Ave Maria L Rev	Ave Maria Law Review
Bl Comm	William Blackstone, *Commentaries on the Laws of England* (1st edn, 1765–1769)
BMCL	Bulletin of Medieval Canon Law, New series
Cath U L Rev	Catholic University Law Review
CIC	*Corpus iuris canonici*
Co Inst	Edward Coke, *First (Second etc.) Part of the Institutes of the Lawes of England (1628)*
CUP	Cambridge University Press
DDC	R. Naz (ed), *Dictionaire de droit canonique* (Librairie Letouzey et Ané 1935-1965) (7 vols)
DMA	JR Strayer (ed), *Dictionary of the Middle Ages* (Charles Scribner's Sons 1982-1989) (13 vols)
EHR	English Historical Review
H	*Decretales pseudo-Isidorianae et Capitula Angilramni* (Paul Hinschius ed, B Tauchnitz 1863)
HP	Wilfried Hartmann and Kenneth Pennington (eds), *The History of Courts and Procedure in Medieval Canon Law* (The Catholic University of America Press 2016)
J Legal Hist	Journal of Legal History
JK, JE, JL	Jaffé, *Regista pontificum romanorum. . .* F. Kaltenbrunner (JK: an.?–590), P. Ewald (JE: an. 590–882), S Loewenfeld (JL: an. 882–1198)
LHR	Law and History Review
LQR	Law Quarterly Review
MGH	*Monumenta Germaniae Historica*
Mich L Rev	Michigan Law Review
ND L Rev	Notre Dame Law Review
n.p.	no pagination
n.s.	new series
ODNB	*Oxford Dictionary of National Biography*
OUP	Oxford University Press
Oxford J Legal Studies	Oxford Journal of Legal Studies
PG	J.-P. Migne (ed), *Patrologiae, cursus completus, Series Graeca* (Parisiorum France: J.-P. Migne 1857-1866) (166 vols)
PGM	George Mason, Robert A Rutland (ed.), *The Papers of George Mason* (3 vols, The University of North Carolina Press 1970) (3 vols)

PJA	LK Wroth and HB Zobel (eds), *Legal Papers of John Adams* (Harvard University Press 1965) (3 vols)
PJM	RA Rutland and others (eds), *The Papers of James Madison* (University Press of Virginia 1979)
PL	*Patrologia Latina*, J.-P. Migne (ed), *Patrologiae cursus competus. Series Latina* (Parisiorum France: J.-P. Migne 1841-1864) (221 vols)
PRO	Public Record Office
RDC	Revue de droit canonique
s.l.	sine loco (no place)
s.n.	sine nomine (no name)
s.v.	sub verbo (under word)
Seipp *Abridgement*	David J Seipp, *Legal History: The Year Books, Medieval English Legal History, an Index and Paraphrase of Printed Year Book Reports, 1268–1535* https://www.bu.edu/law/faculty-scholarship/legal-history-the-year-books/.
SS	Selden Society
St Tr	"A Complete Collection of State Trials and Proceedings for High Treason and Other Crimes and Misdemeanors from the Earliest Period to the Year 1783 / Compiled by T.B. Howell (T.C. Hansard (33 vols)
U Chi L Rev	University of Chicago Law Review
U Toronto LJ	University of Toronto Law Review
Va J Int'l L	Virginia Journal of International Law
X	Decretals of Gregory IX
Yale JL & Hum	Yale Journal of Law and Humanities
Yale LJ	Yale Law Journal
YB	Yearbook
ZRG (KA) (RA)	Zeitschrift der Savigny-Stiftung für Rechtsgeschicte, Kanonistische (Romanistische) Abteilung

List of Abbreviations for the *Ius Commune*

C 1 q.1 c 1	Decretum Gratiani, Causa 1, quastio 1, can 1
CJ 1.1.1	*Codex Justiniani*, lib.1, tit.1, lex 1
Cod Th 1.1.1	*Codex Theodosianus*, lib.1, tit.1, lex 1
De pen	*Tractatus de Penitencia* of Gratian
X 1.1.1	*Decretales Gregorii IX*, lib.1, tit.1, cap1
Dist. 1 c 1	*Decretum Gratiani*, Distinctio 1, can. 1
da	*dictum ante* (a comment of Gratian preceding a canon)
dp	*dictum post* (a comment of Gratian following a canon)
Dig 1.1.1	*Digestum Justiniani*, lib.1, tit.1, lex 1
gl. ord.	*glossa ordinaria*
Nov 1.1.1	*Novellae Justiniani,* lib.1, tit.1, lex 1
Tancred' 1.1	*Ordo* of Tancred, Part 1, Title 1

Table of Roman Citations

JUSTINIAN'S CODE

JUSTINIAN'S NOVELS

Table of Ecclesiastical Citations

IV LATERAN COUNCIL

Table of English Cases

ENGLISH CASES

Table of English Statutes

Table of American Colonial, State, and Federal Laws

Introduction

i.

In the Old Hall of Lincoln's Inn, there hangs a painting by the eminent eighteenth-century artist William Hogarth. Set in its elaborate golden frame, the expansive canvas graces the hall's north wall. The painting depicts the opening stages of a trial of St Paul before a provincial Roman governor in the first century CE when Paul was accused of fomenting discord in the province of Judea.[1]

In 1748, when the painting was hung, the Old Hall was still used as a court of justice. William Murray, then Solicitor General, and later Lord Mansfield, the Chief Justice of the Court of King's Bench, had commissioned his friend Hogarth to adorn the Inn with the painting for the Benchers.[2] Hogarth's subject must have been attractive to Mansfield, who had a deep knowledge of Roman law, as well as familiarity with Scripture. Doubtless, a man of Mansfield's learning was also aware of the role that Paul's trial played in English legal history. Well-known legal figures in the sixteenth and seventeenth centuries had frequently made forensic use of the trial. It served as a rich scriptural authority out of which, and into which, lawyers and defendants could read any number of procedural safeguards for accused persons. In 1607, Nicholas Fuller used the proceedings against Paul to ground a claim that a trial without accusers was against the law of God.[3] Sir Edward Coke, addressing Parliament in 1628, argued that punishing a person without showing cause was against reason, citing the trial of Paul in his support.[4] To make a similar point, John Selden summoned the

---

[1] The full trial is related in Acts of the Apostles, cc 24 and 25.

[2] Thomas Wyndham, the Lord High Chancellor of Ireland, had bequeathed two hundred pounds to the Society of Lincoln's Inn to be expended in decorating the Chapel or Hall, as the Benchers should think fit. William Holden Spilsbury, *Lincoln's Inn: Its Ancient and gestae Modern Buildings* (2nd edn, Reeves and Turner 1873) 55.

[3] Nicholas Fuller in his argument against *ex officio* oaths cited Paul's trial as scriptural authority for a defendant's confrontation with accusers:

> Felix the governor . . . said to Paul, that he would hear him, when his accusers were come; holding it as unjust, without an accuser, to charge him.

Nicholas Fuller, *The Argument of Master Nicholas Fuller in the Case of Thomas Lad, and Richard Maunsell, His Clients* (imprinted William Jones's secret press 1607) (reproduction of original by the Henry E. Huntington Library and Art Gallery) 12.

[4] "I will conclude with the highest authority, that is 25 chap. of the Acts of the Apostles, that last verse, where St. Paul saith, 'It is against reason to send a man to prison without shewing a cause.'" "Proceedings in Parliament Relating to the Liberty of the Subject" in W Cobbett, TB Howell, and TJ Howell (eds), 3 *A Complete Collection of State Trials and Proceedings for High Treason and Other Crimes and Misdemeanors from the Earliest Period to the Year 1783* (1809–1828) (1st edn 1719, TC Hansard 1816) (21 vols) 3. Coke also used the example of Paul's interrogation while in chains to condemn coerced confessions. Edward Coke, 2 Co Inst 54.

Foundations of American Criminal Due Process at Trial. Francis R. Herrmann and Brownlow M. Speer,
Oxford University Press. © Oxford University Press 2025. DOI: 10.1093/9780199364770.001.0001

memory of Paul's trial.[5] In 1629, Richard Chambers invoked Paul's trial to secure his right to be heard personally in Star Chamber against allegations of speaking seditiously. "Doth our law judge any man before it hear him, and know what he doeth?" King Agrippa said unto Paul, "Thou are permitted to speak for thyself."[6] In 1637, John Bastwick, wishing to be heard before Star Chamber in answer to charges of writing libelous books, argued that he ought to "enjoy the same privilege and freedom before Christian Judges, as St. Paul had among Pagans."[7] In the same year, the fearless, twenty-three-year-old John Lilburne, charged with seditious publishing, declaimed that, if even pagan Romans understood what fair trial procedure demanded, must not Star Chamber provide him the same rights? "Why Paul found more mercy before the Heathen Roman Governors"[8] The lawyer and law reporter Sir Thomas Hardres in 1658, arguing on behalf of his client, cited Paul's trial as a scriptural ground for a right to remain silent and not to incriminate oneself:

> The law of God . . . commands every man to preserve himself from hurt and damage; as appears by the case of St. Paul mentioned in the Acts of the Apostles who being accused by Tertullus the orator for sedition and other crimes before the governor answered, I am not careful to answer thee about these things, i.e., I am not bound to answer thereunto.[9]

[5] "Proceedings in Parliament relating to the Liberty of the Subject" in 3 *St Tr* 80 (1628).

[6] "Proceedings against Mr. Richard Chambers in Star Chamber" in 3 *St Tr* 373, 376 (1629).

[7] "Proceedings in Star Chamber against Dr. John Bastwick, Mr. Henry Burton, and William Prynn, esq." in 3 *St Tr* 711, 713–714 (1637).

[8] "The Trial of John Lilburn and John Wharton" in 3 *St Tr* 1315, 1329 (1637). Awaiting his assize trial in 1649, Lilburne again turned to Paul:

> [T]hey commit me to prison without any crime pretended, or without ever letting me see accuser, or accusation, prosecutor or charge; and yet into the bargain, deal worse with me then ever the heathen and pagan Romans dealt with Paul, who had nothing but the depraved light of Nature to guide them, and yet in all his imprisonment never forbad or hindered any of his friends to visit or relieve him, although he were accused for a pestilent fellow, and a turner of the world up side down: but they lock me up in a close room, with centinels at my door, and will not so much as at a distance let me speak with my friends. "A Discourse Betwixt Lieutenant Colonel John Lilburn, and Mr. Hugh Peter: upon May 25, 1649" (London [s.n.] 1649) 3

When brought to trial in 1649, Lilburne again cited Paul's trial:

> Sir, in reference to the Court I shall crave but so much liberty from you as was given to Paul when he pleaded for his life before the heathen Roman judges, which was free liberty of speech to speak for himself; the which I now humbly crave as my right, not only by the Law of God and man, but also by the Law and light of Nature. 4 *St Tr* 1269, 1271

In a 1649 tract, Lilburne once more turned to Paul's trial, appealing to it for the principle that the accused should have notice of the charges and should have pretrial access to supporters. John Lilburne, *The Legal Fundamental Liberties of the People of England, Revived, Asserted, and Vindicated* (2nd edn, London [s.n.] 1649) 1.

See also "The Trial of Mr. Christopher Love before the High Court of Justice, for High Treason," 5 *St Tr* 43, 136 (1651):

> Although I am denied counsel to plead for me in this Court, which is so just and necessary a means for the preservation of my life, yet . . . you have granted me that favour which the Romans did to Paul, that he might answer for himself concerning the crimes laid against him.

[9] *AG v Mico*, 145 Eng Rep 419, 420; Hardres 137 (1658). For other instances of defendants referencing the trial of St Paul, see John Udall in 1 *St Tr* 1271, 1287 (1590); "The Case of Capt. John Streater," 5 *St Tr* 365, 378 (1653) (habeas corpus); "Trial of John Cook," 5 *St Tr* 1077, 1424 (1660) (right to answer for oneself); "Proceedings of the Commissioners, appointed by Oliver Cromwell, for ejecting Scandalous and Insufficient Ministers," 5 *St Tr* 539, 578 (1654) (face-to-face confrontation, burden of proof on accuser).

We can only speculate whether Lord Mansfield bore in mind such moments of English legal history as Hogarth's painting was set above the chancellor's bench in the Old Hall.[10] In any event, from its prominent station there in a principal English courtroom of the day, Hogarth's painting of *The Trial of Paul before Felix* implicitly suggested to anyone who beheld it—lawyers, judges, parties, students of the law, and members of the courtroom audience—to see themselves standing in relationship to legal wellsprings remote from their own time and originating even beyond British shores, yet having affect on them still.[11]

ii.

It has been suggested that "[t]o an American interested in the English antecedents of the Federal Bill of Rights, the obvious starting point is Magna Carta itself" in the early thirteenth century.[12] While the barons' meeting with King John at Runnymede provides one possible point of departure for such an investigation, this book, like Mansfield's picture at Lincoln's Inn, wishes to locate its starting point spatially and temporally before and beyond England itself.

The book will be of interest to any persons, whether lay readers, lawyers, judges, or students, who wish to approach American principles of fair trial from a historical

---

[10] It is not unlikely that Mansfield, who was so involved in the commissioning of the picture, would have played a role in placing Hogarth's work above the Chancellor's dais rather than in the Chapel, as it might have been. Hogarth himself favored the courtroom setting because of the better lighting there. Letter to the Society of Lincoln's Inn, June 28, 1748, reprinted in Austin Dobson, *William Hogarth* (McClure, Phillips & Company; William Heineman 1902) 100.

[11] Both Continental and English historians have argued against an excessive sense of England's legal isolation. See, eg, Kenneth Pennington, "Innocent III and the Ius Commune" in RH Helmholz and others (eds), *Grundlagen des Rechts: Festschrift für Peter Landau zum 65. Geburtstag* (F Schöningh 2000) (observing that "Some English historians will cringe at the thought of 'Romanist' ideas embedded in that palladium of Anglo-Saxon liberties, but eventually even they will have to concede that England too lay within the sphere of the Ius commune." Raoul van Caenegem has advised, "We should not exaggerate the insularity of the English common law, as many of its authors have shown a keen awareness of the products of Continental learning, in Roman, and even, more canon law." RC van Caenegem, "The Modernity of Medieval Law" (2000) 68 Tijdschrift voor Rechtsgeschiedenis/Legal History Review 313, 324. In a similar vein, Charles Donahue Jr has written "the peculiarly insular view of English legal history that is favored by most of those who have written in the field" is "exaggerated." Charles Donahue Jr, "Ius Commune, Canon Law, and Common Law in England" (1991–1992) 66 Tul L Rev 1745, 1758. "The question we must ask is why there are so many parallels in broader principles and method between English and Continental law." Ibid. Richard Helmholz takes the view "that our ancestors, as lawyers, were familiar with international sources of law, that they borrowed from them, and that they did so more than once in a great while, and that this borrowing has been important in the developing of our common law." RH Helmholz, "Continental Law and Common Law: Historical Strangers or Companions" (1990) 1990 Duke LJ 1207, 1208. See also RH Helmholz, "Magna Carta and the Ius Commune" (1999) 66 U Chi L Rev 297. David Seipp observes that "English common law practitioners and judges borrowed much of the conceptual structure for their body of legal knowledge from the legal culture of continental Europe over the centuries." David J Seipp, "The Reception of Canon Law and Civil Law in the Common Law Courts before 1600" (1993) 13 Oxford J Legal Stud 388, 388. See also Anthony Musson, "The Influence of Canon Law on the Administration of Justice in Late Medieval England" in Y Mausen and others (eds), *Der Einfluß der Kanonistik auf die europäische Rechtskultur (Prozeßrecht)* (Böhlau 2014) (Bd 4) 325.

[12] Bernard Schwartz, *The Great Rights of Mankind: A History of the American Bill of Rights* (OUP 1977) 2–3.

perspective. Legal scholars whose works focus on discrete periods of time or on particular elements of due process may also, it is hoped, find useful vantage points from which to consider their own areas of specialization.

The book looks first at ancient Roman law and then at the church's early and medieval canon law, to identify principles of procedural criminal justice that came to be embedded on the European continent. Through a variety of conduits, many of these principles began to become present and accessible in England in the late eleventh and twelfth centuries onward.

Advancing more closely to the horizon of English trial procedure, the book considers defensive protections at criminal trials in England. Among these, the structure of the customary jury trial itself, spare though it was, offered the protection of neighbors against baseless charges or abuse by authority. A set of fourteenth-century statutes yielded assurances of significant due process principles. Yet, other important protections were not guaranteed. For example, the customs of the early jury, and even of later juries, did not assure the presence of witnesses or confrontation with them. In the sixteenth and seventeenth centuries, trials conducted during the reigns of Tudor and Stuart monarchs show some instances of the crown coercing suspects' and defendants' confessions, particularly in the context of treason cases. Fully functioning defense counsel was barred at the trial of felony indictments under the Tudors and Stuarts. Defendants received inadequate notice of charges. Religiously and politically motivated prosecutions, particularly in the seventeenth century, entailed invasions of privacy and conscience. The book will instance such grievances as voiced by prominent defendants. Their complaints contributed to popular and parliamentary pressures for procedural law reform in the mid to late seventeenth century. At the close of the century, parliament finally adopted what amounted to a code of procedural protections for defendants. The statutory reforms were at first limited to persons accused of treason. Eventually, parliament would extend the principles to all felony cases.

With the close of the seventeenth century in England, the book shifts its focus of attention to the American colonies. The political and religious struggles of seventeenth-century England yielded lessons that eighteenth-century British colonists did not forget. From their earliest arrival, colonists, by the authority of the crown, understood themselves to have brought with them the common law of England. An essential element of the common law was the institution of the common-law jury. The book examines the colonial embrace of the jury and the matrix of procedural protections that Americans assumed to be part and parcel of a fair criminal trial.

On the eve of the American Revolution, to the mind of the colonists, jury trials were under severe threat from the British parliament. The book discusses the adoption of state charters and state constitutional provisions to buttress the jury trial rights that the colonists believed they posessed. The American Revolution succeeded in laying to rest the perceived British threats to a jury trial. Yet, even after the Revolution, it remained possible for such hazards to come from an entirely new direction. Many Americans were anxious that the freshly forming federal government, as proposed at the Constitutional Convention of 1787 and ratified in 1789, might itself become the threatening agent. The book examines the further steps that were required to buttress the jury against future erosion. Finally, in ratifying the Sixth Amendment and clauses of the Fifth Amendment, the newly born United States set out the procedural rights deemed by consensus to be indispensable to a fair trial in federal courts.[13] Clearly, the amendments were not an expression of new rights. They were, rather, an American articulation of fair trial rights that flowed from English common law and from ancient traditions of Western law.

iii.

This book is possible only because it draws upon the accomplishments of eminent scholars who have dedicated themselves to the research of such disparate fields as Roman law (both ancient and medieval), canon law, the fusion of laws known as the European *ius commune*, and English and colonial procedure. The names of many such scholars will appear in the course of the text and bibliography.

Historiographers offer several common cautions whenever writers attempt to interpret events occurring over a great expanse of time, culture, and geography. The authors have tried to keep those cautions in mind. First, there is the temptation of "presentism," that is, using the lens of the present to read history backward.[14] We do not wish to suggest, in the instant case, that American due process safeguards at trial represent the culmination of a legal process of inevitable improvement, "a fumbling for the result eventually reached."[15] As any narrative of Western legal tradition will show, including what is set forth in this book, history does not move in straight lines, nor does it have an inexorable arc. Nonetheless, as SFC Milsom observed in his study of the historical foundations of the common law, in "the gulf between the disciplines [of lawyers and historians] there is lost the interest of a story and perhaps the measure of an achievement."[16] So, this book wishes to set out the long story of fair trial procedures. The reader may judge how much has been achieved in the procedural choices that past generations have made.

---

[13] US Const amend V: No person shall be held to answer for a capital, or otherwise infamous crime, unless on a presentment or indictment of a Grand Jury, except in cases arising in the land or naval forces, or in the Militia, when in actual service in time of War or public danger; nor shall any person be subject for the same offence to be twice put in jeopardy of life or limb; nor shall be compelled in any criminal case to be a witness against himself, nor be deprived of life, liberty, or property, without due process of law; nor shall private property be taken for public use, without just compensation.

US Const amend VI: In all criminal prosecutions, the accused shall enjoy the right to a speedy and public trial, by an impartial jury of the State and district wherein the crime shall have been committed, which district shall have been previously ascertained by law, and to be informed of the nature and cause of the accusation; to be confronted with the witnesses against him; to have compulsory process for obtaining witnesses in his favor, and to have the Assistance of Counsel for his defense.

In tracing the historical antecedents of the rights relevant to trial in the Fifth and Sixth Amendments, this book will not make any claims about judicial interpretation of rights based on asserted original meanings or intents, nor does the book seek to follow the delineation of rights after 1791.

[14] For examples of warnings against presentism, see David JA Cairns, *Advocacy and the Making of the Adversarial Criminal Trial 1800–1865* (Clarendon Press; OUP 1998) 35–36; Ilan Wurman, "Law Historians' Fallacies" (2015) 91 ND L Rev 161, 196–201.

[15] SFC Milsom, *Historical Foundations of the Common Law* (2nd edn, Butterworths 1981) ix.

[16] Ibid.

Secondly, historiographers caution that terms appearing the same in two distinct periods of legal cultures may not, in fact, carry the identical meaning or function that they bore in their initial settings. In this text, for example, the maxim *nemo tenetur seipsum prodere* ("no one is held to betray himself") will appear prominently across chronological periods but the phrase's meanings, functions, and purposes will vary as legal contexts and cultures shift over time.[17] Other terms, as well, such as "witness," "counsel," "publicly," "law of nature," "voluntary," and "right," will similarly evolve different meanings or applications at distinct points on the historical canvas.[18]

Thirdly, one cannot assume that the existence of a legally defined norm or articulated doctrine necessarily means that the actual legal practice of its time was consistently in accord with the authoritative texts. This is true of law in every age. Any general principle might be ignored in some period or be accompanied by numerous exceptions. Nonetheless, enduring doctrine ordinarily serves as a guide to practice over the course of time. Continuity is perceptible despite discontinuity.

Fourthly, when surviving evidence offers only limited support for the existence of a fact or practice in a particular period, overly sure conclusions ought to be avoided and the limits of our knowledge admitted. In many periods under examination in this text, surviving legal sources are scarce. In England, for example, fairly reliable and extensive trial reports were not composed until the later seventeenth century. The scarcity of reports is all the more to be borne in mind when one considers practice in medieval and ancient times on the continent. This is not to say that no reliable conclusions can be drawn about the procedural choices of earlier times, but only that we should be cautious not to reach beyond the limits of the evidence.

Finally, a word about translation. Very often, some degree of discretion is required in translating, especially when technical terms or terms with a broad range of possible meanings are involved. The authors believe that including the text of a document in its original language, as we have done throughout, offers readers the opportunity to check the reliability of the English text. The translations here, from both classical and medieval periods, are of the authors' own making.[19]

iv.

Kermit Hall has written that law's history is "a tale of human choices."[20] There is an intrinsic worth in the exploration of that tale. It illuminates the values that generations

---

[17] John Langbein cautions against reliance upon "the powerful searchlight of hindsight" in interpreting the Latin maxim. John H Langbein, "The Privilege and Common Law Criminal Procedure: The Sixteenth to the Eighteenth Centuries" in RH Helmholz, *The Privilege against Self-Incrimination: Its Origins and Development* (University of Chicago Press 1997) 104.

[18] Focusing upon linguistic correspondence can mislead in another way. A particular legal system may not contain vocabulary linguistically similar to another system yet may still possess a functional equivalent expressed through different vocabulary. See Carl-Friedrich Stuckenberg, *Untersuchungen zur Unschuldsvermutung* (Walter de Gruyter 1998) (writing on the term "presumption of innocence") 7.

[19] On the value of including texts in their original language, see Charles Donahue Jr, "Order in the Court: Medieval Procedural Treatises in Translation" (2017) 34 Bull Medieval Canon L (n.s.) 281, 290–291.

[20] Kermit Hall, *The Magic Mirror: Law in American History* (2nd edn, OUP 2009) 4.

and cultures embraced, honored, fought for, and endeavored to hand on. It also sheds light on what principles succeeding generations clung to, altered, or rejected, and what legal lacunae they deplored. There is also a practical value in studying the "tale of human choices." We can evaluate our own choices in a fresh perspective when we set them against the horizon of past achievements, weaknesses, and limitations. Such was the implicit invitation of Mansfield's picture in the Old Hall. It is the invitation of this book, as well.

1

Procedural Norms for Criminal Trials in Roman Antiquity

Classical Roman Criminal Procedure

It is not the custom among the Romans to give up any man before the accused has had the accusers before his face and received opportunity for defense concerning the charge.

Acts. 25:16[1]

Luke, author of the Acts of the Apostles, puts this declaration in the mouth of Festus, the Roman governor of Judea from 60 to 62 CE. Festus had succeeded Governor Felix who sat in the beginning stages of Paul's prosecution. Festus was responding, in his capacity as judge,[2] to the opponents of Paul who wished to punish him for his missionary activity in Jerusalem.

The verse containing Paul's statement is remarkable for two reasons. It expresses elegantly core principles of the Roman criminal law of the day: the necessity of a specific accusation; notice of that accusation to the person accused; the presence of the accused in a court of law; the presence of accusers in court at the same time;

---

[1] "πρὸς οὓς ἀπεκρίθην ὅτι οὐκ ἔστιν ἔθος Ῥωμαίοις χαρίζεσθαι τινα ἄνθρωπον πρὶν ἢ ὁ κατηγορούμενος κατὰ πρόσωπον ἔχοι τοὺς κατηγόρους τόπον τε ἀπολογίας λάβοι περὶ τοῦ ἐγκλήματος." Acts 25:16. The key Greek terms are closely analyzed in Jacques Dupont, "'Aequitas romana.' Note sur Actes 25:16" (1961) 49 Recherches de science religieuse 354, by comparison to other usages of them in the writings of Luke (traditionally accepted as the author of the Gospel according to Luke and the Book of Acts), and elsewhere in the New Testament, in the Septuagint, and in the writings of Flavius Josephus. See ibid at 358–370. Dupont concludes that, uniformly, "the terms of Acts 25:16 . . . are derived from a typically judicial terminology." Ibid 370. The two examples he gives of accounts of criminal cases demonstrating the accuracy of this declaration as a statement of Roman law (see ibid at 379–381 (Cicero's prosecution of Verres) and 381–382 (the trial recounted by Apuleius in the novel *Metamorphoses*)) are set out below in text accompanying nn 17–22.

"In the present passage, the word ἔθος has a . . . technical, legal meaning: 'common practice or use which thereby is law.' . . . When he pronounced the word ἔθος, the governor was not merely mentioning a procedural norm; rather, he was evoking a whole judicial use both ancient and standard." Harry W Tajra, *The Trial of St. Paul* (Mohr 1989) 155, quoting Dupont (n 1) 358.

[2] Provincial governors, such as Festus, exercised a judicial power delegated to them by the emperor and could, in turn, delegate it to others. See Peter Garnsey, *Social Status and Legal Privilege in the Roman Empire* (OUP 1970) 67, 75–82, 90–91; JA Crook, *Legal Advocacy in the Roman World* (Cornell University Press 1995) 59, 68.

Foundations of American Criminal Due Process at Trial. Francis R. Herrmann and Brownlow M. Speer,
Oxford University Press. © Oxford University Press 2025. DOI: 10.1093/9780199364770.003.0001

confrontation between accused and accusers; opportunity to defend against the charge; and the expectation of adhering to a regular procedure.[3]

Second, Luke's verse, in its Latin text,[4] reinforces with the authority of sacred scripture the secular Roman principles it contains. When later inserted into scores of ecclesiastical and secular legal texts, the verse would become an aspirational standard of fair procedure for the trial of persons accused of a crime.

There is no doubt that what Festus enunciated according to Luke were recognized principles of contemporary Roman law. From 149 BCE into the first century CE, the Roman Senate had created a number of permanent criminal courts (*quaestiones perpetuae*), each dedicated to the adjudication of a particular offense.[5] The *lex* establishing each court set out in detail the procedure it was to follow.[6] The text of only one of these *leges*, the *lex Acilia* (123-122 BCE), has largely survived to the present day.[7] The

---

[3] "[N]o Roman legislative text reaching us formulates in precise terms the judicial prescription expressed by Festus; but . . . the declaration of Festus excellently conveys the constant practice of Roman procedure." Dupont (n 1) 373.

[4] The *Vetus Latina* version of the Bible (before 382) gives the first Latin translation of Luke's text: [*N*]*on est consuetudo Romanis donare aliquem hominem, prius quam qui accusatur, praesentes habeat accusatores, et locum excusationis accipiat de crimine* ("It is not the custom among the Romans to give up any man before the accused has the accusers present and receives opportunity for explanation about the charge"). 3 *Bibliorum Sacrorum latinae versiones antiquae, seu Vetus Italica* (Petrus Sabatier ed, Rheims 1743, photo reprint 1976) (3 vols) 582. The word "*donare*" is used to express the idea in the Greek text of yielding Paul up to his accusers. The Latin Vulgate text of Jerome (382/385) follows the *Vetus Latina* in using "*donare*." John Wordworth and Henry J White (eds), 2 *Nouum Testamentum Domini Nostri Jesu Christi latine, secundum editionem Sancti Hieronymi* (OUP 1905) (2 vols) (pt 1) 206. Jerome translates the concluding phrase as "*locumque defendendi accipiat ad abluenda crimina*" ("and receives opportunity for defending in order to purge the charges"). Ibid. Later revisions of the Vulgate use "*damnare*" (condemn) in place of *donare*, see Dupont (n 1) 354 n 1, as do some of the old Latin pre-Vulgate texts.

[5] Richard A Bauman, *Crime and Punishment in Ancient* Rome (Routledge 1996) 22–24. The word *quaestio* in this context denotes an "examination" or "inquiry." Gino Rosmini, "Le *quaestiones perpetuae* nella storia del diritto penale e giudiziario romano (pt. 2)" (1895) 55 Archivio Giuridico 63, 63. *Quaestio perpetua* are the words the ancient Romans used to describe a standing (*perpetua*) criminal court with a specialized jurisdiction, the prototype of which was created in 149 BCE. See AHJ Greenidge, *The Legal Procedure of Cicero's Time* (Lawbook Exchange 1999) 419 & n 2; Rosmini (n 5) 63–64. Each *quaestio* was presided over by a judicial official called a *praetor quaesitor*. See George Mousourakis, *The Historical and Institutional Context of Roman Law* (Ashgate 2003) 87–89. Each was created by a statute (*lex*), which created also a particular statutory crime over which the *quaestio* was to exercise its sole jurisdiction. See Greenidge (n 5) 423–424; Rosmini (n 5) 65–66; Theodor Mommsen, *Römisches Strafrecht* (Duncker & Humblot 1899) 203–204. The enacting *lex*, like almost all Roman *leges*, was designated by the adjectival form of the family name of the magistrate who proposed it. See Giovanni Rotondi, *Leges publicae populi romani* (Società Editrice Libraria 1912) 148. The organization of the *quaestiones* is described in HF Jolowicz and Barry Nicholas, *Historical Introduction to the Study of Roman Law* (3rd edn, CUP 1972) 318–319. The substantive offenses over which they exercised jurisdiction are summarized in detail in JAC Thomas, *The Institutes of Justinian: Text, Translation, and Commentary* (North-Holland Pub Co 1975) 335–338. A full list of Roman criminal *leges*, with the dates of their promulgation, is given in Rotondi (n 5) 105–108. Legislation creating or regulating *quaestiones* continued into the reign of the emperor Augustus. See Rosmini (n 5) 82–83; Jolowicz and Nicholas (n 5) 401.

[6] But there "existed a certain number of general principles, uniformly applied in most criminal trials." Rosmini (n 5) 72. The general procedure of the *quaestiones* is set out at ibid 72–82.

[7] "We have nearly the whole of one such statute, the *lex* . . . commonly known as the *lex Acilia*." OF Robinson, *Penal Practice and Penal Policy in Ancient Rome* (Routledge 2007) 32 n 12. See Susan Ford Wiltshire, *Greece, Rome, and the Bill of Rights* (University of Oklahoma Press 1992) 151. This *lex* created a *quaestio perpetua* for the criminal trials of charges of extortion by provincial officials. Allan C Johnson and others (eds), 2 *Ancient Roman Statutes* (University of Texas Press 1961) (2 vols) 38; Rotondi (n 5) 312–313; Anton-Hermann Chroust and John Richard Murphy, "Lex Acilia and the Rise of Trial by Jury in the Roman World" (1948) 24 Notre Dame Lawyer 1–40; JL Strachan-Davidson, 2 *Problems of the Roman Criminal Law* (1st edn, Clarendon Press 1912, reprint FB Rothman 1991) (2 vols) 6–7; AN Sherwin-White, "The

quaestiones were based on accusatorial procedure.[8] The procedure included a formal accusation specifying the crime charged against the defendant (*reus*);[9] an accuser (*accusator*), who brought the charge, was present in court throughout the proceedings, and was responsible for the prosecution of the case;[10] and a summons to the defendant to appear in court and answer the charge.[11] The accuser presented witnesses (*testes*)[12] and the defendant had opportunity to present witnesses in response.[13] A panel of impartial *iudices* (in modern parlance, jurors)[14] decided the case by majority vote, each casting a ballot marked "C" (for "*condemno*," "I convict"), or "A" (for "*absolvo*," "I acquit").[15]

That the Romans of pre-imperial times perceived these procedural protections as fundamental is apparent from the Roman legal rhetorician Marcus Tullius Cicero's prosecution in 70 BCE of Gaius Verres, the governor of Sicily, for malfeasance in office. In addressing the *iudices*, Cicero stressed, as evidence of Verres' corruption, Verres' contempt for procedural fairness when sitting as a judge. Verres had conducted a trial of one Sthenius in the absence of Sthenius and convicted him in the absence of the accuser. In both respects, Verres had acted contrary to Roman customary procedure.

Lex Repetundarum and the Political Ideas of Gaius Gracchus" (1982) 72 The Journal of Roman Studies 18, 18 & n 2. The surviving portion of it, supplemented in brackets by reconstructions made by the great nineteenth-century scholar of Roman law Theodor Mommsen of words missing from segments of the metal tablets on which the *lex* was set out, is printed in Salvatore Riccobono and others (eds), 1 *Fontes iuris romani antejustiniani* (2nd edn, apud S a G Barbèra Florence 1941) (3 vols) 84. An English translation appears in Johnson and others (n 7) 38–46.

[8] A *quaestio* is also referred to by the "synonymous" term *iudicium publicum*, AHM Jones, *The Criminal Courts of the Roman Republic and Principate* (Blackwell 1972) 45. The adjective *publicum* here signifies an accusation that may be brought by any member of the community in the public interest. Greenidge (n 5) 416–417 and 417 n 1. As to the equivalence of the terms *quaestio* and *iudicium publicum*, see ibid 415–417; Jones (n 8) 46–48, 91; Mommsen (n 5) 180–184, 186–188 (explaining technical distinction between the two terms). The word *iudicium* means "judgment," see Jill Harries, *Law and Crime in the Roman World* (CUP 2007) 23, but in the context of the term *iudicium publicum*, it means the proceeding that results in a judgment, variously translated as "prosecution," see Thomas (n 5) 331 (translating "*[p]ublica iudicia*" as "[p]ublic prosecutions"), or "trial," see David M Walker, *The Oxford Companion to Law* (OUP 1980) 655 s.v. "*Iudicium*." See also Mommsen (n 5) 180 n 2 (*iudicium* in sense of "Prozess").
[9] Harries, *Law and Crime* (n 8) 21; Emilio Costa, 2 *Cicerone Giureconsulto* (2nd edn, Nicola Zanichelli 1927) (2 vols) 133 & n 3; Moriz Wlassak, "Anklage und Streitbefestigung im Kriminalrecht der Römer" in 184 *Sitzungsberichte, kaiserliche Akademie der Wissenschaften* (Alfred Hölder 1917) 6–12; Greenidge (n 5) 465 & n 3, 466; Mommsen (n 5) 384, 385 & nn 1; Jones (n 8) 64, 117.
[10] Mommsen (n 5) 366 & n 1, 373 & nn 3, 4; 2 Costa (n 9) 135 & nn 1–3, 141 & n 2, 143; Greenidge (n 5) 459–460, 463 & n 4, 467–468; Wlassak (n 9) 25–26.
[11] Mommsen (n 5) 425 & n 5, 430 & n 1; Wlassak (n 9) 7; 2 Costa (n 9) 140 & n 5; Greenidge (n 5) 461 & n 7, 463 & nn 2, 4; Jones (n 8) 65.
[12] Jones (n 8) 65, 114; 2 Costa (n 9) 144 & nn 4, 6; Greenidge (n 5) 485 & nn 1, 2, 486 & n 3, 487 & n 1; Mommsen (n 5) 426 & n 5, 430 & n 5.
[13] Mommsen (n 5) 431. The defendant, however, did not have the power to compel their presence. Greenidge (n 5) 485 & n 1; Rosmini (n 5) 80.
[14] The procedure was bifurcated. "[T]he praetor [who controlled the conduct of the trials] deal[t] with the arrangements *in iure* ... the setting up of the matters to be judged ... while the jurors decide[d] the substantive questions of fact, *in iudicio*." Sherwin-White (n 7) 26. The word "jurors" (from the Latin *iurare*, to swear) is an appropriate description of the *iudices* because the *iudices* were "required to swear that they will observe the rules of procedure for the proper trying of the case." Ibid 23.
[15] Greenidge (n 5) 388–389, 497–498; Mommsen (n 5) 445 & n 7; Jones (n 8) 72; Harries, *Law and Crime* (n 8) 19.

[O]penly from the tribunal chair, he proclaims, if anyone would wish to formally accuse the absent Sthenius in a capital matter, he [Verres] himself would accept his name as accused[16] . . . [after one person declines Verres' invitation to make an accusation]. One Pacilius, an indigent and insubstantial man, suddenly approaches; he says, if it would be allowed, he wishes to formally accuse the absent person. This one [Verres] says, indeed, it is allowable and is customarily done, and he would accept it. Therefore, the accusation is presented. He immediately decrees Sthenius be present at Syracuse on the first of December.

[I]n the morning of the first of December, as he had decreed, he orders Sthenius to be summoned . . . .He summons the defendant. He [the defendant] did not answer. He summons the accuser . . . ; the summoned accuser, Marcus Pacilius, for some reason that I do not know, did not answer. He was not present. If Sthenius had been formally accused while he was present, if he were caught red-handed in wrongdoing, nonetheless, since his accuser was not present, it was not proper that Sthenius be convicted.[17]

Cicero mocked this travesty of justice by concluding that "the one whom he [Verres] had made a defendant in his absence, he convicted in the absence of the accuser."[18]

A full century after Paul's appearance before Festus, recorded by Luke, Roman procedure in its accusatorial form is vividly portrayed in the fictional writing of one who had first-hand knowledge of it. Apuleius, a member of a prominent family in the city of Madauros in Rome's province of Africa, had been tried there for the capital offense of magic between 155 and 161 CE. Apuleius successfully defended himself.[19] In his novel, *Metamorphoses,* or *the Golden Ass,* Apuleius describes two trials on capital charges. In one, the accuser so thoroughly inflames the spectators with emotional appeals to sympathy that all the people cry out for the defendant summarily to be stoned to death.[20] But the magistrates insist on adhering to proper procedure:

so that after a trial has been granted in proper form and by the custom of their ancestors and after the allegations on each side have been examined, judgment might be arrived at in a civilized way, lest, in the manner of barbaric savagery or tyrannical

---

[16] The formal act of accusation was called "denunciation of the name" (*nominis delatio*). Its acceptance by the presiding magistrate, the "reception of the name" (*nominis receptio*) made the subject of the accusation a criminal defendant (*reum facere*). 2 Costa (n 9) 133.

[17] [P]alam de sella ac tribunali pronuntiat SI QUIS ABSENTEM STHENIUM REI CAPITALIS REUM FACERE VELLET, SESE EIUS NOMEN RECEPTURUM. . . . Hic tum repente Pacilius quidam, homo egens et levis, accedit; ait, si liceret, absentis nomen deferre se velle. Iste vero et licere et fieri solere, et se recepturum; itaque defertur. Edicit statim ut Kalendis Decembribus adsit Sthenius Syracusis. [M]ane Kalendis Decembribus ut edixerat Sthenium citari iubet. . . . Citat reum; non respondit. Citat accusatorem . . . ; citatus accusator, M. Pacilius, nescio quo casu non respondit, non adfuit. Si praesens Sthenius reus esset factus, si manifesto in maleficio teneretur, tamen, cum accusator non adesset, Sthenium condemnari non oporteret. Marcus Tullius Cicero (ed), 1 *The Verrine Orations in Two Volumes* (LHG Greenwood tr, Loeb Classical Library, Harvard University Press 1966) 392–394, 396–398; II, ii, 38, §94, and 40, §§97–99.

[18] *quem absentem reum fecerat, eum absente accusatore condemnat.* Ibid 400 (40, §99).

[19] HE Butler, "Introduction" in Apuleius, *The Apologia and Florida of Apuleius of Madaura* (HE Butler ed and tr, Greenwood Press 1909) 5, 10–11. See JM Kelly, *A Short History of Western Legal Theory* (OUP 1992) 75.

[20] Apuleius, 2 *Metamorphoses (The Golden Ass)* (J Arthur Hanson ed and tr, Loeb Classical Library, Harvard University Press 1989) (2 vols) 225 (X, 6).

violence, someone might be condemned unheard and in a period of tranquility so horrible an example be produced for a future age.[21]

As soon as the opposing statements were finished, it was agreed that the truth and reliability of the charges be established by proofs that are certain and that so grave a conjecture not be left to suspicions.[22]

Class distinctions in Roman criminal trial procedure

Classical Roman law aspired to assure fundamental fairness to parties. These early principles would endure in the later post-classical empire. Indeed, through a re-birth of Roman law in the Middle Ages, they would prove to be an enduring basis for Western legal culture, not only on the Continent but in England itself.

It must be cautioned, however, that the process of fact-finding in Roman criminal procedure included significant sordid aspects. Fairness was not the sole purpose of the procedural system. A desire to discover truth and to control threats to social order could lead to the use of violent means. The principles of fair procedure might not be applied to members of the lower orders of society charged with common "street crimes" such as theft, robbery, arson, and assault.[23] Persons of lower status were likely

---

[21] *ut, rite et more maiorum iudicio reddito et utrimquesecus allegationibus examinatis, civiliter sententia promeretur, nec ad instar barbaricae feritatis vel tyrannicae impotentiae damnaretur aliquis inauditus et in pace placida tam dirum saeculo proderetur exemplum.* Ibid.

[22] *Simul enim finita est dicentium contentio, veritatem criminum fidemque probationibus certis instrui nec suspicionibus tantam coniecturam permitti placuit.* Ibid (X, 7).

[23] "The city prefect [*praefectus urbi*] was responsible for the public peace, *quies populorum*, for which purpose he stationed special police-soldiers, *milites stationarii*, who were deployed throughout the city and had the duty to report to him about occurrences there [Dig 1.12.1.12]. These reports of his subordinates, *officium*, gave him occasion, where necessary, to initiate criminal proceedings. Further, the prefect of the police watch, *praefectus vigilum*, handed over to him notorious and dangerous arsonists, thieves, and robbers [Dig 1.15.3.1; Dig 1.15.5] and reported to him about capital crimes that had occurred [CJ 1.43.1]. In the provinces, the governor had the mission of ridding them of bad persons [Dig 1.18.3] in order to secure public order and tranquility, and to that end sought out and punished criminals such as shrine desecrators, bandits, robbers, thieves, and receivers [of stolen goods] [Dig 1.18.13. pr; Dig 48.13.4.2; Nov 128, c 2]. Their subordinates, *officium*, spies, *curiosi*, sentries, *stationarii*, and police agents, *agentes in rebus* [CJ 12.20-22(23)], whom they had dispatched and posted for the security of the land, notified them, *denuntiaverunt, nuntiaverunt,* through their reports, *notoria, elogia,* as to what had come to their knowledge about criminal activity [Dig 48.16.6.3; CJ 9.2.7; C Th 16.2.31; CJ 12.22(23).1], and handed over to them apprehended criminals [CJ 9.4.1. pr; CJ 9.4.2]. In the cities in particular, defensors [CJ 1.55.8.1] in part, and irenarchs [Dig 50.4.18.7] in part, with limited jurisdiction, oversaw public order. These officials took into custody dangerous persons and also other criminals caught in the act, handed them over to the competent judge, and informed him in detail in accompanying reports, *notoria, elogia,* of the circumstances that had emerged from the investigation that they had undertaken [CJ 1.55.6,7,8. pr; Dig 48.3.6.1; Nov 15, c 6, §1]. Criminals caught in the act by private persons could also be handed over to the defensors and irenarchs and also to the officers of the magistrates, resulting in a judicial examination against these by reason of office, i.e., without a formal accusation of the alleged offender [CJ 1.55.7; CJ 9.4.2. pr].

"By virtue of this system, magistrates possessing criminal jurisdiction could initiate criminal proceedings by reason of office, on the basis of official denunciations by their officers or other functionaries. The subjects of such [proceedings] were, however . . . only those crimes committed against state institutions with the aim of subverting them, and other crimes dangerous to the public, but other crimes only when the perpetrator was caught in the act by officials or private persons. [See the constitution of the emperors Diocletian and Maximinian appearing at CJ 9.2.8]." Nicholas München, *Das kanonische Gerichtsverfahren und Strafrecht* (Cologne & Neuss 1865) 422–425.

The terms "defensor" and "irenarch" refer to officials whose duties included police functions. See Adolf Berger, *Encyclopedic Dictionary of Roman Law* (American Philosophical 1953, reprint 1991) 428 s.v. "Defensor civitatis" and 516 s.v. "Irenarcha."

to be arrested by police agents on the basis of community notoriety or having allegedly been caught in the act. They would then be delivered to a judge for a speedy and summary determination of guilt or innocence. Typically, the judge began the proceedings by interrogating the defendant with questions that assumed the defendant's guilt of the crime charged. Torture was used to obtain the confessions of suspects and to extract information in criminal cases from slaves.[24] The practice ultimately extended to all free persons, at least in cases of treason (*maiestas*).[25] Additionally, the law treated persons of different social levels unequally in the way their testimony as witnesses was weighed[26] and in the punishments they faced if convicted of a crime.[27]

Notwithstanding these serious flaws, the Roman accusatorial process exhibits numerous specific principles representing important safeguards for criminal defendants. These safeguards appear in writings of the late second- and early third-century jurists (*iuris prudentes*)[28] and in imperial constitutions (*constitutiones*)[29] extending past the fall of the western Roman Empire in 476 into the reign of the eastern Emperor Justinian (Figure 1) in the mid-sixth century.

[24] Garnsey (n 2) 141–147; Olivia Robinson, "Slaves and the Criminal Law" (1981) 98 ZRG (RA) 213, 223, 259; A Esmein, "Le Délit d'Adultère a Rome" (1878) 2 Nouvelle Revue Historique d Droit Français et Étranger 397, 416–419; Yan Thomas, "*Confessus pro iudicato*, l'aveu civil et l'aveu pénal à Rome" in *L'aveu. Antiquité et moyen-âge* (L'École française de Rome 1986) 89, 97; Piero Fiorelli, "Confessione Diritto romano e intermedio," in A Giuffré (ed), 8 *Enciclopedia del diritto* 864, 866 (Varese 1961).

[25] Jones (n 8) 114–115; Robinson, "Slaves" (n 24) 239; Thomas 97; Esmein (n 24) 417; Robinson, *Practice* (n 7) 107–108, 139; Joachim Ermann, "Die Folterung Freier im Römischen Strafprozess der Kaiserzeit bis Antoninus Pius" (2000) 117 ZRG (RA) 424, 425 n 8; PA Brunt, "Evidence Given under Torture in the Principate" (1980) 97 ZRG (RA) 256, 259–261.

[26] Garnsey (n 2) 221–223, 231, 234; Ugo Zilletti, "Sul valore probatorio della testimonianza nella 'cognitio extra ordinem" (1963) 29 Studia et Documenta Historiae et Iuris 150; Jean Gaudemet, "La législation religieuse de Constantin" (1947) 33 Revue d'histoire de l'Église de France 25, 38.

[27] Bauman (n 5) 124–140; Jolowicz and Nicholas (n 5) 403; Robinson, "Slaves" (n 24) 228–230; Garnsey (n 2) 6, 104, 117–118, 121, 124–126, 261–265; Thomas (n 5) 334–335; Robinson, *Penal Practice* (n 7) 195.

[28] As to the role of the *iuris prudens* in the development of Roman jurisprudence, see Crook (n 2) 40–43. "The jurist was the central figure in the Roman legal system . . . His sixth influence lay in his advice to magistrates . . . on the formulation of their edicts and the granting of remedies in individual cases, in his advice also to *iudices* in the making of their decisions, in his teaching, and above all in his writing." Barry Nicholas, s.v. "Jurisprudence" in NGL Hammond and HH Scullard (eds), *The Oxford Classical Dictionary* (2nd edn, Clarendon Press 1970) 569, 570. A judge was expected to include a jurist in his consilium to provide expert advice on the law. Crook (n 2) 193; Jill Harries, *Law and Empire in Late Antiquity* (CUP 1999) 102–103. Foremost among the jurists of the second and third centuries were Aemilius Papinianus (Papinian), Domitius Ulpianus (Ulpian), and Iulius Paulus (Paulus). See Jolowicz and Nicholas (n 5) 391–394; Henry John Roby, *An Introduction to the Study of Justinian's Digest: Containing an Account of Its Composition and of the Jurists Used or Referred to Therein* (CUP 1884) cxci–cxcvi (Papinian), cxcvi–cci (Ulpian), cci–cciii (Paulus).

[29] By the close of the second century CE, "[i]mperial constitutions were firmly established as sources of law." Garnsey (n 2) 175. The term *constitutio* is "the most general word used to describe the various forms" of documents, including the emperor's *rescripta*, by which the emperor legislated. Jolowicz and Nicholas (n 5) 366. A *rescriptum* was the emperor's answer (the word signifies a "writing back") to an official's request for instructions, perhaps on a point of law arising in a particular case in which the writer was functioning as judge, or to a private person's petition for some relief. See ibid 368–370. Tony Honoré, *Emperors and Lawyers* (2nd edn, Clarendon Press; OUP 1994) 24–32. "[A]ll constitutions were recorded in the imperial archives, . . . the date of enactment . . . and of publication . . . being noted." Jolowicz and Nicholas (n 5) 462. See Serena Connolly, *Lives Behind the Laws: The World of the Codex Hermogenianus* (Indiana University Press 2010) 39–41.

Figure 1 Portrait of Emperor Justinian (483–565). A byzantine mosaic in the Basilica of San Vitale, Ravenna, Italy. He arranged for compilations of Roman law in the sixth century.

Credit: Glasshouse Images / Alamy Stock Photo.

Fair Procedures in Imperial Codes of the Fifth and Sixth Centuries CE

A note about chronology

The Roman collections of the emperors Theodosius and Justinian, assembled in the fifth and sixth centuries, drew upon procedural principles that were already centuries old at the times the collections were assembled. Thus, for example, a law confirmed as still valid in Justinian's sixth-century texts would be cited to its second-century source. This method made clear the true antiquity of the principles that the emperors confirmed. To make the same point, the following account will cite both the fifth- and the sixth-century codifications and their much older sources.

The codifications of Theodosius and Justinian

Imperial constitutions were first officially assembled in the Theodosian Code, pro-mulgated in 438 by the Roman senate.[30] In 506, the Visigothic King Alaric II issued an abridged version of the Theodosian Code for his Roman subjects in Spain.[31] This version includes an *Interpretatio*[32] comprised of twenty-four interpretations of many of the constitutions, some cast in a more elegant and lucid Latin than the constitutions themselves.[33] From 529 through 534, the law collections of Justinian appeared,

---

[30] Tony Honoré, "The Making of the Theodosian Code" (1986) 103 ZRG (RA) 133, 164–167; Jolowicz and Nicholas (n 5) 464–465; John Matthews, "The Making of the Text" in Jill Harries and IN Wood (eds), *The Theodosian Code* (Cornell University Press 1993) 19, 19–20; Harries, *Law and Empire* (n 28) 65–66. The Theodosian Code followed two unofficial collections of imperial laws compiled in the late third century, the Gregorian and Hermogenian Codes, and was initiated by a constitution of the emperor Theodosius II in 429. Jolowicz and Nicholas (n 5) 463–64; Matthews (n 30) 22–23; Honoré (n 30) 161–164, 179.

[31] PD King, *Law and Society in the Visigothic Kingdom* (CUP 1972) 10. For many centuries, the abridge-ment was referenced by a wide variety of names, but since the sixteenth century, the terms "Lex Romana Visigothorum" and "Breviarium Alaricianum" have been used interchangeably to describe it. See Jean Gaudemet, "Le Bréviare d'Alaric et les Epitome 5" in Société d'histoire des droits de l'antiquité (ed), *Ius Romanum Medii Aevi* (Société d'histoire des droits de l'antiquité 1965) pt I(2)(b)(*aa*)(β). The Visigothic compilers of the Breviarium omitted provisions of the Theodosian Code that they considered outmoded, including "the great majority of the texts concerning the administrative law of an Empire that had disap-peared." Ibid 24. The redactions are described in detail, ibid 24–33.

The issuance by the Visigothic king in 654 of a new national legal code governing both Goths and Romans effectively deprived the Breviarium of its legal force in Spain. Alfred de Wretschko, "De usu Breviarii Alariciani forensi et scholastico per Hispaniam, Galliam, Italiam regionesque vicinas" in Theodor Mommsen and others (eds), 1/1 *Theodosiani Libri XVI cum constitutionibus Sirmondianis* (apud Weidmannos 1905) CCCVII, CCCXII. But it continued to be widely used in church councils in France and Germany, see ibid CCCXV–CCCXVIII, "and it was one of the main channels through which Roman law [first] entered western European law." Walker (n 8) 151–152 s.v. "*Breviarium Alaricianum.*"

[32] "This *Interpretatio*, as it were, decodes the [Theodosian] Code." Honoré (n 30) 157.

[33] See ibid 159, 209. For a well-supported theory that "the *interpretationes* are to be connected explicitly with the composition of the *Breviarium*" and that "the *interpretationes* were an integral part of the pro-ject" of its issuance, see John F Matthews, "Interpreting the *Interpretationes* of the *Breviarium*" in Ralph W Mathisen (ed), *Law, Society, and Authority in Late Antiquity* (OUP 2001) 11, 15, 17. An alternative pos-sibility is that the Visigothic compilers of the Breviarium assembled the *interpretationes* from multiple

including his Digest and Code.[34] Justinian's Digest, given the force of law by its enacting document in 533,[35] contained the writings of eminent jurists (*iuris prudentes*) of the earlier second and third centuries.[36] Justinian's Code in its 534 edition was a compilation of imperial constitutions dating from the first half of the second century up to its promulgation.[37] Justinian continued to issue new constitutions, collected as the Novels (*Novellae*) until his death in 565.[38] Justinian also ordered the composition of an introductory textbook for law students called the *Institutes*. It came into effect with the Digest in 533.

Normative procedural safeguards for criminal defendants

The imperial collections contain numerous provisions mandating adherence to normative procedural requirements for trial, including safeguards for criminal defendants.

Defendants to be summoned and informed of the specific charges
The early third-century jurist Ulpian, whose voluminous writings the Digest frequently drew upon, stated:

> When anyone wishes to bring an action, he ought to give notice; for it seems most fair that he who will bring the action gives notice so that consequently the defendant (*reus*) may know whether to yield or to contend further; and if he thinks to contend, he may come prepared to act, knowing the action by which he is sued. To give notice means also to provide means for making a copy.[39]

---

preexisting commentaries on the Theodosian Code. See Franz Wieacker, "Lateinische Kommentare zum Codex Theodosianus" in *Symbolae Friburgenses in honorem Ottonis Lenel* (Tauchnitz n.d. [1935]) 259, 291–292. "[U]sually the *Interpretationes* faithfully reproduce the content of the respective constitutions, sometimes with a paraphrase of the text, other times with a summary drawn from the provisions contained in it." Aldo Checchini, "Studi storico-critici sulla 'Interpretatio' al Codice Teodosiano" in 1 *Scritti giuridici e storico-giuridici* (Facoltà di Giurisprudenza dell' Università di Padova 1958) 141, 165. Sometimes they express in impersonal ("*si quis*") form a legal principle drawn either from a personalized example or from an abstractly expressed rule presented by the text. Gaudemet, "La législation religieuse de Constantin" (n 26) 40.

[34] Jolowicz and Nicholas (n 5) 479–480, 493–494.

[35] Ibid 482.

[36] See Roby (n 28) lxxxiii–lxxxviii.

[37] An earlier edition of the Code was published on April 7, 529; it was superseded by the second edition on November 16, 534, which included constitutions of Justinian issued subsequent to the first Code. Alan Watson, "Prolegomena to Establishing Pre-Justinianic Texts" (1994) 62 Tijdschrift voor Rechtsgeschiedenis 113, 116, 124. On Roman jurists as transmitters of doctrine in a time when Roman judges themselves were not professionally trained, see John P Dawson, *A History of Lay Judges* (OUP 1960) 29.

[38] Jolowicz and Nicholas (n 5) 496–498.

[39] *Qua quisque actione agere uolet, eam edere debet: nam aequissimum uidetur eum qui acturus est edere actionem, ut proinde sciat reus, utrum cedere an contendere ultra debeat, et, si contendendum putat, ueniat instructus ad agendum cognita actione qua conueniatur. Edere est etiam copiam describendi facere.* Ulpian, Edict, bk 4; D 2.13.1.

Long before the Digest, the *lex Acilia* (123/122 BCE) had set down the essential require-ment of summoning the defendant before a judge for the defendant to hear the accusa-tion.[40] The rationale for the requirement is expressed in the authoritative work called the *Pauli Sententiae* of the third century:[41]

> accusers are compelled to set out the charges to those they accuse. For it is proper [for the accused] to know to what charges they are to respond.[42]

A charge had to be reduced to writing in a document called an *inscriptio*, signed by the accuser.[43] The jurist Paulus, writing around the turn of the third century CE, gives us the model of an *inscriptio*:

> "Consul and day. Before praetor or proconsul _____, Lucius Titius has declared that he denounces Maevia under the *Lex Iulia Concerning Adulteries* because he says she committed adultery with Gaius Seius in the city of _____, in the home of _____, in the month of _____, in [the year of] consulships of _____."[44]

---

[40] The *lex Acilia* provides that the accuser is to summon before a judge in court ("*ad iudicem … in ious educito*") the person to be accused and there formally make the accusation by "delating [i.e. denouncing] the name" of that person ("*nomenque eius deferto*"). After the accuser has declared on oath that the accusa-tion is made in good faith, the judge is to formally "receive the name" ("*nomen recipito*") of the accused, and the criminal case commences. Lex Acilia repetundarum, lines 19–20, in 1 *Fontes iuris romani antejustiniani* (n 7) 84, 89–90.

[41] The collection called *Pauli Sententiae* appeared not long before 300. Ernst Levy, *Pauli Sententiae: A Palingenesia of the Opening Titles as a Specimen of Research in West Roman Vulgar Law* (Cornell University Press 1945, Rothman Reprints 1969) viii. The "Paulus" to whom the *Sententiae* are attributed is the emi-nent jurist Iulius Paulus, see Roby (n 28) cciii, the author of thirty-four books written between 178 and 235. Hermann Fitting, *Alter und Folge der Schriften römischer Juristen von Hadrian bis Alexander* xi (2nd edn, Max Niemeyer 1908) 81–98. "The title … seems to echo the statement of Gaius [a renowned Roman jurist] that the opinions and views of lawyers of authority have the force of law." Tony Honoré, *Ulpian: Pioneer of Human Rights* (2nd edn, OUP 2002) 217. The *Sententiae* include numerous passages from the works of Paulus, see Paul Krüger, marginal notes to "*Iulii Pauli Sententiarum ad Filium*" in Paul Krüger and others (eds), 2 *Collectio librorum juris anteiustiniani* (Weidmann 1878) (3 vols) 46, but multiple authors revised passages over the following three centuries. See Levy (n 41). A constitution of the emperor Constantine is-sued in 327 or 328 (C Th 1.4.2), officially extolled and declared the *Sententiae* to be of the highest authority. Gaudemet, "La législation religieuse de Constantin" (n 26) 35; Leopold Wenger, *Die Quellen des römischen Rechts* 532 (Adolf Holzhausen NFG 1953). No complete text of the *Sententiae* has survived, but a major portion was incorporated into the Breviarium Alaricianum by its Visigothic compilers in 506. Gaudemet, "La législation religieuse de Constantin" (n 26) 4, 36.

[42] *Reis suis edere crimina accusatores cogendi sunt: scire enim oportet, quibus sint criminibus responsuri. Pauli Sententiae* 5.16.14 in 2 *Collectio librorum juris anteiustiniani* (n 41) 125.

[43] Mommsen (n 5) 384–385. The charging document was also called a *libellus*. Ibid 385 n 1. A prin-cipal purpose of the *inscriptio* was to bind an individual accuser by an "oath against calumny" to produce proofs supporting the accusation. Ibid 386. "Those who bring criminal accusations must not vary from the charge they provided in the *inscriptio*, lest they receive the very punishment they sought to inflict on the de-fendant." Joshua C Tate, "Roman and Visigothic Procedural Law in the False Decretals of Pseudo-Isidore" (2004) 90 ZRG (KA) 510, 514.

[44] The Romans designated the year by the names of the consuls holding office for that year. See EJ Bickerman, *Chronology of the Ancient World* (2nd edn, Cornell University Press 1980) 69, 81. "*Consul et dies. Apud illum praetorem vel proconsulem Lucius Titius professus est se Maeviam lege Iulia de adulteriis ream deferre, quod dicat eam cum Gaio Seio in civitate illa, domo illius, mense illo, consulibus illis adulterium commisisse.*" Iulius Paulus, 3 *De adulteriis* 15 (178/235), Dig 48.2.3.pr. In the same passage, Paulus states that the requirement was established by the "*le[x] Iulia publicorum*," a clear reference to the *lex Iulia iudic-iorum publicorum* of 17 BCE by which the emperor Augustus reorganized criminal procedure. See Rotondi (n 5) 448–450. In Republican times, the accusation (*nominis delatio*) was oral. Wieslaw Mossakowski, "The

Requirement that a criminal case be heard

Roman law set down as a prerequisite to criminal conviction the necessity that a case be "heard" in court. An imperial rescript around the turn of the third century expresses the requirement eloquently and emphatically:

> Let no absent person be punished: and indeed we apply this rule that absent persons ought not to be convicted: for the principle of fairness (*aequitatis ratio*) does not permit anyone to be condemned when the case has not been heard (*inaudita caussa*).[45]

Defendant to be present when accusation is made in court

An imperial constitution of 384 provided:

> It is not proper that anything said by him alone who accuses immediately be considered true against one who is absent, as if against one who is present and convicted.[46]

The *interpretatio* of this constitution focuses upon the necessity for the judge to hear both parties before giving conclusive effect to an accusation:

> However many times an accuser may have suggested anything about his adversary with him absent, he is not to be wholly credited before there is an examination of each party.[47]

Judgment to be made impartially

The *lex Acilia* (123/122 BCE) had provided that the jury panel deciding the case be sifted to exclude anyone even distantly related to one of the parties or associated with him in a club or guild.[48] Under the later *cognitio* procedure, this concern for the

---

Introduction of an Interdiction of Oral Accusation in the Roman Empire" (1996) 43 Revue internationale des droits de l'antiquité (3d ser) 269, 270 & n 6. The term *inscriptio* referred to the inscribing of the accused's name on the list of defendants to be tried in the pertinent *quaestio*. See 2 Costa (n 9) 133, 151–152.

[45] [N]*e quis absens puniatur: et hoc iure utimur, ne absentes damnentur: neque enim inaudita causa quemquam damnari aequitatis ratio patitur.* Rescript of the emperors Severus and Antoninus Magnus (Caracalla) (198/211), quoted in Aelius Marcianus, 2 *De iudiciis publicis* 205 (217/222), D 48.17.1.pr. "Many Roman [literary] texts . . . , without specifically saying that *audi alteram partem* is a rule of law, yet make it clear that its neglect is wrongful." John M Kelly, "*Audi Alteram Partem* Note" (1964) 9 Natural Law Forum 103, 106, citing texts at n 23.

[46] *Non oportet in absentem, quasi in praesentem atque convictum, verum statim putari, quidquid ab eo solo dicitur qui accusat.* Constitution of the emperors Gratian, Valentinian, and Theodosius of December 20, 384, C Th 11.39.9.

[47] *Quotiens quilibet accusator aliquit de adversario suo eo absente suggesserit, ei ante discussionem utriusque partis paenitus non credatur. Interpretatio* to Breviarium 11.14.4 (C Th 11.39.9).

[48] The *lex Acilia* disqualified as a juror anyone who, with respect to either the defendant or the accuser, was a "son-in-law, father-in-law, stepfather, or stepson, . . . or first cousin . . . or anyone more closely related to him, or a member of the same club as he, or a member of the same guild as he." *Lex Acilia*, lines 20 (defendant) ("*[gener socer uitricus pri]uignusue siet, queiue ei sobrinus siet propiusue cum ea cogna[tione] attingat, queiue ei sodalis siet, queiue in eodem conlegio siet*"), 22 (accuser, with slight variation in wording) in 1 *Fontes iuris romani antejustiniani* (n 7) 90 (words and letters in brackets reconstructed by Mommsen).

fact-finder's impartiality was expressed in a maxim that received authoritative sanction in an imperial constitution of 376:

> By universal law, we decree that no one should be a judge for himself.[49]

A constitution of 398 showed imperial concern that favoritism might distort the fact-finding process:

> in a criminal case from humane consideration, we do not deny [to convicted persons] the opportunity for interposing an appeal, if timely, so that it may then be more diligently examined whenever it is supposed that justice was suppressed against the welfare of a man either through error or the favoritism of a fact-finder (*gratia cognitoris*).[50]

An earlier constitution admonished judges in adjudicating criminal cases not to be swayed by popular outcry for or against the accused:

> The empty voices of the public are not to be heard: for it is not proper that their voices be believed when they desire either that a guilty person be acquitted of the charge or that an innocent person be convicted.[51]

Accuser has the burden of proof

Jurists writing in the second and third centuries CE stated the rule:

> Proof lies on him who asserts, not who denies.[52]
> Always the necessity of proof lies on him who brings the action.[53]

---

[49] *Promiscua generalitate decernimus neminem sibi esse iudicem debere.* Constitution of the emperors Valens, Gratian, and Valentinian of December 1, 376, C Th 2.2.1. The prohibition is repeated in Justinian's Code with slight variations in wording: "*Generali lege decernimus neminem sibi esse iudicem vel ius sibi dicere debere.*" CJ 3.5.1. In the constitution as appearing in the Theodosian Code and in the *interpretatio* to the corresponding provision of the Breviarium (2.2.1), this prohibition is linked to the bar on giving testimony in one's own case. In Justinian's Code, however, the witness bar has been severed from the prohibition of being a judge in one's own case and moved to a separate book of the Code (CJ 4.20.10).

[50] *Quibus in causa criminali humanitatis consideratione, si tempora suffragantur, interponendae provocationis copiam non negamus, ut ibi diligentius examinetur, ubi contra hominis salutem vel errore vel gratia cognitoris obpressa putatur esse iustitia.* Constitution of the emperors Arcadius and Honorius of July 27, 398, C Th 9.40.16 and 11.30.57, CJ 7.62.29 (with words "*vel errore*" replaced by "*per errorem*").

[51] *Vanae voces populi non sunt audiendae: nec enim vocibus eorum credi oportet, quando aut obnoxium crimine absolvi aut innocentem condemnari desideraverint.* Constitution of the emperors Diocletian and Maximian (286/305), CJ 9.47.12. The phrase "voices of the public" (*voces populi*) was used here literally. Roman courtroom audiences were noisy, and in criminal cases shouts from the spectators for or against a defendant being tried must have been common. See Leanne Bablitz, *Actors and Audience in the Roman Courtroom* (Routledge 2007) 133–134.

[52] *Ei incumbit probatio qui dicit, non qui negat.* Iulius Paulus, 69 *Ad edictum* 774 (180/195), Dig 22.3.21.

[53] *[S]emper necessitas probandi incumbit illi qui agit.* Aelius Marcianus, 6 *Institutiones* 103 (217/222), Dig 22.3.1.

An imperial constitution of 212 provided that "those who wish to accuse should have proofs."[54] Where such proof is deficient, the burden does not shift to the defendant. An imperial constitution of 294 declared:

> In acknowledging that he cannot prove what he asserted, the moving party does not bind the defendant with the necessity of showing the contrary, because by the nature of things there is no proof of a negative fact.[55]

Ammianus Marcellinus, a fourth-century historian, provided a striking example of this principle in operation in a criminal case tried before the emperor Julian in 359:

> Publicly, with those admitted who wished to be, [Julian] was hearing before the tribunal, with unusually active scrutiny, Numerius, recently the governor of Narbonian Gaul,[56] accused as a thief. And when he defended against the charges by denial and could not be confuted in anything, Delphinius, a very biting orator, assailing him vehemently, exasperated by the lack of proofs, exclaimed, "Is there anyone, most flourishing Caesar, who can ever be guilty, if it will be enough to deny?" In spontaneous rejoinder, says Julian prudently, "Is there anyone who can be innocent, if it will be enough to be accused?"[57]

Julian's principle, in fact, is reflected in an imperial constitution of 380, adopted in both the Theodosian Code and the Justinian's Code. It provided that "[n]o one in jail shall be bound at all before he is convicted."[58]

---

[54] *Qui accusare volunt, probationes habere debent.* Constitution of the emperor Caracalla of March 11, 212, CJ 2.1.4.

[55] *Actor quod adseverat probare se non posse profitendo reum necessitate monstrandi contrarium non adstringit, cum per rerum naturam factum negantis probatio nulla sit.* Constitution of the emperors Diocletian and Maximian of December 25, 294, CJ 4.19.23.

[56] Gallia Narbonensis, the Roman province in present-day southern France named after the city of Narbo (now Narbonne). *A Latin Dictionary* (Charlton T Lewis & Charles Short eds, OUP 1879) 1186 s.v. "Narbo."

[57] *Numerium Narbonensis paulo ante rectorem, accusatum ut furem, inusitato censorio vigore, pro tribunali palam admissis volentibus audiebat, qui cum infitiatione defenderet obiecta, nec posset in quoquam confutari, Delphidius orator acerrimus, vehementer eum impugnans, documentorum inopia percitus, exclamavit: "Ecquis, florentissime Caesar, nocens esse poterit usquam, si negare sufficiet?" Contra quem Iulianus prudenter motus ex tempore, "Ecquis" ait "innocens esse poterit, si accusasse sufficiet?".* Ammianus Marcellinus, *Res Gestae* 18.1.4 (390/391) in John C Rolfe (ed), 1 *Ammianus Marcellinus* (Loeb Classical Library, Harvard University Press 1935) (3 vols) 404.

[58] *Nullus in carcerem, priusquam convincatur, omnino vinciatur* ("Let no one in prison be put in fetters at all before he may be convicted"). Constitution of the emperors Gratian, Valentinian, and Theodosius of December 30, 380, C Th 9.2.3, CJ 9.3.2.
The closely related but distinct principle that an accused person is not properly regarded as a "defendant" (*reus*) until the legal formalities of accusation have been completed is proclaimed in a later constitution appearing in both the Theodosian Code and Justinian's Code: "We command that the order of accusation long since instituted by the laws be observed so that whoever is summoned on a capital charge (*discrimen capitis*) who could be accused shall not immediately be considered *reus*, lest we cause innocence to be undermined." Constitution of the emperors Honorius and Theodosius of August 6, 423, C Th 9.1.19 (*Accusationis ordinem iam dudum legibus institutum servari iubemus, ut quicumque in discrimen capitis arcessitur, non statim reus qui accusari potuit aestimetur, ne subiectam innocentiam faciamus.*), CJ 9.2.17 ("*Accusationibus*" in place of "*Accusationis*").

The placement of the burden of proof in criminal cases was not limited to prosecutions commenced by a private accuser. It extended also to instances in which minor officials with police powers, acting on their own authority, seized suspects without a formal accusation. An imperial constitution of 355 cautioned such officials that they bore a burden of proving their charges in court:

> They whom custom calls upon to be the caretakers [*curagendarii*] or spies [*curiosi*] of the provinces are not hesitating to deliver to the deadly darkness of the prisons those whom they assume on their own authority [*proprio arbitrio*] to be criminals [*reos*]. Therefore, the aforementioned spies and those stationed on the watch [*stationarii*], or those who discharge this duty, should keep in mind the charges must be declared to the judges and that the necessity of proof is incumbent upon them.[59]

Heightened standard of proof in criminal cases
The emperor Trajan (98–117 CE) stated in a rescript to a proconsul that

> No one should be condemned on the basis of suspicions . . . . For it is better that a crime remain unpunished than that an innocent person be condemned.[60]

An imperial constitution of the year 382, included in the Theodosian Code, vividly sets out a standard of proof for criminal cases which emphatically secures Trajan's principle:

> Let all know, bear in mind, and take heed that they should bring into a public proceeding that case which is bolstered by witnesses, supplied with proofs, prepared with items of evidence [*signis*] that are clearer than light for proof.[61]

The compilers of Justinian's Code revised this passage[62] to make unambiguous the high standard of proof it required in accusatory proceedings:

> Let all accusers know that they should bring into a public proceeding that case which is bolstered by *suitable* witnesses, or supplied with *the most evident* proofs, or

---

[59] *Ii, quos curagendarios sive curiosos provincialium consuetudo appellat, proprio arbitrio quos esse reos putaverint, feralibus carcerum tenebris mancipare non dubitant. Memorati igitur curiosi et stationarii vel quicumque funguntur hoc munere crimina iudicibus nuntianda meminerint et sibi necessitatem probationis incumbere.* Constitution of the emperor Constantius of July 22, 355, C Th 6.29.1. A shortened version of the constitution appears in CJ 12.22 (23) 1.

[60] *sed nec de suspicionibus debere aliquem damnari . . . .: sanctius enim esse impunitum relinqui facinus nocentis quam innocentem damnari.* Domitius Ulpianus, 7 *De officio proconsulis* (213), quoting a rescript of the emperor Trajan to Adsidius Severus (98/117 CE), D 48.19.5.pr. For observations on Trajan's rescript in the context of later European and American procedural principles, see Alexander Volokh, "n Guilty Men" (1997) 146 University of Pennsylvania Law Review 173, 178; Mirjan Damaška, *Evaluation of Evidence: Pre-Modern and Modern Approaches* (CUP 2019) 54 & n 23.

[61] *Sciant cuncti praemeditentur, ante praecaveant, eam se rem deferre debere in publicam notionem, quae munita sit testibus, instructa documentis, signis ad probationem luce clarioribus expedita.* Constitution of the emperors Gratian, Valentinian, and Theodosius of May 18, 382, C Th 9.37.3.

[62] The compilers had the authority to alter the wording, though not to change the substantive law, of existing constitutions. See Watson (n 37) 115–116.

prepared with items of evidence [*indiciis*] that are *undoubted* and clearer than light for proof.[63]

Consistent with the high standard of proof required, the Roman jurist Gaius, writing in the second century on a Provincial Edict, clarified that:

Defendants (*rei*) rather than accusers (*actores*) are to be considered more favorably.[64]

Judgment to be made according to conscience
By the end of the second century CE, when the transition from the republic to the empire was essentially complete, the *quaestio* courts with their juries had disappeared.[65] Now, an official in the role of judge heard and decided criminal accusations by exercising *cognitio*, his fact-finding function.[66] *Cognitio* included, in the words of the emperor Hadrian (117–138 CE), "question[ing] the witnesses themselves."[67] Rather than trying to lay down rigid and mechanical evidentiary rules about how factfinders should evaluate evidence, Hadrian provided that judges could freely evaluate the

[63] Emphasis added. *Sciant cuncti accusatores eam se rem deferre debere in publicam notionem, quae munita sit testibus* idoneis *vel instructa apertissimis documentis vel indiciis ad probationem* indubitatis et *luce clarioribus expedita.* CJ 4.19.25. In this recension, the text "brings a particularly rigorous meaning of the burden of proof into the criminal trial." Ugo Zilletti, "Studi sulle prove nel diritto giustinianeo" (1964) 67 Bullettino dell'Istituto di Diritto Romano 167, 213.

[64] *Fauorabiliores rei potius quam actores habentur.* Dig 50.17.125.

[65] Jolowicz and Nicholas (n 5) 439; Garnsey (n 2) 93; Strachan-Davidson (n) 156–158; Jones (n 8) 45, 96; Esmein (n 24) 433–434.

[66] Garnsey (n 2) 90–92; Strachan-Davidson (n 7) 159; Mario Lauria, "Accusatio-Inquisitio" (1933) 56 Atti della Reale Accademia di scienze morali e politiche 304, 305–311; Zilletti, "Sul valore probatorio" (n 26) 124, 137; Ignazio Buti, "La 'cognitio extra ordinem': da Augosto a Diocleziano" in Hildegard Temporini and Wolfgang Haase (eds), 14 *Aufstieg und Niedergang der römischen Welt* II (Walter de Gruyter 1982) 29, 50–51.

Officials exercising the judicial function, from the emperor on down, in effect shared their power of *cognitio* with a *consilium* composed of various dignitaries invited to sit with the judge to hear the case and vote on the judgment. See Honoré (n 30) 5–6, 23; Jones (n 8) 84, 113; Jolowicz and Nicholas (n 5) 339–340; Bauman (n 5) 69; Bablitz (n 51) 107; Wolfgang Kunkel, "Die Funktion des Konsiliums in der magistratischen Strafjustiz und im Kaisergericht" in Wolfgang Kunkel (ed), *Kleine Schriften zum römischen Strafverfahren und zur römischen Verfassungsgeschichte* (H Böhlaus 1974) 151, 153, 234–240. Because these individuals literally "sat" alongside the judge on the elevated tribunal, they were called *residentes* or *adsessores*, Aldo Checchini, *Studi sull' ordinamento processuale romano e germanico. Pt. I, Il processo romano* (Padua 1925) 29–30, 75, 89, 109, 131, in contrast to the *adstantes*, the spectators who remained standing throughout the proceedings and the lawyers, parties, and witnesses who, though seated below, had to stand up when performing their functions. Aldo Checchini, "L'ordinamento processuale romano nell' alto medioevo" (1933) 6 Rivista di storia del diritto italiano 265, 266.

The judicial official could also use his *cognitio* without a formal accusation to investigate and punish criminal activity of all sorts, Jolowicz and Nicholas (n 5) 403; Garnsey (n 2) 103; Jones (n 8) 113–114; Lauria (n 66) 329, 334, 359; Esmein (n 24) 160; Checchini, "Studi storico-critici sulla" (n 33) 44; Jehan Dahyot-Dolivet, "La procédure pénale d'office en droit romain" (1968) 41 Apollinaris 89, 89–91; Robinson, *Penal Practice* (n 7) 64, 76.

[67] *Quod crimina obiecerit apud me Alexander Apro et quia non probabat nec testes producebat, sed testimoniis uti valebat, quibus apud me locus non est (nam ipsos interrogare soleo), quem remisi ad provinciae praesidem, ut is de fide testium quaereret* ("Alexander brought charges against Aper before me [sitting as a judge], and because he did not prove them or produce witnesses, but wanted to use written statements, which have no place before me (for I am accustomed to question the witnesses themselves), I sent him back to him who is presiding in that province, so that he might inquire about the reliability of the witnesses"). Callistratus, 4 *De cognitionibus* 28 (198/211), quoting a rescript of Hadrian to Iunius Rufinus, in D 22.5.3.3. See Zilletti, "Sul valore probatorio" (n 26) 133–139.

evidence according to their own consciences (*ex sententia animi tui*). In a rescript to Valerius Varus about determining the credibility of evidence, the emperor instructed:

> What arguments are sufficient to each matter for a method of proof cannot be satis-factorily defined in any certain way. Often, though not always, the truth can be deter-mined without public records of each matter. Sometimes the number of witnesses, sometimes dignity and authority, at other times a commonly held rumor confirms the credibility of a matter about which there is question. Therefore, in sum, this alone I can reply to you: certainly you should not immediately make a trial [*cognitionem*] depend upon one type of proof, but you ought to draw conclusions from the opinion of your own self what you either believe or consider not sufficiently proven to you.[68]

Similarly, in his response to Vibius Varus, a legate in the province of Cilicia, the em-peror wrote:

> You can know more how much credence is to be placed in the witnesses, who and of what dignity and of what repute they are, who are seen to speak candidly, whether they put forward one and the same studied talk or whether they respond truthfully and instantaneously to those matters which you question them about.[69]

Criminal charge to be prosecuted where crime committed

An imperial constitution of the late fourth century established the venue of criminal prosecutions:

> Permission to accuse shall not extend beyond the boundaries of the province. For it is proper that trials of crimes be conducted in that place where the crime is alleged to have been committed.[70]

The *interpretation* of this constitution states:

> The examination of crimes must be conducted at the place where the crime was com-mitted; for the one accused of crimes is forbidden to be heard elsewhere.[71]

---

[68] *Quae argumenta ad quem modum probandae cuique rei sufficiant, nullo certo modo satis definiri potest. sicut non semper, ita saepe sine publicis monumentis cuiusque rei veritas deprehenditur. alias numerus tes-tium, alias dignitas et auctoritas, alias veluti consentiens fama confirmat rei de qua quaeritur fidem. hoc ergo solum tibi rescribere possum summatim non utique ad unam probationis speciem cognitionem statim alligari debere, sed ex sententia animi tui te aestimare oportere, quid aut credas aut parum probatum tibi opinaris.* Rescript of Hadrian to Valerius Verus (117/38), quoted in Callistratus, De cognitionibus, D 22.5.3.2 (533) 327. For the important function of this rescript in the later context of medieval procedure, see Damaška (n 60) 62 & n 8, 64.

[69] *Tu magis scire potes, quanta fides habenda sit testibus, qui et cuius dignitatis et cuius estimationis sint, et qui simpliciter visi sint dicere, utrum unum eundemque meditatum sermonem attulerint an ad ea quae interrogeueras ex tempore uerisimilia responderint.* Rescript of Hadrian to Vibius Varus. See Callistratus, De cognitionibus, bk 4 in Dig 22.5.3 (533) (quoting Rescript of Hadrian to Vibius Varus, legate to the province of Cilicia).

[70] *Ultra provinciae terminos accusandi licentia non progrediatur. Oportet enim illic criminum iudicia agitari, ubi facinus dicatur admissum.* Constitution of the emperors Valentinian, Valens, and Gratian of November 13, 368 or 373, C Th 9.1.10.

[71] *Criminum discussio ibi agitanda est, ubi crimen admissum est; nam alibi criminum reus prohibetur audiri. Interpretatio* to Breviarium 9.1.5 (C Th 9.1.10).

Accused to be brought to trial expeditiously

A constitution of the emperor Constantine issued on June 30, 320 required that:

> In any case whatsoever, once a defendant is produced, trial ought to happen immediately, so that a guilty person may be punished, an innocent person absolved.[72]

An imperial constitution of August 3, 396 likewise protected defendants against indefinite detention pending trial:

> So that those accused of various crimes detained in jail throughout the provinces might not be more cruelly delayed either by the slothfulness of judges or by some striving for leniency, let all judges be warned to subject defendants, produced from custody, to the trial due and to determine what the laws counsel.[73]

The *interpretatio* stresses the importance of speedy trial of both the innocent and the guilty:

> Accused persons are not to be held for a long time in jail or custody, but speedily either the innocent are to be acquitted or those convicted are to be punished with a criminal judgment.[74]

Legal representation to be available

The jurist Domitius Ulpianus (Ulpian) in his early third-century book *De Officio Proconsulis*, the major source of our information about Roman criminal procedure, wrote that the proconsul:[75]

> ought generally to grant advocates [*advocatos*] to those requesting [them]: to females, or to orphans, or to otherwise weak persons, or to those not in their [right] mind, if anyone requests for them; or, if there is no one who requests, he ought on his own initiative to give [advocates] to them.[76]

Ulpian concludes that this principle applies universally: "And these [directives] are common to all who exercise provincial judicial authority and should be observed by them also."[77]

---

[72] *In quacumque causa reo exhibito...statim debet quaestio fieri, ut noxius puniatur, innocens absolvatur.* C Th 9.3.1; CJ 9.4.1. For commentary on this statute, see Kenneth Pennington, "Torture and Fear: Enemies of Justice" (2008) 19 Revista internazionale di diritto comune 203.

[73] *Ne diversorum criminum rei vel desidia iudicum vel quadam lenitatis ambitione per provincias detenti in carcere crudelius differantur, moneantur omnes iudices productos e custodiis reos disceptationi debitae subdere et quod leges suaserint definire.* Constitution of the emperors Arcadius and Honorius of August 3, 396, C Th 9.1.18.

[74] *Rei non multo tempore in carcere vel custodia teneantur, sed celeriter aut innocentes absolvantur aut, si convicti fuerint, criminosi sententia puniantur. Interpretatio* to Breviarium 9.1.10 (C Th 9.1.18).

[75] At the time Ulpian was writing, a "proconsul" was the governor of a province whose governor was appointed by the Senate. Johnson and others (n 7) 270–271 s.v. "proconsul" and "province."

[76] *Advocatos quoque petentibus debebit indulgere plerumque: feminis vel pupillis vel alias debilibus vel his, qui suae mentis non sunt, si quis eis petat: vel si nemo sit qui petat, ultro eis dare debebit.* Domitius Ulpianus, *De officio proconsulis* (213), Dig 1.16.9.5.

[77] *Quae etiam omnium praesidum communia sunt et debent et ab his observari.* Domitius Ulpianus, *De officio proconsulis* (213), Dig 1.16.9.6. The term *praeses* denoted "the highest official in the province." Berger

The same jurist, writing on the praetorian edict,[78] has the praetor proclaiming the same principle:

> The praetor says: "If they do not have an advocate, I will give [them one."[79] Not only to these persons should the praetor exhibit this humanity, but indeed also if there is some other person who for some reason has not found a *patronus*[80] whether from the effort of the adversary or from fear.[81]

An imperial constitution of the early fourth century sought to protect litigants against the harmful effects of deficient legal representation:

> The mistakes of advocates do not prejudice the parties in the competent court.[82]

Trial and judgment take place in public

Imperial constitutions of the third and fourth centuries declared that judicial proceedings were valid only if held in public. A rescript of 283, later included in Justinian's Code, addressed a complaint that a judgment was defective because it was not announced in public:

> Since you say that judgment of the presiding [judge] was invalid because he did not pronounce his judgment publicly but in a secret place, not present in his official capacity, it is agreed that no prejudice is to be created against you from those things decreed by him.[83]

An imperial constitution of 364, later appearing in the Theodosian Code, emphasized that a judge had to take special care to observe this requirement:

(n 23) 646 s.v. "Praeses provinciae." "Besides his military and administrative duties, he had supreme jurisdiction [in the province] with respect to matters of both civil and criminal law." Mousourakis (n 5) 158.

---

[78] Praetors were officials with various prescribed judicial functions serving one-year terms. See Mousourakis (n 5) 86–89. The two praetors supervising the administration of the law in the city of Rome each issued an edict (*edictum*) at the beginning of his term, Berger (n 23) 449 s.v. "Edictum praetoris," "specif[ying] the principles which he would observe in enforcing the law and the conditions under which he would allow prosecutions and suits." Mousourakis (n 5) 88.

[79] "The announcements of the praetor in the edict are formulated in the first person . . . ." Berger (n 23) 449 s.v. "Edictum praetoris."

[80] There were several Latin words for "advocate," including *advocatus*, but the word "*patronus* ... [was,] in all formal prose, . . . a standard word for an advocate and, . . . in particular, a defence advocate." Crook (n 2) 122.

[81] *Ait praetor: "Si non habebunt advocatum, ego dabo." nec solum his personis hanc humanitatem praetor solet exhibere, verum et si quis alius sit, qui certis ex causis vel ambitione adversarii vel metu patronum non invenit.* Domitius Ulpianus, 6 *Ad edictum* 275 (212/214), Dig 3.1.1.4.

[82] *Advocatorum errores in conpetenti iudicio litigatoribus non praeiudicant.* Constitution of the emperor Constantine of July 28, 320, C Th 2.11.1.

[83] *Cum sententiam praesidis irritam esse dicis, quod non publice, sed in secreto loco officio eius non praesente sententiam suam dixit, nullum tibi ex his quae ab eo decreta sunt praeiudicium generandum esse constat.* Constitution of the emperors Carus, Carinus, and Numerian of November 27, 283, CJ 7.45.6. The requirement of public trial was a "central procedural rule" and a "fundamental principle" in Roman criminal cases. Detlef Liebs, *Vor den Richtern Roms: berühmte Prozesse der Antike* (CH Beck 2007) 87. English translation, Detlef Liebs, *Summoned to the Roman Courts: Famous Trials from Antiquity* (Rebecca LR Garber and Carole Curtin trs, University of California Press 2012).

The judge should have no doubt that a special responsibility is imposed on him in hearing and deciding cases that he not give judgment in the recess of his home . . . but that he hear both civil and criminal controversies with the doors of the *secretarium*[84]open, all persons having been called within, or while he is situated on the tribunal.[85]

The *interpretatio* of this constitution articulates the values promoted when a trial is open to the public. The judge is to render his decision

with the doors of his home open and the crowd let in, so that what he adjudged according to the order of the laws or truth is hidden from no one.[86]

Defendant generally not to be subjected to second trial for the same offense

The *lex Acilia* (123/122 BCE) provided:

There may be no action [against] one who shall have been convicted or acquitted under this law, unless he shall have done [something] thereafter, or unless [the judgment] shall have been produced because of collusion [*praevaricationis caussa*],[87] or in suits for damages, or unless in accordance with the sanction of the law.[88]

The *lex Julia iudiciorum publicorum* (17 BCE), by which the emperor Augustus reorganized criminal procedure,[89] stated a general rule barring the retrial of an acquitted person,[90] with the same exception for collusion:

---

[84] The *secretarium* was that portion of the courtroom that could be closed to the public by the lowering of a curtain so that the presiding judge and the persons sitting with him in the hearing of a case could confer in private, but which was opened to public view by the raising of the curtain whenever the hearing resumed or judgment was to be pronounced. See Checchini, "Studi storico-critici sulla" (n 33) 19–21; Mommsen (n 5) 362.

[85] *Iudex sibi hanc praecipuam curam in audiendis ac discingendis litibus inpositam esse non ambigat, ita ut non in secessu domus . . . sententiam ferat, sed apertis secretarii foribus intro vocatis omnibus aut pro tribunali locatus et civiles et criminales controversias audiat.* Constitution of the emperors Valentinian and Valens of September 19, 364, C Th 1.16.9.

[86] *apertis domus suae ianuis intromissisque turbis, ut neminem lateat, quid secundum legum vel veritatis ordinem fuerit iudicatum. Interpretatio* to Breviarium 1.6.2 (C Th 1.16.9).

[87] The word *praevaricatio* was the technical term for a procedural offense, OF Robinson, *The Criminal Law of Ancient Rome* (Johns Hopkins University Press 1995) 99, consisting of "the conducting, by collusion of the parties, of the criminal proceeding with the aim of achieving the acquittal or milder punishment of the defendant and thereby protecting him against further accusation." Mommsen (n 5) 501, "in particular by the bringing of false evidence which could readily be disproved." Robinson, *Penal Practice* (n 7) 89. "Outside of legal speech, the word was used more generally [to denote] any falsehood or treachery." Ibid.

[88] *[Quei ex h.l. condemnatus] aut apsolutus erit, quom eo [h.]l nisei quod post ea fecerit, aut nisei quod praeuaricationis caussa factum erit, au[t nisei de litibus] aestumandis aut nisei de sanctione hoiusce legis, actio nei es[to . . . .] Lex Acilia*, line 56, in 1 *Fontes iuris romani antejustiniani* (n 7) 96 (words and letters in brackets were reconstructed by Mommsen). This is "[t]he oldest formulation of the rule [a double jeopardy principle] for a particular criminal proceeding." Peter Landau, "Ursprünge und Entwicklung des Verbotes doppelter Strafverfolgung wegen desselben Verbrechens in der Geschichte des Kanonischen Rechts" (1970) 56 ZRG (KA) 124, 124. But the *lex Acilia* covered only charges of extortion by provincial officials and the rule apparently had no application in other criminal proceedings prior to the enactment of the *lex Julia iudiciorum publicorum*. See Detlef Liebs, "Die Herkunft der 'Regel' bis de eadem re ne sit actio" (1967) 84 ZRG (RA) 104, 125–127.

[89] See Rotondi (n 5) 448.

[90] See Liebs (n 83) 127; Landau (n 88) 128.

For if a defendant objects to his accuser in a public trial because he says he was accused of the same charge by another and acquitted, the *lex Julia publicorum* cautions that he not be accused [again] before collusion [*praevaricatio*] of the prior accuser has been established and proclaimed.[91]

A century and a half later, the emperor Antoninus Pius stated the same principle in a rescript:

The *praeses*[92] should not allow the same person to be accused of the same charges of which he has been acquitted.[93]

Rhetoricians[94] of the first through fourth centuries CE expressed the proscription of second prosecutions in a maxim variously worded, which they considered to be a general principle of the criminal law, as quoted by the renowned Quintilian:[95]

---

[91] *Nam si reus accusatori publico iudicio ideo praescribat, quod dicat se eodem crimine ab alio accusatum et absolutum, cavetur lege Iulia publicorum, ut non prius accusetur, quam de prioris accusatoris praevaricatione constiterit et pronuntiatum fuerit* .... Aemilius Macer, 1 *De iudiciis publicis* 19 (212/217), Dig 47.15.3.1. See also CJ 9.2.9.

[92] *Praeses* generally designated a Roman provincial governor. See Berger (n 23) 646.

[93] *Isdem criminibus, quibus quis liberatus est, non debet praeses pati eundem accusari.* Rescript of emperor Pius to Salvius Valens (138/161), quoted in Domitius Ulpianus, 7 *De officio proconsulis* (213), Dig 48.2.7.2. This rescript may represent the emperor Pius's application of the rule established by the *lex Julia iudiciorum publicorum* for the conduct of jury trials to the non-jury trials held in accordance with the *cognitio* procedure. See Liebs (n 83) 129, 130–131; Landau (n 88) 129–130.

One who would bring a criminal charge against a person previously acquitted of the same charge had to show collusion in the prior acquittal. This was the prerequisite to the bringing of the second accusation. The requirement is characterized, in the context of a homicide prosecution, by an imperial constitution of the late third century as having been "salubriously prescribed in the statutes of our ancestral emperors and by the form of law." Constitution of the emperors Diocletian and Maximian of April 6, 292, CJ 9.2.11 (*id enim salubriter statutis principum parentum nostrorum iurisque forma praescriptum est*). However, the reach of the prohibition is uncertain. Ulpian, in the cited passage of *De officio proconsulis* in the Digest (Dig 48.2.7.2) indicates that it is an open question whether the bar is to any second accusation after acquittal or only to a second accusation by the same accuser (*sed hoc, utrum ab eodem an nec ab alio accusari possit, videndum est*). The *Pauli Sententiae*, as appearing in the Breviarium of 506, appears to bar only reaccusation by an unsuccessful first accuser:

As to those criminal charges of which one has been acquitted, the accusation may not be reopened by him who [originally] accused .... A person is not prohibited from bringing a charge from which another has desisted or has gone off defeated.

(*De his criminibus, de quibus quis absolutus est, ab eo qui accusavit refricari accusatio non potest ... Crimen, in quo alius desistit uel uictus discessit, alius obicere non prohibetur*). Pauli Sententiae I. 6B. 1, 3 in 2 *Collectio librorum iuris anteiustiniani* (n 41). See Landau (n 88) 133.

[94] A rhetorician (*rhetor*) or orator (*orator*) spoke in court as an advocate (*advocatus*) for litigants, including criminal defendants, but, unlike the jurists (*iuris prudentes*), was not learned in the law but rather specialized in the art of oral persuasion. See Crook (n 2) 40–41, 62, 120–123, 136–139, 173–174, 196–197. From at least the fourth century CE onward, however, advocates increasingly had jurisprudential training. See ibid 175, 195–196. There is a difference of scholarly opinion, as to whether law and advocacy ever became a unified profession. Tony Honoré, "Roman Law AD 200–400: From Cosmopolis to Rechtsstaat?" in Simon Swain and Mark Edwards (eds), *Approaching Late Antiquity: The Transformation from Early to Late Empire* (OUP 2004) 109, 120–121.

[95] Marcus Fabius Quintilianus (Quintilian), the outstanding teacher and practitioner of advocacy in the first century CE, produced a landmark treatise on oratory, *Institutio oratoria* (c 95 CE), in which he expounds in detail on the forensic skills of the trial advocate. See Roland G Austin, s.v. "Quintilianus" in Hammond and Scullard (eds) (n 28) 907. A summary of Quintilian's teaching on the art of cross-examination is set out in Frank R Herrmann, "The Establishment of a Rule against Hearsay in Romano-Canonical Procedure" (1995) 36 Virginia Journal of International Law 1, 12–13.

There should not be an action twice in the same matter.[96]

Witnesses be present in person to testify in criminal cases

In the century following the fall of the western Roman Empire in 476, the eastern emperor Justinian (527–565) from his capital at Constantinople issued between 527 and 529 a series of constitutions regulating the reception of proof by witness testimony in both civil and criminal cases.[97] A constitution of 527 imposed a general obligation to testify in both civil and criminal cases.[98] In civil cases, persons residing outside the capital city could give their testimony by deposition before a judge in the place of their residence.[99] But an imperial constitution issued on October 1, 539, in Greek, limited deposition testimony to civil cases and created a more exacting rule for criminal cases. The constitution required the production of witnesses in criminal cases both before the defendant and before the judge as fact-finder. This rule emerged from two separate chapters of the constitution.[100] Until the high Middle Ages, this significant provision of law was known in Western Europe only in an unofficial Latin version, the *Epitome of Julian*, made soon after Justinian's promulgation by a professor of law in Constantinople.

[I]n criminal [cases] the very persons of the witnesses are necessary.[101]

---

[96] *Bis de eadem re ne sit actio*. Quintilian, *Institutio oratoria* 7.6.4 (c 95 CE) in Quintilian, 3 *The Institutio Oratoria of Quintilian* (Harvard University Press 1920) (4 vols) 136. In the cited passage, Quintilian refers to the maxim as a written (*scriptum*) principle of law. The maxim is repeated in slightly different wording by rhetoricians of the fourth century. See Liebs (n 83) 108, 113–115. Liebs demonstrates that the maxim does not appear in any surviving Roman legal text. He traces its origin to an abbreviation of an ancient Greek law δὶς περὶ τῶν αὐτῶν δίκας μὴ εἶναι (There are not to be judgments twice concerning the same matters). Ibid 104–106, 115–122.

[97] See Zilletti, "Sul valore probatorio" (n 26) 194–203. Zilletti's opinion is that the constitutions in question represent "the pursuit by Justinian of a policy of reform and normative regulation of trial procedure ... gradually coming to fruition and specifying also structural orientations and revisions." Ibid 196.

[98] Ibid 197–198, citing CJ 4.20.16.

[99] Zilletti, "Sul valore probatorio" (n 26) 199–200 & n 15.

[100] See Nicolaas van der Wal, *Manuale Novellarum Justiniani* 48 (no 348), 137 (no 1114) (2nd edn, Wolters 1964).

[101] *[I]n criminalibus [causis] ipsae personae testium necessariae sunt*. Epitome Iuliani, Const 83, cap 326 (555) in Scholastikos Ioulianos, *Iuliani epitome latina Novellarum Iustiniani* (Gustav Hänel ed, apud Hinrichsium 1873) 111. The "Epitome Juliani" (so called since Hänel's edition, Wolfgang Kaiser, *Die Epitome Iuliani* 173 (Max-Planck-Institut 2004)) is the law professor Julian's abridged version for his Latin-speaking students of Justinian's "new constitutions" (novels), i.e., the constitutions issued in Greek after the promulgation of Justinian's second Code in 534. Ibid 1, 4, 174, 177–178; Friedrich August Biener, *Geschichte der Novellen Justinian's* (Ferdinand Dümmler 1824) 6, 229–230, 232–235. Julian's Constitution 83 is his rendering of Novel 90. The parallel passage in the original reads: "[I]n criminal cases, where there is danger about great matters, it is necessary by all means that witnesses appear before the judges and explain those things that they know" ("ἐπὶ γὰρ ἐγκλημάτων, ἔνθα περὶ μεγίστων ἐστὶν ὁ κίνδυνος, ἀνάγκη πᾶσι τρόποις ὑπὸ τοῖς δικασταῖς παριέναι τοὺς μάρτυρας καὶ τὰ αὐτοῖς ἐγνωσμένα διδάσκειν"). Novel 90.5 (October 1, 539) in Paul Krueger and others, 3 *Corpus Iuris Civilis: Novellae* (apud Weimannos 1954) (3 vols) 451 (hereafter *Novellae*).

The Greek constitution goes on to explain that the physical presence of the witnesses is "necessary" to allow "time both for inquiries under torture and all other observations" ("ἔνθα καὶ βασάνων ἴσως ἔσται καιρὸς καὶ τῆς ἄλλης ἁπάσης παρατηρήσεως"). Novel 90.5. The reference to "torture," however, is absent from Julian's rendering of the substance of this constitution in the Epitome Iuliani (Const 83, cap 326).

> The production of witnesses before judges ... is not valid unless each adverse party is present or contumaciously not coming.[102]

Summary and Conclusions

The imperial collections of Theodosius and Justinian, collecting earlier authoritative statements of jurists, set out fundamental principles for fair accusatorial process. The principles were not organized into a unified, concise statement of procedure. Nonetheless, the principles that the jurists and emperors articulated, when taken together, constituted a sound edifice of safeguards for criminal defendants subject to accusatorial proceedings. A defendant had to be summoned to a formal proceeding to be held expeditiously and in public where the crime was said to have been committed. The accuser, accused, and witnesses were required to be present in court. Legal counsel could assist the defendant. The burden of proof fell upon the accuser who had to present undoubted proof clearer than day to support the charges. The proceedings were to take place before an impartial fact-finder who had the duty to evaluate the evidence according to his conscience. As a rule, though subject to exceptions, an accused was not to be tried twice for the same offense.

Although defendants in lower social classes may have benefitted little from the principles of formal accusatorial procedure, the promulgation by the highest state authority of structural norms for trial provided a repository of legal principles. With the exception of torture, these principles formed a basis for the rational conduct of criminal proceedings. For centuries, however, the potency of the Justinianic norms had to remain mostly latent. As imperial rule deteriorated in the course of the sixth century, Justinian's monumental codification of Roman law fell almost entirely out of sight in Western Europe. It was to remain so for over five hundred years. When rediscovered in the Middle Ages, the texts of Justinian would be highly esteemed and venerated as written reason.

---

[102] *Testium productio apud iudices ... non aliter valeat nisi praesente quoque adversaria parte, vel contumaciter non veniente ....* Epitome Iuliani (n 101) 111. The parallel passage in the original Novel explicitly states that the adverse party must also have opportunity to hear the testimony: "[I]t is fitting that [the adverse party] ... be advised by the judge ... to be present and to hear the testimony. If, indeed, he does not wish to come but declines, so that from [his absence] the testimony ... will be of no effect, we ordain that testimony of this sort will be held ... as if made with [the adverse party] present" ("δεῖ κἀκεῖνον ἐν αὐτῇ τῇ πόλει καθεστῶτα ἔνθα αἱ μαρτυρίαι δίδονται, ὑπομνησθέντα παρὰ τοῦ ἄρχοντος ἢ τοῦ ἐκδίκου παραγενέσθαι καὶ ἀκοῦσαι τῶν μαρτυριῶν. εἰ δὲ μὴ βουληθείν παραγενέθαι, ἀλλὰ διαπτύσειεν, ὥστε ἐκ τοῦ κατὰ μίαν μοῖραν δίδασθαι τὰς μαρτυρίας κατ' αὐτὸ τοῦτο ἀχρήστους εἶναι, θεσπίζομεν τὰς τοιαύτας μαρτυρίας οὕτω κρατεῖν, ὡς ἂν εἰ μὴ μονομερεῖς ἐτύγχανον οὖσαι, ἀλλὰ καὶ αὐτοῦ παρόντος ἐγεγόνεισαν"). Novel 90.9 (October 1, 539) in *Novellae* (n 101) 452.

2

The Formation of Procedural Protections in the Western Church of Late Antiquity and the Early Middle Ages

Judicial Functions of Ecclesiastical Authorities in Late Antiquity

The emergence of Christianity as a state-sanctioned religion within the Roman Empire in the fourth century provided new soil in which Roman law procedural principles could take root. Alongside established Roman secular norms, the church introduced into its nascent ecclesiastical law principles based on scripture and Jewish traditions.

In 313, legislation inspired by the emperor Constantine, known to history as the "Edict of Milan," effectively made the Christian church legal throughout the Roman Empire.[1] Long before that, the church had developed its own internal adjudicatory procedures.[2] These were patterned, at least in part, after the Jewish courts that existed independently of the secular Roman legal system.[3] The church used these internal procedures for the settlement of disputes among its members,[4] for the

---

[1] See Norman Hepburn Baynes, *Constantine the Great and the Christian Church* (2nd edn, OUP for the British Academy 1972) 11, 69–74; Andreas Alföldi, *The Conversion of Constantine and Pagan Rome* (Clarendon Press 1948) 37–38, 54; AHM Jones, *Constantine and the Conversion of Europe* (published by Hodder & Stoughton for The English Universities Press 1948) 84–89. It was Baynes's opinion "that there never was an Edict of Milan: Constantine had previously to [a] meeting [in Milan in February 313 with his co-emperor Licinius, at which the emperors agreed on a written protocol for a policy of complete religious freedom throughout the Roman Empire,] anticipated the protocol of Milan which was itself composed on the basis of those letters." Baynes (n 1) 74. "The Edict of Milan may be a fiction, but the fact for which the term stood remains untouched." Ibid 11.

[2] Yvette Duval, *Les chrétienités et leur évêque au IIIe siècle* (Institut d'études augustiniennes 2005) 259. On the origins of episcopal hearings for the resolution of disputes and the enforcement of ecclesiastical discipline, see Charles Donahue Jr, "The Ecclesiastical Courts: Introduction" in Wilfried Hartmann and Kenneth Pennington (eds), *The History of Courts and Procedure in Medieval Canon Law* (Catholic University Press of America 2016) 247, 251–252. See generally ibid 247–299; Giulio Vismara, *Episcopalis Audientia* (Milan 1937) 97 n 1; Vratislav Bušek, "Episcopalis audientia, eine Friedens- und Schiedsgerichtsbarkeit" (1939) 28 ZRG (KA) 453, 458, 466–467. As to whether Roman or Jewish influences predominated in the early adjudicatory procedures of the church, this "concerns so complex a legal development that one cannot arrive at a single formula to establish the origin of the rules of church procedure." Artur Steinwenter, "Der antike kirchliche Rechtsgang und seine Quellen" (1934) 23 ZRG (KA) 1, 6.

[3] For variations in scholarly assessments of Jewish and Roman influence on the formation of early church procedure, see Steinwenter (n 2).

[4] Vismara (n 2) 7–12; Franz Xaver von Funk, *Die apostolischen Konstitutionen: eine litterar-historische Untersuchung* (Rottenburg am Neckar 1891, reprint Minerva 1970) 32.

Foundations of American Criminal Due Process at Trial. Francis R. Herrmann and Brownlow M. Speer,
Oxford University Press. © Oxford University Press 2025. DOI: 10.1093/9780199364770.003.0002

excommunication of those found to have gravely sinned,[5] and for the deposition of misbehaving or heretical clergy.[6]

Only five years after the Edict of Milan, Constantine in an imperial constitution formally recognized the authority of bishops to conduct hearings in civil matters with the consent of the parties.[7] In 333, the emperor by rescript decreed that the bishops' judgments were to be binding in the secular courts.[8] Subsequently, imperial legislation conferred a criminal jurisdiction on the church by requiring it to decide criminal complaints against bishops in the first instance.[9] This requirement was later applied to criminal complaints against any cleric.[10]

In the exercise of its criminal jurisdiction, the church drew on the principles of Roman criminal procedure.[11] Paramount among these were the requirements that accused persons be present to hear the charges against them and to have the opportunity to be heard in their own defense.[12] A dramatic event in this connection occurred in 355. In a tense head-to-head confrontation between Pope Liberius and Emperor Constantius, the Pope refused the emperor's demand that the Pope endorse the decision of a church synod deposing Athanasius, the bishop of Alexandria, from office. Pope Liberius adamantly contended that the decision had been rendered in Athanasius's absence and was therefore invalid.[13] Ammianus Marcellinus, a contemporary, non-Christian historian, describing the event from a neutral standpoint, vividly summarized the Pope's position:

> [W]hen ordered by the emperor, Liberius, having been cautioned, steadfastly resisted, repeatedly exclaiming it is the ultimate abomination to condemn a

---

[5] Stephen William Findlay, *Canonical Norms Governing the Deposition and Degradation of Clerics: A Historical Synopsis and Commentary* (The Catholic University of America Press 1941) 19–20; Paul Hinschius, 4 *Das Kirchenrecht der Katholiken und Protestanten in Deutschland* (Guttentag 1897, reprint Akademische Druck-und Verlagsanstalt 1959) (4 vols) 691–697.

[6] Findlay (n 5) 3–5, 12–14; Duval (n 2) 311–316. Judeo-Christian doctrine influenced the self-understanding of ecclesiastical judges, emphasizing their duty to be factually accurate in judgments (as a human judge was answerable to the divine judge) and to use discipline as a medicinal measure for the purpose of leading sinners to reform. See Mathias Schmoeckel, *Die Jugend der Justitia: Archäologie der Gerechtigkeit im Prozessrecht der Patristik* (Mohr Siebeck 2013) 103–117, distinguishing the self-understanding of an ecclesiastical judge from that of a pre-Christian Roman judge.

[7] Jones (n 1) 99; Bušek (n 2) 462–465; Vismara (n 2) 13–19.

[8] Jones (n 1) 217–218; Vismara (n 2) 23–26.

[9] R Génestal, "Les origines du privilège clerical" (1908) 32 Nouvelle revue historique de droit français et étranger 161, 163–170. Advocates and jurists could easily be named as bishops. Bishops learned from Roman rhetoric and were acquainted with Roman law. Ambrose and Augustine showed great familiarity with Roman law; Tertullian and Cyprian were probably jurists themselves. Schmoeckel (n 6) 56.

[10] Génestal (n 9) 176–178.

[11] Steinwenter (n 2) 22–34; Vismara (n 2) 97–98 n 1.

[12] Steinwenter (n 2) 46–47. It would be incorrect, at this early stage of the church's legal procedure, to refer to ecclesiastical "courts," in the sense of a modern English or American courtroom. Proceedings took place before church synods. A synod is "[a] general term for ecclesiastical gatherings under hierarchical authority, for the discussion and decision of matters relating to faith, morals, or discipline." William Fanning, 14 *The Catholic Encyclopedia* (Robert Appleton Co 1912) (14 vols) s.v. "synod." The term "ecclesiastical court" became appropriate only in the later Middle Ages. See Barbara Deimling, "The Courtroom: From Church Portal to Town Hall" in Wilfried Hartmann and Kenneth Pennington (eds), *The History of Courts and Procedure in Medieval Canon Law* (The Catholic University of America Press 2016) 30–50.

[13] Johannes Herrmann, "Ein Streitgespräch mit verfahrensrechtlichen Argumenten zwischen Kaiser Konstantius und Bischof Liberius" in Johannes Herrmann (ed), *Kleine Schriften zur Rechtsgeschichte* (Beck 1990) 321, 324–327.

man neither seen nor heard, openly and manifestly resistant to the will of the emperor.[14]

Athanasius himself focused on exactly the same point to convey the injustice of his condemnation, invoking phrases from Paul's trial:

No man is unaware that items of business which are done when one party is absent do not have the slightest force. For this is prescribed even by divine law. . . . "It is not a custom among the Romans casually to give up any man before the accused has had the accusers before his face and received opportunity for defense concerning the charges."[15]

Half a century later, in 417, Pope Zosimus invoked the same principle by quoting the same Lucan text. The Pope refused to accept a synodal judgment of heresy against the priest Caelestius, who, like the apostle Paul, had been accused in his absence:[16]

And in the Acts of the Apostles, the pagan tribune Festus pronounced, against [those] demanding the condemnation of the absent apostle Paul, a most just judgment that it is fitting for us also to set before [Christian] believers to [their] shame, saying: "It is not the custom among the Romans to condemn any man before he who is accused may have the accusers present and receive opportunity of defending to clear himself of the charges."[17]

At the Council of Carthage of 419, the church formally adopted the structural framework of Roman accusatorial procedure.[18] Ultimately, it absorbed into its own adjudicatory proceedings much of the substance of the secular Roman civil and criminal trial practice.[19]

The church appears already to have exercised a significant influence on the standard of proof in Roman criminal law in the form of an important evidentiary

---

[14] "*iubente principe Liberius monitus, perseveranter renitebatur, nec visum hominem nec auditum damnare nefas ultimum saepe exclamans, aperte scilicet recalcitrans imperatoris arbitrio.*" Ammianus Marcellinus, *Res Gestae* 15.7.9 (390/391) in 1 *Ammianus Marcellinus* (John C Rolfe ed and tr, Loeb Classical Library, Harvard University Press 1935) (3 vols) 162, 164.

[15] ὅτι μὲν οὖν τὰ πραττόμενα κατὰ μονομέρειαν οὐδεμίαν ἔχει δύναμιν, οὐδείς ἐστιν, ὅστις ἀγνοεῖ τῶν πάντων ἀνθρώπων. τοῦτο γὰρ καὶ ὁ θεῖος νόμος κελεύει . . . «οὐκ ἔστιν ἔθος Ῥωμαίοις χαρίζεσθαί τινα ἄνθρωπον, πρὶν ἢ ὁ κατηγορούμενος κατὰ πρόσωπον ἔχοι 82.3 τοὺς κατηγόρους τόπον τε ἀπολογίας λάβοι περὶ τοῦ ἐγκλήματος». Athanasius, *Apologia contra Arianos* c 82 (c 357) in 25 PG 239, 396.

[16] The background of the controversy is described in Peter Brown, *Augustine of Hippo* (University of California Press 1967, new edn 2000) 342–344, 359–360.

[17] *Et in Actibus Apostolorum adversus . . . postulantes absentis Pauli apostoli damnationem, justissimam sententiam gentilis Festus tribunus protulit, quam convenit etiam nos in facie credentium objicere ad verecundiam, dicens: "Non est consuetudo romanis, damnare aliquem hominem prius, quam is qui accusatur, praesentes habeat accusatores, locumque defendendi accipiat ad abluenda crimina."* Zosimus, "Epistle to the bishops of Africa" 20 PL 654, 659 para 5.

[18] The second session of the Council formally adopted secular law governing the competence of individuals to accuse and to testify in accusatorial criminal proceedings. Georg May, "Anklage-und Zeugnisfähigkeit nach der zweiten Sitzung des Konzils zu Karthago vom Jahre 419" (1960) 140 Theologische Quartalschrift 163, 166–167, 193–195. "State law was recast by the church legislator [i.e., the Council] as church law and formally enacted anew as church law." Ibid 193.

[19] Jean Gaudemet, *La formation du droit séculier et du droit de l'Église aux IVe et Ve siècles* (2nd edn, Sirey 1979) 224–225; Steinwenter (n 2) 22–27; Eduard Schwartz, *Der Prozess des Eutyches* (Sitzungsberichte der Bayerischen Akademie der Wissenschaften, Philosophisch-historische Abteilung 1929) (Heft 5) 66–69.

principle from outside the Roman law: the "two witness" rule. This rule required for judgment of guilt the testimony of two witnesses to the alleged act.[20] The rule was a staple of Christian practice.[21] The emperor Constantine had incorporated it into the secular law by a constitution issued in 334.[22] The rule may well have derived from the church's Jewish roots, for it had long been a core principle of Jewish law.[23]

The Impact of Augustine on the Criminal Law of the Church

St Augustine's writings and sermons had a profound impact on the ultimate development of the church's criminal jurisprudence. Born in the North African town of Thagaste (now Souk Ahras) in 354, he converted from paganism in 387, was ordained a priest in 391, and was consecrated bishop of Hippo (now Annaba) in 395 or 396. His prolific writings in sermons, letters, and books, together with his rhetorical gifts, made him the central figure of the church in North Africa until his death in 430.[24] Augustine, so far as is known, had no specialized legal education, but he was a vigorous participant in the legal disputes of the church[25] and a keen and insightful observer of secular Roman procedure.[26]

---

[20] Joseph Vogt, "Zur Frage des christlichen Einflusses auf die Gesetzgebung Konstantins des Grossen" in 2 *Festschrift für Leopold Wenger* (Munich 1945) (vols 2) 118, 145. Although a Christian impetus for the adoption of the rule in Roman law has been doubted, see Steinwenter (n 2) 55 & n 2, "no proof can be furnished of the contention that Roman rules of procedure [prior to the legalization of Christianity] excluded the single witness." H van Vliet, *No Single Testimony: A Study on the Adoption of the Law of Deut. 19.15* (Utrecht 1958) 16. See ibid 12–13, 102–103 n 93 (responding to Steinwenter).

[21] van Vliet (n 20) 2–5; Steinwenter (n 2) 54–55.

[22] The constitution provides: "[W]e have ordained that none of the judges shall easily allow to be admitted in any case whatever the testimony of a single person. And now we explicitly ordain that the answer of a single witness shall not be heard at all, even if [the witness] radiates with resplendent official dignity" ("*sanximus, ut unius testimonium nemo iudicum in quacumque causa facile patiatur admitti. Et nunc manifeste sancimus, ut unius omnino testis responsio non audiatur, etiamsi praeclarae curiae honore praefulgeat*"). Constitution of the emperor Constantine of August 25, 334 (C Th 11.39.3; Breviarium 11.14.2; CJ 4.20.9). The *interpretatio* of this constitution, as appearing in the Breviarium, more succinctly states the rule: "But the testimony of a single person, however splendid and suitable the person may seem to be, is not to be heard at all" ("*Unius autem testimonium, quamlibet splendida et idonea videatur esse persona nullatenus audiendum*"). *Interpretatio* to Breviarum 11.14.2.

[23] Boaz Cohen, "Evidence in Jewish Law" in 16 *La Preuve* (Receuils de la Société Jean Bodin, 1964) (pt 1) 103, 106–109; Hasso Jaeger, "La Preuve judiciaire d'après la tradition rabbinique et patristique" in ibid 415, 417 & n 5, 452; van Vliet (n 20) 63–73; Aaron Kirschenbaum, *Self-Incrimination in Jewish Law* (New York 1970) 40; Irene Merker Rosenberg and Yale L Rosenberg, "In the Beginning: The Talmudic Rule against Self-Incrimination" (1988) 63 NYU Law Rev 955, 974–975, 979; Leonard W Levy, "Appendix: Talmudic Law" in Leonard W Levy (ed), *Origins of the Fifth Amendment* (Macmillan Publishing Co 1986) 433–441.

[24] A chronology of the events in the life of Augustine, and of his writings, is given in a table appearing in Pierre-Yves Fux and others (eds), 2 *Augustinus Afer* (Éditions Universitaires 2003) (2 vols) 608–609. His paramount position in the church in North Africa is indicated in May (n 18) 185.

[25] See Caroline Humfress, "A New Legal Cosmos: Late Roman Lawyers and the Early Medieval Church" in Peter Linehan and Janet L Nelson (eds), *The Medieval World* (Routledge 2001) 557, 565–566.

[26] See Noel E Lenski, "Evidence for the *Audientia episcopalis* in the New Letters of Augustine" in Ralph W Mathisen (ed), *Law, Society, and Authority in Late Antiquity* (OUP 2001) 83, 88–89 & n 22. In his *Confessions*, Augustine recalls having taught the "guile" or "wiles" (*dolos*) of the art of rhetoric to "guileless" (*sine dolo*) future legal advocates, "not so that by means of them they might act against the head [life] of an innocent person, but sometimes on behalf of the head [life] of a guilty one" ("*non quibus contra caput innocentis agerent, sed aliquando pro capite nocentis*"). Augustine of Hippo, *Confessions* 4.2.2 (397/401), 27 Corpus Christianorum Series Latina (Turnholt 1983) (65 vols) 40. See Caroline Humfress, *Orthodoxy*

Augustine was a sharp critic of the routine severe tortures that secular procedure significantly relied upon to produce confessions from defendants and testimonial evidence from witnesses.[27] The culture of the day seems to have regarded the judicial use of torture for those purposes as a matter of course, without any sense of moral censure emerging from the extant contemporary sources. Against this cultural background, Augustine's trenchant and detailed critique of judicial torture, set out in *The City of God*, stands in bold relief:

> [What is to be said about] those who make judgments when they cannot discern the consciences of those about whom they are judging? Wherefore, they are often compelled to seek the truth through the torture of innocent witnesses about a case concerning another. What [is to be said] when in his own case someone is tortured and when put to the question whether he is guilty, an innocent person is put on the rack and suffers for an uncertain evil deed the most certain pains, not because it is discovered that he committed it, but because it is not known that he did not commit it? And, so, on most occasions, the ignorance of the judge is the calamity of the innocent. And what is more intolerable and to be lamented and drenched, if that could happen, by fountains of tears than when, on that account, a judge tortures an accused so that he might not unknowingly kill one who is innocent, it happens through his wretched ignorance that he might kill a person both tortured and innocent whom he tortured, in order not to kill an innocent person. For, if ... [the tortured person] should choose to flee from this life rather than withstand those tortures any longer: what he did not commit, he says he committed. After he has been condemned and killed, the judge still does not know whether he killed a guilty or an innocent person, whom he tortured so that he would not unwittingly kill an innocent person; and so, in order to know, he tortured an innocent and, while not knowing, killed him.[28]

and the Courts in Late Antiquity (OUP 2007) 189–190. The passage quoted is reminiscent of the emperor Trajan's rescript, reported in the jurist Ulpian's *De officio proconsulis*, advising acquittal, even of a person who may be guilty in fact, in a case resting on suspicion only. D 48.19.5.pr.

[27] See Gonzalo Martínez Díez, "La tortura judicial en la legislación histórica española" (1962) 32 Anuario de Historia del Derecho Español 223, 225–229. "No fewer than 21 imperial constitutions from the years 312 to 423, collected in [the Theodosian Code] and distributed in 15 different titles [thereof] mention or regulate torture, which for the most part is assumed to be already existing and normally practiced in criminal trials." Ibid 225. See ibid 225 n 1 (listing constitutions). The Roman instruments of torture, and the methods of their application, are described in Piero Fiorelli, 1 *La tortura giudiziaria nel diritto commune* (Milan 1953) (2 vols) 17–19. Less severe forms of corporal abuse applied to defendants and witnesses in criminal trials, collectively known as *verberatio*, are itemized in Angelo Di Berardino, "Christian Liturgical Time and Torture (C Th 9. 35. 4 and 5)" (2011) 51 Augustinianum 191, 200.

[28] *Quando quidem hi iudicant, qui conscientias eorum, de quibus iudicant, cernere nequeunt. Vnde saepe coguntur tormentis innocentium testium ad alienam causam pertinentem quaerere ueritatem. Quid cum in sua causa quisque torquetur et, cum quaeritur utrum sit nocens, cruciatur et innocens luit pro incerto scelere certissimas poenas, non quia illud commisisse detegitur, sed quia non commisisse nescitur? Ac per hoc ignorantia iudicis plerumque est calamitas innocentis. Et quod est intolerabilius magisque plangendum rigandumque, si fieri possit, fontibus lacrimarum, cum propterea iudex torqueat accusatum, ne occidat nesciens innocentem, fit per ignorantiae miseriam, ut et tortum et innocentem occidat, quem ne innocentem occideret torserat. Si enim secundum istorum sapientiam elegerit ex hac uita fugere quam diutius illa sustinere tormenta: quod non commisit, commisisse se dicit. Quo damnato et occiso, utrum nocentem an innocentem iudex occiderit, adhuc nescit, quem ne innocentem nesciens occideret torsit; ac per hoc innocentem et ut sciret torsit, et dum nesciret occidit.* Augustine of Hippo, *Sancti Aurelli Augustini: de civitate Dei* 19.6 (425/427) in 47 Corpus Christianorum Series Latina (Turnholt 1955) (65 vols) 670. Citations to letters of Augustine in which he expresses his opposition to torture are collected by Lenski in Mathisen (n 26) 94 n 52.

It must be granted, however, that, even while Augustine strongly opposed severe secular-style tortures (such as the rack or flames), he did permit the use in bishops' courts of lesser measures (a thrashing with switches or canes) if employed with benevolent intent, as when a parent or teacher might beat a child.[29]

The reason why ecclesiastical views of torture diverged from harsh secular practice cannot be gleaned from the available sources. It is reasonable to surmise, however, that the rejection of secular-style torture in the church's judicial tribunals was, at least in part, another inheritance of long-established Jewish trial procedure. In the earliest known application of a prohibition of self-incrimination, Jewish courts barred the use of any confession of guilt in capital criminal cases.[30] Consequently, Jewish courts were free of any taint of torture.[31]

Augustine displayed a similar heightened sensibility to the elements of just adjudication. He deemed indispensable the absolute impartiality of the judge. In a noteworthy passage from his correspondence, Augustine assails the practice of "selling" justice:

> [A] judge must not ... sell a just judgment [*vendere iustum iudicium*] nor a witness sell true testimony ... When moreover judgments and testimonies which are just and true ought not be sold ... how much more wickedly indeed money is taken when unjust and false ones are sold.[32]

In a sermon *De utilitate agendae poenitentiae* ("On the utility of doing penance," Sermon 351) in 391,[33] Augustine expressed the interrelated principles that adherence

---

[29] See C 23 q. 5 c 1 (*Circumcelliones*). Mathias Schmoeckel observes: "The church fathers, to be sure, recommended mildness above all, but also rigour as a means against sins of the world. In the foreground stood the duty to serve the individual and society through the trials and punishments, not to destroy the offender, but to make him better, that is, to heal him." Schmoeckel (n 6) 99–101. For discussion of the degree to which the later church authorities accepted physical measures in examining defendants, witnesses, and sometimes accusers, see Henry Ansgar Kelly, "Judicial Torture in Canon Law and Church Tribunals: From Gratian to Galileo" (2015) 101 The Catholic Historical Review 754–793. See also Kevin Uhalde, *Expectations of Justice in the Age of Augustine* (University of Pennsylvania Press 2007) 52–53; Steinwenter (n 2) 28, 54; Génestal (n 9) 167–168 n 4; Di Berardino (n 27) 200–201 n 36, 207–208; Leslie Dossey, "Judicial Violence and the Ecclesiastical Courts in Late Antique North Africa" in Mathisen (n 26) 98, 102–104, 107–108, 111.

[30] Kirschenbaum (n 23) 34–36; Rosenberg and Rosenberg (n 23) 984–988.

[31] Kirschenbaum (n 23) 19; Melissa Weintraub, "*Ain Adam Mesim Atsmo Rasha*: The Bar against Self-Incrimination as a Protection against Torture in Jewish and American Law" (*Rabbis for Human Rights— North America* 2005) 8–10 <http://www.rhr-na.org/resource/bar-against-selfincrimination-a-protection-against-torture-jewish-and-american-law>; Isaac Braz, "The Privilege against Self-Incrimination in Anglo-American Law: The Influence of Jewish Law" in Nahum Rakover (ed), *Jewish Law and Current Legal Problems* (The Library of Jewish Law 1984) 161, 163.

[32] *Sed non ideo iudex vendere iustum iudicium, aut testis verum testimonium ... Cum autem iudicia et testimonia, quae nec iusta et vera vendenda sunt, iniqua et falsa venduntur, multo sceleratius utique pecunia sumitur.* Augustine, Letter to Macedonius (Epistle 153 no 23) (414), 33 PL 653, 663–664. For a discussion of this passage in the context of Augustine's teaching on impartial justice, see John T Noonan Jr, *Bribes* (Macmillan 1984) 69–82.

[33] This sermon is conventionally cited as Sermon 351 in accordance with the numbering in the 1683 edition of Augustine's sermons produced by the Benedictines of Saint-Maur. See Pierre-Patrick Verbraken, *Études critiques sur les sermons authentiques de Saint Augustin* (In abbatia S Petri 1976) 20–22, 43, 147. Augustine's authorship of Sermon 351 has been a subject of debate among scholars, see ibid 147; Bernhard Poschmann, "Die Echtheit des augustinischen sermo 351" (1934) 46 Revue Bénédictine 18, 18–19, but the latter author, after an intensely detailed analysis of Sermon 351's content and style, came to "the firm conviction of its authenticity." Ibid 19.

to judicial order is a prerequisite to a valid judgment; that guilt is not to be presumed merely from the fact of a formal accusation; that no one can be both accuser and judge in the same case; that a conviction must be based on sure proofs and not founded on mere suspicion; and that a confession must be the product of free will (*ultro* or *sponte*), if it is to be the basis of punishment. If a confession or conviction cannot be obtained in accordance with these principles, then the presence of a probably guilty person in the church community must simply be tolerated:

> [M]any [sinners] are unknown until the Lord comes who illumines the hidden things of the darkness and makes manifest the thoughts of the heart.... Very many good Christians, moreover, remain silent . . . and suffer the sins of others, which they know, because they are often lacking evidence [*documentis*], and these things, that they themselves know, they cannot prove to the ecclesiastical judges. However much some things may be true, they are, nevertheless, not easily to be believed by a judge unless they shall be demonstrated by sure proofs [*certis indiciis*]. But we cannot exclude anyone from communion . . . unless he has voluntarily [*sponte*] confessed or been convicted in either some secular or ecclesiastical trial.[34] For who would dare to assume to himself that he himself may be both accuser and judge for anyone . . . .[N]ot rashly or in just any manner are evildoers to be removed from the church communion, so that, if they cannot be removed by trial, it is preferable that they be tolerated . . . .For [the apostle Paul] did not want man to be judged by man by an opinion based on suspicion or even by procedure applied out of order: but preferably by the law of God according to the order of the Church, either having voluntarily [*ultro*] confessed or having been accused and convicted . . . Otherwise, why did he say, "If some brother is accused either as a fornicator or an idolator,"[35] et cetera . . . that judgment [should] be pronounced [according to] the judicial order and with integrity [*ordine iudiciario atque integritate*]? For, if accusation suffices, many innocent persons must be condemned because often they are accused with some false criminal charge.[36]

---

[34] Augustine's "confessed or . . . convicted" locution seems to reflect the rule stated in the constitution of the emperor Constantine (issued on November 30, 313, see AIIM Jones and others (eds), 1 *The Prosopography of the Later Roman Empire* (3 vols) (CUP 1971) 187), barring the imposition of sentence on one who has not "been convicted" (*convictus sit*) "either by his confession" (*aut sua confessione*) or by consistent evidence developed by torture or interrogation. The constitution was later included in the Theodosian Code (C Th 9.40.1), the Breviarium (Brev 9.30.1), and Justinian's Code (CJ 9.47.16). The *interpretatio* of the constitution in the Breviarium lacks any reference to torture and is framed in a language not far from Augustine's formulation of the pertinent rule: "A judge trying a person accused of crime shall not impose a capital sentence before the defendant himself has confessed or been convicted, whether by competent witnesses or by associates in his crime" (*Iudex criminosum discutiens non ante sententiam proferat capitalem, quam aut reus ipse fateatur aut convictus vel per innocentes testes vel per conscios criminis sui*). *Interpretatio* to Brev 9.30.1.

[35] The quotation is from 1 Corinthians 5:11.

[36] *[M]ulti nesciuntur, donec veniat Dominus, qui illuminet abscondita tenebrarum, et manifestet cogitationes cordis....Plerique autem boni christiani ... tacent, et sufferunt aliorum peccata quae noverunt, quia documentis saepe deseruntur, et ea quae ipsi sciunt, judicibus ecclesiasticis probare non possunt. Quamvis enim vera sint quaedam; non tamen judici facile credenda sunt, nisi certis indiciis demonstrentur. Nos vero a communione prohibere quemquam non possumus ... nisi aut sponte confessum, aut in aliquo sive saeculari, sive ecclesiastice judicio nominatum atque convictum. Quis enim sibi utrumque audeat assumere, ut cuiquam ipse sit et accusator et judex? ... [N]on temere aut quomodolibet, sed per judicium auferendos esse malos ab Ecclesiae communione: ut si per judicium auferri non possunt, tolerentur potius ... Noluit enim [Apostolus] hominem ab homine judicari ex arbitrio suspicionis, vel etiam extraordinario usurpato judicio: sed potius ex*

There are two aspects of Augustine's teaching that are especially noteworthy. Augustine was the first to focus on the process of adjudication (*ordo iudiciarius*)[37] as having a value distinct from its result. For Augustine, it is even more important that a trial be conducted in adherence to judicial order and with integrity than that it results in the conviction of a person who is factually guilty. Augustine expresses this priority in the phrase "however much some things may be true (*quamvis vera sint quaedam*), they are, nevertheless, not easily to be believed by a judge, unless they shall be demonstrated by sure proofs." Here, Augustine charts the course for a principal strain in Western criminal jurisprudence: insistence on reliable evidence is more important than the punishment of the guilty because without such insistence there is no assurance that only the guilty will be convicted.[38] Public and judicial dedication to Augustine's principle would not be left untested. In the later Middle Ages, security from crime would emerge as a major concern in Western Europe. Society's demands for public safety and for the punishment of criminals would seriously threaten the principle of protection of the innocent.[39]

Augustine is also the first source we have for the assertion that an accused person's confession ought to be voluntary if it is to serve as the basis for any punishment. Roman criminal law, both before and after Augustine, prohibited punishment without the defendant's confession or conviction. But, despite suspicion about the reliability of a coerced confession, Roman law never adopted any requirement that a confession be voluntary.[40]

Pope Gregory I's Articulation of Fundamental Principles of Fair Procedure and Sound Adjudication

A second key figure in the establishment of a fair and enlightened procedure in the nascent criminal jurisprudence of the church was Pope Gregory I (590–604), known to history as Gregory the Great.

---

lege Dei secundum ordinem Ecclesiae, sive ultro confessum, sive accusatum atque convictum. Alioquin illud cur dixit, "Si quis frater nominatur fornicator, aut idolis serviens," et caetera, ... cum sententia ordine judiciario atque integritate profertur? Nam si nominatio sufficit, multi damnandi sunt innocentes, quia saepe falso in quoquam crimine nominantur. Augustine, *De utilitate agendae poenitentiae* (Sermon 351) c 10, 39 PL 1535, 1546–1547.

[37] The term *ordo iudiciarius* appears for the first time in Augustine's Sermon 351. See Linda Fowler-Magerl, *Ordo iudiciorum vel ordo iudiciarius* (Klostermann 1984) 14. See Kenneth Pennington, "Law, Criminal Procedure" in William Chester Jordan (ed), *Dictionary of the Middle Ages, Supplement I* (Charles Scribner's Sons 2004) 316–319, discussing the fundamental importance of the right to a trial.

[38] Augustine's asymmetrical evidentiary view aligns with that of the emperor Trajan. See D 48.19.5.pr. See also Alexander Volokh, "n Guilty Men" (1997) 146 U Pa L Rev 173, 178.

[39] See Richard M Fraher, "The Theoretical Justification for the New Criminal Law of the High Middle Ages: rei publicae interest, ne crimina remaneant impunita" (1984) U Ill L Rev 577; Mirjan Damaška, *Evaluation of Evidence: Pre-Modern and Modern Approaches* (CUP 2019) 82, 85, 90.

[40] See JAC Thomas and Emperor of the East Justinian I, *The Institutes of Justinian: Text, Translation, and Commentary* (North-Holland Pub Co; American Elsevier Pub Co 1975) 109–110, 114 & n 110. Jurists of the second and third centuries CE expressed doubts as to the reliability of confessions compelled by torture, but "imperial constitutions of the fourth century assume to the contrary the hypothesis that a *confessio* obtained under torture always conforms to the truth." Ibid 117 n 122.

Roman criminal law focused on factors that Roman society perceived to be necessary for reliable determinations of guilt or innocence. It did so without any evidentiary principles or unified summary of the procedure to be followed.[41] Gregory's utilization of Roman law to govern the church's criminal proceedings effectively shifted the focal point of Roman law as applied by the church to the individual accused and to the procedural protections on which the accused was entitled to rely.

Gregory was born into a prominent Roman family.[42] Before becoming a monk in 574 or 575,[43] he held a high legal post in the city of Rome, which may have included a substantial criminal jurisdiction.[44] From the evidence of his writings, it is certain that he had a comprehensive knowledge of Roman criminal law. He brought this knowledge with him upon his election as Pope in 590.[45] From the many disparate principles laid down in Justinian's law texts for sound judging in criminal cases, Gregory composed a coherent statement of procedure to be followed in ecclesiastical proceedings of a criminal nature. He did this in letters of instruction collectively known as the *commonitorium*,[46] addressed to the *defensor* Johannes (John the Defensor),[47] a trusted church functionary whom he sent to Spain in 603 with delegated judicial power to determine whether two bishops there, Januarius and Stephen, had been improperly removed from their sees.[48]

In his instructions regarding Stephen's case, Gregory drew on normative principles of Roman criminal law to specify the procedures[49] required for the judgment against Stephen to be valid:

[41] CA Morrison, "Some Features of the Roman and English Law of Evidence" (1958–1959) 33 Tul L Rev 577, 581–583; Fowler-Magerl (n 37) 9; Frank R Herrmann, "The Establishment of a Rule against Hearsay in Romano-Canonical Procedure" (1995) 36 Va J Int'l L 21–22 & n 135.

[42] F Homes Dudden, 1 *Gregory the Great, His Place in History and Thought* (Longmans, Green & Co 1905) (2 vols) 4; Jeffrey Richards, *Consul of God: The Life and Times of Gregory the Great* (Routledge & Kegan Paul 1980) 25.

[43] Dudden (n 42) 107; Richards (n 42) 32.

[44] The secular post held by Gregory is conjectural, but it may have been that of *praefectus urbi* (prefect of the city of Rome), see Richards (n 42) 30–31, who was "the head of the administration [in Rome] and [had] jurisdiction in both civil and criminal matters." Adolf Berger, *Encyclopedic Dictionary of Roman Law* (American Philosophical 1991) 644 s.v. "Praefectus urbi(s)." Although the last Western Roman emperor was deposed in 476, Justinian had successfully, though briefly, reconquered Rome and parts of Italy between 535 and 554.

[45] Unanimously chosen by the papal electors, Gregory was consecrated as Pope on September 3, 590. Richards (n 42) 41–42.

[46] Max Conrat Cohn, 1 *Geschichte der Quellen und Literatur des Römischen Rechts im Frühen Mittelalter* (Leipzig 1891, reprint Scientia Verlag 1963) (7 vols) 8 & n 5. These letters are registered in Philip Jaffé (ed), 1 *Regesta Pontificum Romanorum* (Paul Ewald, rev; 2nd edn, Veit 1885) (2 vols) 590–882. Critical editions of them are included in Paul Ewald and Ludwig M Hartmann (eds), 2 *Gregorii I papae Registrum epistolarum* (MGH Epistolae 1889, 2nd edn, apud Weimannos 1957) (2 vols) 410–412 (Register 13.47), 413–414 (Register 13.49), 414–418 (Register 13.50).

[47] The term *defensor* here signifies a cleric officially appointed to the office of legal "defender" of or "advocate" for the church (*defensor ecclesiae*). Humfress, "A New Legal Cosmos" (n 25) 561–562, 572; François Martroye, "Les 'defensores ecclesiae' aux Vᵉ et VIᵉ siècles" (1923) 2 Revue historique de droit français et étranger (4th ser) 597, 605–607. By the end of the sixth century, the *defensores ecclesiae* had fixed administrative and fiscal duties, see ibid 607, 609–610, and "[b]y special delegation of the authority of the Holy See they were assigned to carry out diverse missions." Ibid 611.

[48] See Albert Gauthier, "L'utilisation du droit romain dans la lettre de Grégoire le Grand à Jean le Défenseur" (1977) 54 Angelicum 417, 417–418 & n 3; Martroye (n 47) 614–616; Richards (n 42) 210; Dudden (n 42) 413–414.

[49] See Gauthier (n 48) 422–426; Conrat Cohn (n 46) 8 n 7.

Therefore, because the bishop Stephen claims that some things were fabricated out of hatred of him and that he was accused of false charges and unjustly convicted, careful investigation must first be made to determine if the trial was held according to proper order, if some were accusers and others witnesses. Then if the type of charges warranted exile or removal. Or if the testimony against him was given under oath with him present, or if [the record] was made in writing, or he himself had opportunity for answering and defending himself.[50]

Gregory paid close attention to how his emissary ought to evaluate witness testimony:

Close examination must be made of the character of the accusers and witnesses, of their type and reputation, or whether they were unfit, or whether they happened to have some animosities against the said bishop, and whether they testified from hearsay or specifically testified that they knew with certainty, or if there was an adjudication in writing and judgment was recited with the parties present. But if it so happened that these things were not solemnly done nor a case proved that was worthy of exile or removal, he should, by all means, be recalled to his church.[51]

In a separate document for John, Gregory quotes the first half of a Latin translation of Justinian's Greek constitution on witnesses of October 1, 539 (now cited as Novel 90.9)[52] requiring a criminal defendant to have the opportunity to be present when opposing witnesses testify. In comments immediately before and after the quotation, Gregory signaled that observance of Justinian's rule was essential to a valid judgment against the defendant:

If what the same bishop [Stephen] says is true, that some witnesses of the worst sort were presented with him absent, it must be acknowledged to be of no moment in the law, under the *constitutio* of the Novel which speaks about witnesses . . . ."[V]ery often . . . those coming before [a court] and making complaint . . . [of having] suffered an illegality at the hands of another . . . want to produce witnesses; and so that it may not afterwards be objected against them that the actions were done unilaterally, it is proper indeed that [the adverse party] . . . be cautioned by the judge·or defensor[53] . . . to come and hear the witnesses.

---

[50] *Quia igitur Stephanus episcopus in odio suo quaedam ficta et de falsis se capitulis accusatum neque aliquid ordinabiliter factum, sed iniuste se asserit condemnatum, diligenter quarendum est primo, si iudicium ordinabiliter est habitum aut si alii accusatores, alii testes fuerunt; deinde causarum qualitas, si digna exilio vel depositione fuit; aut si eo praesente sub iureiurando contra eum testimonium dictum est seu scriptis actum est vel ipse licentiam respondendi et defendendi se habuit.* Gregory I, Register 13.47 (August, 603) in Ewald and Hartmann (eds), 2 *Registrum* (n 46) 410, 411.

[51] *Sed et de personis accusantium ac testificantium suptiliter quarendum est, cuius condicionis cuiusve opinionis aut ne inopes sint aut ne forte aliquis contra praedictum episcopum inimicitias habuissent, et utrum testimonium ex auditu dixerunt aut certe specialiter se scire testati sunt vel si scriptis iudicatum est et partibus praesentibus sententia recitata est. Quod si forte haec sollemniter acta non sunt neque causa probata est, quae exilio vel depositione digna sit, in ecclesia sua modis omnibus revocetur.* Ibid.

[52] As to Novel 90, text to n 101 in ch 1. The text used by Gregory here is taken from a Latin translation of Justinian's Greek Novels whose maker and the place of making are unknown. Friedrich A Biener, *Geschichte der Novellen Justinian's* (bei F Dümmler 1824) 230, 458; Nino Tamassia, "Per la storia dell' Autentico" (1897–1898) 56 Atti del Reale Istituto veneto di scienze, lettere ed arti 535, 595–596.

[53] In this context, the term *defensor* refers to a secular official whose duties included police functions.

But if a defendant absented himself in order to claim he had no chance to see the opposing witnesses, Gregory warned:

> But if he does not wish to come and instead disdains [to do so], so that the testimonies presented unilaterally against him will be of no effect, we ordain testimonies of this sort to be just as valid as if they did not depend upon one party but indeed had been made with him present. For if he refuses and does not wish to come and hear the things being deposed, . . . and is not unable to come on account of some unavoidable necessity, [the testimonies] shall be [treated] the same as if [adverse parties] had come and no advantage shall accrue to him by reason of his contempt, but [the testimonies] shall [be deemed] to have been made in the presence of both [parties].
>
> So, the adversary must always be cautioned to come to hear the witnesses. Because if this is omitted, it is necessary that what has been done against the laws have no force.[54]

In instructions governing other cases, Gregory used his knowledge of the Roman law to formulate two core principles of fair procedure and judgment. With regard to who must bear the burden of proof, Gregory restated the principle of the Roman law clearly and succinctly:

> [R]eason [never] imposes the necessity of proof on him who is accused . . . .[T]hat burden lies not on you [the defendant], but on the accusers . . . .[55]

With regard to the standard of proof, Gregory distilled from the Roman law the concept of "doubt" as the pivot in assessing when conviction is proper. He articulated this concept with elegant simplicity:

---

[54] *Quod autem dicit isdem episcopus, quia se absente aliqui vilissimi sunt testes exhibiti, hoc si verum est, nullius esse momenti lege noscendum est, constitutione Novellae, quae de testibus loquitur, . . . : "Hoc quoque saepius agi novimus, quoniam quidam aut apud locorum defensores aut apud clarissimos provinciarum iudices aut etiam, ut adsolet, hic apud clarissimum magistrum census ingredientes et querentes, tamquam ab alio passi aliquid contra leges aut aliter iniustitiam sustinentes aut damnificati, testes volunt producere; et ne postea obiciatur eis, quia per unam partem gestu confecta sunt, oportet et illum in ipsa civitate constitutum, ubi testimonia dantur, ammonitum a iudice aut defensore advenire et audire testes. Si vero noluerit advenire, sed contempserit, ut ex una parte testimonia adversus eum inutilia sint, sancimus huius modi testimonia ita valere, tamquam si non ex una parte consisterent, sed etiam ipso praesente fuissent facta. Si enim repudiaverit et venire noluerit et audire quae deponuntur, cum utique in publico sint, et non ex inevitabili quadam necessitate venire non possit, aequaliter erunt, tamquam si advenissent, et nulla utilitas ex contemptu suo ei adhibebitur, sed videbuntur quidem ex utriusque praesentia facta.*

Ecce ammonendus est semper adversarius, ut ad audiendos testes adveniat. Quod quia hic omissum est, necesse est, ut, quod contra leges actum est, firmitatem non habeat. Gregory I, Register 13.50 (August, 603) in Ewald and Hartmann (eds), 2 *Registrum* (n 46) 414, 417–418.

The conclusion of the *commonitorium*, which follows, includes an admonition that "the worst sort of witnesses should not be credited without corporal discussion" (*vilissimis testibus sine corporali discussione credi non debeat*). Ibid 418. What the expression *corporalis discussio* means is unclear, but it may indicate the subjection of such prospective witnesses to some form of physical force allowed in church judicial proceedings. See Gauthier (n 48) 425–427 & n 12.

[55] *[Num]quam ratio ei qui accusatur necessitatem probationis imponeret. At postquam non tibi, sed accusantibus hoc onus incumbit.* Gregory I, Register 6.25 (January, 596) [JE 1405] in 1(2) *Gregorii I papae Registrum epistolarum* (n 46) 402, 403.

For it is very grave and unseemly that in a matter that is doubtful, a judgment that is certain should be pronounced.[56]

The Church's Adoption of Exoneration by Oath

After the fall of the Roman Empire in the West, its successor regimes in Western Europe, the Germanic "barbarian states,"[57] did not, for the most part, in their secular courts, follow the Roman law procedure of resolving criminal accusations on the basis of testimonial evidence.[58] Instead they drew upon long-standing folk traditions that relied upon belief in divine intervention in human affairs to determine guilt or innocence when proofs were lacking as to who committed the crime.[59] Accused persons were bound and thrown into water, or made to walk with bare feet on hot coals or carry in their bare hands a hot iron bar, or plunge their bare hands into boiling water to retrieve an object.[60] Such a test, or "ordeal" (Anglo-Saxon *ordal*),[61] was considered to reveal the "judgment of God" (*judicium Dei*) by showing whether the accused floated or sank, or whether the burnt hands or feet became infected.[62]

[56] *Nam grave est satis et indecens, ut in re dubia certa dicatur sententia.* Gregory I, Register 10.11 (May 600) [JE 1779] in Ewald and Hartmann (eds), 2 *Registrum* (n 46) 245, 246. For a study of principles of justice and government in the church contained in Gregory's letters, see Jacques-Yves Pertin, *Justice et gouvernement dans l'Église d'apres les Lettres de saint Grégoire le Grand* (L'Harmttan 2015).

[57] The word "barbarian" in this context signifies only a people whose native language was not Latin or Greek. See William R Trumble and Angus Stevenson, *Shorter Oxford English Dictionary on Historical Principles* (5th edn, OUP 2002) 156 s.v. "Barbarian," citing 1 Corinthians 14:11. The word must have carried some pejorative sense, however. The Visigothic compilers of the Breviarium replaced references to "barbarian" (*barbarus*) in the Theodosian Code with the word "enemy" (*hostis*) in the corresponding *interpretationes*. See John F Matthews, "Interpreting the Interpretationes of the Breviarium" in Ralph W Mathisen (ed), *Law, Society, and Authority in Late Antiquity* (OUP 2001) 18, 21.

[58] A striking exception to this generalization is Visigothic Spain, whose laws reflected, and indeed in a sense increased, the Roman stress on the testimony of percipient witnesses. See Herrmann (n 41) 27–28; Joshua C Tate, "Roman and Visigothic Procedural Law in the False Decretals of Pseudo-Isidore" (2004) 90 ZRG (KA) 510, 513; Alvaro d'Ors, "El Codigo de Eurico" in 2 *Estudios Visigoticos* (Consejo Superior de Investigaciones Cientificas 1960) 62–64; Adolf Helfferich, *Entstehung und Geschichte des Westgothen-Rechts* (Berlin 1858) 132–134. The presentation of witness testimony in Visigothic courts is described in PD King, *Law and Society in the Visigothic Kingdom* (CUP 1972) 102–104. "The Visigoths demonstrated a clear receptiveness to Roman law from the first moments of their settlement in the Roman provinces." d'Ors (n 58) 105.

Also worthy of note, the law of the Lombards in Italy, under the influence of Roman procedure, made provision in the first half of the eighth century for receiving witness testimony. Franca Sinatti D'Amico, *Le prove giudiziarie nel diritto longobardo* (Giuffre 1968) 144, 176, 295–310, 352; Lucas F Bruyning, "Il processo longobardo prima e dopo l'invasione franca" (1984) 57 Rivista di storia del diritto italiano 121, 125, 145–146.

[59] Robert Bartlett, *Trial by Fire and Water: The Medieval Judicial Ordeal* (Oxford Clarendon Press; OUP 1986) 25–30; Paul R Hyams, "Trial by Ordeal: The Key to Proof in the Early Common Law" in Morris S Arnold and others (eds), *On the Laws and Customs of England: Essays in Honor of Samuel E. Thorne* (University of North Carolina Press Chapel 1981) 90, 108.

[60] Bartlett (n 59) 1–2, 10–11; Hermann Nottarp, *Gottesurteilstudien* (Kösel Verlag 1956) 248–256; Federico Patetta, *Le Ordalie* (Fratelli Bocca 1890) 188–192; Karl H Hildenbrand, *Die Purgatio canonica und vulgaris* (Munich Literarisch-artistische Anstalt 1841) 108.

[61] 2 Trumble and Stevenson (n 57) 1459 s.v. "Ordeal." See Peter Browe (ed), "Introduction to Peter Browe" in *De ordaliis* 3, 3 (apud aedes Pont Universitatis Gregorianae 1932).

[62] Nottarp (n 60) 30; Browe (n 61) 3. The ordeals of fire and water "all required that the natural elements behave in an unusual way, hot iron or water not burning the innocent, cold water not allowing the guilty to sink." Bartlett (n 59) 2.

Although priests facilitated the procedures of the ordeals by publicly blessing their rituals,[63] the church never employed those procedures in its own tribunals.[64] With the passage of time, some church officials came to strongly oppose the ordeals because they viewed them as lacking any scriptural foundation and any rationality, and as constituting a "temptation of God" (*tentatio Dei*).[65]

In the opinion of some modern scholars, however, the ordeals had a rational substratum and were not wholly ineffective in determining guilt or innocence.[66] In any event, to the extent that the "rational" Roman procedure depended on torture to reveal the truth, the ordeals represented a somewhat less inhumane approach to criminal adjudication.[67]

---

[63] Claudius von Schwerin, "Rituale für Gottesurteile" (Sitzungsberichte der Heidelberger Akademie der Wissenschaften, Philosophisch-historische Klasse, Abhandlung 3, Heidelberg 1933) 53–58; Hyams (n 59) 110; Hildenbrand (n 60) 105–107. At least at times, priests also derived revenue from their service. See Pipe Roll 14 Henry II (Pipe Roll Soc 12, 1890) 48. The authors are grateful to Professor David Seipp for this reference.

[64] Hildenbrand (n 60) 113.

[65] John W Baldwin, "The Intellectual Preparation for the Canon of 1215 against Ordeals" (1961) 36 Speculum 613, 623–624, 626–628; S Grelewski, *La Réaction contre les Ordalies en France depuis le IXe siècle jusqu'au Décret de Gratien* (thesis presented for the University of Strasbourg, Rennes 1924) 74, 82–83; Jean Gaudemet, "Les Ordalies au moyen âge: doctrine, legislation et pratique canoniques" in 17 *La Preuve* (Recueils de la Société Jean Bodin, 1965) 108–109. Keen to suppress crime, some secular authorities, as well, indicated their misgivings about the results of the ordeals. In England, persons cleared in ordeals were, nonetheless, banished in accordance with the Assizes of Clarendon and Northampton. RC van Caenegem, "Reflexions on Rational and Irrational Modes of Proof in Medieval Europe" (1990) 58 Tijdschrift voor Rechtsgeschiedenis 263, 277; see also Raoul C van Caenegem, "Public Prosecution of Crime in Twelfth-Century England" in CNL Brooke and others (eds), *Church and Government in the Middle Ages: Essays Presented to C.R. Cheney* (CUP 1976); Finbarr McAuley, "Canon Law and the End of the Ordeal" (2006) 26 Oxford J Legal Stud 473.

[66] A recent theory as to the functional effectiveness of trial by ordeal suggests that popular belief in its reliability "created a separating equilibrium. Guilty defendants expected ordeals to convict them. Innocent defendants expected the reverse. Thus only innocent defendants were willing to undergo ordeals. Conditional on observing a defendant's willingness to do so, the administering [judge] knew he was innocent and manipulated the ordeal to find this." Peter T Leeson, "Ordeals" (2012) 55 JL & Econ 691, 692. By contrast, the solemn religious service preceding the ordeal, during which the priest adjured the accused not to come to the altar to receive communion if guilty of the crime charged, must often have induced confessions from guilty persons before the ordeal itself even commenced. See Dominique Barthélemy, "Présence de l'aveu dans le déroulement des ordalies (IXe–XIIIe siècle)" in *L'aveu. Antiquité et moyen-âge* 89, 97 (L'École française de Rome 1986) 191, 195–198.

In one authoritative opinion, trial by ordeal "made sense. Intellectually coherent, not contradicted by the available evidence and well-suited to attaining its avowed ends, it invoked a powerful and omniscient deity to manifest justice through the transformation of the physical elements." Bartlett (n 59) 164. For a particularly thoughtful analysis of the essentially positive role trial by ordeal played in the development of the Western legal tradition, see Hyams (n 59) 125–126; Kenneth Pennington, *The Prince and the Law, 1200–1600* (University of California Press 1993) 132–135.

For an assessment of traditional and revised scholarly opinions on the ordeals, see van Caenegem, "Reflexions" (n 65) 263. Although some scholars see possibilities for rationality in the ordeals, the decretals of Greg IX contain letters of three popes (Coelestinus III, Innocent III, and Honorius III), expressing concern that innocent persons were being convicted and reaffirming that vulgar purgations were to be suppressed. See Decretals Greg. IX, 5.35. i–iii.

[67] Unequivocally inhumane and thoroughly irrational, however, was another means of determining guilt or innocence: trial by battle, in which accuser and accused, or their representatives, mounted or on foot and armed with deadly weapons, fought to the death. See Bartlett (n 59) 110–111; J Declareuil, "Les preuves judiciaires dans le droit franc, du Ve au VIIIe siècle" (1899) 23 Nouvelle Revue historiques de droit français et étranger (pt 6) 313, 351–354; C de Smedt, "Les origines du duel judiciaire" (1894) 63 Études religieuses philosophiques, historiques et littéraires 337, 344. The church barred these vicious proceedings from its own courts, but tolerated resort to them by secular courts. Baldwin (n 65) 621–623; Bernhard Schwentner,

The church for its part maintained for criminal cases the Roman law principles that Pope Gregory I had definitively adopted. These procedures, however, left a problem unresolved. If a clerical defendant were acquitted because witness testimony was lacking and the defendant made no confession, suspicion of his guilt might still linger to scandalize the public. For this reason, Pope Gregory I directed that some persons in this position swear an oath affirmatively asserting their innocence in a holy location.[68] In 726, Pope Gregory II made the public taking of such an oath of purgation a rule for the church courts.[69] This practice ultimately came to be called "canonical purgation" (*purgatio canonica*),[70] as opposed to the "vulgar purgation" (*purgatio vulgaris*) of the ordeals.[71]

Summary and Conclusions

After the emperor Constantine had legitimated the Christian church in the fourth century, the church began to exercise a limited criminal jurisdiction. In doing so, the church adopted key norms of long-standing Roman law. Ecclesiastical procedure, like that of Rome, was accusatorial in nature. At trial, the accused was to be present and to have an opportunity to defend before an impartial judge according to a judicial order of proceeding. Influenced by earlier Jewish principles, the church required two witnesses for conviction. Probably again drawing on its Jewish legal inheritance, the church tried to ameliorate the common Roman use of torturing witnesses or defendants. Augustine made clear that conviction could not rest upon suspicions alone. In the absence of sure proofs of guilt, or alternatively, a confession willingly made, it was better to acquit, even though the accused might be factually guilty.

In the early seventh century, Pope Gregory, reflecting Roman law norms, detailed what constituted a fair ecclesiastical trial. There must be a proper order of proceeding with the accused present and given the opportunity to defend. The burden of proof lay on the accuser. Accusers and witnesses must be legitimate and not motivated by hatred. In sworn testimony, they must speak of what they directly knew and not rely

---

"Die Stellung der Kirche zum Zweikampfe bis zu den Dekretalen Gregors IX" (1930) 111 Theologische Quartalschrift 190, 202, 207–212, 215–217; C de Smedt, "Le duel judiciaire et l'Église" (1895) 64 Études religieuses philosophiques, historiques et littéraires 35, 54–64; E Vacandard, "L'Église et les Ordalies" in J Gabalda (ed), 1 *Études de critique et d'histoire religieuse* (5th edn, Librairie Victor Lecoffre 1913) (4 vols) 189, 199, 207–212.

[68] Hildenbrand (n 60) 41.

[69] Ibid 52. Here the pope was implicitly adopting a practice of the secular courts by which persons of good reputation could clear themselves of suspicion of a crime by solemnly swearing to their innocence. As to that practice, see Bartlett (n 59) 30; Hyams (n 59) 93; Patetta (n 60) 206–208; Declareuil (n 67) (1898) 22 Nouvelle Revue historique de droit français et étranger (pt 2) 457, 479. The content of the oath in the secular proceeding consisted simply of the accused's repeating the precise accusation and declaring, "I am not guilty of it" ("*des byn ich unschuldig*"). Richard Loening, *Der Reinigungseid bei Ungerichtsklagen im Deutschen Mittelalter* (Heidelberg 1880, reprint Ulan Press 2012) 15.

[70] Hildenbrand (n 60) 52, 57–60, 76, 94–97; Édouard Beaudoin, "Remarques sur la preuve par le serment du défendeur dans le Droit franc" (1896) 8 Annales de l'Université de Grenoble 495–503. As to the origin of the term *purgatio canonica* in the twelfth century, see Baldwin (n 65) 617 & n 27.

[71] Hildenbrand (n 60) 121–122; Gaudemet, "Les Ordalies au moyen âge" (n 65) 107–108; Baldwin (n 65) 617 & n 27.

on hearsay. In doubtful matters, the accused ought not to be convicted. Any sentence should also accord with proper order.

Where evidence did not support conviction but suspicion lingered after trial, a defendant could be ordered to swear to his or her innocence and to produce other persons who would swear that they believed in the defendant's truthfulness (canonical purgation). The church's "rational" procedure, predominantly based on Roman law, was distinct from the Germanic custom of trial by "vulgar purgation," that is, by ordeal.

It is noteworthy that, in fashioning its procedural principles for resolving disputes and disciplinary matters, the church did more than simply absorb Roman procedural principles. It rooted them in a new soil of divine authority. St Paul had claimed that judgments made without allowing an opportunity for defense were not "the custom among the Romans." Having thus entered into Christian scripture in the Acts of the Apostles, Christian writers could now consider the Roman procedural norm as more than secular. It was a matter of God's law.[72] Thus, Athanasius, citing Paul's trial, said the conviction of a person in the absence of the other party was "prescribed even by divine law." So, too, the "two witness" rule, rooted in the *Book of Deuteronomy*, carried the authority of sacred scripture.[73] It was "the law of God," Augustine preached, that required any judgment to be based on a voluntary confession or on a conviction supported by sound proof and arrived at through due process (according to judicial order and integrity). The rooting of procedural norms in divine authority would continue to mark the development of judicial procedure in the later Middle Ages and even into seventeenth-century England.

[72] Schmoeckel (n 6).
[73] Deut 19:15.

3

Defensive Protections in the Western Church of the Ninth Century

Hincmar of Rheims's *De presbiteris criminosis*

The ninth century marked a singularly prolific period in the development of norms for ecclesiastical criminal trials.[1] Biblical, patristic, and conciliar texts, along with what Roman texts survived in the West,[2] offered materials that popes, bishops, and even an ingenious group of forgers could draw upon to creatively articulate fair trial procedures.

Hincmar of Rheims (c 806–882), the outstanding ninth-century scholar of both secular and ecclesiastical law,[3] became Archbishop of Rheims in 845.[4] A prolific writer on legal topics, he was heavily involved in public controversies of church and state,[5] exercising enormous influence on the development of the criminal law of the church. In his work, *De presbiteris criminosis* (*Concerning accused priests*), written around 876,[6] Hincmar drew on numerous Roman and canonical authorities to set out comprehensively what he determined should be the procedural requirements for adjudicating criminal charges against clerics. He did this, perhaps, to aid the papacy in its consideration of the appeals by clerics deposed from their posts for misconduct.[7]

De presbiteris criminosis reflects a period of transition in the history of criminal procedure. On the one hand, it affirms fundamental aspects of the evidence-based principles of Roman and canon law practices. On the other hand, it grafts onto those practices a Frankish custom of compurgation. That was a secular practice by which

---

[1] On the significance of ninth-century procedural developments in the church, see Mathias Schmoeckel, *Die Jugend der Justitia: Archäologie der Gerechtigkeit der Patristik* (Mohr Siebeck 2013) 190–209.

[2] On the principal Roman legal materials surviving in the West, see Antonia Fiori, "Roman Law Sources and Canonical Collections in the Early Middle Ages" 34 Bull Medieval Canon L (n.s.) 1, 4.

[3] For biographical material, see Rachel Stone and Charles West, *Hincmar of Rheims: Life and Work* (Manchester University Press 2015); "Hincmar of Reims" in 1 *The New Encyclopedia Britannica* (15th edn, Encyclopedia Britannica 2007) (vol 1) 932–933; HGJ Beck, "Hincmar of Reims" in *New Catholic Encyclopedia* (2nd edn, Gale 2003) (32 vols) 837; Heinrich Schrörs, *Hinkmar, Erzbischof von Reims: Sein Leben und seine Schriften* (1st edn, Herder 1884, reprint G Olms 1967) 389–415; Jean Devisse, *Hincmar et la loi* (Dakar s n 1962) 72–89. For Hincmar's use of Roman law sources, see Simon Corcoran, "Hincmar and His Roman Legal Sources" in Stone and West (n 3) 129–155.

[4] Schrörs (n 3) 38–39.

[5] See, e.g., ibid 136–137, 142–148 (Hincmar's writings on predestination), 188–205 (Hincmar's writings on the divorce of King Lothar and Queen Theutberga). Hincmar's position with regard to the royal divorce is analyzed in detail in Abigail Firey, *A Contrite Heart: Prosecution and Redemption in the Carolingian Empire* (Brill 2009) 13–17, 36–44, 56–58.

[6] Gerhard Schmitz, *De presbiteris criminosis: ein Memorandum Erzbischof Hinkmars von Reims über straffällige Kleriker* (Hannsche Buchhandlung 2004) 1, 4–5.

[7] Ibid 6–7; Schrörs (n 3) 374–375.

multiple oath-helpers (compurgators) supported a defendant's own oath of purgation by swearing to their belief in the defendant's truthfulness.[8] Hincmar borrowed the custom of oath-helpers as a means for bringing to a conclusion matters where guilt or innocence was left in doubt.[9]

Hincmar used provisions of the Theodosian Code, as transmitted through the Breviarium and its *Interpretatio*, to establish that an accuser must personally be present to make the accusation, that it be in writing,[10] and that the trial be conducted in the place where the crime was committed.[11] He quotes the Bible for the principle, also present in Roman law, that one shall not be punished twice in the same matter:[12]

> Of what nature, therefore, the procedure should be in accusation and adjudication, St. Augustine, explaining the opinion of the Apostle [Paul] ... set out: "He says, the Apostle did not want man to be judged by man by an opinion based on suspicion or even by procedure applied out of order, but preferably by the law of God according to the order of the church, either having voluntarily confessed or having been accused and convicted, meaning that [kind of] charge that is made against someone when a judgment is pronounced according to judicial order and with integrity. For, if accusation suffices, many innocent persons must be condemned, because often a charge is alleged falsely against someone.[13]

---

[8] Karl H Hildenbrand, *Die Purgatio canonica und vulgaris* (Munich Literarisch-artistische Anstalt 1841) 56–58. "Oath-helper" is a modern designation of a person who swore in support of the defendant; there was no contemporary description of this individual other than the vernacular term for "witness." Rudolf Ruth, *Zeugen und Eideshelfer in den deutschen Rechtsquellen des Mittelalters* (M. & H. Markus 1922) (pt 1) 4. As to the secular practice, see ibid 225–230; J Declareuil, "Les preuves judiciares dans le droit franc du Vᵉ au VIIIᵉ siècle" (1898) 22 Nouvelle Revue historique de droit français et étranger (pt 1) 220, 256–257; (1899) 23 Nouvelle Revue historique de droit français et étranger (pt 5) 188, 188–190; Édouard Beaudoin, "Remarques sur la preuve par le serment du défendeur dans le Droit franc" (1896) 8 Annales de l'Université de Grenoble 407, 413–416, 464. The oath-helpers swore to their belief that the accused's own oath of innocence was "pure and not false" (*"reyne und unmeyne"*). Richard Loening, *Der Reinigungseid bei Ungerichtsklagen im Deutschen Mittelalter* (Heidelberg 1880, reprint Ulan Press 2012) 17 n 2.

[9] Hincmar, *De presbiteris criminosis* c 5, in *De presbiteris criminosis* (n 6) 85. For a ninth-century application of evidence-based Roman and canon law practices, probably orchestrated by Hincmar himself, in a case where purgation of the defendant by oath was foreclosed, see Frank R Herrmann and Brownlow M Speer, "Facing the Accuser: Ancient and Medieval Precursors of the Confrontation Clause" (1994) 34 Va J Int'l L 481, 500–502.

[10] Hincmar, *De presbiteris criminosis* c [5], quoting *Interpretatio* to Breviarium 9.1.9, in *De presbiteris criminosis* (n 6) 69.

[11] Hincmar, *De presbiteris criminosis* c [7], quoting *Interpretatio* to Breviarium 9.1.5, in *De presbiteris criminosis* (n 6) 71.

[12] "The Lord does not punish twice in the same matter" (*Non vindicabit dominus bis in idipsum*). Hincmar, *De presbiteris criminosis* c 5, quoting Nahum 1:9, in *De presbiteris criminosis* (n 6) 87. As to the equivalent rule in Roman law, see text to n 88 in ch 1.

[13] *Qualis ergo debeat ordo in accusatione et diiudicatione, sanctus Augustinus exponens sententiam apostoli: ... Noluit, inquit, apostolus hominem ab homine iudicari ex arbitrio suspicionis vel etiam extraordinario usurpato iudicio, sed potius ex lege dei secundum ordinem ecclesiae sive ultro confessum, sive accusatum atque convictum, eam nominationem volens intellegi, quae fit in quemquam cum sententia ordine iudiciario et quae cum integritate profertur. Nam si nominatio sufficit, multi damnandi sunt innocentes, quia sepe falso in quemquam crimen nominatur.* Hincmar, *De presbiteris criminosis* c 2, quoting, from word *Noluit* through words *crimen nominator*, from Augustine, Sermon 351, c 10, and from word *Diligenter* through words *sententia recitetur*, from Gregory's *commonitorium* to John the Defensor in *De presbiteris criminosis* (n 6) 77–78.

To specify what Hincmar meant by judicial order, he turned to Pope Gregory's *commonitorium*:

> In what way, however, a judgment ought to be pronounced according to the judicial order and with integrity the sacred canons … and St. Gregory, who in his letters frequently ordered that the cases of ecclesiastical ministers be determined legally and regularly (*legaliter et regulariter*) demonstrated in the *commonitorium* given to John the Defensor going into Spain, saying: It must first be investigated carefully that the trial takes place according to proper order, namely, that some are accusers and others are witnesses. Then if the type of charges warrant exile or removal and that the testimony is spoken under oath with the accused present and the records are made in writing and that the accused has opportunity for answering and defending himself. Close examination must be made of the character of the accusers and witnesses, of their type and reputation, or whether they are unfit, or whether they happened to have had previously some animosities against the accused priest, and whether they are giving testimony from hearsay or testify with certainty that they knew specifically, and that judgment is given in writing and that the judgment is recited with the parties present.[14]

The most striking feature of Hincmar's text is his insightful fusion of the core concepts of Augustine's *Sermo 351* with Gregory's *commonitorium*. Augustine had expressed the teleology of criminal justice as the protection of the innocent and the conviction only of those whose guilt could be established with certainty. Gregory had articulated the procedural elements that must underpin a valid judgment. Hincmar's great achievement was his realization that the consistent application of Gregory's procedural requirements is the effective means to arrive at Augustine's goal.[15] By blending the two sources in a single text, Hincmar set out the first truly holistic view of criminal procedure in Western culture.[16]

---

[14] *Qualiter autem sententia ordine iudiciario et cum integritate proferenda sit, sacri canones, ut supradictum est, et sanctus Gregorius, qui frequenter in epistolis suis causas ministrorum ecclesiasticorum legaliter et regulariter praecipit diffiniri, in commonitorio Iohanni defensori eunti in Ispanias dato demonstrat dicens: Diligenter querendum est primum, ut iudicium ordinabiliter fiat, videlicet ut alii accusatores et alii testes sint. Deinde causarum qualitas, si digna exilio vel depositione sit et ut praesente accusato sub iureiurando contra eum testimonium dicatur seu scriptis acta fiant et ut accusatus licentiam respondendi et defendendi se habeat. Sed et de personis accusantium ac testificantium subtiliter querendum est, cuius conditionis cuiusve opinionis, aut ne inopes sint, aut ne forte aliquas contra accusatum sacerdotem inimicitias ante habuerint, et utrum testimonium ex auditu aut certe specialiter se scire testentur, et ut scriptis iudicetur et partibus praesentibus sententia recitetur.* Ibid. Hincmar in his various writings frequently cites the quoted passage from Augustine's Sermon 351. Pertinent citations are collected by Schmitz in *De presbiteris criminosis* (n 6) 77 n 63.

[15] Later Pope Sylvester II (c 980) employed Hincmar's amalgamation. Julien Havet, *Lettres de Gerbert (983–997)* (Alphonse Picard ed, Librairie des Archives nationales et de la Sociéte de l'École des Chartres 1899, reprint Kessinger Publishing LLC 2010) 217.

[16] The text marks the first designation of the procedure mandated by Gregory as the *ordo iudiciarius*. See Linda Fowler-Magerl, *Ordo iudiciorum vel ordo iudiciarius* in 19 Ius Commune Sonderhefte, Repertorium der Früzeit der gelehrten Rechte (Klostermann 1984) 10 & n 25.

The Pseudo-Isidorian Forgeries of the Ninth Century

Shortly after Hincmar commenced his tenure as archbishop of Rheims, other Frankish clerics in his ecclesiastical province, independent of Hincmar, had begun in secret to work on a massive project of forgeries[17] that would significantly affect the framework of Western criminal procedure. Forgery during the Middle Ages was a wide-spread practice.[18] The forgers were commonly clerics and monks, as they were the most likely to be capable of sophisticated techniques of writing. It was the intention of many forgers to present documentary evidence of truths that they were convinced either were or should be the case.[19]

The pseudo-Isidorian forgers wanted to create procedural protections for bishops, whom secular authorities had been removing without cause or legal process throughout the first half of the ninth century. The forgers intended to make the bishops answerable only to the Pope, removing the bishops from the jurisdiction of secular or lesser ecclesiastical authorities.[20] The production of the corpus of forgeries would prove to be an extremely important, indeed defining, event in the development of Western criminal procedure. It has been said there may hardly be found in all of history a second example of so completely successful yet so blatantly artificial a fiction.[21]

In the first forged product directed at this goal, the forgers created a compendium of maxims designed to safeguard the procedural rights of criminally accused bishops. They assembled these maxims, drawn from preexisting secular and ecclesiastical authorities in a "mosaic" fashion,[22] in a single short document with a heading

[17] The project was carried out in the mid-ninth century in the ecclesiastical province of Rheims in the Western Frankish kingdom. Horst Fuhrmann, "The Pseudo-Isidorian Forgeries" in Detlev Jasper and Horst Fuhrmann (eds), *Papal Letters in the Early Middle Ages* (Catholic University of America Press 2001) 135, 170–172. Because of the huge scope of the project, it is assumed that it was carried out by a team rather than a single individual. See ibid 140. The recent research and analysis of Klaus Zechiel-Eckes have established the abbey of Corbie, lying north of Paris about halfway to Calais, as the likely site of the forgers' activity and its abbot, Paschasius Radbertus, as the likely supervisor of the project. See Zechiel-Eckes, "Auf Pseudoisidors Spur. Oder: Versuch, einen dichten Schleier zu lüften" in Wilfried Hartmann and Gerhard Schmitz (eds), *Fortschritt durch Fälschungen? Ursprung, Gestalt und Wirkungen der pseudoisidorischen Fälschungen* (Hahn 2002) 1, 8–14; Karl-Georg Schon, Einleitung to *Die Capitula Angilramni: Eine prozessrechtliche Fälschung Pseudoisidors* (Hahnsche Buchhandlung 2006) 1, 1. See also Fowler-Magerl (n 16) 13–14. Scholars, for convenience, commonly refer to the group of pseudo-Isidorian compilers as "Pseudo-Isidore." The authors here will follow that convention.

[18] Fuhrmann, "The Pseudo-Isidorian Forgeries" (n 17) 588.

[19] On medieval attitudes toward forgery, see Horst Fuhrmann, *Einfluß und Verbreitung der psuedoisidorischen Fälschungen: von ihrem Auftauchen bis in die neuere Zeit* (Hiersemann 1972) 64–85; TF Tout, *Medieval Forgers and Forgeries* (Longmans, Green & Co 1920); Christopher NL Brooke, "Approaches to Medieval Forgery" (1968) 3 Journal of the Society of Archivists 377–386. On the pseudo-Isidorian forgeries in particular, see Fuhrmann, "The Pseudo-Isidorian Forgeries" (n 17) 135–195.

[20] EH Davenport, *The False Decretals* (BH Blackwell 1916) 28–37; Emil Seckel, "Pseudoisidor" in Albert Hauck (ed), 16 *Realencyklopädie für protestantische Theologie und Kirche* (3rd edn, JC Hinrich'sche Buchhandlung 1905) (24 vols) 265, 280–283; Paul Fournier and Gabriel Le Bras, 1 *Histoire des collections canoniques en Occident depuis les Fausses Décrétales jusqu'au Décret de Gratien* (Recueil Sirey 1931) (2 vols) 129–131.

[21] Fuhrmann, *Einfluß* (n 19) 67, referencing Johann von Döllinger, *Der Papst und das Concil von Janus* (EF Steinacker 1869) 103.

[22] Schon (n 17) 3–5; Fuhrmann, "The Pseudo-Isidorian Forgeries" (n 17) 150; 1 Fournier and Le Bras (n 20) 143–144. The word conveys the combining of pieces of various origins—some authentic, some invented—into a composite that the forgers intended to be accepted as entirely genuine.

describing it as having been given by Pope Hadrian to Bishop Angliramnus of Metz in the year 785.[23] The document, therefore, is called the "Capitula Angilramni."[24]

A parallel project with the same aim, completed in the mid-ninth century, purported to be authentic royal enactments of the deceased emperors Charlemagne (774–814) and Louis the Pious (814–840).[25] The introduction to these supposed enactments, styled "capitularies,"[26] falsely claimed that a deacon of the church at Mainz, one "Benedict Levita," (Benedict the Deacon) had discovered them in the church archives as documents overlooked by the compiler of genuine Frankish capitularies.[27] These "False Capitularies" of Benedict Levita[28] were assumed at the time of their appearance to be authentic normative authorities.

The ultimate forgery initiative, the "False Decretals,"[29] produced between 847 and 852,[30] and presumably stemming from the same group of clerics,[31] was more complex and more ingenious. It purported to be a collection of papal decretals[32] by an Isidore Mercator. The name was probably selected to evoke the authority of the renowned Isidore of Seville, a seventh-century Spanish bishop and writer.[33] The decretals, set out in the chronological order of the popes supposedly issuing them, are a mixture

[23] Fuhrmann, "The Pseudo-Isidorian Forgeries" (n 17) 150; 1 Fournier and Le Bras (n 20) 143; Fuhrmann, Einfluss (n 19) 161–162 (Stuttgart 1972 (pt 1), 1973 (pt 2), 1974 (pt 3)).
[24] The Capitula Angilramni are cited here, by chapter, with reference to the pages on which they appear in the edition of Karl-Georg Schon (n 17) 93–166. The text consists of two series of two consecutively numbered chapters, comprising fifty-one and twenty chapters, respectively. 1 Fournier and Le Bras (n 20) 143. The suggestion has been made that this indicates the joining of two separate texts. See Abigail Firey, "Codices and Contexts: The Many Destinies of the Capitula Angilramni and the Challenges of Editing Small Canon-Law Collections" (2008) 94 ZRG (KA) 288, 296.
[25] F Baix, "Benoit le Lévite" in Alfred Baudrillart and others (eds), 8 Dictionnaire d'histoire et de géographie ecclésiastiques (Letouzey et Ané 1935) (32 vols) 213, 213–214; Davenport (n 20) xxi; Fuhrmann, "The Pseudo-Isidorian Forgeries" (n 17) 152; 1 Fournier and Le Bras (n 20) 146.
[26] "Capitulary" (capitulare) is a term first used in 779 in the Frankish realm of Charlemagne to denote an official document, divided by a separate article or chapter (capitulum), publishing a royal legislative or administrative order. See FL Ganshof, Recherches sur les capitulaires (Sirey 1958) 3–6.
[27] Baix (n 25) 213; Fuhrmann, "The Pseudo-Isidorian Forgeries" (n 17) 151–152; Seckel (n 20) 296; 1 Fournier and Le Bras (n 20) 146–147.
[28] The False Capitularies are cited here, by book and chapter, with reference to the pages on which they appear in the edition of Georg Heinrich Pertz (Pertz ____), Benedicti diaconi capitularia (c 850) in Monumenta Germania Historica, 2 Legum (Hannover 1837) (pt 2) 39–159. The text consists of three books, followed by four supplements called additiones. 1 Fournier and Le Bras (n 20) 147–148, 168–169. The additiones are described in detail in Baix (n 25) 214.
[29] The text is described in detail in Fuhrmann, "The Pseudo-Isidorian Forgeries" (n 17) 162–169. The standard modern print edition (see ibid 157–158) is that of Paul Hinschius in Paul Hinschius (ed), Decretales Pseudo-Isidorianae et Capitula Angilramni (B Tauchnitz 1863). The portions of false decretals quoted or mentioned hereafter are cited by the names of the popes (with the prefix "Ps" for "pseudo") purportedly issuing them, followed by the Jaffé registry number and the page of the Hinschius edition (H ____) at which the text in question appears.
Aspects in which the edition is unreliable are succinctly described in John Gilchrist, The Collection in Seventy-Four Titles: A Canon Law Manual of the Gregorian Reform (Pontifical Institute of Medieval Studies 1980) 241.
[30] Fuhrmann, "The Pseudo-Isidorian Forgeries" (n 17) 170.
[31] Ibid 143, 152–153, 171. "[T]he vast extent and skilled preparation make it unlikely that a single person created the forgeries. Instead, we must assume a circle of forgers." Ibid 140.
[32] "Decretals" are "papal letters that answered questions sent to Rome and that gave responses to legal problems." Wilfried Hartmann and Kenneth Pennington, Foreward to Jasper and Fuhrmann (n 17) ix.
[33] Seckel (n 20) 284; Fuhrmann, "The Pseudo-Isidorian Forgeries" (n 17) 160–161; Davenport (n 20) xxii & n 6.

of false and genuine documents. Of 213 decretals, ninety-four are spurious.[34] The collection sets out fundamental procedural principles, many repeating verbatim the maxims found in the earlier forgeries.

The forgers did not write the false decretals from scratch. They audaciously combined thousands of excerpts from preexisting genuine documents.[35] They ascribed these imaginary decretals to popes from the first century onward. Because the false documents included copious excerpts from the Bible,[36] the Theodosian Code,[37] the Visigothic laws,[38] writings of early Church Fathers,[39] and canons of Church councils,[40] the educated reader would erroneously accept a forged decretal unquestioningly because its language was likely to be familiar and its alleged papal source absolutely authoritative. This collection, now known as the "False Decretals" or "Pseudo-Isidorian Decretals," has justly been called "the greatest deception of world history."[41]

The pseudo-Isidorians themselves set out the overarching theme of their procedural reform in a preface to their Decretals. Borrowing without attribution a dictum of Augustine, they laid down as the cornerstone of their reform that however true allegations of misconduct may be in actual fact, they cannot be the basis of judicial condemnation unless they are established by sure proofs, presented in accordance with a prescribed judicial order.[42] To convey this principle, the forgers blended a passage from the real Isidore—Isidore of Seville—with language from Augustine's Sermon 351:

---

[34] False decretals appear at H 21, 30, 46, 52, 60, 65, 66, 75, 81, 87, 90, 94, 102, 104, 105, 108, 109, 113, 115, 116, 118, 120, 122, 124, 125, 127, 129, 131, 133, 135, 137, 143, 147, 148, 151, 156, 160, 167, 170, 172, 175, 180, 183, 189, 191, 194, 195, 197, 200, 204, 206, 210, 214, 218, 220, 223, 226, 230, 233, 238, 242, 247, 452, 456, 464, 476, 484, 491, 494, 498, 502, 509, 519, 525,526, 561, 628 (two), 684, 694, 695, 697, 701, 703, 705, 706, 708, 712, 715, 718, 720, 725, 730, 749. Genuine decretals appear at H 518, 520, 523, 524, 529, 531, 533, 535, 538, 543, 544 (four), 545 (four), 546 (five), 547 (two), 548 (two), 549 (two), 552, 553, 554 (two), 555 (two), 556, 559, 561, 565, 569, 570, 572, 574 (two), 575, 576, 577 (two), 578, 579, 580 (two), 581, 582, 583 (two), 584, 591, 596, 597, 600, 601, 602 (two), 603 (two), 604, 605 (two), 606, 607 (two), 608 (two), 609 (two), 610, 611, 614, 615 (two), 618, 620, 621, 625, 626, 627, 629, 631 (two), 632, 633, 634, 635 (two), 637, 639, 641, 646, 650, 654 (two), 657, 685, 686, 689 (three), 691 (two), 693 (two), 710, 732, 733, 734, 735, 738, 742.

[35] Fuhrmann, "The Pseudo-Isidorian Forgeries" (n 17) 159.

[36] Seckel (n 20) 273; 1 Fournier and Le Bras (n 20) 180; Fuhrmann, "The Pseudo-Isidorian Forgeries" (n 17) 159 & n 91.

[37] The quotations from or paraphrases of provisions of the Theodosian Code are derived from the Breviarium, its *Interpretatio*, and two of its abridgements. 1 Fournier and Le Bras (n 20) 182; Seckel (n 20) 273.

[38] Seckel (n 20) 274.

[39] Ibid; Fuhrmann, "The Pseudo-Isidorian Forgeries" (n 17) 159 & n 92; 1 Fournier and Le Bras (n 20) 182.

[40] Seckel (n 20) 273; 1 Fournier and Le Bras (n 20) 181.

[41] This is the "famous formulation" of Zechiel-Eckes (n 17) 2 n 4, appearing in Johannes Haller, "Gregor VII. und Innozenz III" in Erich Marcks and Karl A von Müller (eds), 1 *Meister der Politik* (2 vols) (Deutsche Verlags-Anstalt 1922) 323, 350. Fowler-Magerl comments that pseudo-Isidorian literature took the term *ordo iudiciarius* from Augustine's Sermo 351 where it had first appeared c 391. Between Augustine's day and the ninth century, Augustine's Sermo 351 had received little attention. Fowler-Magerl (n 16) 15. The pseudo-Isidorians took the term, used it in their preface, and ascribed the term to three different popes. Ibid.

[42] The forgers otherwise made surprisingly little use of the works of Augustine. See 1 Fournier and Le Bras (n 20) 182.

Very many good Christians ... remain silent ... and bear the sins of others, which
they know, because they are often lacking evidence by which they could prove to
the ecclesiastical judges those things which they themselves know, because, although
some things might be true, nevertheless, they must not be believed by the judges unless they are demonstrated by sure proofs, unless they are convincingly established
by a manifest judgment, unless they are made public according to the judicial order.[43]

Safeguards for the Accused

The Pseudo-Isidorian documents repeatedly sought to emphasize elements protective of defendants in criminal proceedings:

A confession must be voluntary

The pseudo-Isidorians are the first source in Western legal history to maintain that an
involuntary confession has no validity as proof of guilt and should play no part in the
fact-finding process:[44]

[I]f some writings might somehow have been wrung from [*extortae*] ... persons
through fear or fraud or through force ... we declare that this shall result in no prejudice or harm to them ... For every confession that is made from necessity is not to be
credited ... Indeed, a confession should not be compelled in such ways, but should
be voluntary ... For every confession should not be wrung out [*extorqueri*] in such
ways, but rather proffered voluntarily; for the worst thing is to judge anyone on the
basis of suspicion or an extorted confession.[45]

---

[43] *Plerique vero christiani boni ... tacent, et portant aliorum peccata quae noverunt, quia documentis
sepae deseruntur quibus ea quae ipsi sciunt iudicibus ecclesiasticis probare possint, quoniam licet vera sint
quaedam, non tamen iudicibus credenda sunt, nisi quae certis indiciis demonstrantur, nisi quae manifesto
iudicio convincuntur, nisi quae iudiciario ordine publicantur.* Praefatio Sancti Isidori libri huius c 5 (H 18).
   This passage, with minor variations in wording, tracks Augustine's sermon on doing penance through
the word "*demonstrantur.*" The passage concludes with two clauses taken from Isidore of Seville, *Synonyma*
II.86 (c 610), 83 PL 825, 864. Pseudo-Isidore returns at other points in the False Decretals to Isidore of
Seville's restatement of the core principle of Augustine's sermon.
[44] See Piero Fiorelli, "Confessione Diritto romano e intermedio" in A Giuffré (ed), 8 *Enciclopedia del
diritto* (Varese 1961) (64 vols) 864, 866–867.
[45] *[S]i huiusmodi personis quaedam scripturae quoquomodo per metum aut fraudem aut per vim extortae
fuerint, ... ad nullum eis praeiudicium aut nocumentum pervenire censemus ... Confessio vero in talibus non
compulsa, sed spontanea fieri debet ... Omnis enim confessio quae fit ex necessitate fides non est ... Confessio
vero non extorqueri debet in talibus, sed potius sponte profiteri, pessimum est enim de suspitione aut extorta
confessione quemquam iudicare.* Ps-Alexander I c 7 (JK †24; H 97–98).
   The first sentence quoted above draws on language from Lex Visigothorum II.5.9, rubric ("*omnis scrip-
tura ... que per vim et metum extorta fuerit, valere non poterit*") ("every writing ... that is twisted out
through force and fear, cannot have any worth") in Karl Zeumer (ed), *Leges Visigothorum* (MGH, I Legum
Sectio I, Bibiopolii Hahniani 1902).
   The words "*pessimum est*" through "*iudicare,*" without the words "*aut extorta confessione,*" and with the
words "*et periculosum*" ("and dangerous") following "*pessimum,*" appear also in the False Capitularies
III.259 (Pertz 118) and III.464 ("*quempiam*" in place of "*quemquam*; Pertz 132), where they are drawn
from Isidore of Seville, *Synonyma* II.85.864 (n 43) ("*Periculosum est de suspectione quempiam judicare*").

So much of this passage as condemns an involuntary confession appears to be of the forgers' own draftsmanship.

Crime must be charged in writing

The Pseudo-Isidorians adopted the Roman law requirement of a formal written charge:

[B]efore an inscription no one may be adjudged or condemned, the same as, indeed, the secular laws require.[46]

Accusers and the accused must both be present when accusation is formally made

The simultaneous presence in court of accuser and accused was a major concern of Pseudo-Isidorians:

Certainly, the accuser shall not be heard when the adverse party is absent; and a judgment declared by a judge in the absence of the other party shall have no force; and an absent person cannot accuse or be accused through another.[47]

The accused must have opportunity to defend

Drawing on the words of Acts 25:16 (Paul's trial), pseudo-Isidore stressed the need for an accused to have a fair chance to rebut an accusation:

---

[46] *[A]nte inscripcionem nemo debet iudicari vel damnari, cum et saeculi leges hec eadem retineant.* Ps.-Damasus I c 16 (JK †243; H 504). This sentence is derived from the *interpretatio* to Breviarium 9.1.11 (*Ante inscriptionem nemo efficitur criminosus* [Before an inscription no one is made a criminal defendant]).

[47] *Absente vero adversario non audiatur accusator; nec sententia, absente parte alia, a iudice dicta ullam obtinebit firmitatem; neque absens per alium accusare aut accusari potest.* Ps.-Felix I c 13 (JK †143; H 202).
   The first clause of the quoted text is a succinct formulation of the rule stated in C Th 11.39.9 and the *interpretatio* to Breviarium 11.14.4 (C Th 11.39.9). It appears also in the False Capitularies Additio IV.17 (Pertz 148). Expanded versions in different wordings appear in ibid III.238 (Pertz 117), Ps.-Telesphorus c 4 (JK †34; H 111–112), and Ps.-Julius I c 12 (JK †196; H 468).
   The second clause appears also, with a slight variation in wording, in the False Capitularies III.204 (Pertz 115), where it is taken from a paraphrase of Pauli Sententiae 5.5.5 included in an eighth-century epitome of the Breviarium (the epitome of Aegidius) written in what is now France. See Gustav Hänel, Prolegomena to Gustav Friedrich Hänel (ed), *Lex Romana Visigothorum* (apud Guilelmum Besserum 1849) V, XXV–XXVI (describing epitome) and ibid 420 (text of paraphrase).
   The third clause consists of language taken directly from Pauli Sententiae 5.5.9, as included in the Breviarium. See ibid 420. It appears also in the False Capitularies III.354 (Pertz 124) and Additio III.102 (Pertz 144), and its substance, in a different wording, appears in Ps.-Stephen I c 8 (JK †131; H 185).

[I]t is not proper to adjudge or condemn anyone, before he has legitimate accusers present and receives opportunity of defending in order to purge the criminal charges.[48]

The accused must receive a fair trial before an impartial judge

As a device for emphasizing that the trial accorded to an accused person must be "fair," pseudo-Isidore modified *iudicium* with the word *iustum*:

You should condemn no one before a true and fair trial.[49]

As a necessary condition for such a trial, the judge must have no personal interest in the outcome of the proceeding:

Let no one presume to be accuser and at the same time judge or witness.[50]

Nor may the judge be subject to extraneous influence:

To be sure, an unfair trial and an unfair decision pronounced by judges from fear of, or on command of, the king is not valid.[51]

---

[48] *[N]on oportet quemquam iudicare vel damnare, priusquam legitimos habeat praesentes accusatores locumque defendendi accipiat ad abluenda crimina.* Ps.-Marcellus c 9 (JK †161; H 227). This sentence is modeled on Jerome's Latin version of the trial of St Paul in Acts 25:16 which was quoted over four centuries earlier in a genuine writing of Pope Zosimus. The substance of the quoted text appears also, in different wordings, in the False Capitularies I.392 (Pertz 69), II.381 (Pertz 94), and III.184 (Pertz 114); the Capitula Angilramni c 19 (Schon 126); Ps.-Stephen I c 8 (JK †131; H 185); Ps.-Julius I c 17 (JK †196; H 472–473); Ps.-Damasus I c 19 (JK †243; H 505); and Ps.-Damasus I ad episcopos per Italiam constitutos (JK †245; H 520).

[49] *Neminem condempnetis ante verum et iustum iuditium.* Ps.-Melchiades c 2 (JK †171; H 243). The sentence is based on False Capitularies III.259 (Pertz 118) ("*Nullus quemquam ante iustum iudicium damnet*"), where the word "*iustum*" is inserted before the word "*iudicium*" as it appears in Isidore of Seville, *Synonyma* II.85.864 (n 43) ("*Nullum condemnes ante iudicium*"). See Emil Seckel, "Studien zu Benedictus Levita (pt.8[2])" (1916) 40 Neues Archiv 15, 21–22 n 4. The phrase "*iustum iudicium*" in the sense of "just judgment" was used by Augustine. Augustine, Letter to Macedonius (Epistle 153 no 23) (414), 33 Patrologia Latina 653, 663–664. Pseudo-Isidore maintained the position that, even in cases in which the crime was manifest, an *ordo* was necessary. "He granted to the accused the right to a trial—even a very extensive one—in almost every thinkable case. This approach made it next to impossible to proceed judicially against a bishop." Fowler-Magerl (n 16) 13–14.

[50] *Nec ullus umquam praesumat accusator simul esse et iudex vel testis.* Ps.-Fabian c 22 (JK †93; H 165). This page appears to be of the forgers' own draftsmanship, intended to express more emphatically the principle of judicial impartiality reflected in False Capitularies III.152 (Pertz 112) ("*Ut nullus in sua causa iudicet*" ["No one should judge in his own case"]), where it is drawn from the *interpretatio* to Breviarium 2.2.1 (C Th 2.2.1) ("*ut nullus in sua causa iudex sit*").

[51] *Iniustum enim iudicium et definitio iniusta regio metu vel quacum a iudicibus ordinata non valet.* Ps.-Symmachus, sixth synod (entry immediately preceding JK †757; H 683). The source of this text is Lex Visigothorum II.1.29, rubric, in Zeumer (ed), *Leges Visigothorum* (n 45) 76. It appears also in the False Capitularies I.405 (Pertz 69) and the Capitula Angilramni c 18 (bis) (Schon 164), and with a slight variation in wording ("*regis*" for "*regio*") in Ps.-Marcellinus c 4 (JK †159; H 223). The same text, with insertions of other words, is included within Ps.-Calixtus I c 6 (JK †85; H 137).

Judgment must not be based on doubtful proofs

The Pseudo-Isidorians repeated a key phrase that Pope Gregory I had formulated to begin an assertion that the level of proof in criminal cases must be high:

> In a matter that is doubtful, a judgment that is certain should not be pronounced.[52]

Judgment must not be rushed or guilt presumed

Pseudo-Isidore, excerpting a passage from Augustine on Job, but setting it in a false letter of Pope Evaristus, employed the authority of the biblical story of Sodom to warn against presuming to believe evil deeds attributed to anyone are true before they are proven. On hearing reports of evil acts in Sodom, God himself said:

> I shall descend and shall see whether the clamor which has come to me they have done in deed, or whether it is not so as I know.

If even God would investigate before reaching judgment, how much more ought humans to do so:

> God almighty, to whom nothing is hidden but all things are manifest even before they happen, ... deigned himself to inquire [about the truth of evil reports of Sodom] ... to give us an example, lest we be rash in matters that must be investigated and judged, and lest anyone presume to believe bad deeds of any persons rather than to prove them.[53]

In a similar vein, pseudo-Isidore mined Augustine's sermon on penance to require receipt of proofs according to a regular procedure, attributing the insight to pre-Augustinian popes. The passage exemplifies pseudo-Isidore's practice of repeating the same phrases in different documents to convey the sense of an unchallengeable rule of law supported by multiple authorities that reached back almost to the dawn of Christianity:

> For, concerning things hidden in the heart of another, it is a sin to judge rashly and it is unfair to blame on the basis of suspicion one whose works do not seem to be other

---

[52] *Neque in re dubia certa iudicetur sententia.* Ps.-Zepherinus c 4 (JK †80; H 131). The source of this sentence is Gregory I, Register 10.11. It appears also in Ps.-Felix I c 2 (JK †142; H 198) and Ps.-Julius I c 12 (JK †196; H 471).

[53] Letter of Pope Evaristus, H (n 29) 92: *Deus omnipotens, cui nihil absconditum est, sed omnia ei manifesta sunt, aetiam antequam fiant ... per se inquirere dignatus est, nisi ut nobis examplum daret ne praecipites in discutiendis et iudicandis negotiis essemus, et ne mala quorumquam prius quisquam praesumat credere quam probare.* This text was widely received in canonical collections after Ps.-Isidore. See Fuhrmann, "The Pseudo-Isidorian Forgeries" (n 17) III 826. *ne innocentium periclitentur si nimium festinetur sententia.* Fowler-Magerl (n 16) 2 n 4: canonical trials, unlike those of ancient Rome, were to be extended, "in order to impede endangering the rights of innocent" ("um zu verhindern, daß die Rechte 'Unschuldiger' gefährdet würden"). Adopted in C 2, q.1 c 20.

than good, since of those things that are unknown to man, God alone may be a just judge and a true examiner. Wherefore, it is written: let us not judge matters that are uncertain until the Lord, who will illumine the hidden things of the darkness and make manifest the purposes of hearts, comes . . . . And however much these things may be true, they are nevertheless, not to be believed[54] unless they are proven by sure proofs, unless they are established by a manifest judgment, unless they are published according to the judicial order. No one, therefore, whom God has reserved for his own judgment can be convicted by human examination.[55]

Witness testimony must be given orally based on personal knowledge

Pseudo-Isidore appropriated from a law of Chindasvind, King of Visigothic Spain (643–653), a precise limitation on the content of witness testimony. Under the Visigothic formulation adopted by pseudo-Isidore, a witness may testify only orally and only on the basis of first-hand knowledge acquired through direct sensory perception:[56]

[W]itnesses shall not proffer testimony through any writing, but while present shall truthfully speak about what they saw and knew. And they shall not speak testimony

---

[54] Consistent with the forgers' purpose of establishing a high level of proof for conviction, they redact the Augustinian text "easily to be believed" by deleting "easily." Moreover, they adjust the expression from Augustine's sermon from "*certis indiciis*" and substitute "*manifestis indiciis*," strengthening the quantum of proof needed for conviction. See Fowler-Magerl (n 16) 16.

[55] *De occultis enim cordis alieni temere iudicare peccatum est, et eum cuius non videntur opera nisi bona, iniquum est ex suspitione reprehendere, cum eorum quae homini sunt incognita, solus deus iudex sit iustus, inspector et verus. Unde scriptum est: Incerta non iudicemus quoad usque veniat dominus qui et inluminabit abscondita tenebrarum et manifestabit consilia cordium. Et quamvis vera sint, non tamen credenda sunt, nisi que certis inditiis comprobantur, nisi que manifesto iuditio convincuntur, nisi que iudiciario ordine publicantur. Nullus ergo potest humano condemnari examine quem deus suo iuditio reservavit.* Ps.-Sixtus II c 7 (JK †134; H 193).

The first sentence of this passage is taken, with slight variations in wording, from Prosper of Aquitaine, *Liber sententiarum* c 21 (c 440), 51 PL 427, 431. It appears also, with other variations in wording, in Ps.-Zepherinus c 7 (JK †80; H 132) and, through the word "*reprehendere*," in Ps.-Eusebius c 10 (JK †164; H 237) and Ps.-John I, epistle to Archbishop Zacharia (JK †872; H 694).

The second and third sentences of the passage are derived, with variations in wording, from Isidore of Seville, *Synonyma* II.86.864 (n 43), which in turn is, through the word "*convincuntur*," a paraphrase of portions of Augustine's sermon on doing penance. These sentences are repeated, with variations in wording, in the False Capitularies III.259 (Pertz 118), Ps.-Victor I c 4 (JK †74; H 128), and Ps.-Julius I c 12 (JK †196; H 469).

The final sentence of the passage is also derived from Isidore of Seville's *Synonyma*. It appears, with variations in wording, in the False Capitularies III.259 (Pertz 118) and III.373 (Pertz 125), and the Capitula Angilramni c 12 (bis) (Schon 160), Ps.-Alexander I c 7 (JK †24; H 98), Ps.-Eleutherus c 5 (JK †68; H 126–127), Ps.-Fabianus c 17 (JK †93; H 163–164), and Ps.-Julius I c 19 (JK †196; H 474).

[56] The Visigothic formulation and its adoption by pseudo-Isidore are significant events in the development of the rule against hearsay in the Western legal culture. See Joshua C Tate, "Roman and Visigothic Procedural Law in the False Decretals of Pseudo-Isidore" (2004) 90 Zeitschrift der Savigny-Stiftung für Rechtsgeschichte (Kan Abt) 516–518; Frank R Herrmann, "The Establishment of a Rule against Hearsay in Romano-Canonical Procedure" (1995) 36 Va J Int'l L 1, 27–28.

about other cases or matters except about those which are known to have been done in their presence.[57]

Trial must take place where it is claimed the crime was committed

The Pseudo-Isidorians took a rule on trial venue in criminal cases from the Visigothic abridgement of the Theodosian Code:

The case shall always be conducted in the place where the crime is committed.[58]

Many of these elements are joined in a lengthy passage ascribed to Pope Damasus I (366–384) writing to the Italian bishops.[59] The passage memorably expresses a cen-´ tral idea of accusatorial procedure with the vivid phrase *praesens per praesentem*. The simultaneous physical presence of accuser and accused is necessary for the making of a valid criminal accusation:

It has been reported to the Apostolic See that you receive accusations of the brothers through written instruments without a legitimate accuser. Henceforth, by our apostolic authority, we prohibit this from happening, and ask you to correct what has recently been done without any delay and not first to examine through written instruments the case of those who are accused unless, through the procedures of making complaint, they, having been canonically summoned, come to the synod and one personally present learns truly and understands from one personally present what things are charged against him.

In this false letter of Pope Damasus I (366–384), the pseudo-Isidorians have emphasized that the summoning of the accused is an initial and indispensable step for proper procedure. Canonists of the high Middle Ages would view this requirement as a mandate of both divine and natural law. While the summoning of a party was a necessary

---

[57] *[T]estes per quamcumque scripturam testimonium non proferant, sed praesentes quam viderunt et noverunt, veraciter testimonium dicant. Nec de aliis causis vel negotiis testimonium dicant, nisi de his que sub praesentia eorum acta esse noscuntur.* Ps.-Calixtus I c 17 (JK †86; H 141).
These two sentences are modeled, with variations in wording, after False Capitularies II.147 (Pertz 80) and II.345 (Pertz 90), where they are drawn, again with variations in wording, from Lex Visigothorum II.4.5 (*Testes non per epistulam testimonium dicant, sed presentes quam noverunt non taceant veritatem nec de aliis negotiis testimonium dicant, nisi de his tantummodo, que sub presentia eorum acta esse noscuntur*) in Zeumer (ed), *Leges Visigothorum* (n 45) 98. The second sentence appears, with further variations in wording, in Ps.-Damasus I ad episcopos per Italiam constitutos (JK †245; H 519–520).

[58] *Ibi semper causa agatur, ubi crimen admittitur.* Ps.-Sixtus III to the Eastern bishops (JK †397; H 563). This is a paraphrase of the *interpretatio* to Breviarium 9.1.5. Its source is a seventh- or eighth-century epitome of unknown authorship written in what is now France. See Hänel (n 47) XXVI–XXVII (describing epitome), and *Lex Romana Visigothorum* (n 47) (text of paraphrase) 170.
The same rule is stated, in slightly different wording, in the False Capitularies III.365 (Pertz 124), the Capitula Angilramni c 47 (Schon 147), and Ps.-Fabianus c 28 (JK †94; H 168).

[59] Letter of Ps.-Damasus ad episcopos per Italiam constitutos (JK †245; H 519–520).

condition for a fair proceeding, it was hardly sufficient. The letter of pseudo-Pope Damasus continues:

> [T]he secular laws demand that accusers be present and not through written instruments absent. Hence, the canonical laws of the [church] fathers, not once but very often, declare that no accusations nor any testimony whatever can proceed through written instruments, and that none shall give testimony about matters other than those of which they learned in their presence. Similarly, whoever chooses to accuse someone shall accuse while personally present and not through another, an *inscriptio*, of course, having been made first, and no one ever shall be judged before he has lawful accusers present and receives opportunity for defense to clear himself of the charges.[60]

Ps-Damasus made clear that accusers and witnesses had to be personally present and could not merely testify through writings. Moreover, testimony was to be limited to matters within the witness's first-hand knowledge. These requirements were derived ultimately from the Law of the Visigoths.[61] The last clause quoted, requiring the presence of accusers and opportunity for the accused to defend, is based on Acts 25:16 concerning the trial of St Paul.

By gathering legal principles previously fashioned in Roman and ecclesiastical sources and recasting them in an aggressively pro-defense context, Pseudo-Isidore laid the foundation for a later criminal jurisprudence based on protecting specific rights of accused persons. The pseudo-Isidorian principles were transmitted into later collections of canons. There, they were accepted as genuine authoritative pronouncements, just as the forgers had hoped. Consequently, the pseudo-Isidorian literature remained normative for procedural questions in canon law for the ensuing three hundred years.[62]

Papal Legislation in the Ninth Century

The focus on procedural protections underlying the pseudo-Isidorian decretals is manifested also in significant genuine contemporary papal legislation.[63] In the second half of the ninth century, a decretal of Pope Nicholas I (858–867) unequivocally

---

[60] *Relatum est enim ad sedem apostolicam vos accusationes fratrum per scripta suscipere absque legitimo accusatore. Quod deinceps in omni orbe terrarum fieri apostolica auctoritate prohibemus et quod nuper factum est absque ulla retardatione corrigere rogamus, nec umquam prius per scripta eorum qui accusantur causam discutere, nisi per quaerellantium institutiones vocati canonicae ad synodum veniant et praesens per praesentem agnoscat veraciter et intellegat quae ei obiciuntur ... [L]eges enim saeculi accusatores praesentes exigunt, et non per scripta absentes. Unde canonica patrum constituta non semel, sed saepissime clamant nec accusationes nec testimonia ulla per scripta posse proferre, nec de aliis negotiis quicumque testimonium dicant, nisi de his quae sub praesentia eorum esse noscuntur. Similiter et qui accusare alium elegerit, praesens per se et non per alium accuset, inscriptione videlicet praemissa, neque ullus umquam iudicetur, antequam legitimos accusatores presentes habeat locumque defendendi accipiat ad abluenda crimina.* Ibid.

[61] Zeumer, *Leges Visigothorum* (n 45) II.4.5.

[62] Fowler-Magler (n 16) 19–28.

[63] A detailed argument for Nicholas's knowledge of the then recently produced pseudo-Isidorian decretals is set out in AV Müller, "Zum Verhältnisse Nicolaus I und Pseudo-Isidors" (1900) 25 Neues Archiv 652, 654–662.

established as law a rule that lies at the heart of criminal procedure in Western culture: to be valid evidence of guilt a defendant's confession must be voluntary.

In 866, the King of the Bulgarians addressed 106 questions to Pope Nicholas on a broad range of issues touching on doctrine and morals.[64] Among these issues, the King put the question whether it was proper to use force to obtain a confession from a criminal defendant. The pope emphatically disapproved:

> If a thief or bandit shall have been seized and shall have denied what is imputed to him, you assert that, among the Bulgarians [apud vos] the judge beats his head with rods and with other iron goads [and] pierces the flanks of him, until at length he draws out the truth. And that conduct neither divine nor human law admits of at all, since a confession ought not to be unwilling but spontaneous [spontanea] and must not be elicited violently but proeerred voluntarily [voluntarie proferenda]; finally if it should happen that, even with these punishments inflicted, you discover absolutely nothing about the matters which are charged as a crime to the one who suffered, will you not at least blush then and acknowledge how wickedly you render judgment?[65]

The pope warns against the danger of false confessions, making the point that an accused's verbal assertion of guilt cannot be reliable evidence unless the accused is affirming what he or she truly believes to be the truth:

> Similarly, moreover, if a man who has been criminally charged, lacking the power to withstand such things as he has suffered, should say that he committed what he did not commit, upon whom, I ask, should the magnitude of such wickedness devolve, but upon him who forced him to falsely confess such things? However much one proffers something by mouth that he does not hold in his heart he should be known not to confess but [merely] to speak.[66] Therefore, relinquish such things and execrate in the marrow of your bones the senseless things you have practiced up to this point; for what fruit did you have then in those things at which you now blush?[67]

---

[64] The occasion for the Bulgarian inquiries of the pope was the Bulgarian king's consideration of transferring his domain, newly converted to Christianity, from the ecclesiastical supervision of Constantinople to that of Rome. See Lothar Heiser, *Die Responsa ad consulta Bulgarorum des Papstes Nikolaus I (858–867)* (Trierer Theologische Studien, Paulinus Verlag 1979) (Bd 36) 40–46. The content of all the questions and answers is summarized ibid 79–89. Schmoeckel observes that Nicholas's letter summarized what was already characteristic of the church's teachings on procedure and proof. Schmoeckel (n 1) 192.

[65] *Si fur vel latro deprehensus fuerit et negaverit quod ei impingitur, asseritis apud vos, quod iudex caput eius verberibus fundat et aliis stimulis ferreis, donec veritatem depromat, ipsius latera pungat. Quam rem nec divina lex nec humana prorsus admittit, cum non invita, sed spontanea debeat esse confessio, nec sit violenter elicienda, sed voluntarie proferenda; denique si contigerit vos etiam illis poenis illatis nihil de his, quae passo crimen obiciuntur, penitus invenire, nonne saltem tunc erubescitis et, quam impie iudicetis, agnoscitis?* Nicholas I, *Ad consulta vestra*, Responsa to the Bulgarians c 86 (JE 2812, November 13, 866) in Ernst Perels (ed), *Monumenta Germaniae Historica*, 6 Epistolarum (Weidman 1912) 568, 595. Schmoeckel (n 1).

[66] "These thoughts correspond completely with those of Augustine, although Nicholas does not cite him." Heiser (n 64) 234.

[67] *Similiter autem, si homo criminatus talia passus sustinere non valens dixerit se perpetrasse quod non perpetravit, ad quem, rogo, tantae impietatis magnitudo revolvitur nisi ad eum, qui hunc talia cogit mendaciter confiteri? Quamvis non confiteri noscatur, sed loqui qui hoc ore profert quod corde non tenet. Relinquite itaque talia et quae hactenus insipientes exercuistis medullitus execramini; quem enim fructum habuistis tunc in illis, in quibus nunc erubescitis?* Nicholas I (n 65) 595.

If proof fails, the accused shall swear on the gospels that he did not commit the alleged crime:

> Henceforth, when a free man shall have been seized on a criminal charge, unless he has already been found to be guilty [*reus*][68] of some crime, either he submits to punishment after having been convicted by three witnesses or, if he could not be convicted, [then], swearing on the holy Gospel that he did not at all commit what is charged against him, he is acquitted,[69] and thenceforth an end is put to this matter, in the manner that repeatedly the said apostle, teacher of the Gentiles [i.e., the apostle Paul] attests saying, "An oath for confirmation is the end of all their controversy."[70]

Less than three months after Nicholas's response to the King of the Bulgars, the pope again had occasion to address the subject of involuntary confession, this time in a letter to the King of France, who was seeking to divorce the queen Theutberga.[71] The pope had received a letter from Theutberga containing a confession of adultery. He rejected the confession as involuntary:

> [W]ho does not know that Theutberga, subjected to many pressures, declared these things against herself and asserted [them] after being worn down by innumerable harms, even dreading the danger of death? . . . . But, in truth, we do not receive such a confession of hers which not her will but force wrung out [*extorsit*], in any way as a confession.[72]

It is reasonably likely that Nicholas's letter reflects credulity in the pseudo-Isidorian requirement that a confession be voluntary.[73] His use of the verb *extorquere* echoes the use of the verb three times in the pertinent pseudo-Isidorian passage.[74] Although the verb can signify the obtaining of something by physical force, both pseudo-Isidore

---

[68] The term *reus* can be ambiguous and has to be understood according to the context in which it is used. *Reus* can mean "defendant" but here the context makes clear that the term means "a guilty person." On the ambiguity of *reus* and the use of the maxim in the Middle Ages, see Richard M Fraher, "'*Ut nullus describatur reus prius quam convincatur*': Presumption of Innocence in Medieval Canon Law?" in Stephen Kuttner and Kenneth Pennington (eds), Proc. Sixth Int'l Congress Medieval Canon L. (1985) 493.

[69] Nicholas "does not describe the examination of slaves or previously convicted perpetrators, but it does not follow from [his] silence that there is any tolerance of torture in these cases [either]," Heiser (n 64) 236.

[70] *Porre cum liber pridem reppertus est alicuius sceleris reus, aut tribus testibus convictus poenae succumbit aut, si convinci non potuerit, ad evangelium sacrum quod sibi obicitur minime commisisse iurans absolvitur, et deinceps huic negotio finis imponitur, quemadmodum crebro dictus apostolus doctor gentium attestatur: "Omnis," inquiens, "controversiae eorum finis ad confirmationem est iuramentum."* Nicholas I (n 65) 595. Discussed in Schmoeckel (n 1) 191.

[71] The background of the royal divorce controversy is described in Firey, *Contrite* (n 5) 13–14.

[72] *Ceterum quis ignorat Theutbergam haec contra se multis pressuris subactam depromere ad innumeris malis attritam, immo mortis periculum formidantem, . . . asserere? . . . Verum nos talem confessionem eius, quam non voluntas, sed vis extorsit, nequaquam pro confessione recipimus.* Nicholas I. *Audito, revertente* (JE 2873, January 24 or 25, 867), Perels (n 65) 322, 323.

[73] Müller (n 63).

[74] See text to n 45.

and Nicholas apply it in a broader sense to comprehend the obtaining of a confession also by moral or psychological compulsion.[75]

Two decades later, Pope Stephen V (885–891) applied Nicholas's doctrine of voluntariness in a specific factual context presented to him by the archbishop of Mainz:

> You have consulted [me] . . . with regard to infants, who, sleeping in the same bed with their parents, are found dead, whether the parents, by hot iron [ferro cadenti] or boiling water [aqua fervente] or by some other ordeal [examine] should show [se purificare] that they did not suffocate them . . . .[T]he sacred canons do not allow a confession to be wrung out [extorqueri] of anyone by the trial [examinatione] of hot iron or boiling water; and what is not sanctioned by the teaching of the holy fathers must not be presumptuously practiced by means of a superstitious invention. For, crimes made known by voluntary confession [spontanea confessione] or by the proof of witnesses, having the fear of God before [their] eyes, have been committed to our authority to adjudicate; but hidden and unknown [crimes] must be relinquished to the judgment of him who alone knows the hearts of the sons of men.[76]

The ninth century also saw papal adoption of a maxim cautioning against assumption of guilt from the fact of accusation.[77] In his response to the King of the Bulgarians, Nicholas quotes the maxim as it appears in De septem ordinibus ecclesiae (Concerning the seven orders of the Church), a tract of unknown authorship, originating several centuries earlier, that Nicholas thought was the work of St Jerome:[78]

> Before you hear, you should not judge anyone nor, before proof of the accusation alleged, you should suspend no one from your communion because it is not one who is accused who is immediately guilty [reus] but one who is convicted as charged.[79]

---

[75] In both texts, the verb extorquere is used in the classical Latin sense of an "allusion to a 'force' of whatever sort, physical or moral." Emilio Albertario, "L'uso classico e l'uso giustinianeo di 'extorquere'" (1911) 32 ZRG (RA) 307, 311.

[76] Consulisti . . . de infantibus, qui in uno lecto cum parentibus dormientes, mortui reperiuntur, utrum ferro candente an aqua ferrente seu alio quolibet examine parentes se purificare debeant, eos non oppressisse . . . Nam ferri cadentis vel aquae ferventis examinatione confessionem extorqueri a quolibet, sacri non censent canones; et quod sanctorum patrum documento sancitum non est, superstitiosa adinventione non est praesumendum. Spontanea enim confessione vel testium approbatione publicata delicta, habito prae oculis Dei timore, commissa sunt regimin nostro iudicare; occulta vero et incognita illius sunt iudicio relinquenda, qui solus novit corda filiorum hominum. Stephen V, Consuluisti etiam (JL 3443, 887/888) in Erich Caspar (ed), Monumenta Germaniae Historica, 7 Epistolarum (Weidman 1928) 347, 348.

[77] See Fraher (n 68) 493, 495–496.

[78] As to the origins of the tract, see RE Reynolds, "The Pseudo-Hieronymian De septem ordinibus Ecclesiae: Notes on Its Origins, Abridgements and Use in Early Medieval Canonical Collections" (1970) 80 Revue Bénédictine 238, 238–239. See also Fraher (n 68) 495–500.

[79] Priusquam audias, ne iudicaveris quemquam atque ante probationem accusationis illatae neminem a tua communione suspendas, quia non statim qui accusatur reus est, sed qui convicitur criminosus. Nicolas I, Ad consulta vestra c 71 (JE 2812, November 13, 866), Perels (n 65) 592, quoting De septem ordinibus Ecclesiae (Epistola 12) (fourth word in original is judices), 30 Patrologia Latina 152, 154. "In the context of the maxim, reus made sense only if one understood the word to mean 'guilty of crime' or 'accountable for a crime.'" Fraher (n 68) 502, but in other usages it means one who is merely accused of a crime. Ibid 503.

The maxim beginning "non statim qui accusatur reus est . . . " appears to be derived ultimately from an imperial constitution of 423 ("non statim reus qui accusari potuit aestimetur, ne subiectam innocentium faciamus"), where the word reus denotes one who has been formally accused of a crime. This original version of the maxim, with a slight change in word order ("aestimetur" or "estimetur" following "reus") appears

Within a decade, Pope John VIII (872–882) applied the maxim to emphasize the need for hearing before proceeding to punishment or ejection from office:

> [B]ecause no one should be adjudged before a hearing....the [accused] priest ought either to be convicted by witnesses or to be adjudged after having confessed everything....[I]f he should be found innocent, his case should be canonically terminated because it is not one who is accused who is immediately guilty, but one who is convicted as charged.[80]

In another decretal, John links together the concept of "hearing" with the Augustinian principle of fair proceedings even for the possibly guilty and the central themes of canonical procedure that Gregory had articulated: personal presence of accusers; requirement of hearing both parties; and no prejudice to accrue to the accused before conviction:

> For we do not allow him [an accused bishop] to be condemned before a hearing, because we cannot and must not judge one party without the other . . . .Even if he perhaps is charged justly, he must not be stripped of his honors nor his possessions, until, with the accused himself as well as his accusers before us at the same time [*simul*], . . . the case reaches its lawful conclusion.[81]

Summary and Conclusions

In the course of the ninth century, three sets of ecclesiastical writings articulated procedural protections for persons accused before church tribunals. First, Archbishop Hincmar of Rheims's *De presbyteris criminosis* (*Concerning criminal priests*) fused the procedural norms of St Augustine in the fourth century with those of Pope Gregory I in the seventh century. Borrowing Augustine's words, Hincmar declared anew that any conviction must be arrived at "according to judicial order and with integrity." In a second development, the pseudo-Isidorians, working in the Frankish region, produced a massive body of documents falsely attributed to popes, councils, and kings with excerpts from valid legal sources. The documents set out safeguards to protect accused bishops. Circulating broadly, the works were accepted as genuine expressions of proper procedure made by the highest authorities. A third authoritative source for

---

repeated in the pseudo-Isidorian corpus. See False Capitularies III.436 (Pertz 130) and Additio IV.26 (Pertz 138); Capitula Angilramni c 6 (Schon 111); and False Decretals, Ps.-Euticianus c 7 (JK †146; H 211).

[80] [Q]*ua ante audientiam iudicari debet, ... aut a testibus convictus aut iudicari debet presbiter quodcunque confessus ... [S]i innocens repertus fuerit, causa eius canonice terminetur, quia non statim qui accusatur reus est, sed qui convincitur criminosus.* John VIII, Lupenandum presbyterum (JE 2992, 874) in Caspar (n 76) 292, 292.
[81] *Nos enim hunc ante audientiam dampnari non patimur, quia unam partem sine altera iudicare non possumus nec debemus ... Qui etsi iuste forsitan criminatur, non debet ante audienciam nec honoribus nec rebus suis nudari, donec tam ipso accusato quam eius accusatoribus simul coram nobis ... causa finem accipiat.* John VIII, Audquarius venerabilis (JE 3002, 874/875), in Caspar (n 76) 298, 299.

procedural principles flowed from genuine papal pronouncements of Popes Nicholas I, Stephen V, and John VIII made in answer to inquiries made to the papal see.

Viewed collectively, the ninth-century documents presented norms protective of defendants at ecclesiastical tribunals.[82] These safeguards mandated that complaints had to be made in writing with parties summoned to be present to hear the charges. Trial was to take place where the crime was purportedly committed. No presumption of guilt arose from the mere making of an accusation. Any conviction had to be based on witness testimony given at a hearing with accuser and accused simultaneously present. The accused had to be provided an opportunity to make a defense before an impartial judge. To be valid, any confession of guilt was required to be made voluntarily. The same accusation was not to be punished twice.

---

[82] Rachel Stone has characterized the attitude of church authorities of the ninth century toward canonical norms: "The Carolingian church hierarchy regarded canons as persuasive norms, but not necessarily as laying down the law in the modern sense. [fn. omitted]. They weren't the final word, even in theory. Instead, they were a framework within which God-inspired men could hand down a judgement that reflected divine law, which was itself beyond all legal codes." Rachel Stone, "Canon Law before Canon Law: Using Church Canons, 400–900 AD," a paper presented to Cambridge Late Antiquity Network Seminar (February 11, 2014) <https://www.academia.edu/7225232/Canon_law_before_canon_law_usi ng_church_canons_400_900_AD>. See also Mathias Schmoekel, *Die Jugend der Justitia: Archäologie der Gerechtigkeit im Prozessrecht der Patristik* (Mohr Siebeck 2013) 190–209.

4

Formulating Fair Trial Procedures in the Roman and Canon Law of the Late Eleventh and Twelfth Centuries

Medieval Collections of Church Canons

For the church, Gregory's *commonitorium* continued to be the most influential authority governing its disciplinary and criminal proceedings in the tenth and eleventh centuries.[1] Numerous collections of canons (rules)[2] supplemented and refined the *commonitorium*'s central requirement of fair procedures in the trial of an accused. The canonical collections[3] drew upon the pro-defense provisions of

---

[1] Fowler-Magerl, *Ordines iudiciarii and Libelli de ordine iudiciorum (From the Middle of the Twelfth to the End of the Fifteenth Century)* (Turnhout Brepols 1994) 19–28.

[2] The word "canon" comes from "the Greek κανών, meaning a standard measure." Peter Stein, *Regulae Iuris* (Edinburgh University Press 1966) 51. "Canon law is so called because it is a law that has been measured according to an ecclesiastical canon or rule and has been approved in some fashion by the general consensus of the faithful, by an individual either public or private, or by a group or groups of authorities." Roger E Reynolds, s.v. "Law, Canon: to Gratian" in Joseph R Shrayer (ed), 7 *Dictionary of the Middle Ages* (Scribner 1986) 395, 395.

[3] Printed editions of the canonical collections discussed hereafter may be located as follows: Herrmann Wasserschleben (ed), *Regionis abbatis Prumiensis Libri duo de synodalibus causis et disciplinis ecclesiasticis* [App III] (G Engelmann 1840); *Collectio Anselmo dedicata* (882/889) in Jean-Clause Besse, *Histoire des Textes de Droit de l'Église au Moyen-Age de Denys à Gratien: Collectio Anselmo Dedicata, Étude et Textes (Extraits)* (Librairies Techniques 1960); Burchard of Worms, *Decretum* (1008/1012), 140 PL 537; *Collection in 74 Titles* (1051/1076) in John T Gilchrist (tr), *Diusersorum patrum sententie iue Collectio in LXXIV titulos digesta* (Pontifical Institute of Medieval Studies 1980); Anselm of Lucca, *Collectio canonum* (1081/1086) in Friedrich Thaner (ed), *Anselmi episcopi Lucensis Collectio canonum una cum collectione minore* (Innsbruck 1906); Deusdedit, *Liber canonum* (1087) in Victor W von Glanvell (ed), *Die Kanonessammlung des Kardinals Deusdedit* (Paderborn 1905); Ivo of Chartres, *Decretum* (c 1094), 161 PL 59; Ivo of Chartres, *Panormia* (1094/1096), 161 PL 1042.

Foundations of American Criminal Due Process at Trial. Francis R. Herrmann and Brownlow M. Speer, Oxford University Press. © Oxford University Press 2025. DOI: 10.1093/9780199364770.003.0004

the False Decretals[4] and some of them incorporated the writings of Augustine[5] and Gregory.[6]

[4] The magisterial study of the influence of the False Decretals on the development of the canon law from the ninth to the twelfth centuries is Horst Fuhrmann, *Einfluß und Verbreitung der psuedoisidorischen Fälschungen: von ihrem Auftauchen bis in die neuere Zeit* (Hiersemann 1972). Fuhrmann traces the incorporation of passages from the False Decretals in subsequent canonical collections in his table of passages, ibid 784–1005. Fuhrmann's table identifies procedural principles within the pseudo-Isidorian texts migrating into canonical collections. (For printed editions of the collections below, see n 3.)

1. The prohibition of reliance on an "extorted confession" appears in Ivo of Chartres, *Decretum*, pt V, c 241 and Ivo of Chartres, *Panormia*, bk IV, c 118.
2. The requirement of an "inscription" as the prerequisite to criminal prosecution appears in *Collectio Anselmo dedicata*, pt III, c 138; Regino of Prüm, *Libri duo de synodalibus causis*, App III, c 63; *Collection in 74 Titles*, c 101; Anselm of Lucca, *Collectio canonum*, bk III, c 46; Deusdedit, *Liber canonum*, bk IV, c 332; Ivo of Chartres, *Decretum*, pt VI, c 337 (161 PL 514); Ivo of Chartres, *Panormia*, bk IV, c 77.
3. The rule that an accuser "shall not be heard" in the absence of the adverse party appears in *Collectio Anselmo dedicata*, pt III, c 66; *Collection in 74 Titles*, c 55; Anselm of Lucca, *Collectio canonum*, bk III, c 7; Ivo of Chrtres, *Decretum*, pt V, c 248, pt VI, c 331; Ivo of Chartres, *Panormia*, bk IV, c 54.
4. The rule drawn from Acts 25:16 (trial of St Paul) that no one may be adjudged or convicted without "accusers present" and opportunity to defend is stated in Anselm of Lucca, *Collectio canonum*, bk III, c 47; Ivo of Chartres, *Decretum*, pt VI, c 347.
5. The bar to being a judge and accuser or witness at the same time is stated in *Collectio Anselmo Dedicata*, pt III, c 157; Regino of Prüm, *Libri duo de synodalibus causis*, App III, c 62; Burchard of Worms, *Decretum*, bk XVI, c 15; *Collection in 74 Titles*, c 50; Anselm of Lucca, *Collectio canonum*, bk III, c 72; Deusdedit, *Liber canonum*, bk IV, c 36; Ivo of Chartres, *Decretum*, pt VI, c 321; Ivo of Chartres, *Panormia*, bk IV, c 81.
6. The invalidity of a judgment based on "fear" or "command" is stated in Regino of Prüm, *Libri duo de synodalibus causis*, App III, c 36; Burchard of Worms, *Decretum*, bk XV, c 8; Anselm of Lucca, *Collectio canonum*, bk III, c 86; Ivo of Chartres, *Decretum*, pt V, c 235, pt XVI, c 9.
7. The proscription on passing judgment in a "doubtful" matter is stated in *Collectio Anselmo dedicata*, pt III, c 191; *Collection in 74 Titles*, c 66; Anselm of Lucca, *Collectio canonum*, bk III, c 35; Deusdedit, *Liber canonum*, bk I, c 19, bk IV, c 330, bk IV, c 342; Ivo of Chartres, *Decretum*, pt VI, c 329.
8. Isidore of Seville's paraphrase of the "however much these things may be true" passage from Augustine's Sermon 351 appears in Burchard of Worms, *Decretum*, bk I, c 192; Deusdedit, *Liber canonum*, bk IV, c 317; Ivo of Chartres, *Decretum*, pt V, c 244, pt V, c 247; Ivo of Chartres, *Panormia*, bk IV, c 113, bk IV, c 114.
9. The requirement that witnesses testify only from first-hand knowledge appears in *Collectio Anselmo dedicata*, pt III, c 51; Burchard of Worms, *Decretum*, bk I, c 171; *Collection in 74 Titles*, c 48; Anselm of Lucca, *Collectio canonum*, bk III, c 53; Deusdedit, *Liber canonum*, bk IV, c 319, bk IV, c 333; Ivo of Chartres, *Decretum*, pt V, c 289; Ivo of Chartres, *Panormia*, bk IV, c 93.
10. The rule that trial must be had where the crime occurred appears in *Collectio Anselmo dedicata*, pt III, c 125; *Collection in 74 Titles*, c 255; Anselm of Lucca, *Collectio canonum*, bk III, c 79; Deusdedit, *Liber canonum*, bk I, c 73; Ivo of Chartres, *Decretum*, pt VI, c 324; Ivo of Chartres, *Panormia*, bk IV, c 75.

[5] The portion of Augustine's sermon on penitence (Sermon 351) appears in Anselm of Lucca, *Collectio canonum*, c 67. The passage from Sermo 351 barring judgment "based on suspicion" (*ex suspicione*) and the removal from communion of one who has neither "voluntarily confessed" nor been "accused and convicted" (*ultro confessum siue accusatum atque conuictum*) appears in Deusdedit, *Liber canonum*, bk IV, c 81.

[6] For so much of Gregory's *commonitorium* as includes the requirement that "testimony against [the accused] was given under oath with him present" (*eo presente sub iureiurando contra eum testimonium dictum est*), see Deusdedit, *Liber canonum*, bk III c 96; Anselm of Lucca, *Collectio canonum*, bk III c 90; Ivo of Chartres, *Panormia*, c 82 (with the words *qui accusatus est* inserted between *eo presente* and *sub iureiurando*).

Gregory's declaration that "it is very grave and unseemly that in a matter that is doubtful, a judgment that is certain should be pronounced" (*Nam grave est satis et indecens, ut in re dubia certa dicatur sententia*) appears in Deusdedit, bk 4, c 342 and Anselm of Lucca, bk III, c 69.

In shaping the procedural requirements of emerging canon law, the most signifi-cant canonist of the eleventh century was Ivo, bishop of Chartres (c 1040–1115).[7] In a major collection of canons, his *Decretum*, and in many letters responding to legal inquiries, Ivo developed comprehensive and concise requirements for and limitations on witness testimony. To the *commonitorium*'s requirement that witnesses must ap-pear in person and testify orally in the presence of the accused, Ivo fused a require-ment he drew from the pseudo-Isidorian forgeries: witnesses may testify only to matters which they have personally observed.[8]

Ivo lucidly explained this foundational requirement of first-hand knowledge in a letter to a fellow bishop who had inquired whether a woman could be convicted of il-licit sexual intercourse on the basis of testimony from witnesses who had not observed the alleged act:

"No one is to be adjudged guilty unless convicted by the judicial order,"[9] that is, un-less he against whom the crime is alleged either voluntarily [*sponte*] confesses that he is guilty or is proven to be guilty by competent witnesses in some secular or ecclesi-astical trial. But if the accuser . . . uses witnesses who did not see the deed, however much they may be speaking truths, they are, nonetheless, not to be heard, since the laws [*leges*] contain [the requirement that] witnesses must not be admitted against a defendant, except about those things which are known to have been done in their presence.[10]

For Ivo, due process (*iudiciario ordine*) required primary evidence. It would seem that even reliable hearsay was insufficient. However much witnesses might be relaying the truth, their derivative evidence failed to fulfill the strict mandate of the judicial order. This rigidity would pass into further canonical collections, most significantly that of Gratian.

---

[7] For biographical information, see Christof Rolker, "Ivo of Chartres (Yves de Chartres) (c 140–1115)" in Olivier Descamps and Rafael Domingo (eds), *Great Christian Jurists in French History* (CUP 2019) 19–34; Christof Rolker, *Canon Law and the Letters of Ivo of Chartres* (CUP 2010) 1–24; Rolf Sprandel, *Ivo von Chartres und seine Stellung in der Kirchengeschichte* (A Hiersemann 1962) 5–8. On Ivo's significance, see Bruce Clark Brasington, *Order in the Court: Medieval Procedural Treatises in Translation* (Brill 2016) 38–51, 38 n 66.

[8] "[W]itnesses . . . are not to give testimony about cases or matters other than those which are known to have been done in their presence" ([*T*]*estes . . . nec de aliis causis vel negotiis testimonium dicant, nisi de his quae sub presentia eorum acta esse noscuntur*). Ivo of Chartres, *Decretum*, pt V, c 289. See also *Panormia*, a work attributed to Ivo, bk IV, c 93 (sentence beginning "*Nec de aliis causis . . .*" with *facta* in place of *acta*). For recent scholarship indicating that the *Panormia* was likely not from Ivo's own hand, see Brasington (n 7) 38 n 66 and works cited.

[9] This is a paraphrase of a pseudo-Isidorian statement which is itself ultimately a paraphrase of a key portion of Augustine's sermon 351 on doing penance.

[10] "*Neminem reum esse judicandum, nisi judiciario ordine convincatur, id est, nisi ipse in quem crimen intenditur, aut sponte se reum esse fateatur, aut per innocentes testes in aliquo saeculari judicio vel ecclesi-astico reus esse comprobetur. Quod vero accusator . . . testes adhibet qui factum non viderunt, quamvis vera dicant, non sunt tamen audiendi, cum leges contineant testes adversus reum non esse admittendos, nisi de his quae sub praesentia eorum facta esse noscuntur.*" Ivo of Chartres, Epistle 229.

Gratian's *Decretum*: The Definitive Statement of Canonical Procedural Values in the Twelfth Century

In about 1140, Gratian, assumed to be a cleric and teacher of law at Bologna, sought to harmonize discordant provisions of canon law in his *Concordantia discordantium canonum*.[11] The massive work soon became known simply as the *Decretum Magistri Gratiani* after its composer.[12]

Gratian divided the *Decretum* into three parts. The second part extensively covers the trial procedure. It contains thirty-six hypothetical cases composed by Gratian (*causae*), each of which gives rise to a number of specific questions (*quaestiones*) stated in the *causa*. Each *quaestio* is then treated separately, prefaced by a comment (*dictum*) of Gratian stating his view of the correct answer. In support of his view, Gratian assembled rules (*canones*) drawn from earlier canonical collections.[13]

The *Decretum*'s impact on Western legal culture cannot be overemphasized.[14] Methodical and analytical, it synthesized the writings of the pseudo-Isidorians, Augustine, Gregory, and the ninth-century popes. Incorporating Gregory's *commonitorium* to John the Defensor,[15] portions of Augustine's sermon on penance,[16] and Acts 25:16 (the trial of St Paul), as transmitted through the False Decretals,[17] Gratian set out a coherent trial procedure. It was enlightened in its search for truth and humane in its insistence on protections for accused persons, not limited to proceedings against bishops.[18]

The *Decretum* requires that every criminal case commence with an accusation made in writing.[19] The accused is not to be regarded as guilty from the fact of the

---

[11] Little is known about the details of Gratian's life. For what biographical information there is, see Kenneth Pennington, "The Biography of Gratian, the Father of Canon Law" (2014) 59 Villanova Law Review 679–706; "*Graziano*" in Italo Birocchi and others (eds), 59 *Dizionario biografico dei giuristi italiani (XII–XX Secolo)* (Il Mulino 2013) 1058–1061 (with bibliography); Anders Winroth, *The Making of Gratian's* Decretum (CUP 2004) 5–8, 194–195.

[12] As to the dates of composition of Gratian's Decretum, see Winroth (n 11), fixing the first recension of the *Decretum* not before 1139 and the second recension not later than 1150. See also Peter Landau, "Gratian and the Decretum Gratiani" in Wilfried Hartmann and Kenneth Pennington (eds), *The History of Medieval Canon Law in the Classical Period, 1140–1234 from Gratian to the Decretals of Pope Gregory IX* (Catholic University of America 2008) 22–54.

[13] More than half of the *capitula* in the second and third *causae* dealing with criminal procedure against clerics are rooted in the False Decretals, not counting eight uses of pseudo-Isidore in *dicta*. Fuhrmann (n 4) 572.

[14] For a comprehensive analysis of the *Decretum*'s critical significance in the history of Western jurisprudence, see Harold J Berman, *Law and Revolution* (Harvard University Press 1983) 144–148.

[15] C 2 q. 1 c 7 in 1 Emil Friedberg and Emil Richter (eds), *Decretum Magistri Gratiani* (B Tauchnitz 1879, reprint Akademische Druck- u Verlagsanstalt 1959) 439–442.

[16] C 2 q. 1 c 18 in 1 Friedberg and Richter (n 15) 446–447.

[17] "It is not proper to adjudge or condemn anyone before he has legitimate accusers present and receives opportunity of defending in order to purge the criminal charges" (*Non oportet quemquam iudicari uel dampnari prius, quam legitimos habeat presentes accusatores, locumque defendendi accipiat ad abluenda crimina.*) C 3 q. 9 c 5 in 1 Friedberg and Richter (n 15) 530.

[18] ZN Brooke, *The English Church and the Papacy* (The University Press 1931, Cambridge reprint 1968) 98.

[19] "An accusation must always be made in written form" (*Accusatio semper debet fieri in scriptis*). Rubric to C 2 q. 8 c 3 in 1 Friedberg and Richter (n 15) 503.

accusation alone.[20] Trial must take place where the alleged crime was committed.[21] The accused must not have been previously punished for the offense.[22] Both accuser and accused must be present when the accusation is made.[23] The accused must receive a fair trial[24] with time to prepare his defense.[25] Truly manifest and heinous offenses, by way of exception, could be punished without a trial, but Gratian restricted the category narrowly.[26] The judge must have no personal interest in the outcome,[27] nor be subject to any external compulsion to rule in a certain manner.[28]

[20] "[I]t is not he who is accused who is immediately guilty, but he who is convicted as criminal" ([N]on statim qui accusatur reus est, sed qui conuincitur criminosus). C 15 q. 8 c 5 in 1 Friedberg and Richter (15) 761.

[21] "A case is always acted upon in the place where the crime is committed" (Ibi semper causa agatur, ubi crimen admittitur). C 3 q. 6 c 1 in 1 Friedberg and Richter (n 15) 519.

[22] "'God will not adjudge twice in the same matter . . .' Therefore, those who have been punished shall not be punished afterwards)" ("'Non iudicabit Deus bis in id ipsum . . .' Ergo qui puniti sunt postea non punientur"). C 23 q. 5 c 6 in 1 Friedberg and Richter (n 15) 931. The reference to divine judgment is drawn from the biblical Book of Nahum I. 9. Richard H Helmholz has extensively studied what in modern terms may be called the canonical principle against double jeopardy and its exceptions. RH Helmholz, The Spirit of Classical Canon Law (University of Georgia Press 1996) 284–310. Other expressions of the canonical principle may be found in Dist 81 c 12; C 2 q. 1 c 14; C 13 q. 2 c 30; D pen Dist 3 c 44 dp; De pen. Dist 3 c 39 dp. See Helmholz (ibid) 287–288.

[23] "Unless the defendant is present, the accuser shall not be heard" (Nisi reo presente accusator non audiatur). Rubric to C 3 q. 9 c 1 in 1 Friedberg and Richter (n 15) 529. "An absent person can neither accuse nor be accused" (Absens nec accusare, nec accusari potest). Rubric to C 3 q. 9 c 18 in 1 Friedberg and Richter (n 15) 533.

[24] "[Y]ou may condemn no one before a just and true trial" ([N]eminem condempnetis ante iustum et uerum iudicium). C 2 q. 1 c 13 in 1 Friedberg and Richter (15) 444.

[25] "and receives opportunity of defending, that is, ecclesiastical delays for purging the charges" (locumque defendendi accipiat, id est inducias ecclesiasticas ad abluenda crimina). C 3 q. 1 c 6 in 1 Friedberg and Richter (n 15) 530. The reference to inducias is to judicially mandated continuances for preparation of one's case. See Jan Frederik Niermeyer (ed), Mediae latinitatis lexicon minus (2nd rev edn, Brill 2002) 529 s.v. "indutiae." Stephen of Tournai in his summa of Gratian explains continuances are necessary for obtaining documents (instrumenta) and witnesses of the parties. ("iudex ex necessitate propter instrumenta requirenda vel testes litigantium postulanti concedit inducias." Stephen of Tornai, Summa des Stephanus Tornacensis in Johannes Friedrich von Schulte (ed), Die Summa des Stephanus Tornacensis über Das Decretum Gratiani (Emil Roth 1891) 190.

[26] C 2 q. 1 c 17 in 1 Friedberg and Richter (n 15) 445. According to Gratian, a defendant accused of murdering a person in the very eyes of the judge and in sight of many others could not be convicted without due process, so long as the defendant denied guilt. C 2 q. 1 c 20 dp. Only if the defendant's repeated, public behavior was tantamount to a confession of guilt could he be condemned without full due process. See Richard M Fraher, "'Ut Nullus Describatur Reus Prius Quam Convincatur': Presumption of Innocence in Medieval Canon Law?" (1985) Proceedings of Sixth International Congress Medieval Canon Law 494. On the history of "notorious" crimes, see ibid 496–500. Ecclesiastical summary process, as later developed, did not dispense with a defendant's fundamental right to due process. Kenneth Pennington, "The Jurisprudence of Procedure" in Wilfried Hartmann and Kenneth Pennington (eds), The History of Courts and Procedure in Medieval Canon Law (Catholic University of America Press 2016) 133.

[27] "No one can be at the same time accuser and judge in one and the same case" (In una . . . eademque causa nullus simul potest esse accusator et iudex). C 2 q. 1 c 17 dp in 1 Friedberg and Richter (n 15) 446. "One cannot be at the same time accuser, witness, and judge" (Accusator, testis uel iudex aliquis simul esse non potest). Rubric to C 4 q. 4 c 1 in 1 Friedberg and Richter (n 15) 541.

[28] "An unfair trial and an unfair decision pronounced by judges for fear of, or on command of, the king, shall not be valid" (Iniustum iudicium et diffinitio iniusta, regio metu vel iussu a iudicibus ordinata, non ualeat). C 25 q. 1 c 8 in 1 Friedberg and Richter (n 15) 1009.

The burden of proof is on the accuser, not the accused.[29] Witnesses must testify under oath orally,[30] only as to matters they personally observed,[31] and they must give the testimony in the presence of the accused.[32] If a confession of the accused is relied on, it must be voluntary, that is, not the product of torture, fear, or fraud.[33] No judgment can be imposed if the proofs leave the matter in doubt.[34]

These procedural norms of the *Decretum* were principally based on Roman law, but Gratian also incorporated the procedure of purgative oaths which the church had adopted several centuries before, perhaps under the influence of Germanic custom.[35] Thus, where proofs were insufficient and public suspicion of the accused remained, the *Decretum* directed that the accused must purge himself of the suspicion by his innocence under oath with the aid of oath-helpers.[36] The procedure of compurgation did not fit easily with Gratian's emerging judicial order drawn from principles of

[29] "The burden of proof does not lie upon the defendant" (*Onus probationis reo non incumbit*). Rubric to C 6 q. 5 c 1 in 1 Friedberg and Richter (n 15) 565.

[30] "Witnesses shall give testimony after having proffered an oath in person" (*Testes corporaliter prestito sacramento testimonium dicant*). Rubric to C 3 q. 9 c 20 in 1 Friedberg and Richter (n 15) 533.

[31] "Witnesses shall not proffer testimony through any writing, but while present shall truthfully testify about what they saw and knew. And they shall not testify about other cases or matters except about those which are known to have been done in their presence" (*Testes per quamcumque scripturam testimonium non proferant, sed presentes de his que uiderunt et nouerunt, ueraciter testimonium dicant. Nec de aliis causis uel negotiis testimonium dicant, nisi de his, que sub eorum presentia acta esse noscuntur*). C 3 q. 9 c 15 in 1 Friedberg and Richter (n 15) 532. Commenting on this portion of Gratian, Stephen of Tournai in his *summa* states: "in a criminal case, witnesses are not admitted, except those who say they themselves saw; in a civil case, however, he [Gratian] says hearsay testimony is valid ... Very few however are the cases in which hearsay testimony is admitted" (*in criminali causa non admittendos testes, nisi eos, qui vidisse se dicerent; in civili autem dicit, valere testimonium ex auditu ... Paucissimi autem sunt casus, in quibus admittatur testimonium ex auditu*). An exception was made, for example, for testimony about family blood relationships. Stephen of Tournai (n 25) 198.

[32] "if with him present, the testimony against him was given under oath" (*si eo presente, sub iureiurando testimonium contra eum dictum est*). C 2 q. 1 c 7 §3, quoting the *commonitorium* of Gregory I in 1 Friedberg and Richter (n 15) 440. See Erwin Jacobi, "Der Prozess im Decretum Graziani und bei den ältesten Dekretisten" (1913) 3 ZRG (KA) 223, 306.

[33] "If from priests or from authorities of the church any writings in some way through fear or fraud or through force were extorted ... we ordain that it shall not count to any prejudice or harm to them ... For a confession in such matters must not be compelled but made voluntarily. For every confession which is made from necessity is not to be credited. A confession therefore in such matters must not be extorted, but proffered willlingly" (*Si sacerdotibus uel auctoribus ecclesiae quedam scripturae quoquo modo per metum aut fraudem, aut per uim extortae fuerint, ... ad nullum eis preiudicium uel nocumentum ualere censemus ... Confessio enim in talibus non compulsa, sed spontanea fieri debet. §1. Omnis enim confessio, que fit ex necessitate, fides non est. §2. Confessio ergo in talibus non debet extorqueri, sed sponte profiteri*). C 15 q. 6 c 1 in 1 Friedberg and Richter (n 15) 754–755.

[34] "[I]n doubtful matters there ought not be an absolute judgment" (*[I]n rebus ambiguis absolutum non debet esse iudicium*). Dist 33 c 7 in 1 Friedberg and Richter (n 15) 124.

[35] C 2 q. 5 cc 1–26 in 1 Friedberg and Richter (n 15) 455–465. To what extent Gratian's adoption of compurgation was rooted in Germanic custom has been disputed. See RH Helmholz, "The Law of Compurgation" in RH Helmholz (ed), *The* Ius Commune *in England: Four Studies* (OUP 2001) 90–91. For in-depth study of compurgation, see ibid 82–134.

[36] Designed as a means for resolving charges that were not proven at trial, in fact, "canonical purgation was not a form of proof at all. It was instead a substitute where there was no proof[.]" Ibid 95. Compurgation was not itself a trial procedure but rather a demonstration of innocence. Ibid 92, 94. In his decretal X 5.34.5, Pope Gregory IX made clear that purgation was to be employed only in cases where legitimate proofs failed to establish guilt, yet public scandal lingered. In instances such as adultery, an assertion of innocence under oath supported by oath-helpers was deemed sufficient to restore an accused's reputation and to dispel scandal. Helmholz, "The Law of Compurgation" (n 35) 93–95. On the nature of the oath of the accused, see ibid 101. The person who failed in compurgation was treated "as if" convicted. The consequences were the

Roman jurisprudence.[37] The requirement that the accused take an oath as to his innocence would be transformed in the next century into a requirement that the accused speak under oath to the merits of the accusation against him.[38] On the continent of Europe, the transformation would shift criminal procedure away from its traditional accusatorial form into a new inquisitorial structure.

The Revival of Roman Law

Even before Gratian's canonical work in the mid-twelfth century, the legal landscape of continental Europe had begun to change dramatically in secular law. Toward the end of the eleventh and beginning of the twelfth century, the gradual recovery of Justinian's Digest and complete versions of his Code and Novels spurred the teaching of Roman law as an academic subject centered at the University of Bologna.[39] The revived Roman law, adapted to medieval circumstances, gradually became a living law throughout much of Italy where it supplemented the statutes of Italian city-states. It also came gradually to influence strongly local and national law across the rest of continental Western Europe.

The Roman law revival blended with the developing ecclesiastical law. Gratian's Decretum represented a successful attempt to create a corpus of canon law equivalent in scope to the texts of the revived Justinianic corpus. Gratian himself cited Roman law in his Decretum. Both secular and canon laws were taught at universities. Scholars of each body of law—legists and canonists—frequently drew upon one another's sources to explicate and develop concepts and procedures common to both. Thousands of law students from across Europe, including England, studied the texts of both laws. The amalgam of the two laws became known as the *ius commune*[40] (common law) of Europe, also referred to as "the learned law" in distinction from the ordeals.[41]

---

same. Ibid 112. See also RH Helmholz, "Crime, Compurgation and the Courts of the Medieval Church" in RH Helmholz (ed), *Canon Law and the Law of England* (Hambledon Press 1988) 119–144.

[37] Helmholz, "The Law of Compurgation" (n 35) 110–116; Pennington, "Procedure" (n 26) 134.

[38] Helmholz, "The Law of Compurgation" (n 35) 101.

[39] On the recovery of the full Digest in the West after its disappearance for over five hundred years, see Wolfgang P Muller, "The Recovery of Justinian's Digest in the Middle Ages" (1990) 20 Bull Medieval Canon L (n.s.) 1–29.

[40] On the formation of the *ius commune*, see Michael Höflich and Jasonne M Grabher, "The Formation of Normative Legal Texts: The Establishment of the Ius commune" in Hartmann and Pennington (eds), *Classical Period* (n 12) 1–21. Raoul van Caenegem comments: "The ius commune (particularly the Roman law side . . .) originated in twelfth-century Italy in the context of an intellectual passion for the four great texts of Antiquity. It originally was an academic pursuit, in the hands of scholars who were dazzled by the sheer brilliance of the classical jurists and their writings. At first, the masters restricted themselves to the literal explanation of the *Corpus Iuris* . . . Later schools broadened their vision, took the living customary law into account and made use of the ancient texts to help judges, advocates and administrators with their practical concerns." RC Van Caenegem, "The Modernity of Medieval Law" (2000) 68 Tijdschrift voor Rechtsgeschiedenis/Legal History Review 313, 324.

[41] Fowler-Magerl (n 1) 12. The ordeals were already fading. Kenneth Pennington, *The Prince and the Law, 1200–1600: Sovereignty and Rights in the Western Legal Tradition* (University of California Press 1993) 135. For suspicion about the deficits of the ordeals in England, see Eleanor Rathbone, "Roman Law in the Anglo-Norman Realm" (1967) 11 Studia Gratiana 255, 265.

Wherever it was received, the revived Roman law had a profound impact on secular criminal procedure. Accusatorial in form, it presented a rational approach to the determination of disputed facts based on witness testimony. The dominant expositor of the Roman law at the turn of the thirteenth century was the Bolognese professor Azo (1150–1230). He expressed a central principle of the revived procedure in his university lectures:

> And although in civil matters where there is a dearth of proofs, an oath is tendered [citation to Justinian's Code 58.2.3], here, however, in criminal cases where the accuser fails to prove, the defendant is acquitted. [Citation to Justinian's Digest.] For it is more just [*sanctius*] that the crime of a guilty person be left unpunished than to convict an innocent person.[42]

Rational and enlightened though such a formulation plainly is, the reappearance of Roman criminal law carried with it a deleterious element. Medieval and early modern writings on passages in Justinian's *Digest* commonly contained extensive regulations about the use of torture.[43] Where the testimony of two eyewitnesses could not be obtained,[44] but where there was nevertheless a quantum of well-based public suspicion about an individual, a judge could subject the suspect to torture in an effort to obtain a confession. Such a confession alone could not justify a conviction. The defendant had to repeat the confession in open court in the physical absence of the instruments of torture in order for the confession to be deemed "voluntary" and supply the basis for a full conviction. If the defendant were disinclined to repeat the confession "voluntarily" in court, the judge could order the defendant to be tortured anew. Such practice utterly hollowed out the *ius commune*'s doctrinal insistence on the voluntariness of confessions.

The *ordines iudiciarii*: Medieval Guides to Trial Procedure

The need for orders of procedure

Neither the procedural statements scattered in Justinian's corpus nor the trial requirements of Gratian's *Decretum*, nor even summaries of either, offered a clear and usable

---

[42] *Et licet in ciuilibus inopia probationum deferatur sacramentum* [Citation to CJ 58.2.3] *hic tamen in criminalibus accusatore non probante absoluitur reus. sanctius est enim impunitum relinqui facinus nocentis, quam innocentem condemnare* [Citation to Trajan's rescript in Dig 48.19.5.pr] Azo, *Lectvra Azonis et Magni Apparatvs ad Singvlas Leges Dvodecim Librorvm Codicis Ivstiniani* (apud Sebastianum Niuellium 1581) (commenting on CJ 4.19.25 "*testibus idoneis*") 286.

[43] Kenneth Pennington has emphasized that the *ius commune* imposed legal restrictions on the conditions under which torture could be used. Pennington disputes whether torture was as extensively employed as historians have traditionally assumed. See Kenneth Pennington, "Introduction" in Hartmann and Pennington (eds), *Courts and Procedure* (n 26) 13; and Chapter 5, "The Jurisprudence of Procedure" in ibid 157–158.

[44] Kenneth Pennington has questioned how rigidly the two-witness rule was followed from the thirteenth century onward. See Pennington, "Procedure" (n 26) 155. When crime increased, the rigor of the two-witness rule became a serious impediment to crime's suppression. Mirjan R Damaška, *Evaluation of Evidence: Pre-Modern and Modern Approaches* (CUP 2019) 4, 22–25.

design for legal practice. Judges, lawyers, and litigants, consequently, found themselves in need of methodical statements of judicial procedure that could serve to guide them in the conduct of trials. To meet that need, medieval writers began to compose "orders of procedure" (*ordines iudiciarii*) during the closing decades of the twelfth century.[45] Some authors drew principally on the revived Roman texts,[46] others predominantly on ecclesiastical sources. By the thirteenth century, the writers often intermingled both secular and canon authorities.[47] Legists, that is, the scholars of the revived Roman law, often referred to canon works. Canonists cited Roman-law texts alongside their preferred biblical authorities, papal decretals, and conciliar documents.[48] Ecclesiastical influence over procedure became increasingly important.[49]

While variations in local customs created differences among the many *ordines*,[50] as a whole, the *ordines* set out a well-organized system of procedure, exhibiting a consensus concerning essential elements of a fair and rational trial.

Tancred's *ordo*

Tancred of Bologna (c 1185–c. 1236) studied Roman law under Azo and taught canon law at the University of Bologna from 1210 onward. It is universally agreed that Tancred's *ordo* (c. 1216) towered above all others in his time.[51] Drawing together

---

[45] On the formation of the *ordines*, see Kenneth Pennington, "Law, Criminal Procedure" in William Chester Jordan and Joseph R Strayer (eds), *Dictionary of the Middle Ages: Supplement 1* (Charles Scribner 2004) 310–312; Pennington, "Procedure" (n 26) 125, 134–148; Brasington (n 7) 214–251; Wieslaw Litewski, "Mündliche Klage und Klageschrift in den ältesten ordines iudiciarii" in Gerhard Köbler and Hermann Nehlsen (eds), *Wirkungen europäischer Rechtskultur: Festschrift für Karl Kroeschell zum 70, Geburtstag* (CH Beck 1997) 666–667. Not all *ordines* were designed for practice. See A-M Stickler, "Ordines judiciarii" in R Naz (ed), 6 *Dictionnaire de droit canonique* (Librairie Letouzey et Ané 1957) 1134. The term *ordo iudiciarius* (*ordines iudiciarii*) gradually came to designate procedural literature describing the trial process as a whole, as opposed to other juridical kinds of literature that addressed only particular portions of the trial process. Knut Wolfgang Nörr, "Ordo Iudiciorum und Ordo Iudicarius" (1967) 11 *Studia Gratiana* 327, 334–337.

[46] Bulgarus de Bulgarinis, writing between 1123 and 1141, was the first to base his *ordo* on the revived Roman law. Charles Donahue Jr, "Procedure in the Courts of the Ius Commune" in Hartmann and Pennington (eds), *Courts and Procedure* (n 26) 83. Responding to a request from the papal chancellor, Bulgarus gathered into a short treatise the material concerning procedure which was scattered throughout the *Corpus* into a short treatise. Rathbone (n 41) 263.

[47] Ken Pennington, "Canonical Jurisprudence and Other Legal Systems in the Medieval and Early Modern Periods" in Jesús Miñambres (ed), *Diritto Canonico e Culture Giuridiche nel Centenario Del* Codex Iuris Canonici *del 1917* (EDUSC 2019) 109, 110–116; Antonio García y García, "Ecclesiastical Procedure in Medieval Spain" in Hartmann and Pennington (eds), *Courts and Procedure* (n 26) 418–419.

[48] Fowler-Magerl (n 1) 11.

[49] "The norms of courtroom procedure were developed primarily in canonical jurisprudence, but secular courts very quickly adopted the same norms and practices." Kenneth Pennington, "Introduction to the Courts" in Hartmann and Pennington (eds), *Courts and Procedure* (n 26) 9 n 6; Stickler (n 45) 1134.

[50] See Brasington (n 7) xiv.

[51] Nörr, "Ordo" (n 45) 339. Pennington, "Procedure" (n 26) 144; Donahue, "Procedure" (n 46) 83; Brasington (n 7) xiv. Internal references in Tancred's text suggest its composition was taking place between 1214 and 1216. See Bergmann (n 48) iv–v. The suggestion has also been made that Tancred may have completed his *Ordo* before 1214 and updated it after Pope Innocent III's death in 1216. Fraher, "*Ut Nullus*" (n 26) 28 & n 21. For biographical note and a list of Tancred's writings, see <https://amesfoundation.law.harvard.edu/BioBibCanonists/Report_Biobib2.php?record_id=a552>.

canon and Roman sources, Tancred presented a clear and usable order of trial. Hundreds, perhaps thousands, of lawyers paid to have his *ordo* copied.[52]

Tancred's *ordo*[53] laid down, as an initial matter, that a party was to be summoned to be present at trial.[54] Upon responding, a defendant was to be presented a written bill of the charges against him or her, signed by the accuser,[55] including the name of the accuser and the accused, the crime alleged, and the month the crime was said to have been committed.[56]

If the defendant denied the charges and chose to challenge them, the defendant was free to do so.[57] A defendant could also challenge the judge for lack of impartiality[58] or

[52] Charles Donahue Jr, "Order in the Court: Medieval Procedural Treatises in Translation" (2017) 34 Bull Medieval Canon L (n.s.) 281, 286.

[53] For the text of Tancred's *ordo*, see Tancredus Bononiensis, *Ordo iudiciarius* in Friedrich Christian Bergmann (ed), *Pillii, Tancredi, Gratiae Libri de iudiciorum ordine* (apud Vandenhoeck et Ruprecht 1842, photo reprint Scientia Verlag 1965). In the introduction to his *ordo*, Tancred states he is responding to colleagues' requests for guidance. Ibid 89. Tancred's *ordo* will here be cited by Part and Title with a parenthetical reference to where his text may be located in Bergmann's edition. For example, "Tancred," Part 1, Title 1 = "Tancred" 1.1 (Berg --).

[54] "Tancred" 2.2 (Berg 131): "and the judge should summon the defendant so that he may come" (*et iudex statim reum citare debet*) and see "Tancred" 2.14 (Berg 174): "and summon the defendant that he may come" (*et citat reum ut veniat*). Concerning the summons, see also the ordo *De edendo* in Brasington (n 7) 134. Even, in cases of manifest or notorious crimes, though procedures were abbreviated, essential elements of fair procedure had to be retained: the defendant was to be summoned to be present and the matter investigated. "Tancred" 2.7 (Berg 151–152): "but nevertheless a certain judicial procedure must be maintained in cases of notorious crimes . . . because a defendant must be summoned and questioned, and sentenced with him being present or contumaciously absent . . . because if he is not summoned, the decision does not hold . . . . But if the crime is not notorious, although it is public, the judicial order must be maintained" (*Verumtamen quidam ordo iudiciarius in notoriis criminibus est servandus . . . quia reus debet citari et interrogari, et eo praesente vel per contumaciam absente debet sententiari . . . , quoniam si non citaretur, non teneret sententia . . . . Si vero crimen non est notorium, licet sit publicum, servandus est ordo iuris*). A judge could know a crime was notorious if its notoriety was proven to him by two witnesses and everyone proclaimed the crime was notorious. On notorious crimes, see Pennington, "Procedure" (n 26) 132–133, 146–147; Richard M Fraher, "Preventing Crime in the High Middle Ages: The Medieval Lawyers' Search for Deterrence" in James Ross Sweeney and Stanley Chodorow (eds), *Popes, Teachers, and Canon Law in the Middle Ages* (Cornell University Press 1989) 224–225 & n 49.

[55] "Tancred" 2.7 (Berg 157–158): "because it is a criminal matter, an *inscription* is necessary . . . and indeed it generally is true that no one is heard to accuse unless a bill of inscription is put forward" (*quia criminaliter agitur, est inscriptio necessaria . . . .et hoc quidem generaliter verum est, quod nullus auditur accusans, nisi libello inscriptionis porrecto*). Inscription was not necessary for charitable denunciations or, later, for inquisitorial procedure. "Tancred" 2.7 (Berg 152–153). For a detailed study of the requirement of inscription in the *ordines*, see Wieslaw Litewski, "Mündliche Klage und Klageschrift in den ältesten ordines iudiciarii, Wirkungen europäischer Rechtskultur" in *Festschrift für Karl Kroeschell zum 70. Geburtstag* (CH Beck 1997) 667. Toward the end of the twelfth century, it was accepted as a general principle that in trial a written complaint was indispensable. Ibid 670.

[56] "Tancred" 2.8 (Berg 162): "Because having been summoned to court, he [the accuser] ought to offer a bill in which he must certify what he charges or what he seeks from him [the defendant], so that he [the defendant], upon continuances, may consider whether to concede or contend" (*Quoniam vocato ad iudicium offerri debet libellus, in quo certificandus est, quid sibi obiicitur, vel quid ab eo petitur, ut habitis induciis deliberet, utrum velit cedere vel contendere*). See also the Ordo *Bambergensis* in Brasington (n 7) 203–204, stating that the charge must be clear and complete so as not to ensnare the accused.

[57] "Tancred" 2.5 (Berg 139–146).

[58] "Tancred" 2.5 (Berg 141): "or because he [the judge] is for some reason suspect to the defendant, seeing that he [the judge] is his enemy, a relative or very much a friend of his adversary" (*vel quia est reo certa ratione suspectus, utpote inimicus suus, vel adversarii consanguineus vel multum amicus*). And see "Tancred" 2.6 (Berg 148–149). See also the ordo *De edendo*, stating that "since it is just to try cases without any suspicion, one who considers a judge suspect could be permitted to recuse him before the trial begins" in Brasington (n 7) 167.

jurisdiction.[59] At trial, the defendant was entitled to be present when the opposing witnesses were sworn with the other party also present.[60] The defendant could raise objections to the suitability of the opposing witnesses to testify. Those who could not be witnesses included, slaves, women, persons under twenty (in criminal cases), persons with impaired judgment or mental incapacity, defamed persons, paupers, infidels, criminals, persons testifying in their own case, judges, lawyers, executors, children against their parents and vice versa, members of the household, and domestics.[61] All of these categories admitted of exceptions that would at times allow testimony from persons generally unsuitable. By the thirteenth and fourteenth centuries, objections to the suitability of witnesses could be based on a wide variety of reasons, including enmity toward the defendant or association with, and therefore presumed partiality toward, the accuser.[62] If the witnesses were permitted to testify, they would do so under oath to tell the whole truth about the matter to the judge or to whomever the judge delegated to question them.[63] The oath was to be given in the presence of both parties.[64] Advocates for parties could compose questions to be put to the opposing party in writing and asked by the judge or the judge's delegate.[65] The witnesses were restricted to testifying about what they personally saw and was done in their presence. They were not simply to report what they had heard from others.[66] Although the judge or delegate was to examine the witnesses separately and apart

---

[59] "Tancred" 2.1 (Berg 142); 2.17 (Berg 181). And see *De edendo* in Brasington (n 7) 162. A summons from a judge without proper jurisdiction was invalid. Brasington (n 7) 189.

[60] "Tancred" 3.8 (Berg 235): "Witnesses must be received with both parties present, otherwise their introduction counts for nothing" (*Recipiendi sunt testes praesente utraque parte aliter introducti non valerent*) (citing CJ 4.20.19 and Nov 90.9). On the history of the Justinianic confrontation requirement, see Frank R Herrmann and Brownlow M Speer, "Facing the Accuser: Ancient and Medieval Precursors of the Confrontation Clause" (1994) 34 Va J Int'l L 481. *De edendo* does not mention the presence of opposing party. Brasington (n 7) 154.

[61] "Tancred" 3.6 (Berg 222–228): *Servi, mulieres, minor quatordecim annis, minor viginti annis in causa criminali, indiscretus sive mente captus, infames, pauperes, infideles, omnes criminosi, quis in causa propria, iudices, advocate, exsecutores, liberi pro parentibus et e contra, familiares et domestici, suspecti et inimici contra inimicum suum.*

[62] Ibid. See *De edendo* in Brasington (n 7) 153 and the *Ordo Bambergensis* in Brasington (n 7) 231–233. For an account of objections to witnesses in the secular and ecclesiastical courts of the *ius commune*, Donahue, "Procedure" (n 46) 83–94. For a study of witnesses in the church courts of England, see Charles Donahue Jr, "Proof by Witnesses in the Church Courts of Medieval England: An Imperfect Reception of Learned Law" in Morris S Arnold and others (eds), *On the Laws and Customs of England: Essays in Honor of Samuel E. Thorne* (University of North Carolina Press 2017) 127–158. A comprehensive list of the specific objections a criminal defendant might make to witnesses against him is set out in Giorgio Zordan, *Il diritto e la procedura criminale nel Tractatus de maleficiis di Angelo Gambiglioni* (CEDAM 1976) 358–360. For a detailed study of the grounds of rejection and acceptance of witnesses for and against a criminal defendant, see Bernard Schnapper, "Testes inhabiles, Les témoins reprochables dans l'ancien droit pénal" (1965) 33 Tijdschrift voor Rechtsgeschiendenis 575, 578–594; Heinrich Himstedt, inaugural dissertation, "Die neuen Rechtsgedanken im Zeugenbeweis des oberitalienischen Stadtrechtsprozesses des 13. und 14. Jahrhunderts" (Zivilprozeßrecht. Forschungen H. 5 1910) 122–138.

[63] "Tancred" 3.9 (Berg 236): "that they would tell the whole truth to the judge or to the one commissioned by him for inquiring" (*quod ipsi dicent iudici vel ei, cui iudex hoc commiserit inquirendum, totam veritatem*).

[64] "Tancred" 3.9 (Berg 237).

[65] "Tancred" 3.3 (Berg 208).

[66] "Tancred" 3.9 (Berg 239): "The witness, moreover, ought to testify about those things which he saw and knew and were done in his presence" (*Testis autem dicere debet de his, quae vidit et novit et sub eius praesentia acta sunt*). See also the *Ordo Bambergensis* in Brasington (n 7) 242. There were, of course, exceptions. On the history of the romano-canonical rule against hearsay, see Frank R Herrmann, "The

outside the parties' presence,[67] the trial was, nonetheless, a public matter. The witnesses' written testimonies would be published with both parties present and provided with a copy before the judge made a decision.[68] Parties could raise challenges to the witnesses' statements and to the witnesses who made them.[69]

The *ordo* provided that a defendant must be allowed ample time for preparation of his defense.[70] The judge was to grant the defendant time to produce witnesses in his or her favor.[71] Witnesses could be compelled to appear personally in a criminal case.[72] In civil cases, an advocate and friends could be consulted, but not in criminal matters where a lawyer's intervention was not permitted.[73]

Parties were not obliged to produce witnesses or evidence against themselves.[74] Any confession in court was to be made willingly (*sponte*). If twisted out (*extorta*) through

---

Establishment of a Rule against Hearsay in Romano-Canonical Procedure" (1995) 36 Virginia Journal of International Law 1; Mirjan Damaška, "Hearsay in Cinquecento Italy" in Michele Taruffo (ed), *Studi di Onore di Vittorio Denti* (CEDAM 1994) 59; Mirjan Damaška, "Of Hearsay and Its Analogs" (1992) 76 Minn L Rev 425.

[67] "Tancred" 3.9 (Berg 237): "The oath having been offered and taken by the witnesses in the presence of the parties, the judge withdraws with a single witness separated from the others to some place, so that no one hears them, and reduces to writing the individual statements or the witness, or has them reduced . . . . And this separation of witnesses was introduced through Daniel, as one reads in the story of Susanna and the very vile priests" (*Recepto supra dicto iuramento a testibus coram partibus praestito, iudex cum uno solo teste ab aliis separato secedat in aliquem locum, ita quod nullus eos audiat, et singula dicta testis per ordinem redigat in scriptis vel redigi faciat. . . . Et haec separatio testium per Danielem introducta est, sicut legitur in historia de Susanna et nequissimis sacerdotibus*).
[68] "Tancred" 3.10 (Berg 240–243).
[69] "Tancred" 3.11 (Berg 243).
[70] "Tancred" 2.17 (Berg 181): "And at least six months to a year in a criminal case" (*Et sunt in causa criminali ad minus sex mensium, ad plus vero unius anni*). And see *De edendo* in Brasington (n 7) 150–151; *Ordo Bambergensis* in Brasington (n 7) 209.
[71] "Tancred" 2.17 (Berg 181): "For seeking witnesses, preparing proofs, finding advocates and seeking the counsel of friends" (*ad testes quaerendos, instrumenta preparanda, advocatos inveniendos et consilia amicorum pentenda*).
[72] "Tancred" 3.8 (Berg 233): "For in criminal cases especially the witnesses, who know about the matter, are compelled to appear before the judge" (*nam in criminalibus praecise cogendi sunt testes venire ad iudicem, qui de causa cognoscit*). Citing Nov 90.5. And see *De edendo* in Brasington (n 7) 152, 154.
[73] "Tancred" 1.6 (Berg 118): "But if the case is criminal, there is no ground for a procurator to intervene" (*Si vero causa est criminalis, frustra intervenit procurator*). Canon law took the view that the intervention of counsel might frustrate the discovery of truth. RH Helmholz, "Introduction" in RH Helmholz and others (eds), *The Privilege against Self-Incrimination: Its Origins and Development* (The University of Chicago Press 1997) 13–14.
[74] "Tancred" 3.5 (Berg 215): "the burden of proof lies on the moving party because proof lies on the one who speaks, not on the one who denies . . . . The moving party and the accuser who say something ought to make proof, if the defendant denies, because, if the moving party does not prove, the defendant, even if he has produced nothing, is acquitted" (*onus probationis incumbit actori, quoniam ei incumbit probatio, qui dicit, non qui negat* [citing Justinian's Digest] . . . *Probare debet actor et accusator, qui aliquid dicunt, si reus negat quoniam actore non probante reus, etsi nil praestiterit, absolvetur*). A Bolognese *ordo* from the third quarter of the thirteenth century deals with the matter expressly: "therefore witnesses are to be produced by those who think they will be of benefit to themselves, because no one ought to be compelled to produce witnesses or proofs against himself or harmful to himself" (*producendi ergo sunt testes ab hiis qui ex[is]timant eos sibi profuturos, quia non debet quis compelli ut testes vel instrumenta contra se vel sibi nocitura producat*). For the dating of the Bolognese *ordo*, see Knut W Nörr, "Bologna and the Court of Admiralty, a Latin Text in the Black Book" in Peter Linehan (ed), 8 *Proceedings of the Seventh International Congress of Medieval Canon Law* (Monumenta iuris canonici Series C, Subsidia 1988) 475, 477. On the burden of producing evidence, see also *De edendo* in Brasington (n 7) 152 and *Ordo Bambergensis* in Brasington (n 7) 233–234.

fear, a confession was not to prejudice the one confessing.[75] At trial, the burden of proof lay on the accuser. The proof was to be clear and transparent.[76] Two witnesses, at least, were required to make sufficient proof.[77] In matters of doubt, a defendant was to be favored.[78] Nevertheless, although not convicted or confessed, accused persons were compelled to purge themselves canonically, if they had been "spattered upon by bad reports" (mala fama respersus), but in no case if they had not been defamed.[79] If defendants failed in purgation, they were to be punished as though they had been convicted.[80]

Judgment had to be pronounced in a dignified public place.[81] If the order of judicial procedure (ordo iudiciarius) was omitted, the decision (sententia) of the court was a nullity (non valet).

In his ordo, Tancred dealt with a circumscribed exception to a judicial order that Gratian had allowed for crimes so manifest that they admitted of no dispute.[82] Tancred noted that a certain judicial order (quidam ordo iudiciarius) had to be followed even in a case where the crime was notorious. Defendants had to be summoned and present; they had to be questioned; no sentence was valid unless defendants willingly absented themselves.[83] Controversy over whether persons charged with notorious crimes were entitled to trial in accord with the ordo was settled by the late thirteenth century, when it was commonly agreed that everyone had a right to a trial, no matter what the crime.[84] Judgments made outside of the ordo were invalid.

[75] "Tancred" 3.4 (Berg 211): "Many things are necessary for a confession to prejudice someone . . . 'Willing,' it has been said, because a confession twisted out through fear does not prejudice" ('Sponte' ideo dictum est, quia confessio per metum extorta non praeiudicat, citing Gratian). See also Ordo Bambergensis in Brasington (n 7) 263–264. Tancred, relying on Gratian, explains that a confession must be voluntary "because a confession twisted out through fear does not prejudice" the defendant (quia confessio per metum extorta non praeiudicat). Ibid citing C 15 q. 6 c 1. And Dig 48.18.1. Tancred's citation to the Justinian's Digest is striking because the Digest's Book 48 acknowledges the customary Roman use of torture. But, at the same time, Dig 48.18.1.27 cautions that confessions made in fear are not trustworthy. Perhaps Book 48 offered the best approximation Tancred could find in a Roman text to support the ordinary canonical principle of voluntariness of confessions.

[76] "Tancred" 2.7 (Berg 161): "in a criminal case the proofs must be clear and open (in causa criminali clarae debent esse probationes et apertae," citing Gratian and Justinian's Code. See also De edendo in Brasington (n 7) 152.

[77] "Tancred" 2.7 (Berg 228): "in any case two witnesses are sufficient" (in qualibet causa duo testes sufficient), citing Gratian and the Digest, unless the law or canons expressly required more. And see De edendo in Brasington (n 7) 154; Ordo Bambergensis in Brasington (n 7) 240.

[78] "Tancred" 3.12 (Berg 247): "But if there are as many [witnesses] for one party as for the other and equally good . . . , what should the judge do then? I answer, then he should acquit the defendant, in that we should be more inclined to acquit than to condemn" (Sed si tot sunt pro una parte, quot pro altera, et aeque boni . . . quid facere debet tunc iudex? Respondeo, absolvat tunc reum . . . eo quod proniores esse debemus ad absolvendum, quam ad condemnandum), citing Gratian and Justinian's Digest.

[79] "Tancred" 2.7 (Berg 161–162).

[80] Ibid.

[81] "Tancred" 4.2 (Berg 280); De edendo in Brasington (n 7) 161.

[82] C 2 q. 1 c 20 dp.

[83] "Tancred" 2.7 (Berg 151). On Tancred's requirement of basic procedural protections even in cases of crimen notorium, see James A Brundage, "Full and Partial Proof in Classical Canonical Procedure" (2007) 67 Jurist 58, 65–66.

[84] Pennington, "Procedure" (n 26) 146–147, citing the thirteenth-century canonist Guillelmus Durantis's maxim that "even the devil if he is in court should not be denied" his right to judicial process.

Attributing divine and natural authority to fair procedure

To show how God proceeds in justly determining disputes between parties, Gratian set out in his Decretum the text of a decretal letter which he believed was written by Pope Evaristus in the early second century.[85] The letter was, in fact, a mosaic of sources that the pseudo-Isidorian forgers of the ninth century had cobbled together. By Gratian's day, the decretal was thought to be genuine. The false ascription of the letter, however, did not affect the valid point the letter was meant to prove: God shows how to make a sound judgment. The letter recites an incident from the Book of Genesis, c 18. When complaints reached God's ears that the people of Sodom were wicked, God did not rush to judgment. Even though God was all-knowing, God did not punish the people without first investigating and requiring proof of the complaints made against them.[86] God did this, not because God was ignorant of the truth, but that he might give us an example, lest we be hasty in deciding and in judging matters, and lest anyone presume to believe the bad deeds of neighbors before proving them:

> By this example, we are warned against ever being impetuous in arriving at judgment or rashly and carelessly judging in any way any matters without examination . . . . For bad reports should move no one, and no one should believe words spoken indiscriminately without certain proof . . . For if the lord, knowing everything, did not wish to believe or to judge all the evils of the people of Sodom, reports (*clamor*) of whom had arrived even in heaven, before himself carefully with faithful witnesses investigating the matters he heard . . . so much more should we, humans and sinful men, to whom the judgments of God are unknown, avoid these things and not judge or condemn any one before there is true and just proof.[87]

Gratian's canon shows that God's own way of proceeding served as a model for fundamental principles of proper procedure.[88] Later commentators on Gratian's work developed the theme. Paucapulea, the first to gloss Gratian's Decretum, recalled another biblical story to make the point that proper order was rooted in a divine prototype. According to the Book of Genesis 3: 8–9, God encountered Adam and Eve after they

---

[85] C 2 q. 1 c 20.

[86] Paul Hinschius (ed), *Decretales Pseudo-Isidorianae et Capitula Angilramni* (B Tauchnitz 1863) 92. The real source of the text quoted above was a passage from a work of Pope Gregory the Great ("Moralia in Job," bk 19, 25 no 45). Given Gregory's sharp consciousness of proper order, as shown in his very genuine *commonitorium*, it is not surprising that Gregory should have seen in the Genesis story a divine legal lesson for just human procedure. Gregory may well have been the first to have interpreted the Genesis story in such a fashion.

[87] Hinschius (n 86) 92. *Deus autem omnipotens, ut nos a praecipitante sententiae prolatione compesceret, cum omnia nuda et aperta sint oculis eius, mala tamen Sodomae noluit audita iudicare priusquam manifeste agnosceret quae dicebantur, unde ipse ait: Descendam et videbo, utrum clamorem, qui venit ad me, opere compleverint, an non est ita ut sciam. Deus omnipotens, cui nihil absconditum est, sed omnia ei manifesta sunt, aetiam antequam fiant, non ab aliud haec et alia multa, quae hic prolixitatem vitantes non inseruimus, per se inquirere dignatus est, nisi ut nobis exemplum daret ne praecipites in discutiendis negotiis essemus, et ne mala quorumquam prius quisquam praesumat credere quam probare. Cuius exemplo monemur, ne ad proferendam sententiam umquam praecipites simus, aut timere indiligenterque indiscussa quaeque quoquomodo iudicemus.* See C 2 q. 1 c 20 in 1 Friedberg and Richter (n 15) 448.

[88] Pennington, *Prince* (n 41) 142.

had tasted of the forbidden fruit in Paradise. God did not punish the couple without first having summoned them.[89] Stephen of Tournai (c 1128–1203),[90] who had studied at Bologna, developed Paucapalea's biblical reference. In his *summa* (1166/1169)[91] of Gratian's *Decretum*, Stephen laid out the biblical story of Adam and Eve in technical terms of legal procedure, as though a trial were taking place.[92] After having summoned Adam and Eve, God gave them the opportunity to raise challenges and objections (*exceptiones*) and to be heard in their defense. Adam was able to make answer that he was innocent. He defended himself by blaming his wife, who also pleaded innocent. She raised the defense that it was all the serpent's fault.[93] By means of his biblical analysis, Stephen was, in effect, anchoring essential procedural principles of judicial order in divine law.[94] Stephen's work began to spread quickly.[95]

By the mid-thirteenth century, where the canonists saw a divine basis to the *ordo*, the jurists spoke of it as natural law or as the law of nations.[96] Although distinctions were drawn among them, the concepts of divine law, scriptural authority, and natural law were closely allied. Referring to God as "highest nature," Stephen of Tournai held that natural law embraced and was harmonious with human and divine law.[97]

---

[89] Ibid 143. On the *ius commune*'s view of the necessity of citing parties, see Richard Helmholz, "Citations and the Construction of Procedural Law in the Ius Commune" in John W Cairns and Paul J du Plessis (eds), *The Creation of the Ius Commune: From Casus to Regula* (Edinburgh University Press 2010) 257–259 and generally 247–275.

[90] For biography of Stephen of Tournai, see von Schulte (n 25) xxii–xxi; Kenneth Pennington, "Stephen of Tournai (Étienne de Tournai)" in Olivier Descamps and Rafael Domingo (eds), *Great Christian Jurists in French History* (CUP 2019) 35–51. Stephen studied at Bologna and influenced early French schools. He "was definitely responsible for the spread of the new science in the Western countries." Stephan Kuttner and Eleanor Rathbone, "Anglo-Norman Canonists of the Twelfth Century: An Introductory Study" (1949–1951) Traditio VII, 279, 293.

[91] For the dating, see Herbert Kalb, *Studien zur Summa Stephans von Tournai, Ein Beitrag zur kanonistischen Wissenschaftsgeschichte des späten 12. Jahrhunderts* (Universitätsverlag Wagner, Innsbruck 1983) 112.

[92] Pennington, *Prince* (n 41) 143–144.

[93] "Some say divine law had its origin in the beginning of the world. For when Adam was charged by the Lord with disobedience, as a defense to the action, he threw the charge back against his wife; indeed, he turned into a plaintiff of his wife, saying, 'the woman whom you gave me as a companion, she herself deceived me and I ate', and so the form of litigating or, as we commonly say, of pleading seems to have arisen in paradise" (*Diuini iuris originem quidam a principio mundi cepisse dicunt. Cum enim Adam de inobedientia argueretur a domino, quasi actioni exceptionem obiciens relationem criminis in coniugem, immo in coniugis actorem conuertit dicens: Mulier, quam didisti michi sociam, ipsa me decepit et comedi sicque litigandi, uel, ut uulgariter dicamus, placitandi forma in paradiso uidetur exorta*). Stephan of Tournai, "Prologue to the 'Summa of Stephan of Tournai'" in Kalb (n 91) 114–115.

[94] Pennington, "Procedure" (n 26) 137. The myth that the *ordo iudiciarius* was rooted in the biblical account of Adam and Eve "retained its explanatory force until the sixteenth century." Ibid.

[95] von Schulte (n 25) xxi.

[96] "In the middle of the thirteenth century, . . . the jurists began to reshape their thinking about the origins of the judicial process and about the rights of defendants . . . [T]heir tentative gropings for rights exploded into a passionate embrace during the second half of the thirteenth century. [cite omit] Theories of inviolable individual rights to . . . due process were spawned in the deep pools of juristic thought." Pennington, *Prince* (n 41) 148; Fraher, "Preventing Crime" (n 54) 230–231. For discussion distinguishing the modern view of fair trial procedure from the view of the medieval *ius commune*, see RH Helmholz, "Natural Human Rights: The Perspective of the Ius Commune" (2003) 52 Cath U L Rev 301, 316–318.

[97] "The law is termed natural, sometimes the law of peoples, because it derived its beginning from human nature alone, as conceived with it. The divine law is also said to be natural because our highest nature, that is God, has taught us both through the law and the prophets, and he has bestowed his gospel upon us. Therefore, the law is termed natural because it at once comprehends human and divine law" (*Dicitur ius naturale quandoque ius gentium, quod ab humana solum natura, quasi cum ea incipiens, traxit*

It was undisputed that any positive law must yield in the face of divine or natural law.[98]

Ordines in Anglo-Norman realms

As the romano-canonical procedure of the *ordines* spread across Western Europe,[99] many such *ordines* and other forms of procedural literature were authored in English and Norman regions.[100] The earliest English treastise on Gratian was the *Summa de multiplici iuris divisione* (1160–1170). It was largely based on Stephen of Tournai's *summa*.[101] Oxford served as the chief center for legal study. Even students from the Continent came there, just as English students went to Bologna to study. Besides at Oxford, the law was also a subject of attention in the cathedral schools of Exeter, Lincoln, and Northampton.[102]

---

exordium. Ius etiam diuinum dicitur naturale, quod summa natura nostra, id est deus, nos docuit et per legem et prophetas et euangelium suum nobis obtulit. Dicitur enim ius naturale, quod simul comprehendit humanum et diuinum). Stephan of Tournai, *Summa*, commenting on Gratian's Dist 1 pr v. "Humanum genus." Kalb (n 91) 41 n 58.

[98] Natural law, it was agreed, held predominance over any conflicting positive law. Gratian repeated the point forcefully in distinguishing human law from divine and natural. "But the natural law prevails of course in dignity over custom and statute. For whatever is received through custom or contained in writings, if they are contrary to the natural law, they must be held void and erroneous" (*Dignitate uero ius naturale simpliciter preualet consuetudini et constitutioni. Quecunque enim uel moribus recepta sunt, uel scriptis comprehensa, si naturali iuri fuerint aduersa, uana et irrita sunt habenda*). Dist 8 c 1 dp in Friedberg and Richter (n 15) 13. Similarly: "Clearly, therefore it appears that statute is subordinate to natural law" (*Liquido igitur apparet, quod consuetudo naturali iuri postponitur*). Dist 8 c 9 dp in Friedberg and Richter (n 15) 16. "But that a *constitutio* must yield place to natural law is proven by much authority" (*Quod autem constitutio naturali iuri cedat multiplici auctoritate probatur*). Dist 9 da in Friedberg and Richter (n 15) 16. "*Constitutiones* therefore, whether ecclesiastical or secular, are utterly to be excluded, if they are contrary to natural law" (*Constitutiones ergo uel ecclesiasticae uel seculares, si naturali iuri contrarie probantur, penitus sunt excludendae*). Dist 9 c 11 dp in Friedberg and Richter (n 15). For a detailed explication of the views of canonists and legists on the preeminence of natural law, see Rudolf Weigand, *Die Naturrechtslehre der Legisten und Dekretisten* (Max Hueber Verlag 1967).

[99] On the new procedure's slow advance in parts of Europe, see Pennington, "Procedure" (n 26) 134–135. The *ordines* were attractive to litigants who thereby could protect themselves against being tried by ordeal. Ibid.

[100] "[E]ver since Stephen of Tournai introduced the methods of Gratian's school in his native country, French canonists—basing themselves of course on a thorough study of Bolognese work—produced in their glosses, *summae, distinctiones, questiones,* etc. an impressive literature of their own [footnote omitted] . . . The influence of French teaching became apparent as a determining factor at the moment when English canonistic learning turned from the receptive stage into that of productive scholarship, i.e., when an English school properly speaking began to take shape." Kuttner and Rathbone (n 90) 290. These genres of procedural literature were concerned "to raise the knowledge of law from a professional technique to a scholastic science." Ibid 292.

[101] Kuttner and Rathbone (n 90) 293. Other Anglo-norman *ordines* include: *Ulpianus de edendo* (1140–1170); *Nunc primo nobis adversarius* (after 1153, in England or Scotland); *Quia iudiciorum quedam sunt preparatoria* (after 1182, for use in Ireland or England); the *Practica legum et decretorum* of William Longchamp (before 1189); *Magistri Ricardi Anglici ordo iudiciarius* (before 1190); *Iudicium est trinus actus trium personarum, scilicet actoris et rei et iudicis* (after 1198); *A.,B.,C., iudices, T. rectori talis ecclesiae* (end of 1100s); *Abbas cuiusdam monasterii* (after 1210); *Modus procedendi in causa et super actionem civilem et criminalem* (after 1234).

[102] Kuttner and Rathbone (n 90) 323. "There is therefore evidence of some degree of familiarity with the principles and doctrines of Roman law in a fairly wide stratum of the educated class in England about 1180 and of a marked infiltration in court and council by men with specialist knowledge." Rathbone (n 41) 263.

Because England, however, had already formed central royal courts before the composition of the *ordines*, the *ius commune* orders of procedure did not govern English common-law procedure.[103] In contrast to the Continent where romano-canonical procedure entered quickly into secular law, in the British Isles, it was the English church that absorbed the principles of the *ordines*. Ecclesiastical courts had done so by the early fourteenth century.[104] Romano-canonical procedure, however, also exercised a marked influence on the procedural principles of those secular courts of England that did not strictly follow the procedures of the common law.[105] These courts included the courts of equity, admiralty, and prerogative royal courts, such as Star Chamber. Through these non-common-law courts, as well as through the ecclesiastical courts, the romano-canonical principles of the *ordines* continued to abide in the English realm.[106]

Summary and Conclusion

In the course of the late-eleventh century and into the twelfth, individual bishops compiled canons for the conduct of ecclesiastical affairs. The canons included procedures to govern trials in church courts. Ivo of Chartres produced the most capacious of these collections. Concerning trials, Ivo's works drew upon Pope Gregory's

---

[103] "England was one of the oldest nation states in Europe and from the twelfth century onwards its royal courts developed one common law for the whole land." Van Caenegem (n 40) 315. English common law "took shape in the royal courts in the twelfth century, well before the rediscovery of the classical Roman law and its study in the School of Bologna started to lead to the 'reception' of Roman law by Continental lawyers and judges. England was early in the modernization of its legal system and, as the neo-Roman model was not yet available, resorted to the adoption of existing elements of customary origin and the invention of native solutions." RC van Caenegem, "L'histoire du droit et la chronologie: Reflexions sur la formation du 'Common Law' et la procédure romano-canonique" in 2 *Études d'histoire du droit canonique dédidiées à Gabriel Le Bras* (Sirey 1965) (2 vols) 1459–1470. See also RC van Caenegem, *The Birth of the English Common Law* (2nd edn, CUP 2012) 85–110; John Langbein, "Trinity Hall and the Relations of European and English Law from the Fourteenth to the Twenty-first Centuries" in *The Milestones Lectures* (Trinity Hall Cambridge 2001) 76; Charles Donahue, Jr.,I "The Courts of the Ius commune" in Hartmann and Pennington, *Courts and Procedure* (n 26) 96.

[104] Donahue, "Witnesses" (n 62) 141; Hartmann and Pennington, *Courts and Procedure* (n 26) 96.

[105] "The new procedure [of Gratian and the *ordines*] was not immediately or universally accepted. Procedural norms die hard in human society. In England, for example, ecclesiastical courts used the *ordo* but the secular courts did not. There the ordeal flourished until 1215." Pennington, "Procedure" (n 26) 134. As to the Continent, "[t]he new procedure took root slowly in some parts of Europe. Although jurists produced scores of treatises that described the rules and procedures of the *ordo iudicarius*, old customs were often resistant to change." Ibid 136.

[106] Church courts were the principle conduit for romano-canonical procedure in England. See generally Charles Donahue, "Proof by Witnesses in the Church Courts of Medieval Europe: An Imperfect Reception of the Learned Law" in Morris S Arnold and others (eds), *On the Laws and Customs of England: Essays in Honor of Samuel E. Thorne* (The University of North Carolina Press 2017). Even after the Reformation, "canon law, together [with] the Roman law that was a necessary component of the *ius commune*, would continue to provide the basic rules of decision in the courts of the English church." RH Helmholz, "Introduction" in RH Helmholz (ed), 127 *Three Civilian Notebooks (1580–1640)* (Selden Society 2011) x. See generally David J Seipp, "The Reception of Canon Law and Civil Law in the Common Law Courts before 1600" (1993) 13 Oxford J Legal Stud 388–420.

instructions in his *commonitorium* of the early seventh century and on the pseudo-Isidorian productions of the mid-ninth century, including the requirement (originally set out in the seventh-century laws of the Visigoths) that witnesses testify from first-hand knowledge about deeds done in their presence.

Around 1140, Gratian sought to make concordant the many canonical collections circulating in his day. Relying often on Ivo, together with the works of Augustine, Gregory, pseudo-Isidore, and papal legislation of the ninth century, Gratian set out coherent principles of trial procedure.

Somewhat in advance of, but later overlapping with Gratian's ecclesiastical endeavors, secular legal scholars at universities devoted themselves to expounding and adapting for medieval needs the full corpus of Justinian's Roman law, now including the *Digest* of Justinian, which had been, for the most part, lost in Western Europe during the previous five hundred years. Azo at the University of Bologna was the leading expositor of the revived Roman law. The two streams of law, Roman and ecclesiastical, blended into a common law (*ius commune*). This "learned law" (as opposed to the so-called "vulgar" ordeals derived from customary or local law) spread over time into the European courts.

The sheer enormity of the legal texts of Justinian and of the church made it difficult for practitioners and judges to grasp and apply the doctrines of the *ius commune* at trial. To respond to their needs, legal scholars began to compose orders of procedure which, drawing upon Gratian and Roman texts, set out orderly stages and detailed principles for trials. Among the proliferation of *ordines*, Tancred's came to be widely accepted as the best and most influential. In most important respects, the various *ordines* agreed on the elements of proper procedure, including presence of parties and witnesses at a public trial at which the accused had the opportunity to defend against the charges. Even at a summary proceeding, the due process principles of summoning defendants and according them an opportunity to defend were observed. Although examination of witnesses took place in secret, their testimonies were published and subject to response by the adverse party.

Employing another practical legal genre, Stephen of Tournai composed a widely influential summary of procedure. In his *summa*, Stephen grounded in biblical and natural law the right of defendants to be summoned and to be accorded a formal trial according to a set order of procedure. The conviction that divine and natural law grounded proper procedure would remain an abiding element of Western legal consciousness.

By the end of the thirteenth century, ecclesiastical courts and the secular courts of the continental *ius commune* employed the main features of the *ordines* across Western Europe.[107] In England, which had developed a common law of its own

---

[107] James A Brundage, "Full and Partial Proof in Classical Canonical Procedure" (2007) 67 The Jurist 58, 58; Kenneth Pennington, "The Fourth Lateran Council, Its Legislation, and the Development of Legal Procedure" in John Witte Jr and others (eds), *Texts and Contexts in Legal History: Essays in Honor of Charles Donahue* (Robbins Collections Publications 2016) 179, 198.

under the influence of a centralized royal government, the principles of the *ordines* did not enter directly into the English common law courts. Nonetheless, romano-canonical doctrines and procedures continued to be well known and practiced in the English church courts, as well as in the courts of admiralty, equity, Star Chamber, and other courts where the *ius commune* remained procedurally influential.

5

Principles of Criminal Procedure
in Inquisitorial Proceedings

The Inception of Inquisitorial Procedure:
Innocent III and the Fourth Lateran Council

Tancred's *ordo* and many like it, along with the *summa* of Stephen of Tournai, reflect the work of legal scholars as they integrated the principles of the revived Roman law with those of the canon law in the latter twelfth and thirteenth centuries. Principles of accusatorial procedure, as contained in Gratian's Decretum, suffused their works. But a most consequential alternative to accusatorial procedure had begun to take root in ecclesiastical forums some sixty years after Gratian's work (c 1140). Even while Tancred was writing his *ordo* (c 1216), "a sea change in court procedure"[1] was already under way in canon law. It would soon be absorbed into a secular criminal procedure. The new way of proceeding would profoundly alter the position of any person suspected of a crime.

This new method of procedure was *inquisitio* or "inquest," so called from the verb *inquirere*, "to inquire." In the late twelfth and early thirteenth centuries, elements of the new procedure had been emerging in church tribunals. Pope Innocent III (pontiff from 1198–1216) (Figure 2) first introduced inquisitorial procedure as a device for attacking corruption in the obtaining of church offices and in other administrative matters.[2] *Inquisitio* offered an efficient method for resolving allegations of wrongdoing. Accusatorial procedure continued as an option,[3] but it required an accuser

---

[1] Kenneth Pennington, "The Fourth Lateran Council, Its Legislation, and the Development of Legal Procedure" in Gert Melville and others (eds), *The Fourth Lateran Council: Institutional Reform and Spiritual Renewal Proceedings of the Conference Marking the Eight Hundredth Anniversary of the Council* (Didymos-Verlag 2017) 18. Pennington understands inquisitorial procedure "as having organically emerged out of practice rather than as a mode of proof imposed on ecclesiastical courts by Rome." Ibid.

[2] *Licet Heli* X 5.3.31 (1199) in Emil Friedberg and Emil Richter (eds), 2 *Decretalium Collectiones, Corpus Iuris Canonici* (B Tauchnitz 1879, reprint Akademische Druck- u Verlagsanstalt 1959) (2 vols) 760–761. The decretal *Qualiter et Quando* followed in February 1206 (ibid 738–739). Contrary to common belief, *inquisitio* was not an institution primarily designed to suppress heresy. HA Kelly, "Inquisition and the Prosecution of Heresy: Misconceptions and Abuses" (1989) 58 Church History 439, 440–441. The inquisitional proceedings against "heretical depravity" (*inquisitiones heretice pravitatis*) should be kept distinct from inquisitorial procedure (*inquisitio*) itself. Ibid 441. Heresy inquisitions, as they developed, truncated opportunities for defense by keeping the names of witnesses secret and other measures. "The abusive practices that came to prevail in the special heresy tribunals do not merit the name of inquisition but rather should be identified as a perversion of the inquisitorial process caused by overzealous and underscrupulous judges." Ibid 450–451.

[3] "Inquisitorial procedure took its place alongside accusatorial, and both remained important for the next four centuries." Kenneth Pennington, "Introduction to the Courts" in Wilfried Hartmann and Kenneth Pennington (eds), *The History of Courts and Procedure in Medieval Canon Law* (The Catholic University of America Press 2016) 7.

Foundations of American Criminal Due Process at Trial. Francis R. Herrmann and Brownlow M. Speer,
Oxford University Press. © Oxford University Press 2025. DOI: 10.1093/9780199364770.003.0005

Figure 2 Relief of Pope Innocent III (1161–1216). Under his authority and that of the Fourth Lateran Council (1215), inquisitorial procedure spread in ecclesiastical and secular courts. This marble relief was carved by Joseph Kiselewski in 1950 and is one of 23 marble relief portraits over the gallery doors of the House Chamber in the U.S. Capitol, which depict historical figures noted for their work in establishing the principles that underlie American law.

Credit: Architect of the Capitol.

to commence a criminal proceeding. This requirement could present an obstacle to prosecution, for an accuser might be loathe to come forward or might be otherwise unavailable. In such instances, there was a danger that unknown crime or corruption might remain unpunished.[4] The new inquisitorial procedure dispensed with the need for an accuser in any traditional sense. It provided for an ecclesiastical judge to initiate a proceeding by virtue of his office (*ex officio*) against a particular cleric, provided that public suspicion (*fama*) of his misconduct had accumulated. No individual accuser was required to make the complaint.[5]

On its face inquisitorial procedure appeared to transgress the time-honored Roman and canon law rule that one cannot be accuser and judge in the same case.[6] The Fourth Lateran Council of 1215 anticipated this objection when it institutionalized the inquisitorial procedure of Innocent's earlier decretal *Qualiter et Quando*. The public *fama* or *clamor* that had to precede the initiation of any inquisition fulfilled the role of an accuser.[7] Frequently repeated reports had to have arisen from prudent and honest persons, and not from ill-willed or slandering ones.[8]

While the method was novel, it was not intended to eliminate the due process values that the *ordines* expounded.[9] Indeed, Canon 8 emphasized due process procedures.[10]

---

[4] Canonists, drawing from Roman law, formulated the phrase "lest crimes remain unpunished" (*ne crimina remaneant impunita*) to reflect the fact that crime was not merely a private matter but one of public concern requiring effective prosecutorial procedures. See Richard M Fraher, "The Theoretical Justification for the New Criminal Law of the High Middle Ages: Rei Publicae Interest, Ne Crimina Remaneant Impunita" (1984) 1984 U Ill L Rev 577, 581–584; Kenneth Pennington, "The Jurisprudence of Procedure" in Wilfried Hartmann and Kenneth Pennington (eds), *The History of Courts and Procedure in Medieval Canon Law* (Catholic University of America Press 2016) 133, 140–144; Kenneth Pennington, "Law, Criminal Procedure" in William Chester Gordon (ed), *Dictionary of the Middle Ages, Supp I* (Charles Scribner's Sons 2004) 312–313.

[5] By 1210, Tancred included a description of *inquisitio* in his "*Summula de criminibus*." For the text, see Richard M Fraher, "Tancred's Summula de Criminibus: A New Text and a Key to the Ordo Iudiciarius" (1979) 9 Bull Medieval Canon L (n.s.) 23, 29–35.

[6] Pennington, "Procedure" (n 4) 142–143; Kelly, "Misconceptions" (n 2) 446.

[7] X 5.1.24, *Qualiter et quando* in 2 Friedberg and Richter (n 2) 745–747 ("not as though the same person is accuser and judge, but, as if with *fama* denouncing and *clamor* accusing, let him fulfill the duty of his office" (*non tanquam idem sit accusator et iudex, sed quasi denunciante fama vel deferente clamore officii sui debitum exsequatur*").

[8] *a malevolis et maledictis.* X 5.1.24.

[9] "The pope insisted that all the procedural protections that were granted to defendants in accusatorial procedure were also given in this procedure. Defendants had the right to defend themselves with testimony, witnesses, and exceptions as well as replications (judicial replies to specific charges). The defendant should also be present at the trial." Pennington, "Procedure" (n 4) 143. "The defendant had to be present, and the chapters of inquiry (that is, the charges) had to be given and explained to him and all rights of defense allowed." Kelly "Misconceptions" (n 2) 446; HA Kelly, "The Fourth Lateran *Ordo* of Inquisition Adapted to the Prosecution of Heresy" in Donald S Prudlo (ed), *A Companion to Heresy Inquisitions* (Brill 2019) 73, 103–104; Walter Ullmann, "The Defense of the Accused in the Medieval Inquisition" (1950) 73 The Irish Ecclesiastical Record 481.

"Although *Qualiter et quando* made it easier both to initiate criminal charges and to secure conviction on them, it preserved the most basic element of the *ordo iuris*. The defendant must be summoned to appear; he must be informed of the charges and given an opportunity to defend himself. The constitution specified that he must be told who had testified against him and what they had said. He must likewise be permitted to enter objections and rebut their evidence, 'lest the suppression of the names of a hostile witness or the exclusion of exceptions present an insolent person with the chance to bear false witness.'" James A Brundage, "Full and Partial Proof in Classical Canonical Procedure" (2007) 67 The Jurist 58, 59.

[10] Fourth Lateran Council c 8 in Antonio García y García, *Constitutiones Concilii quarti Lateranensis una cum Commentariis glossatorum* (MIC Series A: Corpus Glossatorum 2; Biblioteca Apostolica Vaticano 1981).

The presence of the defendant at trial was required.[11] Charges had to be revealed to him so that he would have opportunity to defend himself.[12] Not only the statements but also the names of the witnesses were to be provided him so that both what was said and by whom might be clear.[13] Legitimate defenses were to be admitted.[14]

The canon defended against the possible objection that the new inquisitorial procedure failed to keep the role of judge and criminal investigator distinct and thereby compromised the disinterestedness of the judge. To justify the judge's investigative initiatives, the canon cited two biblical bases. In Luke's gospel, the property owner in the parable of the unjust steward called the suspected steward in and asked him, "What is this I hear about you? Give an account of your management, because you cannot be manager any longer."[15]"And did not God himself investigate whether there was any truth to the people's outcry over wrongdoing in Sodom and Gemorrah?"[16]

A new emphasis on combatting crime may have impelled the shift in procedure, as the prosecution of offenses became a matter of public and not merely private interest.[17] *Inquisitio* was quickly adopted as the primary means for prosecuting serious offenses in secular jurisdictions, where the secular law also empowered judges to torture the suspect in an effort to obtain a confession.[18]

Voluntary confessions and freedom from compulsory self-incrimination

The great paradox of medieval Continental criminal jurisprudence is that, while torture of a suspect to obtain a confession of guilt was permitted under certain conditions, the jurisprudence never abandoned in theory the principle that a confession must be "voluntary" in order to serve as the basis for a conviction.

---

[11] "Therefore, he ought to be present against whom the inquisition is made, unless he has absented himself through contempt" (*Debet igitur esse praesens is, contra quem facienda est inquisitio, nisi se per contumaciam absentaverit*). Ibid.

[12] "Those charges about which inquisition will be made must be to explained to him, so that he may have the ability to defend himself" (*exponenda sunt ei illa capitula, de quibus fuerit inquirendum, ut facultatem habeat defendendi se ipsum*). Ibid.

[13] "And not only the statements but also the very names of the witnesses must be published to him in order that what was said and by whom might appear" (*Et non solum dicta, sed etiam nomina ipsa testium sunt ei, ut quid et a quo sit dictum appareat, publicanda*). Ibid.

[14] "And legitimate exceptions and replications must be allowed."(*nec non exceptiones et replicationes legitimae admittendae*). Ibid. The canon's *ordo* did not have to be followed in every detail in cases against lesser religious non-prelates who could be removed from office more easily (*facilius et liberius*). Ibid.

[15] Ibid, referencing Lk 16:1–13; see also X 5.1.17 in 2 Friedberg and Richter (n 2) 746.

[16] Canon 8 (n 10), referencing Gen 18:21; see also X 5.1.17 in 2 Friedberg and Richter (n 2) 746. For discussion, see RH Helmholz, *The Ius Commune in England: Four Studies* (OUP 2001) 117. On judge taking place of accuser, see Walter Ullmann, "Some Medieval Principles of Criminal Procedure" (1947) 59 Juridical Review 1, 23.

[17] See Fraher, "Theoretical Justification" (n 4) 577.

[18] In turn, Pope Innocent IV (1243–1254) in 1252, breaking with the Church's previous teachings that rejected involuntary confessions as bases of guilt, required authorities to coerce confessions from suspected heretics, so long as there was no danger of loss of member or death. *Ad extirpanda*, lex 25 in A Tomassetti and others (eds), *Bullarum, Diplomatum, et Privilegiorum Sanctorum Romanorum Pontificum Taurensis editio* (Tomus III) (Seb Franco, H Fory et H Dalmazzo 1858) 552–558.

The *ordines* insisted that a confession must be voluntary (*sponte*) to be valid proof of guilt.[19] The revived Roman law adopted the requirement of voluntariness but manipulated the concept to make it compatible with the practice of torture. When a defendant had confessed in the torture chamber, the defendant would be brought before a judge after a lapse of time. There, publicly in the presence of witnesses and in the absence of any immediate threat of imminent physical harm the defendant would be invited to repeat the confession.[20] Thus, in the thinking of medieval Continental jurists, the in-court confession was purged of the use of force and qualified as "voluntary."

Related to the requirement that a confession be voluntary, there emerged a distinct principle that, under certain conditions, one need not answer an incriminating question in a judicial proceeding. In the mid-thirteenth century, the Latin maxim "*nemo tenetur seipsum prodere*" (No one is held to betray himself.) originated in the canon law on the continent of Europe.[21] Various strands of earlier canon law and practice contributed to its crystallization in the medieval era. Three deserve mention here:

(1) *The seal on sacramental confession.* Pope Leo I in 459 had recognized that sacramental confession, if not confined to the internal forum[22] of the church, risked a penitent's being subjected to public shame and disgrace or exposure to ecclesiastical or secular criminal jurisdictions. Leo opposed such public confession and emphasized that guilty consciences should be revealed only to priests in a secret confession. Otherwise:

> [M]any may be prevented from approaching the remedies of penance, so long as they grow red with embarrassment or fear their deeds will be revealed to

---

[19] See Tancredus Bononiensis, *Ordo iudiciarius* in Friedrich Christian Bergmann (ed), *Pillii, Tancredi, Gratiae Libri de iudiciorum ordine* (Göttingen 1852, photo reprint Scientia Verlag 1965); "Tancred" 3.3 (Bergmann 211). See text to n 75 in ch 4.

[20] "Someone can be definitively convicted not only on the basis of witnesses but from a confession willingly made in court" (*[N]edum ex testibus, sed ex confessione in iudicio sponte facta potest quis diffinitive damnari*). Alberto da Gandino, *Tractatus de maleficiis* in Hermann Kantorowicz, 2 *Albertus Gandinus und das Strafrecht der Scholastik* (Walter De Gruyter & Co 1926) (2 vols) 95. But a confession "willingly made in court" did not exclude torture *before* the defendant's "willing" confession before a judge. "If, however, one confesses in tortures or in the fear of tortures, then his confession does not stand nor is he taken as if having confessed and the reason is that torture is a delicate matter, so that the judge should make the criminal come before him and ask of him whether he wishes to persevere in his confession or retract or contradict. And if he should persevere, the confession holds, otherwise not" (*Si autem confiteatur quis in tormentis vel formidine tormentorum, tunc confessioni non statur nec pro confesso habetur* [citing to Justinian's Code] *et est ratio, quia questio fragilis res est* [citing Justinian's Digest] *ut iudex faciat coram se criminosum venire et querat ab eo, utrum velit perseverare in confessione sua an retractare vel contrarium dicere. et si perseveraverit tenet confessio, alias non*). Ibid 161–162.

[21] Bernard of Parma, X 2.20.37 s.v. "*de causis*" (1241). The maxim did not originate in the common law of England as is sometimes thought. See RH Helmholz, "Introduction" in RH Helmholz and others (eds), *The Privilege against Self-Incrimination: Its Origins and Development* (University of Chicago Press 1997) 7–9 and passim.

[22] Joseph Goering defines the distinction between the internal and external forum: "In general, the external forum is concerned with public and manifest transgressions of the Church's law or of divine law, while the internal forum is the court of conscience ('*forum conscientiae*') where even secret crimes and sins are considered, along with manifest sins against God, neighbor, and self." Joseph Goering, "The Internal Forum and the Literature of Confession" in Wilfried Hartmann and Kenneth Pennington (eds), *The History of Medieval Canon Law in the Classical Period, 1140–1234: From Gratian to the Decretals of Gregory IX* (The Catholic University of America) 379, 380.

their enemies by whom they can be destroyed by means of the establishment of the laws.[23]

John Chrysostom, bishop of Antioch in the fourth century, expressed the same concern in pithier language, translated to the Middle Ages into a Latin version as: *Non tibi dico ut te prodas in publico* ("I do not tell you to betray yourself in public").[24] Gratian used Leo's passage and that of Chrysotom.[25] Peter Lombard's *Sententiae* (c 1150), a work central to the curricula of medieval universities, referenced Gratian's use of both Leo and Chrysostom.[26]

The Lateran Council of 1215 decreed that the seal of confession absolutely protected against any public revelation a penitent's statements made in the course of confessing sins to a priest.[27]

(2) *Oaths of innocence suffice to end prosecutions of clerics.* In pre-inquisitorial canonical criminal procedure, an accused cleric never had the burden of explaining or giving his version of the facts alleged against him. This factor may have fostered a belief in a right not to answer questions seeking a disclosure of one's turpitude or criminality. All that practice required of the accused cleric was his oath that he was innocent, buttressed by the oaths of other clerics in support of him.

(3) *The emergence of a limited principle against self-betrayal.* The secrecy of sacramental confession and the sufficiency of oaths of purgation to establish innocence suggest a consciousness that one should not be forced to speak publicly about one's alleged misconduct. However, to the extent that an individual may have been able to refuse to respond to any question put to him, two new legal developments introduced in the first half of the thirteenth century curtailed that ability.

It was assumed that Lateran Council IV's Canon 8 (*Qualiter et Quando*) required a defendant to take an oath to tell the truth about the subject under investigation and then to respond truthfully to whatever questions the inquisitorial judge put to him.[28]

Around the same time, civil procedure in romano-canonical practice introduced the custom of pretrial interrogatories known as *positiones*.[29] By a party's

[23] *[N]e multi a poenitentiae remediis arceantur, dum aut erubescunt aut mituunt inimicis suis sua facta reserari, quibus possint legum constitutione percelli.* Epist 168, in J-P Migne and others (eds), 1 *Sancti Leonis Magni Romani Pontificis Opera Omnia* in 54 PL 1211.

[24] 63 PG 216.

[25] De pen Dist 1. c 87 dp in 1 Friedberg and Richter (n 2) 1184; De pen Dist 1. c 89 in 1 Friedberg and Richter (n 2) 1189.

[26] 192 PL 884–885.

[27] X 5.38.12 (= Canon 21 of Lateran IV's decrees in Johannes Domenicus Mansi and others (eds), 22 *Sacrorum Conciliorum nova, et amplissima collectio* (Venetiis apud Antonium Zatta 1778) 1007–1010). See Goering (n 22) 379–428.

[28] Innocent III's decretal *Cum delecti*, X 5.1.18 (1205) required defendants to answer truthfully to the charges laid against them (*ad inquisita veraciter responderet*). Commentators took the oath of *Cum delecti* to be the oath required by Canon 8. Kelly, "*Ordo*" (n 9) 79.

[29] On the origin of *positiones*, see William P Sullivan, "Admissibility in Roman-Canon Procedure: The Emergence of the Law of Positions" (Dissertation submitted to the Faculty of the Division of the Humanities Department of Classics and the Faculty of the Division of the Social Sciences Department of History, University of Chicago, ProQuest LLC 2020).

stating a *positio* for the adversary to agree or disagree with, the factual issues of a case were narrowed. Under this procedure in its inception, the adversary might be called upon to respond to a *positio* requesting him to acknowledge his own turpitude in the subject matter of the litigation. A passage in Tancred's *Ordo iudiciorum* shows there was resistance to this infringement of a perceived right not to answer an incriminating question:

> If indeed the person interrogated does not respond in any manner, some say he is to be held just as if he confessed. [citations]. Indeed, the truth is he neither acknowledges nor denies . . . And therefore, I say he must not be condemned as having confessed, but is to be punished at the discretion of the judge as contumacious.[30]

Tancred here is relying on the Digest of Justinian where the maxim about the implications of silence appears in the concluding book as one of the *regulae iuris*. While the maxim obviously does not articulate an unfettered right to remain silent in the face of interrogation, it, nonetheless, carefully makes the point that silence is not to be equated with confession.[31]

The same point is made on the same authority in a somewhat later *ordo*, Gratia's *Summa de iudiciario ordine*:

> Next let us see about the punishment of persons unwilling to respond to a *positio* that was made. And it is known that the practice of cases in this is common that if someone does not respond to a *positio* he is considered as convicted as to that *positio*. But according to the law it seems to be otherwise, because one who is silent does not always affirm; because one who is silent does not altogether confess but it is true he does not deny. [Citation to Justinian's Digest 50.17.142] Whence some say that he ought not to be proceeded against as one confessing but as against one who is contumacious. And this opinion pleases me greatly, because it contains fairness (*equitatem*). Nevertheless, the common practice is against the law as has been said.[32]

What is not present in the *ordines* of Tancred and Gratia is a straightforward statement of a right to remain silent in the face of an incriminating question. Bernard of Parma (Bernardo Bottoni) (d. 1266) offered such a statement, hedged by an express limitation, when he compiled his glosses (i.e., short explanations) on the decretals

---

[30] *Si vero interrogatus nullo modo respondeat, dicunt quidam eum perinde teneri ac si confiteretur . . . Verum quidem est, quod nec fatetur, neque negat . . . ; et ideo dico illum non condemnandum tamquam confessum, sed tamquam contumacem ad arbitrium iudicis puniendum.* "Tancred" 3.3 (Bergmann 209–210)". See Sullivan (n 29) 146, discussing Tancred's interpretation of silence.

[31] See Christoph Krampe, "Qui tacet, consentire videtur: Über die Herkunft einer Rechtsregel" in Dieter Schwab and others (eds), *Staat, Kirche, Wissenschaft in einer pluralistischen Gesellschaft: Festschrift zum 65. Geburtstag von Paul Mikat* (Duncker & Humblot 1989) 367.

[32] *Deinde videamus de poena nolentium respondere positioni factae. Et est sciendum, quod usus causarum ad hoc communis est, quod si quis non respondeat positioni, pro convicto habeatur quantum ad illam positionem. De iure vero secus videtur, quia non semper, qui tacet, affirmat; quia, qui tacet, omnino fatetur, sed verum est eum non negare.* [Dig 50.17.142]. *Unde dicunt quidam, quod non debet procedi contra eum tamquam confitentem, sed tamquam contra contumacem.* Gratia Aretinus, *Summa de iudiciario ordine* (after 1234), *De positionibus* 2.3 in Bergmann (n 19) 365.

which Pope Gregory IX had collected and issued as an authoritative text of the canon law in 1234. Bernard's glosses came to be regarded as the *glossa ordinaria* to the decretals and were regularly published with them.

His gloss on the decretal *Cum causam* addressed the need for careful examination of witnesses and the foundation of their proffered testimony.[33] In this context, Bernard took up the question whether a witness could be asked possibly incriminating questions. Bernard began by observing that witnesses who are questioned about their qualifications are analogous to persons about to become clerics. By canon law, a person who was doing penance could not be ordained a cleric. Before ordination, the person had to truthfully disclose to the bishop the fact that he was doing penance. If the candidate failed to reveal the fact, and the bishop then in ignorance ordained him, the man was to be deposed from the clerical state due to his failure to disclose. Bernard suggests that a witness, similarly, has to be honest about his qualifications. Thus, at first glance, it seems the witness would have to answer whether he was criminous or otherwise be disqualified from testifying:

> [W]hether a witness is held to respond whether he is criminous, a person who has perjured himself, or such as cannot testify? And it seems so: because these are circumstances about which question is being made, [citation to Digest] and because the witness in a criminal case and man being ordained are equivalently situated [citation]. But a man being ordained is held to speak his crime [Gratian Dist 50. c 55].[34]

Bernard, however, further observes that there appears to be contrary authority. He cites what may have been a familiar maxim "no one is held to betray himself" (*nemo tenetur se ipsum prodere*), derived from Chrysostom's sermon on sacramental penance: "I do not tell you that you should betray yourself in public" (*non tibi dico ut te prodas in publico*):

> But it seems to the contrary that he is not held to respond: because no one is held to betray oneself. [Citation to *non tibi dico* in Gratian].[35]

Bernard then focuses on the original sacramental context of the maxim and limits the reach of its application:

> This authority speaks about him who confesses in the court of his soul, and he is not held to confess publicly what is secret.[36]

---

[33] *Cum causam* (X. 2.22.37) was a decretal of Innocent III. For the text of the decretal see, 2 Friedberg and Richter (n 2) 330 & n 2. The earliest known copy of Bernard's gloss is Oxford University's manuscript BL MS Lat th b 4ms (1241).

[34] *Sed numquid testis tenetur respondere an sit criminosus, periurus, vel talis qui non possit testificari? Et videtur quod sic: quia istae sunt circumstantiae de quibus quaeritur . . . & quia testis in causa criminali & ordinandus aequiparantur . . . sed ordinandus tenetur dicere crimen suum* [cite to Dist 50 c 55]. Gloss on X 2.20.37, s.v. *"de causis"* in *Decretales D. Gregorij Papae IX suae integretati una cum glossis* (Venetiis apud Socios Aquilae Renouantis 1605) 523.

[35] *Sed contra videtur, quod non teneatur respondere: quia nemo tenetur prodere se* [citation to Chrysostom's *non tibi dico* as incorporated in Gratian]. Ibid.

[36] *Haec autoritas loquitur de eo, qui in iudicio animae confitetur, & ille non tenetur crimen suum occultum publicè confiteri.* Ibid.

Bernard struggles to harmonize two competing lines of thought. How can the church, dependent upon qualified witnesses in its investigation of clerical misconduct, assure itself that proffered witnesses are non-criminous without compelling the witnesses to reveal publicly their own wrongdoing? He concludes, with some apparent hesitation, the maxim should not operate to impede the investigation of the witness's qualifications:

> What therefore shall we say? It is enough to be able to say that he ought to respond at least to those things which are under discussion [citations to Gratian and Digest]. And it seems fair enough that they not be interrogated except about those matters about which mention is made in the aforesaid laws:[37] because such things are not to be enlarged but restricted.[38]

Pope Innocent IV, before assuming the papacy in 1243, was the distinguished legal scholar Sinibaldo dei Fieschi. He took a clearer position on the issue of when a person might be compelled to answer an incriminating question. In commenting on the decretal *Dudum*, involving the legality of a single cleric holding several church benefices simultaneously. Innocent first stated a principle against such compulsion broadly:

> [B]ut about crimes he [the target of the proceedings] ought not to swear to tell the truth [*de veritate dicenda*], since if inquiry is made of anyone about his secret crimes, hardly anyone would be found without crimes [cite to Gratian on penance] because again no one should be told that he should betray himself in public [C 2, q. 1 c 19].[39]

The principle even shields him from having to give answers, which, although not directly incriminating, would inexorably lead to proof of guilt; that is, tend to incriminate him.[40]

Innocent, however, circumscribes the principle with a critically important limitation. It does not apply to facts that are already "notorious":

> [As to] facts that are notorious, we say, nevertheless, he is required to answer whether he has been defamed about any crime or convicted ... Likewise, some say, and not badly, that about all matters which impede the execution of office after penance has been done interrogation should be made since thus his good is cared for [citation to C 23 q.5 c 4.]. Likewise, he does not betray himself in public [*nec iste prodest se in*

---

[37] Apparently the laws concerning witness qualifications.

[38] *Quid ergo dicemus? Satis potest dici, quod debet respondere saltem ad ea de quibus traditur ... Et satis videtur honestum, quod non interrogentur nisi de his, de quibus fit mentio in legibus praedictis: quia talia non sunt amplianda sed restringenda.* Ibid.

[39] *[S]ed super criminibus non debet iurare de veritate dicenda, cum si a quolibet inquireretur de suis criminibus occultis, vix quisquam sine criminibus reperiretur* [citation to Gratian on penance] *quia item nemini dicendum est, vt se prodat in publicum* [C 2 q.1 c 19]. Innocent IV, *Apparatus in quinque libros Decretalium* (Frankfurt 1570, reprint Frankfurt am Main 1968) commentary on "*Dudum ecclesia*" (X 1.6.54) 78v at s 11.

[40] "Just as he is not held to respond whether he is criminous, so neither [is he held to respond] to those *positiones* through which that conclusion is reached" ([S]*icut non tenetur respondere, an sit criminosus, sic nec illis positionibus, per quas pervenitur ad illud.*) Ibid. Of course, so long as he was not forced (*coactus*), the subject of questioning could respond voluntarily (*voluntarius*). Ibid.

publicum] because he is inquired of only about those things which are known, that is by infamy and conviction, not about secret crime . . . I believe also that the principal persons (*principales personae*) are not required to answer, if the matter has to do with a punishment other than spiritual.[41]

Thus, Innocent maintained that inquisitorial procedure does not violate the principle against self-betrayal when infamy had already attached to the target of the inquiry. In his commentary on the decretal *Cum super*,[42] Innocent equates a defamed person's obligation to swear that he is innocent under the older purgative procedure with the obligation of a defamed *inquisitus* to answer truthfully whether he, in fact, committed the crime. Innocent poses the problem of whether a judge can require a defamed person to admit to the crime charged (simony) in light of the principle against self-betrayal expressed in the quotation from John Chrysostom *non tibi dico, ut te prodas in publicum*:

> But it seems to be to the contrary [citation to Gratian, C.2.q.1.c.19] where it says I do not tell you that you should betray yourself in public [*non tibi dico, ut te prodas in publicum.*] Solution: wherever it is put in a *positio* that one was publicly apprehended, or convicted, or confessed, he must answer . . . Likewise also, if it was certain that someone has been defamed, even if it is not put forward in a *positio*, he can be publicly interrogated, if he is proceeded against by accusation, or by inquisition . . . or also in another manner criminally or civilly.
>
> This I show thus, a purgation can be imposed on him where he ought to deny through his oath and purging that he committed the crime. [C 2 q.5 c13]. All the more strongly, before purgation is imposed, it can be asked of him whether he committed the crime . . . but if he was not defamed, or convicted, or confessed, or apprehended, then the judge does not force him to respond.[43]

Here Innocent IV explicitly recognizes the principle against self-betrayal, even as he drastically circumscribes its scope in inquisitorial proceedings.[44] An *ordo iudiciorum*,

---

[41] *[Q]ualiter autem facti, talis notoria sunt, dicimus tamen eum cogendum respondere, an sit infamatus de aliquo crimine, vel condemnatus . . . Item dicunt quidam, & non male, quod, de omnibus, quod impendiunt executionem officij post actam poenitentiam interrogari debent, cum sic bonum eius procuretur* [cite omitted]. *Item nec iste prodest se in publicum, quia tantum de his quae nota sunt quare. s. infamia & condemnatione, non de crimine occulto . . . credo etiam quod principales personae non coguntur respondere, si ad aliam poenam quam spirituale agatur.* Ibid.

[42] Ibid commentary on *Cum super* (X 2.18.2) 246v. The decretal mandates that a person incriminated by the confession of another must purge himself of the resulting infamy.

[43] *Sed videtur contra* [citation to Gratian], *ubi dicit, non tibi dico, vt te prodas in publicum. Solu. vbicumque in positione ponitur quod publicè fuit deprehensus, vel conuictus, vel confessus respondere debet* [citation to X 3.2.7, 349v]. *Item etiam si certum esset, quod quis infamatus est, etiam si in positione non apponatur, publicè poterit interrogari, si agitur contra eum accusando, vel inquirendo . . . vel etiam alio modo criminaliter vel ciuiliter.*

Quod probo sic, potest ei indici purgatio, vbi per iuramentum suum, & purgatorium oportet negare se crimen commississe [C 2 q. 5 c 13] *multofortius antequam indicatur purgatio, potest ab eo quaerere an crimen commiserit, . . . si verò non sit infamatus siue conuictus, nec confessus, nec depraehensus, tunc non coget eum iudex repondere.* Ibid.

[44] Henry Ansgar Kelly remarks: "[M]erely indicating that an oath had to be taken by persons established to be suspect and ordered to undergo purgation was hardly sufficient justification for imposing such an

published in Innocent's lifetime, cited Innocent as the primary authority for the principle itself:

> Concerning criminal matters, however, according to the teaching of the Lord Pope Innocent the Fourth, *positiones* should not be made because no one is obligated to betray himself [citation to Gratian *non tamen dico ut te prodas*] except in two cases: one is when he against whom *positiones* are made has been defamed [*infamatus*] about that crime that is posed.[45]

Thomas Aquinas (1224/1225–1274), the central figure of medieval theology, closely analyzed the principle against self-betrayal in his *Summa Theologiae*, composed between 1266 and 1273. In a theological context, Aquinas first sets out a contention that the principle is universally applicable and allows an accused person to deny the truth that would lead to his conviction:

> It seems that an accused, without sinning mortally, can deny the truth that would lead to his conviction. For Chrysostom says...I do not say to you that you should betray yourself in public, nor accuse yourself before another (*Non tibi dico ut te prodas in publicum, neque apud alium accuses*). But if an accused were to confess the truth in court, he would betray and accuse himself. Therefore, he is not held to speak the truth; and thus he does not sin mortally, if he lies in court.[46]

Aquinas, however, distinguishes between an accused's independent disclosure of his own guilt and the disclosure required by an interrogating judge. In the latter case, it is the judge, and not the accused, who is the agent of "betrayal":

> [To this contention] it must, therefore, be said that when someone is interrogated by a judge according to the rule of law [*secundum ordinem iuris*], he does not betray

oath [to answer truthfully to questions] on a defendant in an inquisition, because in the latter case it went beyond registering mere denial. It obligated him to tell the truth in response to additional questions about the denied crime." Henry Ansgar Kelly, "Oath Taking in Inquisitions" (2018) 35 Bull Medieval Canon L (n.s.) 215, 224–225.

[45] *Super criminalibus autem secundum doctrinam Domini Pape Innocentii Pape quarti non debent fieri positiones quia nullus debet se prodesse ... nisi in duobus casibus: unus est quando ille contra quem fiunt positiones infamatus est de illo crimine tali ponatur ... de quibus habes Extra, De acc. in qui, Si communis* [X. 5.1.21]. Martinus da Fano, *De positionibus* in Ugo Nicolini, *Trattati "De positionibus" attribuiti a Martino da Fano in un codice sconosciuto dell'Archiginnasio di Bologna (B 2794, 2795)* (Vita e Pensiero 1935) (Orbis Romanus 4) 81. The second exception applied where there was some continuing harm to the Church even after penance has been done, as when a judicial office or reception of a benefice is impeded ("*post actam penam impeditur executio iudici vel receptio benefitij*"). See RH Helmholz, *The Privilege against Self-Incrimination: Its Origins and Development* (University of Chicago Press 1997) 22, discussing X 5.1.21.

[46] *Videtur, quod absque peccato mortali possit accusatus veritatem negare, per quam condemnaretur: dicit enim Chrys...:'Non tibi dico ut te prodas in publicum, neque apud alium accuses': sed si veritatem confiteretur in judicio accusatus, seipsum proderet, et accusaret; non ergo tenetur veritatem dicere: et ita non peccat mortaliter, si in iudicio mentiatur.* Question 69, article 1 in *Divi Thomae Aquinatis, Summa Theologica, Secunda Secundae Partis* (Romae ex typograhia Forzani et S. 1894) 506.

himself, but is betrayed by another; provided that the necessity of responding is imposed on him through whom he is held to obey.[47]

Aquinas draws the conclusion that a person may remain silent about his guilt, but not if a judge of competent authority compels him to speak in response to an interrogation for which a factual foundation exists. Then, he may not resist the interrogation by remaining silent. In that case, the accused, who owes obedience to the judge, sins mortally by withholding the truth:

[F]or no one is held to confess the whole truth but only that which a judge can and should require from him according to the rule of law [*ordinem iuris*]: for example, when infamy [*infamia*] about some crime has preceded, or manifest evidence [*expressa indicia*] has appeared, or also a half-proof has preceded [*probatio semiplena*] ... So, therefore, a defendant who is accused may defend himself by hiding the truth which he is not bound to confess through some appropriate means, for example, if he does not respond to matters to which he is not held to respond.[48]

As a matter of canon law, the contours of the principle against self-betrayal were set out in Guillaume Durand (Durantis)'s encyclopedic *Speculum Iudiciale* (1271–1291), a comprehensive and widely used treatise on practice and procedure in the canon law courts. Durantis first takes up the matter in the context of the *positiones*. He asks whether a party can be obliged to answer the opposing party's *positio* when it would entail an admission of criminality by the party questioned. He answers that one is not compelled to respond to a criminous *positio*:

[I]t must be considered whether a *positio* should be made about a crime of him against whom it is made: that it ought not to be, whether the proceeding is in the manner of accusation, or inquisition, or exception. For no one is forced to answer that he is criminous, according to *Non tibi dico, ut te prodas* ... But what if it is put that someone committed a crime? and that it is *notorius*? and that there is *fama*? I respond he must answer about notoriousness and *fama* ... and if he denies *fama* and notoriousness, he is not held to respond whether he committed the crime, since he is not held to accuse himself [*se publicare*] ... But if he confesses that he is defamed, or it is otherwise proven, then it is inquired of him whether he committed the crime.[49]

---

[47] [D]icendum, quod quando aliquis secundum ordinem iuris a judice interrogatur, non ipse se prodit, sed ab alio proditur; dum ei necessitas respondendi imponitur per eum, cui obedire tenetur. Ibid 507.

[48] [N]on enim aliquis tenetur omnem veritatem confiteri, sed illam solum, quam ab eo potest, et debet requirere judex secundum ordinem iuris; puta cum praecessit infamia super aliquo crimine, vel aliqua expressa indicia apparuerunt, vel etiam cum praecessit probatio semiplena ... sic ergo reo, qui accusatur, licet se defendere veritatem occultando, quam confiteri non tenetur, per aliquos convenientes modos, puta quod non respondeat, ad quae respondere non teneatur. Ibid 508.

[49] [C]onsiderandum est, an positio fiat super crimina eius, contra quem fit: quod esse non debet, siue agatur de crimine per modum accusationis, siue inquisitionis, siue exceptionis. non enim cogitur aliquis respondere se criminosum, iuxta illud, Non tibi dico, ut te prodas ... Sed quid se ponatur, quod aliquis crimen commiserit? Item quod illum est notorium? Item quod est fama? Respondeo de notorio & de fama debet respondere ... et si neget famam & notorium, non tenetur respondere, an crimen commiserit, cum non teneatur se publicare ... Si autem confessus fuerit se diffamatum, uel aliàs probatum fuerit, tunc quaeritur ab eo, an crimen commiserit. Gvl. Durandi Episcopi, 1 *Speculum iudicale* (Basel 1574. reprint Scientia Verlag Aalen 1975) (hereafter *Speculum*) (2 vols) (pt 2 no 40–41) 594–595.

Subsequently in his text, however, Durantis addresses how the principle against self-betrayal provisionally survives in the context of inquisitorial procedure. If the judge is acting on the basis of his office, in the absence of an accusing party, and *fama* about the crime supplies reason for inquiry, the judge can compel the defendant to respond under oath to his questions. Referring to the basic rule against criminous *positiones*, Durantis wrote:

> The inquisitors . . . should not require an oath from the defendant because he is not held to swear against himself, as above concerning *positiones* . . . But the moving party [*promouens*] should conduct the inquisition, [and introduce] witnesses, and proofs . . . But where there is no one prosecuting but inquiry is made based on the office of a superior [*ex superioris officio*], then he [the defendant] shall swear on account of the infamy that has arisen against him.[50]

An authoritative fourteenth-century commentator on the secular law minimized the application of the canonical principle against self-betrayal outside the canon law itself. Bartolo da Sassoferrato (1313–1357), whose influence as an interpreter of the revived Roman law was immense, recognized the existence of a dispute over the reach of the principle.

> [T]here is doubt whether one can be compelled to respond because the canon laws say that one should not betray himself . . . Likewise, our *glossae ordinariae* say that one ought not be compelled to respond to these interrogations through which someone's turpitude is detected . . . But I say to the contrary that he is held to respond. That is proven through the civil laws.[51]

Notwithstanding Bartolo's preeminent position as a commentator on the secular laws, his negative evaluation of the principle against self-betrayal did not prevail. His former pupil, Baldo degli Ubaldi (1327–1400), took the contrary view that the principle had general application except where the law sanctioned torture of a defendant to obtain a confession. It became the accepted opinion (*communis opinio*) and a general rule of the legal scholars of the *ius commune* that a party had no obligation to respond to an incriminating *positio*. Baldo, sharply disagreeing with Bartolo, wrote:

> But Bartolo speaks wrongly [citation to Innocent IV on *Dudum*] because a person is not held to confess a crime, nor even deny; because perhaps by denying he would be perjurious . . . And therefore a person is not forced to respond about a crime of which he is accused except on two occasions, to wit, on the occasion when the issue is

---

[50] *Inquisitores . . . nec a reo exigent iuramentum: quia non tenetur contra se iurare ut super de positio. Sed promovens inquisitionem, testes & probationes inducat . . . Ubi vero nullo prosequente, sed ex superioris officio inquiritur, tunc iurabit propter infamiam contra eum ortam.* 2 *Speculum* 3.1.3 (n 49) 35.

[51] *[A]n possit cogi respondere, dubium facit, quia jura canonica dicunt, quod quis non deberet se prodere . . . Item dicunt glo. nostrae, quod istis interrogationibus, per quas alicuius turpitudo detegitur non debet cogi respondere . . . Sed contra dico quod respondere tenetur. Hoc probatur per iura civilia.* Lib 1, Consilium 194, Bartolus, *Consilia, quaestiones et tractatus Bartoli à Saxoferrato* (Compania della Stampa 1589) 54r, 54v.

joined because one ought to respond to the legal complaint [*super libello*], and on the occasion of torture, whatever Bartolo may say.[52]

The exception for torture, that even Baldo allowed, was clearly repugnant to the principle underlying the maxim against self-betrayal and to the general rule that no one was obliged to answer a criminous *positio*. An early seventeenth-century author of a tract on confessions in the *ius commune* nicely summed up the long-standing yet irresolvable tension between its allowance of torture and its disapproval of self-incrimination:

> [A]lthough torture may be permitted both by the Constitutions of the civil law and by the sanctions of the Canons . . . [n]evertheless it seems repugnant to all reason and to both natural equity and directly contrary to many rules of the *ius commune*, founded in natural justice and equity . . . Secondly, it is repugnant to the law which admonishes that no one may be held to betray himself [*se ipsum prodere nemo teneatur*]. [Citation to Gratian *non tibi dico*]. It is well-grounded that no one may be held to answer a criminous *positio* containing his own crime [citations] . . . if a witness interrogated about some crime committed by him from which his own turpitude can be discovered ought not be forced to respond [citation] . . . so much the less ought the defendant be forced to confess to a crime by means of tortures, whence he may cut his throat with his own sword.[53]

The *ius commune*'s maxim against self-betrayal was clearly not universally honored in practice. Nonetheless, at its core, the maxim encapsulated a persistent principle and useful formula that could serve anyone who would protest against compelled self-incrimination, wherever and whenever needed.

Physical production of accusing witnesses before a criminal defendant

The revival of Justinian's Roman law in late eleventh- and early twelfth-century Italy did not occasion a uniform revival of Roman trial procedure. In classical Roman practice, as preserved in Justinian's Code, trials, including the presentation of witness

---

[52] *Sed Bart[olus] male dicit . . . quia non tenetur quis confiteri crimen, nec etiam negare, quia forte esset periurus negando . . . et ideo de crimine intentato non cogitur quis respondere, nisi duobus temporibus scilicet tempore, quo lis contestatur, quia oportet respondere super libello, & tempore torturae, quicquid dicat Bar[tolus].* Consilium 326 in Baldo degli Ubaldi and Girolamo Polo, 2 *Baldi Vbaldi de Perusini, Consiliorum, sive responsorum* (apud Hieronymum Polum 1575) 92r, 92v.

[53] *Quamvis tortura & iuris ciuillis Constitutionibus & Canonicis sanctionibus sit permissa . . . , Nihilominus repugnare videtur omni rationi, & naturali aequitati, & dedirecto contraria multis iuris comunis regulis, in naturali iustitia & aequitate fundatis . . . Secundo, repugnat legi, qua cauetur, vt se ipsum prodere nemo teneatur . . . Non tibi dico* [de pen. Dist 1. c 87 dp.] . . . *[F]irmatum est, vt positioni criminosae continenti proprium delictum nemo respondere teneatur . . . [S]i testis interrogatus de aliquo crimine à se commisso, vnde propria turpitudo detegi possit, cogi non debet ad respondendum . . . multò minus mediis cruciatibus cogi debet reus ad fatendum delictum, vnde proprio gladio iuguletur.* Vincenzo Mancini, *Vincentii Mancini, De confessionibus . . . in causis Civilibus, Criminalibus, & mixtis Tractatus* (apud Iacobum Mascardum 1611) 123–124.

testimony, were fully open to the public. However, absent witnesses might give testimony through written depositions. In his Novel 90, Justinian introduced a significant reform by barring deposition testimony from absent witnesses in criminal cases. Henceforth, witnesses in criminal cases were to appear in person with full opportunity for the defendant to be present and hear their testimony. Examination of witnesses in public dropped out of the revived medieval Roman practice. The impetus for this radical change arose before the advent of inquisitorial procedure. It is linked to the biblical story of Daniel and Susanna (Daniel 13: 1–64), which, as early as the ninth century, was regarded as a model for the examination of witnesses so as to promote the discovery of truth in disputed matters.

In the story, Susanna spurns the lecherous advances of two elders. In retaliation against her, they falsely claim they saw her commit adultery with a young man in a garden underneath a tree. In the ensuing trial, Daniel, moved by the spirit of God, intervenes. He is granted leave to question each of the elders separately and out of the presence of the other. He then asks each under what kind of tree he saw the adultery take place. One answers under a mastic tree. The other replies under an oak tree. The discrepancy between the testimonies convinces the assembly that the elders are lying. Susanna is found innocent.

The story of Daniel and Susanna offered strong biblical support for the sequestration of witnesses as a device for revealing truth. The account, however, does not justify the examination of witnesses out of public view and in the absence of the defendant. Nonetheless, the narrative of Daniel and Susanna came to serve as the authority for examining witnesses separately and in secret and for doing so outside of the presence of the defendant and his counsel.[54] This practice may have arisen at Bologna around the end of the twelfth century.[55] Azo, the preeminent Bolognese scholar of the law in the early thirteenth century, described the practice in his authoritative *Summa codicis*:

> [I]n criminal [cases] witnesses are absolutely compelled to appear ... And [the] oath is undergone with both parties present ... But the testimony is given before the judge alone with the other witnesses having been separated, unheard by any party, as was introduced through Daniel.[56]

[54] See A Esmein, "Le jugement de Daniel" (1907) 31 Nouv Rev Hist de Droit Français et Étranger 729, 751–754; James Austin Hughes, *Witnesses in Criminal Trials of Clerics: An Historical Synopsis and Commentary* (The Catholic University of America 1937) 16–17; Erich Genzmer, "Eine anonyme Kleinschrift de testibus aus der Zeit um 1200" in 3 *Festschrift Paul Koschaker zum 60. Geburtstag* (Hermann Böhlaus 1939) (3 vols) 381–384, 391–392; Giuseppe Salvioli, "Storia della procedura civile e criminale" in Pasquale Del Giudice (ed), 3 *Storia del diritto italiano* (U Hoepli 1927) (3 vols) (pt 2) 284. For the historical background of the story, see Bernard S Jackson, "Susanna and the Singular History of Singular Witnesses" (1977) 2 Acta Juridica 37, 38–40; David Golinkin and others, "Susanna and the Singular History of Singular Witnesses" in David Golinkin and others (eds), *Essays on Halakhah in the New Testament* (Brill 2008) 89–110.

[55] See Frank R Herrmann and Brownlow M Speer, "Facing the Accuser: Ancient and Medieval Precursors of the Confrontation Clause" (1994) 34 Va J Int'l L 516–522.

[56] *Nam in criminalibus [causis] praecise cogendi sunt testes uenire ... Et subitur hoc iusiurandum utraque parte presente ... Sed testimonium feretur soli iudici, separatis alijs testibus, nulla partium audiente, ut per Danielem inductum est.* Azo, Summa Codicis 4, de Probationibus 9 nos 18, 22 (1208/10) in Azo, *Azonis Summa* (Venice, sub signo Angeli Raphaelis 1581) fol 323. Azo's view that witnesses are to be examined out of the parties' presence after having been produced before them effectively became the law by its adoption

The requirement that the witnesses be present was taken directly from Justinian's Novel 90. That Novel, however, required further that the defendant have the opportunity to hear the witnesses' testimony. Medieval scholars held that this requirement was satisfied merely by defendants having the opportunity to see adverse witnesses sworn[57] so that the defendants might object to the witnesses' competence to testify against them. This residual right might seem minimal, but it could prove to be critically important because there was a broad range of reasons for barring the testimony of many categories of persons proferred as witnesses:[58]

> The accused therefore must be summoned in definite terms in order that he may come to see the witnesses swear who are produced against him, so that, if the accused should be present and see their very persons, if he knows they are impeded in so far as bearing testimony, he may immediately make exception against their persons. For example, if he knows some one of them is his mortal enemy, or conspirator, servant, or is defamed, perjurious, or excommunicated, or heretical, or other such, he may immediately make exception against their persons.[59]

The right was taken seriously and its violation was a ground for reversing a conviction.[60]

The *glossa ordinaria* to Justinian's texts, compiled by Accursius (1182–1263) in the mid-thirteenth century, effectively established the "Daniel practice" as the procedural law in the *ius commune*. In glossing chapter nine of Novel 90, Accursius construed its rule that adverse parties must have the opportunity to be present when witnesses testify against them to mean:

> that they should hear the attestations, that is, the oath, when [the witnesses] swear . . . and also can put questions . . . [they can] not, however, hear the answers, but it must

in the Magna Glossa or Glossa ordinaria of Accursius ("the Accursian Gloss"), which was regarded, from the thirteenth century on, as the definitive interpretation of the Corpus Iuris Civilis in the law schools and in the courts. See Herrmann and Speer (n 55) 519 n 201.

[57] See Herrmann and Speer (n 55) 518–522.

[58] A comprehensive list of the specific objections criminal defendants might make to the witnesses is set out in Giorgio Zordan, *Il diritto e la procedura criminale nel Tractatus de maleficiis di Angelo Gambiglioni* (CEDAM 1976) 358–360. For a detailed study of the grounds of rejection and acceptance of witnesses for and against a criminal defendant, see Bernard Schnapper, "Testes inhabiles-Les témoins reprochables dans l'Ancien Droit Pénal" (1965) 33 Tijdschrift voor Rechtsgeschiedenis 575, 578–594.

[59] *Citari ergo debet reus expresse, ut veniat videre testes iurare, qui contra se producuntur, ut si reus fuerit praesens et videat personas ipsorum, si scit eos esse impeditos quoad testimonium ferendum, statim excipiat contra personas eorum. Puta, si scit aliquem eorum inimicum suum capitalem, vel conspiratorem, servum, vel infamem, periurum, vel excommunicatum, vel haereticum, vel alia huiusmodi; statim excipiat contra eorum personas.* Gratiae Aretini, *Summa de iudiciario ordine* 2. 6, de testibus in Bergmann (n 19) 370.

[60] Albertus Gandinus in his treatise on criminal law and procedure, the *Tractatus de maleficiis* (1301) states that if "witnesses . . . have deposed without being sworn or have sworn with the other party absent and not summoned . . . their statements are as a matter of law a nullity" (*[P]onamus, quidam testes . . . deposuerunt non iurati vel iuraverunt parte absente et non citata, . . . ita quod eorum dicta ipso iure sunt nulla*). Albertus Gandinus, "Tractatus de maleficiis, De falsariis et falsitatibus" (1301) in Kantorowicz, 2 *Gandinus* n 20) §26, 335. When the witnesses swore in the defendant's presence, the defendant had the opportunity to make "reproach" (*reprobatio*) or of "objection" (*objectio*) to the witnesses; that is, to seek to bar the reception of their testimony. See Herrmann and Speer (n 55) 521.

be said to the judge in secret with the adversary and other witnesses absent, as was introduced through Daniel.[61]

Under the "Daniel practice," the judge examined each of the competent witnesses privately, usually on the day of their appearance to be sworn, with only a notary present to take down the testimony. After all witnesses had been examined, the notary made "publication" (*publicatio*) of their testimony by reading it aloud in open court.

The "Daniel practice," with its partial preservation of Justinian's rule that accusing witnesses must be produced physically before the defendant, arose in the context of accusatorial procedure. This principle, even in its reduced form, was perceived as so fundamental that it ultimately survived in inquisitorial procedure, as well. The leading medieval authority on the criminal law and "the father of criminal jurisprudence," [62] Alberto da Gandino [c. 1250–1310] made this clear in his magisterial *Tractatus de maleficiis* (1301).

Gandino drew a distinction between a "general inquisition" (*inquisitio generalis*) and a "special inquisition" (*inquisitio specialis*). In the former, the inquisitor "may be inquiring generally about a crime and who may have committed it."[63] There the inquisitor does not summon any potential target to be present.[64] But in the latter, the inquisitor "is inquiring against some single and individual and named person."[65] There the defendant must be summoned to see the witnesses swear:[66]

> But when the general inquisition has been completed, if the inquisitor shall have found someone inculpated in that crime, he shall cause that person to be summoned to him and shall furnish to him . . . the names of the witnesses whom [the inquisitor] intends to examine about that crime, and he shall cause to be summoned to the swearing of those witnesses that one who was so inculpated in the first and general inquisition.[67]

The rule as stated by Gandino leaves open the question of whether an inculpated defendant could be tortured to produce his confession without having seen the witnesses against him swear. Bartolus, writing on Justinian's Digest in 1341 or 1342,[68] answered the question in the negative:

---

[61] *quod testationes debeant audire, id est sacramentum, quando iurant . . . et etiam facere quaestiones possunt . . . non tamen responsiones audire: sed in secreto iudici debet dici absente adversario et aliis testibus: ut per Danielem inductum est.* Accursius, Glossa ordinaria, gl "Presentem" on Nov 90.9 (1228/60) in Novellae Constitutiones Divi Caesaris Iustiniani (Venice, Nicolo Bevilacqua 1569) 250.

[62] Hermann Kantorowicz, "Introduction" in 2 Kantorowicz, *Gandinus* (n 20) xvi.

[63] *an inquirat generaliter de maleficio, quis illud maleficium fecerit.* Kantorowicz, 2 *Gandinus* (n 20) 39.

[64] Ibid 40.

[65] *inquirit contra aliquam singularem et specialem et nominatam personam.* Ibid 39.

[66] *legitime citato per [name] nuntium, ut continue esset ad videndum testes iurare.* Kantorowicz, 1 *Gandinus* (n 20) 117.

[67] *Sed hac generali inquisitione completa, si ipse inquisitor invenerit aliquem de ipso crimine infamatum, faciet illum ad se citari et edet sibi . . . nomina testium, quos super illo crimine examinare intendit, et ad iuramentum illorum testium faciet citari istum in prima et generali inquisitione taliter infamatum.* Kantorowicz, 2 *Gandinus* (n 20) 40.

[68] These are the dates of Bartolus's lectures on the Digestum Novum (bks 39–50 of interpretum Justinian's Digest) as a professor at the University of Pisa. See F Calasso, "Bartolo da Sassaferrato" in Alberto Maria Ghisalberti (ed) 6 *Dizionario biografico degli Italiani* (1966) 642.

Query, whether evidence received on the general inquisition prejudices the defendant, so that he may be tortured when there is a special inquisition or accusation? I think not, because those witnesses were not examined after he himself was summoned, and he himself was there to speak in opposition, therefore they do not prejudice him. [Citation to Code]. Thus, they must be examined a second time.[69]

In the following century, the rule that inculpating witnesses take the oath in the presence of the defendant was repeated in the *Tractatus de maleficiis* (1438/44) of Angelo Gambiglioni (Angelus Aretinus):

[W]itnesses examined on the general inquisition do not prejudice the malefactor against whom inquiry is later made specially, if the malefactor is not summoned when the witnesses swore in the general inquisition … [A]nd if he denies [guilt], they [the judge and his assistants] examine the witnesses again with the defendant summoned and coming into court so that he sees the witnesses swear, and he or his advocate can then make interrogatories.[70]

Citing Angelus Aretinus and Bartolus as authorities, Hippolytus de Marsilliis in his *Practica causarum criminalium* (1528) affirms that a defendant's opportunity to see the witnesses against him take the oath is a prerequisite to torture of the defendant to obtain a confession:

[T]he judge himself must have the defendant summoned and brought before him and similarly have before him those witnesses whom he first examined for the taking of evidence and tender to them the oath in the presence of the defendant himself, and recall and examine them again; otherwise, unless he shall first have done this, the judge may not proceed to torture on the strength of the first deposition of the said witnesses, since the defendant himself was not summoned to see the witnesses against him swear, as is required. And as a consequence, their statement effects nothing.[71]

---

[69] *Quaero, an indicia habita super generali inquisitione praeiudicent reo, vt possit torqueri, quando fit inquisitio vel accusatio specialis? puto quod non, quia illi testes non fuerunt examinati ipso citato, et ipso existencte contradictore, ergo non praeiudicant sibi … Vnde debebant iterum examinari.* Bartolus, In Secundam Digesti Novi Partem on Dig 48.18.22 (21) no 9 (1341/42) in Bartoli à Saxaferrato, 6 *Omnium Iuris Interpretum Antesignani Commentaria* (Giunta Lucantonio 1602) (9 vols) fol 183v. As authority, Bartolus cites CJ 4.20.19.

[70] *[T]estes examinati super inquisitione generali, non praeiudicant malefactori, contra quem specialiter postea inquiritur, si malefactor non fuit citatus, quando testes iurauerunt in inquisitione generali … [E]t si negat iterato examinant testes reo citato et in iudicium veniente vt videat iurare testes, et potest tunc ipse vel eius aduocatus interrogatoria facere.* Angelus Aretinus, "Tractatus de maleficiis, Quod fama publica praecedente et clamosa" (1438/44) in *Angeli Aretini De Maleficiis Tractatus* (Venetiis, apud Cominum de Tridino Montisferrati 1573) fol 73rv, no 11.

[71] *[I]pse iudex debet facere citare reum et eum ducere coram se et similiter habere coram se illos testes quos primo examinavit pro indiciis habendis et eis deferre iuramentum in praesentia ipsius rei et eos iter-mum repetere et examinare alias nisi primo hoc fecerit non posset iudex procedere ad torturam vigore prime depositionis dictorum testium: eo quia ipse reus non fuisset citatus ad videndum iurare testes contra eum: vt requiritur. et per consequens dictum eorum nihil operaretur.* Ippolito Marsili, "Nunc videndum" in *Practica causarum criminalium domini Hippolyti de Marsilijs* (apud Iacobum Giuncti in vico Mercuriali 1538) fol 29r, no 29.

A Presumption of Innocence

Even after the advent of inquisitorial procedure, both secular and canon law continued to emphasize principles that by the first quarter of the fourteenth century may be called a presumption of innocence in modern terms.[72] The foundation for formulating such a presumption was already present in antiquity.[73] Roman law, both in its classical and revived forms, clearly placed the burden of proof, and not merely the burden of making an accusation, on the accuser.[74]

> We command that the order of accusation long since instituted by the laws be observed so that whoever is summoned on a capital charge (*discrimen capitis*) who could be accused shall not immediately be considered *reus*, lest we cause innocence to be undermined.[75]

Consistent with the secular law, Pope Nicholas I had written to the Bulgars that "someone who is accused is not to be immediately judged guilty [*reus*]."[76]

Twelfth-century scholars of Justinian's corpus, as well as scholars of decretal letters of Pope Gregory IX, began to introduce the language of "presumptions" into legal theory. It was Accursius who first wrote of a presumption of goodness.[77] Glossing the phrase "good soldier" (*bonus miles*) in a rescript of the Emperor Hadrian (and citing no authority), Accursius wrote "if he was good, he is presumed to be good."[78] The Accursian presumption of present goodness was based on empirical facts about the person's past character. Obviously, however, on the same ground, the presumption could readily be defeated. Accursius added "so also if he was bad" (*sic etiam si malus*).[79]

In contrast to the fragile factual foundation of character on which legists based their presumption of goodness, canonists set their presumption on what was for them the firm

---

[72] Kenneth Pennington, "Innocent until Proven Guilty: The Origins of a Legal Maxim" (2003) 63 Jurist 106, 115; Carl-Friedrich Stuckenberg, *Untersuchungen zur Unschuldsvermutung* (Walter de Gruyter 1998) 14–15.

[73] Richard M Fraher, "'*Ut nullus discribatur reus priusquam convincatur*: Presumption of Innocence in Medieval Canon Law?'" in Stephan Kuttner and Kenneth Pennington (eds), *Proceedings of the Sixth International Congress of Medieval Canon Law* (Città del Vaticano 1975) 493, 494.

[74] Dig 22.3.2. "The burden of proof lies upon him who speaks, not who denies" (*Ei incumbit probatio qui dicit, non qui negat*).

[75] Constitution of the emperors Honorius and Theodosius of August 6, 423, CTh 9.1.19 (*Accusationis ordinem iam dudum legibus institutum servari iubemus, ut quicumque in discrimen capitis arcessitur, non statim reus qui accusari potuit aestimetur, ne subiectam innocentiam faciamus.*), CJ 9.2.17 ("*Accusationibus*" in place of "*Accusationis*").

[76] See text to n 70 in ch 3. It is clear from its context that the term here means "guilty person" rather than defendant. Fraher, "*Ut nullus*" (n 73) 502.

[77] Rolf-Jürgen Köster, *Die Rechtsvermutung der Unschuld: historische und dogmatische Grundlagen* (Rheinische Friedrich-Wilhems-Universität 1979) 9 & n 5.

[78] *si bonus fuit, et bonus praesumitur.* Accursian gloss h to "*bonus miles*" on Dig 49.16.5. §6 in *Digestum Nouum, sev Pandectarvm Ivris Civilis, Tomus Tertius, ex Pandectis Florentinis* ([s.n.] Lvgdvni 1604) 1686.

[79] Ibid. See Köster (n 77) 12. In his tract on crimes, Gandinus added that, "if someone has been born of good lineage or has had good parents, he is presumed to be good" (*si aliquis sit natus ex bona progenie vel bonos habuerit parentes, praesumitur esse bonus*). Kantorowicz, *Gandinus* (n 20) 79. Gandinus lists this as a presumption of nature (*presumptio naturae*). Ibid.

and universal ground of divine and natural law.[80] For the canonists, every person, regardless of past character and independent of social status, was entitled to a presumption of goodness. God was all good and accordingly had made all things good in their very nature. Bernard of Parma, glossing a decretal from Innocent III to the archbishop of Milan,[81] set down a general norm that anyone is presumed to be of good faith (*bonae fidei*) unless the contrary is proven.[82] An anonymous French jurist's work c 1270 moved the presumption of goodness an important step further.[83] The jurist used the term *innocens* in the context of presumption.[84] In doing so, the unnamed writer cited the first-century Roman emperor Trajan's rescript stating that it is better to let a guilty person's crime go unpunished than to convict a person on the ground of suspicions alone.[85]

Johannes Monachus (Jean Lemoine) (d. 1313), a French canonist and bishop, glossed a decretal of Pope Boniface VIII.[86] Monachus, too, used the phrase "*presumitur innocens*" ("presumed innocent").[87] Discussing defendants' trial rights, Monachus alluded to St Paul's trial in Acts 25:16, as a scriptural basis for requiring that an accused person have the opportunity to defend himself.[88] Monachus then rooted a presumption of innocence in divine law. God, who knew all things, did not convict Adam, until God had investigated the case against him. By implication, it was clear that even God presumed Adam innocent absent proof to the contrary.[89] Other canonical sources evidence the presumption of innocence, as well.[90]

---

[80] Köster (n 77) 14, 23, 25.

[81] Gloss h ("*praesumatur ideoneus*") on X 2.23.16 in *Decretales D. Gregorii Papae IX svae integritati, vna cvm glossis* (Venetiis Apud Iuntas 1615) 565. Bernard composed his *glossa ordinaria* on the Decretals between 1241 and 1266.

[82] "So, everyone is presumed to be of good faith, unless the contrary is proven" (*sic praesumitur quis bonae fidei, nisi probetur contrarium*). Ibid note h.

[83] Responsa doctorum Tholosanorum (Rechtshistorisch Instituut, Leiden 2.8; Haarlem 1938), cited in Kenneth Pennington, *The Prince and the Law, 1200–1600: Sovereignty and Rights in the Western Legal Tradition* (University of California Press 1993) 157 n 146. Pennington has found this to be "[t]he first explicit formulation of the presumption of innocence" known to him. Ibid.

[84] "About a charge, anyone is presumed innocent who is not proven very clearly to have committed the crime" (*super crimine quilibet innocens presumatur qui comisisse facinus clarissime non probatur*). See Pennington, *Prince* (n 83) 157 & n 146, citing Responsa doctorum Tholosanorum (Rechtshistorisch Institut, Leiden 2.8; Haarlem 1938) quaestio 50, 116–120.

[85] Dig 48.29.5 (rescript of Trajan to Julius Fronto). See text to n 60 in ch 1.

[86] Extravagantes communes 2.3.1 (Rem non novam) in *Extraaugantes tum viginti Ioannis vicesemisecuvdi, tum commvnes cum glossis* (apud Hugonem à Porta, & Antonionum Vincentium 1553) 161, 164. For scholarship on the gloss, see Pennington, *Prince* (n 83) n 168.

[87] "Everyone is presumed innocent unless proven guilty... and the law is more prompt in acquitting than in convicting" (*quilibet presumitur innocens nisi probetur nocens... et ius promptius ad absoluendum quam ad condemnandum*). For the proposition that the law is more prompt in absolving, see the letter of Pope Lucius III (c 1097–1185), X 2.19.3, to the bishop, or to the archdeacon, of Chichester: *promptiora sint iura ad absolvendum quam ad condemnandam* in Friedberg and Richter (n 2) 307. For the editing of Lucius's letter, see Edward Andrew Reno III, *The Authoritative Text: Raymond of Penyafort's Editing of the Decretals of Gregory IX* (Columbia University 2011) 200–203.

[88] Monachus cites Gratian's C 3 q.9 c 5, referencing Paul's demand, based on Roman law that accused persons have a right to make a defense in order to clear themselves of the charges against them (*locus defendendi ad abluenda crimina quae sibi obijciuntur*).

[89] Pennington, *Prince* (n 83) 162.

[90] Monachus's gloss "circulated in hundreds of manuscripts and scores of printed until the seventeenth century... It was a primary vehicle for transmitting the principle to later generations of jurists." Pennington, "Innocent" (n 72) 116. See also Françoia Quintard-Morénas, "The Presumption of Innocence in the French and Anglo-American Legal Traditions" (2010) 58 The American Journal of Comparative Law 107, 114–115.

In the early seventeenth century, the widely influential Italian jurist Menochius (1532–1607) devoted extensive attention to the presumption of innocence in his tract concerning presumptions.[91] Menochius first recalled that God created all things good by nature. "By our law both pontifical and imperial, it is clearly shown a man is and is presumed to be by his nature good."[92] From this presumption, he said, "flows that one by which we say everyone is presumed innocent."[93] Menochius's tract on presumptions was known in the civil law faculties of England and in the spiritual courts of England by the early seventeenth century.[94]

The importance of protecting a person's innocence against false conviction came later to be expressed in the Continental maxim *in dubio pro reo* (in doubt, for the defendant), giving the benefit of doubt to the defendant.[95] The maxim echoes roman and canonical passages which provided that when defendants' assertions were in equipoise with the assertions of prosecutors, those of the defendant were to be considered more favorably.[96]

Summary and Conclusion Regarding Protections in the Ius Commune

By the first quarter of the fourteenth century, jurists of the *ius commune* had delineated critically important due process safeguards for criminal trials. These first developed in the setting of accusatorial procedure. When Pope Innocent III and the Fourth Lateran Council adopted inquisitorial procedure, it, too, had careful regard for due process. Although there were exceptions to almost any *ius commune* procedural rule, certain standards remained normative. A defendant had to be accorded a trial.[97] The

---

[91] Jacobus Menochius, *Iacobi Menochii Tractatus De Praesumptionibus, Coniecturis, Signis, & Indiciis, Commentaria in sex distincta libros* (first published Cologne 1587; apud Io. Dominicum Tarinum 1594). Menochius treats presumptions concerning innocence in presumptions I and II of the fifth book of *De praesumptionibus* 237r–239v.

[92] *Iure autem nostro vel Pontificio vel Caesareo hominem sui natura bonum esse, & praesumi manifestè probatur.* (bk 5, *praesumptio* 1, 15). Ibid 237v.

[93] *Ex hac praesumptione fluit & illa qua dicimus, quemlibet praesumi innocentem.* Ibid 237v. In Book 5, *praesumptio* 2, Menochius continues: "From the above presumption flows this noble and outstanding [presumption] by which we say no one is presumed to have committed a crime: since to offend and to sin are not of the nature of a good man but of an evil and bad one" (*Ex superiore praesumptione fluit haec notabilis & egregia, qua dicimus, neminem deliquisse praesumi: Cum delinquere et peccare viri boni non sit, sed mali et nequam*). Ibid 238v.

[94] See RH Helmholz, *Roman Canon Law in Reformation England* (CUP 1990) 146; RH Helmholz, *The Oxford History of the Laws of England: The History of the Canon Law and Ecclesiastical Jurisdiction* (OUP 2004) 244, 331.

[95] For studies of the maxim, see Peter Holtappels, *Die Entwicklungsgeschichte des Grundsatzes "in dubio pro reo"* (Hamburg Cram, de Gruyter & Co. 1965); Kenneth Pennington, "Procedure" (n 4) 153–154 & n 3.

[96] The second-century Roman jurist Gaius wrote that defendants are to be considered more favorably than plaintiffs, Dig 50.17.125. See text to n 64 in ch 1. For canonical statements, see the letter of Pope Lucius III (the laws are more prompt in absolving than in condemning; especially, where the witnesses of each party are of equal weight, a judgment (*sententia*) should favor liberty. X 2.19.3. See also Gullielmus Durandus: "And it is safer to absolve one who ought to be condemned than to convict one who ought to be acquitted . . . since everyone is presumed to be good" (*Et tutius est condemnandum absoluere, quam absoluendum condemnare . . . cum quilibet praesumatur esse bonus*). 1 *Speculum* (n 49) 1.4.8.1.

[97] On the retention of basic due process principles at summary procedure, see Pennington, "Introduction" (n 3) 24–29; Pennington, *Prince* (n 83) 164–164, 229–230.

exact charges had to be disclosed to the defendant, including the names of witnesses and their statements. (At inquisitions for heresy, however, testimony could be given anonymously.) The testimony of at least two eyewitnesses was required to meet the *ius commune*'s demanding standard of proof clearer than the light of day in order to justify conviction in the absence of a defendant's confession. The defendant was to be given opportunity to prepare. A defendant was entitled at the swearing in of the witnesses to see the opposing witnesses take their oaths. A defendant could object to a witness's suitability to testify. Although witnesses at trial were questioned separately and apart from one another and from the parties in inquisitorial procedure, the defendant could submit to the court written questions to be put to opposing witnesses. Answers of witnesses were published to the defendant. Witnesses had the right not be questioned about and not to incriminate or disgrace themselves regarding crimes or behavior not already publicly known. Any confession of guilt made in court was deemed invalid if it was not proffered "voluntarily." Although the allowance of torture subverted the *ius commune*'s concept of voluntariness, the core belief that an involuntary confession was invalid for conviction remained an indispensable element of procedure. At least by the third quarter of the fourteenth century, a defendant was to be presumed innocent unless convicted by proof clearer than the light of day. A judge was to resolve any doubt he had about a defendant's guilt in favor of the defendant.[98]

From the study of canon and Roman texts at European universities, the due process principles the "learned" law infused the rational procedures of church tribunals. This was true in the ecclesiastical forums both on the Continent and in England. In secular courts, however, the picture was more complicated. Although the study of Gratian's and Justinian's works was spreading as the twelfth century came to its close, there were still secular courts which had not yet received the learned doctrines. Trial by ordeal continued to be a means of deciding cases. In the first quarter of the thirteenth century, however, a single catalytic event was about to shift the legal landscape of the secular courts, both on the Continent and in England.

---

[98] In evaluating a witness's testimony, a *ius commune* judge could assess credibility. Two persons might testify that they were eyewitnesses to a crime (thus potentially satisfying the *ius commune*'s demand for proof clearer than day), but if one or the other was not believable, the judge could not mechanically find the defendant guilty. See Mirjan Damaška, *Evaluation of Evidence: Pre-Modern and Modern Approaches* (CUP 2019) 59–65. Damaška notes that the emperor Hadrian's rescript allowing a fact-finder to judge according to conscience (*ex sententia animi sui*), when applied by medieval jurists and canonists, rendered more flexible the seemingly mechanical hierarchy of roman-canon rules of proof. Mirjan R Damaška, *Evaluation of Evidence: Pre-Modern and Modern Approaches* (CUP 2019) 62 & n 8, 64. While *ius commune* doctrine always honored Hadrian's rescripts, it was the English jury that forthrightly practiced free evaluation.

6

Due Process Protections for the Accused
in Early English Jury Trials

The Demise of Trial by Ordeal and the Rise
of the English Trial Jury

In 1215, the Fourth Lateran Council in its eighth *constitutio* declared that clerics were henceforth barred from the common practice of blessing ordeals[1] in which suspects were made to purge themselves of guilt by plugging their hands into boiling water or by being bound and thrown into cold water, or made to carry red-hot irons.[2] Having been deprived of their theological oxygen, the ordeals withered after the Council's decree. The demise of trial by ordeal presented a difficult conundrum regarding criminal procedure both on the Continent and in England. Each had to develop methods apart from the ordeals to determine the guilt or innocence of criminal suspects.

The Continent turned to its already nascent inquisitorial procedure.[3] In order to initiate an inquisitorial proceeding against an individual suspect, repeated, reliable reports (*fama*) from local community members were needed to establish probable cause of a crime and of the suspect's commission of it. In order to guide judges in evaluating evidence, *ius commune* doctrine developed an elaborate hierarchy of what could constitute full proof, half-proof, or even quarter-proof.[4]

---

[1] See text to n 57 in ch 2 and works cited.

[2] "nor shall anyone give any sort of blessing or consecration to a purgation of boiling or frigid water or the glowing iron (*nec quisquam purgationi acquae ferventis vel frigidae, seu ferri candentis, ritum cujuslibet benedictionis aut consecrationis impendat*)." IV Lateran Council (1215) c 18 in A Garcia y Garcia (ed), *Constitutiones Concilii quarti Lateranensis una cum Commentariis glossatorum* (Biblioteca Apostolica Vaticana 1981) 18. In 1220, Pope Honorius explicitly extended the bar on trial by ordeal to secular tribunals. *Dilecti filii*, X 5.35.3.

[3] Transition from the ordeal to inquisitorial procedure on the Continent had begun earlier than 1215. Kenneth Pennington, "The Jurisprudence of Procedure" in Wilfried Hartmann and Kenneth Pennington (eds), *The History of Courts and Procedure in Medieval Canon Law* (The Catholic University of America Press 2016) 125; Charles Donahue Jr, "The Courts of the Ius commune" in ibid 95. Although inquisitorial procedure came to predominate, accusatorial procedure continued to be available in both ecclesiastical and secular law. Kenneth Pennington, "Introduction to the Courts" in ibid 7. For descriptive accounts of *ius commune* procedure, see Charles Donahue Jr, "Procedure in the Courts of the Ius commune" in ibid 74–124; Kenneth Pennington, "Law, Criminal Procedure" in William Chester Jordan (ed), *DMA (Supp 1)* (Charles Scribner's Sons 2004) 309–315; A Esmein, 5 *A History of Continental Criminal Procedure* (John Simpson tr, Little, Brown and Co 1913) 78–144.

[4] For explication of the hierarchy of proofs, see Jean-Phillipe Lévy, *La Hierarchie des preuves dans le droit savant du Moyen-Âge depuis la renaissance du droit romain jusqu'à la fin du XIVe siècle* (Librairie du Recueil Sirey 1939). Mirjan Damaška has shown that this hierarchy was not nearly as mechanical or restrictive as scholarship has traditionally understood it to be. A *ius commune* judge was still free to factor the credibility of witnesses into his considerations, both as to *fama* before trial and testimony at trial. See Mirjan Damaška, *Evaluation of Evidence: Pre-Modern and Modern Approaches* (CUP 2019) 51, 59–65, 132–137 and passim. The judgment of a *ius commune* judge was subject to supervision on appeal to guard against any conviction in the absence of sufficient evidence or contrary to the evidence submitted. Ibid 65, 139–140.

Foundations of American Criminal Due Process at Trial. Francis R. Herrmann and Brownlow M. Speer,
Oxford University Press. © Oxford University Press 2025. DOI: 10.1093/9780199364770.003.0006

England did not adopt the Continent's inquisitorial model.[5] Instead, England expanded the ways in which it had been using jurors well before 1215. Even prior to the end of the ordeals, the local community had been playing a vital role in gathering information and determining disputes concerning land possession and title. Extending the use of jurors, Henry II (1154–1189) began to employ the inquest as a prosecutorial device to bring charges against criminal suspects.[6] The Assise of Clarendon (1166) established that groups of twelve lawful men of a county subdivision ("hundred") together with four lawful men of a township ("vill") should make an initial determination whether "any man has been charged or published" to have committed certain serious crimes in their vicinity.[7] The justices would scrutinize the reports. If the jurors themselves suspected the accused of crime, the suspect went to the ordeal; but if the jurors themselves did not suspect the person, then the accused avoided the ordeal. A defendant charged by a private person ("appellor") might also avoid the ordeal or

[5] The account of the institution of the jury given here is intended to set out a context for exploring procedural strengths and weaknesses at criminal jury trials up until the late sixteenth century. For broader commentary on the beginnings of jury trial, see generally John H Langbein, Renée Lettow Lerner, and Bruce P Smith (eds), *History of the Common Law: The Development of Anglo-American Legal Institutions* (Aspen Publishers/Walters Kluwer 2009) 3–84; John Hamilton Baker, *An Introduction to English Legal History* (4th edn, Buttersworth LexisNexis 2002) 72–76; Mike Macnair and others, "The Origins of the Jury: Forum" (1999) 17 LHR 537; RC van Caenegem, *The Birth of the English Common Law* (CUP 1973) 62–84; Theodore FT Plucknett, *Concise History of the Common Law* (5th edn Little, Brown and Co 1956) 106–138; WS Holdsworth, 3 *A History of English Law* (5th edn, Little, Brown and Co 1956) (17 vols) 607–623; James Fitzjames Stephen, 1 *A History of the Criminal Law of England* (Macmillan and Co 1883) (3 vols) 51–74, 244–272. On the possible relation of the English jury to Continental institutions, see Ralph V Turner, "The Origins of the Medieval English Jury: Frankish, English, or Scandinavian?" (1968) 7 Journal of British Studies 1; RC van Caenegem, *The Birth of the English Common Law* (2nd edn, CUP 1988) 71. For synopses of scholarly views on the historical roots of inquests and juries, see generally Patrick Wormald, 1 *The Making of English Law: King Alfred to the Twelfth Century* (Blackwell Publishers 1999) 3–28; James Masschaele, *Jury, State, and Society in Medieval England* (Palgrave Macmillan 2008) 18–20; Mike Macnair, "Vicinage and the Antecedents of the Jury" (1999) 17 LHR 537; Charles Donahue Jr, "Biology and the Origins of the English Jury" (1999) 17 LHR 591; Patrick Wormald, "Neighbors, Courts, and Kings: Reflections on Michael Macnair's Vicini" (1999) 17 LHR 597. On the use of jurylike procedures in the ecclesiastical courts in the twelfth century, see Charles Donahue Jr, "Proof by Witnesses in the Church Courts of Medieval England: An Imperfect Reception of the Learned Law" in Morris S Arnold (ed), *On the Laws and Customs of England, Essays in Honor of Samuel E. Thorne* (The University of North Carolina Press 1981) 129, 136, 140.

[6] Scholarly views diverge concerning Continental predecessors to the English inquest. See Ralph V Turner, "The Origins of the Medieval English Jury: Frankish, English, or Scandinavian?" (1968) 7 Journal of British Studies 1. See also Wormald, "Neighbors" (n 5); RC van Caenegem, *The Birth of the English Common Law* (CUP 1973) 71–72.

[7] The term "assise" derives from Norman-French for a "sitting down." It here means the legislation enacted at the "sitting down" of kings and nobles at Clarendon. In other contexts, "assise" may refer to the "sitting down" of royal court justices. See Daniel R Coquillette, *The Anglo-American Legal Heritage: Introductory Materials* (2nd edn, North Carolina Academic Press 2004) 60 n 3, 69. For English texts of the Assize of Clarendon, see ibid 69–71; David C Douglas and GW Greenway (eds), 2 *English Historical Documents 1042–1189* (2nd edn E Methuen, OUP 1979) (2 vols) 407–410; Carl Stephenson, 1 *Sources of English Constitutional History: A Selection of Documents from A.D. 600 to the Present* (Harper & Brothers 1972) (2 vols) 76–80. For the Latin text of the Assize of Clarendon, see William Stubbs and HW Carless Davis, *Select Charters and Other Illustrations of English Constitutional History from the Earliest Times to the Reign of Edward the First* (9th edn, FB Rothman 1985) 170–173. The Assize of Northampton (1176), in the main, repeated the provisions for presenting jury laid down at the Clarendon assize, but added forgery and arson to the crimes subject to presentment. Elizabeth Papp Kamali and Thomas A Green, "A Crossroads in Criminal procedure: The Assumptions Underlying England's Adoption of Trial by Jury for Crime" in Travis R Baker (ed), *Law and Society in Later Medieval England and Ireland: Essays in Honour of Paul Brand* (Taylor & Francis Group 2017) 54.

trial by combat by seeking a writ *de odio et atia.* Jurors would be convened to deter-mine whether "hatred and spite" lay at the heart of the appellor's charge; if so, no trial took place.[8]

The use of local persons thus provided both a means to control criminal miscon-duct and a restraint against the initiation of baseless prosecutions.[9] The canon law analogously used neighbors to establish the common fame (*fama*) of suspects as a condition preliminary to initiating an inquisitorial trial.[10] In fact, the ecclesiastical procedure may have contributed to the formation of the English secular procedure.[11]

By the beginning of the thirteenth century, the jury of accusation, also termed the presenting jury, and later known as the grand jury,[12] would issue a "true bill" (*vere-dicta*), known as a presentment (if based on the jurors' own suspicions), or indict-ment (if based on other reports).[13] Prior to 1215, the jury accusing a suspect did not

---

[8] A private party ("appellor") could make an "appeal" against a defendant ("appellee"). A writ *de odio et atia* was intended to protect against malicious prosecution, but it inevitably entailed an exploration of the primary issue of guilt or innocence. If the verdict of the jury regarding the appellor's motive was unfavor-able to the defendant, then proof would be made by combat or ordeal. Kamali and Green (n 7) 51, 60. If either party were unable to fight, trial would be by ordeal. Roger D. Groot, "The Early Thirteenth-Century Criminal Jury" in JS Cockburn and Thomas A Green (eds), *Twelve Good Men and True? The Criminal Trial Jury in England, 1200–1800* (Princeton University Press 2014) 8.

Trial by wager of law offered another method of proof. It required compurgators to swear to the truth of a suspect's denial of guilt. The Assize of Clarendon's requirement of trial by ordeal put an end to wager of law in the royal courts. See Baker, *Introduction* (n 5) 507. For a study of the similarities between wager of law and canonical purgation, see RH Helmholz, *The Ius Commune in England: Four Studies* (OUP 2001) 82–134.

[9] Kamali and Green conclude that well before 1215 "the role of juries was actively expanding beyond their intitial role as presenters. Thus, by the time of Lateran IV, not only were juries routinely employed in criminal cases, but their scope was actively expanding beyond their initial role as presenters. As a result, officials in a post-ordeal England may have viewed trial juries as a natural extension of the use of juries in other aspects of criminal adjudication." Kamali and Green (n 7) 60.

[10] RH Helmholz, "The Early History of the Grand Jury and the Canon Law" (1983) 50 U Chi L Rev 613, 620, 625–627. The English and the Continental systems shared an intent to restrain authorities from initiating baseless accusations. RH Helmholz, Charles M Gray and others, *The Privilege against Self-Incrimination: Its Origins and Development* (University of Chicago Press 1997) 7, 29, 44. In Richard Helmholz's view, the parallels between the ecclesiastical and secular procedures support the thesis of RC van Caenegem that "the canon law influenced the Assize of Clarendon." Helmholz, "Early History" (n 10) 625. See RC van Caenegem, "Public Prosecution of Crime in Twelfth-Century England" in CNL Brooke and others (eds), *Church and Government in the Middle Ages: Essays Presented to C. R. Cheney* (CUP 1976) 41, 72–73. Helmholz further concludes that "it is at least possible that ideas and practices percolated back and forth throughout the medieval period between criminal prosecution in the canon law and the common law . . . The correspondence between *ex officio* procedure in the Church courts and much of the early history of English procedure should therefore be no surprise. It fits within a habit of mind that saw no radical disjunction between the correction of secular and spiritual offenses." Helmholz, "Early History" (n 10) 627. See also Karl Blaine Shoemaker, "Criminal Procedure in Medieval European Law: A Comparison Between English and Roman-Canonical Developments After the IV Lateran Council" (1999) 85 ZSS (KA) 174, 180–181, 202.

[11] Helmholz, "Early History" (n 10) 626–627.

[12] On the institution of the presenting jury, see Roger D Groot, "The Jury of Presentment before 1215" (1982) 26 Am J Legal Hist 1, 1–24; Roger D Groot, "The Jury in Private Criminal Prosecutions before 1215" (1983) 27 Am J Legal Hist 113; Groot, "Thirteenth-Century" (n 8) 3–35; Naomi D Hunard, "The Jury of Presentment and the Assize of Clarendon" (1941) 56 English Historical Review 374; SFC Milsom, *Historical Foundations of the Common Law* (2nd edn, Butterworth 1981) 357.

[13] The indictment system, generally considered to have been formally initiated in 1166, was perhaps a development of still earlier uses of the community to report crime. See Milsom (n 12) 357; JM Kaye, "The Making of English Criminal Law" (1977) The Criminal Law Review 4, 5. The system of private per-sons ("appellors") bringing complaints to the presenting jury was well established by the middle of the reign of Edward I (1272–1307). See John G Bellamy, *The Criminal Trial in Later Medieval England: Felony*

decide whether its accusation was finally true. Trial by ordeal decided the ultimate issue of guilt or innocence when a suspect denied.[14]

A new method, however, for arriving at the final verdict was required after the Fourth Lateran Council theologically decertified the ordeals in 1215. Between 1216 and 1222, the true trial jury was born, eventually known as the petit jury.[15] Where neighbors were earlier mandated to report suspicions, they now were called upon to render final verdicts.[16] In the time of transition from the ordeals, jury verdicts may have been considered inferior to the judgment of God rendered through the ordeals.[17] Defendants had to consent to trial by human judgment by placing themselves "upon the country" for trial. If they resisted doing so and stood mute, they were put under duress until they assented.[18] Despite any initial resistance to the petit jury, by 1275, a jury's declaration of guilt or innocence had become the established method for adjudicating criminal cases across England.[19]

As representatives of the community where an alleged crime was committed, these early jurors, it was presumed, already knew the relevant facts that led to a criminal

---

before the Courts from Edward I to the Sixteenth Century (University of Toronto Press 1998) 19, 21, 22. Presentments were indictments made on the basis of the jurors' own knowledge. Not all presentments, however, were indictments. John Hamilton Baker, The Legal Profession and the Common Law: Historical Essays (Hambledon Press 1986) 264 n 19. By the second quarter of the fourteenth century, indictment had become the normal method of initiating prosecution. See Anthony Musson, Public Order and Law Enforcement, the Local Administration of Criminal Justice, 1294–1350 (Boydell Press 1996) 185. By the early fourteenth century, the terms indictment and presentment had become interchangeable. The indictment was treated as a suit by the Crown. John H Baker, "Criminal Procedure" in Baker, Introduction (n 5) 505. Public rather than private prosecutions developed later. See John H Langbein, "The Origins of Public Prosecution at Common Law" (1973) 17 Am J Legal Hist 313.

[14] Assize of Clarendon (n 7) para 2: "And whoever is found by the oath of the aforesaid men to have been accused or publicly known as a robber or murderer or thief, or as a receiver of them ... shall go to the ordeal of water and swear that ... so far as he knows, he has not been."

[15] Groot, "Thirteenth-Century" (n 8) 34.

[16] The need for the extension of the accusing jury's function is apparent in a decree that Henry III (1216–1272) sent to his itinerant justices in 1219, just four years after Lateran Council IV signaled the end of the ordeals. Henry acknowledged that "the Roman Church prohibited the judgment of fire and water" (cum prohibitum sit per ecclesiam Romanam iudicium ignis et aquae). Letter patent of January 26, 1219, printed in Thomas Rymer and Robert Sanderson (eds), 1 Foedera, conventiones, litterae ... (London 1816) (3 vols) 154. The King offered, however, no alternative method for determining a final judgment. The problem was solved when, beginning around 1219, the voice of the petit jury replaced the voice of God that was said to assure the reliability of the ordeals.

[17] Kamali and Green (n 7) 55, 62. The jury may also have met resistance because it represented an intrusion of powerful central government into local affairs. See Sara M Butler, "Rejecting the Jury, Rejecting the Common Law, Rejecting the King" in Sara M Butler, Pain, Penance, and Protest: Peine Forte et Dure in Medieval England (CUP 2022) 348, 352, and passim. On the difficulty of accepting trial by jury as a mode of proof, see Milsom (n 12) 359; Langbein, Lerner, and Smith (n 5) 59; Shoemaker (n 10) 174–202; George Fisher, "The Jury's Rise as Lie Detector" (1997) 107 Yale LJ 575, 587–602.

[18] For study of peine forte et dure and the motivation of some defendants to reject the jury as a protest against the intrusion of royal power into the local community, see Sara M Butler, Pain, Penance, and Protest: peine forte et dure in Medieval England (CUP 2022) 348–397 and passim.

[19] Milsom (n 12) 359. Trial by battle, already a disfavored method, withered in criminal cases after the new method of trial by petit jury advanced after 1219. John H Baker, "Criminal Procedure" in Baker, Introduction (n 5) 507. No trial by battle was possible when the Crown was the prosecuting party, as the King could always decline to do battle. Trial by appeal (a private prosecution by a victim or victim's kin) remained possible, though increasingly less used. Royal justices began to intervene in the prosecution of private appeals when the appellor abandoned the suit. This became standard practice under Henry III (1216–1272). Kamali and Green (n 7) 60.

charge. They likely knew the reputation of a suspect, even before the trial took place. Indeed, the jurors were selected for that very reason. The jury could reflect communal attitudes.[20] If the petit jury lacked sufficient personal knowledge, they could investigate for themselves by going about and inquiring of local witnesses.[21] In the course of the Middle Ages, however, the petit jury ceased being self-informing. The process by which this occurred is unclear.[22] In early modern England, the jury came to assume the function of hearing evidence from witnesses presented to it in court.[23] The jury, nonetheless, maintained its essential character as a group of local community members.

Magna Carta and the Statutes of Magna Carta

Magna Carta

In June 1215, the same year that the Fourth Lateran Council deprived trial by ordeal of the church's blessing, an assembly of English barons met with King John at the meadow of Runnymede to solicit from him written assurances against his infringing upon their traditional feudal liberties as landholders.[24] No sooner did John seal the Great Charter (*Magna Carta*) than he repudiated it.[25] From Rome, Pope Innocent

---

[20] Kamali and Green (n 7) 60.

[21] Elizabeth Papp Kamali, "Trial by Ordeal by Jury in Medieval England, or Saints and Sinners in Literature and Law" in Kate Gilbert and Stephen W White (eds), *Emotion, Violence, Vengeance and Law in the Middle Ages* (Brill 2018) 49–79.

[22] On the self-informing jury, see David J Seipp, "Jurors, Evidences, and the Tempest of 1499" in John W Cairns and Grant McLeod (eds), *The Dearest Birth Right of the People of England* (Hart Publishing 2002) 75–92; Thomas Andrew Green, *Verdict According to Conscience: Perspectives on the English Criminal Trial Jury, 1200–1800* (The University of Chicago Press 1985) 105–106. See Daniel Klerman, "Was the Jury Ever Self-Informing" (2003) 77 S Cal L Rev 123, addressing doubts raised by some historians about the extent to which the English jury was self-informing.

[23] "By the late fourteenth century ... the duty of the jury was to try sworn evidence in court, although they could still rely on personal knowledge." Anthony Musson, "Twelve Good Men and True? The Character of Early Fourteenth-Century Juries" (1997) 15 LHR 115, 126. On the composition of early juries, see ibid 118–126.

[24] William C Koch Jr, "Magna Carta's Enactment" in Randy J Holland (ed), *Magna Carta, Muse and Mentor* (Reuters in association with the Library of Congress 2014) 39. For indications of the *ius commune*'s influence on some of Magna Carta's provisions, see RH Helmholz, "Magna Carta and the ius commune" (1999) 66 U Chi L Rev 297; RH Helmholz, "Continental Law and Common Law: Historical Strangers or Companions?" (1990) 1990 Duke LJ 1207, 1209–1214; Kenneth Pennington, "Reform in 1215: *Magna Carta* and the Fourth Lateran Council" (2015) 32 BMCL 97–125; Ken Pennington, "Canonical Jurisprudence and Other Legal Systems in the Medieval and Early Modern" in Jesús Miñambres (ed), *Diritto Canonico e Culture Giuridiche nel Centenario del Codex Iuris Canonici del 1917* (Edizione Santa Croce 2019) 109, 117–118; John Hudson, "Magna Carta, the *ius commune*, and English Common Law" in Janet S Loengard (ed), *Magna Carta and the England of King John* (Boydell & Brewer 2010) 99–117.

[25] The document did not bear the title *Magna Carta*. In order to distinguish it from a much shorter accompanying charter, the Charter of the Forest was issued in 1217; the longer document became known thereafter as *magna carta*. AB White, "The Name Magna Carta" (1915) EHR 472, 473; Bryan A Garner, "A Lexicographic Look at Magna Carta" in Holland (ed) (n 24) 89. From his seventeenth-century viewpoint, Edward Coke described "*Magna Charta*" as "the fountaine of all the fundamental lawes of the realme; and therefore it may truly be said of it, that it is *magnum in parvo*." Edward Coke, *The First Part of the Institutes*

III annulled it on the ground that the King's consent had been coerced.[26] When John died in the autumn of 1216, he was succeeded by his nine-year-old son, Henry III. In 1225, the then seventeen-year-old Henry reissued the charter with some modifications. Need for financial support from his barons in his battle against the French may have induced Henry to be agreeable.[27] Successor monarchs repeatedly confirmed the 1225 Charter.[28]

In the 1225 version, two chapters from the 1215 document (cc 39 and 40) were combined, renumbered, and renewed. Although many of Magna Carta's provisions soon fell into desuetude, its newly numbered c 29 proved to possess an enduring potency for future legal development:

> No freeman shall be taken or imprisoned or disseised of any freehold, or liberties, or free customs, or outlawed, or banished, or in any other way destroyed, nor will we go upon him, nor send upon him, except by the legal judgment of his peers or by the law of the land. To no one will we sell, to no one will we deny, or delay right or justice.[29]

By the fourteenth century, the clause was emerging as "the most important of the provisions of Magna Carta."[30]

No definitions accompanied the words of c 29/39. "Freeman" may not have meant broadly "everyman" but rather only those who were not villeins (peasants obligated to perform services for a lord).[31] "Peers" was understood then to refer to temporal lords of Parliament.[32] A "legal judgment" appears to have been one made by peers or according to the "law of the land," that is, according to the rule of law and not by the whim of the king. Some historians have understood Magna Carta's "law of the land" to refer to trial by ordeal or battle.[33] Chronology alone, however, can dispel one common misinterpretation: "legal judgment of his peers" could not have meant criminal trial

---

of the Laws of England (Francis Hargrave and Charles Butler eds, 14th edn, printed for James Moore 1791) Lib 2, sec 108, at 81a. Coke listed other titles by which *Magna Carta* was commonly known: *Charta Libertatum, et Communis Libertas Angliae, or Libertates Angliae, Charta de Libertatibus.* Ibid.

[26] On the role of the Pope in annulling Magna Carta, see Richard Helmholz, "Pope Innocent III and the Annulment of Magna Carta" (2018) 69 Journal of Ecclesiatical History 1.

[27] William C Koch, "Magna Carta's Enactment" in Holland (ed) (n 24) 45.

[28] For centuries, Magna Carta was credited to Henry III rather than to his father John. It is Henry's 1225 version, and not the repudiated 1215 version, that entered into the English statute books. Sir John Baker, "The Legal Force and Effect of Magna Carta" in Holland (ed) (n 24) 67; Garner (n 25) 92–94.

[29] Magna Carta 1225 c 29 [1215 cc 39–40]. The 1215 document did not operate as law after its annulment. John Baker, *The Reinvention Magna Carta 1215–1616* (CUP 2017) 3. The petit jury did not exist in 1215. Baker, *Introduction* (n 5) 472 & n 34. Only through anachronistic interpretation did Magna Carta's c 29 come to apply to the jury. Ibid 508 & n 41.

[30] Baker, *Reinvention* (n 29) 40. On the historiography of Magna Carta, see ibid 442–451; Jack N Rakove, *Declaring Rights: A Brief History with Documents* (Bedford Books 1998) 7–8.

[31] The point is discussed in William Sharp McKechnie, *Magna Carta: A Commentary on the Great Charter of King John* (2nd edn, J Maclehose & Sons 1914) 118–119, 386; Baker, *Reinvention* (n 29) 247.

[32] Two centuries later, judgment by peers meant the privilege of members of the House of Lords to be tried by the nobility and bishops summoned as lords to parliament. David J Seipp, "Magna Carta in the Late Middle Ages: Over-Mighty Subjects, Under-Mighty Kings, and a Turn Away from Trial by Jury" (2016) 25 William and Mary Bill of Rights Journal 665, 676 n 78.

[33] Bryan A Garner, "A Lexicographic Look at Magna Carta" in Holland (ed) (n 24) 149.

by jury. Criminal jury trials did not yet exist in 1215.[34] Not until the late sixteenth century would lawyers begin to see in c 29/39 a basis for procedural protections for defendants at jury trial.[35] It was only in 1581 that William Lambarde became the first to link "peers" with trial jurors.[36]

The Due Process Statutes of Edward III

During King Edward III's fifty-year reign (1327–1377), Magna Carta's c 29/39 supplied "the spiritual source"[37] for a series of statutes that his parliaments issued.[38] The statutes had the effect of specifying and codifying the vague language of c 29/39.

In 1351, Parliament enacted 25 Edw III, stat 5, c 4. It contained a set of foundational statutory protections for defendants:

> Whereas it is contained in the Great Charter of the Franchises of England, that none shall be imprisoned nor put out of his Freehold, nor of his Franchises nor free Custom, unless it be by the Law of the Land; It is accorded, assented, and established, That from henceforth none shall be taken by Petition or Suggestion made to our Lord the King, or to his Council, unless it be by Indictment or Presentment of good and lawful People of the same neighborhood where such Deeds be done (*de bones et loialx de visnee ou tiele fair se face*) in due Manner or by Process made by Writ original at the Common Law; nor that none be out of his Franchises, nor of his Freeholds, unless he be duly brought to answer (*sil ne soit mesne duement en respons*), and forejudged of the same by the Course of the Law ("*per voie de lei*"); and if anything be done against the same, it shall be redressed and holden for none (*tenue pro nul*).[39]

Indictment by reliable neighbors

The statute of 25 Edw III, stat 5, c 4 insulated persons against abusive assertions of power by royal authority. Accusations could not be made directly by the Crown or

---

[34] Baker, *Reinvention* (n 29) 37, 247.

[35] On the relationship between Magna Carta and the English jury, see Thomas J McSweeney, "Magna Carta and the Right to Trial by Jury" in Holland (ed) (n 24) 139–157.

[36] Baker, *Introduction* (n 5) 472 n 34; Sir John Baker, "The Legal Force and Effect of Magna Carta" in Holland (ed) (n 24) 73. See William Lambarde, *Eirenarcha: Or of the Office of the Iustices of Peace in Two Bookes: Gathered 1579 and Now Reuised* (R Tottell and Chr Barker 1582) 436.

[37] John H Baker, "Introduction" in JH Baker (ed), *The Reports of Sir John Spelman Part II* (SS 1978) 71. See also Baker, *Reinvention* (n 29) 41, 50–51.

[38] 2 Edw III, c 8; 5 Edw III, c 9; 14 Edw III, stat 1, c 14; 25 Edw III, stat 5, c 4; 28 Edw III, cc 3 and 5; 42 Edw III, c 3. Most of the statutes restrained the extraordinary jurisdiction of the King's Council. See JH Baker, "Personal Liberty under the Common Law, 1200–1600" in *The Common Law Tradition: Lawyers, Books, and the Law* (Hambledon Press 2000) 319 n 3.

[39] 25 Edw III, c 4. The phrase "by the Course of the Law" may have been a paraphrase of Magna Carta's "by the law of the Land" (*per legem terrae*). CH McIlwain, "Due Process of Law in Magna Carta" (1914) 14 Col L Rev 27, 49.

its council, or by royally appointed judges.[40] Rather, the statute required that an accusation depend upon an indictment or presentment issuing from an accusing jury composed of local community members.[41] By requiring that only a group of "good and lawful people" could make presentment or indict, the act shielded defendants from baseless accusations. As a possible added protection for defendants, a careful judge might dismiss an indictment that was too vague or failed to conform to required technicalities of wording.[42]

Edward's statute specifically required jurors to be "of the same neighborhood where such deeds be done" (*de visnee ou tiele fair se face*). This provision served to assure that a jury would be ordinarily composed of neighbors with adequate knowledge of the persons and circumstances involved in the crime. In addition, the local venue made it likely that parties and witnesses would be available at trial without undue burden.

Requirement of trial and opportunity to defend

Of signal importance, 25 Edw III, stat 5, c 4 required that a defendant must be able to respond to the indictment ("brought to answer"). Edward's statute expressed for English justice a principle that had deep roots in Continental law, as well. The mandate already appeared in England before Edward's reign. The *Leges Henrici Primi* (1114/1118) required that accused persons must be present in a proper judicial forum before any action could be taken against them and the accused must be given the opportunity to defend:

> And it is not fitting that anyone be judged or condemned before he has legitimate accusers present and receives an opportunity of defending for washing away crimes.[43]

[40] John H Baker, "Criminal Courts and Procedure 1550–1800" in Sir John Baker, 2 *Collected Papers on English Legal History* (CUP 2013) (3 vols) (hereafter Baker, *Collected Papers*)1015.

[41] Private parties could still accuse by prosecuting an "appeal" of felony. Baker, *Introduction* (n 5) 503, 506. On prosecutions by private parties before 1215, see Roger D Groot, "The Jury in Private Criminal Prosecutions" (1983) 27 Am J Legal Hist 113, 117–125. False accusations by private parties could be contested on the ground that the prosecution was the product of an enemy's "hatred and malice." If a jury of inquest agreed with the defendant's objection, the suit against the defendant was ended. See Susanne Jenks, "The Writ and the Exception *de odio et atia*" (2002) 23 J Legal Hist 1, 2, 16 n 45; James Masschaele, *Jury, State, and Society in Medieval England* (Palgrave Macmillan 2008) 23–24.

[42] "By the middle of Edward III's reign, the courts would strike down the indictment itself for generality." JH Baker, "Some Early Newgate Reports 1315–1328" in Baker, 2 *Collected Papers* (n 40) 975. In effect, "no one could be put on trial for his life except upon a specific charge, made either by appeal or indictment. This salutary rule came to be cherished as one of the greatest liberties of the subject." Baker, *Introduction* (n 5) 506. On indictments, see T.F.T. Plucknett, "A Commentary on the Indictments" in Bertha H Putnam (ed), *Proceedings Before the Justices of the Peace in the Fourteenth and Fifteenth Centuries* (Spottiswoode & Ballantyne 1938) cxxxiii. For exceptions to the indictment requirement, see Baker, 2 *Collected Papers* (n 40) 973.

[43] *Nec oportet quemquam iudicari uel damnari priusquam legittimos accusatores habeat presentes locumque defendendi accipiat ad abluenda crimina. Leges* 5, 9a in LJ Downer (ed and tr), *Leges Henrici Primi* (Clarendon Press 1972) 86. Downer traces the source of the requirement to the pseudo-Isidorian *Capitula Angilramni*. Ibid 309. The ultimate source of phrases is Acts of the Apostles 25:16, narrating the trial of St Paul. The *Leges Henrici Primi* also repeat St Augustine's caution in his Sermo 351 that a suspect's guilt must be established by proper procedure, that is, by a willing confession (*sponte confessum*) or by conviction

And let whatever is done against absent persons (in every place and undertaking), or is conducted by those who are not his judges, be completely nullified.[44]

These portions of the *Leges Henrici* were adopting verbatim the language of the pseudo-Isidorian forgeries composed in mid-ninth-century Frankish regions and introduced into England by Lanfranc, the first Norman archbishop of Canterbury (1070–1089) immediately after the Norman invasion.[45] The summoning of an accused to trial was considered a basic element of natural and divine law.[46]

An impartial jury

In the early years of the jury's institution, impartiality of jurors could be compromised because accusing jurors were able to sit on the petit jury. This danger was eliminated by 25 Edw III, stat 5, c 3 (1351), which provided that a defendant could challenge any petit juror who had previously sat on the jury of accusation.[47] In addition to removal for cause, a defendant could challenge up to thirty-five jurors in a felony case peremptorily.[48]

Observance of "due process" of law

In 1354, another of Edward's parliaments passed a statute emphasizing that persons could be punished only according to the rule of law. 28 Edw III, c 3 responded to a parliamentary concern that some persons had been subjected to summary proceedings

in a court (*iudicio convictum*) by proper procedure (*ordine iudiciario*). *Leges Henrici* 5, 18a in Downer (n 43) 90.

[44] *Et quidquid adversus absentes (in omni loco vel negotio) uel a non suis iudicibus agitur, penitus euacuetur. Leges* 31, 7b in Downer (n 43) 134. Downer traces the source to pseudo-Isidore. Ibid 310.

[45] See ZN Brooke, *The English Church and the Papacy* (CUP 1952) 60, 72, 77, and passim. The manuscript was copied and widely distributed throughout the cathedral libraries of England. Ibid 83. By the mid-twelfth century, complete copies of the False Decretals were available. Ibid 85. They became the basis for the study of canon law in England. Ibid 60. See also RH Helmholz, 1 *The Oxford History of the Laws of England: The Canon Law and Ecclesiastical Jurisdiction from 597 to the 1640s* (OUP 2004) (12 vols) 26–27; MG Gibson, *Lanfranc of Bec* (Clarendon Press 1978) 139–140. Evidence of pre-Conquest canon law collections in England, though quite spare, shows evidence of Continental influence. See Michael D Eliot, "Canon Law Collections in England ca 600–1066" (doctoral thesis for the Centre for Medieval Studies, University of Toronto 2013) 1.

[46] See Gillian Evans, "Lanfranc, Anselm and a New Consciousness of Canon Law in England" in Norman Doe and others (eds), *English Canon Law* (Cardiff 1998) 11.

[47] 25 Edw III, stat 5, c 3: "It is accorded, that no indictor shall be put to inquests upon the deliverance of the indictees of felonies or trespass, if he be challenged for that same cause by him which is so indicted." See Bellamy, *The Criminal Trial* (n 13) 28; Musson, "Twelve Good Men" (n 23) 141. For an example of a defendant making such a challenge, see David J Seipp, *Legal History: The Year Books, Medieval English Legal History, an Index and Paraphrase of Printed Year Book Reports, 1268*-1535 (hereafter Seipp's Abridgement: <https://www.bu.edu/phpbin/lawyearbooks/display.php?id=1151>.

[48] See Baker, *Introduction* (n 5) 508 n 42, 509. Musson, "Twelve Good Men" (n 23) 133. Under Henry VIII, the number of challenges was reduced to twenty. Whether challenges applied in cases of treason was questionable. Baker, *Spelman* (n 37) 108 & n 10.

without adequate provision for defense. The case of Roger Mortimer may have contributed to parliament's action. Mortimer had been captured, imprisoned, and condemned by attainder in his absence after he led a revolt against Edward III's father. Mortimer was hanged in 1330 without having received an opportunity to defend himself. Parliament reversed the attainder in 1354.[49] 28 Edw III, c 3 employed a phrase that subsequently became renowned in legal history:

> That no man of what estate or condition that he be, shall be put out of land or tenement, nor taken, nor imprisoned, nor disinherited, nor put to death, without being brought in answer by due process of law. (*saunz estre mesne en respons par due proces de lei*).[50]

This first mention of the term "due process" within a statute reinforced the principle that proceedings must be held in accord with the ordinary procedures of the common law and not undertaken at the whim of authorities.[51] As used within the statute, "due process" expressed the principle that "people must not be treated arbitrarily, but only in accordance with the regular procedures of the day. It had been used in that sense well before 1354.[52]

Concerned to protect its own members against biased and false accusations, Commons in 1368 repeated the "due process" requirement:

---

[49] For discussions of *Mortimer*, see Baker, *Reinvention* (n 29) 56; Baker, 2 *Collected Papers* (n 40) 974; Keith Jurow, "Untimely Thoughts: A Reconsideration of the Origins of Due Process of Law" (1975) 19 AJLH 265, 267; RR Davies, *ODNB*, 'Mortimer, Roger, first earl of March (1287–1330) https://doi.org/10.1093/ref:odnb/19354.

[50] 28 Edw III, c 3 (1354). Similar procedural complaints arose around the same time in the cases of John Maltravers and the Earl of Arundel. See Baker, *Reinvention* (n 29) 56–57. In voiding attainders against the accused, Parliament seems to have accepted the argument "that even Parliament could not override the requirement of natural justice." Ibid 57. Judicialized summary procedure did not survive the due process statutes of Edward. JH Baker, "Some Early Newgate Reports 1315–1328" in Baker, 2 *Collected Papers* (n 40) 974.

[51] Baker, *Reinvention* (n 29) 52."The right to be heard, and 'due process of law' were easier to understand than the obscure language of 1215 and 1225, though they only codified the previous understanding . . . These statutes were to prove important in the seventeenth century . . . [T]here are no learned commentaries on 'due process,' though it is apparent from conciliar petitions that it was merely an encapsulation of the received sense of chapter 29 as protecting what is now known as the rule of law . . . Due process was not an arcane constitutional mystery, but the ordinary procedure of the common law as opposed to the arbitrary whim of those in power." Ibid 51–52.

[52] Ibid 41. The phrase "due process" did not yet carry with it the broad expanse of meaning attached to the term in modern times, particularly in the United States. See also Jurow (n 49) 272: the phrase meant a procedural writ summoning a defendant to answer before the court and the writs necessary for the execution of judgments. See also Faith Thompson, *Magna Carta: Its Role in the Making of the English Constitution, 1300–1629* (University of Minnesota Press 1948) 92. According to Kenneth Jurow, "The term 'due process of law' never played a crucial role in the development of English law. It was to chapter twenty-nine of Magna Carta and the phrase 'by the law of the land' that men turned during the great crises of English liberty." Kenneth Jurow, "Untimely Thoughts: A Reconsideration of the Origins of Due Process" (1975) 19 AJLH 265, 279. Kenneth Pennington has found that "[t]he term 'due process' entered the English language as an invention of fourteenth-century French jurists." Pennington, "Introduction" (n 3) 4 n 2. Medieval jurists captured the concept in the phrase "*secundum ordinem iudiciarium.*" Ibid 4. "It meant that the full rights of the defendant were respected by the court. The rights of defendants—and plaintiffs—were of paramount importance in the medieval courtroom." Ibid.

At the request of the commons by their petitions put forth in this parliament, to es-
chew the mischiefs and damages done to divers of his Commons by false accusers,
which oftentimes have made their accusations more for revenge and singular benefit, than for the profit of the King, or of his people, which accused persons, some
have been taken, and [sometime] caused to come before the King's Council by writ,
and otherwise upon grievous pain against the law: it is assented and accorded, for
the good governance of the Commons, that no man be put to answer without presentment before Justices, or matter of record, or by due process and writ original,
according to the old law of the land: and if any thing from henceforth be done to the
contrary, it shall be void in the law and holden for error.[53]

A unanimous verdict based on conscience

In 1367, the court of Common Pleas settled beyond question that a jury's verdict had
to be unanimous.[54] The decision is recorded in the Year Books:[55]

In another Assize before the same Justices at North' the jury (l'Assise) were sworn,
and they were all in agreement (accord) except one, who did not want to agree with
the eleven. Then they were sent back (remand), and remained there the whole day
and the next day without drinking or eating. Then he was asked by the Justices if
he wanted to agree with his companions, and he said never, because he would die
first in prison. Therefore they took the verdict of the eleven, and commanded him
to prison, and upon this gave a day upon the same verdict in the Common Pleas.
The plaintiff prayed judgment on the verdict. Thorp CJCP said that they were all in
agreement that this was not a verdict taken of eleven; a verdict could not be taken
of eleven .... And then by assent of all Justices it was the opinion that this was not
a verdict. Therefore, it was awarded that this panel was quashed and annulled, and
that he who was in prison was released, and that the plaintiff sued a new Venire fa-
cias of a jury (d'Assise) .... Note, that the Justices said that they should have carried
the jury (l'Assise) with them in a cart until they were in agreement.[56]

---

[53] 42 Edw III, c 3 (1368).

[54] See Baker, *Introduction* (n 5) 76, citing YB Mich, 41 Edw III, fo 31, pl 36; Lib Ass, 41 Edw III, pl 11.
The same case is more extensively reported in 11, fol 253b–254a. Leonard Levy suggests that the rule of
unanimity may have its roots in the old form of trial by compurgation where sworn witnesses had to be in
agreement. Leonard Williams Levy, *Origins of the Fifth Amendment: The Right against Self-Incrimination*
(Ivan R Dee 1999) 36–37. Pollock and Maitland ascribed unanimity to the belief that the "country," as
representing the voice of the community, needed to speak with one voice. Fredrick Pollock and Frederic
William Maitland, 2 *The History of the English Law before the Time of Edward I* (2nd edn, CUP 1898) (2
vols) 626.

[55] Originating in the 1250s or 1260s, the Year Books (so-named for regnal years) were brief and unoffi-
cial abridgements in Anglo-French of proceedings observed in courts. Anonymous authors, perhaps students as well practitioners, drew up the reports for purposes of legal education and practice. John Hamilton
Baker, *The Common Law Tradition: Lawyers, Books, and the Law* (Hambledon Press 2000) 136–164;
Baker (n 5) 179–181. For an electronically searchable database with index and paraphrase of printed Year
Book reports, see Seipp's Abridgment (n 47): https://www.bu.edu/law/faculty-scholarship/legal-history-
the-year-books/. For a study of criminal matter in the Year Books, see David Seipp, "Crime in the Year
Books" in Chantal Stebbings (ed), *Law Reporting in England* (Hambledon Press 1995).

[56] Seipp, *Abridgement* (n 47) fol 253b–254a.

No rules of evidence determined what jurors could or could not consider in arriving at their verdict.[57] They were to reach their decision according to whatever satisfied their consciences.[58] As juries assumed their role of hearing witnesses and other evidence presented to them in court, they might feel themselves in need of instruction on how to evaluate the credibility of what they heard, but until at least sometime in the seventeenth century, judges typically limited themselves to repeating that jurors should judge according to conscience.[59] The jurors were placed under oath to give a true verdict. The new procedure of jury trial, thus, caused a critical moral shift from the ordeals.[60] Where the *vox Dei* (at least in concept) decided innocence or guilt in an ordeal, the Crown now imposed that responsibility upon community members.[61] The jury's verdict was irreversible.[62]

Trial in public

Sir Thomas Smith, describing the customary English trial in the mid-sixteenth century, noted that the trial was always held:

> openlie in the presence of the Iudges, the Iustices, the enquest, the prisoner, and so manie as will or can come so neare as to heare it, and all depositions and witnesses given aloude, that all men may heare from the mouth of the depositors and witnesses what is saide.[63]

Smith contrasted this openness with the Continental *ius commune* trial where the examination of witnesses took place separately and apart from the parties. In fact, however, except for the examination of the witnesses, the Continental trial was in public and the testimony of witnesses was published publicly and subject to replies from opponents.

---

[57] The very imprecision of the standard supplied an impetus for the accused to speak and explain his knowledge of the charges. John H Langbein, *The Origins of Adversary Criminal Trial* (OUP 2003) 57.

[58] See David J Seipp, "Jurors, Evidences, and the Tempest of 1499" in John W Cairns and Grant McLeod (eds), *The Dearest Birth Right of the People of England* (Hart Publishing 2002) 84 & n 41 (citing fifteenth-century cases). See Thomas A Green, *Verdict According to Conscience: Perspectives on the English Criminal Jury Trial 1200–1800* (University of Chicago Press 1985) 1–27 (discussing early jury's power to base its verdict inscrutably upon conscience); Barbara Shapiro, *"Beyond Reasonable Doubt" and "Probable Cause": Historical Perspectives on the Anglo-American Law of Evidence* (University of California Press 1991) (tracing the movement of the English law from "satisfied conscience" standard in the time of the early jury to the development of proof "beyond reasonable doubt" in the later eighteenth century).

[59] Shapiro (n 58) 6.

[60] James Q Whitman, *The Origins of Reasonable Doubt: The Theological Roots of the Criminal Trial* (Yale University Press 2008) 56–59.

[61] Ibid 56–57, 133. Whitman states that jurors were aware of the "spiritual danger entailed by passing judgment" and that this apprehension contributed to the eventual establishment of a reasonable doubt standard to "ease the fears of jurors who might otherwise refuse to pronounce the defendant guilty." Ibid 186.

[62] See Baker, *Introduction* (n 5) 509.

[63] Thomas Smith, *De republica anglorum. The Maner of Gouernement or Policie of the Realme of England* (printed by Henry Midleton for Gregorie Seton 1584) Second booke, c 23, 81–82. On the public nature of the criminal trial under the English common law, see also John G Bellamy, *The Tudor Law of Treason, an Introduction* (Routledge & Kegan Paul, University of Toronto Press 1979) 133–137.

Hostility to Repeated Trials and Punishments for the Same Indictments

In 1164, King Henry II issued the Constitutions of Clarendon. They limited clerical privileges and the jurisdiction of church courts, permitting the royal court to punish ecclesiastical clerks (clerics) charged with serious crimes after an ecclesiastical tribunal had found the clerics guilty and degraded them from the clerical state. Thomas à Becket, archbishop of Canterbury from 1162 to 1170), opposed this subjection of criminous clerks to royal authority. In support of his argument, Becket cited the biblical phrase *nec enim Deus iudicat bis in idipsum* (for God does not judge twice in the same matter).[64] Becket could have relied on Roman law, as well. Justinian's Digest had declared "the governor must not allow a man to be charged with the same offenses of which he has already been acquitted."[65]

In the aftermath of Becket's struggle with royal authority, the troublesome archbishop was murdered, perhaps by agents of the king, although Henry always denied any role in the killing. The prominence of the persons and events involved in the controversy over criminous clerks was unparalleled. Becket's invocation of the biblical maxim lent authority for opposition to repeated trials.[66]

Procedural restrictions on subjecting persons to repeated trial or punishment for the same crime appear in the common law at least by the start of the thirteenth century.[67] It is possible that the restrictions may have existed independently of the canonical maxim.[68] Most often, private parties ("appellors"), who were victims or kin the victims, prosecuted the case.[69] Defendants could claim protection against repeated prosecutions by the same private party for the same crime by pleading *autrerfois acquit* (acquitted at another time) or *autrefois convict* (convicted at another time). In

---

[64] The biblical passage is Book of Nahum 1:9. For proceedings in the Becket controversy, see Craigie Robertson and others (eds), 4 *Materials for the History of Thomas Becket* (Longman 1875–1885) (7 vols) 202. Also used in the controversy was the maxim "*non iudicabit Deus bis in idipsum*" (God will not accuse twice in the same matter). Ibid 96. See Martin L Friedland, *Double Jeopardy* (Clarendon Press 1969) 326 n 5; Jill Hunter, "The Development of the Rule Against Double Jeopardy" (1984) 5 J Legal Hist 3, 5–7; Baker, "Liberty" (n 38) 504.

[65] *isdem criminibus, quibus quis liberatus est, non debet praeses pati eundem accusari.* Dig 48.2.7. See text to n 93 in ch 1.

[66] See, eg, *Hudson v Lee* (1589) 4 Co Rep 43a, 76 Eng Rpt 989, 990, cited in Friedland (n 64) 328 n 5. Richard Helmholz points out that in the hands of later generations of lawyers the canonical maxim may have attained a greater significance in application than it originally possessed. Richard H Helmholz, "The Law of Double Jeopardy" in Richard H Helmholz (ed), *The Spirit of Classical Canon Law* (University of Georgia Press 1996) 309.

[67] Select Pleas of the Crown, Shropshire Eyre, No 76 (1203) and Warwickshire Eyre, No 158 (1221), 1 SS (1887), cited in Hunter (n 64) 16 n 3. And see Doris Mary Stenton (ed), 2 *Pleas before the King or His Justices, 1198–1202* (4 vols) pl 737 (1949) 68 SS 217 (Somerset 1201), cited in David S Rudstein, "A Brief History of the Fifth Amendment Guarantee Against Double Jeopardy" (2005) 14 William and Mary Bill of Rights Journal 193. Cornish Eyre, No 6 (1201). See also William Craddock Bolland, "Introduction" in William Craddock Bolland, *The Year Books of Edward II: The Eyre of Kent, 6 & 7 Edward II (1313–1314)* (Bernard Quatrich 1919) xc: "The Roll shows that it was no uncommon thing for a man to be brought up for a second time for trial on a charge of which he had already been acquitted. Of course, he was at once discharged on proving the validity of his previous acquittal."

[68] Hunter discusses a possible Anglo-Saxon origin. Hunter (n 64) 4.

[69] See David J Seipp, "The Distinction Between Crime and Tort in the Early Common Law" (1996) 76 Boston Univ L Rev 59–87; Bellamy, *The Criminal Trial* (n 13) 15, 19–56.

1202, for example, a complainant offered to prove in court that a defendant had fe-
loniously killed a man. In his defense, the defendant asserted that "on a former occasion" he was accused and acquitted of being an accessory to the same murder. The
second "appeal" was deemed "null."[70]

The procedural rules for applying *autrefois acquit* shifted over time and were inconsistent in outcomes.[71] They may have been motivated by a concern for the efficient
use of judicial resources rather than a solicitude for the welfare of an individual defendant.[72] Nonetheless, from the standpoint of the accused, the pleas could provide
a shield against abuse by private parties. A former judgment could form a barrier to
re-prosecution, even though a hostility to re-trial did not amount to a clear and absolute bar against it.[73] The safeguard against re-trial at the suit of private accusers did
not, however, provide protection against the power of the state.[74] When, in the later
Middle Ages, the Crown increasingly assumed the role of prosecutor, *autrefois acquit*
was not available for use against the state.[75] It did not constitute a fundamental right of
an individual, but it staked out a basic principle of procedure charged with the possibility of growth and refinement.[76]

Conclusions

After the Fourth Lateran Council (1215) banned clerics from blessing the ordeals,
England found an alternative method for determining guilt or innocence. Building
upon preexisting uses of local persons to settle civil disputes and to issue criminal
accusations, a petit jury of twelve neighbors was employed to render final verdicts,
replacing the traditional trial by ordeal. By the last quarter of the thirteenth century,
the petit jury was the established method of trial throughout England. The system of
trial by jury soon came to be a dominating method for proceeding against individuals
accused of crime. The institution would later be embraced as one of the fundamental
rights of English persons. In its infancy, it was not.[77]

[70] Shropshire Eyre (n 67) 33. Hunter (n 64) cites additional examples: YB of Edward II (vol 5), The
Eyre of Kent, 6 & 7 Edward II (1313–1314) (SS, xxiv London 1910) 67, 74, 127; YB of Edward II (vol
3) (1309–1310) (SS, xx 1910) 153; YB of Edward II, Eyre of London, 14 Edw II (1321) (SS, lxxxv 1910) 66,
86. See also David J Seipp, "Crime in the Year Books" in Chantal Stebbings (ed), *Law Reporting in England*
(Humbledon Press 1995) 27 nn 76–81 (citing double jeopardy cases in the fourteenth and fifteenth centuries) 31–32.
[71] The rules were "replete with exceptions and compromises," at least up until the end of the sixteenth
century. Hunter (n 64) 4. Learning surrounding the pleas could be "arcane and apparently contradictory."
Helmholz, "Double Jeopardy" (n 66) 286.
[72] Hunter (n 64) 7.
[73] See Jay A Sigler, "A History of Double Jeopardy" (1963) 7 Am J Legal Hist 285, 292.
[74] Ibid 289–290, 293, 308; Hunter 4 (n 64).
[75] Sigler (n 73) 292; Hunter (n 64) 8.
[76] Hunter (n 64) 4.
[77] Sara Butler has written that both the presenting jury and the petit jury, at their inception, were unwelcome extensions of central royal authority into local communities. At least in the fourteenth century,
the jury was not embraced as a "bulwark of liberty," as viewed in later centuries. Butler sees the choice of
defendants to stand mute as a passive protest against the king's common law. Butler, "Rejecting" (n 17) 352,
354, and passim.

In chapter 39 (1215), and again in chapter 29 (1225), Magna Carta set out protections for nobles against arbitrary royal actions. (Only in the seventeenth-century
did lawyers interpret the charter's language to apply to jury trials.) Magna Carta's
chapter provided inspiration for several fourteenth-century parliaments of Edward
III to issue a set of statutes assuring important due process protections for all individuals against possible abuse by the Crown. These safeguards included a requirement of indictment or presentment by neighbors from the vicinity where the alleged
crime occurred; an opportunity to appear and answer the charges; and a trial before
twelve impartial jurors according to the ordinary procedures of the common law. By
custom, the common-law trial was always public. Verdicts were to be arrived at unanimously according to what satisfied the jurors' consciences. Consistent with biblical
texts, English procedure, like that of the *ius commune*, generally rejected placing a
defendant in jeopardy of repeated trials or punishments.

The matrix of customs that comprised jury trial constituted a robust protection for
defendants against unsubstantiated accusations and unfair convictions. Judgments
could not be based on the arbitrary authority of the Crown, the vindictiveness of
accusers, or the bias of jurors. Local, impartial neighbors, sworn to tell the truth,
considered the evidence they already knew or was presented in court. What kind
or amount of evidence was not specified. Unlike *ius commune* procedure, which restricted a judge's ability to find guilt in the absence of two credible eyewitnesses to the
crime, England had no such requirement. Jurors were free to evaluate the evidence
as they wished. They were to deliberate together until they decided that the evidence
satisfied each of their individual consciences unanimously. Only then did they render
a verdict.[78]

The jury's protective power is suggested in the high acquittal rates recorded.[79] In the
thirteenth century, only fifteen percent of homicide suspects and thirty percent of alleged thieves are thought to have been convicted.[80] The rates of conviction rose in the
sixteenth and seventeenth centuries.[81] Nevertheless, a jury, using its power to render a
general verdict or a partial verdict, could act to a defendant's advantage. In any event,
defendants continued to "place themselves upon the country," that is, upon the jury,
for its protection.[82] Even at treason trials under the Tudor and Stuart governments,

---

[78] Mirjan Damaška carefully analyzes the *ius commune*'s approach to decision-making at its criminal
trials and compares that approach to the English jury system's procedures. Damaška shows that the *ius
commune*'s rules for evaluation of evidence was not nearly as mechanical and rigid as scholarship has regularly portrayed it. Emperor Hadrian had set out that a Roman fact-finder was free to evaluate evidence
in his rescript *tu magis scire potes* ("you can know better"). See text to nn 68–69 in ch 1. Medieval jurists
often cited the ancient rescript to free *ius commune* judges, acting as fact-finders, from an overly mech-
anistic scheme of evaluating evidence. Damaška (n 4) 62, 64. But a *ius commune*'s judge's freedom was
circumscribed. He had to state in writing the reasons for disbelieving evidence, so that appeals could be
made. Ibid.

[79] Bellamy, *The Criminal Trial* (n 13) 69.

[80] Thomas Andrew Green, *Verdict According to Conscience: Perspectives on the English Criminal Trial
Jury 1200–1800* (University of Chicago Press 1985) 22–27. For a detailed analysis and dissection of jury
verdicts in first half of the fourteenth century, see Musson, *Public Order* (n 13) 208–222.

[81] Musson, *Public Order* (n 13) 106.

[82] Baker, "Criminal Courts" (n 40) 1027. From the sixteenth to the eighteenth centuries, one-quarter to
one-half of those indicted were acquitted. Ibid.

conviction was "by no means automatic" and "there were quite a number of acquittals," despite the Crown prosecutors' best efforts.[83]

Yet, for all the valuable protections the early English jury trial offered against erroneous convictions, there were procedural lacunae that impeded the defense of accused persons and risked the conviction of the innocent. These deficits will be the subject of the next chapter.

[83] Bellamy, *Treason* (n 63) 171.

7

Confronting Opposing Witnesses
in Sixteenth-Century England

An Absence of Evidentiary Rules

Sir John Fortescue (c 1395–c. 1477) believed the English jury system offered a defendant robust protections that were clearly superior to Continental trial procedure. In *De laudibus legum Angliae* (*Concerning the Praises of the Laws of England*), Fortescue bragged:

> Who, then, in England can die unjustly for a crime, when he can have so many aids in favour of his life, and none save his neighbours, good and faithful men, against whom he has no manner of exception, can condemn him? I should, indeed, prefer twenty guilty men to escape death through mercy, than one innocent to be condemned unjustly.[1]

The rates of acquittal were significant, in so far as records show.[2] The institution of the jury itself, combined with the due process procedures of Edward III's statutes, offered defendants important protections against the risk of false accusation or erroneous conviction. Yet, at the same time, the common-law trial that Fortescue praised was virtually devoid of evidentiary principles. No rules limited what jurors could take into consideration in arriving at a verdict.[3] Granted, it is true that a fourteenth-century

---

[1] Sir John Fortescue, *De laudibus legum Angliae* (*In Praise of the Laws of England*) c 27 in Shelley Lockwood (ed), *On the Laws and Governance of England* (CUP 1997) 41. Fortescue's preference for acquittal of the guilty over the risk of convicting the innocent echoes the Roman Emperor Trajan's rescript "for it is more honorable that the crime of a guilty person remain unpunished than an innocent person be condemned" (*sanctius enim esse impunitum relinqui facinus nocentis quam innocentem damnari*). Rescript of the Emperor Trajan to Adsidius Severus (98/117 CE), Dig 48.19.5.pr. See also Kenneth Pennington, "Innocent until Proven Guilty: The Origins of a Legal Maxim" (2003) 63 Jurist 106. On variations of the maxim, see Alexander Volokh, "n- Guilty Men" (1997) 146 U Pa L Rev 173.

[2] Information about jury procedures is scarce before the mid-sixteenth century. "The trial...was very far from being a matter of course, and was perhaps the weakest link in the common-law system." John H Baker, "Introduction" in John H Baker (ed), *The Law Reports of Sir John Spelman* (Selden Society 1997) 103."We have only fleeting glimpses of the proceedings before the jury, and must be wary of assuming that a 'trial,' with witnesses, was essential or even usual." John H Baker, "Some Early Newgate Reports 1315–1328" in Sir John Baker, 2 *Collected Papers on English Legal History* (CUP 2013) (2 vols) 974. See John G Bellamy, *The Criminal Trial in Later Medieval England: Felony before the Courts from Edward I to the Sixteenth Century* (University of Toronto Press 1998) 199–200; John Hamilton Baker, *An Introduction to English Legal History* (4th edn, Butterworths Lexis Nexis 2002) 509; Thomas Andrew Green, *Verdict According to Conscience: Perspectives on the English Criminal Trial Jury 1200–1800* (University of Chicago Press 1985) 16.

[3] Regarding jurors using their personal knowledge, see David J Seipp, "Jurors, Evidences, and the Tempest of 1499" in John W Cairns and Grant McLeod (eds), *The Dearest Birth Right of the People of England* (Hart Publishing 2002) 84; Green (n 2) 16–19. On the transformation of the jury to its modern function of hearing witnesses presented to it in court, see John H Langbein, "Historical Foundations of

Foundations of American Criminal Due Process at Trial. Francis R. Herrmann and Brownlow M. Speer,
Oxford University Press. © Oxford University Press 2025. DOI: 10.1093/9780199364770.003.0007

note in the Year Books urged "when a man has been arrested on suspicion and indicted as a common thief, and arraigned for this, the Justices shall tell the jury not to find him guilty unless they are certain of his guilt."[4] Nothing, however, limited the evidence that might serve as a foundation for such certainty. The jury could base its verdict on whatever satisfied its conscience,[5] including knowledge gained extrajudicially.[6] Eyewitnesses were not required; nor any witnesses, at all, for that matter. Although it is unlikely that jurors would convict where no victim or other witnesses appeared,[7] no rule prevented the jury from doing so.[8] It was not unambiguously clear that the burden of proof lay upon the prosecution to prevail in its case. Thomas Smith, *De Republica Anglorum* (1589), recounts:

> When the Judge hath heard them [the witnesses] say ynough, he asketh if they can say nay more: if they say no, then he turneth his speeche to the enquest. Good men (saith he) ye of the enquest, ye haue heard what these men say against the prisoner, you have heard what the prisoner can say for himselfe, have an eye to your othe, and to your duetie, and doe that which God shall put in your mindes to the discharge of your consciences, and marke well what is saide.[9]

---

the Law of Evidence: A View from the Ryder Sources" (1996) 96 Colum L Rev 1168, 1170–1172; John H Langbein, "The Criminal Trial before the Lawyers" (1978) 45 U Chi L Rev 263, 299 n 105; Bellamy, *Criminal Trial* (n 2) 101–102, 104, 111.

[4] "*Nota qe home pris pur suspeccion ou endite cor comune laron e de ceo arene les justices dirroit a la dorein qil ne les soilent pas sil ne soit pas certain fait.*" William Craddock Bolland and others (ed and tr), *The Year Books of Edward II: The Eyre of Kent, 6 & 7 Edward II (1313–1314)* (vol 5, Bernard Quatrich 1910) vol 1, 24 SS, 140–141.

[5] Seipp, "Jurors" (n 3) 84. For the emergence of the "satisfied conscience" into "proof beyond reasonable doubt" in the seventeenth and eighteenth centuries, see generally Barbara J Shapiro, *"Beyond Reasonable Doubt" and "Probable Cause": Historical Perspectives on the Anglo-American Law of Evidence* (University of California Press 1991); Barbara J Shapiro, *A Culture of Fact: England, 1550–1720* (Cornell University Press 2000) 22–23.

[6] Bellamy, *Criminal Trial* (n 2) 112. On the likelihood of jurors knowing something of the facts of a case even into the sixteenth century, see Baker, *Spelman* (n 2) 109. Even in the late seventeenth century, jurors were not restricted to considering only the evidence presented to them. In his *Enchiridion legum* (1673), John Brydell explained: "[T]he jury is not tied only to the evidence of two men or of more witnesses, but may find *veritatem facti* upon circumstances, or by witnesses, or sometimes (especially for want of manifest or probable evidence) upon their own knowledges." John Brydell, *Enchiridion legum* (printed by Elizabeth Flesher 1673) 109.

[7] Bellamy, *Criminal Trial* (n 2) 117.

[8] " 'Witnesses' appearances at trials are not recorded before the sixteenth century." Ibid 25–26. "For the historian what is lacking before the later fifteenth century is an unequivocal reference to a non-victim, an observer of the crime who was not a law officer, giving testimony to a petty jury. That they in fact frequently did so, however, seems very likely." Ibid 102.

[9] Thomas Smith, L Alston (ed), *De Republica Anglorum: A Discourse on the Commonwealth of England* (CUP 1906) 100. Langbein comments that "the imprecision of the standard of proof was another of the many factors that put pressure on the accused to speak in his own defense about his knowledge of the charges and the events," citing Stephen's remark that "[t]he jury expected from him [the defendant] a clear explanation of the case against him; and if he could not give it, they convicted him." John H Langbein, *The Origins of Adversary Criminal Trial* (OUP 2003) 57. The *ius commune*, by contrast, clearly stated that the burden of proof (*onus probandi*) rested on the party initiating suit. Charles Donahue Jr, "The Courts of the Ius commune" in Wilfred Hartmann and Kenneth Pennington (eds), *The History of Courts and Procedure in Medieval Canon Law* (The Catholic University of America Press 2016) 86; Kenneth Pennington, "The Jurisprudence of Procedure" in ibid 129.

A defendant's right to call witnesses against the Crown was seriously disputed in the Tudor and Stuart era.[10] Even when a defendant was allowed to call witnesses in his or her favor, they would not speak under oath.[11] Nor was there any legal mechanism for criminal defendants to compel the appearance of witnesses in their favor.[12] In the Tudor and Stuart monarchies in felony cases brought on indictment, defendants were not allowed the assistance of counsel as to matters of fact.[13] Hearsay evidence was permitted, although it may have been given less weight.[14] No statute guaranteed that defendants would be able to face the witnesses against them. Although a judge would not reasonably allow irrelevant evidence, no rules of evidence in a modern sense existed.[15]

Sixteenth-Century Piracy Prosecutions: *Ius commune* Procedure vs. the English Jury

The absence of any requirement for confrontation at common law could work to the prosecution's advantage. An act of Henry VIII's parliament in 1536 vividly illustrates the point.[16] At the time, piracy threatened English maritime commerce. Such cases fell under the jurisdiction of the admiralty courts.[17] Because maritime disputes often involved non-English parties unfamiliar with the customs of English common law, admiralty followed the romano-canonical procedures of the *ius commune*.[18] The *Black Book of the Admiralty (Niger Librum Admiralitatis)*[19] set out those procedures

---

[10] Baker, *Introduction* (n 2) 509; Sir John Baker, 6 *The Oxford History of the Laws of England* (OUP 2003) (12 vols) 519: "Although defence witnesses were not unknown, by the middle of the sixteenth century there seems to have been a prevailing notion—perhaps influenced by the Civil law—that witnesses ought not to give evidence to contradict clear evidence for the Crown... The question was not settled until later in the century, and even then defence witnesses were unsworn," citing J Dalison, that when defense witnesses were allowed, it was "always without oath."

[11] Baker, 6 *Oxford History* (n 10) 519.

[12] As to subpoenas of witnesses in civil cases, see Baker, *Spelman* (n 2).

[13] Professor David Seipp has shown that prior to 1500, and even for some time thereafter, defense counsel actively engaged with matters of fact as well as law in cases of felony indictment. See David Seipp, "Crime in the Yearbooks" in Chantal Stebbings (ed), *Law Reporting in England* (Hambledon Press 1995) 15, 23–27 (collecting cases).

[14] Baker, *Spelman* (n 2) 110.

[15] Ibid. John Langbein traces the beginnings of rules of evidence to the eighteenth century. Langbein, *Adversary Criminal Trial* (n 9) 4, 178–280. See generally ibid 178–251.

[16] 28 Hen VIII, c 15. See also 27 Hen VIII, c 4 (1535).

[17] "The Admiralty was probably the most important of the English civil law (as opposed to canon law) courts." Charles Donahue Jr, "Ius Commune, Canon Law, and Common Law in England" (1991–1992) 66 Tul L Rev 1745, 1773. Since 1361, piracy cases were not to be tried before common law judges (*coram iusticiariis nostris ad communem legem*) but before the admirals according to maritime law (*coram Admirallis nostris iuxta legem marittimam*). See Reginald G Marsden (ed), 1 *Select Pleas in the Court of Admiralty* (Bernard Quaritch 1894) xlv; Reginald Marsden, "Introduction" in MJ Prichard and DEC Yale (eds), *Hale and Fleetwood on Admiralty Jurisdiction* (SS 1993) xxx.

[18] William Senior, *Doctors' Commons and the Old Court of Admiralty: A Short History of the Civilians in England* (Longmans, Green and Co. 1922) 11–12.

[19] The *ordo iudiciorum* is printed in Travers Twiss (ed), 2 *Monumenta Juridica. The Black Book of the Admiralty, with an Appendix* (Longman & Co, and Trubner & Co, 1871–1876) (4 vols). The Black Book itself was likely completed around 1400 or shortly thereafter. Knut W Nörr, "Bologna and the Court of Admiralty, a Latin Text in the Black Book" in Peter Linehan (ed), 8 *Proceedings of the Seventh International Congress of Medieval Canon Law* (Monumenta iuris canonici Series C, Subsidia 1988) 475, 476.

by adopting an *ordo iudiciarius* from thirteenth-century Bologna.[20] The *ordo*'s methods of proof were far more detailed and demanding than the customary procedures of the common-law jury. Drawing on Roman law principles, the *ordo* required the testimony of at least two eyewitnesses for sufficient proof of guilt.[21] The witnesses had to be produced in person before the court.[22] They were required to base their testimony on what was done in their presence and not on what the witnesses may have learned from other persons.[23] Hearsay was discounted in principle.[24] To support conviction, the prosecution bore the burden of presenting proofs "clearer than light" (*luce clariores*).[25]

Under these demanding evidentiary requirements, convictions were difficult to secure in admiralty.[26] As could be expected, in piracy cases, eyewitnesses were often unavailable because either pirates had killed them or the witnesses had dispersed over the high seas. Parliament deftly removed the hindrances to conviction that Admiralty's procedures presented.[27] It transferred the trials of pirates to special

---

[20] Knut Nörr has identified the text as a section of the *Summa artis notariae* of Rolandus Rodulphini Passagerii, dating from the third quarter of the thirteenth century. Nörr (n 19) 477. The *ordo* is "one of the clearest and most concise descriptions of romano-canonical procedure that exists." Ibid 478. The *ordo* itself is printed in *Summa totius artis notariae Rolandini Rodulphini Bononiensis* (apud Iuntas 1546, anastatic reprint Bologna 1977).

[21] "For sufficient proof by witnesses, two witnesses are necessary [where number not otherwise defined]" (*ad sufficientem probacionem per testes… necessarii duo testes*). Twiss (n 19) 196.

[22] "In criminal cases specifically witnesses must be forced to come" (*in criminalibus precise cogendi sunt testes venire*). Ibid 197. On the requirement for confrontation in romano-canonical law, see Frank R Herrmann and Brownlow M Speer, "Facing the Accuser: Ancient and Medieval Precursors of the Confrontation Clause" (1994) 34 Va J Int'l L 481.

[23] "But if he says he was not present, but that he heard it said by others, the aforesaid interrogatories are not be be made … Whence, interrogatories are customarily formed if witnesses of the opposing party say that they themselves were present" (*set si dixerit se non fuisse presentem, set hoc audivisse ab aliis dici, non sunt predicatae interrogaciones ei faciendae. … Unde interrogaciones ita formari solent si testes adversae partis dixerint se presentes fuisse*). Twiss (n 19) 195.

[24] "witnesses ought to depose that they themselves were present and saw, for it is not sufficient to depose about hearsay … it is not sufficient if one says he himself heard it said that so-and-so struck so-and-so" (*deponere debent testes se interfuisse et vidisse, non enim sufficit deponere de auditu … non sufficit si dicat se audivisse dici quod talis percussit talem*) (exceptions in contractual cases). Ibid. On the development of the romano-canonical rule against hearsay, see Frank R Herrmann, "The Establishment of a Rule against Hearsay in Romano-Canonical Procedure" (1995) 36 Va J Int'l L 1; Mirjan Damaška, "Of Hearsay and Its Analogues" (1992) 76 Mimm L Rev 425, 434–441.

[25] "The accuser ought to persist in an accusation, especially of public crime, and ought to produce proofs of it clearer than light" (*Accusator debet in accusacione, presertim publici criminis… persistere, et super ipsa probaciones afferre luce clariores*). Twiss (n 19) 214.

[26] The *ordo* of the admiralty's book sets out additional robust protections for defendants. A summons had to be issued to the defendant to assure his presence in court. Ibid 178. The charge (*libellus*) had to be shown to the defendant so that he could defend against it. Ibid 181. The fact-finder had to be impartial. Ibid 182. There has to be a reasonable time provided for continuances. Ibid 189. The burden of proof lay unambiguously on the accuser. Ibid 191. Both parties had to be present to one another at the taking of an oath to tell the truth. Ibid 192. There was no compulsion to produce evidence against oneself. Ibid 193. The complaint (*libellus*) had to contain the names of accuser and accused, the crime alleged, the time alleged, and the place alleged. Ibid 213. There had to be an accuser except if the crime was notorius or manifest. Ibid 214. A principle of double jeopardy protected defendants. Ibid 216. No counsel was permitted in cases of felony. Ibid 217. In cases of doubt, it was better to acquit the guilty than condemn the innocent. Ibid 218. If any confession was made under torture, it was invalid unless later persevered in "voluntarily" in court before the inquisitional judge. Ibid 218.

[27] See Sir John Baker, 6 *Oxford History* (n 10) 212. GR Elton observes: "The assertion that the civil law was too careful of accused's interests should be taken into account when considering the usual encomia

commissions.[28] These commissions proceeded according to English common law, which did not require proof to be made by any eyewitnesses, the jury being free to evaluate evidence as it wished and to convict so long as any kind of evidence satisfied the jurors' consciences. In a preamble to its statute, parliament made no attempt to hide its motivation for the change in jurisdiction:

Where traitors, pirates, thieves, robbers, murderers and confederators upon the sea many times escape unpunished because the trial of their offences hath hereto-fore been ordered, judged and determined before the admiral... after the course of the civil laws, the nature whereof is that before any judgment of death can be given against offenders, either they must plainly confess their offences (which they will never do without torture or pains), or else their offences be so plainly and directly proved by witness indifferent, such as saw their offences committed, which cannot be gotten but by chance at few times because such offenders commit their offences upon the sea, and at many times murder and kill such persons being in the ship or boat where they commit their offences which should witness against them in that behalf, and also such as should bear witness be commonly mariners and shipmen... which depart without long tarrying and protraction of time... for reformation whereof be it enacted... that all treasons, felonies, robberies, murders... hereafter to be com-mitted in or upon the sea... shall be tried... in like form and condition as if any such offence... had been committed... upon the land; And such commissions shall be had under the King's great seal and directed to the admiral... to hear and determine such offences after the common course of the laws of this land, used for treasons, felonies, robberies, murders... committed upon this land with this realm.

ii. And be it enacted... that trial of such offence or offences, if it be denied by the offender... shall be had by 12 lawful men inhabited in the shire limited within such commission...[29]

Hangings significantly increased under the new common-law commissions.[30]

on the common law's protection of the innocent." GR Elton, *The Tudor Constitution: Documents and Commentary* (2nd edn, CUP 1982) 153.

[28] The commissions were composed of both civilians and common lawyers sitting alongside one another. Marsden, "Introduction" (n 17) cxxxix–cxl.
[29] 28 Hen VIII, c 15 (1536). The 1536 act added treason to the list of offenses at sea listed in the 1535 statute. See Baker, 6 *Oxford History* (n 10) 212, 512; JH Baker, "Criminal Courts and Procedure at Common Law, 1500–1800" in 2 *Collected Papers on English Legal History* (CUP 2013) (3 vols) (hereafter Baker, *Collected Papers*) 1015; Bl Comm IV 269.
[30] It was challenging to convict pirates under any circumstances, but all the more so when requirements for witnesses stood in the way. Before the shift to the common-law commissions, no records show a pirate hanged after trial in admiralty, and only three were hanged at common law. After the shift to the commis-sions, twenty-two pirates were hanged from 1549 to 1551 and 113 from 1561 to 1583. Reginald G Marsden (ed), 1 *Documents Relating to the Law and Custom of the Sea* (printed for Navy Records Society 1915) (2 vols) 149. See also Neville Williams, *Captains Outrageous: Seven Centuries of Piracy* (Barrie & Rockcliff 1961) 45–46; Theodore FT Plucknett, *A Concise History of the Common Law* (5th edn, Little, Brown and Co 1956) 662 n 4; Sir John Baker, 2 *Collected Papers on English Legal History* (CUP 2013) (2 vols) 1024, 1066–1067 & n 2. Elton observes: "On the interesting grounds that the civil law procedure of Admiralty, with its demand for witnesses' evidence, allowed piracy to be committed with impunity if only it was san-guinary enough, an act of 1536 transferred the criminal jurisdiction of the court to special commissions." Elton, *Tudor Constitution* (n 27) 153. The commissioners were usually common law judges. ibid.

The Inception of Statutory Mandates for
Confrontation at Treason Trials

Prosecutions under Henry VIII's treason acts

For the prosecution of pirates, the common law's freedom from the constraints of *ius commune* methods of proof proved to be a virtue. Yet, a jury's power to convict in the absence of any defined quantity or quality of evidence was not limited to cases of piracy. Political or religious opponents of the Crown, just as well as pirates, stood at risk of prosecution without having the opportunity to confront their accusers.[31]

The danger was apparent in prosecutions for treason under Henry VIII. Frustrated by the narrow definitions of treason in an old 1351 treason act, Henry VIII had his parliament pass additional acts, declaring it treason to slander the King's marriage,[32] or to deprive the King of his titles.[33] Parliament further provided that any treasons committed outside the realm could be tried in any county within the realm.[34] None of Henry's treason statutes made mention of the use of witnesses to prove any alleged treason.[35] There was no requirement that any person testify that he or she personally heard the treasonous words spoken. Nothing in the statute prevented mere rumors from sufficing as proof of treason.

Prosecution under Henry's treason legislation was swift and lethal.[36] In April and June 1535, a total of seven monks were tried, convicted, and sentenced to death for refusing to acknowledge Henry as supreme head of the Church of England. Bishop John Fisher was tried and beheaded in June. Later the same month, a grand jury indicted Henry's chancellor, Sir Thomas More, for maliciously attempting to deprive the King of his rightful title by remaining silent when asked whether he acknowledged the King as supreme head of the church and for aiding Fisher in his refusal to recognize the same title. More was convicted and beheaded.[37] Accusations of heresy could also prove deadly. Protestants, as well as Roman Catholics, stood at risk.

---

[31] With respect to prosecutions on religious grounds, see Henry Ansgar Kelly, "Mixing Canon and Common Law in Religious Prosecutions under Henry VIII and Edward VI: Bishop Bonner, Anne Askew, and Beyond" (2015) 46 Sixteenth Century Journal 927.

[32] 25 Hen VIII, c 22 (1534).

[33] 26 Hen VIII, c 13 (1534). Discussed in GR Elton, *Policy and Police: The Enforcement of the Reformation in the Age of Thomas Cromwell* (CUP 1972) 286–287.

[34] 26 Hen VIII, c 13, s 1 (1534).

[35] See John Bellamy, *The Tudor Law of Treason: An Introduction* (Routledge & Kegan Paul 1979) 154. An Act for Punishment of Heresy, 25 Hen VIII, c 14 (1533–1534) required witnesses to make accusations, but was silent about their appearing before the accused. The Act forbade an ecclesiastical ordinary "on the basis of any suspicion conceived of his own fantasy without any due accusation or presentment" to place a person at risk of his life. Provision for witnesses was provided in two statutes that promoted religious obedience, 34 & 35 Hen VIII, c 1, s 19, and 35 Hen VIII, c 5 (1542–1542). See Bellamy, *Treason* (ibid) 154.

[36] "After 1534, opponents of the royal supremacy were executed not for heresy but for treason." Bellamy, *Treason* (n 35). On the oppressive severity of Henry VIII's last years, see AF Pollard, *England under Protector Somerset: An Essay* (Russell and Russell 1966, first published 1900) 44–45.

[37] For a detailed analysis of the trial of Thomas More, see Henry Ansgar Kelly and others (eds), *Thomas More's Trial by Jury: A Procedural and Legal Review with a Collection of Documents* (The Boydell Press 2011). See also Elton, *Policy* (n 33) 409–417.

In a stinging commentary on the situation under Henry VIII, the French ambassador, Charles de Marillac, in August 1540, wrote to his King Francis I, attacking the unfairness of both treason and heresy trials in England. He reported that two days after Thomas Cromwell was executed:

> six more were put to death; three were hanged as traitors. . . for having spoken in favour of the Pope; three were burnt as heretics. . . . They had never been called to answer for their supposed offences; and Christians under grace, they said were now worse off than Jews under the law. The law would have no man die unless he were first heard in his defence and Heathen and Christian, sage and emperor, the whole world except England, observed the same rule.
>
> Here in England, if two witnesses will swear and affirm before the council[38] that they have heard a man speak against his duty to his King, or contrary to the articles of religion, that man may be condemned to suffer death, with the pains appointed by the law, although he be absent or ignorant of the charge, and without any other form of proof. Innocence is no safeguard when such an opening is offered to malice or revenge. Corruption or passion may breed false witness; and the good may be sacrificed, and the wicked, who have sworn away their lives, may escape with impunity. There is no security for any man, unless the person accused is brought face to face with the witnesses who depose against him.
>
> Of the iniquity of the system no other evidence is needed than these executions just passed.[39]

Henry's treason legislation between 1534 and 1536 was regarded as "the zenith of severity."[40] Reaction against his ferocious treason prosecutions promptly set in after his death in 1547.[41]

Two Treason Acts of Edward VI

At Henry's demise, the Crown passed to his nine-year-old son, Edward VI. The executors of Henry's will elected Edward Seymour, Duke of Somerset, to act as Lord Protector (1547–1549) during Edward's minority. Somerset took steps to rein in the broad reach of the Henrician treason acts. He told the imperial ambassador that some of Henry's laws were "extremely rigorous and indeed almost iniquitous in

[38] As to the procedures and legal business of the Privy Council, see Baker, 6 *Oxford History* (n 10) 200–203.

[39] Letter of August 6, 1540 from Charles de Marillac to Francis I, printed in James Anthony Froude and William Thomas (eds), *The Pilgrim: A Dialogue on the Life and Actions of King Henry VIII by William Thomas, Clerk of the Council to Edward VI* (1554) (Parker, Son, and Bourn 1861) 152; James Gairdner and RH Brodie (eds), 15 *Letters and Papers, Foreign and Domestic, of the Reign of Henry VIII* (published for Her Majesty's Stationery Office (1896) (21 vols) 483 no 953.

[40] Bellamy, *Treason* (n 35) 37. On Henry's despotic nature, see Lacey Baldwin Smith, "English Treason Trials and Confessions in 16th Century" (1954) 15 Journal of the History of Ideas 471, 475; Baker, 6 *Oxford History* (n 10) 512, citing barbarity of Henry's statutes.

[41] "[T]he rigour of H. VIII's reign compelled a reaction upon his death." ML Bush, *The Government Policy of Protector Somerset* (E Arnold 1975) 2.

their severity."[42] A few months after Henry's death, parliament passed 1 Edw VI, c 12 (1547), the first treason act of Edward's reign.[43] The act repealed many of the broad and draconian portions of Henry's treason legislation and laws relating to religious opinion, which "to men of exterior realms and many of the King's Majesty's subjects" might have seemed "very strait, sore, extreme and terrible."[44]

Edward's repeal act barred indictment, arraignment, or conviction of treason defendants without prosecution witnesses to support the accusations "unless the same offender... be accused by two sufficient and lawful witnesses, or shall willingly without violence confess the same."[45] The Act's provision for witnesses furnished some assurance that an accusation of treason would be reliably based. The Act, however, was unclear whether accusers had to be personally present before the court at arraignment or trial; or whether defendants had a right to know who was accusing them, or to know what the accusers might have to say against them. Nor did the statute explicitly require that accused and their accusers must be present simultaneously to each other before the court.[46]

The Duke of Somerset himself, the King's Protector and uncle, encountered the problems that the 1547 statute's ambiguities raised. In 1551, Somerset was tried for treason partly under the 1547 repeal act.[47] At his arraignment, he asserted that, because he had "many things against the witnesses," he "desired they be brought face to face."[48] His request was denied. He was, instead, tried on the basis of depositions

---

[42] Ibid 135–136 (remarking that the abolition under Edward VI "was initiated by men whose religious beliefs had made them potential victims").

[43] For discussion of the Act, see ibid 2, 131–136, 145–146. Bush observes the Act was one "of revulsion against a history of oppression in the cause of self-preservation." Ibid 136. See also WK Jordan, *Edward VI: The Young King: The Protectorship of the Duke of Somerset* (Harvard University Press 1968) 172–175; Bellamy, *Treason* (n 35) 48–51 (stating the Act showed that there was widespread dissatisfaction with the Henrician laws).

[44] 1 Edw VI, c 12, s 1 (1547). Elton observes that new reigns always started with a relaxation of rigour and attempts to gain popularity for the new regime. GR Elton, "Review: The Good Duke" (1969) Historical Journal xii, 4, 702, 705. In effect, the repeal put an end, for the time being, to executions for treason and for heresy. Pollard (n 36) 59. See also Plucknett (n 30) 324.

[45] 1 Edw VI, c 12, xxii (1547). Provision for "two witnesses" had been previously adopted in Heresy Act, 25 Hen VIII, c 14, s 6 (1534) in the context of trials before ecclesiastical ordinaries. In 1539, parliament inserted the two-witness requirement in the Act of Six Articles. The requirement was not a product of English law but a borrowing from romano-canonical law. Kelly, "Canon and Common Law" (n 31) 953. On the history of the two-witness rule in English treason trials, see generally LM Hill, "The Two-Witness Rule in English Treason Trials: Some Comments on the Emergence of Procedural Law" (1968) 12 Am J Legal Hist 95.

[46] Baker, 6 *Oxford History* (n 10) 518 n 75. A similar ambiguity caused dispute in the *ius commune*, where it was eventually settled that a defendant and witnesses had to be present to each other at the same time at the initial stage of the proceeding where the witnesses swore to tell the truth.

[47] Bellamy, *Treason* (n 35) 50.

[48] 1 St Tr 515, 520–521. See Bellamy, *Treason* (n 35) 155. Likewise, Somerset's brother, Sir Thomas Seymour, Lord Seymour of Sudeley, at his pretrial examination in the Tower of London on February 23, 1549, said that he expected to see his accusers face-to-face. "[T]he said Lord Admiral would answer to nothing laid to his charge, neither yea nor nay, except he had his accusers brought before him, and except he were brought in upon trial of arraignment, where he might say before all the world what he could say for his declaration." John Roche Dasent (ed) 2 *Acts of the Privy Council of England* (n.s.) (published for Her Majesty's Stationery Office 1890–1964) (45 vols) 256. This answer seemed to the Council "very strange." The admiral answered further when he was proceeded against by parliamentary bill of attainder several days later. He was voted guilty. His own brother signed the death warrant. Ibid 260–263.

read against him in court. Although acquitted of treason, Somerset was convicted of a felony. Thereupon, he was executed.[49]

In 1552, Parliament strengthened the protection of the 1547 repeal act.[50] The new act, 5 & 6 Edw. VI, c 11, ix (1552),[51] explicitly required that an accused must be able personally to confront at least two lawful accusers at the time of arraignment so that the accused could hear whatever proof the accusers could offer in support of the indictment:

> [N]o person or persons. . . shall be indicted, arraigned, condemned, convicted or attainted for any of the treasons or offenses aforesaid. . . unless the same offender or offenders be thereof accused by two lawful accusers, which said accusers at the time of the arraignment of the party accused, if they be then living, shall be brought in person before the party so accused, and avow and maintain that that they have to say against the said party to prove him guilty of the treasons or offences contained in the bill of indictment laid against the party arraigned; unless the said party arraigned shall willingly without violence confess the same.[52]

An examination of the Act's legislative history makes clear how critically important the confrontation procedures were to the Act's adoption.[53] Commons was apparently

---

[49] About his uncle, the fifteen-year-old Edward VI wrote in his journal: "The Duke of Somerset had his head cut off upon Tower Hill between eight and nine o'clock in the morning." WK Jordan (ed), *The Chronicle and Political Papers of King Edward VI* (Cornell University Press 1966) 107. Jordan remarks: "[T]here remains unexplained the young King's incredible coldness and the fact that at no time did he require a sifting or a fair appraisal of the evidence gathered to destroy Somerset." WK Jordan, *Edward VI: The Threshold of Power* (Harvard University Press 1970) 103. Sir Thomas Palmer and John Dudley, the Duke of Northumberland, later admitted that the charges against Somerset were false. Ibid. See also Pollard (n 36) 297–298.

[50] Bellamy, *Treason* (n 35) 77, 154.

[51] The act may have been intended to supply a remedy to Somerset's demand for confrontation, although the statute came too late for him. As a reporter of the trial noted:

> [W]hen the duke of Somerset came to be tried both for treason and felony, he had not the benefit of the accusers being brought face to face, but was proceeded against by depositions read in the court. He was acquitted for the treason, but cast for felony; and that occasioned the act which the commons grafted upon a bill sent down by the lords in the subsequent sessions, viz. 5 and 6 Edw. VI.

1 *St Tr* 521 note *g*, attributed to William Rastell. Concerning Rastell's account, see Bellamy, *Treason* (n 35) 155.

[52] The statute spoke not of "witnesses," as the 1547 statute had, but rather of "accusers." The term "accusers" was not a common-law term. Consequently, its meaning caused confusion. In 1556, at a judges' conference at Serjeants Inn, two judges opined that "accusers" meant the same as "witnesses." But it was resolved that "accusers" was a term taken from the civil law and meant something "like parties and not witnesses." See Brook's report of the conference, 109 SS (1993) 18; Baker, 6 *Oxford History* (n 10) 518. Edward Coke in his *Institutes* wrote that the two terms "witnesses" and "accusers" were synonymous: "Two lawful accusers in the Act of 5 E. [1552] are taken for two lawful witnesses; for by two lawful accusers, and accused by two lawful witnesses (as is said in 1 E. 6) [1547] is all one: which word [accusers] was used, because two witnesses ought directly accuse, that is, charge the prisoner, for other accusers have we none in the Common Law, and therefore lawful accusers must be such accusers as the Law allows." Edward Coke, *The Third Part of the Institutes of the Laws of England Concerning High Treason, and Other Pleas of the Crown, and Criminal Causes* (4th edn, London, printed for A. Crooke and others 1669) c 2, 25.

[53] On the legislative history, see WK Jordan, *Edward VI: The Threshold of Power* (Allen & Unwin 1970) 336, 337 n 3; James Anthony Froude, 5 *History of England from the Fall of Wolsey to the Death of Elizabeth* (Scribner, Armstrong, & Co 1872) (12 vols) 371–372.

dissatisfied with an initial version of the bill as proposed in the House of Lords. The Lords' draft did not provide sufficient protections for defendants. Commons added the new requirement that the "two lawful accusers. . . be brought before the party so accused" at the time of the arraignment, unless the defendant freely confessed. Consequently, a person accused of treason under the 1552 statute, as adopted, had the protection of seeing accusers and the benefit of hearing them before trial "maintain that that they have to say against the said party to prove him guilty of the treasons or offenses contained in the bill of indictment."[54]

Limited though the confrontation requirement was to treason charges brought under the particular act, the 1552 statute constituted "one of the most important constitutional provisions which the annals of the Tudor family afford."[55]

Confrontation in the treason acts of Mary and Elizabeth

After the death of Edward at age fifteen in 1553, successor parliaments under both Mary and Elizabeth continued to provide for confrontation. As will be seen, however, the requirement could be subverted in a variety of ways. Mary's second[56] treason act, 1 & 2 Ph & Mary, c 10 (1554) affirmed that prosecutions brought under it required at least two prosecution witnesses to "be brought forth in person before the party arraigned, if he require same, and object and say openly in his hearing what they or any of them can against him."[57]

After the close of Mary's reign in 1558, another treason statute under Elizabeth unambiguously required confrontation. At least two "lawful and sufficient" witnesses for the prosecution had to "be brought forth in person before the party so arraigned face to face, and there. . . avow and openly declare all they can say against the said party so indicted."[58] Previous treason statutes had not used the phrase "face to face."[59] Elizabeth's second treason act in 1571, likewise, required "face to face" confrontation of prosecuting witnesses with treason defendants at arraignment.[60]

By requiring that the witnesses be "lawful and sufficient," present "face to face" with the defendant, and that the witnesses declare "all they can say against" the accused in his hearing, the treason acts offered defendants assurance that they would, at the least, see their accusers and hear the details of their accusations. Defendants might then

---

[54] 5 & 6 Edw VI, c 11, ix (1552).

[55] Henry Hallam, 1 *The Constitutional History of England* (W J Widdleton 1871) (2 vols) 54.

[56] Mary's first treason act, 1 M st 1, c 1 (1553) abrogated earlier treason statutes and restricted treason to the terms of 25 Edw III (1351). Mary's first act made no mention of any procedures concerning witnesses.

[57] 1 & 2 Ph & M, c 10, xi (1554). The statute speaks of "persons" rather than "witnesses" or "accusers."

[58] 1 Eliz, c 5, s 10 (1558–1559). This general treason act of Elizabeth "was intended, so it said, to take the place of the Marian act 1 & 2 Ph. & M, c 10, because the latter only extended its protection to Queen Mary and her issue." Bellamy, *Treason* (n 35) 62. 1 Eliz, c 1, s xxi (1558–1559) also required confrontation with two witnesses.

[59] The phrase appeared in legal parlance before its adoption into the statute. In 1549, Lord Seymour told his examiners that his accusers should be brought "face to face" with him at an open trial. In 1551, the Duke of Somerset demanded at his arraignment that the witnesses "be brought face to face" before him. His request was denied. See Bellamy, *Treason* (n 35) 155.

[60] 13 Eliz, c 1, ix (1571). See also 23 Eliz, c 2, xiii (1580–1581) (requiring witnesses at indictment and face-to-face confrontation at arraignment); 13 Chas II, st 1, c 1, s v (1661) (repeating face-to-face requirement).

have a basis to challenge the witnesses on grounds of unlawfulness, or otherwise dispute with them at the trial proper, which usually followed promptly after arraignment.

Diminishing the mandates for confrontation

The procedural protection that Edward's, Mary's, and Elizabeth's statutes tendered was soon seriously undermined. In 1554, the very year that 1 & 2 Ph & M, c 10 was enacted, judges agreed in *Thomas* that a hearsay accuser, even at third- or fourth-hand, was acceptable as one of the two required accusers.[61] Moreover, the witness-requirements of a particular treason act could be understood to apply only to treason proceedings brought under that act. The Crown could still indict persons under the thirteenth-century act of 25 Edw III, stat 5, c 2.[62] That statute contained no requirements regarding the presence of witnesses or confrontation protections. To make the status of witness-confrontation more complex, 1 & 2 Ph & M, c 10, vi, explicitly provided that treason prosecutions were henceforth to be conducted according to the "common law."[63] Sixteenth-century judges interpreted the provision as having repealed the confrontation requirement of Edward VI's statute.[64] Thus, the protective provisions of Edward VI's and of Mary's statutes mandating two accusers and the requirement of Elizabeth's statutes for confrontation "face to face" with accusers

---

[61] *Thomas* (1554) in *Reports of Cases in the Reigns of Hen. VIII. Edw. VI. Q. Mary, and Q. Eliz. Taken and Collected by Sir James Dyer* (printed for Mssrs P Byrne and others 1794) 99b. See Baker, 6 *Oxford History* (n 10) 518, commenting that the decision to allow an accuser by hearsay emasculated the two-accuser protection. Bellamy, however, questions whether the *Thomas* decision had lasting influence. Bellamy, *Treason* (n 35) 158. Edward Coke rejected the view that a hearsay accuser could substitute under the statute: "And the strange conceit . . . that one may be an accuser by hearsay, was utterly denyed by the Justices in the *Lo. Lumley's* case." Edward Coke, 3 Co Inst cap 2, 25.

[62] Bellamy surmises that Throckmorton was indicted in Mary's reign in part under the 1351 treason act out of "a desire to avoid having to produce certain witnesses in court." Bellamy, *Treason* (n 35) 156. Similarly, Elizabethan practice sometimes brought treason indictments under the 1351 act or as common-law treason, "thereby depriving the accused of any right to face witnesses against him." Ibid 157. "The response of the Elizabethan government, when it found it had no liking for the appearance of witnesses as demanded by some of the new treason laws, was really one of subterfuge. When the duke of Norfolk in 1571 asked for [witnesses] to be brought face to face with him, he was told by Sgt. Barham that that particular provision of the law 'hath been repealed.'" Ibid 155.

[63] 1 & 2 Ph & M, c 10 seemed to contain conflicting clauses. Cl xi required at least two witnesses at the arraignment, yet cl vi placed treason prosecutions under the common law which did not require witnesses. At a conference of the judges at Serjeants Inn in 1556, it was agreed that "for any treason charged under the statute of 25 Edw III, there is no need for accusers at the trial, because it is enacted by the statute of 2 Mar I, c 10 [1 & 2 Ph & M, c 10], that all trials for treason shall be by the order of the common law, and not otherwise; and the common trial at common law is by jury and by witnesses, not by any accusers. . . But for all treasons made by the said act of 2 Mar I, c 10 [1 & 2 Ph & M I, c 10], there ought to be witnesses or accusers both at the indictment and at the arraignment, according to a clause at the end of the said statute." Brook's report of the conference, 109 SS (1993) 18. See Saunders report of the same conference, ibid 19. See also Bellamy, *Treason* (n 35) 77. It is not clear whether a defendant could be present at the indictment. Ibid 127.

[64] Jordan, *Threshold* (n 49) 337. Edward Coke, upon considering the thicket of treason statutes, concluded that "the statute of 5 Edw. 6 cap 11 is a general law and extends to all high treasons as well as by the common law declared by the statute of 25 Edw 3." 3 Co Inst 25. For a survey of divided opinions on whether 1 Ph & M, c 10 repealed Edward VI's treason statutes, see John Reeves and William Francis Finlason, 5 *Reeves' History of the English Law: From the Time of the Romans to the End of the Reign of Elizabeth* (M. Murphy 1880) (5 vols) 120–128.

proved deficient in application.[65] Treason defendants, like any other common-law defendants, were left without statutory or other assurance that they would see the witnesses against them.

Summary

The institution of the common-law trial jury, together with the due process legislation of Edward III's reign, offered criminal defendants significant protections against arbitrary accusations and unjust verdicts. The customs governing the common-law trial, however, were few and undefined compared to the elaborate evidentiary demands of the *ius commune*. In deciding to transfer piracy trials to common-law jurisdiction, Henry VIII's parliament showed it understood that convictions under common-law procedure could be easier to obtain, since a jury could convict without the testimony of eyewitnesses or any witnesses, at all. After Henry's death, Tudor and Stuart parliaments passed treason acts intended to assure that charges against treason defendants would be supported by the testimony of reliable witnesses and that defendants would see their accusers "face to face" and hear what they had to say against them in person. Judicial statutory interpretations, however, soon undermined the parliamentary mandates.

[65] Dyer 132, 73 Eng Rep 287 (1555). The judges inferred that at least at the trial two witnesses were no longer needed. "The practice of the courts seems to have been established in pursuance of this opinion given by all the judges; for in all the state trials during the subsequent reigns, the statutes of Edward VI are either forgotten, or, when any argument is attempted to be grounded on them, they are pronounced by the judges repealed, and no longer in force." Reeves and Finlason (n 64) 120. But Coke in 3 Co Inst 24 (published after his death) "expresses himself of the opinion that the statutes of Edward VI are still in force." Ibid. Because Mary put treason prosecutions under the common law, and judges by judicial construction allowed hearsay accusers, JH Wigmore considered the provisions for confrontation contained in Edward's and Mary's statutes to have had "only a short life" and be a "dead letter" until the end of the seventeenth century. John H Wigmore, 5 *Evidence in Trials at Common Law* (Little, Brown and Co 1974) 21.

8

Requiring Confessions at Common Law to Be Made Voluntarily

Common-Law Repudiation of Involuntary Confessions

The earliest statement in English law against the use of coerced confessions can be traced to *ius commune* texts. The *Leges Henrici Primi* (*Laws of Henry I*), composed c 1114–1118,[1] contained the rule that "a confession twisted out through fear or fraud is invalid."[2] The original source of the text was not English law but rather the pseudo-Isidorian false decretals, authored in Reims in the mid-ninth century. The pseudo-Isidorians attributed their bar against coerced confessions to a spurious letter of Pope Alexander I (c 107–c. 115).[3] Ivo of Chartres (1040–1115) accepted the pseudo-Isidorian passage as genuine law. The bar was inserted into the *Decretum* (c 1094) and into the widely influential *Panormia* (1094/1096) (attributed to Ivo). Both works became important sources of later canon law. The *Leges Henrici* incorporated the pseudo-Isidorian rule, transmitted through the *Panormia*. Gratian, too, in his own *Decretum* (c 1140) adopted the pseudo-Isidorian text.[4] The canonical rule supplied an authoritative resource to buttress a principle of voluntariness in the common law. The *Leges Henrici Primi* themselves, although circulated in manuscripts, received

---

[1] The *Leges Henrici Primi* were not legislation introduced by Henry but a collection of laws drawn from Anglo-Saxon and ecclesiastical sources and from actual laws of Henry's reign. The composition was the work of an unknown compiler, perhaps working in Winchester. See LJ Downer, "Introduction" in LJ Downer (ed and tr), *Leges Henrici Primi* (Clarendon Press 1972) (hereafter *Leges Henrici*) 1–37, 42–45. Lanfranc, the first Norman archbishop of Canterbury, accepting as genuine the pseudo-Isidorian false decretals, introduced his version of them into England, making a gift of his copy to the English church in 1070. Whoever compiled the *Leges Henrici* accessed a different manuscript than Lanfranc's. "[H]ow much of the *Leges* was taken from conduct of legal practice, how much from knowledge of texts, and how far practice was dictated by knowledge of texts . . . is a question that remains unanswerable from the *Leges* alone." Patrick Wormald, 1 *The Making of English Law: King Alfred to the Twelfth Century* (Blackwell Publishers 2000) 414.

[2] *Confessio vero per metum uel fraudem extorta non ualet. Leges Henrici Primi*, 5, 16b in *Leges Henrici* (n 1) 88–89. The immediate source for the sentence is Ivo of Chartres, *Decretum* (pt V, c 241; 161 PL 396–397), and *Panormia* (bk IV, c 118; 161 PL 1208) (traditionally attributed to Ivo). Ivo adopted the material from the pseudo-Isidorian forgeries.

[3] Ps.-Alexander I c 7 (JK †24). See Paul Hinschius (ed), *Decretales pseudo-Isidorianae et Capitula Angilrmani* (B Tauchnitz 1863) 97–98.

[4] C 15 q. 6 c I pars. "Truly, a confession must not be twisted out by tortures" (*Quod vero confessio cruciatibus extorquenda non sit*). See also C 15 q. 6 c 1: "For a confession in such matters is not compelled, but ought to be willingly made. For every confession that is made out of necessity is not credible. A confession, therefore, in such matters should not be twisted out, but willingly professed. For it is the worst thing to judge anyone on the basis of suspicion or a tortured confession" (*confessio enim in talibus non compulsa, sed spontanea fieri debet. §1. Omnis enim confessio, que fit ex necessitate, fides non est. §2. Confessio ergo in talibus non debet extorqueri, sed sponte profiteri. Pessimum enim est de suspicione aut extorta confessione quemquam iudicare*). The *Leges Henrici* predate the composition of Gratian's Decretum.

Foundations of American Criminal Due Process at Trial. Francis R. Herrmann and Brownlow M. Speer,
Oxford University Press. © Oxford University Press 2025. DOI: 10.1093/9780199364770.003.0008

little attention from English legal authorities until a full text of the *Leges* appeared in print for the first time in 1644.[5]

Additional evidence that the coercion of confessions was repugnant to the English common law is evident in *De Legibus et Consuetudinibus Angliae*, composed sometime before 1235 by Henry Bracton (1210–1268) and others.[6] The Bracton treatise warned that a captured suspect produced before the judges (*iustiiarii*) "ought not be presented with his hands bound," except where there is danger of escape. He explained "and that is so that he does not appear to be forced to make any purgation."[7]

From the *Leges Henrici Primi*, therefore, and from the Bracton work, both of which exhibit continental roots, there appears to have existed in England an expectation that confessions (pleas of guilt) would be voluntarily made.

The Year Books report a case showing the expectation being realized. In 1301/1302, judges expressed concern about a confession that may have been coerced. The report relates that Richard, suspected of theft, homicide, and other crimes, was captured and led to York. "Harshly and with great torment, he was led to prison," where "in order that he might be relieved of his straits," he acknowledged to the coroner that he was a thief. Appearing before the judges, the coroner said he had written down Richard's confession word for word and that Richard had confessed to being a thief, murderer, and rapist. He handed over the written confession to the judges. The judges sent for Richard "to see if he wished to admit what he acknowledged before the coroner." Appearing before them, Richard "acknowledged his confession, but he said that he made it under the severity (*rigore* and *dirricione*) which he withstood in prison." He only did it to "relieve himself from pain."

Richard's claim troubled the judge enough that they investigated whether his complaint was true. They summoned before them three companions of Richard from the prison, listed only as P, O, and W:

---

[5]   *Leges Henrici* (n 1) 73. The printing coincided with a renewed interest by seventeenth-century legal historians in "the ancient constitution." On the ancient constitution, see generally JGA Pocock, *The Ancient Constitution and the Feudal Law: A Study of English Historical Thought in the Seventeenth Century* (CUP 1957, reprint 1987); John Philip Reid, *The Ancient Constitution and the Origins of Anglo-American Liberty* (Northern Illinois University Press 2005).

[6]   The work is traditionally attributed to Bracton, but "the bulk of the work was written in the 1220's and 1230's by persons other than Bracton himself . . . [T]he author of later editions was probably Bracton himself." "Bracton Online Home Page," Harvard Law School Library (vol 2) 2 <https://amesfoundation. law.harvard.edu/Bracton/> accessed 8 June 2023. On the authorship of the Bracton treatise, see Thomas McSweeney, *Priests of the Law: Roman Law and the Common Law's First Professionals* (OUP 2019).

[7]   "When, however, such captured person shall be brought before the justiciars, he ought not to be lead forth with his hands bound unless sometimes shackled because of the danger of escape, and this is so lest he seem coerced to undergo some purgation" (*Cum autem taliter captus coram iustitiariis producendus fuerit, produci non debet ligatis manibus quamvis aliquando compeditus propter periculum evasionis, et hoc ideo ne videatur coactus ad aliquam purgationem suspiciendam*). Henry Bracton, *On the Laws and Customs of England* in George E Woodbine (ed) and Samuel E Thorne (tr), *Bracton on the Laws and Customs of England* (William S Hein & Co 1997) 385. See Edward Coke, citing the same passage of Bracton, 3 Co Inst c 2. Bracton, who used Roman law extensively, seems to have drawn on a passage of Justinian's Code which prohibited placing a defendant in chains before trial: "No one incarcerated should be chained at all before he may be convicted" (*Nullus in carcerem, priusquam convincatur, omnino vinciatur*). CJ 9.3.2; see also Constitution of the emperors Gratian, Valentinian, and Theodosius of December 30, 380, C Th 9.2.3.

Judge: What things did he suffer? Is there such harshness in prison among you as
   he says?
P, O, and W: No.
Judge to Richard: Behold, your companions in prison are testifying before you.

The judges then sent for the custodian of the prison, who swore that he would tell
the truth.

Custodian (angered by what Richard claimed): It was never true.
Judges to Richard: Do you want to say anything more?
Richard: I am a good and faithful person, and I know nothing bad about anyone, and
   that confession that I made, I made on account of the harshness of the prison.

Whereupon, Richard, pleading not guilty, placed himself for trial upon the country
for good or for ill.

Judges: Let him be sent back to prison.[8]

Clearly, the judges found the defendant's claim not credible. Nonetheless, from the
judges' clear concern, one may infer that a forced confession would have called for
some action on their part. The brief Year Book account, however, gives no indication
of what measures, if any, the judges might have taken if they had believed the prisoner's claim.

The Year Books contain a further case bearing on the voluntariness of a defendant's
in-court confession of guilt. In 1353, a woman was arraigned for stealing bread.[9] In

---

[8] YB, Edw 30, 31 Ed.I (RS) in Alfred J Horwood (ed), 3 *Year Books of the Reign of Edward the
First: Years XXX and XXXI (1302–1303)* (London Longman and others) 1863) 543–545; David J Seipp,
*Legal History: The Year Books, Medieval English Legal History, an Index and Paraphrase of Printed Year
Book Reports, 1268–1535,* https://www.bu.edu/law/faculty-scholarship/legal-history-the-year-books/.
1295.023rs. (*Robertus le Botiler de Skelebroke habuit quendam filium suum primogenitum R. nomine, qui
captus et ductus apud Eboracum propter suspectionem furti, homicidii, et aliorum maleficiorum, et adhuc
vivo patre, R. filius quia rigide et cum magna angaronia deducebatur ad prisonam, ut revelaret ab Anglia* [sic;
may be "*revelaretur ab angustia*"] *recognovit seipsum esse latronem, et cepit homines indictare: misso &c.
coronatore super cum cognovit corum eo se furem esse, homicidam et raptorem, et cepit ut prius &c. Et coro-
nator scripsit confessionem suam de verbo ad verbum, et eam tradidit sic scriptam Justiciariis. Et Justiciarii
miserunt pro ipso Ricardo ad videndum si fateri vellet quod cognovit coram coronatore. Qui quidem Ricardus
in curia comparens cognovit confessionem suam, sed dixit quod eam facit rigore et dirricione quam sustinuit
in prisona, ut sic relevari posset ab angustia.—JUSTICIARIUS. (Vocatis tribus scilicet P.O.W.) Quae patie-
batur? ne esse in prisona talem duritiam inter vos qualem dicit?—qui dixerunt quod non.—JUSTIARIUS.
Ecce, socii vestri in prisona testificantur coram vobis. Et ultra hoc, Justiciarii miserunt pro prisone custode
carceris, et fecerunt ipsum jurare quod verum diceret de eo unde peteretur, et ipse—furato proposito quod
dicto gravamine per ipsum R. in proposit in prisona—dixit quod nunquam fuit verum.—JUSTICIARIUS. R.,
vis tu aliud aliquid dicere.—R. Sum bonus et fidelis, et nil mali scio de aliquo, et illam confessionem quam feci
[feci] propter duritiam prisonae; et clericus sum, unde do bono et male, solvo meo privilegio clericali, me pono
in patriam.—JUSTICIARIUS. Remittatur prisonae.*) For discussion of the case, see Elizabeth Papp Kamali,
Felony and the Guilty Mind in Medieval England (CUP 2019) 193–194; WS Holdsworth, 9 *A History of
English Law* (Little, Brown and Co 1926) 183 n 4; Frederic Pollock and Frederic William Maitland, 2 *The
History of English Law before the Time of Edward I* (The University Press 1898) 653–654.
[9] 27 Edw 3, Lib Ass pl 40, fol 137b; David J Seipp, *Legal History: The Year Books, Medieval English Legal
History, an Index and Paraphrase of Printed Year Book Reports, 1268–1535,* 1353.165ass https://www.
bu.edu/law/faculty-scholarship/legal-history-the-year-books/.

offering to plead guilty at her arraignment, the woman asserted that she committed the alleged theft only because her husband made her do so. Out of mercy, the judges declined to accept her plea. In fact, as is evident, the case did not involve an involuntary confession of guilt, at all, but rather a possible defense of coercion. Nonetheless, later sixteenth-century legal authorities would cite the stolen-bread case as a precedent for instructing justices to reject coerced confessions (pleas of guilt).[10]

English legal writers extolled the jury trial's freedom from coerced confessions. Fortescue's *De laudibus legum angliae* (*In Praise of the Laws of England*) (c. 1467–1468) maintained that in the jury trial, in contrast to a *ius commune* trial, "nothing is cruel, nothing inhuman; an innocent man cannot suffer in body or members. Hence he will not fear the calumny of his enemies because he will not be tortured at their pleasure. Under this law, therefore, life is quiet and secure."[11] Thomas Smith's *De Republica Anglorum* (1562/65) similarly condemned involuntary confession: "[T]orment or question which is used by the order of the civill lawe and custome of other countreis to put a malefactor to excessive paine, to make him confesse of him selfe, or of his felowes or complices, is not used in England, it is taken for servile."[12] Fortescue maintained that, in addition to being cruel, tortured confessions were unreliable. "But who is so hardy that, having once passed through this atrocious torment, would not rather, though innocent, confess to every kind of crime, than submit again to the agony of torture already suffered, and prefer to die at once, since death is the end of terrors."[13] Likewise, Smith wrote: "And therefore he will confesse rather to have done any thing, yea, to have killed his own father, than to suffer torment."[14]

The salient reason why the English common law did not employ torture to produce confessions probably lay not so much in the unreliability of the resultant confession or in the inhumanity of the torture, but, rather, in the simple fact that confessions were unnecessary in England to obtain a conviction. An English jury was free to convict on whatever basis it wished.[15] As Smith asked, "And to say the truth, to what purpose is it

[10] For examples of later uses of the case, see William Staunford, *Les Plees del Coron* (Richard Tottell 1557) in PR Glazebrook (ed), *Les Plees del Coron* (photo reprint, Professional Books Ltd 1971) 142v; William Lambard, *Eirenarcha of the Office of Justices of Peace* (1581/1582, photo reprint Professional Books Ltd 1972) 426; Ferdnando Pulton, *De Pace Regis et Regni* (London, Companie of Stationers 1609, photo reprint 1973) fol 184; *Attorney General v Mico*, 145 Eng Rep 419, 420; Hardres 137, 139 (1658).

[11] Sir John Fortescue, *De laudibus legum angliae* in Shelley Lockwood (ed), *On the Laws and Governance of England* (CUP 1997) 41.

[12] Thomas Smith, *De republica anglorum. The Maner of Gouernement or Poicie of the Realme of England* (printed by Henrie Midleton for Gregorie Seton 1583) (bk 2, c 24) 85.

[13] Fortescue (n 11) 32.

[14] Smith (n 12) 85. Sir Edward Coke, late in his career, claimed that the rack was a creature of the civil law. "There is no law to warrant tortures in this land, nor can they be justified by any prescription being so lately brought in." 3 Co Inst 35. This statement of Coke in the 1620s obscures the fact that he himself was named as Solicitor General or Attorney General in six torture warrants between 1593 and 1603. Lord Toulson, "Fundamental Rights and the Common Law: Keynote Address given at the Fundamental Rights Conference: A Public Law Perspective, LSE" (October 10, 2015). "At the time of his writing [in 1620s] there is evidence that the manacles and rack were still being used on occasion, although it seems that the practice had by then become rare and there is no evidence of torture in that sense after 1640." Ibid. For detailed study of torture and torture warrants in England, see John Langbein, *Torture and the Law of Proof: Europe and England in the Ancien Régime* (University of Chicago Press 2006).

[15] "The jury standard of proof made it unnecessary to provide for extensive and refined evidence-gathering." Langbein, *Torture* (n 14) 138. Langbein's is the most significant modern study of the use of torture in England during the Renaissance. For an early and influential study of torture in England, see David Jardine, *A Reading on the Use of Torture in the Criminal Law of England Previously to the Commonwealth*

to use torment? For whether the malefactor confesse or no, and whatsoever he saith, if the enquest of xij. do find him guiltie, he dyeth therefore without delaye."[16]

Treason Statutes Requiring a Plea of Guilt to Be Voluntary

If the common law, in contrast to *ius commune* practice, did not employ violence to twist out confessions of guilt from defendants, what need was there, then, for Edward VI's 1547 repeal statute and successor treason acts to specify, as they repeatedly did, that any confession must be made "willingly and without violence" in order to be valid?[17]

In actuality, the boasts of Fortescue and the later claims of Smith and Coke that the English common law did not engage in torture left an important fact in the shade. True enough, common-law procedure itself did not employ torture, as a rule.[18] The crown's privy council, however, could and did order examination of treason suspects under torture in order to obtain their confessions or to make suspects implicate accomplices.[19] The council would issue a warrant authorizing examination of a suspect under torture. The examiners recorded in writing the suspect's answers and any confession. The transcribed confession could later be read out against the defendant at trial. Torture at the behest of the council became more frequent in the later years of Henry VIII's reign.[20] Nor did the council always restrict its authorization of torture solely to matters of state importance. On occasion, the council ordered the torture of persons involved in common felonies.[21] The preamble to Henry VIII's Piracy Act may

---

(Baldwin and Cradock 1837). For other studies of English torture, see James Heath, *Torture and English Law: Administrative and Legal History from the Plantagenets to the Stuarts* (Greenwood Press 1982); Danny Friedman, "Torture and the Common Law" (2006) 2 European Human Rights Law Review 180–199.

[16] Smith (n 12) 86. By contrast with England, the *ius commune*'s rigid standard of proof obliged a Continental judge to acquit unless a defendant confessed in court or two suitable and reliable eye-witnesses offered sufficient testimony against him.

[17] 5 & 6 Edw VI, c 11, s 9 (1552); 1 & 2 Ph & M, c 10 (1554) ("willingly confess"; the phrase "without violence" is absent); 1 Eliz, c 5, s 10 (1558–1559); 13 Eliz, c 1, s 9 (1571); 13 Car II, st 1, c 1, s 5 (1661). 1 Edw VI, c 12, s 22 (1547) "may be regarded as a collateral antecedent of the involuntary confession rule." Lawrence Herman, "'The Unexplored Relationship between the Privilege against Compulsory Self-Incrimination and the Involuntary Confession Rule (Part I)" (1992) 53 Ohio St LJ 101, 115.

[18] The preambles to 27 Hen VIII, c 4 and 28 Hen VIII, c 8 (concerning trials of felonies committed on the high seas) criticized torture under admiralty procedure. By transferring criminal jurisdiction from admiralty to common law commissions, the legislature "end[ed] the last possibility of lawful torture in England." John H Baker, 6 *The Oxford History of the Laws of England* (OUP 2004) 512.

[19] Langbein suggests that the power to torture did not flow affirmatively from the royal prerogative (the crown's reserved powers), but defensively through the prerogative power of sovereign immunity which protected the crown and its agents from liability for criminal and civil trespass. Langbein, *Torture* (n 14) 129–130.

[20] John G Bellamy, *The Tudor Law of Treason: An Introduction* (Routledge & K Paul; University of Toronto Press 1979) 120–121.

[21] Langbein records 81 torture warrants issued between 1540 and 1640 for examinations predominantly involving treason, sedition, or religious dissent; and sporadically for common felonies of robberies, horse-stealing, murder, embezzlement, and burglary. Langbein, *Torture* (n 14) 91–124. See also Bellamy (n 20), commenting with respect to the use of torture in treason cases: "No doubt the handling of treason started a trend in regard to other crimes as well and it is important evidence that the study of sedition should not be divorced from the study of the history of English criminal law as a whole." Ibid 111. The register in 1587 referred to the rack as the "accustomed torture." John H Baker, *The Reinvention of Magna Carta 1216–1616*

be read as casting aspersions upon the use of torture in Continental procedure, but the king's council, composed of the king's closest and most trusted advisors, did not scruple at ordering torture within the English realm if the council deemed necessary, especially in the absence of other evidence of guilt.

It was in reaction to the use of torture under Henry VIII that Edward VI's repeal act required that any confessions be made "willingly and without violence."[22] In the absence of a voluntary confession, proof had to rest on the accusations of "two sufficient and lawful witnesses."[23]

Tudor and Stuart monarchs, however, did not scrupulously heed the repeal act's mandate or those of successor statutes. Using its prerogative powers, the crown's council continued the practice of torture when judged necessary to support a treason prosecution.[24] Both Thomas Smith and Edward Coke signed warrants authorizing torture.[25] Coke, however, without referencing his past, unambiguously asserted by at least 1620 that no statute or judicial ruling in common law ever tolerated torture:

> [I]it is against Magna Carta cap.29 *Nullus liber homo, etc., aliquo modo destruatur, nec super eum ibimus, nec super eum mittemus, nisi per legale iudicium parium suorum, aut per legem terrae.* And accordingly all the said ancient authors are against any paine, or torment to be put or inflicted upon the prisoner before attainder, nor after attainder, but according to the judgement. And there is no opinion in our books, or judicial record (that we have seen and remember) for the maintenance of tortures or torments, etc.).[26]

Coke's assertion that there is "no opinion in our books, or judicial record" permitting torture may have been his way to screen the ugly truth that tortures were performed at the behest of the king's council.[27]

Any lingering doubt about the illegality of torture at common law was put to rest in 1628. When, reportedly in connection with Felton's case, King Charles I inquired of the judiciary whether the common law permitted torture.[28] Meeting at the Inns of Court to respond to the royal inquiry, all the judges of England advised that the

---

(CUP 2017) 170. Nonetheless, the common law itself never permitted torture. "It was done outside the law, under the absolute royal prerogative, on grounds of national emergency." Ibid 171.

[22] Coke interpreted the phrase to apply to confessions made out-of-court under torture: "And it was resolved by all the justices in Rolston's case . . . that these words [shall willingly without violence confess the same] are to be understood where the party accused upon his examination before his arraignment, willingly confessed the same without violence, that is willingly without any torture: and is not meant of any confession before the judge, for he is never present for any torture, neither upon his arraignment was any torture offered." Coke, 3 Co Inst 25.

[23] 1 Edw VI, c 12, s xxii.

[24] See Langbein's chart of torture warrants from 1540 to 1640. Langbein, *Torture* (n 14) 128. See also Bellamy (n 20) 109–121; Baker, *Reinvention* (n 21) 170–174.

[25] Langbein, *Torture* (n 14) 73.

[26] Coke, 3 Co Inst 35.

[27] The authors are grateful to Prof David Seipp for this observation.

[28] Whether Charles I, in fact, made the inquiry is disputed. See Alastair Bellany, "The Torture of John Felton, 1628" in Lorna Hutson (ed), *The Oxford Handbook of English Law and Literature: 1500–1700* (OUP 2017) 548–565.

common law did not authorize the use of torture. As real or imagined plots against the crown subsided by the later Stuart years, the use of torture at the behest of the council eventually ceased.[29]

Excursus: the influence of the *ius commune* on Tudor treason acts

The vocabulary and function of the defensive safeguards of confrontation and voluntary confession, as set out in the 1547 and 1552 treason acts, suggest that Edward VI's parliaments may have consciously drawn upon *ius commune* doctrine in formulating the English protections.

At first blush, the *ius commune* appears to be an unlikely resource for such safeguards. As to confrontation, after all, under *ius commune* practice, witnesses were examined apart from one another and in private. In fact, however, the *ius commune* always insisted that an inquisitorial proceeding against a particular defendant was invalid unless the court provided the defendant the opportunity at the beginning of proceedings to see the witnesses against him in person swear their oaths (*ad videndum iurare testes*).[30] Without such confrontation, a conviction was deemed a nullity. The confrontation procedure in the 1552 treason act functioned similarly. It was a preliminary to trial. "The accusers" were to be "brought in person before the party accused ... at the time of the arraignment of the party accused," and "avow what they have to say to prove him guilty."[31]

As to Edward's requirement that confessions in court be made voluntarily, the *ius commune* again appears to be an improbable source, given the Continent's frequent use of torture to produce confessions. Paradoxically, however, even while it tolerated torture, the *ius commune* never abandoned the principle that any confession had to be made willingly in order to be valid.[32] Thirty-seven years before Edward VI's repeal act first laid down the English requirement that a confession be given "willingly and without violence," Philips Wielandt in his *Practijcke criminele*,[33] written in Holland in 1510, wrote that a confession had to have been made willingly (*gewillicht*) and "without all bonds of irons," if it was to serve as full proof for conviction in *ius commune* procedure.[34] Similarly, Edward VI's requirement that "two sufficient and lawful witnesses" support an accusation corresponds with the *ius commune*'s requirement that two sufficient and not reproachable witnesses[35] are needed for full proof. The

---

[29] Langbein, *Torture* (n 14) 138–39.

[30] See text to n 66 in ch 5.

[31] 5 & 6 Edw VI, c 11, s 9 (1552).

[32] See text to n 19 in ch 5.

[33] Philips Wielant, *Practijcke Criminele (c. 1510)* (first published Gent 1872, Scientia Verlag Aalen 1978).

[34] "Confession by the parties given in judgment willingly and without all bonds of iron also makes full proof" (*Confessie vanden partien gedaen in jugemens gewillicht ende buijten allen banden van ijsere, maect oock volle preuve*). Ibid 71.

[35] "Two sufficient [witnesses], in accord, not reproachable, living, speaking of matters seen and well known, make full proof in criminal matters" (*Twee suffisanten oocorden niet reprochable, levende, sprekende vanden stucke van ziene ende wel weetene*). Ibid. See also Joss Damhouder, *Praxis rerum criminalium* (Antwerp 1556, a Latin version without ascription of Wielandt's work) 143. In the *ius commune*, a confession "willingly" made in court often meant that defendants "willingly" ratified their extrajudicial confessions already coerced under torture.

requirement of two witnesses had long been well-rooted in romano-canon law and Scripture.[36]

English civilian lawyers may have had a hand in drafting the Edwardian protections. Protector Somerset was keenly interested in developing the study of civil law.[37] William Cook, one of the six prominent lawyers appointed to draft the 1552 act, was himself a civilian.[38] He also served in reforming the canon law. Cook was later High Judge of the Admiralty whose procedures bore the influence of the *ius commune*.[39] When Edward VI's parliaments in 1547 and again in 1552 wanted to formulate new protective devices for defendants in treason cases, it would not have been unreasonable to reach out to continental ideas to fill its need.[40] The vocabulary of the 1552 statute, moreover, suggests just such a connection. The act's use of the word "accusers" puzzled English judges. The term was unfamiliar to them. In a conference together at Serjeants Inn in 1556, the judges concluded that the parliamentary drafters must have been using a term from civilian law.[41]

To summarize, both the English statutes and the *ius commune* set confrontation at an initial stage of trial proceedings; both insisted that any confession be willingly made; both adopted two lawful witnesses as an alternative proof to confession. This close coincidence in function and vocabulary, together with the *ius commune*'s

[36] Deuteronomy 19:15 requires at least two witnesses. Roman law sources rejected single witnesses. C Th 11.39.3; CJ 4.20.9. Twelfth-century jurists demanded two credible eye-witnesses for full proof. James A Brundage, "Full and Partial Proof in Classical Canonical Procedure" (2007) 67 Jurist 58, 60. See John H Wigmore, "Required Numbers of Witnesses: A Brief History of the Numerical System" (1901) 15 HLR 12, 12; LM Hill, "The Two-Witness Rule in English Treason Trials: Some Comments on the Emergence of Procedural Law" (1968) 12 Am J Legal Hist 95.

[37] ML Bush, *The Government Policy of Protector Somerset* (E Arnold 1975) 54–55. Bellamy thinks "quite possibly the act was drafted by Protector Somerset himself." Bellamy (n 20) 49.

[38] For thorough study of English civilian lawyers, see Daniel R Coquillette, *The Civilian Writers of Doctors Common* (Duncker & Humblot 1988).

[39] Bellamy (n 20) 51 & n 7. See also WK Jordan (ed), *Chronicle and Political Papers of King Edward VI* (Cornell University Press 1966) 110–111 & n 33.

[40] For England to look to the *ius commune* would not have been novel. The Year Books in the fifteenth century show Yelverton advising: "The common law takes notice of the civil law, in the court of Admiralty, and court of the constable and marshal: and of the law among merchants; and of the canon law in the Ecclesiastical courts. And if any case happens at common law, for which there is no precedent; the Common Law will judge according to the law of nature and the public good." Seipp, *Legal History* (n 9) 1430.006 (8 Hen VI fol 18b). For explorations of the interrelationships of the *ius commune* and English common law, see RH Helmholz, "Continental Law and Common Law: Historical Strangers or Companions" (1990) 1990 Duke LJ 1207; Charles Donahue Jr, "Ius Commune, Canon Law, and Common Law in England" (1991–1992) 66 Tul L Rev 1745; David J Seipp, "The Reception of Canon Law and Civil Law in the Common Law Courts before 1600" (1993) 13 Oxford J Legal Stud 388. Seipp comments that "[o]ver the period from 1400 to 1600, common lawyers came to invoke these other bodies of law [civil and canon] in more and different circumstances. Common lawyers also came into more and more frequent contact with the exponents of those other laws, the doctors of civil law and canon law. This increasing interest in the bodies of law shared with Continental Europe is one sign that the community of English common lawyers gradually adopted a more sophisticated, cosmopolitan outlook. Their growing acquaintance with the other laws led English common lawyers to engage in a more reflective and comparative study of their own law." Ibid. 392.

[41] On the judges' conference, see Baker, 6 *Oxford History* (n 18) 528 & n 76; John H Baker, *The Reports of Sir John Spelman* (Selden Society 1977) 110; Bellamy (n 20) 77; James Fitzjames Stephen, 1 *A History of the Criminal Law of England* (Macmillan and Co. 1883) (2 vols) 336. Coke believed the two words meant the same, 3 Co Inst cap 2, 25.

chronological priority in articulating the requirements, is strong evidence that parliament was looking beyond English common law in formulating its defensive safeguards.[42]

Voluntary Confessions in Star Chamber

Despite popular historical myths reflecting negatively on the Star Chamber's proceedings, the Court[43] for much of its history enjoyed an excellent reputation.[44] Litigants considered it a fair forum where a party could receive justice, often more efficiently than at common law. According to William Hudson, its most eminent practitioner, Star Chamber practice required any confession be made "freely and voluntarily":

> For when some dangerous persons attempt some unusual, and perhaps desperate inventions, which, in short time, may be very like to endanger the very fabric of the government, these persons are apprehended by a pursuivant[45] or messenger, and privately examined, without oath, or any compulsory means, concerning the fact. If he shall deny the accusation, then cannot the court proceed against him *ore tenus*; but if he confess the offense freely and voluntarily, without constraint, then he may be brought to the bar.[46]

Only after a voluntary confession could the Chamber resort to a summary proceeding (*ore tenus*) which in essence amounted to a plea colloquy before the court.[47]

There is no evidence that the Chamber itself ever engaged in torture to produce confessions of guilt.[48] Yet, its methods of punishing misdemeanors and contempts

---

[42] See RH Helmholz, *The Oxford History of the Laws of England: The History of the Canon Law and Ecclesiastical Jurisdiction, 597–1649* (OUP 2004) 311. See also Richard Helmholz, *The Privilege against Self-Incrimination: Its Origins and Development* (University of Chicago Press 1997) 45 (Continental influence on an English statute does not exclude the existence of differences); Helmholz, "Strangers" (n 40) 1220–1221; Donahue (n 40)1760.

[43] The King's Council, when acting judicially, became known as the Court of Star Chamber, taking its name from the starred ceiling of the room in which it ordinarily sat.

[44] On the myth that Star Chamber was always a dreadful court, see Michael Stuckey, *The High Court of Star Chamber* (Gaunt, Inc 1998) 79–88; Thomas G Barnes, "Star Chamber Mythology" (1961) 5 Am J Legal Hist 1–11.

[45] A pursuivant was an agent of the crown empowered to execute warrants.

[46] William Hudson, *A Treatise of the Court of Star Chamber* in Francis Hargrave (ed), *A Treatise of the Court of Star Chamber by William Hudson* (first published London 1792, reprint The Legal Classics Library 1986) 127.

[47] When the defendant appeared before the bar, having confessed in an out-of-court examination, "his confession is shewed to him; and if he acknowledge it, then who can doubt but that the court may justly proceed *ex ore suo*, and give judgment against him: but with the defendant confessing, the matter is handled more speedily, *sed cum confitente reo citius est agendum* . . . although it be subscribed with his hand, and in the presence of the king's council, which are present to testify the same, yet is the rule so strictly held, that they must proceed upon confession; and Pye so denying his confession was remitted from the bar, and the court afterwards proceeded against him in a formal manner by witnesses." Ibid.

[48] "Not a single example is known in which Star Chamber employed the rack to extract confessions or obtain information from accomplices, and statements to the contrary arise from a total confusion between Star Chamber and Privy Council, between this court of law and the security services of the state." GR Elton, *The Tudor Constitution: Documents and Commentary* (2nd edn, CUP 1982) 169–170. As to procedure in Star Chamber, see Stuckey (n 44) 55–65; John H Langbein, *History of the Common Law: The Development of Anglo-American Legal Institutions* (Aspen Publishers/Wolters Kluwer & Business 2009) 575–576. As

became unquestionably cruel, especially in its lattermost period under the Stuart kings.[49] In that period, Star Chamber imposed whippings, chopping off ears, mutilations, public humiliations, and imprisoning in chains. By that point, the Chamber appeared little less savage than a *ius commune* torturer seeking a "voluntary" confession, or an English torturer acting under the protection of the royal prerogative. Such cruelty contributed greatly to an act of parliament dissolving Star Chamber in 1641, declaring that its proceedings had become "an intolerable burden to the subjects, and the means to introduce an arbitrary power and government."[50]

Voluntariness of Confessions in English Legal Commentaries

Close to the time that parliament set out its requirement that confession in treason cases be made "voluntarily and without violence," writers of English legal literature began to devote attention to the principle of voluntariness.

In 1557, William Staunford authored *Les Plees del Coron*. He had participated in the parliamentary arguments for Edward VI's 1552 treason act that required face-to-face confrontation or a voluntary confession.[51] Staunford's treatise came to serve as an important guide to assize judges.[52]

In his treatise, Staunford restated the Bracton treatise's admonishment that defendants should not be brought before the bar in chains so as to avoid any suggestion that defendants were forced or constrained to give a response except from their free will (*forsque lour frank volunte*).[53] Staunford admonished that, if a defendant at his arraignment on an indictment wished to confess, the judge should be sure that the confession did not proceed from "fear, menace, or duress" (*pauour, manace, ou dures*).[54] For authority, Staunford reached back to the Year Book's 1353 case of the woman arraigned for stealing bread:

> If one be indicted or appealed for felony, and upon his arraignment he confesses this, it is the better and more sure response that can be in our law, to quiet the conscience of the judge and to make a good and firm conviction, if it is true that the said confession did not proceed from any fear, threat, or duress, that if it did and the judge perceived it, he should not take or record this confession, but cause him to plead not

to the Chamber's origin and legal business, see Baker, 6 *Oxford History* (n 18) 195–200; John H Baker, *An Introduction to English Legal History* (3rd edn, Butterworths 1990) 117–119.

[49] Stuckey (n 44) 65

[50] 16 Car I, c 10.

[51] John Strype, 2 *Ecclesiastical Memorials Relating Chiefly to Religion and the Reformation of it* (Clarendon Press 1822) (3 vols) 554. See PR Glazebrook, "Introduction" in Staunford (n 10) iii (unnumbered). Glazebrook suggests that Staunford may have taken a prominent part in the drafting of Edward's two treason acts. Ibid.

[52] JH Baker, "Introduction" in JH Baker (ed), *Reports from the Lost Notebooks of Sir James Dyer* (109 SS 1993) xcv.

[53] Staunford (n 10) 78.

[54] Ibid 142–142v.

guilty and take an inquest to try this, as was done in the 27th year, Liber Assisarum plea 40.[55]

Staunford's vocabulary regarding involuntariness bore a marked resemblance to terms that had long been standard in the *ius commune*. "*Menace, pauour, dures*" (threat, power, or force) parallels the familiar canonical wording that the confessions of accused must not be "*per metum aut fraudem, aut per vim extortae*" (through fear, fraud, power, or twisted out by force).[56] As in the *ius commune*, Staunford also speaks of the need for defendants to be presented free of chains lest they appear to be pleading involuntarily.[57] Staunford may have deemed citation to civilian materials inappropriate in a common-law treatise. Perhaps, the bread case was the closest, or even the only common-law precedent that could serve his purpose.

The close coincidence in time between the parliamentary acts concerning voluntariness in treason procedure and Staunford's articulation of a broadly stated rule of voluntariness concerning any plea may indicate that the issue of involuntary confessions had become a matter of some concern in the mid-sixteenth century. In any event, Staunford's language became the staple of successor legal handbooks.[58]

After Staunford, the eminent Edward Coke, as noted previously, took up the subject of voluntariness of confessions in the *Third Part of the Institutes on the Laws of England*. Without alluding to any possible tension between his previous manifest tolerance of torture under the royal prerogative and his position in the *Institutes*, Coke maintained that the common law rejected coerced confessions. "All tortures and torments of parties accused were directly against the Common Laws of England . . . So as there is no law to warrant tortures in this land, nor can they be justified by any prescription, being lately brought in."[59] Commenting on Edward VI's requirement of voluntariness of confessions in treason cases, Coke remarked:

"willingly and without violence confessed the same," that is, willingly without any torture: and is not meant of any confession before the judge, for he is neither present at any torture, neither upon his arraignment was any torture offered.[60]

[55] Ibid 142v.
[56] The phrases can be traced from the pseudo-Isidorian false decretals into the canon law and from thence into the *Leges Henrici*. See Paul Hinschius (ed), *Decretales Pseudo-Isidorianae et Capitula Angilramni* (B Tauchnitz 1863) 94, 95 (spurious letter of Pope Alexander V) (*metu, vi, fraude*); Ivo of Chartres, *Decretum* (c 1094), 161 PL 396 (*per metum aut fraudem, aut per vim extortae*); C 15 q. 6 c 1; *Leges Henrici* 5, 16b in *Leges Henrici* (n 1) 118 (*metu, vi, fraude*).
[57] See *Bracton* (n 7) 385, drawing on CJ 9.3.2.
[58] See, eg, Pulton (n 10) 184 (confession to indictment must "proceed freely, and of his own good will, without any menace, threats, rigor, or other extremities"); Walter Yonge, *A Vademecum . . . together with an Epitome of Master Staniford's Plees of the Crowne* (printed for R.B. 1643) 132: "Though a man confesseth the cryme yet if the confession doth appeare unto the Court to proceed of feare, threatening or imprisonment; that he did it, he ought not to record his confession, but cause him to plead not guiltie, Stamf.142." Matthew Hale, *Historia Placitorum Coronae: The History of the Pleas of the Crown* (printed by E and R Nutt and others 1737) c 38 (confession of defendant upon examination must be done "freely, without any menace, or undue terror imposed upon him") 284; William Hawkins, *Treatise of the Pleas of the Crown* (first published 1716; 8th edn, John Curwood (ed), S Sweet 1824) (judge not to record a confession [plea of guilt] that proceeds "from fear, menace, or duress, or from weakness or ignorance") (bk 2, c 31, s 2) 333.
[59] 3 Co Inst cap 2. Coke maintained the use of the rack in England sprang from the Continent. Ibid.
[60] Ibid 25. Coke appears to be referring to those confessions that might be made in pretrial examinations, for it was there, and not in front of the court, that torture was employed. John Wigmore, citing sources in

Summary

Evidence from the early twelfth century onward indicates that a defendant's confession in court was to be made without compulsion and voluntarily. The *Leges Henrici Primi* drew on earlier roman-canon sources to express the principle. The Bracton treatise *De legibus* and two reports in the Year Books confirm common-law hostility to involuntary confessions. The works of both Fortescue and Smith condemned compelled confessions. By statute, Edward VI mandated that in treason cases, confessions had to be made "willingly and voluntarily." Successor statutes repeated the requirement. Star Chamber and legal commentaries, including that of Edward Coke, likewise rejected forced confessions. Certainly, as English legal sources emphasized, torture was never inflicted during official, public court proceedings. Nonetheless, the royal council ordered the torture of suspects, particularly in cases of treason. Despite such instances, the judiciary unambiguously declared that torture was illegal under the common law.

conflict with Coke, maintained the term "confession," as used in the period of the 1500s and 1600s, meant only pleas of guilt made before a court and had no application to out-of-court inculpatory admissions. John H Wigmore, "Confessions: A Brief History and a Criticism" (1899) 33 Am L Rev 376, 376–380. The *ius commune* courts similarly evaded the principle of meaningful voluntariness. If a defendant repeated as "voluntary" in court a confession first made under torture out of court, the ratified confession would be held valid.

9

Silence and Self-incrimination in England Before the Late Seventeenth Century

No Legal Obligation for Suspects or Defendants to Speak at Common Law

The common law did not compel criminal suspects or defendants to speak, either against themselves or for themselves, except for the specific purpose of entering a plea and choosing whether to be tried by jury.[1] Potential suspects had no obligation to initiate accusations against themselves. This accorded with the canonical principle that "no one is held to accuse himself" (*nemo tenetur seipsum accusare*). If defendants chose to speak, they were not permitted to "testify," that is, to speak under oath. English common law presumed that parties would be strongly tempted to lie in their own interest. If they did so under oath, they would endanger their own souls. From this point of view, the bar against defendants speaking under oath ("testifying") was a protection against their perjuring themselves.

While the common law did not inflict any legal punishment on a person's silence or compel answers to incriminating questions, neither did it surround the exercise of silence with any protective safeguards. The choice of a criminal suspect or defendant to remain silent or not to answer incriminating questions could come at a high practical cost, even though silence was permissible by law.[2]

---

[1] Under the procedure of *peine forte et dure*, a defendant was required to elect to "place himself upon the country," that is, upon the jury, for his trial. Originally, by the Statute of Westminster 1, c 12 (1275), a defendant who declined to accept trial by jury was to be taken to a harsh prison (*prison forte et dure*) until he or she consented. Over time the word *prison* was understood to mean *peine*, which is pain. Consequently, a recalcitrant defendant would be placed on the ground with heavy weights put upon his chest until he "consented" or died. Sara Butler has argued that the refusal of defendants to consent to trial by jury was a form of protest against the unwelcome expansion of royal power into localities through the institution of the jury. Sara M Butler, "Rejecting the Jury, Rejecting the Common Law, Rejecting the King" in Sara M Butler (ed), *Pain, Penance, and Protest: Peine Forte et Dure in Medieval England* (CUP 2022) 355, 396–397. See also George Fisher, "The Jury's Rise as Lie Detector" (1997) 107 Yale LJ 575, 588–589; John H Langbein, *Torture and the Law of Proof: Europe and England in the Ancien Regime* (University of Chicago Press 2006) 75–76, 184 n 20 (1977); HRT Summerson, "The Early Development of the Peine Forte et Dure" in EW Ives and AH Manchester (eds), *Law, Litigants, and the Legal Profession* (Royal Historical Society 1983) 116, 116–125. The procedure was not designed to elicit confessions or evidence from defendants. Matthew Hale advised, in case where a defendant stands mute, "let the judge hear the witnesses upon oath to give a testimony of his probable guilt, for though his malicious silence carries with it a presumption of guilt, yet it is good to have some concurrent testimony." Matthew Hale, 2 *Historia Placitorum Coronae, the History of the Pleas of the Crown* (printed by E and R Nutt and R Gosling for F Gyles 1736) (2 vols) (c XLIII) 321.

[2] See John Langbein, "The Privilege and Common Law Criminal Procedure: The Sixteenth to the Eighteenth Centuries" in RH Helmholz and others (eds), *The Privilege against Self-incrimination: Its Origins and Development* (University of Chicago Press 1997) 82; John H Langbein, "The Criminal Trial before the Lawyers" (1978) 45 U Chi L Rev 263, 283. Initial indications of limits against self-incrimination appear only in the mid- to late seventeenth century concerning witnesses. Not until the end of the mid-eighteenth century did a criminal defendant enjoy a legally defined privilege against self-incrimination in the jury courts.

Foundations of American Criminal Due Process at Trial. Francis R. Herrmann and Brownlow M. Speer,
Oxford University Press. © Oxford University Press 2025. DOI: 10.1093/9780199364770.003.0009

The customary form of the jury trial presented the first risk to a defendant who wished to remain silent. Once juries evolved to receiving evidence in court, the trial consisted principally of an "altercation," to use Sir Thomas Smith's term, between the prosecuting party (by Smith's time, the king on behalf of the victim or a dead victim's kin) and the accused.[3] The presentation of the prosecution case intermingled with that of the defense. There was no clear demarcation between the two. Even when official prosecutors represented the interests of the crown in trials of signal importance, such as treason, the "altercation" format was followed. Under that format, defendants were likely to speak for practical reasons. After all, in felony cases brought pursuant to indictment, at least by the sixteenth century, there was no counsel allowed to speak for them as to matters of fact.[4] (Cases reported in the Year Books show that this rule was not followed, if it existed at all, in the fourteenth and fifteenth centuries.)[5] In addition, if a defendant declined to answer questions, a judge might well tell a jury that it could consider the accused *pro confesso* as to the matter.[6] Compounding the danger, it was not clear which party had the burden of producing evidence and persuading the jurors.[7] In short, on the whole, it might be wiser to speak.

The second risk to a defendant wishing to remain silent or refusing to answer questions flowed from two statutes governing pretrial investigation. The statutes of Phillip and Mary (1554 and 1555)[8] directed a justice of the peace to interrogate suspects and prosecution witnesses before trial and to transcribe their responses. (No provision was made for questioning defense witnesses.)[9] The justice of the peace delivered the

---

[3] To capture the nature of the "altercation" trial, John Langbein has used the apt phrase "the accused speaks" trial. Langbein, "Privilege" (n 2) 82–84, 90–92, 95–96; Langbein, "Before the Lawyers" (n 2) 283–284. Langbein notes that the shift from the self-informing jury to the "altercation" style turned the defendant into an informational resource at trial. Langbein, "Privilege"(n 2) 86–87; John H Langbein, *The Origins of Adversary Criminal Trial* (OUP 2003) 20, 39, 48–61.

[4] Under the system of private appeals, however, all felony defendants could have counsel to argue fact, law, or other relevant matters, so long as the party could afford counsel. In misdemeanor cases, as well, defendants were permitted the assistance of counsel. See David J Seipp, "Crime in the Year Books" in Chantal Stebbings (ed), *Law Reporting in Britain* (Hambledon Press 1995) 15, 23.

[5] From 1300 to 1500, the restriction of counsel, even as to felony cases brought by indictment, may not have existed, or at least was not uniformly observed. See ibid 16, 22–32 (collecting Year Book cases in which counsel was active on behalf of defendants, and not only as to matters of law). After 1500, a rule against defense counsel in indictments was justified by German, Smith, and Staunford. Ibid 25. Seipp opines that "the rule forbidding counsel for criminal defendants really had effect only in the more repressive Tudor and Stuart regimes." Ibid 26. See JB Post, "The Admissibility of Defence Counsel in English Criminal Procedure" (1984) 5 Journal of Legal History 23.

[6] This will be recognized as a romano-canonical doctrine. The effect of silence admitted of ambiguity. D 50.17.142: "One who remains silent, certainly does not admit, but, nevertheless it is true, he does not deny" (*Qui tacet, non utique fatetur: sed tamen verum est eum non negare*). See text to n 31 in ch 5.

[7] "There was as yet no articulation of prosecution and defense 'cases,' hence the burdens of production and proof had yet to be developed." John H Langbein, "Shaping the Eighteenth-Century Criminal Trial: A View from the Ryder Sources" (1983) 50 U Chi L Rev 1, 124. "When the concept of the prosecution case had been clarified for purposes of sequence, the party burdens of proof could be recognized and the motion for directed verdict at the conclusion of the prosecution case could come into play." Ibid 131.

[8] 1 & 2 Ph & M, c 13 (1554–1555); 2 & 3 Ph & M, c 10 (1555). For extensive analysis of the statutes, see Langbein, "Privilege" (n 2) 40–47; John H Langbein, *Prosecuting Crime in the Renaissance: England, Germany, France* (Harvard University Press 1974) 5–125. Langbein has shown that the examination of suspects was not an innovation brought on for the first time by the Marian statutes. Ibid 73–74. See also John H Langbein, "The Origins of Public Prosecution at Common Law" (1973) 17 Am J Legal Hist 313, 317–324.

[9] The statutes are silent about examining any witnesses for the defense. This may be explained by the purpose of the Marian statutes: the pretrial examination was not intended to establish guilt or innocence,

written answers of the prosecution witnesses and of the defendant, if any were made, to the trial court where they might be read into evidence.[10] Defendants would be likely to think that answering questions from the justice of the peace was probably in their best interest.

For all of that, it remained true that in a common-law court no legally punitive consequences were attached to a suspect's or to a defendant's refusal to answer questions, either in a pretrial investigation or at trial. A defendant could refuse to answer an incriminating question and the law itself would inflict no legal punishment for doing so. In contrast, a *ius commune* defendant who refused to answer a judge's legitimate questions might well be tortured to produce a confession; a defendant before a church court could be excommunicated for refusing to answer; and a defendant before Elizabeth's High Commission could be held in contempt and imprisoned.[11] The common law's approach represents a significant societal value judgment: it would not require accused persons to be the unwilling instruments of their own destruction.

Resistance to defendants speaking under oath at common law

The common law's repugnancy toward using punitive measures to overcome a defendant's silence[12] can be discerned in the long tradition of the common law against placing defendants under oath. This sharply contrasted with the practice of those English courts whose procedures were significantly influenced by the *ius commune*. Among the principal courts following such procedures were the Court of Chancery and Equity (addressing issues on equitable principles); the King's Council; the Court of Star Chamber (derived from the King's Council and exercising an important misdemeanor jurisdiction); the Court of Admiralty; and the ecclesiastical courts. In 1415, Commons protested against Chancery's practice of subpoenaing defendants to answer questions under oath "according to the form of civil law and canon law" (*examination et serement . . . solonc la fourme de ley cyvle et ley de Seinte Eglise*). Commons told King Henry V that this practice was "in subversion of your common law" (*en subvercion de vostre commune ley*) and was "against the form of the common law of your Kingdom" (*encountre la fourme de la commune ley de vostre Roialme*).[13]

The resistance to placing common-law defendants under oath is also apparent in commentaries concerning the Marian statutes. As we have seen, pursuant to the

but only to secure the appearances of the prosecuting party and prosecution witnesses, so that the charges would be brought to trial.

[10] Langbein, "Privilege" (n 2) 41 & n 156. By the mid-eighteenth century, it was no longer routine to read the pretrial examinations at trial, but they could be used to impeach. Ibid.

[11] See MRT Macnair, "The Early Development of the Privilege against Self-Incrimination" (1990) 10 Oxford Journal of Legal Studies 66, 82 & n 127.

[12] Apart, once again, from requiring an accused to decide whether to choose a jury trial under the procedure of *peine forte et dure*. On the methods of and reasons for the procedure, see Sara M Butler, *Pain, Penance, and Protest: Peine forte et dure in Medieval England* (CUP 2022).

[13] 4 *Rotuli Parliamentorum; ut et Petitiones, et Placita in Parliamento* (London s.n. 1767–1768) (7 vols) 84. See DM Kerly, *An Historical Sketch of the Equitable Jurisdiction of the Court of Chancery* (CUP 1890) 43–44.

investigative procedure the statutes ordered, the justices were to examine suspects and prosecution witnesses brought to them. But the statutes did not alter the common law's aversion to requiring a defendant to speak under oath. Anthony Fitzherbert's *L'office et Aucthoritie de Justices de Peace* (1538) gave instructions on how the justices of the peace were to implement the statutory requirement for taking a suspect's statement. Drawing on the romano-canonical protection against self-incrimination under oath, Fitzherbert advised:

> One is not to be examined on his oath about a matter which sounds to his reproach, *et nullus tenetur seipsum perdere* (no one is held to lose himself), as that he committed such felony, or that he was a perjurer, or such like etc. for the law presumes that one does not want to discredit or accuse himself in such a case.[14]

Fitzherbert makes clear the justices were not to administer an oath to the suspect. He does not appear to object to the suspect being questioned, so long as the suspect was not sworn. William Lambarde also commented on the statutory procedures that justices of the peace were to follow.[15] His critique of the Marian statutes may be read more broadly than Fitzherbert's. Lambarde appears to have objected to the very practice of examining a suspect, irrespective of any oath. In the first edition of his *Eirenarcha* (1581), Lambarde observed that judicial examination of a suspect constituted a departure from the traditional common law:

> There [in 2 & 3] Philip & Mary c. 10 (1555)] also you may see (if I bee not deceived) the time when the examination of the Felon himselfe, was first warranted by our Law. For at the Common Lawe, his faulte was not to bee wrung out of himself but rather to be proved by others.[16]

In his second edition in 1588, Lambarde, like Fitzherbert before him, turned to the canonical maxim *nemo tenetur seipsum prodere*. In using the maxim, however, Lambarde tellingly put it in the past tense, in light of the recent establishment of the Marian procedures:

---

[14] *Home ne serra examine sur son serement de chose que sounde a son reproche, et nullus tenetur seipsum perdere, come lequel il fist tiel felony, ou le que il fuit periure, ou tiel semble etc. car le ley intend quehome ne voile luy mesme discrediter ou accuser in tiel case.* Anthony Fitzherbert, *L'Office et Aucthoritie de Justices de Peace* (Richard Tottell, R Crompton rev 1584, photo reprint 1972) fol 152r. See Macnair, "Development" (n 11) 66, 70 & n 24 (citing Fitzherbert and observing that maxim also appears in canon law sources). One might infer from Fitzherbert's caution that at least some justices needed clarification about not imposing an oath on a suspect under the novel Marian statutory procedures.

[15] William Lambarde (1536–1601) was educated in the common law at Lincoln's Inn. In 1592, he was appointed master in Chancery. Retha M Warnicke, *William Lambarde: Elizabethan Antiquary, 1536–1601* (Philmore 1973) xiv–xv.

[16] William Lambard, *Eirenarcha: Or of the Office of the Iustices of Peace in Two Bookes: Gathered. 1579. and Now Reuised, and Firste Published* . . . (London, Imprinted by Ralph Newbery and H Bynneman 1581) (c 21) 208–209. Lambarde discusses a difference of legal opinion as to whether those who bring a suspect to the justice of the peace should speak under oath. He makes no suggestion that the suspects themselves be placed under oath. Ibid 209–210.

Here [in 1 and 2 Ph. & M.] one may see (if I be not deceived) when the examination of a Felon began first to be warranted among us. For at the common Law, *Nemo tenebatur prodere seipsum* (No one was being held to betray himself), and then his fault was not to be wrung out of himselfe, but rather to be discovered by other meanes and men.[17]

Lambarde appears to have viewed questioning a suspect by judicial authority as *per se* compulsory, whether a suspect was under oath or not. "Twisted out" could be an allusion to the oath, but that seems unlikely since Lambarde nowhere refers to the suspect being placed under oath, unlike the prosecution witnesses ("the bringers"). "Discovered by other means and men" suggests it was not customary or fitting for the law to require a suspect to destroy himself, whether under the compulsion of an oath or simply under the compulsion of judicial questioning. Michael Dalton, in his 1618 *Country Justice*, another popular handbook for justices of the peace, explicitly states that a suspect shall not be placed under oath at the pretrial examination. Dalton repeats Lambarde's salient point that, at least until the Marian statutes, a man's fault was not to be wrung out of him. Rather, it was for the prosecution to prove its case without compelling an offender to cooperate under questioning:

> The Offender himself shall not be examined upon Oath: For by the Common Law, *Nullus tenetur seipsum prodere*. Neither was a Man's fault to be wrung out of himself (no not by Examination only) but to be proved by others, until the Stat. 2&3 P&M. cap. 10 gave Authority to the Justices of the Peace to examine the Felon himself.[18]

Lambarde's and Dalton's apparent opposition to the questioning of defendants, even without being under oath, could not, of course, prevail against the statutes. Consequently, suspects continued to be examined by justices, though not on oath.[19] But, a suspect's refusal to answer, however injudicious, did not trigger contempt or other legal punishment.

In sum, a pretrial suspect, or a defendant at trial, could remain silent and not incur legal punishment for doing so. To that degree, it may be truly said a defendant had a right to remain silent. *Nemo tenetur seipsum prodere*, embedded in manuals for justices of the peace and spread throughout England, encapsulated the core procedural principle that no one had to participate in his own undoing. As Lambarde said, the

---

[17] William Lambard, *Eirenarcha: Or of the Office of the Iustices of Peace in Foure Bookes: Gathered 1579: First Published 1581: And Now Reuised, Corrected, and Enlarged* . . . (London, Printed by Ralph Newbery 1588) (bk 2, cap 7) 213.

[18] Michael Dalton, *The Country Justice: Containing the Practice of the Justices of the Peace* (first published 1618, printed for John Walthoe 1715) (c 191) 411.

[19] See Macnair, "Development" (n 11) 79 n 99. Not until the Jervis's Act, 11 & 12 Vic 42 (1848) was there an end to the practice of pretrial examination. Under the Act, suspects were not to be asked any questions at all, although they could make statements if they so chose. The magistrate was to instruct a suspect: "Having heard the evidence, do you wish to say anything in answer to the charge? You are not obliged to say anything unless you desire to do so, but whatever you say will be taken down in writing and may be given in evidence against you at trial." Ibid. See James Fitzjames Stephen, *A History of the Criminal Law of England* (Macmillan & Co 1883) 220–221.

burden was on the accuser and proof was not to be "twisted out" of the accused. But that is not to say that silence might not be costly. The statutory practice of justices of the peace questioning defendants pretrial inevitably had the effect of prompting them to respond. The customary altercation style of trial, too, would have imposed a risk. A judge might instruct jurors they could consider a silent defendant as having confessed (*pro confesso*).[20] A felony defendant, having no counsel to speak in his stead, might conclude that silence was not worth the price.[21]

Self-incrimination in non-common-law courts

Romano-canonical procedures exercised a pronounced influence in admiralty, chancery, the ecclesiastical courts, Star Chamber, and the conciliar courts.[22] In these courts, parties initiated cases by bill and submitted written *positiones* requiring the opposing party to answer. Written interrogatories (*interrogationes*) were put to witnesses. Both *positiones* and *interrogatories* were answered under oath.

In these non-common-law courts, the romano-canonical principle against self-incrimination offered witnesses and defendants a limited degree of protection. Parties and witnesses, all of whom testified under oath, did not have to answer questions that required them to divulge their secret crimes or disgraceful behavior not already publicly known. Several closely related romano-canonical maxims were used to express the protective principle: "no one is held to betray himself" (*nemo tenetur seipsum prodere*); "no one is held to uncover his own shame" (*nemo tenetur detegere turpitudinam suam*); and "no one is to be punished without an accuser" (*nemo puniri sine accusatore*).[23]

Self-incrimination in chancery

The Court of Chancery can be found applying the romano-canonical anti-self-incrimination protection at least by 1580.[24] There, it was readily accepted that a

[20] Macnair, "Development" (n 11) 82.

[21] At misdemeanor proceedings, however, counsel was permitted and, consequently, a defendant's silence was shielded. Langbein, *Adversary Trial* (n 3) 36.

[22] Besides Star Chamber, other conciliar courts were the Court of Requests and local councils. Admiralty was not a conciliar court, but was heavily influenced by the romano-canonical procedure of the *ius commune* since it dealt often with cases of foreigners. See Daniel Coquillette, *The Anglo-American Legal Heritage* (2nd edn, North Carolina Academic Press 2004). "Everything procedurally particular to Star Chamber also obtained in Chancery, save that in Chancery the defendant usually was not examined." Thomas G Barnes, *Shaping the Common Law: From Glanvill to Hale, 1188–1688* (Stanford Law Books 2008) 156.

[23] Using each of the maxims as a scaffolding, Richard Helmholz has analyzed the romano-canonical rule against self-incrimination which was absorbed into the *ius commune*. RH Helmholz, "The Privilege and the Ius Commune: The Middle Ages to the Seventeenth Century" in RH Helmholz and others (eds), *The Privilege against Self-incrimination: Its Origins and Development* (University of Chicago Press 1997) 20–28. See also Albert W Alschuler, "A Peculiar Privilege in Historical Perspective" in ibid 185–190.

[24] Macnair, "Development" (n 11) 75. Macnair shows that the anti-self-incrimination principle was applied to witnesses and later to defendants in the chancery and equity courts where romano-canonical influence was significant. Only in the seventeenth century did traces of the principle begin to appear in the common-law courts.

defendant was not compelled to answer an incriminating question.[25] In *Fenton contra Blomer* (1580),[26] Chancery prevented the civil defendant from being compelled to answer a question concerning usury where the answer might have made him criminally liable. Similarly, in *Vice-Countess Montague* (c 1599),[27] Chancery safeguarded the defendants against being obliged to answer questions concerning an abduction where their answers might have subjected them to criminal penalties ("and it seemed they should not answer to charge themselves criminally; especially in this case, where so great a punishment as abjuration may follow").[28] It is noteworthy that parties in Chancery could be represented by counsel, if they could afford to do so. Counsel would have been knowledgeable enough to object to questions that tended to violate the rule against self-incrimination. Parties or witnesses themselves may well not have been aware of such a rule.

Self-incrimination in Star Chamber

Romano-canonical procedure also heavily influenced practice in Star Chamber.[29] Like Chancery, the Chamber, which had jurisdiction only over misdemeanors,[30] acknowledged the validity of a principle against self-incrimination as to answers that

[25] The Chancery is one of a variety of venues where common-law lawyers and justices may have become knowledgeable in *ius commune* principles. "In the Elizabethan Chancery, as in other courts, it was an accepted maxim that the defendant need not answer to incriminate himself... The Court of Chancery was presided over by the Lord Chancellor, technically its only judge. After the fall of Wolsey in 1529 had terminated an ecclesiastical tradition, Lord Chancellors or Lord Keepers of the Great Seal were almost always common lawyers." William J Jones, "Due Process and Slow Process in the Elizabethan Chancery" (1962) 6 Am J Legal Hist 123, 123. "By the end of [the sixteenth century], with increasing frequency, common law justices are to be found on the Chancery bench." Ibid 128.

[26] Fenton *contra* Blomer, 21 Eng Rpt 126; Tothill, 70 (1579–1580).

[27] Anon, 21 Eng Rpt 5; Cary, 9 (c 1599).

[28] *Vice-Countess Montague.* Anon, 21 Eng Rpt 5; Cary 9. Michael Macnair discusses the cases of Vice-Countess Montague and Fenton contra Blomer in Macnair, "Development" (n 11) 73–75. Macnair observes further: "The right not to answer incriminating or defamatory questions is consistent with the canon law rules." Michael RT Macnair, *The Law of Proof in Early Modern Equity* [Comparative Studies in Continental and Anglo-American Legal History] (Duncker & Humblot 1999) 242. "*Nemo tenetur seipsum prodere* was readily conceded to apply without significant exceptions to persons produced as witnesses in the canon law." Ibid 236.

[29] Star Chamber was held in high regard for much of its existence. The court's later negative reputation in the mid-seventeenth century and ever since obscures its historical status as a highly respected and efficient venue for doing justice, at least through the time of the early Tudors. GR Elton, *Star Chamber Stories* (Methuen Library; Barnes and Noble 1974) 11–12. In 1635, William Lambarde lauded Star Chamber as "the most noble and praiseworthy court . . . the beams of whose bright justice . . . do blaze and spread themselves as far as the realm is long and wide." Michael Stuckey, *The High Court of Star Chamber* (Gaunt 1998) 108. Edward Coke viewed the Chamber as "the most honorable court (our Parliament excepted) that is in the Christian world, both in respect of the judges of the court, and of their honourable proceeding." 4 Co Inst c 5. Francis Bacon saw the Chamber as "one of the sagest and noblest institutions of this kingdom." Michael Stuckey, *The High Court of Star Chamber* (Gaunt, Inc 1998) 124. The Chamber, however, became clearly harsh and abusive by the 1630s. In terminating the Chamber's existence in 1641, Parliament's act of dissolution, after recounting the fourteenth-century due process statutes of Edward III, dissolved the Chamber, effective 1641. 16 Car 1, c 10 (1640).

[30] 75 Selden Society (1956) xcv. Conviction of misdemeanors could result in severe punishments, especially in the Chamber's lattermost days, such as imprisonment, fine, whipping, pillory, branding, or loss of ears. Ibid xciv.

might cause a person to incriminate himself in a felony.[31] William Hudson addressed the subject in *A Treastise of the Court of Star Chamber* (c 1621):[32]

> But I observe that the court, in all these cases which trench to felony,[33] never examined it further than the party's confession; for in these cases *nemo tenetur prodere seipsum*, but upon voluntary confession without oath.[34]
>
> [S]ometimes . . . the matter in charge tendeth to accuse the defendant of some crime which may be capital; in which case *nemo tenetur prodere seipsum*[35]
>
> [N]either must it [the court] question the party to accuse him of a crime, for it is an high contempt to make the justice of this court an instrument of malice, and hath been punished by fine and imprisonment, and now always by imprisonment and costs.[36]

The rule also sheltered witnesses from having to answer questions that tended to uncover their own turpitude or to bring them into disgrace concerning matters not already publicly known. Hudson advises strongly against witnesses relinquishing the rule's protection:

---

[31] CG Bayne and William Dunham, "Introduction" in CG Bayne and William Dunham (eds) "Council in the Star Chamber: The Introduction" (1956) 75 SS xi, xcv. "Hudson, probably writing around 1620–21, applies the rule to witnesses in Star Chamber . . . clear common law authority on this point starts from the 1640s." Macnair, *Proof* (n 28) 236.

[32] Hudson was the most eminent practitioner of his day in the Chamber, "the leader par excellence of the specialized bar practicing in Star Chamber . . . more highly practiced than any contemporary and probably any other barrister in the court's history." TG Barnes, "Introduction" in William Hudson, 2 *A Treatise of the Court of Star Chamber* in Francis Hargrave (ed), *Collectanea Juridica* (printed for E. and R. Brooke 1792, The Legal Classics Library reprint 1986) (2 vols) vi.

[33] The Star Chamber could not impose capital punishment. Technically, its jurisdiction could include any offense the king wished to prosecute there. But, given the limitation on its sentencing power, the Chamber's jurisdiction, as a practical matter, was limited to trespasses and misdemeanors. Ibid 63. Both private parties and the King's Council could initiate suits in the Chamber. In the latter case, the king's attorney appeared for the Crown. Ibid 126, 134.

[34] Ibid 64. Hudson's reference shows that *nemo tenetur* was recognized in Star Chamber as applying at least to felonies. In *Tresham*, the judges in Star Chamber agreed that "where a man should lose life or limb, that there he is not bound to accuse hymself . . . one of the judges beginning with this, that *nemo tenetur seipsum prodere*, which is an universal proposition." Ibid at 108. Tresham had objected to taking the compelled oath because it was contrary to the natural law: "For, if I swear falsely, I am perjured; if by my oath I accuse myself, I am condemned to the penalty of the law and displeasure of my prince, which is contrary to the law of nature *seipsum prodere*." "Observations upon certain Proceedings in the Star Chamber against Lord Vaux, Sir Thomas Tresham, Sir William Catesby, and others for refusing to swear that they had not harbored Campion the Jesuit" in 30 *Archaeologia: or Miscellaneous Tracts relating to Antiquity* (Society of Antiquaries of London 1844) 64, 87, 92. Although Tresham was technically before the Chamber for misdemeanor contempt, all of the judges "helde it a great matter of estate, and some judged yt lytle differing from treason, that there he is not bound to accuse hymselfe . . . one of the judges beginning with this, that *nemo tenetur seipsum prodere*, which ys an universall proposition." Ibid 108. Consequently, supporters of the accused claimed the maxim against self-incrimination should apply to them, even though charged technically only with a misdemeanor. For discussion of self-incrimination in *Tresham*, see Lawrence Herman, "The Unexplored Relationship between the Privilege against Compulsory Self-Incrimination and the Involuntary Confession Rule (Part 1)" (1992) 53 Ohio St LJ 101, 118–125, 145, 177. On the examinations and trials of Campion, Vaux, Tresham, and companions, see "A Morning in the Star-Chamber" [Sir Thomas Tresame's Trial (1581), Harleian Ms. 859] 7 Rambler (n.s.) 15 (1857); Leonard W Levy, *Origins of the Fifth Amendment* (2d edn, Macmillan Publishing Company) 93–94, 100–107, 182, 184.

[35] Hudson (n 32) 164.

[36] Ibid 208.

[A]nd it is the folly of the witness if he shall give any answer to any such scandalous and impertinent question; for the oath ministered to the witness is, "You shall make true answer to such interrogatories as shall be ministered unto you as a witness concerning this cause, without partiality or affection to either of the parties"; so that if the question concern not the cause he need not answer it, whether it be scandalous to himself or to any other, if not concerning that crime in question[37]

And it hath been ever held, that the witness's testimony must be truly voluntary, and not constrained . . . and therefore if a witness conceive that the answering of a question may be prejudice to himself, it seemeth that he need not to answer; for he is produced to testify betwixt others, and not to prejudice himself, where he is produced as a witness . . . [Lord Egerton said] he knew no law to compel a witness to speak more than he would of his own accord.[38]

Self-incrimination before the Ecclesiastical Court of High Commission

English ecclesiastical procedure, as opposed to common-law procedure, was inquisitorial. Like other non-common-law courts, the procedure acknowledged the romano-canonical rule against self-incrimination together with limits and exceptions.[39]

Pursuant to statute and by letters patent,[40] Elizabeth I in 1559 authorized crown commissioners for the policing of a church settlement that was intended to reduce religious strife.[41] Seeking to lay to rest questions about the so-called High Commission's controversial practice of using oaths *ex officio*[42] in its proceedings, nine learned doctors of the civil law in 1590 described the principal features of ecclesiastical inquisitorial procedure as it existed then and from "time out of mind" in England.[43] First, they stated the canonical rule that "[n]o man may be urged to bewray himself in hidden

---

[37] Ibid 208–209. This seems to be a reference to *nemo detegere turpitudinem suam*. At the same time, it is a bar against immaterial questions. See Macnair, "Development" (n 11) 75 & n 63 (citing cases on protection against scandalous questions in Chancery) and Helmholz, "Privilege and the Ius Commune" (n 23) 26–32 (on protection for witnesses against having to answer questions tending to their disgrace).

[38] Hudson (n 32) 209. See Levy discussing the Star Chamber's view of the principle against self-incrimination and self-defamation, in Levy (n 34) 105–107.

[39] For the rule in English ecclesiastical courts, see Francis Clerke, *Praxis Francisci Clarke in curiis ecclesiasticis* (printed Nathaniel Thompson 1666) 409: where no *fama* had been shown, a defendant was not held to answer to criminous positions. Ibid Tit 314. See also ibid Tit 318, Tit 322. Having been written in the 1590s, Clerke's work circulated widely in manuscript before publication. See RH Helmholz, *Roman Canon Law in Reformation England* (CUP 1990) 128–131. See also HC Conset, *The Practice of the Spiritual or Ecclesiastical Courts* (first edn 1681; 2nd edn, W Battersby 1700) 100 (defendants are not by law to answer to criminal and captious positions without preceding *fama*).

[40] 1 Eliz, c 1 (1559).

[41] The High Commission was intended for "the conservation of the Peace and Unity of this Realme." GR Elton, *The Tudor Constitution: Documents and Commentary* (2nd edn, CUP 1982) 217–227; John H Baker, *The Reinvention of Magna Carta 1216–1616* (CUP 2017) 353–375; Macnair, *Law of Proof* (n 28) 69–70. Before Elizabeth, Edward VI and Mary had initiated similar commissions.

[42] An oath *ex officio* was one imposed by virtue of the judge's duty or office (*officium*).

[43] *A Short Discourse, Being the Judgment of Several of the Most Learned Doctors of the Civil Law, Concerning the Practice of Their Courts, and the Oath Ex Officio*, printed in Appendix, bk III, no II in John Strype, *The Life and Acts of . . . John Whitgift* (London, printed for T Horne and others 1718) 136–137. Noted in Levy (n 38) 455 n 16.

and secret crimes, or simply therein to accuse himself."[44] The doctors noted, however, that the rule ceased to offer its haven against self-incrimination when "that which was secret before is found to be so public." Vehement suspicions and "fame" repeatedly reported to the ordinary by credible persons, or by presentment of churchwardens, or by neighbors examined as witnesses could render a crime no longer secret, if it ever was. The public nature of the suspected offensive conduct imposed a duty on the ordinary (usually a bishop) to proceed "by Enquiry, especially *ex officio*." "[T]ho' no other Man will prosecute," the ordinary was to do so on account of the "public Trust reposed in him" lest crimes remain unpunished (*ne maleficia remaneant impunita*).[45] Once the prerequisite probable cause was established, a judge could initiate an inquisitorial trial and require the defendant to purge himself, "at which time of purgation, the defendant had to directly answer, clearing or convicting himself" of the truth or falsity of the crime charged.[46] If he failed in his purgation, he was taken to be guilty by fiction of law. Thus, the rule was encapsulated:

> Although no one is held to betray himself, nevertheless, having been betrayed by *fama*, he is held to show whether he can display his innocence and purge himself.[47]

Inquisitorial *ex officio* procedure was justified, according to the doctors, because the "penances" enjoined after findings of guilt were not "taken in Law" to be criminal punishments but rather medicinal remedies (*medicinae*), "tending to the reformation of the delinquent." Consequently, defendants "are not to make scruple to discover themselves after fame."[48] In fact, the "medicinal" consequences of a finding of guilt included forfeiture of property and imprisonment. A third offense constituted high treason and could result in death. Even a refusal to take the oath *ex officio* could result in a finding of contempt, triggering severe conditions of confinement until the suspect acquiesced and submitted to the oath.

Puritans, Catholics, and other dissenters who found themselves the regular targets of the High Commission's inquisitions did not agree to swallow their medicine. They attacked the Commission's procedural practices. The Commission, they protested, sought to invade the privacy of their consciences, probing into their religious convictions and practices. The oath *ex officio*, they said, compelled them to reveal the religious beliefs hidden in their hearts, thereby violating the very core of the ecclesiastical

---

[44] Whitgift (n 43) 136. This was in keeping with the church's long-standing position that it did not judge hidden crimes. Text to n 54 in ch 3; text to n 126 in ch 5.

[45] If a private party chose to prosecute, the party charged was required to testify under oath, but he was "not bound to answer upon Oath any Articles of the very crime it self." Ibid 137.

[46] The defendant was to be supported by others (compurgators) who would swear to his credibility (*de credulitate*). Ibid 137.

[47] *Licet nemo tenetur seipsum prodere, tamen proditus per famam tenetur seipsum ostendere utrum possit suam innocentiam ostendere et seipsum purgare.* Ibid 137. A defendant canonically purged himself by taking an oath that he was innocent. The procedure was intended to rehabilitate a person's reputation after a trial in which proof of guilt had failed. Requiring a defendant to "directly answer, clearing or convicting himself" concerning the truth or falsity of the charge at the time of purgation was said to be justified by the supposedly medicinal nature of any ecclesiastical chastisement.

[48] Ibid 137.

rule that sheltered them against self-betrayal of their secret crimes.[49] Compounding the abuse, the Commission, according to opponents, acted purely on the basis of its own unsupported suspicions ("suspiciously to conceive it of his own fantasie"). This practice contravened the canonical requirement that "fame" (*fama*) or some other publicly grounded basis serve for the initiation of proceedings against individuals.[50]

James Morice (1539–1597),[51] a lawyer and sometimes member of Parliament, attacked the oath *ex officio* as contrary to both canon and common law. He did so, first, in a treatise against compelled oaths and later in a speech in Commons. Referring to ecclesiastical judges, Morice argued in *A Briefe Treatise of Oathes Exacted by Ordinaries and Ecclesiastical Iudges*:[52]

> [S]uch judges sometimes not knowing by any due proof that such as have to do be-fore them are culpable, will enforce them by an oath to detect themselves in opening before them their hearts. In this so doing, I cannot see that men need to condescend in their requests, for as it is in the law, *Nemo tenetur prodere seipsum*.[53]

[49] The High Commission agreed that *nemo tenetur* applied only to secret crimes. But once well-founded *fama* was established, the crime was no longer hidden. The suspect then had the obligation to take an oath to tell the truth and to respond to questions relating to the alleged crime. See Nine Commissioners, "Oaths in Ecclesiastical Courts," State Papers, Domestic, Elizabeth, PRO P.12/238, no 47. Also in Strype, *Whitgift*, III, 232–235. See Levy (n 38) 179 & n 11.

[50] Objection to the ecclesiastical oath *ex officio* had a history before the reign of Elizabeth. In 1532, the priest John Lambert, during the reign of Henry VIII, complained of being questioned by ecclesiastical judges who "sometimes, not knowing by any due proof that such as have to do before them are culpable, will enforce them, by an oath, to detect themselves, in opening before them their hearts . . . I cannot see that men need to condescend to their requests." Josiah Pratt (ed), 5 *The Acts and Monuments of John Foxe* (4th edn, The Religious Tract Society 1877) (8 vols) 221. Lambert cited *nemo tenetur* twice. Ibid 184, 221. On Lambert's resistance to the oath, see Henry Ansgar Kelly, "Oath-Taking in Inquisitions" (2018) 35 Bull Medieval Canon L (n.s.) 215, 234–235. In the same year, Commons brought a complaint to Henry VIII. Ordinaries (bishops and others with a power to govern) were imposing oaths by virtue of their office. In its "Supplication against the Ordinaries," Commons sought relief from *ex officio* oaths which, it was said, often trapped people into speaking at their peril "so that every your subjects, upon the only will and pleasure of the Ordinaries . . . without any accuser, proved fame or presentment, sometime is and may be infamed, vexed and troubled to the peril of their lives, their shames, costs and expenses." Printed in Arthur Ogle, *The Tragedy of the Lollards' Tower* (Pen-in-Hand 1949) 324. In 1534, 25 Hen VIII, c 14, protected persons suspected of heresy from being prosecuted on the mere suspicion of bishops. For discussion of the Supplication, see Baker (n 41) 124. Levy (n 38) 64–69. Richard Helmholz found that in England the medieval use of inquests to establish *fama* had come to an end in the latter half of the sixteenth century. Helmholz, "Privilege in Ius Commune" (n 23) 41–42.

[51] For biography of Morice, see Christopher W Brooks, "Morice, James" in David Cannadine (ed), *Oxford Dictionary of National Biography* (hereafter *ODNB*) (OUP 2004).

[52] James Morice, *A Briefe Treatise of Oathes Exacted by Ordinaries and Ecclesiasticall Iudges, to Answere Generallie to All Such Articles Or Interrogatories, as Pleaseth Them to Propound and of Their Forced and Constrained Oathes Ex Officio, Wherein is Proued that the Same are Vnlawfull* (Middelburg, printed by Richard Schilders 1590). Morice's manuscript was secretly printed in 1590. His treatise was published abroad in 1598 and reprinted in 1600. Levy (n 38) 172, 194. He delivered his speech in Commons in 1593.

[53] Morice (n 52) 17. Pointing to Star Chamber and Chancery procedure, Morice comments: "But who hath ever seen in these Courts any subject of this land, in a cause concerning himself, brought forth and compelled to depose or make answer upon his oath, no bill of complaint or information formerly exhibited against him. Nay on the contrary, these Courts observing the due form of Justice, enforce no man to an-swer, but where he hath a known accuser, and perfect understanding of the cause or crime objected, and therewithal is permitted to have a copy of the bill of complaint or information (being not *ore tenus* [that is, where the defendant has not already confessed]). And allowed moreover both time convenient and counsel learned well to consider and advise of his oath and answer . . . [I]f the interrogatories ministered be imper-tinent to the matter of complaint, the defendant without offence to the Court may refuse to make answer to the same." Ibid 38–39.

Drawing on canon-law principles, Morice maintained an inquisition was not orderly undertaken unless *fama* or sufficient indicia, based on reports of suitable witnesses preceded.

> A judge who fails to abide by this condition and acts on his own suspicion makes himself both judge and accuser, forfeiting his impartiality in violation of the rule that every trial must have three independent actors: a judge, a moving party, and a defendant.[54]

Defendants complained that the Commission obliged them to swear to answer truthfully any questions *before* the details of any charges were shown to them. This manner of proceeding by "general" oaths, Morice argued, trespassed upon the romano-canonical rule, practiced both in Chancery and in Star Chamber, which limited questions to specific charges shown to a suspect in advance:

> the forcing of Oaths by Ordinaries and Iudges Ecclesiastical generally to answer unto all such questions or interrogatories as they shall demand or minister touching either the thoughts, words or deeds of him that is to depose, is contrary to the honorable institution, lawful use, and true ende of an oathe.[55]

He complained that such general oaths were often used "before notice or understanding (for the most part) of the crime objected. And the extorting by oath of the ground and foundation of the inquisition from the party convented showed that the examiners "have no good or sufficient warrant by the lawto demand the oath."[56] Instead, with the defendant not knowing the cause of the inquisition before he is "by his oath fast bound," he is subject to the discretion or indiscretion of the ecclesiastical judge who has "straightly tied and snared this seelie subject" and "enforcing him by the bound of his oath to accuse himself even of the most secret and inward thoughts."[57]

Morice further deplored such a way of proceeding because it invited "the great hazard and peril of willful perjury."[58] In this conundrum, Morice said, the defendant "thinketh to make answer."[59]

To protect themselves against such alleged abuses of the High Commission, defendants at times sued in the common-law courts for writs of prohibition or *habeas corpus*. In 1568, the High Commission prosecuted the attorney Thomas Leigh for being present at a Mass. When the court demanded that Leigh take an oath to tell the truth in response to questions put to him, he refused.[60] The Commission imprisoned him for his refusal. On a writ of *habeas corpus*, the Court of Common Pleas

---

[54] Ibid 19. Levy analyzes Morice's argument against the *ex officio* oath, Levy (n 38) 193–195. See generally, ibid 173–204.

[55] Morice (n 52) 7.

[56] Ibid 22. Morice summarizes the teaching of canonists on the oath, ibid 19.

[57] Ibid 10.

[58] Ibid.

[59] Ibid.

[60] *Leigh* (aka *Lee*). The case is not printed but referred to by Coke in "Burrowes and Others v. The High Commission" 81 Eng Rep 42 (1616). 23 Eliz I, c 1 declared it a crime to celebrate or attend a Mass. Baker (n 41) 128.

discharged Leigh on the ground of the canonical rule *nemo tenetur seipsum prodere*.[61] Likewise, in *Hynde* (1576), the defendant, charged with pretense of usury, refused the oath the commissioners demanded of him. Common Pleas discharged him, again on the canonical ground that no one is held to betray himself.[62] In 1589, in *Collier v Collier*, Edward Coke sought a prohibition because an ecclesiastical judge had required a party implicated for adultery to "answer upon his oath if he ever had carnal knowledge of such a woman."[63] The defendant refused, asserting the protection of the rule *nemo tenetur seipsum prodere*. The Court of Common Pleas appears to have granted the prohibition.[64]

In seeking interventions from the common-law courts, petitioners were not relying upon any existing common-law rule against self-incrimination. (There was none.) They were claiming that the High Commission was abusing its own ecclesiastical principles that governed the appropriate use of the oath *ex officio*.[65]

In his treatise against ecclesiastical oaths, Morice sought to buttress his canonically based argument with common-law arguments that he sought to fashion.[66] Although the common law itself had no rule against self-incrimination, Morice drew inspiration from the fact that the common law never required defendants in criminal cases to testify under oath:

> For in wisdom it was foreseen that the frailty of man for the safety of life, the preservation of liberty, credit, and estimation would not spare to profane even that which is most holy, and by committing sinful perjury, cast both soul and body to eternal perdition. ... Therefore in causes capital or otherwise criminal, these our laws neither urge by oath nor force by torment any man to accuse or excuse himself, but reject the oath as unbeseeming a well governed state or commonwealth: and condemn the torture as a thing most cruel & barbarous.[67]

For further support, Morice turned to Magna Carta and the due process statutes of Edward III. He was at the forefront of lawyers in the late sixteenth and seventeenth

---

[61] Dyer's Notebooks i, 143. Baker cites *Leigh* as "the first clear decision affirming the privilege against self-incrimination. It was frequently followed by Coke, CJ, in the following century." Baker (n 41) 160. See Coke's account, 81 Eng Rep 42, 43 (1616). Leonard W Levy sees Justice Dyer's use of the *nemo* maxim in the Court of Common Pleas as the first instance where the romano-canonical phrase was "wrenched" out of the conditions imposed on it in its ecclesiastical context and given "independent life." Levy (n 38) 96–97.

[62] Not printed but reported by Coke, 81 Eng Rpt 42, 43. Coke lists usury as among the "secret" crimes. See "Of Oaths Before an Ecclesiastical Judge *Ex officio*" 77 Eng Rep 1308, 12 Co Rep 26 (1607).

[63] *Collier v Collier*, 74 Eng Rep 816, 4 Leo 194.

[64] See Baker (n 41) 138 n 153.

[65] RH Helmholz, "Introduction" in Helmholz and others (eds), *Privilege* (n 23) 7–9. Common-law courts acknowledged that ecclesiastical courts, when acting within their proper jurisdiction, could use the procedures of the civil law. In *Dr. Hunt*, the common-law judges agreed that "where the knowledge of the matter did belong to the Court Christian, they may proceed according to the civil law." 78 Eng Rep 518, Cro Eliz 263.

[66] On Morice's arguments, see "James Morice and the High Commission" in Baker (n 41) 270–275; Levy (n 38) 193–195.

[67] Morice (n 52) 30–31. Morice comments favorably on the practice of Star Chamber and Chancery regarding oaths, ibid 38.

centuries who began to raise the profile of the Charter's c 29/39 as a bulwark of individual liberties, reviving it from centuries of relative quiescence.[68]

> [B]y the statute of *Magna Charta* (containing many excellent laws of the liberties and free customs of this Kingdom), it is ordeyned that no free man be apprehended, imprisoned, distrained or impeached, but by the law of the land: and by the statute made Anno 5. Ed. 3. ca. 9. It is enacted, That no man shall be attached vpon any accusation contrarie to the forme of the great Charter, and the lawe of the Realme. Moreouer it is accorded by Parliament Anno 43. E. 3. ca. 9. for the good gouernement of the Communaltie, That no man be put to aunswere, without present|ment before Iustices, or matter of recorde, or by due processe, or by writt originall, after the auncient lawe of this Lande. And howe then shall that kinde of proceedinge *ex officio* by forced oathes, & the vrging of this general oath, and streight imprisoning of such as refuse to sweare, bee justifiable.[69]

Morice was well aware that English ecclesiastical procedure had attached to the phrase *nemo tenetur seipsum prodere* a further clause restricting the maxim's application. That clause, as set out by the nine doctors, asserted that, although no one is held to betray himself, "nevertheless having been betrayed through *fama*, he is held to show whether he can show his innocence and purge himself" (*tamen proditus per famam tenetur seipsum ostendere utrum possit suam innocentiam ostendere & seipsum purgare*). The "nevertheless" appendage, Morice saw, constituted such a capacious exception to the anti-self-incrimination maxim that, in practice, the qualifier ordinarily rendered the antecedent part of the maxim nugatory. Once *fama* was established according to proper standards, an ecclesiastical judge was warranted in imposing on a suspect an oath to tell the truth concerning the issues. Morice attacked the escape clause head-on:

> [I]f it be a true and sound principle or maxim in law, not denied by themselves [the ecclesiastical judges] that *Nemo tenetur seipsum prodere,* where should the benefit thereof be had or taken but in their courts and consistories. But if it should be granted that this rule faileth where a man is *proditus per famam* [betrayed by *fama*], doeth not that as a gloss confounding the text wholly and altogether destroy that rule or principle, except for some relief this narrow shift may be used.[70]

Additionally, Morice denounced the clause that required a defendant to demonstrate his innocence by an oath of purgation when the proof of his guilt failed:

> Know we not that all, or the most part of men ... will rather hazard their souls then put their bodies to shame and reproach: presume the law never so much that after same they should not make scruple to discover themselves. If the like course of

---

[68] Baker (n 41) 250 and passim; Faith Thompson, *Magna Carta: Its Role in the Making of the English Constitution, 1300–1629* (University of Minnesota Press 1948) 68–69.
[69] Morice (n 52) 47.
[70] Ibid 22.

purgation should be used at the common law upon indictments of felony or other criminal causes, what doubt were to be made, but that perjury in short time would overflow the whole land and shall we not think that the same is not frequent in these kinds of purgations?[71]

Morice proposed a better way:

Why rather do not these ordinaries . . . free the people from these pernicious oaths and deadly purgations and proceed . . . not by feigned offices and fictions of law, but by good proof and lawful witnesses? And again, absolve the party defamed where such sufficient proof doeth fail them.[72]

Morice clearly did not lift the *nemo tenetur* maxim out of its ecclesiastical context through inadvertence. He explicitly rejected the qualifying clause, arguing that the principal clause of the maxim should stand on its own. He maintained, as Lambarde had, that it was not for the accused to supply the prosecution's proof. That was the role of witnesses.

Morice's argument against the *ex officio* oath was not the last word. Richard Cosin, an ecclesiastical lawyer,[73] published a seven-hundred-page rebuttal to Morice in 1593.[74] Against Morice's view that the *tamen* (nevertheless) clause was a gloss on the core principle, Cosin replied: "yet is it not any gloss, but aswell warranted by law; as the rule it self. Neither doth it confound, but shew, how that rule is (truely) to be understood: so that one part of the law (without any antinomie) may stand with another."[75]

The controversy over the *ex officio* oath continued. King James himself at a Conference at Hampton Court in 1604 discussed with the Archbishop of Canterbury and many other bishops and the lords of the Privy Council the High Commission's manner of proceeding. An unnamed lord complained:

The proceedings in that court [of High Commission] are like the Spanish Inquisition, wherein men are urged to subscribe more than law requireth, and by the oath *ex officio*, forced to accuse themselves, being examined upon twenty, or twenty-four Articles on a sudden, without deliberation, and for the most part against themselves.[76]

---

[71] Ibid 24.

[72] Ibid.

[73] For biography of Cosin, see Martin Ingram, "Cosin, Richard" in *ODNB* (n 51).

[74] Richard Cosin, *An Apologie for Sundrie Proceedings by Jurisdiction Ecclesiastical* (by the deputies of Christopher Barker 1593). Cosin agreed that generally *fama* had to precede an *ex officio* inquisition against a particular individual, but he listed numerous exceptions to the *fama* requirement. Ibid 59–66. Richard Helmholz analyzes Cosin's response, Helmholz, "Privilege and the Ius Commune" (n 23) 23. See generally Ethan H Shagan, "The English Inquisition: Constitutional Conflict and Ecclesiastical Law in the 1590s" (2004) 47 The Historical Journal 541, 544–565.

[75] Cosin (n 74) 129.

[76] "Proceedings in a Conference at Hampton Court" in 2 *St Tr* 69–92 (1604). Discussed by Levy (n 38) 210–213.

The Archbishop sought to refute the charge: "Your lordship is deceived in the manner of proceeding; for, if the Article touch the party for life, liberty, or scandal, he may refuse to answer[.]"[77]

Given the passionate division of opinion about the oath *ex officio* and its relation to self-incrimination, it is not surprising that the Commons felt itself in need of clarification concerning the matter. In 1607, the Privy Council, upon a motion of Commons, requested Sir Edward Coke, Chief Justice of the Court of Common Pleas, and Sir John Popham, Chief Justice of the King's Bench, to advise "in what cases the Ordinary may examine any person *ex officio* upon oath."[78] Coke and Popham answered, first, that a suspected person must be informed of the charges against him before being asked to take an oath:

> The Ordinary cannot constrain any man, ecclesiastical or temporal, to swear generally to answer to such interrogatories as shall be administered unto him; but ought to deliver to him the articles upon which he is to be examined to the intent that he may know whether he ought by the law to answer to them.

As Coke observed, such adequate notice of charges was "the course of the Star Chamber and Chancery."

Secondly, Coke emphasized that, even when examinations under an oath *ex officio* were permissible, there was a boundary to what questions were permissible:

> No man, ecclesiastical or temporal shall be examined upon the secret thoughts of his heart, or of his secret opinion: but something ought to be objected against him what he hath spoken or done.[79]

This view faithfully reflected the core of the *nemo tenetur* maxim as it had been understood from its first recorded mention in canon law.[80] It applied to non-public crimes. Coke wrote that, because issues of heresy and faith belonged quintessentially to the internal forum, "the ecclesiastical judge ought not to examine the *partem ream* (suspect party) upon their oath: for as a civilian said, that this was *inventio diaboli ad destruendas miserorum animas ad infernum* [an invention of the devil for casting the souls of the wretched into hell]."[81]

As to whether an *ex officio* oath could be imposed where there was no probable cause for initiating an ecclesiastical inquisition, Coke held that:

---

[77] 2 *St Tr* 86.

[78] "Of Oaths Before an Ecclesiastical Judge *Ex Officio*" (n 62).

[79] Ibid. An exception to the bar against imposing oaths on lay persons existed for cases of matrimony and testamentary matters. "And the reason that the ecclesiastical judge shall examine them in these two cases, is for this, that contracts of matrimony, and the estates of the dead, are many times secret; and they do not concern the shame and infamy of the party, as adultery, incontinency, usury-, simony, hearing of mass, heresy, &c." Ibid.

[80] See text to n 21 in ch 5.

[81] In support of his opinion, Coke cited *Leigh* and *Hynde*. He expressed the fear that uneducated laymen might be "inveigled and entrapped" into incriminating themselves. 77 Eng Rep 1308–1309.

it is not reasonable that any Ordinary upon suspicion conceived of his own fancy without due accusation or presentment should put any subject of this realm in infamy and slander of heresy, to the peril of his life, loss of good name or goods.[82]

Just as Coke and Popham were answering Parliament's questions, Nicholas Fuller (1543–1620),[83] an ardent defender of Puritans, appeared as counsel in 1607 on behalf of two Puritans, Richard Maunsell and Thomas Ladd.[84] The High Commission had imprisoned both for religious offenses. Without being permitted to see the charges against them before they were sworn, both had refused the oath *ex officio* to answer questions truthfully, as the Commission had demanded. Fuller sought to restrain the High Commission on a writ of *habeas corpus* granted by the King's Bench. Fuller's argument, much like Morice's, sought to delegitimize the compelled oath altogether.[85] Fuller interpreted Magna Carta's c 29 to buttress his argument. Such use of the chapter was striking in Fuller's day and foreshadowed its further emergence after the chapter had been largely dormant since 1225. Fuller maintained against the High Commission that

the laws of England did so much regard and preserve the liberty of the subjects, as that none should be imprisoned, *nisi per legale iudicium parium suorum aut legem terrae*, as it is said in *Magna Charta cap. 29* which Charter, by divers other statutes after, is confirmed, with such strong enforcements in some of them, as to make void such statutes, as should be contrary to *Magna Charta*.[86]

In additional support of his attack on the oath, Fuller reached further into the common law. He instanced the example of prospective jurors challenged on *voir dire*. It was long-accepted law, he said, that at common law jurors could not be forced to answer questions that lessened their credibility or threatened a loss because *nemo tenetur prodere seipsum*.[87] Again employing the common law to subvert the High Commission, Fuller claimed the Commission's proceedings were contrary to the due process statute of 42 Edw III, c 3, which provided that "no man may be put to answer

---

[82] Ibid 1309. An ecclesiastical judge could initiate an inquisitorial proceeding in response to a person bringing a complaint (procedure *ex officio promoto*) or purely on his own authority (*ex officio mero*). It was this latter procedure initiated on the suspicions or knowledge of a judge alone that was the target of Coke's remark. See Macnair, *Law of Proof* (n 28) 79–80. Coke was quoting Henry VIII's Heresy Act, 25 Hen VIII, c 14 (1533–1534), 3 Stat Realm 454, which restrained ordinaries from initiating inquisitions on the basis of their mere suspicions.

[83] For biography of Fuller, see Stephen Wright, "Fuller, Nicholas" in *ODNB* (n 51).

[84] On *Maunsell and Ladd*, see Baker (n 41) 356–363; Levy (n 38) 233–238.

[85] Nicholas Fuller, *The Argument of Master Nicholas Fuller, in the Case of Thomas Lad, and Richard Maunsell, His Clients Wherein It is Plainly Proved, that the Ecclesiasticall Commissioners Haue no Power, by Vertue of Their Commission, to Imprison, to Put to the Oath Ex Officio, or to Fine Any of His Maiesties subiects* (imprinted at William Jones's secret press 1607) 11. For analysis of Fuller's argument, see Charles M Gray, "Self-Incrimination in Interjurisdictional Law: The Sixteenth and Seventeenth Centuries" in Helmholz, *Privilege* (n 23) 70–77; Baker (n 41) 356–363; Levy (n 38) 232–239.

[86] Fuller (n 85) 5.

[87] "And to prove the old law of England to be so, the ordinary case of daily experience, touching the challenge of jurors, doth sufficiently declare . . . [I]f the challenge do tend to touch the juror in any way in his credit, or loss, he shall not be forced upon his oath to answer, although his answer might tend to further justice, *quia nemo tenetur seipsum prodere*." Ibid 10.

without presentment before Iustices, or thing of Record, or by due process and writ original according to the old law of the land."[88]

Besides transgressing the common-law protections, Fuller argued, the oath *ex officio* "to force a man in a criminal cause to accuse himself, was directly against the rule of the law of God," citing scriptural texts that required proof by witnesses.[89] Fuller said that "without any witness or accuser to establish the matter, upon the inforced oath of the partie, hath no coherence with the rule of Gods law."[90] He turned to the trial of St Paul in support:

> *Felix* the governor of the Jews under the Emperor, when Paul the Apostle was brought before him, said to Paul that he would hear him, when his accusers were come; holding it as unjust, without an accuser, to charge him.[91]

Indeed, the oath *ex officio* violated not just divine law, but "hath no coherence with the law of nature"[92] and the law of nations.[93]

Like Coke, Fuller maintained that the Commission had no authority to force defendants "to answer upon suspicion conceaved upon the fantasye of the Ordinaries," that is, without probable cause manifested through reliable *fama* or other indicia.[94]

Fuller's attack on the High Commission, which he also made in parliament, caused such consternation that the High Commission ordered his imprisonment. In 1608, after printed copies of his argument were seized, Star Chamber charged him with sedition, but he was later permitted to resume the practice of law.

Conclusions Regarding Self-incrimination in England prior to the Late Seventeenth Century

The canonical rule against self-incrimination could offer limited protection to defendants and witnesses in those courts influenced by romano-canonical procedures. In Chancery, the rule was applied in civil cases to parties and witnesses. Star Chamber acknowledged the protection as it applied to self-incriminating answers involving felonies. Before the High Commission and ecclesiastical courts, *nemo tenetur* imposed restraints on self-incrimination, even though broad exceptions weakened the protection. Yet, where no probable cause justified a judge in imposing the oath, or where

---

[88] Ibid 10. The oath, Fuller argued, conflicted even with the very statute that established the High Commission. 1 Eliz 1, c 1 required witnesses at the time of arraignment to be brought face to face to declare what they had to say against the party arraigned. Fuller (n 85) 32.

[89] Fuller (n 85) 11. See Deut 19:15; Mt 18:16; 2 Cor 13:1.

[90] Fuller (n 85) 11.

[91] Ibid 12.

[92] Ibid. For a study of the place of the law of nature in the courts of the *ius commune*, of England, and of the United States, see RH Helmholz, *Natural Law in Court: A History of Legal Theory in Practice* (Harvard University Press 2015); RH Helmholz, "Natural Law and Human Rights in English Law: From Bracton to Blackstone" (2005) 3 Ave Maria L Rev 1; RH Helmholz, "Natural Human Rights: The Perspective of the Ius Commune" (2003) 52 Cath U L Rev 301.

[93] Fuller (n 85) 12, citing Trajan's letter to Pliny the Younger forbidding anonymous accusations.

[94] Ibid 9.

questioning might force witnesses or defendants to reveal their hidden crimes or other matters tending to their disgrace, the rule had force, shielding them against having to answer. It is noteworthy that all parties and witnesses testified under oath in those courts. Protection against self-incrimination was associated with having to incriminate oneself *under oath*.

Defendants in the common-law jury courts, however, did not give their statements under oath. None of the controversy surrounding the oath *ex officio* directly touched the conduct of their trials. The arguments that Morice and Fuller aimed against the oath *ex officio* would have been moot in a jury court. Defendants there did not have to face the psychological and moral dilemma the oath could trigger. They had no need to balance the salvation of their souls against their freedom and earthly welfare. Defendants before a jury faced a practical dilemma rather than a moral one. They had to weigh any refusal to speak against the likely loss of the opportunity to defend themselves.

While *nemo tenetur* was not a rule birthed in the jury courts, knowledge of the rule did not remain sealed up within the non-jury courts where it was acknowledged. Trials in all courts were public events. Lay audiences, parties, and witnesses at proceedings in courts influenced by romano-canonical procedure had the opportunity to learn of the principle against self-incrimination, at least in a general way. The *nemo tenetur* principle would have been known, as well, among those common-law judges who sat in the Court of Star Chamber. Relationships across the legal community offered further conduits.[95] Doctors of the civil law conversed with common lawyers.[96] The libraries of some common lawyers, including that of Sir Edward Coke, held Continental law books, which likely contained the rule.[97] Coke cited the principle himself using canonical phrases.[98] In the context of common-law pretrial investigation, manuals for justices of the peace repeated the *nemo tenetur* maxim, even while the Marian statutes existed in tension with it. Trials of prominent defendants before the High Commission and Star Chamber may well have contributed to a public mentality that compelling persons to betray themselves by their own words

[95] Exchanges of ideas between common lawyers and civilians took place. RH Helmholz observes: "Meetings between ecclesiastical and common lawyers, held to work out lawyers' problems, were not infrequent in Tudor and Stuart England. The 'Doctors of the Arches' appeared with some regularity in the common law courts, called there to answer questions about the Roman canon law that were pertinent to doubtful cases.[fn omitted] They were listened to with respect, though not always with agreement. Informal discussions also occurred . . . Regular discussion among professionals requires listening, and listening can lead to the exchange of ideas." RH Helmholz, *Roman Canon Law in Reformation England* (CUP 1990) 190. See also Helmholz, "Privilege and the Ius Commune" (n 23) 45 & n 139; RH Helmholz, "Continental Law and Common Law: Historical Strangers or Companions" (1990) 1990 Duke LJ 1207, 1215.

[96] David J Seipp, "The Reception of Canon Law and Civil Law in the Common Law Courts before 1600" (1993) 13 Oxford J Legal Stud 388, 390.

[97] The library of Sir Edward Coke, for example, contained many *ius commune* texts, including Gratian's Decretum, the decretals of Gregory IX and of Boniface VIII, Justinian's Digest and Code, Cosin's *Apologie*, the canons of the Church, the rules of civil law, and a lexicon and opinions of both canon and secular law. See WO Hassall (ed), *A Catalogue of the Library of Sir Edward Coke* (Yale University Press 1950) 38–41; Helmholz, *Privilege* (n 23) 222 n 141. "[T]he last quarter of the sixteenth century and the first third of the seventeenth was an 'age of flourishing canonical and civilian scholarship,' comparable to that of the twelfth century." Helmholz, *Reformation* (n 95) 49.

[98] See Coke's opinion in *Burrowes et al against the High Commission Court*, 81 Eng Rep 42, 3 Bulstrode 49 (1616); *Roy v Dighton et al*, 81 Eng Rep 445, 1 Rolle 220 (1616).

offended a sense of fairness in proceedings, at least when an imposed oath coerced one to tell the truth.[99] Morice and Fuller, on behalf of puritans,[100] had argued as much from divine law and the law of nature and from implications of Magna Carta and Edward III's "due process statutes."[101] The target of their arguments was the oath *ex officio*. It was not their purpose at the time to apply their arguments to unsworn statements, such as those that parties could make at criminal common-law trials. But if, as Morice and Fuller (and Lambarde) maintained, proof ought to be produced from prosecution witnesses and not twisted out of defendants' own mouths, why should *nemo tenetur seipsum prodere* not protect against defendants' unsworn incriminating statements, as well as sworn ones? In short, why should the oath not drop out of the self-incrimination calculus all together?[102]

---

[99] Macnair, "Privilege" (n 28) 84. "[S]eventeenth century common lawyers inhabited much the same 'mental universe' as the civilians in the matter of self-incrimination." Ibid.

[100] The role of puritans in reviving the significance of Magna Carta is discussed in Baker (n 41) 255–261. See also, cited by Baker, Faith Thompson, *Magna Carta: Its Role in the Making of the English Constitution, 1300–1629* (University of Minnesota Press 1948) 144, 198.

[101] "[T]he most striking feature of counsels' argument is their successful attempt to show that the common law contained 'a privilege against self-incrimination' in a sense specific enough to manage. They argued from Magna Carta and the law of nature." Charles M Gray, "Prohibitions and the Privilege against Self-Incrimination" in Delloyd J Guth and John McKenna (eds), *Tudor Rule and Revolution: Essays for G R Elton from His American Friends* (CUP 1982) 362.

[102] Richard Helmholz observes that men and women of the time did not think to apply the rule against self-incriminatory oaths to unsworn, as well as to sworn, statements. Helmholz, *Privilege* (n 23) 12.

10

Weaknesses of Defensive Safeguards in the Sixteenth and Seventeenth Centuries

A Note on Trial Reports

Apart from Thomas Smith's account of a hypothetical common-law trial set out in *De republica anglorum*, knowledge of trial procedure in the Tudor and Stuart periods derives principally from unofficial reports based on contemporary manuscripts[1] and pamphlets that private persons composed. Those narratives subsequently supplied the basis for the *State Trials* series, first compiled and published in 1719.

The *State Trials* focus predominantly on treason cases. These cases were unusual in several regards.[2] Not infrequently, they entailed political matters and passionately held religious convictions in an age when religion and politics intertwined. Unlike the case in ordinary trials, in treason trials, the government itself, and not private parties, undertook the prosecutions, with the crown appointing prosecutors to represent royal interests.[3] The crown's prosecuting agents engaged in extensive pretrial examinations of suspects, sometimes using torture, to produce depositions from them and from other potential witnesses for use at trial. Commissions appointed by the crown presided over the trials. Pressure from the crown may have affected the exercise of judicial discretion. That pressure may have compromised the independence of jurors. Particularly, in the later Stuart period, some verdicts proved to be clearly untrustworthy.[4] Given the important issues at stake in the exercise of state power against individuals of great prominence, the trials received widespread public attention.

---

[1] See, eg, Theodorus Varax's prefatory note to his account of the 1649 trial of John Lilburne: "being exactly penned and taken in Short-Hand, as it was possible to be done in such a Crowd and Noise, and Transcribed with an Indifferent and Even Hand, both in Reference to the Court, and the Prisoner; that so Matter of Fact, as it was there Declared, might truly come to Publick View." To this statement, Lilburn himself added a declaration, dated November 28, 1649, hardly more than a month after the close of the trial, confirming that he had read Varax's "discourse" and that it was accurate. John Lilburne and Clement Walker, *The Tryal of Lieutenant Colonel John Lilburn . . . October 1649 by Theodorus Varax* (2nd edn, printed for H Hills 1710) [np].

[2] See John H Langbein and others (eds), *The History of the Common Law: The Development of Anglo-Saxon Legal Institutions* (Aspen Publishers; Wolters Kluwer Law and Business 2009) 606; John H Langbein, *The Origins of Adversary Criminal Trial* (OUP 2003, reprint 2005) 14. For cautions concerning possible deficiencies of the reports, see John H Langbein, "The Criminal Trial before the Lawyers" (1978) 45 U Chi L Rev 263, 264–267; George Fisher, "The Jury's Rise as Lie Detector" (1997) 107 Yale LJ 575, 602–603. In addition to Smith's account of the jury trial, Sir John Baker discovered a brief description of sixteenth-century trial procedure in an unprinted manuscript, *Modus intrandi deliberationem gaole*. Baker observes: "Little is known of the courtroom procedure used at a trial on indictment before Tudor times . . . but the procedure described in the sixteenth century had quite probably been in use for at least a century and perhaps longer." John H Baker, 6 *Oxford History of the Laws of England* (OUP 2004) (12 vols) 509.

[3] On the late emergence of the public prosecutor at ordinary trials, see John H Langbein, "The Origins of Public Prosecution at Common Law" (1973) 17 Am J Legal Hist 313.

[4] Langbein and others (n 2) 648–659.

Foundations of American Criminal Due Process at Trial. Francis R. Herrmann and Brownlow M. Speer,
Oxford University Press. © Oxford University Press 2025. DOI: 10.1093/9780199364770.003.0010

Although the exceptional aspects of the state trials must be borne in mind when reading the trial reports, the common-law customs governing the conduct of state trials were the same as those at ordinary felony trials.[5] With those cautions in mind, the state trials can offer vivid illustrations of the common law's lack of robust procedural protections. The account following here will make reference to and draw distinctions from ordinary trials where relevant. Besides the illustrative value they offer, state trials are uniquely important for two further reasons. It was they, rather than non-treason felony trials, that provided an impetus for legislative procedural reform at the close of the seventeenth century. Secondly, through their being memorialized, many of the state trials entered into and "became part of England's political memory,"[6] a memory that British colonists would inherit.

Impediments to Full Defense at Criminal Trials under Tudor and Stuart Monarchs

No assistance of counsel as to matters of fact at felony trials by indictment

According to customary legal thinking in the sixteenth century, the intrusion of counsel into a felony trial brought by indictment impeded the discovery of truth. Truth would best emerge from the spontaneous "altercation" of the parties. Consequently, no counsel was permitted to assist defendants at treason or ordinary felony trials by indictment as to matters of fact.[7] Edward Coke approvingly set out the thinking of the day:

> Where any person is indicted of treason or felony and pleadeth to the Treason or felony, not guilty, which goeth to the fact best known to the party; it is holden that the party in that case shall have no councel to give in evidence, or alledge any matter for him.[8]

---

[5] Langbein comments: "The major treason trials preserved in the State Trials differed from ordinary criminal trials in various respects, especially in having prosecution counsel, but they share the dynamic of Sir Thomas Smith's altercation-style trial." Langbein, *Adversary Trial* (n 2) 15; John Langbein, "The Criminal Trial before the Lawyers" (1978) 45 U Chi L Rev 263, 266; William Staunford, *Les Plees del Coron* (PR Glazebrook ed, np, Richard Tottell 1557, photo reprint Professional Books Ltd 1971) (not different in kind) 587.

[6] Barbara J Shapiro, *Political Communication and Political Culture in England, 1558–1688* (Stanford University Press 2012) 264. For an account of the process of composing the *State Trial* volumes, along with commentary on prominent Stuart trials, see Brian Cowan and Scott Sowerby (eds), *The State Trials and the Politics of Justice in Later Stuart England* (The Boydell Press 2021).

[7] But counsel was permitted in "appeals," that is, prosecutions conducted by appellors (usually victims or their kin) and in misdemeanors. In addition, in cases of felony indictment, where prosecution was by the crown, the restriction on counsel did not prevent lawyers from assisting defendants outside of trial and in preparation for trial.

[8] 3 Co Inst 3, 137.

Judges, in their discretion, might permit counsel's assistance on questions of law, but it was the defendant who had to identify the question. Not surprisingly, that task was beyond the capacity of most defendants.[9]

Although the rationale limiting counsel was routinely accepted, it was the subject of criticism in the early sixteenth century. In *Doctor and Student* (1530), a set of dialogues between a doctor of divinity and a student of the laws of England, the Doctor questions whether the English law is not unreasonable in prohibiting counsel in felony cases. The student admits it would be "a great unreasonableness" to put a person in jeopardy of his life without counsel; but, by "a great favour of the law," the judges will protect defendants against mispleading and, in cases of indictment, the king's justices "shall help forth the offenders according to the truth as far as reason and justice may suffer."[10] Thus, the common law is "saved from the stain of unreasonableness."[11]

The denial of the assistance of counsel was a primary and frequent complaint of the defendants. When the Duke of Norfolk requested counsel to advise him on answering the indictment against him, the Lord Chief Justice told him "that in case of High-Treason he cannot have counsel allowed: and that he was to answer to his own fact only, which he himself best knew, and might without counsel sufficiently answer."[12] Custom charged the judges themselves with aiding defendants in understanding the law and protecting them against abuse. Compelled to defend without counsel on factual matters, defendants faced a further disadvantage that could give the prosecution an upper hand: the crown could designate official prosecutors to represent its interests both as to matters of fact and law, whereas defendants had to rely on themselves as to fact.

Defendants chafed under the exclusion of the assistance of counsel in factual matters along with the uncertainty of a judge granting them assistance as to legal issues.[13] The Duke of Norfolk complained at trial in 1572:

[9] A fortunate defendant might have had family, friends, and other supporters who could have paid for legal advice.

[10] Christopher Saint German and William Muchall, *The Doctor and Student: Or, Dialogues between a Doctor of Divinity and a Student in the Laws of England, Containing the Grounds of Those Laws Together with Questions and Cases Concerning the Equity Thereof* (R Clarke 1886) (Second dialogue) 256–259.

[11] For a positive assessment of the role of judge as counsel for defendants, see David J Cairns, *Advocacy and the Making of the Criminal Trial, 1800–1865* (Clarendon Press 1998) 27–28; Douglas Hay, "Property, Authority, and the Criminal Law" in Douglas Hay, *Albion's Fatal Tree: Crime and Society in Eighteenth Century England* (Allen Lane 1975) (describing the extreme solicitude of judges for the rights of the accused) 17, 32, 33. See also David J Seipp, *Legal History: The Year Books, Medieval English Legal History, an Index and Paraphrase of Printed Year Book Reports, 1268–1535*, https://www.bu.edu/law/faculty-scholarship/legal-history-the-year-books/. 1321.124ss (judge advises woman who claimed self-defense to plead not guilty; convicted and hanged), cited in Sara M Butler, *Pain, Penance, and Protest: Peine forte et dure in Medieval England* (CUP 2022) 124.

[12] "Duke of Norfolk's Trial," 1 *St Tr* (hereafter "Norfolk") 957, 965. On the likely ineptitude of many felons to make their own defense, Langbein comments: "The fallacy in this reasoning was the assumption that because the accused may have been close to the events, he is therefore adept at explaining the circumstances of his own conduct, or at cross-examining the testimony of mistaken or malevolent accusers." Langbein, *Adversary Trial* (n 2) 34.

[13] The absence of counsel "caused more criticism than nearly every other feature of the English criminal trial." John G Bellamy, *The Tudor Law of Treason: An Introduction* (Routledge and K Paul, University of Toronto Press 1979) 142. "The worst defect was that, in capital cases, the defendant was not allowed counsel except to argue a point of law—which had to be specified first." John H Baker, *Collected Papers on English Legal History* (CUP 2013) 937.

I have had very short warning to provide to answer so great a matter; I have not found fourteen hours in all, both day and night, and now neither hear the same statute alleged and yet I am put at once to the whole herd of laws, not knowing which particularity to answer unto. The indictment containeth sundry points and matters to touch me by circumstance . . . therefore with reverence and humble submission I am led to think I may have counsel . . . I am hardly handled, I have had short warning, and no books; neither Book of Statutes, nor so much as the Breviate of Statutes. I am brought to fight without a weapon.[14]

But Dyer, as chief justice, answered: "[A]ll our books do forbid allowing of counsel in the point of treason; but only it is to be answered guilty or not guilty."[15] (The same rule applied to ordinary felony trials by indictment.) Hampered, Norfolk sought to present his defense to the jury as best he could: "I am unlearned, unable to speak, and worst of all to speak for myself."[16] The Puritan John Udall (1560–1592/3) likewise sought counsel in 1590 but was denied.[17] Any ordinary felon would have met with the same denial.

At the forefront of his procedural demands at his treason trial in 1649, John Lilburne pleaded for the appointment of counsel along with other safeguards:

I desire nothing but Council and a little time to consult with them, and to produce my Witnesses and a Copy of my indictment; if not, I am willing to die as the Object of your Indignation and Malice, do your will and pleasure.[18]

Upon the judge telling him "if the matter is proved, there needs no counsel," Lilburne tartly responded, "Sir, by your favor, it may be too late to desire counsel after the fact is proved."[19]

Robert Persons (Parsons) (1546–1610), a Jesuit priest who previously had been a fellow and tutor at Oxford,[20] maintained that the denial of counsel in England compared poorly to Continental practice:

And for England it is evident that divers points of our Common Law, . . . touching life and death . . . do favour much of tyranny and seem to be against not only all laws of other countries, but also against very reason and justice it self, and against all law of nature also; which law of nature doth permit to every man a just and reasonable defence of life and innocency . . . But in England it seemeth that the defence it self is taken away, or at least the true liberty, means, and possibility thereof. For how is it possible, for example sake, that a man standing at the bar for his tryal upon life and

---

[14] "Norfolk" (n 12) 965–966.
[15] Ibid 966.
[16] Ibid 969.
[17] "Trial of John Udall," 1 *St Tr* (hereafter "Udall") 1271, 1277.
[18] "Trial of Lieut. Col. John Lilburne," 4 *St Tr* (hereafter "Lilburne") 1269, 1309.
[19] Ibid 1313.
[20] For biography of Persons, see Victor Houliston, "Persons [Parsons], Robert," in David Cannadine (ed), *Oxford Dictionary of National Biography* (hereafter *ODNB*) (OUP 2004). See generally Victor Houliston, *Catholic Resistance in Elizabethan England: Robert Persons's Jesuit Polemic, 1580–1610* (Ashgate; Institutum Historicum Societatis Iesu 2007).

death, feared on the one side with terrour of that may happen unto him; and on the other side, astonished with the sight of such a court and company set against him, and with the many accusations, exaggerations, and amplifications of the Prince's attorneys, and other officers that pleas against him: how is it possible, I say, that such a man, especially if he is bashful, and unlearned, in so short a time, as there is allotted him for answering for his life without help of a lawyer, proctor, or other man, that may direct, counsel, or assist him in such an agony; how can he see all the parts or points that may be alleged for his defence, being never so innocent?

The Imperial Laws confirmed by Justinian, and other Emperors, after many hundred years of proof, and received by all Christian nations saving ours, do allow to every man that is accused for his life, all lawful and reasonable means of defence, with sufficient time and deliberation for the same.[21]

Likewise protesting against the denial of counsel in England, Sir Edwin Sandys alluded to Continental practice when he moved in parliament in 1607:

that the Scotchmen treyyd in England shold have advocats and counsell to plead for them alledging the hardness of our lawes in that point in regard of all the lawes of christendom and howe in Venice the most Eminent persons tooke upon them that office to defend such as were accused of Capitale cryimes wherin he seem he wold wish that liberty permitted all over England. But that was answered by Mr. Atturney to be the removing of a corner stone and soe it was put off to the tyme when ther shold be a tretying of the conformitye of lawes of both Kingdomes.[22]

In his Institutes of the Laws of England, Sir Edward Coke undertook to justify the English practice of denying counsel to the defense as to matters of fact:

And after the plea of not guilty, the prisoner can have no counsel learned assigned to him to answer the king's counsel learned, nor to defend him. And the reason thereof is, not because it concerneth matter of fact . . . but the true reasons of the law in this case are: First, that the testimonies and the proofs of the offence ought to be so clear and manifest, as there can be no defence of it. Secondly, the court ought to be in stead of counsel for the prisoner.[23]

---

[21] Robert Persons, *The Jesuit's Memorial of the Reformation of England under the First Popish Prince Published from the Copy Presented to the Late King James II* (Richard Chiswel 1690) 248–249. Edward Coke wrote that the Jesuits slandered the law because, in fact, counsel as to questions of law was allowed by permission of court.

[22] Robert Bowyer, *The Parliamentary Diary of Robert Bowyer, 1606–1607* (The University of Minnesota Press; H Milford, OUP 1931) 307. "For reasons that are not wholly clear," Continental writers in the sixteenth century "opened the gates a little wider to the admission of lawyers in criminal causes, and English lawyers followed their lead." RH Helmholz, *Roman Canon Law in Reformation England* (CUP 1990) 118. The predictable result of admitting lawyers (proctors) in church courts was increased objections to the imposition of oaths without the required probable cause (*fama*). Ibid 119.

[23] 3 Co Inst 29. Langbein observes that paradoxically "the ostensibly high standard of proof, intended as a safeguard for the accused, was effectively turned against him, and used as a justification for denying him counsel." Langbein, *Adversary Trial,* (n 2) 33.

The reassurance that no innocent person could possibly be convicted, or that judge would be solicitous, may have sounded hollow to an accused person trying to defend himself. In any case, the defendants continued to complain and to insist that they be represented by counsel, just as the prosecution was.

Inadequate opportunity to prepare for trial

By established custom, criminal defendants in common-law courts were not permitted to receive any copy of their indictments in advance of trial.[24] At trial, a defendant would only hear the indictment read. Often, details were set out at great length. He could not obtain a copy.[25] As a rationale for keeping the indictment from the accused before trial, contemporary legal thinking held that truth would best emerge if the altercation between prosecution and defense took place spontaneously.[26] At times, persons accused received notice that their trial would begin only a few hours beforehand.[27] Defendants might not even know under what statute they were charged, nor what specific acts or words were alleged against them. The Duke of Norfolk (1571), unsure under which treason act he was indicted, had to ask the court for clarification. He expostulated, "I was told before I came here, that I was indicted upon the Statute of 25th Edw. 3d."[28]

Sir Walter Raleigh was caught in similar straits at his trial in 1603. Although the clerk read out the accusation against him, Raleigh had no written copy of the lengthy indictment. He protested that at least two witnesses were required to prove guilt of treason and that, under Elizabethan statutes, they had to be brought face to face with the accused at the arraignment.[29] But the Chief Justice told him that statutes requiring two witnesses had been repealed.[30]

In 1649, John Lilburne (1615?–1657), a committed supporter of the Puritan cause who enjoyed broad public support, was accused under a newly enacted treason statute of authoring *The Second Part of England's New Chains*. Parliament deemed the tract a treasonable attack impugning the government.[31] The lieutenant of the Tower where Lilburne was held in custody had, in fact, shown him a copy of the lengthy

[24] Donald Veall, *The Popular Movement for Law Reform, 1640–1660* (Clarendon Press 1970) 18; Langbein, *Adversary Trial* (n 2) 27, 51 n 198. In contrast, a copy of the articles was provided in the prerogative courts, consistent with *ius commune* procedure. Ibid 22.

[25] Indictments were composed in Latin, but translated for the defendant at arraignment. Langbein, *Adversary Trial* (n 2) 51 n 198.

[26] Bellamy, *Treason* (n 13) 143–144. See also Veall (n 24) 18 (supplying copy of indictment might allow defendant to take advantage of technical errors, or waste court time, or be acquitted).

[27] Bellamy, *Treason* (n 13) 137, citing, eg, "Storey's Trial," 1 *St Tr* 1091 (1571), where the defendant protested that he had been informed at 7 AM that his arraignment and trial would begin that same day.

[28] "Norfolk" (n 12) 965–966, 971.

[29] "Raleigh's Trial," 2 *St T* (hereafter "Raleigh") 1, 15 (1603).

[30] Ibid.

[31] For biography of Lilburne, see Andrew Sharp, "Lilburne, John" in *ODNB* (n 20); Michael Braddick, *The Common Freedom of the People: John Lilburne and the English Revolution* (OUP 2018); MA Gibb, *John Lilburne, the Leveller: A Christian Democrat* (Lindsay Drummond 1947); Pauline Gregg, *Free-born John: A Biography of John Lilburne* (George G Harrap & Co 1961). For modern commentary on Lilburne's trials, see Leonard W Levy, *Constitutional Opinions: Aspects of the Bill of Rights* (OUP 1986) 14–39; Leonard W Levy, *The Origins of the Fifth Amendment* (2nd edn, Macmillan Publishing Co 1986) 266–332.

indictment, but it was written in Latin. Neither Lilburne nor the lieutenant could understand it.[32] At trial, Lilburne complained:

> And truly, Sir, I heard but by uncertain common fame of my trial now. Some parliament men told my wife and friends that my chiefest crime was corresponding with the Prince; and to defend my self against that, I fitted my self, never dreaming that only Books should be laid to my charge, and therefore I could not as to that come prepared: and therefore do humbly desire counsel, a copy of my Indictment, and time to bring in my witnesses.[33]
>
> My prosecutors have had time enough to consult with counsel of all sorts and kinds to destroy me, yea, with yourselves, and I have not had any time at all, not knowing in the least what you would charge upon me, and therefore could provide no defence for that which I knew not what it would be.[34]

State trials, and ordinary trials all the more so, could be rushed affairs. There was little or no delay from indictment to arraignment, from arraignment to trial, and from the beginning of the trial to its conclusion.[35] A grand jury indicted Thomas More on June 28, 1535, for high treason. On July 1, he was arraigned and had the contents of the indictment read to him for the first time. He was, he said, "scarcely able to remember a third of the things that were objected against him."[36] Having pled not guilty, More was tried by jury. After no more than fifteen minutes of deliberation, the jury found him guilty. The court sentenced him to death. The entire procedure from arraignment to sentence took place in one day.[37] Raleigh's jury in 1603 likewise retired for only fifteen minutes before returning a verdict of guilt.

No guarantee of confrontation with opposing witnesses

Hearsay witnesses were allowed, although a jury might give their testimony less credit. This was true at ordinary trials where no two-witness rule applied. It was even true at treason trials despite the language of statutes that appeared to require the presence of two prosecution witnesses. The prosecution could resort to using a hearsay witness to fulfill the mandates of such statutes. In 1554, the judges in *Thomas* interpreted the two-accuser provision of 5 & 6 Edw VI, c 11, to mean "if one be an accuser of his own

---

[32] "Lilburne" (n 18) 1284.

[33] Ibid 1312.

[34] Ibid 1307.

[35] See RB Pugh, "The Duration of Criminal Trials in Medieval England" in EW Ives and AH Manchester (eds), *Law, Litigants and the Legal Profession* (Royal Historical Society; Humanities Press Inc 1983) 104–110; JG Bellamy, *The Criminal Trial in Later Medieval England: Felony before the Courts from Edward I to the Sixteenth Century* (University of Toronto Press 1998) 110, 113–115; Langbein, *Adversary Trial* (n 2) 16–25.

[36] Henry Ansgar Kelly and others (eds), *Thomas More's Trial by Jury: A Procedural and Legal Review with a Collection of Documents* (Boydell Press 2011) 198.

[37] Ibid 5. Such brief trials were typical for an ordinary criminal trial. See Pugh (n 35) 104–108; Langbein, *Adversary Trial* (n 2) 22 (often jurors did not retire to deliberation room); John H Langbein, "The Criminal Trial before the Lawyers" (1978) 45 U Chi L Rev 263, 274–275.

knowledge, or of his own hearing, and he relate it to another, the other may well be an accuser."[38] A hearsay witness, therefore, who merely repeated what an accuser had told the witness could constitute the second required "accuser." The Duke of Norfolk complained in vain that a hearsay witness was counted as one of the required two witnesses against him:

> It is said [by the prosecution] that there are two or three witnesses against me; all this two or three are but one witness: for Rodolph said it to the bishop of Ross, and of his mouth the bishop told it to Barker, and so from mouth to mouth; they are all but one witness.[39]

Crown prosecutors could also circumvent whatever face-to-face requirements there were by bringing charges under alternative treason statutes that did not contain any such requirement. Had the Duke of Norfolk in 1571 been indicted under 13 Eliz, c 1, he would have been able to rely on the statute's face-to-face requirement. Instead, he was charged under 25 Edw III which contained no such mandate.[40] The Duke protested that he had no opportunity to examine witnesses against him because the prosecution did not produce them at trial.[41] Only their depositions were read in court. "[I]f I might have had them face to face, and been allowed to bring forth my proofs, I would have brought forth direct matter and proofs, and therewith made them remember themselves."[42] So also, Edward Abington sought confrontation by relying on the Elizabethan treason statutes requiring production of at least two witnesses face to face with the accused at arraignment. But he was told, "True it is, had you been indicted on the Statute of the 1st and 13th of this queen, two Witnesses ought to have been produced; but you stand indicted by the common law, and the Statute of 25 Edw. 3 ... and in that statute is not contained any such proof."[43]

In 1590, shortly after Elizabeth's statute used the phrase "face to face," the Puritan preacher and writer John Udall (1560–1592/3)[44] was tried for seditious libel under 23 Eliz, c 2 for authoring a book that demeaned the Church of England and was offensive to Queen Elizabeth. At his trial, Udall sought to confront a prosecution hearsay declarant whose deposition was read into evidence. "My Lords, I answer thus, denying it to be his Testimony; for if it be, why is he not present to verify it face to face, according to the law?"[45] The judges

---

[38] *Thomas*, 73 Eng Rep 218, 218–219; 1 Dyer 99b–100a (1554). See Baker, 6 *Oxford History* (n 2) 518, commenting that the judges' interpretation emasculated the two-accuser requirement.

[39] "Norfolk" (n 12) 1011 (1571).

[40] Bellamy discusses the possibility that the prosecution could avoid statutes requiring confrontation. Bellamy, *Treason* (n 13) 155–156. On the prosecution's deliberate use of confusing treason statutes, see Allen D Boyer, "The Trial of Sir Walter Ralegh, the Trial of Treason and the Origins of the Confrontation Clause" (2005) 74 Miss LJ 869, 883.

[41] "I would they might, in our private Examinations, have been brought face to face with me." "Norfolk" (n 12) 1012.

[42] Ibid.

[43] "Trial of Edward Abington," 1 *St Tr* 1141, 1148 (1586).

[44] For Udall's biography, see Claire Cross, "Udall, John" in *ODNB* (n 20).

[45] "Udall" (n 17) 1271, 1281 (1590). Udall also used the phrase "face-to-face" at his arraignment. The statute required at least two prosecution witnesses to be brought face-to-face with a defendant at that point.

denied that any law required such confrontation. No witness appeared against Udall.[46]

In 1603, Raleigh complained that no witness appeared against him face to face, even though statutes appeared to require at least two.[47] He reached out to the authority of Scripture, romano-canonical principles, and the *ius commune* for support:

> [I]f by the Canon, Civil Law and God's Word, it be required, that there must be two Witnesses at the least; bear with me if I desire one.[48]

But, the Chief Justice refused to acknowledge such guarantee under the common law of England.[49] Raleigh replied that he hoped, at least, the equity of the repealed statutes remained and would supply a law for posterity.[50] "[L]et Cobham be here, let him speak it. Call my accuser before my face, and I have done."[51] Since no statute supported his claim ("You have no law for it"),[52] the judges considered Raleigh's demands for confrontation as "things of favour and grace" which "cannot be granted for then a number of Treasons would flourish: the Accuser may be drawn in practise, whilst he is in person."[53] In the same vein, Warburton, as judge, tellingly explained to Raleigh, "My lord Cobham hath, perhaps, been labored withal; and to save you, his old friend, it may be that he will deny all that which he hath said."[54] While confrontation under the common law may have been a frequent and preferred method for persuading juries of a defendant's guilt, it was clearly not assured.

No provision for defendants to summon favorable witnesses or have them testify under oath

The law did not provide accused persons any means to compel witnesses to appear on their behalf.[55] Moreover, the ability of defendants to secure by their own power

---

"[I]n case of Life," Udall said, "the Evidences ought to be pregnant, and full living witnesses (I am sure by the Word of God, and I trust also by the Law of this Land) were to have been produced Face to Face to charge me." Ibid 1299.

[46] Ibid 1299. It was Nicholas Fuller, a defender of Puritans, who advised Udall, but the court evicted Fuller for his objection to the judge's instruction. Ibid 1289.

[47] "Raleigh" (n 29) 15 (1603).

[48] Ibid 15–16.

[49] Justice Gawdy said the requirement of two witnesses was "found to be inconvenient, therefore by another law it was taken away." Ibid 18. Whether the Edwardian statute had been repealed was a disputed issue. See LM Hill, "The Two-Witness Rule in English Treason Trials: Some Comments on the Emergence of Procedural Law" (1968) 12 Am J Legal Hist 95, 95–96 (concluding it was a mistake for the justices to think the statute was repealed).

[50] "Raleigh" (n 29) 15.

[51] Ibid 16.

[52] Ibid 19.

[53] Ibid 18.

[54] Ibid.

[55] See, eg, "The Trial of Colonel James Turner" and others, 6 St Tr 565, 570 (1664) ("the law will not admit to summon any witnesses; you see when any they come against the kind, we cannot put them to their oaths, much less can we precept them to come"). On summoning defense witnesses, see Baker, 6 *Oxford History* (n 2) 509–511; Kenneth Pennington, "The Development of Criminal Procedure in England" in

the presence of favorable witnesses was severely impeded whenever a defendant was held in custody before trial.[56] Lilburne, who had been kept in prison for six months awaiting his 1649 trial, complained to his judge that he needed "time to bring them [his witnesses] in, and also subpoenas . . . some of them . . . will not come without compulsion."[57] The judge told him he could have until seven the next morning. Lilburne requested ten days, or at least eight days, to gather his witnesses, protesting that he could not have acted sooner because he did not know the charges against him. The judge refused his request.[58]

Indeed, whether defendants could present witnesses against the crown, at all, has been a subject of dispute.[59] The reliability of reports of Nicholas Throckmorton's case[60] in 1554 and John Udall's case in 1590 has been the cause of controversy. Throckmorton in his defense reportedly wanted to call one John Fitzwilliams, who is "here even now, who can testify . . . I pray you, my Lords, let him be called to depose in this matter what he can." The proffered witness drew up to the bar "and presented himself to depose his knowledge in the matter in open court." The crown's attorney objected to the witness's testifying. Throckmorton argued:

> Why should he not be suffered to tell the truth? And why be ye not so well contented to hear truth for me, as untruth against me? . . . I called him, and do humbly desire that he may speak and be heard as well as Vaughn [a witness for the prosecution], or else I am not indifferently used; especially seeing master Attorney doth so press this matter against me.[61]

Throckmorton told the court that Queen Mary herself had instructed judges that:

> notwithstanding the old error amongst you which did not admit any witness to speak or any other matter to be heard in the favour of the adversary, her majesty being

---

Joseph R Strayer and William Chester Gordon (eds), *Dictionary of the Middles Ages: Supplement I* (Charles Scribner's Sons 2004) 315; Langbein, *Adversary Trial* (n 2) 51, 53 (citing two state trials as examples) 56, 96. On the development of the compulsory process in England, see Peter Westen, "The Compulsory Process Clause" (1974) 73 Mich L Rev 73, 78–90.

[56] This was certainly a condition shared with ordinary defendants. See Langbein, *Adversary Trial* (n 2) 48, 50–51. At least, however, defendants accused of felonies other than treason rarely faced torture. The Privy Council continued to warrant pretrial examinations under torture when it deemed desirable against state trial defendants, but very rarely against ordinary felons. The Tudor treason acts that insisted on voluntary confessions could be and were circumvented. Edmund Campion was racked before trial in 1581. At Raleigh's trial in 1603, he suggested that one prosecution witness's examination was produced by the threat of torture. "[T]his poor man [Kemish] hath been close prisoner these 18 weeks; he was offered the rack to make him confess." "Was not the Keeper of the Rack sent for, and he threatened with it?" Sir W Wade responded, "When Mr. Solicitor and myself examined Mr. Kemish, we told him he deserved the Rack, but did not threaten him with it." The Commissioners appeared unconcerned: "It was more than we knew." "Raleigh" (n 29) 22. It appears that, so long as a defendant affirmed his confession in open court, it was deemed voluntary enough to comply with the statutory requirement. This was redolent of the *ius commune*'s approach to "voluntary" confession.

[57] "Lilburne" (n 18) 1312 (1649).

[58] Ibid.

[59] Baker, 6 *Oxford History* (n 2) 509.

[60] "Trial of Nicholas Throckmorton," 1 *St Tr* 869 (hereafter "Throckmorton") (1554).

[61] Ibid 884–885.

party, her highness's pleasure was that whatsoever could be brought in favour of the subject should be admitted to be heard.[62]

But Bromley, one of Throckmorton's judges, said the Queen's remark was addressed to the court of common pleas and did not apply. He told Throckmorton "you have no cause to complain, for you have been suffered to talk at your pleasure."[63] For a defendant to talk at his pleasure was, of course, quite different from having a witness testify on the accused's behalf. Nonetheless, Southwell, sitting as judge, ordered the witness to "[g]o your way ... the court hath nothing to do with you." The witness then "departed the court and was not suffered to speak."[64]

Similarly, at his trial in 1590, John Udall sought to present several witnesses in his defense. They purportedly could have contradicted an affidavit of one Thompkins that incriminated Udall:

Here are some witnesses that upon their oaths will testify, how diversely he [Thompkins] hath reported of his Confession to this thing, if it please your lordships to accept them. And the witnesses offering themselves to be heard, were answered, that because their Witness was against the queen's majesty, they could not be heard.[65]

After his conviction, Udall complained of the court's decision "that no Witnesses might be heard in my behalf, seeing it was against the queen." The ruling, he said, "seemeth strange to me; for methinks it should be for the queen, to hear all things on both sides, especially when the life of any of her subjects is in question."[66]

At his 1603 trial, Walter Raleigh encountered the same problem. He wanted to call Lord Cobham as a witness. The Lord Chief Justice, however, considered it impermissible to produce a witness against the King. "There must not such a gap be opened for the destruction of the king, as would be if we should grant this."[67]

When defense witnesses did appear, they were not permitted to present evidence under oath. In contrast, prosecution witnesses were always sworn.[68] Sir Edward Coke

---

[62] Ibid 887–888. See Bellamy, *Treason* (n 13) 161.

[63] "Throckmorton" (n 60) 888.

[64] Ibid.

[65] "Udall" (n 17) 1281.

[66] Ibid 1304. John Langbein has argued that the reports of restrictions on defense witnesses at Throckmorton's and Udall's trials "even if accurately reported, do not in my view justify inferring that a rule against defense witnesses had formed in early modern criminal procedure. Had so important a point of practice as this supposed prohibition been in effect, it would have been evidenced in the legal literature." Langbein, *Adversary Trial* (n 2) 55. Langbein also found "no evidence that a rule against defense witnesses was ever applied in a trial for ordinary felony." Ibid. On the examination and trial of John Udall, see also Levy, *Origins* (n 31) 150, 164–170.

[67] "Raleigh" (n 29) 19.

[68] John Hamilton Baker, *An Introduction to English Legal History* (4th edn, Buttersworth LexisNexis 2002) 509. "Although defence witnesses were not unknown, by the middle of the sixteenth century there seems to have been a prevailing notion—perhaps influenced by the Civil law—that witnesses ought not to give evidence to contradict clear evidence for the Crown ... The question was not settled until later in the century, and even then defence witnesses were unsworn" (citing Dalison, J, that when defense witnesses were allowed it was "always without oath"). Baker, 6 *Oxford History* (n 2) 519. As to defendants not testifying under oath, see Langbein, *Adversary Trial* (n 2) 38, 52, 96. As to prosecution witnesses testifying under oath, see ibid 51. On the critical importance of the oath, versus unsworn testimony, in the jury's assessment of credibility, see Fisher (n 2) 602–609 and passim.

believed there was no legal justification for depriving defense witnesses of the oath. In support of his position, Coke cited the authority of 4 James 1, c 1 (1606–1607). The statute assured that for certain felonies witnesses favorable to the accused could present evidence and could even do so under oath "for the better discovery of the truth" and "for the information of the consciences of the jurie and justices."[69] Coke opposed any custom to the contrary, saying that:

> as witnesses are produced and sworne against him [a defendant], so he may have witnesses produced and sworne for him, for *jurato creditur in judicio* (by having been sworn one is believed in court), and to say the truth we never read in any act of parliament, ancient author, book case, or record, that in criminall cases the party accused should not have witnesses sworne for him; and therefore there is not so much as *scintilla iuris* against it.[70]

In any event, when a judge allowed defense witnesses, their appearance depended upon the court's "grace and favor." A judge's reply to the Duke of Norfolk at his trial in 1572 indicated as much. When the Duke complained that he was not allowed to produce proofs in his favor, Burleigh, sitting as judge, told him:

> My lord, did you ever desire to have any proofs or witnesses produced for your part, to prove anything that might make for you? And were you denied? . . . I ask it, because I have not heard it reported to her majesty [Queen Elizabeth] that you made any such request, to have any special witnesses examined or proofs heard, on your part.[71]

Well after Coke's statement in favor of defense witnesses testifying under oath, the defendant Colonel Turner in 1664, indicted for felony and burglary, requested the court to summon his witnesses and have them sworn. The Lord Chief Justice told the defendant:

> We will help what the law will do, but this cannot be done; those that will come voluntarily, may; the law will not permit us to summon any witnesses; you see when they come against the king we cannot put them to their oaths, much less can we precept them to come.[72]

Sir Matthew Hale observed in his *Pleas of the Crown* (first published 1678) that "[r]egularly the evidence for the prisoner in cases capital is given without oath, tho the reason thereof is not manifest."[73] Hale adds:

---

[69] 3 Co Inst 79 (first published 1644), quoting 4 James 1, c 1 (1606–1607). For Coke's views on evidence at treason trials and his sometimes inconsistent practices, see Gerald P Bodet, "Coke's Third Institutes: A Primer for Treason Defendants" (1970) 20 U Toronto LJ 469–477.

[70] 3 Co Inst 79.

[71] "Norfolk" (n 12) 995–996.

[72] "Capt. Turner's Trial," 6 *St Tr* 570, 570 (1664).

[73] Matthew Hale, *Historia Placitorum Coronae. The History of the Pleas of the Crown II* (E and R Nutt 1736) 283.

Nay, it is manifestly against all reason, that the prisoner should not be allow'd the same liberty to make out his innocence, as is allowed to prove his guilt, and tho it has been the usual practice not to suffer witnesses for the prisoner in capital cases to be examined under oath, ... yet as Lord Coke observes ... there is not so much as a *scintilla juris* for it.[74]

In 1679, Thomas Whitebread, one of the Jesuit defendants accused of high treason in the Popish Plot cases, requested the court to have defense witnesses sworn. Chief Justice Scroggs responded: "In no capital case against the king can the witnesses for the prisoner be sworn."[75] Protesting, the defendant Gavan cited Coke's opinion that there was no reason against it. Unmoved, Justice North answered:

We know that the constant usage and practice is so, and you cannot produce any man, that in any capital case had his witnesses sworn against the king.[76]

Justice Scroggs added that Coke himself held there was no danger to a treason defendant if his witnesses were not sworn since the prosecution evidence had to be "so plain that nothing could be answered to it."[77]

No protected right against self-incrimination for criminal defendants at common law

Controversy over whether the High Commission and Star Chamber employed the oath *ex officio* properly in their proceedings was definitively mooted in 1641 when Parliament dealt a death blow to both Star Chamber and the Commission by abolishing them entirely.[78] Simultaneously, Parliament banned the use of the oath *ex officio* in all ecclesiastical courts.[79]

The abolition of the compelled oath *ex officio*, however, did not affect the questioning of common-law suspects (required by the Marian committal statutes) nor the questioning of criminal defendants at trial. Since neither suspects[80] nor defendants at

---

[74] Ibid.
[75] "Trial of Thomas Whitebread," 7 *St Tr* 311, 359 (1679).
[76] Ibid.
[77] Ibid 360.
[78] 16 Car I, cc 10–11 (1640, effective 1641).
[79] 16 Car I, c 11, s 2 (no person exercising spiritual power shall administer any corporal oath by which anyone shall be obliged "to confess or to accuse him or her selfe of any crime ... by reason whereof he or she shall or may be liable or exposed to any censure, pain, penalty or punishment whatsover"). In 1661, after the restoration of the monarchy, the ecclesiastical courts regained their criminal jurisdiction, but did not regain the oath *ex officio*. The Roman church abolished the oath *ex officio* in 1725 after a papal commission determined that the oath was a form of spiritual torture. See Eugene J Moriarty, *Oaths in Ecclesiastical Courts* (Catholic University of America 1937) 33.
[80] The widely used manuals of Fitzherbert, Lambarde, and others, written for justices of the peace in the 1500s, used the maxim *nemo tenetur seipsum prodere* only to caution justices conducting pretrial examinations against compelling criminal suspects to answer investigative questions under oath. The manuals did not apply the maxim in the context of the criminal trial itself.

trial made any statements under oath,[81] persons prosecuted under the common law never had to confront the acute moral dilemma that the oath *ex officio* had triggered. Rather, common-law defendants faced practical risks. If they did not answer a justice of the peace at pretrial investigation, their silence would be duly recorded and might be used against them at trial. If, at trial, they did not voluntarily enter into "altercation" with the prosecution, a judge might comment to the jury that the defendant was implicitly admitting the matter in issue and might be considered *pro confesso*.

Records disclose at least two prominent persons who chose to take those risks. (Perhaps, other defendants did, as well, but their cases are unreported.) In 1590, John Udall was put on trial at a common-law assize for "maliciously publishing a slanderous and infamous libel against the Queen's majesty."[82] The publications were religious books offensive to the Church of England. Udall refused at trial to answer whether he made the books alleged. He argued to the court, as he had earlier to the privy council in their pretrial investigation, that because "the thing was accounted criminal, . . . by Law I was not to answer."[83] Whether he was under oath or not, he told the trial judges, "[i]t is all one, I make a conscience of my word as of my oath, for I must give account for both."[84] It is significant that Udall insisted the law protected him against self-incrimination even when being pressed to make an unsworn statement. In effect, Udall disregarded any tie there was between the oath and self-incrimination. The salient point, he emphasized, was that the burden of proof rested on the prosecution. It was not for him to supply proof against himself. "My Lord, I answer, that according to my Indictment I am not guilty, every point whereof must be proved, or else the whole is false."[85] Udall paid a price for his intransigence. While not outrightly rejecting Udall's right to remain silent, the judge instructed the jury, "[t]he Evidences are manifest . . . that he is the author of the book."[86] Upon conviction, the court sentenced him to death. He died in prison two years later, while hoping for a royal pardon that never came.[87]

The situation had not essentially changed when the Puritan John Lilburne came to trial in 1649. Lilburne was criminally accused of treason for publishing libelous materials of a religious nature.[88] He presented to the court a panoply of procedural

---

[81] Defendants in England were forbidden to testify under oath until 1898. An Act to Amend the Law of Evidence, 61 & 62 Vict, c 36 (1898). In the United States, the first state to let criminal defendants testify under oath was Maine in 1864. Fisher (n 2) 575, 658, 668.

[82] "Udall" (n 17) 1277.

[83] Ibid 1289.

[84] Ibid 1282. Levy proposes that Udall "was probably the first defendant in a common-law trial who claimed a right against self-incrimination, at least in a capital case, even though he had been duly indicted." Levy, *Origins* (n 31) 168. Nicholas Fuller, who had attacked the *ex officio* in the High Commission, was present at Udall's trial and attempted unsuccessfully to act as counsel for him. "Udall" (n 17) 1239. Fuller may have encouraged Udall, who was no lawyer, to resist any self-incrimination. See Levy, *Origins* (n 31) 186.

[85] "Udall" (n 17) 1282.

[86] Ibid 1289.

[87] Ibid 1316.

[88] Lilburne at first refused to enter a plea. In his 1645 tract, *England's Birthright Justified*, Lilburne had addressed the problem of "whether to answer to an Indictment, when a man is demanded Guilty or not Guilty, be not a criminall Interrogatory, concerning a man's self, and so a man not by law bound Answer to it, especially seeing to a Conscientious man, who dare not lie, it is a great snare, who if he be indicted of a thing he hath done or spoken, dare not plead, Not Guilty, for feare of lying, and if he plead guilty, he shall become a self-destroyer (contrary to the law of Nature, which teacheth a man to preserve, but not

demands, including the removal of his chains; assurance the trial would be public; appointment of counsel and time to consult; a copy of the indictment; time to bring in favorable witnesses; and the right to be fully heard in his defense. At the very outset, he told Lord Keble, one of the judges: "[B]y the laws of England, I am not to answer to questions against or concerning myself."[89] The judge assured him, "You shall not be compelled."[90] When the prosecutor pressed Lilburne to admit that handwriting on the offending publication was the defendant's own, Lilburne refused to answer. "Sir, I am too old with such simple gins to be catch'd, I will cast mine eyes upon none of your papers, neither shall I answer to any questions that concerns my self."[91] The judge told him that "[y]ou may answer a question whether it be true or false and confess and glorify God." Just as Udall had, Lilburne refused to confess and insisted that the burden of proof lay on the prosecutor. "I have said, Sir, prove it, I am not to be catch'd with such Fooleries." When the crown attorney argued that Lilburne's refusal to answer was an implicit confession of guilt,[92] the defendant retorted, "Sir, I deny nothing: and what now can be I have a life to lay down for the justification of it, but prove it first."[93]

For his acquittal, Lilburne appealed to the consciences of the jury, whose satisfaction was the traditional standard for conviction. "Truly, I hope the Jury hath more conscience in them, than to go about to take away my life for giving away a single sheet and a half of paper, that no man swears I was the author of, or the cause of it to be printed and published."[94] His prosecutor looked to the same standard, arguing he had presented enough evidence "as to make it plain and clear, to your judgments and consciences" that Lilburne was guilty.[95] The judge, too, appealed to the consciences of the jury. "Therefore, my masters of the jury, look into your conscience and see what it saith unto you, which he [Lilburne] stands so much upon: The Witnesses testimonies are now plain and good in law, in this cause they are multiplied . . . you are the proper

destroy himself) in declaring that which peradventure all his Adversaries would never be able to prove against him." John Lilburne, *England's Birthright Justified* (London [s.n.] 1645) 7. James Fitzjames Stephen reflected on Lilburne's refusal: "Indeed, our own practice of calling the prisoner to plead cannot be reconciled with absolute adoption of the rule that a man is not to be questioned as to his guilt, and one of the most consistent and earliest advocates of that principle (Col. Lilburne) long refused to plead upon that very ground." James Fitzjames Stephen, 1 *A History of the Criminal Law of England* (Macmillan and Co 1883) (2 vols) 460. The grounds for Lilburne's protest may be further explained in a later pamphlet advocating law reform: "It seems to be not only against the law of God and Nature, but even of common reason to ask a prisoner at the Barr whether he be guilty or not guilty. 1. In respect that if he answer guilty, he condemns, or rather murthers himselfe, as much, if he were truly guilty, as if he were innocent. 2. If he be guilty, and answers not guilty, he tells a lye." Henry Robinson, *Certaine Considerations, in Order to a More Speedy, Cheap, and Equall Distribution of Justice throughout the Nation* (Matthew Simmons 1651) 1.

[89] "Lilburne" (n 18) 1292.

[90] Ibid 1293.

[91] Before Star Chamber in 1637, Lilburne, then twenty years old, had taken a similar stance when asked whether he would submit to the oath *ex officio*. He resisted. "The Trial of John Lilburne and John Warton for Printing and Publishing Seditious Books, in the Star Chamber," 3 *St Tr* 1315 (1637).

[92] The prosecutor remarked, "he will not own his own hand although I must desire you, gentlemen of the jury, to observe, that Mr. Lilburn implicitly confesseth it." "Lilburne" (n 18) 1269.

[93] Ibid 1341.

[94] Ibid 1384.

[95] Ibid 1332.

judges of the matter of fact, being of the country....And so in God's name, as the prisoner doth lead to your consciences, so go and do."[96]

In the event, the jury declined the prosecutor's invitation to draw an inference of guilt from Lilburne's silence. His acquittal was greeted with cheers and celebratory bonfires throughout London.[97] Fortunately, Lilburne's hazarding silence proved not to have cost him before the jury. Nonetheless, it remained true, for Lilburne and any other criminal defendant, that courts of the mid-seventeenth century, while not compelling answers, offered no shield for accused persons who declined to respond to incriminating questions, either in pretrial investigations or at trial.

At about this time, however, the originally canonical principle against self-incrimination began to make its appearance at common law in other contexts. Not surprisingly, the principle arose where witnesses were called to give sworn testimony (unlike criminal suspects and criminal defendants, who were unsworn). The principle is, first, used to enable witnesses in civil cases to avoid incriminating themselves.[98] The *Regestum Practicale* ("The Accomplish'd Lawyer") reports a court ruling in 1648 that a civil witness:

> may not be compelled to answer upon a *voire dire* touching a trespass done, for the doing whereof he may himself be liable to an action, Mich. 23 Car. B.r. For *nemo tenetur prodere seipsum*; for it is against the very Law of Nature.[99]

Chancery, influenced by roman-canon procedures, had long acknowledged this principle.[100]

In the same period, the privilege was applied to protect prosecution witnesses in a criminal case, all of whom testified under oath. At the 1649 trial of King Charles I,[101] the court spared a prosecution witness from answering "questions intended to be asked him that tended to accuse himself."[102] The trial of Sir Nathaniel Reading

---

[96] Ibid 1402. See Barbara Shapiro, *"Beyond Reasonable Doubt" and "Probable Cause": Historical Perspectives on the Anglo-American Law of Evidence* (University of California Press 1991) (tracing the movement of the English law from "satisfied conscience" standard in the time of the early jury to the development of proof "beyond reasonable doubt" in the later eighteenth century).

[97] "Lilburne" (n 18) 1405.

[98] MRT Macnair, "The Early Development of the Privilege against Self-Incrimination" (1990) 10 Oxford J Legal Stud 66, 78–79. In his study of self-incrimination, Macnair argues that limitations on self-incriminating questioning "were applied (in their general conception rather than in specific detail) by those courts which used roman-canon procedure, the church and equity courts, in the late sixteenth and early seventeenth centuries; were used as an objection to the procedure of the church courts by common lawyers; and one of them, the privilege against self-incrimination as applied to witnesses, was applied in the common law courts from the 1640s at the latest." Ibid 70. "It is only in the very late seventeenth century or early eighteenth centuries that there are signs *in the cases* of the idea of a general right to silence in the face of charges of a crime, distinctive to the common law" (emphasis in original). Ibid 67.

[99] The case is noted in William Style, *Regestum practicale, or The Practical Register of Rules... Concerning the Common-Laws, and the Practice thereof... in Matters Criminal as Civil* (printed by A.M. for Charles Adams 1657) 355. The case is cited in Macnair (n 98) 78 n 93, who points out that the case pre-dated Lilburne's 1649 trial.

[100] See *Fenton contra Blomer* (1580) and *Vice-Countess Montague* (c 1599). See text to n 28 in ch 9. This application of the privilege "to witnesses in civil trials and to allegations of crime in civil proceedings, came into English law from the common family of european laws and particularly the canon law." Macnair (n 98) 67.

[101] "The Trial of Charles Stuart, King of England," 4 *St Tr* 989 (1649).

[102] Ibid 1101.

offers another instance of the privilege protecting a prosecution witness.[103] Reading, charged with trespass and misdemeanor (and told his offense "looks rather like treason"), wanted to cross-examine a witness for the prosecution. The chief justice told the defendant, "[I]f you offer to ask him any question upon his oath, to make him accuse himself, we must oppose it . . . You shall not make him calumniate himself."[104] Judge Wild enjoined, "No, you should never object it against him to accuse himself."[105]

The same safeguarding of a sworn prosecution witness was evident in the case of Sir John Freind.[106] The prosecution wished to call Captain Porter as a witness. The defendant attempted to ask Porter whether he was a Roman Catholic. The prosecutor asked the court to intervene and protect the witness from the question. The judge, the prosecutor entreated, ought to acquaint Porter "with the danger [that by] turning Roman Catholic, he subjects himself to a very severe penalty."[107] The judge advised that "answering the question may subject him [the witness] to several penalties; at least he is liable to prosecution upon several acts of parliament that are very penal; and therefore it is by no means to be asked."[108] The very putting of the question, the Chief Justice said, would contravene the rule that "[n]o man is bound to answer any question that tends to make him accuse himself, or subject him to any penalties."[109] When consulted upon the issue, the two other judges showed no hesitation in agreeing with the Chief Justice's refusal. Treby, J. opined: "No man is bound to answer any questions that will subject him to a penalty or to infamy. If you should ask him, whether he were a deer-stealer, or whether he were a vagabond, or any other thing that will subject him to punishment, either by statute or by common-law, whether he be guilty of a petty larceny, or the like, the law does not oblige him to answer any such questions."[110]

It is worthy of note that neither in the case of the civil witness nor of the prosecution witnesses did the judges or parties or counsel make any mention of the oath as the reason for invoking protection against self-incrimination. Perhaps, in the context, there was no reason to draw attention to the obvious fact that the witnesses were testifying under oath. The judge at Freind's trial simply stated as a rule that the witnesses must be protected against incriminating themselves. No reason is given for the application of the rule. The case cited in the *Regestum Practicale* reported that being compelled to incriminate oneself was against the law of nature. If that was all there was to the matter, the rule would apply to any compelled self-incrimination, irrespective of an oath.

At this point, one can see some common-law courts in the mid-seventeenth century applying the *nemo tenetur* principle to civil and prosecution witnesses. These applications, however, did not yet extend to criminal suspects or defendants. Justices of the peace continued their pretrial investigative questioning, seeking to elicit

---

[103] "The Trial of Nathaniel Reading," 4 *St Tr* 296 (1679).
[104] Ibid.
[105] Ibid.
[106] "The Trial of John Freind," 13 *St Tr* 1 (1696).
[107] Ibid 16.
[108] Ibid.
[109] Ibid 17.
[110] Ibid.

incriminating evidence in accord with the Marian statutes. At trial, the "altercation" style of questioning continued with the expectation that defendants would be drawn to speak, as there was no counsel as to matters of fact to speak for them, at least in felony trials by indictment. If a defendant chose to remain silent at the pretrial investigative stage, or at trial proper, the exercise of that "right to remain silent," while not subject to punishment, might well come at a price higher than they wished to pay.

Summary and Conclusions

State trials, though unusual in regard to their public prominence and possibly subject to political pressures, were conducted according to customary common law. Providing the most replete accounts of trials in the sixteenth and first half of the seventeenth centuries, the trial reports illustrate how the common law of the time could leave criminal defendants indicted for felonies without important procedural safeguards.

If defense counsel had any role at all at trial, it was restricted to advising on questions of law and not on matters of fact. Trial judges charged with protecting defendants against abuse or confusion may have been conscientious in their solicitude, yet it is hard to imagine even a dutiful judge could fill the role of a zealous defense counsel who would be cognizant of possible defenses and prepared to exploit prosecutorial weaknesses. In any event, judging from reports of repeated pleas for counsel, defendants appear not to have been satisfied with this arrangement.

No rule of evidence prevented hearsay testimony. A jury, of course, might not credit it. Or, it might. As Raleigh and others found out, they had no ability to require face-to-face confrontation with their accusers. Then hearsay could be a defendant's undoing. The earlier guarantees of confrontation contained in the statutes of Edward VI, Mary, and Elizabeth had been judicially circumvented (and, in any case, applied only to treason under those statutes).

Even in trials of great import, defendants had little time to prepare their defenses. They had no right to compel the attendance of favorable witnesses. There is controversy over whether defense witnesses could be heard against the crown. When favorable witnesses appeared, it was as a matter of judicial grace and favor rather than of right. The witness for the accused did not speak under oath, nor did the accused. The absence of the oath could seriously impair the credibility of both in the eyes of the jury.

Defendants, such as Udall and Lilburne, could legally choose to remain silent and call for the prosecution to prove its case. But in the "altercation"-style of trial, where the burden of proof was not clearly delineated, juries may have anticipated that defendants would speak and prove their innocence. A silent defendant was unlikely to meet the jury's expectations.

11

Popular Efforts to Bolster Due Process Protections at Criminal Trials in the Later Seventeenth Century

John Lilburne, the Levellers, and Law Reform

John Lilburne did not confine his many procedural objections to the courtroom. His public prominence enabled him to become a champion in a loosely structured popular movement for social and legal reforms. Opponents dubbed the agitators "Levellers" because, it was said, the adherents sought to make law treat all social classes equally.[1] Amid the turmoil surrounding the English civil wars (1642–1651), the Levellers advocated an expansive program calling for radical reforms in the political and economic structures of English government and society.[2] They also advocated for procedural and substantive reform of the criminal law.

The Levellers drew followers from London, as well as from towns and villages.[3] The reformers often set out their wide-reaching proposals in tracts, "agreements of the people," and petitions signed by thousands of citizens and submitted to Parliament.[4]

[1] On the origins, thought, and agenda of the Levellers, see Gary S DeKrey, *Following the Levellers: Political and Religious Radicals in the English Civil War and Revolution, 1645–1649* (Palgrave Macmillan 2017) (2 vols); Rachel Foxley, *The Levellers: Radical Political Thought in the English Revolution* (Manchester University Press 2013); Donald Veall, *The Popular Movement for Law Reform 1640–1660* (OUP 1970); HN Brailsford, *The Levellers and the English Revolution* (Christopher Hill ed, Stanford University Press 1961). For printed texts of many Leveller tracts, see David M Hart and Ross Kenyon (eds), *Tracts on Liberty by the Levellers and Their Critics (1638–1660)* (Liberty Fund 2014–2018) (7 vols); Andrew Sharp (ed), *The English Levellers* (CUP 1998); William Haller and Godfrey Davies (eds), *The Leveller Tracts 1647–1653* (Columbia University Press 1944); Don M Wolfe (ed), *Leveller Manifestoes of the Puritan Revolution* (T Nelson 1944).
[2] Their demands for law reform included manifestoes for participatory government, liberty of conscience, religious toleration, improvements in civil litigation, changes in laws of land ownership, socio-economic reform, and improvement in prison conditions. On other movements, both radical and moderate, urging law reform and often joining in Leveller demands, see Veall (n 1) 97–126. See generally Stuart E Prall, *The Agitation for Law Reform During the Puritan Revolution, 1640 to 1660* (Martinus Nijhoff 1966).
[3] Leveller support came largely from the middle class, especially from trades people and artisans. The movement was particularly strong in London, but not confined there. For analysis of the movement's social and the geographical dimensions, see DeKrey, 1 *Following* (n 1) 17–26 and passim; 2 DeKrey *Following* (n 1) 325–326.
[4] On the development of the popular agreements of the people, see Philip Baker and Elliot Vernon (eds), *The Agreements of the People, the Levellers, and the Constitutional Crisis of the English Revolution* (Palgrave MacMillan 2012).

Foundations of American Criminal Due Process at Trial. Francis R. Herrmann and Brownlow M. Speer,
Oxford University Press. © Oxford University Press 2025. DOI: 10.1093/9780199364770.003.0011

Lilburne (Figure 3) and fellow Puritans, William Walwyn, Richard Overton, and Thomas Price, separately or jointly, produced a stream of pamphlets. One of the most prominent was their *Agreement of the Free-People of England*[5] which, in effect, proposed a new constitution for England after the civil war.[6] By including due process demands in their petitions, they raised public awareness of the need for the trial protections they advocated. Many thousands of citizens and whole communities joined as signatories.[7] Leveller petitions usually carried about 10,000 names. *The Large Petition* of September 11, 1648 may have had 40,000.[8] The *Remonstrance of Many Thousands of the Freeborn People of England* claimed 98,000.[9]

As one part of their far-reaching agenda, Levellers, with Lilburne prominently in front, called for strengthening defensive safeguards at jury trials.[10] In reaction against prosecutions of religious dissenters before the High Commission and Star Chamber, Leveller publications, of which Lilburne alone authored more than sixty,[11] stressed repeatedly the sacredness of the common-law jury. A defendant's best protector was "that great and strong hold of our preservation, the way of trial by twelve sworn men of the neighbourhood."[12] Lilburne insisted that it be the sole means for judgment in criminal cases.[13]

---

[5] John Lilburne, William Walwyn, Richard Overton, and Thomas Prince, *An Agreement of the Free People of England* (printed for Gyles Calvert at the black spread-Eagle at the West end of Paul's 1649). For commentary of the 1649 Agreement, see DeKrey, 1 *Following* 238–244.

[6] John Witte Jr, *The Reformation of Rights: Law, Religion, and Human Rights in Early Modern Calvinism* (CUP 2007) 215–220. On the theological foundations of the rights asserted, see John Witte Jr, "A New Magna Carta for the Early Modern Common Law: An 800th Anniversary Essay" (2015) 30 Journal of Law and Religion 428, 434–436.

[7] On Leveller use of petitions as a means of presenting the demands of large crowds to Parliament, see Barbara J Shapiro, *Political Communication and Political Culture in England, 1558–1688* (Stanford University Press 2012) 210–215.

[8] Brailsford (n 1) 574.

[9] Veall (n 1) 73. On the basis of George Thomason's catalogue of publications relating to the English Civil War, Veall reports almost 22,000 pamphlets concerning law reform were published from 1642 to 1649 and 8,631 from 1650 to 1660. "The normal impression of a pamphlet was about 1,500 copies, with an estimated ten readers for every copy." Ibid.

[10] "There was no one Leveller theory regarding the criminal trial jury. Nonetheless, there may have been more agreement regarding the institution than any other." Thomas Andrew Green, *Verdict According to Conscience: Perspectives on the English Criminal Jury Trial 1200–1800* (University of Chicago Press 1985) 158. Disagreement arose particularly around the question whether jurors were judges of law as well as of fact. See ibid c 5, "Conscience and the True Law: The Ideology of Jury Law-Finding in the Interregnum," 153–199.

[11] Forty of them between 1646 and 1649. See Andrew Sharp, "Lilburne, John" in David Cannadine (ed), *Oxford Dictionary of National Biography* (hereafter *ODNB*) (OUP 2004) <https://doi.org/10.1093/ref:odnb/16654> (accessed October 27, 2024)

[12] John Lilburne, *Englands New Chains Discovered* ([s.l.] [s.n.] 1648) 7.

[13] John Lilburne, *The Legall Fundamentall Liberties of the People of England, Revived, Asserted and Vindicated* (London [s.n.] 1649) 67. See also William Walwyn, *The Bloody Project* (London [s.n.] 1648) 13; John Lilburne, *The Humble Petition of Many Thousands Earnestly Desiring the Glory of God* (London 1647) 4; Lilburne, *New Chains* (n 12) 16; Lilburne and others, *Agreement of the Free People* (n 5) 6–7; John Lilburne, *The Just Defence of John Lilburn* (London [s.n.] 1653) 4. See also Anonymous, *The Fundamental Lawes and Liberties of England, Claimed, Asserted, and Agreed upon* (London [s.n.] 1653) 3 ("That no other ways of trials be in England for life, limb, liberty, or estate but by juries of any person of what quality soever"); William Walwyn, *Juries Justified, or, a Word of Correction to Mr. Henry Robinson for His Seven Objections against the Trial of Causes, by Juries of Twelve Men* (Robert Wood 1651) 5 ("What more fundamental liberty than the trial of causes by Juries of twelve men? What more constant, more glorious administration of Justice and Righteousness?").

Figure 3 Portrait of John Lilburne (1615?–1657) by George Glover. A leader of the Leveller movement and a prolific author of political tracts, including many calling for law reform. Justice Hugo Black of the U.S. Supreme Court believed that Lilburne influenced the formation of the American Bill of Rights.

Credit: George Glover, Public domain, via Wikimedia Commons.

For the Levellers, a common-law jury trial encompassed far more than the mere assembling of twelve persons to decide guilt or innocence. Long-established common law attached to the jury a cluster of principles and procedures that the Levellers understood to be indispensable to a jury trial. In a flood of tracts, Lilburne and his followers laid out those elements: notice of charges beforehand;[14] a right to

---

[14] Anonymous, *The Humble Petition of Divers Wel-affected Persons Inhabiting the City of London* (London [s.n.] 1648) 5 ("That you would have … mitigated and made certain the charge therof in all particulars"). John Lilburn, *The Afflicted Man's Outcry against the Injustice and Oppression Exercised…* (London [s.n.] 1653) 7 ("the charge and accusation by the law of Nature ought to be cleer, distinct, and particular [with the time and place, or other circumstances] else the party accused cannot discharge himself").

defend[15] with assurance that any pleas would be voluntary;[16] that trials not be unreasonably delayed;[17] that they be conducted in public[18] before an indifferent jury,[19] chosen from the vicinage[20] with witnesses produced face to face with defendants;[21]

Levellers repeatedly protested against laws applied *ex post facto*. See John Lilburn, *A Plea at Large for John Lilburn, Gentleman, now a Prisoner at Newgate* (London [s.n.] 1653) 13 (complaining he was to be tried "for a fact done before there was a law in being"); Edward Billing, *A Mite of Affection Manifested in 31 Proposals* (printed for Giles Calvert 1659) 3 ("[A]nd to the end that they [the laws] may be truly known to every individual person, let the Law be printed, that every one may know that Law, which he is to be subject to, to the intent that no man may be condemned by a Law he neither knowes, nor ever heard of, nor understands; neither indeed can he, when as it lyes in the brest of other men: And further that the Law be read to every person (called or summoned before any Judicature as concerns the person or persons so summoned"); Lilburne, *Agreement of the Free People* (n 5) 5, s XIIII ("where there is no law, there is no transgression"); Anonymous, *Fundamental Lawes* (n 13) 4 ("that no man is to be judged . . . by a law made after the fact committed").

[15] Writing from prison, Lilburne advocated that fair procedure ought to assure "[f]or a free-man to have a charge laid against him, and his Adversaries brought face to face to prove it, and then the Accused to have liberty to make the best defence for himself he can, which was the practise amongst the very Heathen Romans, who had no light but the light of Nature to guide them, Act. 25.16 [trial of St Paul]. Yea, Christ himself, when his enemies endeavoured to catch him by Interrogatories, he puts them off, without an Answer [citing the gospel of Luke]." John Lilburne, *England's Birthright Justified: Against All Arbitrary Usurpation* (Larner's Press at Goodman's Fields 1645) 7.

[16] John Lilburne, *Liberty Vindicated against Slavery . . . Published for the Use of All Free-Borne of England . . . by a Lover of His Country and Sufferer for the Common Liberty* (London [s.n.] 1646) 16 (drawing on Bracton and roman law to argue "that prisoners for criminall causes, . . . when they are brought forth . . . as men to receive judgement of Law, neither ought to be fettered, lest they seeme to be inforced to answer"). See also Richard Overton, *An Appeale from the Degenerate Representative Body* (London [s.n.] 1647) 34; Anonymous, *The Only Right Rule for Regulating the Lawes and Liberties of the People of England* (London [s.n.] 1652) 8.

[17] Petitions for speedy trials were repeatedly made to Parliament. Lilburne, *Humble Petition* (n 13) 5 ("That all prisoners may have a speedy trial, that they be neither starved, nor their families ruined, by long and lingering imprisonment; and that imprisonment be used onely for safe custody until time of trial, and not as a punishment for offences"). See also Anonymous, *The Humble Petition of Divers Constant Adherers* (London [s.n.] 1652) 1; Anonymous, *Fundamental Lawes* (n 13) 4; *The Earnest Petition of Many Free-Born People of this Nation*, appended to *A Declaration of Some Proceedings of Lt. Col. John Lilburn, and His Associates* (printed for Humphrey Harward 1648) 30 ("Whereas according to Iustice, and the equitable sense of the Law, Goals and Prisons ought to be only used as places of safe custody, until the constant appointed time of tryall and now they are made places of torment and punishment of supposed offenders: that therefore be enacted henceforth no supposed offender whatsoever may be denied his legal trial, at the first sessions, assizes, or goal delivery after his commitment").

[18] Anonymous, *Fundamental Lawes* (n 13) 4 ("all Courts to be publicke and open").

[19] Ibid 5 ("That it is the English-man's liberty, concerning Iuries, upon any Tryal, to make his challenge or exception against 35, without shewing cause, and against as many more as just cause can be alledged against, until the party do evidently see, that his Tryers do stand indifferent").

[20] Billing (n 14) 2 ("that no person or persons whatsoever, be tryed for Life, Limb, Liberty, or Estate, but by a Jury of twelve men of the Neighbour-hood, or others who shall well know each other, reserving the right of just exception against any Judge, Jury-man, or Witnesse, if any justly can be made"). See also Lilburne, *New Chains* (n 13) 3, 7; Lilburne, *Agreement* (n 5) 6, XXV; Anonymous, *The Remonstrance of Many Thousands of Free-People of England* (London [s.n.] 1649) 6.

[21] *A Discourse Betwixt Lieutenant Colonel John Lilburn, Close Prisoner in the Tower of London, and Mr. Hugh Peter* (1649) 3 ("they commit me to prison without any crime pretended, or without ever letting me see accuser, or accusation, prosecutor or charge; and yet into the bargain, deal worse with me then ever the Heathen and Pagan Romans dealt with Paul, who had nothing but the depraved light of Nature to guide them, and yet in all his imprisonment never forbad or hindered any of his friends to visit or relieve him, although he were accused for a pestilent fellow, and a turner of the world up side down: but they lock me up in a close room, with centinels at my door, and will not so much as at a distance let me

and that defendants be able to produce favorable witnesses who would testify under oath.[22] The Levellers advocated for two trial elements that common-law courts had not yet broadly come to acknowledge: protection against self-incrimination[23] and an opportunity for the full assistance of counsel.[24]

speak with my friends"); Anonymous, *Fundamental Lawes* (n 13) 12 ("That upon all Tryals Witnesses on both sides may be sworn, the Accuser and the Accused brought face to face, and all Courts to be publicke and open"). See also Anonymous, *Divers Constant Adherers* (n 17) 1; Billing (n 14) 2; William Walwyn, *Englands Lamentable Slaverie* (London [s.n.] 1645) 5.

[22] Anonymous, *Fundamental Lawes* (n 13) 4 ("That upon all Tryals Witnesses on both sides may be sworn"); Lilburne, *Agreement of the Free People* (n 5) 6 ("That it shall not be in their [Parliament's] power to continue or make any Law, to deprive any person, in case of Tryals for Life, Limb, Liberty, or Estate, from the benefit of witnesses, on his, or their behalf"); Anonymous, *Diverse Constant Adherers* (n 17) 5 ("and that witnesses may be sworn in behalf of the accused, as well as for the prosecutor"); John Cooke, *The Vindication of the Professors and the Profession of the Law* (London 1646) 22 ("I conceive there are many defects in our Law, both in matters Criminall on the Crown side and Civill, As that witnesses should not be examined upon oath for the prisoner as well as for the King, that Counsell is not allowed as well for matter of life, as for estate").

[23] Lilburne, *Liberty Vindicated* (n 16) 28–29 (complaining that honest persons, committed "for some triviall matter, as refusing to answer interrogatories against themselves (a custome now of late growne a thing which Law and nature abhorres that any should bee a self-destroyer, according to the maxime of Law, *Nemo tenetur prodere seipsum*, No man is bound to betray himselfe, frequent and common . . . are disrespected")); Anonymous, *Fundamental Lawes* (n 13) 4 ("That no man is to be compelled to swear or answer to Questions, to accuse himself or Relations"). See also Anonymous, *The Case of the Army Truly Stated* (London [s.n.] 1647) 19; Anonymous, *Divers Wel-affected Persons* (n 14) 5; Anonymous, *Divers Constant Adherers* (n 17) 3; Overton, *An Appeale* (n 16); John Lilburne, *Foundations of Freedom; or an Agreement of the People* (London, published for the satisfaction of all honest interests 1648) 13; Lilburne, *Agreement of the Free People* (n 5 s XVI) 5 ("We agree and Declare, XVI. That it shall not be in the power of any Representative, to punish, or cause to be punished, any person or persons for refusing to answer questions against themselves in Criminall cases"); Walwyn, *Slaverie* (n 21) 5 ("[F]or a man to be examined in criminall cases against himselfe, and to be urged to accuse himselfe is as unnatural and unreasonable, as to urge a man to kill himselfe, for though it be not so high a degree of wickednesse, yet it is as really wicked"); A Booth (attributed), *Examen Legum Angliae: Or the Laws of England* (London, printed by James Cottrel 1656) 49–50 ("For the very exacting this Oath is against the Law of Nature, whose dictates are the same with those of the Law of God written; from which are derived undeniable Maximes and Principles, whereof this is one: *Nemo tenetur accusare seipsum*: This Maxime is agreed by all men; and the Lawyers allow it. The reason of it is . . . because every man is nearest to himself; and it's against Nature, for him to be a means of his own punishment: a man ought to preserve himself, although to the hurt of another: it were better to kill another, then to kill himself, or to suffer himself to be killed; if of necessity the one must needs be. Therefore, to exact this Inquisitory Oath against a mans ownself, is against the Law of Nature, and so against the Law of God").

[24] Cooke (n 22) 22 ("I conceive there are many defects in our Law, both in matters Criminall on the Crown side and Civill, as that witnesses should not be examined upon oath for the prisoner as well as for the King, that Counsell is not allowed for matter of life, as for estate"). See also Booth (n 23) 93 ("the prisoner hath not liberty either to have witnesses sworn for his defence, to clear him; nor admitted to have any Counsel, if he deny the fact, although there be a lawyer as eloquent as Tertullus [the prosecutor of St Paul] against him . . . ; however, the judge will hear his witnesses without oath: But all the witnesses who are to give evidence for the Commonwealth are sworne . . . [E]very man ought to have as much favour, & means allowed to clear himself, as his Accuser hath to charge him"); Anonymous, *The Laws Discovery, or a Brief Detection of Sundry Notorious Errors and Abuses, Contained in Our English Laws . . . by a Well-Wisher to His Countrey* (London, printed by R I 1653) 7 ("That persons accused for life, be permitted Councel, in regard their fears render them often, both speechless and unadvised; bare accusations are not such sufficient condemnations, as to deprive any (though innocent) of Councel in such extremity").

Asserting bases for rights

Levellers sought to secure their procedural demands against parliamentary denials and the unpredictability of judicial discretion.[25] To that end, they increasingly cast their claims as rights, anchoring those rights variously in common law, divine law, fundamental law, natural law,[26] a mythical pre-Norman ancient constitution, the mutual consent of the people, or Magna Carta.[27] The approaches did not necessarily contradict one another. Each served, alone or in combination, to justify and make unalterable the procedures sought. Take what approach one would, the rights for whose recognition the Levellers and like-minded seventeenth-century reformers petitioned were distinctly not rooted in governmental grace, favor, or indulgence. They were not to be limited to a particular class of persons, but broadly based. Terms such as "liberties and privileges" and "franchises" might carry with them a suggestion that trial procedures were the product of parliamentary or royal grant, which could always shift, and that they might not include all people. "Rights" offered a more stable and egalitarian foundation.[28]

Lilburne did not limit himself to resting his claims for procedural rights on only one basis. He could appeal to "those ancient laws and ancient rights of England."[29] Or, he might invoke Magna Carta's c 29[30] and the due process statutes of Edward III that specified it, referring to the Charter as "the English man's legal birth-right and inheritance."[31]

When speaking of Magna Carta in this manner, Lilburne found support in the recently emerging legal trend to resuscitate c 29's significance.[32] Ever since 1225, monarchs had faithfully confirmed the Great Charter, but many of its chapters became

[25] Anonymous, *Fundamental Lawes* (n 13) 3 ("These following, as our Fundamentals, we claim and expect ... For our liberties are our own, and our Childrens after us; they are not of Grace or Favour: And therefor we crave them not as an Almes, but claim them as Our and our Childrens Right"). The fundamental laws were intended to be fixed and inalterable. Ibid 5 ("That the grand Councels or Parliaments of England, have not power to diminish, violate or alter any of these Fundamentals ... [T]hese being the only bars against Monarchy and arbitrary power"). DeKrey suggests that *The Fundamental Lawes* is "a compilation of proposals from the previous Agreements" and "a digest of previous Leveller tracts and petitions." DeKrey, 2 *English Civil War* (n 1) 40.

[26] For the importance of natural law to the Levellers, see Richard A Gleissner, "The Levellers and Natural Law: The Putney Debates 1647" (1980) 20 Journal of British Studies 74.

[27] For a comprehensive investigation of Magna Carta's role in English law from the charter's thirteenth-century birth as an agreement between king and nobles to its seventeenth-century talismanic importance, see the magisterial work of Sir John Baker, *The Reinvention of Magna Carta, 1216–1616* (CUP 2017). Jack Rakove observes "for Magna Carta to attain its exalted stature ... it had to acquire meanings it did not originally possess. It was not written as a beacon of liberty to shine across the ages, but as a negotiated settlement." Jack N Rakove, *Declaring Rights: A Brief History with Documents* (Bedford Books 1998) 8.

[28] See Rakove (n 27) 29, drawing and elaborating upon these distinctions. The emerging use of the term "right" is evidenced in titles such as the "Petition of Right" (1628), the English "Bill of Rights" (1689), and in many Leveller pamphlets. For Lilburne's intent that rights be inclusive, see Rachel Foxley, "John Lilburne and the Citizenship of 'Free-Born Englishmen'" (2004) 4 The Historical Journal 849, 853–854, 870–871.

[29] John Lilburne, *The Just Defence of John Lilburne* (London [s.n.] 1653) 4.

[30] Ibid. Magna Carta, c 29 (1225): "No free-man shall be taken, or imprisoned, or dispossessed, of his free tenement, or liberties, or free customs, or be outlawed, or exiled, or in any way destroyed; nor will we condemn him, nor will we commit him to prison, excepting by the legal judgement of his peers, or by the laws of the land. To none will we sell, to none will we deny, to none will we delay right or justice."

[31] John Lilburne, *The Free-man's Freedom Vindicated* (London [s.n.] 1646) 6.

[32] Baker, *Reinvention* (n 27) 335.

obsolete over time. C 29 generally lay dormant until the 1580s.[33] Then, Puritans took it up as a weapon against the High Commission's oath *ex officio*.[34] Prominent lawyers, such as James Morice and Nicholas Fuller, discovered in the chapter a touchstone for claiming common-law protections.[35] Edward Coke soon followed, interpreting expansively the protections of c 29:

> in as much as everything that anyone has in this world, or that concerns the freedom and liberty of his body or his freehold, or the benefit of law to which he is inheritable, or his native country in which he was born, or the preservation of his reputation or goods, or his life, blood and posterity; to all these things this act extends.[36]

Coke appeared to understand the term "lawful judgement of his peers" to mean trial by jury (as Lambarde had done before him). No one's "free-birth right" was to be infringed, said Coke,

> unlesse it be by the lawfull judgement, that is, verdict of his equals (that is, of men of his own condition) or by the law of the land (that is, to speak it once for all) by the due course, and processe of law.[37]

Lilburne, embracing the new learning, eagerly endorsed Coke's view:

> And now, Sir, that I and all the Commons of England, may not be mistaken in expounding of Magna Charta, and what is meant by a tryall of our Peers, we have learned Sir Edward Cook (our own approved Oracle of the law) ... expressly saith, that by a tryall of our Peers, is meant Equalls, men of our own condition, Commons, as being the only Peers to Commons.[38]

Lilburne noted that in 1642, Commons had twice ordered Coke's work published "unto the whole kingdom for good law."[39]

---

[33] Ibid 259. Thereafter, "enthusiasm for it spread like wildfire." Ibid.

[34] Ibid 335.

[35] Ibid.

[36] Edward Coke, "Memorandum on Chapter 29 (1604)" in John H Baker, *Selected Readings and Commentaries on Magna Carta 1400–1604* (Selden Society 2015) 394, 394. On Edward Coke's expansive interpretation of Magna Carta, see ibid 335–409.

[37] Co Inst ii, 46. Soon after Coke, Francis Ashley, lecturing on c 29 at the Middle Temple in 1616, referred to the chapter as "the law of laws," "the ground," "the base," and "the statute of statutes." Baker comments, "Ashley's exposition of chapter 29 could fairly be described as representing the apotheosis of the new learning about Magna Carta. Barely a hint of that learning can be detected in any readings prior to Morice's in 1578, and yet little of it was Ashley's own invention, since it was largely derived from cases decided since the 1580s, from current professional thinking and from majority opinions in the House of Commons ... Ashley managed to stretch the interpretation of the statute to its uttermost limits." Baker, *Selected Readings* (n 36) 428.

[38] John Lilburne, *Two Letters Writ by John Lilburne, Prerogative Prisoner in the Tower of London, to Col Henry Martin* (London [s.n.] 1647) 2–3.

[39] Ibid 3. Overton likewise relied upon Coke's interpretation of "judgment of his peers" as meaning trial by jury "for all manner of persons, aswell Noblemen as Commons." Richard Overton, *Vox Plebis, or the People's Outcry against Oppression, Injustice, and Tyranny* (London [s.n.] 1646) 10.

William Walwyn, Lilburne's friend and fellow Leveller, took a markedly less positive view of the Great Charter. In *England's Lamentable Slaverie*, a letter of support written to the captive Lilburne, Walwyn granted that Lilburne was "the first indeed, that ever raised this new doctrine of Magna Charta to prove" that it was unlawful to examine persons "upon questions, tending to their own accusations and imprisonment." But, in Walwyn's opinion, Magna Carta "hath been more precious in your esteeme then it deserveth." To Walwyn, Magna Charta was just a "messe of pottage." In the end, however, with seeming reluctance, he admitted "its the best we have."[40]

Lilburne looked beyond Magna Carta for additional grounds for rights. In *The Afflicted Man's Outcry against the Injustice and Oppression*,[41] he elaborated on the theme of what is required for fair process. He composed the work while in custody awaiting trial in Newgate prison, having returned from an imposed exile after his 1649 acquittal. *Outcry* took the form of a letter penned to a London minister. Claiming he had been denied due process when he was not summoned or provided the opportunity to defend against charges, Lilburne employed the scriptural passage that the twelfth-century canonists Paucapalea and Stephen of Tournai had used to base fair procedures upon divine law.[42] In their vein, Lilburne wrote:

> Although God knew well enough that he [Adam] had so done; yet he abhorred to deal unjustly with him, and condemn him without summoning him to answer for himself; and therefore he fits him by, saying, *Adam where art thou?* as much as if he said, *Come forth and stand up for thyself, and answer to the Bill of Indictment against thee . . . and speak the utmost that thou canst why thou should not be condemned.*[43]

Any law or custom incompatible with this divinely established right to be summoned and defend was invalid:

> The best and chiefest of the law books of England do aver and glory in it, that the foundations of the true law of England, is built on the pure law of God . . . And therefore against this Law, Prescription, Statute, nor Customs, may not prevail: And if any be brought against it, they be no Prescriptions, Statutes, nor Customs, but things void and against justice.[44]

---

[40] Walwyn, *Slaverie* (n 21) 3–4.

[41] Lilburne, *Outcry* (n 14).

[42] See Kenneth Pennington, "The Jurisprudence of Procedure" in Wilfried Hartmann and Kenneth Pennington (eds), *The History of Courts and Procedure in Medieval Canon Law* (The Catholic University of America Press 2016) 137–139. For English translations of the texts, see Paucapalea, "Preface to the *Summa* of Paucapalea on Gratian's Decretum, c. 1150" in Robert Somerille and Bruce C Brasington (eds and trs), *Prefaces to Canon Law Books in Latin Christianity* (Yale University Press 1998); and Stephen of Tournai, "Preface to the *Summa* of Stephen of Tournai on Gratian's *Decretum*, Second Half of the 1160s" in ibid 195.

[43] Lilburne, *Outcry* (n 14) 2, referring to Book of Genesis 3:9. See Kenneth Pennington, discussing Paucapalea's and Stephen of Tournai's development of the biblical text as a divine model for fair procedure. Pennington (n 42) 137–138.

[44] Lilburne is relying here on the language of Christopher Saint-Germain, *Doctor and Student*, c 2, Dialogue 1. Lilburne had a copy with him in his cell.

In his concern for fair procedure, Lilburne found a kindred soul in John Sadler, a contemporary advocate of legal reform.[45] While preparing *Outcry*, Lilburne had with him in his cell John Sadler's recently published principal work, *Rights of the Kingdom*.[46] Fair procedure, Sadler's work emphasized, was indispensable to arriving at a just result. "The very form and life and power or substance of the justest lawes doth much consist in processe."[47] In passages praised by Lilburne, Sadler stressed the right to a trial, even for notorious crimes;[48] the need for clear and particular information about charges;[49] the simultaneous presence of defendants with accusers and legitimate witnesses at trial;[50] the right to make a full defense;[51] the need for impartial judges;[52] the right to challenge witnesses and jurors;[53] acquittal in doubtful matters;[54] the aid of counsel allowed by law;[55] a presumption of innocence;[56] and judgment made by an accused's equals.[57]

Rhetorically, Sadler asked (and Lilburne with him), "Are these the Laws of England; or of Nature, rather?"[58] Answering his own question, Sadler wrote, "These we owe to Beauclerk . . . " that is, to Henry the First (1100–1135).[59] In truth, most of the *Leges* that Sadler cites were not original to England. The Pseudo-Isidorian forgers had composed the texts in the ninth century in Frankish regions for the protection of bishops against unjust accusations.[60] From there, the norms had passed into canonical collections, most significantly into the widely influential *Panormia*, attributed to Ivo of Chartres, and into Ivo's *Decretum*. Brought to England shortly after 1066 by Lanfranc of Bec, the first Norman Archbishop of Canterbury, the pseudo-Isidorian procedural

[45] For Sadler's biography, see Richard L Greaves, "Sadler, John" in *ODNB* (n 11) (OUP 2004) <https://doi.org/10.1093/ref:idnb/24459> (accessed October 27, 2024); Janelle Greenberg, *The Radical Face of the Ancient Constitution* (CUP 2001) 230–236. After studying law at Lincoln's Inn, Sadler was later appointed to be master in chancery, to the high court of justice, and to the admiralty court. A member of the Council of State, he was a moderate, distinguished lawyer, Oxford professor, and member of parliament. He was appointed to the Hale Commission on law reform, and later commissioner for law reform by appointment of parliament. John Milton and Thomas Hobbes cited Sadler's *Kingdom*. His writings were considered so important that they were published at public expense.

[46] John Sadler, *Rights of the Kingdom or, Customs of Our Ancestours* (London, printed by Richard Bishop 1649).

[47] Ibid 161. On the fundamental role of due process in Lilburne's thinking, see Diane Parkin-Speer, "John Lilburne: A Revolutionary Interprets Statues and Common Law Due Process" (1983) 1 LHR 276.

[48] Sadler (n 46) 176, 182.

[49] Ibid 123, 175.

[50] Ibid.

[51] Ibid (referencing St Paul's trial, Acts 25:16).

[52] Ibid 123, 179.

[53] Ibid 176. Sadler ascribes the right to challenge to the Law of Nature and the Law of the Kingdom.

[54] Ibid 123, 176.

[55] Ibid 177. See JB Post, "The Admissibility of Defence Counsel in English Criminal Procedure" (1984) 5 J Legal Hist 23, 24.

[56] Sadler (n 46) 176 ("But judges should suppose all men to be good till they be proved to be evil"). See text accompanying n 76 in ch 5.

[57] Sadler (n 46) 123, 162.

[58] Ibid 124.

[59] Ibid.

[60] Ibid 123. Sadler may have been working from a manuscript of Henry's *Leges*. They first appeared in print in 1644, only five years before Sadler wrote. He was enthusiastic about the *Leges* being published, but he seemed not yet to have a printed copy. "Henry the First, is yet alive, in his Lawes, and Charters . . . They are now in print . . . I must but runne, and glance." Ibid 122.

safeguards were incorporated into the *Leges*. Sadler and Lilburne were advocating for norms originally developed on the Continent.[61]

But one of the *Leges* Sadler relied upon probably has a truly English feudal origin, not attributable to continental sources. "Each one must be judged by his equals (*pares*)."[62] Sadler had the word "*pares*" printed in capital letters. It fits well with the new interpretation of "judgement by peers." *Pares*, in fact, could not have referred to trial jurors in Henry's time, as there were no juries in the early 1110s when the *Leges* was composed. But Sadler and Lilburne could latch onto the *Leges* term to give historical reinforcement to their seventeenth-century interpretation of trial by jury.

Sadler's account of due process rights naturally enkindled Lilburne's enthusiasm. He praised *Kingdom's* principles as "worthy to be written in letters of gold"[63] and as constituting "the Basis, or Foundation, or our Law Processe."[64] Absent these procedural fundamentals, Lilburne said, repeating Sadler's words, a defendant was like one condemned "to be sliced and fryed with exquisite tortures."[65]

The Hale Commission

In 1652, while Leveller proposals for law reform were still fresh, parliament formed a commission under the leadership of Matthew Hale to study "what inconveniences there are in the law" and "the speediest way to reform" them. Among the commissioners was John Sadler, whose *Rights of the Kingdom* Lilburne so admired.[66] The commission proposed that defendants should be allowed to have counsel in any criminal cases where the prosecution was represented by counsel. Counsel's role was not to be limited to questions of law, but should include factual issues, as well. The commission further proposed that defense witnesses be able to testify under oath, placing them on par with prosecution witnesses whose testimony was always taken under oath.[67] Parliament, however, failed to act on most of the Commission's proposals.[68] With the

---

[61] Through Ivo's text, the same norms were adopted into Gratian's *Concordantia discordantium* (or *Decretum*) (c 1140), the decretals of Gregory IX (1234), and the *ordines iudiciales* of the late-twelfth and thirteenth centuries, all of which were known in England and contributed to the procedures of English ecclesiastical courts.

[62] "*Unusquisque per pares suos iudicandus est.*" *Leges Henrici*, 31, 7; Sadler (n 46) 123. On the feudal meaning of "pares," see Sir Frank Stenton, *The First Century of English Feudalism: 1066–1166* (2nd edn, Clarendon Press 1961) 60–61, cited in LJ Downer (ed and tr), *Leges Henrici Primi* (Clarendon Press 1972) 308 n to *Leges* c 5, 6; 343 n to *Leges* c 31, 7.

[63] Lilburne, *Outcry* (n 14) 3.

[64] Ibid 4.

[65] Ibid 10. See Sadler (n 46) 185.

[66] On criminal law reform from 1640 to 1660, see Veall (n 1) 127–166; Mary Cotterell "Interregnum Law Reform: The Hale Commission of 1652" (1968) 83 EHR 689–704; GB Nourse, "Law Reform under the Commonwealth and Protectorate" (1959) 75 LQR 512–529.

[67] The Hale Commission's proposals are printed in John Somers, 6 *A Collection of scare and valuable tracts* (13 vols) Somers Tracts, "Several Draughts of Acts" 177–245. For the Hale Commission's proposals touching on criminal causes, see ibid 234–235.

[68] On the Hale Commission's failure to succeed with its proposals, see Veall (n 1) 84. On the reasons for the failure of many law reform proposals, see Veal (n 1) 228–235.

return of the monarchy in 1660, movement for legislative law reform lost much of its momentum.

Conclusion: Aftermath of Law Reform Movement

Much of the visionary agenda of the Levellers for broad social and economic reform proved too radical for adoption in its day.[69] But, by the time the movement waned during the 1650s, tens of thousands of citizens had read Leveller pamphlets, signed Leveller agreements, and endorsed Leveller petitions. These tracts heightened public awareness of the sacredness of the jury-trial right and, at the same time, the deficits in procedural protections for defendants at trial. The efforts of the Hale Commission, likewise, had sharpened recognition that jury trial procedure needed to be a more balanced contest between prosecution and defense.

While Parliament rejected Leveller petitions and took no action on the Commission's reform proposals, a perceptible improvement was emerging in judicial practice.[70] Although courts continued to deny the full assistance of counsel, accused persons came to be treated with more humanity.[71] Defendants were commonly confronted with the witnesses against them. Judges on occasion permitted defense witnesses to be sworn. In a first occurrence in 1649, Lilburne obtained a copy of the indictment against him and additional time to prepare his defense. Assertions of claims against self-incrimination, although still unusual, were treated with less judicial resistance.[72] It is probably impossible to determine to what extent reformist

---

[69] By 1649, much but not all of the movement's energy was drained when Oliver Cromwell defeated Leveller supporters in the army. In addition, Parliament passed an act restricting the publication of any opinions suggesting that the government was "tyrannical, usurped, or unlawful" or challenged the supremacy of Commons in parliament. "An Act Declaring What Offences Shall be Adjudged Treason" (1649) in *Acts and Ordinances of the Interregnum, 1642–1660* (London 1911) 193–194. See James S Hart Jr, *The Rule of Law, 1603–1660* (Pearson Education Ltd 2003) 247–248, 271 n 42; Nourse (n 66) 517. Law reform pamphlets continued to be published, but the impetus for law reform ebbed with the return of the monarchy in 1660. See TA Davies, *The Quakers in English Society, 1655–1725* (Clarendon Press 2000). Still, the movement's force was not entirely spent. From 1650 to 1660, some fifty-eight further Leveller publications appeared.

The movement's influence on individuals in successor generations, though hard to trace, was felt at least into the 1680s. For a thorough study of Leveller influence well after 1649, see Gary S DeKrey, 2 *Following the Levellers: Political and Religious Radicals from the Commonwealth to the Glorious Revolution, 1649–1688* (Palgrave Macmillan 2018). DeKrey concludes that Levellers "imparted some of their ideas to more mainstream Whigs", including Leveller demands for safeguarding trial by jury. Ibid 328.

Rachel Foxley observes, "the legacy of the Levellers is disputed and it seems fair to say it has been fragmented and discontinuous." Foxley, *Levellers* (n 1) 233. See also Brailsford (n 1) 625–641. Particularly among Quakers and dissenters, Leveller influence was welcome. Lilburne himself became a Quaker in his latter years. Brailsford (n 1) 15. "Many Levellers found a spiritual refuge in the Society of Friends." Ibid 640. Edward Billing and William Penn were both Quakers, as the Society became known by some. Billing, who fought in the English Civil War, later authored the West Jersey concessions (1677). Ibid 639. Penn authored the Democratic Frame of Government for Pennsylvania (1682). See Peter Westen, "The Compulsory Process Clause" (1974) 73 Mich L Rev (Pt 1) 91 & n 80, 92 & n 85. Brailford remarks, "What was England's loss was America's gain." Brailford (n 1) 640.

[70] Veall (n 1) 160–166, 226–228.

[71] James Fitzjames Stephen, 1 *A History of the Criminal Law of England* (Macmillan and Co. 1883) 357–368.

[72] See Crook, 6 *St Tr* 201, 205–206, 218, 222 (1662); Penn and Mead, 6 *St Tr* 951, 957–958 (1670).

trends in the broader society of the time may have influenced judges in making their discretionary decisions. In any event, the judicial developments began to show more compatibility with reformist desires. Parliament, however, would finally reform trial procedure only after further politically and religiously based trials prompted political and public fears of unjust verdicts.[73]

[73] See George Fisher, "The Jury's Rise as Lie Detector" (1997) 107 Yale LJ 618, observing, in the context of seventeenth-century trials, that "treason trials had peculiar power to spur reform because of the status of those charged."

12

The 1696 Treason Act's
Recognition of Fair Procedures

Genesis of the 1696 Treason Act

After the restoration of the monarchy in 1660, the Stuarts used accusations of treason to defeat political opponents.[1] For its part, Parliament prosecuted treason by means of impeachment or attainder to suppress enemies. In these trials, judges might use their discretion to permit defendants procedural advantages, such as access to counsel outside the courtroom, or even in it (for matters of law), or to receive copies of indictments. But these were matters of grace and favor, not of right.[2] Defense counsel, when there was such, was prevented from arguing factual matters, even while the crown was able to prosecute its case with counsels' assistance. Defendants continued to have no right to obtain copies of their indictments despite growing criticism of the denials.[3] Defense witnesses, if allowed at all in crown cases, did not testify under oath, while prosecution witnesses always did. Prosecution witnesses were shielded against self-incrimination in their testimony,[4] but nothing protected defendants or defense witnesses, since none of them testified under oath.[5]

The consequent danger of unreliable verdicts became the subject of broad consternation in the century's latter half.[6] Parliamentarians and royalists, protestants and papists, Whigs together with Tories came to fear that each one's vengeful opponents would instigate prosecutions against their enemies. [7] The shortcomings of a defendant's position were clear to Thomas Roswell (Rosewell). Preaching in Westminster

---

[1] James R Phifer, "Law, Politics, and Violence: The Treason Trials Act of 1696" (1980) 12 Albion 235, 237.

[2] Samuel Rezneck, "The Statute of 1696: A Pioneer Measure in the Reform of Judicial Procedure in England" (1930) 2 The Journal of Modern History 5, 9–10.

[3] See "Trial of Roswell," 10 St Tr 147, 267 (1684) (Chief Judge Jeffreys, refusing defense request for at least so much of an indictment "as may be enough for us to know the foundation on which we are to go").

[4] See "Trial of Nathaniel Reading," 7 St Tr 259, 296 (1679) (the court cautioned the defendant, "[i]f you offer to ask him [the prosecution witness] any question upon his oath, to make him accuse himself, we must oppose it . . . you shall not make him calumniate himself"); "Trial of Roswell" (n 3) 168 (the court forbidding the defendant to question the witness about her attending a conventicle, "No, no; that you must not ask her, that is to accuse herself . . . You must not ask her any thing that may make her obnoxious to any penalty").

[5] On the critical importance of the oath, versus unsworn testimony, in a jury's assessment of credibility, see George Fisher, "The Jury's Rise as Lie Detector" (1997) 107 Yale LJ 585, 602–609 and passim.

[6] See John H Langbein, The Origins of Adversary Criminal Trial (OUP 2003) 32.

[7] John Langbein reviews the major politically and religiously motivated trials of the late Stuart period. See ibid 68–78; for his critique of the trials' procedures, see ibid 78–86; John Langbein and others (eds), History of the Common Law: The Development of Anglo-American Legal Institutions (Wolters Kluwer 2009) 649–654. For further commentary on late Stuart trials, see Fisher (n 5) 575–624; Sir James Fitzjames Stephen, 1 A History of the Criminal Law of England (Macmillan & Co 1883) (3 vols) 369–416. On the resolve of parliament to avoid a cycle of vengeful political trials, see Phifer (n 1) 235.

Foundations of American Criminal Due Process at Trial. Francis R. Herrmann and Brownlow M. Speer,
Oxford University Press. © Oxford University Press 2025. DOI: 10.1093/9780199364770.003.0012

Cathedral in 1684, he proclaimed that the monarchy had papist sympathies. Thereupon, he was arrested. Tried for treason, he, like many defendants before him, petitioned the court to allow him the assistance of counsel; to provide him a copy of the indictment; and to permit witnesses favorable to him to testify under oath. Lord Jeffreys, a trial judge notorious for his partiality to the crown, who was described as "perhaps the worst judge who ever disgraced Westminster Hall,"[8] denied Roswell's requests. Yet, even to Jeffreys, the unfairness of the defendant's predicament was apparent. He told the accused:

> Look ye, if ye speak to me privately, as to my own particular opinion, it is hard for me to say, that there is any express resolution of the law in this matter; but the practice has always been to deny a copy of the indictment ... I think it a hard case, that a man should have counsel to defend himself of a two-penny trespass, and his witnesses examined on oath, but if he steal, commit murder ... nay, high treason, where life, estate, honor, and all are concerned, he shall neither have counsel nor his witnesses examined on oath: But yet you know as well as I, that the practice of the law is so but the law is so; and the practice is the law.[9]

Sir John Hawles trenchantly criticized the inadequacies of defense safeguards. Intending to show that the guilty verdicts against Colledge, Wing, Russell, and others were unjust,[10] Hawles took direct aim at the denial of counsel:

> Tis true, no counsel are allowed for the prisoner in a trial upon an indictment of any capital matter, but in an appeal [i.e. a private suit not brought by the crown] for capital matters, counsel are allowed even on the trial. The reason given that the indictment is the suit of the King, and no counsel or witness is allowable in a capital matter against the King, is foolish ... and as vain is the reason that the judges are counsel for the prisoner, which they ought to be, but I doubt it will be suspected, that in this case and many others they did not make the best of their clients case; nay, generally have betrayed their poor client, to please, as they apprehended, their better client, the King[.][11]

Hawles censured, as well, other procedures that prevented an accused from preparing and presenting a defense. He denounced the absence of face-to-face confrontation, recollecting how Chief Justice Popham at Sir Walter Raleigh's trial infamously refused Raleigh's demand to confront Cobham.[12] Hawles decried the

---

[8] 11 *St T* 371 (note).

[9] "Rosewell's Trial," 10 *St Tr* 147, 267.

[10] John Hawles, *Remarks upon the Tryals of Edward Fitzharris, Stephen Colledge, Count Coningsmark, the Lord Russel, Collonel Sidney, Henry Cornish and Charles Bateman* (London, printed for Jacob Tonson 1689).

[11] Ibid 22. Hawles believed the true reason impeding counsel for defendants arose from the inability of defendants to pay for lawyers. "[B]ut the true reason in probability is that the prisoners in indictments are generally so very poor that they could not be at the charge of having counsel, and so non-usage gave colour of a law." Ibid 23.

[12] Ibid 10. Hawles pointed out that treason defendants were worse off than common criminals who at least had the right to see their accusers face to face at commital hearings and hear the accusations made against them under oath. Ibid 30. Judicial interpretation had rendered ineffective the mandates of earlier treason statutes that had required confrontation. See text to n 38 in ch 10.

inability of Colledge to have free and private access of all persons, "as is used in all other capital matters."[13] Hawles deplored the fact that "generally the prisoner never knows what he is accused of, and consequently cannot know his accuser, nor know how to provide a counter-evidence, till he comes to be arraigned, and then it is too late; for generally he is presently tried after his arraignment."[14]

A particular target of Hawles's criticism was the accepted expectation that a defendant could make his innocence apparent out of his own mouth without the aid of counsel:

> I would fain know how the prisoner shall escape; is it that his innocence shall appear in his forehead, or shall an angel come from heaven to disapprove the accuser? neither of which we have observed, though all have said, and I believe, that some persons have been very innocently executed. Or shall the accuser be detected by the bare questions of the prisoner? that I think will not be neither.[15]

Hawles objected that the prisoner, who was "tried as soon as he comes into the court," was not provided any list of the jurors, although the crown counsel had access to their names.[16] Without such a list, wrote Hawles, the defendant could not intelligently use his peremptory challenges. While no counsel was permitted to assist defendants in presenting their cases, the prosecution might have a number of counsel allowed to present the crown's case.[17] No defense witness was permitted to testify under oath, while prosecution witnesses were sworn.[18]

With defendants laboring under such procedural disadvantages, Hawles asked how they could possibly defend themselves:

> Let any person consider truly these circumstances, and it is a wonder how any person escapes; it is downright tying a man's hands behind him, and baiting him to death ... The trial of ordeal, of walking between hot iron bars blindfold, which was abolished for the unreasonableness of it; though it had its saying for it too, that God would lead the blind so as not to be burnt, if he were innocent, was a much more advantageous trial for the suspected than what of late was practised.[19]

Writing in the same year as Hawles, Sir Robert Atkyns authored *A Defence of the Late Lord Russel's Innocency*.[20] With the purpose of instructing uncounseled defendants in capital cases "how to manage their defence,"[21] Atkyns reflected:

---

[13] Hawles (n 10) 29.
[14] Ibid.
[15] Ibid 31.
[16] Ibid 32.
[17] Ibid 32.
[18] Ibid 33.
[19] Ibid 32.
[20] Sir Robert Atkyns, *A Defence of the Late Lord Russel's Innocency* (London, printed for Timothy Goodwin 1689). In 1684, Atykins had advised Lord Russell before trial as to how he might make a defense.
[21] Ibid 2.

And I ever thought it a severity in our law, that a prisoner for his life is not allowed the assistance of a grave and prudent lawyer or some other friend to make his defence for him, even as to matter of fact, as well as to law. I know 'tis said the court is of councel for the prisoner, but for my part, I should never desire to depend upon that onely. I know what this is by experience.[22]

Perhaps motivated by Hawles's and Atykins's explications of defense deficits at trial, the House of Lords moved to legislate procedures that would eliminate, or at least diminish, the cycle of politically vengeful treason trials with their increasingly suspect verdicts. In 1689, the Lords composed a draft "for the better regulation of trials." It was designed to effect "more equal and indifferent trials" of all peers.[23] The provisions of the draft responded to the repeated demands of treason defendants. The draft provided "that the party accused, whether Lord or Commoner, may have a copy of his indictment a week before his arraignment, and of the panel [of jurors] two days before his trial"[24] and "that counsel be allowed to the party accused in case of treason."[25] It further provided that counsel could address issues of both fact and law. Additionally, defense witnesses would testify under oath, correcting a customary hindrance to their credibility in the eyes of jurors:

And be it further enacted that in all cases of high treason the defendant and defendants shall be admitted to have counsel to advise them before and at their trials in matter of fact as well as law, which counsel, if the party demands it, shall be assigned by the Court. And be it further enacted ... that in all criminal cases, evidence shall be given upon oath for the defendant.[26]

Lords and Commons, however, could not agree on a final bill. Only after seven more years of debates, compromises, and re-drafts did parliament finally pass a new act for regulating trials in cases of treason and misprision of treason, 7 & 8 Will. III, c 3 (effective March 1696).[27]

---

[22] Ibid 8.

[23] "Trial of the Peers Bill" in *Manuscripts of the House of Lords 1689–1690* (Twelfth Report, Appendix pt VI, Historical Manuscripts Commission) (Eyre & Spottiswoode 1889) 31.

[24] Ibid 32.

[25] Ibid. The draft was amended to have gender-neutral language and provided that indictments be "translated into English." Ibid.

[26] Ibid 34.

[27] For commentary on the 1696 act and its background, see Langbein, *Adversary Trial* (n 6) 67–105; John Langbein, "Criminal Trials before the Lawyers" (1978) 45 U Chi L Rev 263, 307–310; JM Beattie, *Crime and the Courts of England, 1660–1800* (Princeton University Press 1986) 357–359; Phifer (n 1) 235–256; Rezneck (n 2) 5–26; Alexander H Shapiro, "Political Theory and the Growth of Defensive Safeguards in Criminal Procedure: The Origins of the Treason Trials Act of 1696" (1993) 11 Law & Hist Rev 215, 215–256.

The Terms of the New Treason Act

In its preamble, the Treason Act, noted that "nothing is more just and reasonable than that persons prosecuted for high treason and misprision of treason . . . should be justly and equally tried and that persons accused as offenders therein should not be debarred of all just and equal means for defence of their innocencies in such cases." With the phrases "equally tried" by "equal means," Parliament signaled its intention to set the procedural postures of defense and prosecution in equilibrium.[28] Consequently, the new act declared that defendants:

- "shall have a true copy of the whole indictment but not the names of the witnesses delivered unto them . . . five days at the least before he or she shall be tried";[29]
- "for the same to advise with counsel thereupon to plead and make their defence";[30]
- "and that every such person so accused and indicted, arraigned, or tried for any such treason . . . shall be received and admitted to make his and their full defense by counsel learned in the law";[31]
- "and to make any proof that hee or they can produce by lawful witness or witnesses who shall then be upon oath for his and their just defence in that behalf";[32]
- "and in case any person or persons so accused or indicted shall desire counsel, the court before whom such person or persons shall be tried . . . is required immediately upon his or their request to assign to such person and persons such and so many counsel not exceeding two as the person or persons shall desire to whom such counsel shall have free access at all seasonable hours;"[33]
- "noe person or persons whatsoever shall be indicted tryed or attainted of High Treason . . . but by and upon the Oaths and Testimony of Two lawful Witnesses . . . unlesse the Party indicted and arraigned or tryed shall willingly without violence in open Court confesse the same or shall stand Mute or refuse to plead."[34]
- "no person . . . shall be indicted, tried, or prosecuted for any such treason . . . unless the same indictment be found by a grand jury within three years next after the treason or offence done."[35]
- "all Persons so accused and indicted for any such Treason as aforesaid shall have the like Processe of the Court where they shall be tried to compel their witnesses

---

[28] Langbein and others (n 7) 663–664.

[29] 7 & 8 Will III, c 3, s 1 (1696). The names of the prosecution witnesses who testified at the grand jury were usually written on the back of an indictment. Langbein, *Adversary Trial* (n 6) 91.

[30] 7 & 8 Will III, c 3, s 1 (1696).

[31] Ibid.

[32] Ibid.

[33] Ibid. JB Post observes that "well before the 1696 act the secretaries of state were issuing warrants for counsel to visit prisoners for private consultation." JB Post, "The Admissibility of Defence Counsel in English Criminal Procedure" (1984) 5 J Legal Hist 23, 28.

[34] 7 & 8 Will III, c 3, s 2 (1696).

[35] Ibid s 5.

to appear for them at any such trial or trials as is usually granted to compel witnesses to appear against them."[36]

The Act contained no provision against self-incrimination for treason defendants. It may have been thought that such protection attached only to persons speaking under oath, and criminal defendants did not. The principle that one was not obliged to incriminate oneself had long been an accepted protective device (with limits) in the non-common-law courts, where defendants and witnesses testified under oath. Religious dissenters, with the aid of common-law lawyers, vigorously asserted the privilege against the abuses of the High Commission. The original canon privilege began to seep into the common-law courts, where it offered protection to prosecution witnesses and defense witnesses testifying under oath at treason trials (as the 1696 Act allowed). Treason defendants themselves remained unsworn. Even so, by providing counsel to speak for them, the Act strengthened the right to remain silent. Indeed, through counsel, the Act opened a path for the old canon-law *nemo tenetur* maxim to function in a new common-law environment.[37]

Effect of the 1696 Treason Act on the Structure of Treason Trial

The 1696 Act's provision for the assistance of defense counsel quickly began to affect the structure of the treason trial. The "accused speaks" or "altercation" style of trial had theretofore impeded defendants at common law from remaining silent. Once the Act opened the door to a broader role for defense counsel, treason defendants no longer had to establish their innocence by words out of their own mouths. No longer did the accused stand alone before a court "fighting without a weapon," as the Duke of Norfolk had once complained. Now, after each prosecution witness testified, defense counsel, sometimes in combination with the defendant himself, conducted examination and cross-examination. Counsel could emphasize that the burden of producing proof rested on the prosecution.[38] At the treason trial of Capt. Thomas Vaughn

---

[36] Ibid s 7. In the British colonies, the Province of Massachusetts Bay enacted in whole the Treason Statute of 1696, 7 Will III, c 3, s 1 and specifically provided for the accused "the benefits and privileges in and by the said act granted and declared." Acts and Laws of the Province of Massachusetts Bay in New England, c 36 in *Charters and General Laws of the Colony and Province of Massachusetts Bay* (Boston, T B Wait and Co. 1811) 294. The Massachusetts Act is evidence that the reforms of the 1696 Treason Act were known in the colonies, at least in Massachusetts, in the same year Parliament passed the Act in England.

[37] John Langbein maintains the right against self-incrimination "seeped into" the common law from its original canon setting first as a protection for witnesses. Langbein, *Adversary Trial* (n 6) 284. Michael Macnair holds "in the 1690s and 1700s the strands of legal limitations on self-incriminatory questioning and of religious/political objections began to flow together into the idea of a general right not to be compelled to give evidence against oneself and the rule began to spread into areas in which it had not previously been applied." MRT Macnair, "The Early Development of the Privilege against Self-Incrimination" (1990) 10 Oxford J Legal Stud 66, 69–70. John Wigmore holds that only by "a gradual perversion of function" from its canonical, oath-based context did the *nemo tenetur* maxim come to assume its modern function "not earlier than the latter half of the seventeenth century." John H Wigmore, "*Nemo Tenetur Seipsum Prodere*" (1891) 5 HLR 71, 72.

[38] Beattie, summarizing trial procedure in the early 1700s, observes the "severe limitations of the ability of the accused to prepare for trial would have been defended as essential to a form of trial that did not presume the innocence of defendants, but rather that the best indication of innocence was provided by the

conducted just days after the effective date of the act, Vaughn's counsel moved to dismiss the indictment for insufficiency of proof without the defense needing to present any evidence at all.[39] No longer did the admission of favorable witnesses depend on judicial grace and favor. By force of law, the witnesses were to be admitted. If defense witnesses declined to appear, the law could compel them to do so. Upon appearing, they would testify under oath on equal footing with prosecution witnesses.[40] Counsel could sum up the defendant's case to the jury. If an accused wished to plead guilty, the law assured, as it had since Edward VI, that his plea would be invalid unless voluntarily made.

Conclusion Regarding the 1696 Act

The 1696 Treason Act stands as a signal parliamentary recognition of fair trial principles.[41] It was arguably the most significant statutory statement of due process protections in England since the fourteenth-century statutes of Edward III which specified the implications of Magna Carta for trials.[42] The 1696 Act responded, in effect, to the major procedural complaints that English treason defendants had made for over a hundred years. In his *English Liberties, or the Free-born Subject's Inheritance*, Henry Care (1646–1688), a successor of the Levellers, critiqued the unfairness of trial

---

defendant's immediate and unrehearsed responses to the evidence as it was presented . . . In such a trial, defense counsel was not only unnecessary, but positively harmful." JM Beattie, "Scales of Justice" (1991) 9 LHR 221, 223.

[39] "Trial of Capt. Thomas Vaughn," 13 *St T* 485, 506 (1696) ("We are in your Lordship's judgment, whether we need give any evidence; for we think they have not proved their indictment"). By contrast, just *two* days before the effective date of the new act, Sir John Friend asked for the assistance of counsel. The court denied the request except as to matters of law, assuring the defendant the court would be his counsel. The absence of counsel proved costly. When speaking to the jury, the defendant admitted he was present at two meetings, just as the prosecution alleged. The prosecutor then seized upon the defendant's statement as an "affirmation of a thing unlikely in defence of himself, and what is deposed upon oath by the king's witnesses to the contrary."

Sir William Parkyns met the same fate just *one* day before the Act's effective date. The court denied Parkyns the assistance of counsel at trial:

> Court: We cannot allow counsel . . . You are not ignorant, sir William, that counsel has always been refused when desired in such cases.
>
> Parkyns: My lord, there is a new act of parliament that is lately made which allows counsel.
>
> Court: But that does not commence yet, sir William.
>
> Parkyns: My lord, it wants but one day.
>
> Court: That is as much as if it were a much longer time: for we are to proceed according to what the law is, and not what it will be. ("Trial of Sir William Parkyns," 13 *St Tr* 63, 72)

The trial then proceeded as an altercation between the crown prosecutor and the defendant with the judge intervening to join in questioning the defendant.

[40] 7 & 8 Will III, c 3, s 1. See Langbein, *Adversary Trial* (n 6) 102. For the development of a right to assistance of counsel in England, see Post (n 33) 23.

[41] Langbein and others (n 7) 660 ("a charter of defensive safeguard"); the Act was "the entering wedge of a more modern and a more liberal procedure," Rezneck (n 2) 26.

[42] See Langbein and others (n 7) 660–661 (the Act was "a turning point in the history of Anglo-American criminal procedure," observing that the Act's provisions for a right to counsel and a right to compel witnesses were later absorbed into the American Constitution).

procedure as it had previously existed and set out the Act's remedying provisions.[43] Welcoming the reforms of the 1696 Act, Care commented, "one would wonder that amongst a people so jealous of their liberties, that it had not been done before; or indeed that in these cases, where the punishment is so great, the criminal should not have the same benefit of defending himself, as he hath for a common trespass."[44]

The procedures Care critiqued at treason trials remained in place for ordinary felony trials in England.[45] No right to counsel, to a copy of the indictment, to compulsory process, or to sworn favorable testimony was assured there. Sentiment in favor of allowing counsel as to matters of fact at all felony trials was widespread but did not prevail.[46] Only gradually did the impact of defense counsel on the structure of the treason trial extend to the trial of other felony cases.[47] But a process had begun. By the 1730s, English judges were increasingly allowing counsel to appear in felony cases and to undertake a broad range of functions, including cross-examination, with the sole exception of addressing the jury.[48] Nonetheless, not until the 1780s was it common to see counsel at felony trials in England.[49]

---

[43] Henry Care, *English Liberties or the Free-born Subject's Inheritance* (4th edn, in the Savoy 1719) 89–92. Care's first edition was published c 1680 in London for Benjamin Harris. Crown officers in England confiscated five thousand copies of the work. Harris was forced to flee to America where the work continued to be published up to 1774. John B Nann and Morris L Cohen, *The Yale Guide to Research in American Legal History* (Yale University Press 2018) 87.

[44] Care (n 43) 89.

[45] For analysis of the reasons restricting the safeguards of the 1696 Act to treason, see Langbein, *Adversary Trial* (n 6) 97–102. Logic might suggest that the newly secured safeguards should not have been restricted within the narrow boundary of treason trials. Several reasons, however, may have underlay parliament's limitation of its procedures to treason. Treason, being a singularly complex charge to defend against, warranted the assistance of counsel more than the ordinary felony did. See Sollom Emlyn commenting: "In Cases of High-Treason the English subject has peculiar advantages: This is a Charge of a general nature, and therefore more difficult to make a Defence to; it subjects the offender to a severer punishment, than other crimes; the crown is more nearly concerned, by reason whereof the Prisoner has a more powerful adversary to contend with." Sollom Emlyn, "Preface to the Second Edition" in 1 *St Tr* xxvi.

[46] Beattie, *Crime* (n 27) 358.

[47] Beattie suggests that an argument made in favor of including all felony trials may have failed "because while defendants in treason trials were usually gentlemen, even peers, the accused in most felonies were poor. Nonetheless, the branching out of the rule that prohibited accused in high treason cases from engaging counsel almost certainly made it easier for the judges to allow accused felons the same priviliege when the balance in the courtroom appeared to shift against them." Beattie, "Scales" (n 38) 223.

[48] Judicial discretion in favor of allowing defense counsel may have been influenced by the increasingly common appearance of attorneys for the prosecution. Beattie, *Crime* (n 27) 359; Beattie, "Scales" (n 38) 226. Langbein comments, "The most important connection between the reforms of the 1690s and the 1730s is that the judges of the 1730s understood the enduring lesson of the Stuart treason trials—that there might lurk within common law criminal procedure the potential for convicting the innocent." Langbein, *Adversary Trial* (n 6) 172.

[49] Not until 1836 was the process of full assistance of counsel complete. The Prisoner's Counsel Act ("An Act for enabling Persons indicted of Felony to make their Defence by Counsel or Attorney") 6 & 7 Will IV, c 114 (1836).

13

Colonial Esteem of Trial by Jury

Colonial Charters

In 1578, as Sir Humphrey Gilbert set out to explore the Atlantic coast of North America, he carried with him letters patent that Queen Elizabeth had granted. The Queen assured:

> to the said sir Humphrey, his heirs and assigns, and to all and every other of them, and to all and every other person and persons, being of our allegiance . . . and to their and every of their heirs . . . [that they] shall and may have and enjoy all the privileges of free denizens[1] and persons native to England, and within our allegiance.[2]

Elizabeth further provided that the future colonists could draw up "statutes, laws, and ordinances," provided that they "may be as near as conveniently may, agreeable to the laws and policies of England."[3] The Queen made similar assurances in letters patent[4] to Sir Walter Raleigh[5] before his fall from grace. Likewise, James I on April 10, 1606, in granting the First Charter of Virginia, declared that all subjects and those born to them within the colonies and plantations:

> shall have and enjoy all liberties, franchises, and immunities, within any of our other dominions, to all intents and purposes, as if they had been abiding and born within this our Realm of England, or any of our other said dominions.[6]

---

[1] According to Blackstone, "[a] denizen is an alien born, but who has obtained *ex donatione regis* letters patent to make him an English subject: a high and incommunicable branch of the royal prerogative. A denizen is in a kind of middle state between an alien, and natural-born subject, and partakes of both of them." Bl Comm c 45. For discussion of the term "free denizens," see Mary Sarah Bilder, "Charter Constitutionalism: The Myth of Edward Coke and the Virginia Charter" (2016) 94 NC L Rev 1545, 1561, 1563.

[2] Letter Patent to Sir Humfrey Gylberte, June 11, 1578, in Francis Newton Thorpe (ed and compiler), 1 *Federal and State Constitutions Colonial Charters, and Other Organic Laws of the States, Territories, and Colonies Now or Heretofore Forming the United States of America* (GPO 1909, reprint Buffalo 1993) (7 vols) 49, 51. Even before Gilbert received his charter, it was clear from practice and from earlier letters patent that English liberties extended to children born overseas, thus guaranteeing that children born in the colonies shared the same liberties as those born in England. Bilder, "Charter" (n 1) 1546–1553 and passim. On the history of the first Virginia charter, see ibid 1563–1564. See generally Mary Sarah Bilder, *The Transatlantic Constitution: Colonial Legal Culture and Empire* (Harvard University Press 2004).

[3] 1 Thorpe (n 2) 49.

[4] For discussion of the terms "letters patent" and "charters," see Mary Sarah Bilder, "English Settlement and Local Governance" in Michael Grossberg and Christopher Tomlins (eds), *The Cambridge History of Law in America* (CUP 2008) 63, 65–66.

[5] 1 Thorpe (n 2) 53.

[6] The First Charter of Virginia (1606) in 7 Thorpe (n 2) 3783. The second and third charters of Virginia made similar provision, 7 Thorpe (n 2) 3790, 3802. On the myth that Sir Edward Coke authored the first charter of Virginia, see Mary Sarah Bilder, "Charter" (n 1) 1545 and passim. On other colonies enjoying the

Foundations of American Criminal Due Process at Trial. Francis R. Herrmann and Brownlow M. Speer,
Oxford University Press. © Oxford University Press 2025. DOI: 10.1093/9780199364770.003.0013

From the beginning of British settlements in North America, colonists firmly believed that they possessed the same legal rights as any other British subjects.[7] The crown authorized colonies to adapt English common law to the fresh circumstances of each in their new environments, as varying practical concerns might suggest to them, so long as the laws they enacted were not "repugnant" to the statutes and traditions of England.[8] Accordingly, the manner and details in which one colony received the common law differed in its implementation from another, as well as from aspects of practice in England.[9] It was clear, in any case, that the colonies guarded their right to common law.[10]

Colonial Esteem for Trial by Jury

From the very beginnings of the colonies, James I (1603–1625) implanted trial by jury. The King issued "Articles, Instructions and Orders" (November 20, 1606) for the subjects in "the country commonly called Virginia and America between thirty-four and forty-five degrees from the aequinoctial line" (a territory spanning present-day northern South Carolina to the northern border of New Hampshire and mid-Maine). "[F]or the good government of the people to be planted in those parts and for the good ordering and disposing of all causes happening within the same (and the same to be done for the substance thereof as neer to the common lawes of England and the equity thereof as may be)," James directed that the resolution of serious crimes was to be resolved:

> within the precinct of their several colonies, in manner and forme following, that is to say, by twelve honest and indifferent persons sworne upon the Evangelists . . . and the twelve persons shall, according to their evidence to be given unto them upon oath and according to the truth, in their consciences, either convict or acquit every of the said persons so to be accused and tried by them.[11]

"rights of Englishmen," see Charter of New England (1620) in 3 Thorpe (n 2) 1827, 1839; Massachusetts Bay (1629) in 3 Thorpe (n 2) 1846, 1856–1857; The Charter of Maryland (1632) in 3 Thorpe (n 2) 1677, 1681; Grant of the Province of Maine (1639) in 3 Thorpe (n 2) 1625, 1635; Charter of Connecticut (1662) in 1 Thorpe (n 2) 533; Charter of Rhode Island and Province Plantations (1663) in 6 Thorpe (n 2) 3220; Charter of Carolina (1633) in 5 Thorpe (n 2) 2743, 2747; Charter of Georgia (1732) in 2 Thorpe (n 2) 765, 773. See Richard L Perry (ed), *Sources of Our Liberties: Documentary Origins of Individual Liberties in the United States Constitution and Bill of Rights* (revised edn, American Bar Foundation 1978) 35 & n 12.

[7] Eben Moglen, "The Privilege in British North America: The Colonial Period to the Fifth Amendment" in RH Helmholz and others (eds), *The Privilege against Self-Incrimination: Its Origins and Development* (The University of Chicago Press 1997) 129; BH McPherson, *The Reception of English Law Abroad* (Brisbane 2007) 224–225.

[8] Mary Sarah Bilder comments: "The central principle—that a colony's laws could not be repugnant to the laws of England but could differ according to the people and place—bound all the American colonies." Bilder, *Transatlantic* (n 2) 1. On the principles of repugnancy and divergence, see ibid 40–50.

[9] Moglen (n 7) 110–111.

[10] See John Phillip Reid, *Constitutional History of the American Revolution: The Authority of Rights* (The University of Wisconsin Press 1986).

[11] "Articles, Instructions, and Orders" (November 20, 1620), printed in William Waller Hening, 1 *The Statutes at Large, being a Collection of All the Laws of Virginia from the First Session of the Legislature in the Year 1619* (New York, printed for the editor 1823) (13 vols) 67–68. The instructions provided for jury trial for "the offences of tumults, rebellion, conspiracies, mutiny and seditions . . . together with murther,

James's order provided that, as in England, any confession to a charged crime must be made "voluntarily."[12] Although surviving reports are scarce, if they existed at all, it appears the criminal trial in the early decades of the British colonies generally mirrored that of England. It was an "altercation" between accused and accuser.[13]

The *Ordinances for Virginia* (1621) specifically required trial as in England:

> [W]e require ... the said General Assembly, as also the said Council of State, to imitate and follow the Policy of the Form of Government, Laws, Customs, and Manner of Trial, and other Administration of Justice, used in the Realm of England, as near as may be.[14]

Successor charters and agreements throughout the seventeenth century repeatedly affirmed trial by jury.[15] The frequency of use of the jury, however, varied among

---

manslaughter, incest, rapes, and adulteries committed in those parts within the precincts of any of the degrees above mentioned (and noe other offences) shall be punished by death." Ibid 69. The minutes of judicial proceedings in 1633 report a jury convicting a woman for manslaughter in the death of her child (ibid 209) and a conviction by jury for homicide per misadventure in 1654/55 (ibid 406). See also Act XXIV, 1661/1662 in 2 Hening (n 11) 63–64 (allowing some jurors in some criminal cases to be chosen outside vicinage contrary to the laws of England because "the remoteness of our habitations do not allow us so fully to practice as we desire, yet that we may come as neere to them as we possibly may"). For reports of jury trials from 1660 to 1666–1667, see ibid 549–553. Less serious crimes were customarily tried by summary procedure. Perry (n 6) 34–35. Jury trials in the seventeenth century were few. Michael Meranze, "Penalty and the Colonial Project: Crime, Punishment, and the Regulation of Morals in Early America" in Grossberg and Tomlins (eds) (n 4) 193. See also Susan C Towne, "The Historical Origins of Bench Trial for Serious Crimes" (1982) 26 Am J Legal Hist 123, 124–145, 151.

[12] "and that all and every person or persons which shall voluntarily confesse any of the said offences to be committed by him shall, upon such his confession thereof, be convicted of the same as if he had been found guilty of the same by the verdict of any such twelve jurors." 1 Hening (n 11) 70. Anyone "who shall stand mute or refusing to make direct answer [to the charges] shall be and be held convicted of the same as if he had been found guilty by the verdict of such twelve jurors, as aforesaid." Ibid.

[13] Moglen (n 7) 110, 112–114, 121–122.

[14] The *Ordinances of Virginia* (1621) in 7 Thorpe (n 2) 3810, 3812.

[15] *Laws of the Colony of New Plymouth* (1623) in William Brigham (ed), *The Compact with the Charter and Laws of the Colony of New Plymouth* (Dutton and Wentworth 1836) 28 ("It was ordained 17 day of December Ano. 1623 by the court then held that all criminall facts, and also all matters of trespasses and debts betweene man and man should be tried by the verdict of twelve honest men to be impanelled by authority in forme of a jury upon their oath").

The *Charter of Maryland* (1632) made no express mention of jury, but the power was given to resolve criminal matters in a manner "(so far as conveniently may be) agreeable to the Laws, Statutes, Customs, and Rights of Our Kingdom of England." 3 Thorpe (n 2) 1681. So also New Hampshire (1680) in 4 Thorpe (n 2) 2515.

Massachusetts Body of Liberties, para 29 (1641): Plaintiffs and defendants may choose bench or jury trial. "The like libertie shall be granted to all persons in Criminall cases." See also paras 30, 31, 49, 50, 76, pertaining to juries. William H Whitmore, *Colonial Law of Massachusetts. Reprinted from the Edition of 1660 ... Containing also the Body of Liberties of 1641* (Rockwell and Churchhill 1889) 39.

The *Government of Rhode Island* (1641) in 6 Thorpe (n 2) 3208–3209 (regulating quarter sessions courts and referring to the jury).

The *Fundamental Constitutions of Carolina* (1669), c 111: "No cause whether civil or criminal, of any freeman shall be tried in any court of judicature, without a jury of his peers." William MacDonald (ed), *Select Charters and Other Documents Illustrative of American History 1606–1775* (Macmillan Co 1906) 167.

Concessions and Agreements of West New Jersey, c XVII (1676): "That no ... inhabitant of the said Province of West New Jersey, shall be deprived or condemned of life, limb, liberty, estate, property or any ways hurt in his or their privileges, freedoms or franchises, upon any account whatsoever, without a due tryal, and judgment passed by twelve good and lawful men of his neigborhood first had: And that all causes to be tryed, and in all tryals, the person or persons arraigned may except against any of the said

the colonies. Capital offenses were most likely to entail juries; minor offenses less so. Rhode Island accorded jury trials for virtually all offenses with the exception of drunkenness.[16]

Consistent with the charters' assurances, legal literature available in the colonies emphatically extolled the right to a jury trial. In *The Excellent Privilege of Liberty & Property Being the Birth-Right of the Free-born Subjects of England* (1687), William Penn wrote that the "Birth-right of English-men shines most conspicuously" in "two grand pillars of English liberty," parliaments and juries.[17] Many colonial lawyers possessed *English Liberties, or the Free-born Subjects Inheritance* of Henry Care (1646– 1688) in its London editions or later American ones.[18] Care was a successor of the Levellers.[19] Thomas Jefferson's second library contained two copies of Care's *English Liberties*, as did the library to which George Mason had access.[20] Colonial lawyers would have read Care's praise for trial by jury as an "advantage Englishmen enjoy . . . above any other nations under heaven."[21] In the same vein, Giles Duncombe's *Trials per pais: or, The Law of England concerning juries by nisi prius*, also familiar in the colonies, spoke of jury trial:

> You know that in the whole Practice of Law, there is nothing of greater Excellency, nor of more frequent Use than Trials by *Juries*. In this, our Common Law (and not without just Cause) values itself beyond the Imperial Law, before the Canon Law, or any other Laws in the World . . . .For without Victory at the Trial, to what Purpose is the Science of Law?[22]

The *Conductor Generalis*, a leading practice manual throughout the colonies, similarly emphasized the centrality of the jury right for British subjects:

neighborhood, without any reason rendered (not exceeding thirty five) and in case of any valid reason alleged, against every person nominated for that service." 5 Thorpe (n 2) 2549.

The Fundamental Constitutions of the Province of East New Jersey in America, c XIV (provisions for jury trial by twelve proprietors) in 5 Thorpe (n 2) 2579.

Frame of Govt of Pennsylvania (1682), para VIII: "That all trials shall be by twelve men, and as near as may be, peers or equals, and of the neighborhood, and men without just exception . . . But reasonable challenges shall be always admitted against the said twelve men, or any of them." 5 Thorpe (n 2) 360.

[16] Albert W Alschuler and Andrew G Deiss, "A Brief History of the Criminal Jury in the United States" (1994) 61 U Chi L Rev 867, 871 n 17.

[17] William Penn, *The Excellent Privilege of Liberty and Property Being the Birth-right of Free-born Subjects of England* (Philadelphia, printed by William Bradford [n.p.] 1687).

[18] Henry Care, *English Liberties, or the Free-born Subjects Inheritance* (In the Savoy, printed by Eliz. Nutt and R. Gosling 1719). Care's text was first published in London c 1680 for Benjamin Harris "who was forced to flee to America in 1686 in part for his publication of this book." John B Nann and Morris L Cohen, *The Yale Law School Guide to Research in American Legal History* (Yale University Press 2018) 87. Care's text was republished in Boston 1721 and Providence 1774 "and many colonial lawyers had copies of the several earlier London editions." Ibid.

[19] Gary S DeKrey, 2 *Following the Levellers* (Palgrave Macmillan 2017) (2 vols) 328.

[20] H Trevor Colbourn, "Thomas Jefferson's Use of the Past" (1958) 15 The William and Mary Quarterly 56, 62 n 30. Mason had access to Care's work in the library of John Mercer, Mason's uncle and guardian.

[21] Care (n 18) 244.

[22] Giles Duncombe, *Trials per pais, or the Law of England Concerning juries nisi prius, &c.* (London in the Savoy [n.p.] 1718).

Trial by juries is the Englishman's birth right, and is that happy way of trial, which notwithstanding all revolutions of times, hath been continued beyond all memory to this present day; the beginning whereof no history specifies, it being contemporary with the foundation of this state, and one of the pillars of it, both as to age and consequence.[23]

In Virginia, George Webb's very popular *Office of the Justice of the Peace* (1736) spoke of:

this invaluable Privilege of being tried by their Peers; which they [British subjects] enjoy at this Day, so that none of them can suffer in his Life, Liberty, or Property, until he is found Guilty, by the Verdict of 12 of his Neighbours, or Equals, upon their Oath. A happy security! Peculiar to the British Subject, envied perhaps, but not enjoyed by any other Nation in the World.[24]

In sum, "[W]e cannot capture the extreme euphoria of British and colonist alike when they thought of jury trial."[25]

The Elements of Trial by Jury

Besides reading imported English legal texts or those printed in the colonies and collected in private libraries,[26] those interested in the law, whether professional lawyers or "legal literates" could receive education by tutoring from or clerking with lawyers.[27]

[23] James Parker, *Conductor Generalis, or the Office, Duty and Authority of Justices of the Peace* (James Parker 1764) 261. The 1764 edition was "compiled chiefly from Burn's *Justice*, and the several other books on those subjects, as far as they extend and can be adapted to these American Colonies," quoting Duncombe (n 22) 3 Dalton c 186.

[24] George Webb, *The Office and Authority of a Justice of the Peace ... Collected from the Common and Statute Laws of England ... Adapted to the Constitution and Practice of Virginia* (Williamsburg, printed by William Parks 1736) 195.

[25] 1 Reid (n 10) 47, quoted in Moglen (n 7) 130.

[26] As to the availability of English legal literature imported into the colonies, see Herbert A Johnson, *Imported Eighteenth-Century Law Treatises in American Libraries, 1700-1799* (The University of Tennessee Press 1978). As to English legal literature printed in the colonies, see Eldon Revare James, "A List of Legal Treatises Printed in the British Colonies and the American States Before 1801" in Morton Carlisle Campbell and others, *Harvard Legal Essays: Written in Honor of and Presented to Joseph Henry Beale and Samuel Williston* (Harvard University Press 1934) 159-211. Much research on the contents of colonial legal libraries has focused on Virginia. See, eg, William Hamilton Bryson, *Census of Law Books in Colonial Virginia* (University Press of Virginia 1978); Warren M Billings and Brent Tarter (eds), *"Esteemed Books of Law" and the Legal Culture of Early Virginia* (University of Virginia Press 2017); WH Bryson, "Private Libraries before 1776" in W Hamilton Bryson (ed), *Virginia Law Books: Essays and Bibliographies* (American Philosophical Society 2000) 479-499. On colonial private libraries in general, see Joe W Kraus, "Private Libraries in Colonial America" (1974) 9 The Journal of Library History 31-53. Kraus observes that "the books that formed the libraries of Virginia and in North and South Carolina were not markedly different from those found in libraries in the Northern Colonies." Ibid 44. "The personal libraries of colonists from different regions did not differ as much as one might expect." Ibid 50. See also Moglen (n 7) 114-117 on English JP manuals imported in the colonies and on American manuals produced in the colonies.

[27] Mary Sarah Bilder employs the phrase "legal practiioners and legal literates" to capture broadly the variety of colonists knowledgeable in law besides professional attorneys. Bilder, *Transatlantic* (n 2) 15-30. Bilder disestablishes "the myth of the seventeenth-century colonies as being a world of 'law without lawyers.'" Ibid 15. See also Mary Sarah Bilder, "The Lost Lawyers: Early American Legal Literates and

It was also common, for those who could afford to do so, to send their sons to study law at the Inns of Court.[28] Those who did so returned to the colonies with a know-ledge of the reforms of trial procedure legislated in the 1696 Treason Act as to wit-nesses and counsel for the accused.[29]

Legal tracts and manuals available in the colonies made clear that jury trial comprised much more than a bare determination of guilt or innocence by twelve jurors. It encom-passed, as well, a group of elements that custom or statute firmly attached to the trial.[30] Care's popular *English liberties* set out the elements:

> by a fundamental law in our government, no man's life ... shall be touched for any crime whatsoever, but upon being found guilty on two several trials (for so may that of the Grand and Petty Jury be called) and the judgment of twice twelve men at least, all of his own condition and neighborhood, and upon their oaths ... that is to say, twelve or more to find the bill of indictment against him, and twelve others to give judgment upon the general issue of *not guilty*; all which jurors must be honest, substantial, impartial men, and being neighbours of the party accused, or place where the supposed fact was com-mitted, cannot be presumed to be unacquainted either with the matters charged, the prisoner's course of life, or the credit of the evidence; and all these must first be fully satisfied in their consciences that he is guilty, and so unanimously pronounce him upon their oaths, or else he cannot be condemned.[31]

For Care, trial by jury included rights to an indictment by grand jury, impartial petty jurors drawn from the vicinage, and a verdict of guilt unanimously reached upon ev-idence fully satisfying the jurors' consciences.[32] It also included a right to challenge "thirty-five in case of treason and twenty of them in felony, without showing any

---

Transatlantic Legal Culture" (1999) 11 Yale JL & Human 47. On the legal environment of the colonies, see Nann and Cohen (n 18) 76–83 and works cited.

[28] Helen Hill Miller, *The Case for Liberty* (University of North Carolina Press 1965) 148. Colonial atti-tudes varied concerning formal legal education at the English Inns of Court. New York considered it useless and expensive; South Carolina required it for admission to the bar. Johnson (n 26) xxv.

[29] Francis H Heller (Francis Howard), *The Sixth Amendment to the Constitution of the United States: A Study in Constitutional Development* (University of Kansas Press 1951) 21.

[30] Moglen (n 7) 128–130, citing 1 Reid (n 10) 47.

[31] Care (n 18) 245–246.

[32] That a jury's verdict based on the jurors' consciences is inviolable was authoritatively decided some ten years before Care composed his work. In 1670, a jury acquitted William Penn and William Mead, both Quaker preachers, who were prosecuted for unlawful assembly and disturbance of the peace. The trial court, convinced that the verdict was against the facts and the law, ordered the jurors held in prison until they paid a fine. Edward Bushel, one of the jurors, sought a writ of habeas corpus. Vaughn, J, in the Court of Common Pleas ruled that inquiry into a jury's verdict is barred, absent ministerial abuse. *Bushel*, 84 Eng Rpt 1123 (1670); Jones T, 13 (1670). For discussion of the case, see Thomas A Green, "Light Hidden Under *Bushel's Case*" in John Witte Jr and others, *Texts and Contexts in Legal History: Essays in Honor of Charles Donahue* (The Robbins Collection 2016) 397–412; James Q Whitman, *The Origins of Reasonable Doubt: Theological Roots of the Criminal Trial* (Yale University Press 2008) 176–178, 188–189 and passim; George Fisher, "The Jury's Rise as Lie Detector" (1997) 107 Yale LJ 575, 706; Thomas Andrew Green, *Verdict According to Conscience: Perspectives on the English Criminal Trial, 1200–1800* (University of Chicago Press 1985) 236–249 and passim.

cause; and as many more as he can assign cause against."[33] "Deservedly therefore is this trial by juries ranked amongst the choicest of our fundamental laws."[34]

Care did not include the assistance of counsel as one of the elements of trial by jury. The 1719 edition of *English Liberties*, however, taking note of the 1696 Treason Act and welcoming its provision for counsel, argued in favor of extending assistance of counsel to all felony cases. Care pointed out the inconsistency of allowing counsel for misdemeanors but not for capital offenses.

> Now as to trials of treason, there hath been a considerable alteration in the law for the benefit of subject in late years; and one would wonder that amongst a people so jealous of their liberties, it had no done before; or indeed, that in these cases, where punishment is so great the criminal should have the benefit of defending himself, as he hath for common trespass.[35]

Manuals for justices of the peace also explained the elements of a jury trial as then understood.[36] The *Conductor Generalis*, available in repeated editions, described trial by jury as requiring that twelve men of the county "come and say the truth upon which the issue is joined";[37] that they be of the vicinage;[38] impartial, not being kindred of any party, or having declared an "opinion beforehand that the party is guilty, or will be hanged, or the like."[39] Parties could exercise peremptory challenges and challenges for cause;[40] the defendant was to be summoned and given opportunity to be heard, as a matter of "natural justice."[41] "[A] witness" was "not be asked any question, the answering to which might oblige him to accuse himself of a crime."[42]

In *The History of the Common Law of England*, Matthew Hale (1609–1676), the Lord Chief Justice of the Court of King's Bench and chair of the law reform Hale

---

[33] Care (n 18) 247.

[34] Ibid.

[35] Care (n 18) 90. Sollom Emlyn's critique of the denial of counsel in felony cases would also have been familiar to those who read his preface to the 1730 edition of *State Trials*. Commenting on the 1696 Treason Act's improved defensive safeguards, Emlyn took the occasion to suggest improvements in ordinary jury-trial procedure: "Hitherto the Law allows no copy of the Indictment, nor of the names of Jurors, nor the assistance of Counsel as to matter of fact for any Indictments of Felony, yet it is the opinion of many it would never be the worse if it did; for it seems very strange to allow a man these assistances in defence of his property, and deny them to him, when his life lies at stake." Sollom Emlyn, "Preface," 1 *St Tr* 31 (1719). England, however, continued to deny defense counsel on matters of fact in felony cases until 1836, although judges before then increasingly relaxed the rule. See generally JB Post, *The Admissibility of Defence Counsel in English Criminal Procedure* (1984) 5 J Legal Hist 23, 23.

[36] See, eg, Webb (n 24) 192–200; *Conductor generalis* (New York [s.n.] 1711) 155; Michael Dalton, *The Countrey Justice . . . Gathered for the Better Help of Such Justices of the Peace, as Have Not Been Much Conversant in the Study of the Laws of This Realm* (printed for John Walthoe 1715) cc 186–187; Richard Starke, *Office and Authority of a Justice of Peace: Explained and Digested, under Proper Titles* (Williamsburg, printed by Alexander Purdie and John Dixon 1774) 233. The manual was particularly popular in Virginia. On summary procedure in the colonies, see Moglen (n 7) 122–128.

[37] Richard Burn, *The Conductor Generalis* (Hugh Gaine 1788) vii.

[38] Ibid 247.

[39] Ibid 251.

[40] Ibid 251-254.

[41] Ibid 189.

[42] Ibid 169

Commission, summarized elements of jury trial.[43] The 1713 edition's account of jury trial sets out that jurors "are to be of the neighbourhood of the Fact to be inquired, or at least of the county or baileywick."[44] Parties must have "notice of the jurors and their sufficiency, and indifferency."[45] The jurors can be challenged until indifferent.[46] The evidence on either part is "given in upon the oath of witnesses . . . and other evidence in open court and in the presence of the parties, the attorneys, counsel, and by-standers, and before the judge and jury."[47]

> [b]y this course of personal and open examination, there is opportunity for all persons concern'd, *viz.* the judge, or any of the jury, or parties, or their council or attornies, to propound occasional questions personal appearance and testimony of witnesses, there is opportunity for confronting the adverse witnesses, of observing the contradiction of witnesses sometimes on the same side and by this means great opportunities are gain'd for the true and clear discovery of the truth.[48]

Unanimity of the twelve jurors is required. "When the whole twelve men are agreed upon, then, and not until then, is their verdict to be received . . . but if any one of the twelve dissent, it is no verdict, nor ought it to be received":

> And indeed this give a great weight, value and credit to such a verdict, wherein twelve men must unanimously agree in a matter of fact, and none dissent; though it must be agreed that an ignorant parcel of men are sometimes governed by a few that are more knowing, or of greater interest or reputation than the rest.[49]

William Hawkins's *Treatise of the Pleas of the Crown*,[50] frequently annotated with references to the State Trials, extensively explicated the principles of jury trial. His work could be found in colonial libraries in many editions. Hawkins interpreted the statute of 1 Anne st 2, c 9 (1702), which allowed witnesses for a defendant to be sworn, to include allowance of process to compel their appearance in any case whatsoever.[51] Hawkins also laid out the common-law doctrines relating to double jeopardy, namely, the pleas of *autrefois acquit* ("that a man shall not be brought into danger of his life for one and the same offence, more than once")[52] and *autrefois attaint* or *convict* ("wherever a man is attained of felony either by judgment upon a verdict or outlawry . . . it is against a maxim of law to bring a man into such danger more than once for one and the same offence").[53]

---

[43] Matthew Hale, *The History of the Common Law of England* (E Nutt 1713) 252–264. The text was available in the colonies. See Johnson (n 26) 27.

[44] Ibid 252–253.

[45] Ibid 253–254.

[46] Ibid 256–257.

[47] Ibid 256.

[48] Ibid 258.

[49] Ibid 261.

[50] William Hawkins, 2 *Treatise of the Pleas of the Crown: Or, a System of the Principal Matters Relating to That Subject* (London 1739) (2 vols).

[51] Ibid 435. See Peter Westen, "The Compulsory Process Clause" (1974) Mich L Rev 71, 90.

[52] 2 Hawkins (n 50) 368.

[53] Ibid 375.

Colonial Criminal Trial Procedure

In the early period of the colonies, pretrial and trial procedure generally accorded with the common-law format of the "accused speaks."[54] In pretrial procedure, the manuals followed the Marian statutes for questioning suspects and prosecution witnesses.[55] A justice of the peace was to reduce all statements of prosecution witnesses to writing. They were made under oath. A principal against self-incrimination protected witnesses under oath because *nemo debet seipsum accusare*.[56] The depositions of the prosecution witnesses could be used at trial if there were excusing circumstances, such as death, inability to travel, or procurement of the witness's absence by the defendant, provided that the suspect was present at the deposition and could have cross-examined.[57] Grand jury indictments were used in many colonies. At trial proper, as in England, defendants were not placed under oath, but could speak in their own defense. While there was no legal punishment if they chose not to speak, their silence in the face of incriminating questions could be taken as evidence of admission. Witnesses testifying under oath were protected against self-incrimination, as had long been the rule in England, regarding their own crimes or moral turpitude.[58] A Virginia grand assembly in 1677 shows the common-law tradition in operation there:

> Upon motion from Acomack county, sent by their burgesses, It is answered and declared, that the law has provided that a person summoned as a witness against another, ought to answer upon oath, but no law can compel a man to swear against himself in any matter wherein he is liable to corporal punishment.[59]

As to whether witnesses for a defendant testified under oath, the record is incomplete. Virginia allowed for summoning defense witnesses and taking their testimony under oath. And in New York, as well, defense witnesses were sworn.[60]

Legal treatises composed in England, even when printed in the colonies, did not include the full assistance of counsel within the matrix of elements constituting jury trial. The 1749 *Conductor Generalis* took note of the 1696 Treason Act's improvements on defense safeguards at trial, including the right to full defense by counsel for persons accused of treason;[61] but, as to all other felony trials, the *Conductor* stated the familiar rule that "[i]n trials of criminals the court is to be of counsel with the prisoner, and ought to advise him for his good, not taking advantage too strictly against him."[62]

---

[54] Moglen (n 7) 112. See Albert W Alschuler, "A Peculiar Privilege in Historical Perspective" in RH Helmholz and others (eds), *The Privilege against Self-Incrimination: Its Origins and Development* (The University of Chicago Press 1997) 194.

[55] See, eg, Starke (n 36) 143–144. The manual was particularly popular in Virginia.

[56] James Parker, *Conductor Generalis* (2nd edn, printed by J Parker 1749) 100.

[57] Starke (n 36) 143–144, relying on 2 Hawkins (n 50) 430.

[58] Starke (n 36) 145–146.

[59] 2 Hening (n 11) 422.

[60] Randolph N Jonakait, "The Origins of the Confrontation Clause: An Alternative History" (1995) 27 Rutgers LJ 77, 99.

[61] Parker, *Conductor Generalis* (n 56) 302.

[62] Ibid 279. For an example of a colonial court in 1692 denying counsel but assuring it would assist a defendant at a felony trial, see H Clay Reed and George J Miller (eds), *Burlington Court Book: A Record of Quaker Jurisprudence in West New Jersey, 1608–1709* (American Historical Association1944) (upon

Hawkins expressed no doubt about the traditional view that the court would act as counsel or would appoint counsel, if needed, as to questions of law. Hale noted that the 1696 Act had made the law "more tender than it was in former times" respecting counsel for treason defendants, but passed over the issue of felony defendants.[63] As late as 1765, Blackstone acknowledged that the exclusion of defense counsel in felony cases was still "a settled rule of common law." He took the occasion to remark that the rule "seems to be not at all of a piece with the rest of the humane treatment of prisoners by the English law."[64]

Whatever may have been the judicial practice regarding counsel in England, the American colonies, as we have seen, were free to adapt their inherited common law to colonial needs, so long as not "repugnant" to the laws of the mother country. Colonists exercised that flexibility in the matter of defense counsel. Although there was variation among them, colonies adopted a more liberal stance regarding counsel at criminal trials than was customarily granted in England.[65] As early as 1641, the Massachusetts *Body of Liberties* provided that "every man that findeth himself unfit to plead his owne cause in any Court shall have Libertie to imploy any man against whom the Court doth not except, to helpe him."[66] Rhode Island was early in expanding a right to counsel. Even before England extended that right in treason cases, Rhode Island allowed counsel by statute in 1669, although, like the mother country, it limited counsel's role "to plead any point of law."[67] William Penn's Charter of 1701 for Pennsylvania extended to "all criminals . . . the same privileges of witnesses and council as their prosecutors."[68] The Charter covered Delaware, as well. By 1731, South Carolina's legislature provided for the assignment of counsel upon request of the defendant.[69] Virginia in 1734, in a statute for "enabling all persons brought to trial for capital cases, to make their best defence," provided "in all trials for capital offences, the prisoner, upon his petition to the court, shall be allowed counsel."[70] Given the

requesting counsel, defendant told "if he want to know any particular in law touching the premises, he shall be informed; but if it be a matter of fact, counsel against the king cannot be allowed him") 138.

[63] Matthew Hale and Giles Jacob, *Pleas of the Crown* (J N Assignee of Edw Sawyer 1716) 6.
[64] 2 Bl Co 354.
[65] See Randolph N Jonakait, "The Origins of the Confrontation Clause: An Alternative History" (1995) 27 Rutgers L J 77, 94–97 and passim (colonies were in advance of England in extending a full right to the assistance of counsel, thus enabling opportunity for robust cross-examination); Randolph N Jonakait, "The Rise of the American Adversary System: America before England" (2009) 14 Widener L Rev 323, 327–332; William M Beaney, *Right to Counsel in American Courts* (University of Michigan Press 1955) 15; Felix Rackow, "The Right to Counsel: English and American Precedents" (1954) 11 William & Mary Quarterly 3, 12–21. For the development of cross-examination in England in the eighteenth century, see Stephan Landsman, "Rise of the Contentious Spirit: Adversary Procedure in Eighteenth Century England" (1990) 75 Cornell L Rev 496; John Felipe Acevedo, "The Ideological Origins of the Right to Counsel" (2016) 68 S C L Rev 87, 88.
[66] William H Whitmore, *Colonial Laws of Massachusetts. Reprinted from the Edition of 1660, with the Supplements to 1672. Containing also, the Body of Liberties of 1641* (Rockwell and Churchill 1889) 39.
[67] See Moglen (n 7) 112.
[68] "Charter of Privileges granted by William Penn, Esq. to the Inhabitants of Pennsylvania and Territories, 1701, Art. V" in 5 Thorpe (n 2) 3079. By statute in 1718, Pennsylvania provided that in all capital trials "learned counsel" would be "assigned defendants." Act of May 31, 1718, c CCXVII, s 4, I *Laws of Penn.* 134 (Dallas 1700–1781). See Rackow (n 65) 18 n 65.
[69] No 552, s XLIII, enacted August 20, 1731 (Grimke, *Public Laws of South Carolina, 1682–1790*) 129. See Rackow (n 65) 20.
[70] Laws of Virginia, 8th Geo II (1734) in 4 Hening (n 11) 404.

scarcity of trial records, it is not possible to judge how much practice was in accord. New York ordinarily followed the common-law limiting counsel, yet at Peter Zenger's 1735 trial for seditious libel, four defense counsel appeared on the defendant's behalf. North Carolina in a 1777 statute provided that "every person accused of any crime or misdemeanor whatsoever, shall be entitled to council in all matters which may be necessary for his defence, as well as to facts as to law."[71] Where counsel did appear, cross-examination was most likely to occur. Without counsel, the defendant was left in the position of the traditional trial by altercation.

Important insights into colonial trial practice in Massachusetts can be gained from the trial of eight British soldiers accused of murder in the Boston Massacre. In 1770, John Adams appeared on their behalf as counsel. First, the very fact that Adams was acting as defense counsel in a non-treason felony case and was cross-examining witnesses is itself sound evidence that the right to counsel was recognized in Massachusetts at the time. In contrast, Adama's legal assistance concerning matters of fact might have been disallowed in England where full assistance of counsel was not extended to felony cases until 1836. Even in New York, counsel's assistance as to matters of fact might not have been permitted.[72] A Massachusetts statute of 1701, however, allowed for counsel in civil matters, and this was extended to criminal cases.[73]

The trial is particularly significant for an additional reason. Adams's recorded summation to the jury, as well as the prosecutor's argument and the instruction of the judges, shines light on the standard of proof expected to justify a criminal conviction. The traditionally accepted standard, both in the colonies and in England, was that of the "satisfied conscience." In the sixteenth century, Thomas Smith described a standard judicial instruction to the jury. It was brief: "Doe that which God shall put in your mindes to the discharge of your consciences." No records show that any judge or party questioned the standard. Yet, neither judges nor counsel, when counsel were permitted, are recorded elaborating upon the meaning of the standard. In that regard, the record of the soldiers' trial is singular. All the legal actors expand upon the degree of confidence in the evidence that jurors ought to possess before reaching their verdict. For his part, Adams arguing on behalf of the soldiers told the jury:

> [I]n the rules laid down by the greatest English judges, who have been the brightest of mankind; We are to look upon it as more beneficial, that many guilty persons should escape unpunished, than one innocent person should suffer . . . [T]he best rule in doubtful cases, is rather to incline to acquittal than conviction.[74]

After drawing on Fortescue's Praise of the Laws of England (1467) to make the same point, Adams added:

---

[71] Session Laws of North Carolina, 1777, c 115, s 85 in I *North Carolina Revised Laws, 1715–1796*, 316. See Rackow (n 65) 19.

[72] See L Kinvin Wroth and Hiller B Zobel (eds), 2 *Legal Papers of John Adams* (The Belkap Press 1965) (hereafter PJA) (3 vols) 402–403 n 40. Counsel was not only allowed, but was appointed by the court.

[73] Ibid.

[74] " 'Adams' Argument for the Defense" in 3 PJA (n 72) 242, 243.

Indeed this rule is not peculiar to the English law,[75] there never was a system of laws in the world, in which this rule did not prevail; it prevailed in the ancient Roman law, and which is more remarkable, it prevails in the modern roman law, even the judges in the Courts of Inquisition who with racks, burnings and scourges, examine criminals, even there, they preserve the maxim, that it is better the guilty should escape punishment, than the innocent suffer. *Satius esse nocentem absolvi quam insentem damnari*, this is the temper we ought to set out with; and these the rules we are to be governed by.[76]

Adams had studied not only English law but a good deal of Roman law, as well.[77] He may well have known from his familiarity with Justinian's Digest that the Latin maxim he employed was a quote from the emperor Trajan's second-century rescript.

The prosecutor Robert Treat Paine spoke in similar terms but even more explicitly about the role of doubt, arguing that the evidence for the prosecution was sufficient to satisfy the jurors' consciences:

Ld Coke's Observation on Our Law in General that it is the *Ultima Ratio* the last improvement of Reason which in the nature of it will not admit any Proposition to be true of which it has not Evidence, nor determine that to be certain of which there remains a doubt; if therefor In the examination of this Cause the Evidence is not sufficient to Convince beyond a reasonable Doubt of the Guilt of all or any of the Prisoners by the Benignity and Reason of the Law you will acquit them, but if the Evidence be sufficient to convince you of their Guilt beyond a reasonable Doubt the Justice of the Law will require you to declare them Guilty and the Benignity of the Law will be satisfied in the fairness and impartiality of their Tryal.[78]

[75] The term "doubt" had long played a central role for fact-finders' considerations. The emperor Hadrian (second century) had called for judgments to rest on proofs that were "undoubted." Augustine (fourth century), drawing on Roman law, determined that no person should be excommunicated, even if the charges might be true, unless "sure evidence" (*certis indiciis*) demonstrated guilt. Otherwise, he said, the innocent would be convicted. Pope Gregory (seventh century) had focused on the concept of "doubt" in guiding judicial judgment: "For it is very grave and unseemly that in a matter that is doubtful, a judgment that is certain should be pronounced." The pseudo-Isidorians (ninth century) had repeated Gregory's caution. Gratian's Decretum (twelfth century) did so, as well. "[I]n doubtful matters there ought not be an absolute judgment" ([I]n rebus ambiguis absolutum non debet esse iudicium). Tancred's *ordo iudiciorum* (twelfth century), drawing on romano-canonical law, had set out the principle that "in matters of doubt" where the evidence was in equipoise, a decision should favor the accused. It was fitting that this be so, Tancred wrote, because the law should be more prompt in acquitting than in convicting. The *ius commune* captured the essence of the matter in its maxim *in dubio pro reo*.

Surely, all of this was long known in England, particularly through ecclesiastical law. In fact, in secular law, the *Leges Henrici Primi* (eleventh century) served as a vehicle for importing into England the term "doubt" used by pseudo-Isidore in relation to making judgments. Certainly, any English jury when determining whether evidence satisfied their consciences weighed their doubts. Yet, no rules in England limited jurors in their evaluation of evidence. Still, neither for the self-informing jury of early times nor for later jurors in altercation-style trials did any instructions guide them apart from an injunction from a judge to "do that which God shall put in your minds to the discharge of your consciences, and marke well what is saide."

[76] Adams Argument (n 74) 243.

[77] On Adams's knowledge of and use of Justinian, see Daniel R Coquillette, *Justinian in Braintree: John Adams, Civilian Learning, and Legal Elitism, 1758–1775* (Colonial Society of Massachusetts 1984).

[78] 3 PJA (n 72) 271.

In his instructions to the jury, Judge Oliver adopted comparable language: "[If] upon the whole, ye are in any reasonable doubt of their guilt, ye must then, agreeable to the rule of law, declare them innocent."[79]

In using the language of reasonable doubt in addressing the jury, counsel and the court do not appear to have been replacing the traditional standard of the "satisfied conscience." Rather, they were explaining how the jury might arrive at a satisfied conscience on the basis of the evidence and in keeping faith with the principle that it is better to acquit the guilty than convict the innocent.[80]

Conclusion

The colonists jealously guarded their jury trial "birth-right" in all its dimensions.[81] In words that colonists on the eve of the American Revolution might well have borne in mind, Henry Care had warned that:

> [W]hoever shall go about openly to suppress [trials by juries], or craftily to undermine, and render only a formality, does *ipso facto* attack the government, [and] brings in an arbitrary power ...; for which reason English Parliaments have all along been most zealous for preserving this great jewel of liberty.[82]

---

[79] Ibid 309.

[80] Barbara Shapiro comments: "Reasonable doubt was simply a better explanation of the satisfied conscience standard that resulted from increasing familiarity with the moral certainty concept." Barbara J Shapiro, *"Beyond Reasonable Doubt" and "Probable Cause": Historical Perspectives on the Anglo-American Law of Evidence* (University of California Press 1991) 21. Randolph Jonakait, agreeing, states: "[R]easonable doubt was just another formulation of a long-utilized standard that did not demand absolute certainty but did require a strong certitude based on reason." Randolph N Jonakait, "Finding the Original Meaning of American Criminal Procedure Rights: Lessons from Reasonable Doubt's Development" (2012) 10 The University of New Hampshire Law Review 97, 147. James Whitman, referring to Adams's argument, states: "There is nothing novel about this: ... many Continental and English moral theologians ... had spoken, almost verbatim, in the same terms during the same years, and indeed for centuries." James Q Whitman, *The Origins of Reasonable Doubt: Theological Roots of the Criminal Trial* (Yale University Press 2008) 193.

[81] On the significance of the jury right to American colonists, see Reid (n 10) 47–59.

Colonial enthusiasm for the jury did not extend to the trials of slaves. Virginia established a special court for the prosecution for them. There was no jury. Other colonies also established special courts for slaves. See Lawrence M Friedman, *A History of American Law* (OUP 2019) 56. See generally ibid 54–57. Thomas Morris, reviewing the relationship of slaves to the law in early America, concludes "for persons of color, and especially for those who were held as property, the rules were never fair. There had even been times when slaves were not only unprotected at law—they were not even admitted to the mysteries of the criminal side of the legal order, unless the case were minor, or they confessed." Thomas D Morris, "Slaves and the Rules of Evidence in Criminal Trials-Symposium on the Law of Slavery: Criminal and Civil Law of Slavery" (1992) 68 Chi-Kent L Rev 1209, 1239–1240. See also Mary Frances Berry describing "how the Founding Fathers had excluded Afro-Americans from political protection and had attempted to establish a rationale for their worthlessness, powerlessness, and lack of humanity by recognizing them as passive objects to be acted upon", Mary Frances Berry, "Slavery, the Constitution, and the Founding Fathers", in *Afro-Americans and the Evolution of a Living Constitution: A Symposium of the Smithsonian Institution and the Joint Center for Political Science* (Smithsonian Institution 1988) 3, 5.

[82] Care (n 18) 247.

The sixth edition of Care's work, published in Providence, Rhode Island, in 1774, added a footnote borrowed from Blackstone's *Commentaries*. The note emphasized the "duty which every man owes his country ... to guard, with the utmost jealous circumspection, against the introduction of new and arbitrary methods of trial, which, under a variety of plausible pretences, may in time imperceptibly undermine this best preservative of English liberty."[83] The following year, Moses Mather, a Yale graduate and Congregational minister, published in Hartford, Connecticut, *America's Appeal to the Impartial World. Wherein the Rights of the Americans, as Men, British Subjects, and as Colonists ... are stated and considered and, the Opposition made by the Colonies to Acts of Parliament, their resorting to arms in their necessary defence ... vindicated* (1775). This work stressed the jury as a central right of the colonists:

> And no mode of trial would so effectually do this [guard the rights of the subject], be so unimpeachable, by reason of equality, and the impartial manner in which they are taken and impanelled; so advantageous, on account of their knowledge of the parties, the credibility of the witnesses, and what weight ought to be given to their testimony, as that by our peers, a jury of the vicinity.[84]

Quoting Blackstone, Mather warned that every colonist was obliged to guard this "most transcendant privilege which any subject can enjoy" against any dilutions.[85] This "glorious constitution" guaranteed that English subjects could not be judged "but by unanimous consent of twelve of his neighbors and equals."[86] It was "worthy to be engraved in capitals of gold, on pillars of marble; to be perpetuated through all time, a barrier, to circumscribe and bound the restless ambition of aspiring monarchs, and the palladium of civil liberty."[87]

[83] Henry Care and William Nelson (compilers), *English Liberties, or the Free-Born Subject's Inheritance* (Providence, John Carter 1774) 216, quoting 3 Bl Co 381.

[84] Moses Mather, *America's Appeal to the Impartial World* (Ebenezer Watson 1775) reprinted in Gordon S Wood (ed), *The American Revolution: Writings from the Pamphlet Debate: II: 1773–1776* (The Library of America 2015) 595, 600–601. Mather became so outspoken an American patriot that he was twice imprisoned by the British. Ibid 844.

[85] Ibid 601.

[86] Ibid.

[87] Ibid 602.

14

Colonial Fears of the Erosion of
Right to Trial by Jury

Perceived British Threats to the Jury

In the last third of the eighteenth century, specific reasons emerged for colonists to be concerned about their jury birthright. A series of parliamentary acts, either adopted or contemplated, threatened the continued enjoyment of the rights commonly understood, to inhere in "trial by jury."

The Sugar Act

As a result of Queen Anne's War (1702–1713), Great Britain found its treasury severely drained. To raise revenue toward paying off the war debt and to bring its expenditures in the North American colonies into balance, Parliament passed the American Revenue Act of 1764.[1] Among colonists, the act became known as the Sugar Act because it enforced taxes on molasses and imposed duties on the importation of foreign sugar, as well as other products.[2] Prosecutions for violations of the Act could be brought in a court of vice-admiralty. The Act included a provision, later withdrawn, to move the trial from the vicinage to a vice-admiralty court sitting in Halifax, Canada.[3] In admiralty proceedings at that time, an admiralty judge appointed by the crown decided cases, and not a jury. Colonists protested against this feared infringement on their right to trial by jury, including its provision that trials could take place out of the vicinage.[4]

The Stamp Act

In a further attempt to raise needed revenue, Parliament enacted the Stamp Act of 1765 "towards further defraying the expences of defending, protecting, and securing" British colonies and plantations in North America.[5] The act levied taxes on many

---

[1] 4 Geo III, c 15 (1764).

[2] The Act's lengthy title describes its purpose: "An act ... for applying the produce of such duties, and of the duties to arise by virtue of the said act, towards defraying the expences of defending, protecting, and securing the said colonies and plantations." Ibid.

[3] Carl Ubbelohde, *The Vice-Admiralty Courts and the American Revolution* (Chapel Hill 1960) 60–63.

[4] In the colonies, admiralty courts were known as vice-admiralty courts. On colonial reaction to the transfer of jurisdiction to the vice-admiralty court, see ibid; Bernard Bailyn, *The Ideological Origins of the American Revolution* (reprint of 1967 edn, The Belknap Press of Harvard University 2017) 108–109; Jack N Rakove, *Declaring Rights: A Brief History with Documents* (Bedford Books 1998) 32.

[5] 5 Geo III, c 12 (1765).

Foundations of American Criminal Due Process at Trial. Francis R. Herrmann and Brownlow M. Speer,
Oxford University Press. © Oxford University Press 2025. DOI: 10.1093/9780199364770.003.0014

varieties of paper and legal instruments. It also imposed rules on the sale of liquor. Any tampering with the required stamp was made a felony punishable by death.[6] The Stamp Act authorized any prosecutor to bring a case in the vice-admiralty courts, sitting without a jury.[7] Prosecutions for failure to pay the stamp taxes would affect many businesses and citizens who had no relation to maritime trade itself.

Colonists raised the constitutional argument that the Stamp Act eroded their right to trial by jury. Daniel Dulany, a member of the Maryland governor's council, promptly attacked the act on procedural grounds, claiming that "the substitution of an arbitrary Civil Law Court [the vice-admiralty court], in the Place of the legal Judicatories, and that deserved Favourite, the Common-Law Trial by Jury ... hath stripped the Colonies of the Guards and Securities provided by the Constitution against Oppression in the Execution of the Laws."[8] Together with its imposition of taxes, "the Stamp Act hath not left them [the colonists] even the Shadow of a Privilege." In New York, the Stamp Act Congress, with representatives from nine of the thirteen colonies, convened. In its Declaration of Rights and Grievances, the Congress declared "[t]hat trial by jury is the inherent and invaluable right of every British subject in these colonies"[9] and that the Act "by imposing taxes on the inhabitants of these colonies, and the said Act, and several other Acts, by extending the jurisdiction of the courts of Admiralty beyond its ancient limits have a manifest tendency to subvert the rights and liberties of the colonists."[10] In London, Benjamin Franklin testified for three hours before the House of Commons urging it to repeal the Stamp Act. He told the Commons that the impositions of the Stamp Act and the "taking away, at the same time, trials by juries" "greatly lessened" the colonists' traditional high respect for Parliament.[11]

The Stamp Act was repealed within a year, but its damaging provisions remained in the colonial memory.[12] In October and November 1772, the freeholders and inhabitants of Boston assembled at Faneuil Hall under the chairmanship of John Hancock. They resolved "to state the Rights of the Colonists" and "to Communicate and Publish the same . . . to the World, as the Sense of this Town, with the Infringements and

---

[6] Ibid para XVIII.

[7] Ibid para LVIII provided "all the forfeitures and penalties hereby inflicted, and which shall be incurred, in the said colonies and plantations, shall and may be prosecuted, sued for, and recovered, in any court of record, or in any court of admiralty, in the respective colony or plantation where the offence shall be committed, or in any court of vice admiralty appointed or to be appointed, and which shall have jurisdiction within such colony, plantation, or place, (which courts of admiralty or vice admiralty are hereby respectively authorized and required to proceed, hear, and determine the same) at the election of the informer or prosecutor."

[8] Daniel Dulany, "Considerations on the Propriety of Imposing Taxes in the British Colonies, for the Purpose of raising a Revenue, by an Act of Parliament" in Gordon S Wood (ed), *The American Revolution: Writings from the Pamphlet Debate II: 1773–1776* (The Library of America 2015) 270.

[9] Proceedings of the Congress at New York (Jonas Green 1766, photofacsimile Boston 1938) 15, para VII. An exact copy of the Congress's complete journal is printed in CA Weslager, *The Stamp Act Congress* (University of Delaware Press 1976) 181–223.

[10] Proceedings of the Congress at New York (n 9) 16, para VIII.

[11] Benjamin Franklin, "The Examination of Doctor Benjamin Franklin, before an August Asssembly, relating to the Repeal of the Stamp Act" in Gordon S Wood (ed), *The American Revolution: Writings from the Pamphlet Debate I: 1764–1772* (The Library of America 2015) 335, 340.

[12] See Bernard Knollenberg, *Growth of the American Revolution, 1776–1775* (Liberty Fund 2003) 19. On the Stamp Act, see Pauline Maier, *Colonial Radicals and the Development of American Opposition to Britain, 1765–1776* (Alfred A Knopf 1972) 51–76; Ubbelohde (n 3) 55–80; Edmund S Morgan and Helen M Morgan, *The Stamp Act Crisis: Prologue to Revolution* (3rd edn, Chapel Hill 1995).

Violations thereof that have been, or from Time to Time may be made."[13] Among the infringements the freeholders complained of was "[t]he extending the power of the Courts of Vice-Admiralty to so enormous a degree, as deprives the people in the colonies, in a great measure, of their inestimable right to trials *by Juries*; which has ever been justly considered as the grand Bulwark and Security of English property."[14]

An act concerning treasons committed out of the King's Majesties Dominions

As the relationship between the colonists and Parliament unraveled, another particularly ominous threat to jury trial shook the colonies. Members of Parliament were making suggestions that American colonists who were suspected of treason or misprision of treason should be transported to England for trial. To accomplish this, Parliament contemplated applying to the colonies the terms of a treason act originally passed in the reign of Henry VIII.[15] The statute allowed for treasons "perpetrated or commytted . . . out of this Realme of Englande" to be tried within England. Motivating this proposed action was the belief among some members of Parliament that colonial treason trials had to be held in England in order to avoid biased colonial juries who would not convict any American charged with treason. From the American point of view, however, the application of Henry's act would directly imperil untold numbers of colonists. Royal governors could potentially interpret "treason" and "misprision of treason" to apply to assemblies, street protests, tumults, and any resort to arms.

On December 15, 1768, a resolution was moved in the House of Lords that an address be made to King George III beseeching him to direct the governor of Massachusetts Bay to "take the most effectual methods for procuring the fullest Information that can be obtained, touching all Treasons and Misprision of Treason . . . and to transmit the same, together with the Names of the Persons who were most active in the Commission of such Offences."[16] So informed, the King could form a special commission of inquiry, "pursuant to the Provisions of the Statute of the Thirty-fifth Year of the Reign of Henry the Eighth." The Lords passed the resolution and sent it to Commons.

The subsequent proceedings in Commons deserve attention because they demonstrate with a force even greater than any colonial pamphlets the sanctity of the jury trial, on both sides of the Atlantic, and the serious nature of the threat posed against it. Members of Commons heatedly debated the explosive question of removing colonial

---

[13] "The Votes and Proceedings of the Freeholders and other Inhabitants of the Town of Boston" in Wood (ed), *Writings* (n 11) 763.

[14] Ibid 776.

[15] 35 Hen VIII, c 2, s 1 (1543–1544): "Be it enacted . . . that all manner of offenses . . . declared . . . to be Treasons mysprisions of Treasons . . . and done perpetrated or commytted . . . by any person or persons out of this Realme of Englande, shalbe from henceforth inquired of herd and determyned before the Kings Justice of his Benche . . . by good and lawful men of the same Shire where the saide Benche shall sytt . . . as if suche treasons mysprisions of treasons or concelements of treasons had been done perpetrated and commytted within the same Shire where they shalbe so inquired of harde & determyned as is aforesaid."

[16] RC Simmons and PDG Thomas (eds), 3 *Proceedings and Debates of the British Parliament Respecting North America, 1754–1783* (Kraus International Publications 1984) (4 vols) 47–48.

treason trials to England. Mr. Dowdeswell warned that "[i]t will be most cruel to them [the colonists], most destructive to ourselves," if 35 Henry VIII were carried into execution.[17] Although the jury itself, as a group of twelve persons, would be preserved, the rights clustered around it would be destroyed and the full nature of the jury right hollowed out:

> [H]e [an American] is a subject of Great Britain, and entitled to the laws of his country, which say that crimes are local, and shall be tried where they are committed.[18]

Dowdeswell brought out the real damage that would be done in depriving colonists of the proper venue for trial:

> If tried in America he has neighbours around him, he is tried by a jury. What is the case, if you bring him here? You separate him from his relations, from his native place, from his witnesses. In what manner are you to proceed? Will you put him upon his trial, when he says he has not his witnesses, or will you put him off from time to time? In one case the law will be evaded, in the other he will have an unfair trial. Are his witnesses to come from America?

Absence of the home venue compounded the procedural problems:

> When is he to know the charge? How is he to be indicted? He finds another witness still wanting: he is tried at three thousand miles' distance, at least with this melancholy reflection; had the court given a little time more he might have brought his witnesses at three thousand miles from home, and his cause might have been supported. His condition is deplorable, the witnesses can't now be had.[19]

Dowdeswell saw any removal of colonial trials to England as an indignity to Commons and a provocation to colonists:

> [I]t becomes us, a British House of Commons, to consider, whether we can justify putting men upon their trial in this manner. It will give them a reason to complain. Gentlemen say you can't trust a jury in America. Where does that go? What, not find a jury of twelve men! If so there is something wrong in the conduct of this country, that has alienated the affections of the people in America.[20]

Edmund Burke, in a similar vein, cautioned:

---

[17] Ibid 65. Dowdeswell argued that Henry VIII's act was never intended to and could not apply to the colonies: "In the first place, I question much in law, that there is any man whatever, who thinks that Act ought to be applied to the colonies. The Act could not at the time it was made apply to the colonies. We had no colonies at that time." Ibid.

[18] Ibid 66.

[19] Ibid 66.

[20] Ibid 67. The Attorney General replied in part: "Suppose the whole colonies are in rebellion; will it be said, that such persons shall be tried by persons as guilty as themselves?" He favored the resolution because "It may awe. It may deter . . . It may save the colonies from entering into rebellion." Ibid 69.

If the remedy should be such as is not probable to appease America, but to exasperate them, you fire a cannon upon your enemy to react upon yourselves ... Why? Because you can't trust a jury in that country; that word must convey horror to every mind. If you have not a party among two millions people, you must change your plan of government, or renounce the colonies forever ... Suppose you do call over two, or three, what will become of the rest? If you break through rules, you unhinge human society. If the Americans see justice not observed, they will fall into despair.[21]

Like Dowdeswell, Burke saw that merely providing twelve people to decide guilt or innocence did not constitute what British subjects meant by a jury trial:

The law applied to America is inequitable; it can't annihilate the laws of nature. Suppose a man is brought over for high treason. Governor Bernard [the royal governor of Massachusetts] may transmit the account; let him be as implacable as Henry VIII. Some other governors may send over reports full of falsehood. They are all men of business in that country; he is brought over; he sends for witnesses; what process can bring the witnesses here? If they don't appear, he can't have a fair trial. If not, the law is eluded. God and nature oppose your doing it justly. Whatever you do in America will react upon yourselves.[22]

Burke railed against the inevitable failure to provide an impartial jury for colonists transported to England. He warned, as well, that defendants would not know the specifics of charges against them:

I am brought from America to an inflamed English jury to be tried, not upon the known ground of high treason ... Sir, I am pleading the cause of our ancient constitution, of our charters, of everything that is dear. There is a serpent creeping in the grass. Misprisions of treason, and the definitions of them; no man can say what they are. They may signify a neglect, or oversight, negligence in not revealing treason.[23]

Joining against the resolution, Mr. Montagu argued, "That part which directs that the statute of Henry VIII shall be put in execution I look upon to be a most dangerous measure.... As to the history of this Act of Parliament, it was passed in the worst time of the worst reign that ever disgraced our annals."[24] Sir William Meredith added, "If I were an American, rather than have that Act of Henry VIII, I would undergo any suffering. It is giving an horrid impression of the government of this country to be raking into acts of arbitrary times."[25]

Trying to bring down the temperature of the debate, Grey Cooper, Esq., assured the House there was no intention to actually put the proposal into execution, "but only to show to America, what government could do if pushed to it."[26] Whereupon, Captain

[21] Ibid 71.
[22] Ibid 72.
[23] Ibid.
[24] Ibid 92.
[25] Ibid 94.
[26] Ibid 110.

Phipps in opposition told the House, "Measures such as these are more calculated to raise the rebellion, they are pretended to be pointed at, than to quell it, did it exist."[27]

In a peroration, Phipps declaimed:

> A trial by jury in its utmost extent is too inherent a right, too sacred a privilege to be trifled with, and explained away by any forced constructions upon an obsolete statute . . . . It is, Sir, by the whole tenor of our laws, their inheritance as Englishmen— it is, I thank God, by the spirit of our constitutions their birth-right as men.[28]

The House voted 161 for the Address [i.e. resolution] and 65 against it on February 8, 1769.[29] A year later, on January 9, 1770, the ministry was called upon "to say what other means besides the terrors of an old Act of Henry VIII had been made use of to reconcile the minds of the subjects in America to acknowledgement of legal authority."[30] On March 5, 1770, Governor Pownell of Massachusetts, addressing Commons, advised:

> If it be asked, Whether it would remove those apprehensions and fears, which your resolutions of last year, and your Address and advice of sending for the subjects in *America*, on the supposition of treasons, in order to be tried here, have spread throughout the colonies?—I answer, No. If it be asked, If this commercial concession would quiet the minds of the *Americans*, as to the political doubts and fears which have struck them to the heart throughout the continent?—I answer, No.[31]

On April 26, 1770, Mr. Trecothick again addressed the Commons:

> We have acted the parts of bullies in America. Where is the minister, that would dare to put that into execution, subversive of every right natural and constitutional, to drag a man from his vicinity across an ocean of 1000 leagues to be tried before judges who can't have competent knowledge. We have shown the Americans, that we are not incapable of adopting ideas, and even systems of despotism. They think it is in the will of this country if in the power to enslave them.[32]

The Dockyards Act and Administration of Justice Act

Parliament invoked a similar threat to the jury in passing *An Act for the better securing and preserving His Majesty's Dock Yards, Ships, Ammunition, and Stores.*[33] The act punished as a felon and subjected to death any person "within the Realm or areas thereunto belonging" who willfully and maliciously destroyed his Majesty's ships.

---

[27] Ibid 111.
[28] Ibid 112.
[29] Ibid 112.
[30] Ibid 169.
[31] Ibid 236.
[32] Ibid 256–257. On the impact in the colonies of the unfulfilled threat to remove treason trials to England, see Neil L York, "Imperial Impotence: Treason in 1774 Massachusetts" (2011) 29 LHR 657–702.
[33] 12 Geo III, c 24 (1772).

The act provided that such persons might be indicted and tried "in any Shire or County within the Realm, in like manner and form, as if such Offence had been committed within the said Shire or County ... where such Offence shall have been actually committed, as His Majesty ... may deem most expedient for bringing such Offender to Justice; any Law, Usage, or Custom notwithstanding."[34] Driven by the same concern that colonial juries were biased against the crown, Parliament also passed The Administration of Justice Act,[35] providing that the trials of royal officials be transferred to England, when the officials were charged with a crime, including murder, in the course of dutifully enforcing the law or quelling riots, such as had occurred in Boston. Colonists referred to the statute as the Murder Act. By moving the trials out of the vicinage, colonists believed British jurors favorable to the crown would acquit even factually guilty officials.[36]

Conclusion

The cumulative effect of Parliament's ominous acts added a volatile ingredient to the cause for revolution. Members of Parliament on both sides of the debate understood well that the threat to restrict colonial rights to jury trial would trigger a powerful counter-reaction in America. Parliament, for its part, hoped its threats would induce the colonies to obey the British measures. American responses, however, would run distinctly in the opposite direction.[37]

---

[34] Ibid. On the history of the act, see Gwenda Morgan, "Arson, Treason and Plot: Britain, America and the Law, 1770–1777" (2015) 100 History 374–391.

[35] 14 Geo III, c 39 (1774). In 14 Geo III, c 45 (The Massachusetts Government Act), Parliament further alienated the colonists by providing that jurors, who were popularly elected, would henceforth be summoned by the sheriffs because such elections "afford[ed] occasion for many evil practices." The act was repealed in 1778.

[36] For commentary on the impact of the British acts, see Helen Hill Miller, *The Case for Liberty* (University of North Carolina Press 1965) 163–183.

[37] See York (n 32) 660.

15

Reinforcing Jury-Rights

Reactions to Parliamentary Threats

On July 7, 1769, the Massachusetts General Court resolved:

> That all Trials for Treason, Misprision of Treason, or for any Felony or Crime what-
> soever, committed or done in this his Majesty's Colony, by any Person or Persons
> residing therein, ought of Right to be [held] and conducted in and before his Majesty'
> Courts held within the said Colony, according to the fixed and known Course of
> Proceedings; and that the seizing any Person or Persons residing in the Colony, sus-
> pected of any Crime whatsoever, committed therein, and sending such Person or
> Persons to Places beyond the Sea, to be tried, is highly derogatory of the Right of
> British Subjects; as thereby the inestimable Privilege of being tried by a Jury from
> the Vicinage, as well as the Liberty of summoning and producing Witnesses on such
> Trial, will be take away from the Party accused.[1]

In 1772, a meeting of freeholders of the town of Boston, moderated by John Hancock, similarly opposed any attempt to sabotage jury trial by use of the vice-admiralty court or by transporting alleged colonial traitors to England.[2] In support of Hancock's resolutions in Massachusetts, the Virginia House of Burgesses joined in registering its protest.

Thomas Jefferson, too, protested against any attempt to apply 35 Henry to the colonies. In "A Summary View of the Rights of British North America" in 1774, Jefferson attacked an act permitting "the suppression of riots and tumults in the town of Boston" to be transferred to Great Britain for trial.[3]

> [W]ho does his majesty think can be prevailed on to cross the Atlantic for the sole
> purpose of bearing evidence to a fact? . . . who are to feed the wife and children whom
> he leaves behind, and who have had no other subsistence but his daily labour? . . . And

---

[1] 45 *Journals of the House of Representatives of Massachusetts* (Massachusetts Historical Society 1919–1990) (55 vols) 171–172. See also Ebenezer Baldwin, "An Appendix, Stating the Heavy Grievances the Colonies Labour under from Several Late Act of the British Parliament . . . " in Gordon S Wood (ed), *The American Revolution: Writings from the Pamphlet Debate II: 1773–1776* (The Library of America 2015) 343, 359–360, 363.

[2] "The Votes and Proceedings of the Freeholders and Other Inhabitants of the Town of Boston" (Edes and Gill [n.d.]) in Gordon S Wood (ed), *The American Revolution: Writings from the Pamphlet Debate I: 1764–1772* (The Library of America 2015) 763, 776–778.

[3] In Wood, *Writings, Pamphlet Debates II* (n 1) 100. For a consideration of the American Revolution as treason, see Bradley Chapin, "The American Revolution as *Lese Majesty*" (1955) 79 The Pennsylvania Magazine of History and Biography 310. See generally, Bradley Chapin, "Colonial and Revolutionary Origins of the American Law of Treason" (1960) 17 William & Mary Law Quarterly 3.

the wretched criminal, if he happen to have offended on the American side, stripped of his privilege of trial by peers of his vicinage, removed from the place where alone full evidence could be obtained, without money, without counsel, without friends, without exculpatory proof, is tried before judges predetermined to condemn. The cowards who would suffer a countryman to be torn from the bowels of their society, in order to be thus offered as a sacrifice to parliamentary tyranny, would merit that everlasting infamy now fixed on the author of the act![4]

Finally, the First Continental Congress in 1774, spurred by parliament's acts which were "impolitic, unjust, and cruel, as well as unconstitutional, and most destructive of American rights," drew together the sentiments of "the good people of the several colonies of New-Hampshire, Massachusetts Bay, Rhode-Island and Providence Plantations, Connecticut, New-York, New-Jersey, Pennsylvania, Newcastle, Kent and Sussex Delaware, Maryland, Virginia, North-Carolina, and South-Carolina." In a unified statement, the Congress set out the rights of the colonists including their being "entitled to the common law of England, and more especially to the great and inestimable privilege of being tried by their peers of the vicinage, according to that law."[5] The Congress determined that among the "many infringements and violations of the foregoing rights" were parliament's extension of power to the vice-admiralty courts for trials and deprivation of "the American subject of a constitutional trial by jury of the vicinage, authorizing the trial of any person, charged with the committing any offence described in the act, out of the realm, to be indicted and tried for the same in any shire or county within the realm." So offensive were the parliamentary acts that Congress moved aggressively beyond simply asserting rights. It resolved concretely to "enter into a non-importation, non-consumption, and non-exportation agreement or association" among themselves until the offending acts were repealed.[6]

---

[4] Wood, *Writings, , Pamphlet Debates II* (n 1) 100. See also "Instructions for the Deputies Appointed to Meet in General Congress on the Part of this Colony" [Virginia] (1774) (Early American Imprints, Series I: Evans, 1639–1800).

In England, the colonial fears did not disturb the famous Dr Samuel Johnson. Arguing on behalf of British policy, he declared, "If they [colonists] are condemned unheard, it is because there is no need for a trial. The crime is manifest and notorious. All trial is the investigation of something doubtful. An Italian philosopher observes, that no man desires to hear what he has already seen." Samuel Johnson, *Taxation No Tyranny: An Answer to the Resolutions and Address of the American Congress* (4th edn, T Cadell 1775) in Wood, *Writings* (n 2) 485.

[5] "First Continental Congress: Declaration and Resolves (October 14, 1774)" in Jack N Rakove (ed), *Founding America: Documents from the Revolution to the Bill of Rights* (Barnes & Noble Classics 2006) 39–49. Francis Heller comments: "the common law so appealed to must be understood to include not only trial by jury of twelve men of the vicinage but also publicity of the proceedings, and the right to witnesses and to the assistance of counsel; in short, all the recognized rights of the accused." Francis H Heller, *The Sixth Amendment to the Constitution of the United States: A Study in Constitutional Development* (University of Kansas Press 1951) 21–22. To make the same point, Eben Moglen cites the 1774 Congress's message to the Quebecois for its summary of rights attaching to jury trial. Eben Moglen, "The Privilege in North America" in RH Helmholz and others (eds), *The Privilege against Self-Incrimination: Its Origins and Development* (The University of Chicago Press 1997) 130.

[6] See also *A Declaration by the Representatives of the United Colonies of North-America, Now Met in General Congress at Philadelphia, Setting Forth of the Causes and Necessity of Taking up Arms* (printed by William Thomas Bradford 1775) 6. Parliament's attempts, whether real or feigned, to interfere with the jury trial formed the basis in the Declaration of Independence for two charges against George III "for depriving us in many cases of trial by jury: for transporting us beyond the Seas to be tried for pretended offenses." Pauline Maier, *American Scripture: Making the Declaration of Independence* (Knopf 1997) 116–118.

State constitutions and state bills of rights

After the non-importation agreement, peaceful attempts to resolve conflicts with parliament continued to founder. The colonial representatives assembled again. On May 10, 1776, the Second Continental Congress resolved that it be recommended to "the assemblies and conventions of the United Colonies where no government sufficient to the exigencies of their affairs have been hitherto established" that they should "adopt such government as shall, in the opinion of the representatives of the people, best conduce to the happiness and safety of their constituents in particular, and America in general."[7] Virginia soon took the lead in responding to Congress's recommendation. The Virginia convention on May 15, 1776, resolved to prepare "a Declaration of Rights, and such a plan of Government as will be most likely to maintain peace and order in this Colony, and secure substantial and equal liberty to the people."[8]

To compose a bill of rights, the Virginia convention appointed a committee of delegates. George Mason (Figure 4) quickly emerged as the most influential member.[9] Mason was not a lawyer. He had many opportunities, however, to have absorbed legal learning even from his youth. He received private education at the Marlborough home of his uncle and guardian John Mercer, an eminent lawyer, avid collector of legal books, and fierce opponent of the Stamp Act. Mercer's library contained one of the most prominent and extensive legal collections in the colonies.[10] Among its holdings were many justice of the peace manuals, including Parker's *Conductor Generalis*, the manuals of Webb, Stark, Burns, and others; Henry Care's *English*

---

[7] 4 *Journals of the Continental Congress, 1774–1789* (Government Printing Office 1904) (34 vols) 342. On the formation of state governments and their interdependence in responding to Congress's request, see Craig Green, "United States: A Revolutionary History of American Statehood" (2020) 119 Mich L Rev 1, 17–26 and passim.

[8] *The Proceedings of the Convention of Delegates, Held at the Capitol in the City of Williamsburg in the Colony of Virginia, on Monday the 6th of May, 1776* (Ritchie, Truehart & Du-Val 1816) 16.

[9] Robert A Rutland, "Note" in Robert A Rutland (ed), 1 *The Papers of George Mason, 1725–1792* (University of North Carolina Press 1970) (3 vols) (hereafter *PGM*) 274. For biography of George Mason, see "Mason, George" in Brent Tarter, *American National Biography* (OUP 2018) 1–7; Pamela C Copeland and Richard K MacMaster, *The Five George Masons, Patriots and Planters of Virginia and Maryland* (University of Virginia Press 2016); Jeff Broadwater, *George Mason, Forgotten Founder* (The University of North Carolina Press 2006); Helen Hill Miller, *George Mason: Gentleman Revolutionary* (University of North Carolina Press 1975); Kate Mason Rowland, *The Life of George Mason, 1725–1792: Including His Speeches, Public Papers, and Correspondence* (G P Putnam's Sons 1892) (2 vols).

[10] Mercer's library is held in the Henry E Huntington Library, San Marino, California. On the contents of Mercer's collection, see William Hamilton Bryson, *Census of Law Books in Colonial Virginia* (University of Virginia Press 1978) 482, 487. Bryson characterizes Mercer's legal collection as "one of breadth and depth; it was the working library of a practicing lawyer who could and did handle any sort of lawsuit." Ibid xviii. The collection included 101 copies of reports and state trials, 191 copies of a wide range of treatises, and 18 copies of legislative compilations. Mercer's entire library, beyond its strictly legal holdings, contained approximately 1,800 volumes. Bennie Brown, "John Mercer: Merchant, Lawyer, Author, Book Collector" in Warren M Billings and Brent Tarter (eds), *"Esteemed Bookes of Lawe" and the Legal Culture of Early Virginia* (University of Virginia Press 2017) 109. Regarding Mason's access to legal knowledge, Helen Hill Miller comments, "[T]he foundations in constitutional law and in history for George Mason's later work in modeling new political institutions, the classics of legal and political theory, the case books, and the compilations of statutes were available at Marlborough, and so was his uncle's practical legal experience." Miller (n 9) 31. For an account of private law libraries in the colonies before 1776, see WH Bryson, "Private Law Libraries before 1776" in W Hamilton Bryson (ed) *Virginia Law Books, Essays and Bibliographies* (American Philosophical Society 2000) 479–499.

Figure 4 Portrait of George Mason (1725–1792) by Dominic W. Boudet. He drew up the Virginia Bill of Rights which became the basis of the U.S. federal Bill of Rights. Thomas Jefferson wrote that Mason was "one of our really great men, and of the first order of greatness."
Credit: Dominic W. Boudet, public domain, via Wikimedia Commons.

Liberties; Coke's *Institutes*, including Part Three on criminal law; Duncombe's *Trials per pais; or, Law Concerning Juries Nisi Prius*; collections of English statutes and cases, including reports of the Tudor and Stuart state trials, and many other treatises on English, Continental, and ecclesiastical law. How much Mason, as a pupil, may have familiarized himself with his uncle's legal library offerings is unknown.[11] In any event, his acquaintance with the law certainly deepened in his adult years. As a successful gentleman planter,[12] he was appointed in 1769 justice for Fairfax County "according

[11] Hugh Grigsby describes Mason as "thorougly skilled not only in general history, but especially in the political history of England ... from an early period of life devoting his leisure to study, he had become so deeply versed in the knowledge of our early charters and in the lore of the British constitution, that, in the midst of men whose lives had been devoted to law, his opinions on a great political question had almost a conclusive authority." Hugh Blair Grigsby, *The Virginia Convention of 1776* (J W Randolph 1855) 155.
[12] Miller (n 9) 39, 55–56.

to common Law and in Chancery."[13] In that capacity, he would certainly have been familiar with trial procedures and with manuals composed for the guidance of justices of the peace. In 1774, he and George Washington were the principal authors of Virginia's *Fairfax Resolves* in which the burgesses listed among their complaints parliament's threat to undermine jury trial by applying 35 Hen VIII, c 2 to the colonies.

Both Jefferson and Madison credited Mason as the author of the Virginia Declaration.[14] Mason's draft was said to "swallow up all the rest."[15] Judging from his ability to compose a first draft of the Virginia Bill of Rights within five days (May 20–24, 1776),[16] including its clause on trial rights, he possessed a sound knowledge of criminal jury trial procedure. Mason set down fundamental rights he believed to be constitutive of "the ancient Tryal by Jury" which "is preferable to any other and ought to be held sacred."[17] His first draft of "A Declaration of Rights ... recommended to Posterity as the Basis and Foundation of Government" declared:

> That in all capital and criminal Prosecutions a Man hath a right to demand the Cause and Nature of his Accusation, to be confronted with the Accusers or Witnesses, to call for Evidence in his favour, and to a speedy Tryal by Jury of his Vicinage; without whose unanimous Consent, he cannot be found guilty; nor can he be compelled to give Evidence against himself. And that no Man, except in times of actual invasion or insurrection, can be imprisoned upon suspicion of crimes against the state, unsupported by legal evidence.[18]

The select committee reported out Mason's draft declaration to the delegates on May 27. On June 12, the convention unanimously adopted Mason's draft as the Declaration's Section 8 with few changes.[19]

---

[13] Ibid 77.

[14] Letter of Thomas Jefferson to Augustus Elias Brevoort. Woodward, April 3, 1825: "The fact is unquestionable that the Bill of Rights, and the Constitution of Virginia, were drawn originally by George Mason, one of our really great men, and of the first order of greatness." Thomas Jefferson, 12 *Works of Thomas Jefferson* (Paul Leicester Ford ed, G.P. Putnam's Sons 1904–1905) (12 vols) 407. See also Maier (n 6) 182–183, quoting Jefferson's letter.

[15] Edmund Randolph, quoted in 1 *PGM* (n 9) 274, 296 (editor's note).

[16] Ibid 279.

[17] Ibid 278.

[18] 1 *PGM* (n 9) 277–278 (proposition 7). While admiring Mason's draft as "genuinely creative" and "far more comprehensive than the British precedents," Leonard Levy finds in Mason's text "a certain carelessness." It lacked any reference to a grand jury indictment, or to representation by counsel, or to a bar against double jeopardy. Additionally, its language was imprecise: to "demand" the cause and nature of accusation was weaker than to "know"; taken literally, the self-incrimination bar was superfluous because it protected defendants rather than witnesses, and defendants were not permitted to testify, in any case); and to "call" for favorable evidence fell short of true compulsory process. Leonard W Levy, *Origins of the Fifth Amendment: The Right against Self-Incrimination* (Macmillan 1986) 407–409. See 1 *PGM* (n 9) 280–281 (editor's note) responding to Levy.

[19] The Committee's changes were: the addition of "impartial" to modify "jury"; the phrase "accusers *and* witnesses, instead of *or*"; and the insertion of "nor ... can he be deprived of his liberty except by the law of the land, or the judgment of his peers." The committee also dropped Mason's exception for imprisonment without evidence in times of invasion or insurrection. 1 *PGM* (n 9) 284–285. On June 29, the Convention passed the Virginia constitution as a separate document. In 1830, the Declaration was combined with the Virginia constitution.

Newspapers broadcast the adopted Declaration throughout the colonies which were, like Virginia, in the midst of responding to the call of the Continental Congress to draw up frames of government for themselves. Virginia's Declaration quickly became a model for other colonies,[20] including those that drew up their declarations in the ensuing decade.

The state bills of rights and constitutions were not in strict conformity with one other.[21] That disparities would appear was not surprising since the statutes and practices of one colony varied from another. Moreover, the colonies were composing their declarations of rights and constitutions in the press of events on the eve of revolution.

Those states that composed constitutions, as well as the independent republic of Vermont,[22] unanimously assured the right to a jury trial.[23]

Specific rights clustering around the jury trial were not uniform across the states. Nine states asserted a right to trial and judgment "according to the law of the land."[24] Seven states and Vermont expressly provided that trials be of the vicinage.[25] Eight states and Vermont expressly guaranteed defendants a right to be informed of the accusation.[26] Six and Vermont provided for speedy trial or trials without delay.[27] Seven and Vermont specified the right of an accused to confront prosecution witnesses.[28] Seven and Vermont made provision for assistance of counsel.[29] Seven assured the

[20] Levy (n 18) 409. Virginia's Declaration was promptly sent to Philadelphia where the *Pennsylvania Evening Post* printed it on June 6, 1776. 1 *PGM* (n 9) 286, 438 (editor's notes); Jack N Rakove, *Declaring Rights: A Brief History with Documents* (Bedford Books 1998) 77 & n 9; Maier (n 6) 286 n 59, 269 n 63.

[21] Connecticut and Rhode Island did not compose constitutions but continued government under their colonial charters.

[22] Admitted to the union in 1791.

[23] Declarations referenced here can be found in Francis Newton Thorpe (ed and compiler), *Federal and State Constitutions Colonial Charters, and Other Organic Laws of the States, Territories, and Colonies Now or Heretofore Forming the United States of America* (GPO 1909, reprint Buffalo 1993) (7 vols): Virginia (June 12, 1776), Declaration of Rights, s 8 (7 Thorpe 3813); New Jersey (July 3, 1776), Const XXII (5 Thorpe 2598); Delaware (September 11, 1776), Declaration of Rights, ss 13, 14 (Richard L Perry (ed), *Sources of Our Liberties: Documentary Origins of Individual Liberties in the United States Constitution and Bill of Rights* (revised edn, American Bar Foundation 1978)); Pennsylvania (September 28, 1776), Declaration of Rights IX (5 Thorpe 3083); Maryland (November 11, 1776), Declaration of Rights XIX (3 Thorpe 1688); North Carolina (December 18, 1776), Declaration of Rights IX (refers to "no freeman" tried without jury) (5 Thorpe 2787); Georgia (February 5, 1777), Const, Art LXI (2 Thorpe 785); New York (April 20, 1777), Const XLI (5 Thorpe 2637); independent republic of Vermont (December 24, 1777) X (6 Thorpe 3741); South Carolina (March 19, 1778), Const XLI ("no freeman" tried without jury) (6 Thorpe 3257); Massachusetts (March 2, 1780), Declaration of Rights, Art XII (3 Thorpe 1891); New Hampshire (January 2, 1784), Bill of Rights, Art XVI (4 Thorpe 2453).

[24] Delaware, Massachusetts, Maryland, New Hampshire, New York, North Carolina, Pennsylvania, South Carolina, Virginia.

[25] Delaware, Georgia, Maryland, Massachusetts, New Hampshire, Pennsylvania, Virginia, (Vermont) (parentheses acknowledge Vermont was not a state until March 1791).

[26] Delaware, Maryland, Massachusetts, New Hampshire, New Jersey, North Carolina, Pennsylvania, Virginia, (Vermont).

[27] Delaware, Massachusetts, Maryland, New Hampshire, Pennsylvania, Virginia, (Vermont).

[28] Delaware, Maryland, Massachusetts, New Hampshire, North Carolina, Pennsylvania, Virginia, (Vermont).

[29] Delaware, Maryland, Massachusetts, New Hampshire, New Jersey, New York, Pennsylvania, (Vermont).

accused a right to present favorable witnesses and evidence.[30] Seven and Vermont protected witnesses against compelled self-incrimination.[31] Five and Vermont stated the jury must be "impartial."[32] Five and Vermont required unanimous verdicts.[33] Four and Vermont guaranteed a speedy trial.[34] Two required grand juries.[35] Two forbade double jeopardy.[36]

The fact that a state did not expressly include a particular right, for example, unanimity, in its constitution or bill of rights did not necessarily mean that the state did not observe the right in practice. North Carolina and Vermont expressly articulated that trials were to take place in public. Yet, it was unheard of that any state would conduct its trials in secret. The states that did not expressly declare that trials were to be "according to the law of the land" surely recognized the due process as an essential guarantee for British subjects dating back to the statutes of Edward III in the fourteenth century. The matrix of state constitutional trial protections provided a ready source for any future federal composition of rights.

Criminal Jury Trial in the Federal Constitution and Bill of Rights

The states' unsatisfying experience with the Articles of Confederation in the years following independence eventuated in the convening of delegates from each state in Philadelphia in 1787. Meeting from May to mid-September to address the inadequacies of the Articles that had bound them together, the delegates scrapped the Articles entirely and proposed a new federal constitution.

Article Three, section two, of the draft constitution secured the right to jury trial in all federal criminal cases.[37] The federal guarantee, however, lacked any specification of what protections, if any, a defendant at a jury trial would be entitled to enjoy. Those who were opposed to the new constitution, the Anti-Federalists, raised as a principal objection its failure broadly to include a bill of rights that would protect individuals from possible abuse by a federal government. Not surprisingly, it was George Mason, the principal author of the Virginia Bill of Rights, who fastened on the lacunae in the federal draft. Only a bill of rights, he asserted, could protect individual rights against possible abuses by the federal government. Mason proposed that the federal constitution should contain a statement of rights, just as the states offered protections in

---

[30] Delaware, Maryland, Massachusetts, New Hampshire, New Jersey, Virginia, (Vermont).

[31] Delaware, Maryland, Massachusetts, New Hampshire, North Carolina, Pennsylvania, Virginia, (Vermont).

[32] Delaware, Maryland, New Hampshire, Pennsylvania, Virginia, (Vermont).

[33] Delaware, Maryland, North Carolina, Pennsylvania, Virginia, (Vermont).

[34] Delaware, Maryland, Pennsylvania, Virginia, (Vermont).

[35] Georgia, Massachusetts, North Carolina, and New York made reference to indictments without express mention of grand juries.

[36] New Hampshire, Pennsylvania (1790 Constitution).

[37] As later ratified, US Const, Art III, s 2, states: "The trial of all crimes, except in cases of impeachment, shall be by jury; and such trial shall be held in the state where the said crimes shall have been committed; but when not committed within any state, the trial shall be at such place or places as the Congress may by law have directed."

their state constitutions and bills of rights.[38] Mason thought such a bill of rights could be drawn up in a matter of hours with the aid of the state declarations.[39] His motion, however, was defeated unanimously probably because most delegates believed the state constitutions were sufficient to guarantee individual rights. The rejection did not deter Mason. When the convention referred the proposed federal constitution to the states for ratification in September 1787, Mason determined to oppose the ratification of the constitution in the state of Virginia.

It was clear that ratification of the constitution hinged on Virginia's acceptance. James Madison had opposed any federal bill of rights, believing it unnecessary in light of the existing state bills and constitutions. But, hoping to garner Virginia's ratification of the draft federal constitution and to avoid the risk of a second constitutional convention, as well as to make himself a stronger candidate for election to Congress from Virginia, Madison assured anti-federalist objectors that he would urge Congress to adopt a federal bill of rights promptly after the sufficient number of states ratified the Constitution.[40]

Madison held true to his word. In May 1789, he announced to the House of Representatives his intention to introduce the subject of amendments to the Constitution. In June, he did so. In his speech to the House, he explained why, despite his earlier thought that such a declaration would be a useless "paper parchment," he had now concluded that such a bill would perform important and lasting functions. "So far as a declaration of rights can tend to prevent the exercise of undue power, it cannot be doubted but such declaration is proper."[41] Emphasizing the need to protect against a majority of the people abusing the rights of a minority, Madison continued:

> It may be thought all paper barriers against the power of the community, are too weak to be worthy of attention ... yet, as they have a tendency to impress some degree of respect for them, to establish the public opinion in their favor, and rouse the attention of the whole community, it may be one mean to controul the majority from those acts to which they might be otherwise inclined.[42]

---

[38] 3 *PGM* (n 9) 981. His fears and those of like-minded representatives were similar to those the Levellers expressed when they proposed "An Agreement of the People" in 1647: "But if any shall inquire why we should desire to join in an agreement with the people to declare these to be our native rights—and not rather petition parliament for them—the reason is evident: No Act of parliament is or can be unalterable, and so cannot be sufficient security to save you or us harmless from what another parliament may determine if it should be corrupted." Anonymous, *An Agreement of the People for a Firme and Present Peace, upon Grounds of Common-Right and Freedom* (London [s.n.] 1647) 9.

[39] 3 *PGM* (n 9) 981.

[40] See Madison's letter to the Virginia Baptist minister George Eve, January 2, 1789, confirming that, despite initially thinking a bill of rights was unnecessary, Madison's view post-ratification had developed to the point that "it is my sincere opinion that the Constitution ought to be revised, and that the first Congress meeting under it, ought to prepare and recommend to the States for ratification, the most satisfactory provisions for all essential rights, particularly the rights of Conscience in the fullest latitude, the freedom of the press, trials by jury, security against general warrants &c." JCA Stagg (ed), 11 *The Papers of James Madison Digital Edition* (Congressional Series, University of Virginia Press 2010) (hereafter *PJM*) 404–405.

[41] 12 *PJM* 204 (n 40) 204.

[42] Ibid 204–205.

In composing his list of rights, Madison looked to those repeatedly expressed in the state constitutions and in other amendments proposed at state ratifying conventions.[43] Among these, he told the House on June 8, he considered jury trial itself to be indispensable to liberty:

> Trial by jury cannot be considered as a natural right, but a right resulting from the social compact which regulates the action of the community, but it is essential to secure the liberty of the people as any one of the pre-existent right of nature.[44]

To express the rights of defendants at criminal jury trials, Madison turned to the broad consensus of safeguards already articulated in state constitutions. Madison's Fourth Amendment proposed to the House stated:

> No person shall be subject, except in cases of impeachment, to more than one punishment, or one trial for the same office; nor shall be compelled to be a witness against himself; nor be deprived of life, liberty, or property without due process of law.
>
> . . .
>
> In all criminal prosecutions, the accused shall enjoy the right to a speedy and public trial, to be informed of the cause and nature of the accusation, to be confronted with his accusers, and the witnesses against him; to have a compulsory process for obtaining witnesses in his favor; and to have the assistance of counsel for his defence.

Madison's Seventh Amendment elaborated further:

> The trial of all crimes (except in cases of impeachments, and cases arising in the land or naval forces, or the militia when on actual service in time of war or public danger) shall be by an impartial jury of freeholders of the vicinage, with the requisite of unanimity for conviction, of the right of challenge, and other accustomed requisites; and in all crimes punishable with loss of life or member, presentment or indictment by a grand jury, shall be an essential preliminary, provided that in cases of crimes committed within any county which may be in possession of an enemy, or in which a general insurrection may prevail, the trial may by law be authorised in some other county of the same state, as near as may be to the seat of the offence.

These were not new procedural rights, but ones that were, with variations, long cherished in the colonies.[45] That fact explains Congress's swift approval of Madison's amendments with very little substantive alteration or discussion.

In a major instance, however, the House chose to reject one of Madison's amendments. It was the one he considered "to be the most valuable amendment on the whole

---

[43] On August 13, 1789, Madison told the House that he wanted his proposed amendments to be inserted in the Constitution itself, but the House rejected the proposal in favor of a separate Bill of Rights appended to the Constitution. See 12 *PJM* (n 40) 333 and editorial note.

[44] 12 *PJM* (n 40) 204.

[45] Rakove, *Founding America* (n 5) 33.

list."[46] Not trusting state legislatures to faithfully adhere to their own constitutions and bills of rights, Madison proposed that the federal constitution contain a "double security,"[47] which would guarantee that the states, as well as the federal government, would adhere to the federal amendments. "No State shall violate the equal rights of conscience, or the freedom of the press, or the trial by jury in criminal cases."[48] The Senate later rejected the proposed amendment.

After revision and Senate approval, Madison's rights became numbered as the first ten amendments to the Constitution. Congress submitted the Bill to the states for ratification. In December 1791, Virginia gave the final vote needed for ratification of the amendments.[49]

Conclusion

The ratification of the Fifth and Sixth Amendments dampened fears that a powerful federal government might abuse the people's procedural trial rights. The rights themselves relating to criminal trials were ones the founders believed they had been entitled to, or ought to have been, as part of their inheritance of the common law and statutes of England. Having been fixed in a constitution, procedural safeguards at trial were no longer to be subject to the vicissitudes of custom, or statutory change, or shifting political preference, as they had been at times in England and as they might have been in the new United States absent the Bill of Rights.[50] The ratifying generation bequeathed its principles of fair trial to Americans today. The challenge of preserving those rights is ours.

---

[46] "Mr. Madison conceived this to be the most valuable amendment on the whole list. If there was any way to restrain the government of the United States from infringing upon these essential rights, it was equally necessary that they be secured against the state governments; he thought that if they be provided against the one, it was necessary to provide against the other, and was satisfied that it would be equally grateful to the people." "Speech of August 17, 1789" in Congressional Register, II, 227; 12 *PJM* (n 40) 344.

[47] 12 *PJM* (n 40) 208.

[48] Art I, s 10.

[49] As adopted, the Fifth Amendment states: "No person shall be held to answer for a capital, or otherwise infamous crime, unless on a presentment or indictment of a Grand Jury, except in cases arising in the land or naval forces, or in the Militia, when in actual service in time of War or public danger; nor shall any person be subject for the same offence to be twice put in jeopardy of life or limb; nor shall be compelled in any criminal case to be a witness against himself, nor be deprived of life, liberty, or property, without due process of law; nor shall private property be taken for public use, without just compensation."

The Sixth Amendment states: "In all criminal prosecutions, the accused shall enjoy the right to a speedy and public trial, by an impartial jury of the State and district wherein the crime shall have been committed, which district shall have been previously ascertained by law, and to be informed of the nature and cause of the accusation; to be confronted with the witnesses against him; to have compulsory process for obtaining witnesses in his favor, and to have the Assistance of Counsel for his defence."

[50] James Madison, "Speech Introducing Amendments in the House of Representatives" (June 8, 1789) in Rakove (ed), *Founding America* (n 5) 614.

Epilogue

Reflections on the Foundations

i.

Sir Edward Coke believed the English common law represented the "perfection of reason."[1] Coke was quick to explain that the kind of "reason" he meant was not a process detached from history. He was not referring to "every man's natural reason" but, rather, to an "artificial" kind of reasoning, "gotten by long study, observation, and experience."[2] Such reason, Coke said, is an "art"[3] which "by many successions of ages . . . hath been fined and refined by an infinite number of grave and learned men."[4]

Twenty-first-century Americans have so long been accustomed to their inherited trial rights that the safeguards they enjoy may seem to be no more than a set of common-sense procedural choices.[5] With George Mason, they may believe that their constitutionally protected rights could have been drawn up in a few hours of reflection. But, when Mason declared he could compose a bill of rights in so short a time, his offer was possible only because he was the inheritor of legal traditions much older than himself and his revolutionary generation. They were the product of "many successions of ages."

This book has attempted to illuminate the struggles, reasoning, and judgments of a very broad span of generations regarding their procedural choices for criminal trials. Each society sought to determine what protections were proper for persons accused of crimes. The choices were not the result of an abstract legal reasoning disassociated from the beliefs, values, and pressing controversies of their respective times. Answers to procedural questions were hammered out in the forge of contemporary conflicts.

---

[1] 1 Co Inst bk 2, c 6, s 138.

[2] Sir Edward Coke, *Commentary Upon Littleton* (first edn 1628, Charles Butler ed, 18th edn, Legal Classics Library 1985) 97b. Lilburne echoed his point. See John Lilburne, *The Afflicted Man's Outcry against the Injustice and Oppression* (London [s.n.] 1653) 3.

[3] Coke's word "art" has been often misprinted as "act." Sir John Baker, *The Reinvention Magna Carta 1215–1616* (CUP 2017) 367 & n 165.

[4] On Coke and his theory of "artificial reason," see JW Tubbs, *The Common Law Mind: Medieval and Early Modern Conceptions* (Johns Hopkins University Press 2000) 162–167; JU Lewis, "Sir Edward Coke (1552–1688): His Theory of Artificial Reason as a Context for Modern Basic Legal Theory" (1968) 84 LQR 330–342; Allen D Boyer, *Sir Edward Coke and the Elizabethan Age* (Stanford University Press 2003) 83–107; Baker (n 3) 367.

[5] Paul Hyams observes many rights Western culture deems fundamental are not so viewed by non-Western cultures. Such rights "are now so deeply engrained into our [Western] culture that I for one frequently espouse the illusion of their indisputable rightness as passionately as anyone else and experience angry frustration at the inability of outsiders to see the truth. So hard is it to see them for what they are, as context-dependent as any other aspect of our culture." Paul Hyams, "Due Process versus the Maintenance of Order in European Law: The Contribution of the Ius Commune" in Peter R Coss, *The Moral World of the Law* (CUP 2000) 62–63.

Foundations of American Criminal Due Process at Trial. Francis R. Herrmann and Brownlow M. Speer, Oxford University Press. © Oxford University Press 2025. DOI: 10.1093/9780199364770.003.0016

When reason influenced a society's choices, it was a reason schooled in the "experience" of culture, politics, religion, and historical events.

A society's blend of experiences yields differing procedural conclusions in one age and in another.[6] What was reasonable yesterday may seem quite unreasonable today, and whether what is reasonable today will appear so tomorrow is uncertain. Consider, for example, how social norms about torture and confession shifted—and may yet shift—back and forth across cultures and times. Ancient Roman law permitted torture to coerce confessions, although it harbored some doubts about the reliability of such confessions. The canon law, however, conscious of both the dignity of the individual and the need for truth, repeatedly asserted that confessions must be made voluntarily. But the views of Augustine and many other church authorities in favor of voluntariness failed to prevail in a meaningful sense in the secular courts of the ius commune. Society's desire to secure the common good against crime rendered the torture of individuals acceptable when deemed necessary. England, too, engaged in torture, when the security of the crown (and, therefore, of the state) needed protection, even while English legal writers took pride in the common law being torture-free. A society's choice to use or forswear torture depended upon the lessons it drew from the contingencies of its historical experiences. Perhaps, we are not so far removed from such considerations today.

Political pressures, too, contribute to the molding of procedural choices. King John acquiesced in signing Magna Carta only when the barons pressed the charter upon him at Runnymede in 1215. Through the Charter's chapter 39 (c 29, 1225), nobles restrained the crown from undertaking arbitrary prosecutions. Likewise, a fear of abusive power led Edward III's fourteenth-century parliaments to specify key procedural safeguards in a set of due process statutes. It was the political and religious trials of the seventeenth century that breathed new life into chapter 39/29 of Magna Carta after it had largely lain dormant for some four hundred years. Lawyers for defendants transformed the chapter into a touchstone for procedural protections, interpreting it anachronistically to apply to jury trials.

The treason legislation of the Tudor and Stuart statutes offers another telling instance of political events exercising an impact upon procedural choices. In 1547, the perilous experience of Henry VIII's recent treason prosecutions caused Edward VI's parliament to legislate that persons accused of treason make any confessions of guilt voluntarily. Members of parliament, themselves possibly at risk of prosecutions, felt a new urgency to assure confessions were made without force or violence. Successor Tudor and Stuart parliaments reinforced such defensive protections at treason trials, attempting to assure that a defendant would see accusing witnesses face to face and hear what they had to say against the accused. But, as Walter Raleigh found out to his dismay, what arises in one political setting can disappear in another. Raleigh's judges claimed the statute requiring confrontation was repealed by an act of Queen Mary. The initial requirements for confrontation and eyewitness testimony proved insecure. Through statutory interpretation, the safeguards evanesced.

---

[6] See EP Thompson observing: "The greatest of all legal fictions is that the law itself evolves, from case to case, by its own impartial logic, true only to its own integrity, unswayed by expedient considerations." EP Thompson, *Whigs and Hunters* (Allen Lane 1975) 250.

Instances of religion's effect on procedural principles are legion. By the fourth century, the western church's choice to adopt ancient Roman procedure for adjudicating ecclesiastical disputes affected not only the subsequent history of canonical trials but secular trials, as well. The ninth-century pseudo-Isidorian forgeries offer a particularly consequential instance of religion's role. To protect bishops from possibly ungrounded accusations, the forgers produced rafts of spurious documents containing defensive safeguards, including the requirement that confessions of guilt be voluntary. Accepted as genuine, many of the forgeries' principles found a place in early canonical collections. In turn, those collections influenced canonical trial procedures and contributed to developing European *ius commune*.

As a further instance of religion's impact on procedural choices, the Fourth Lateran Council's decrees cannot be overestimated. When the Council discontinued the church's blessing of ordeals, it thereby hastened their end and created a need for alternative trial procedures. The Council's canon 8 laid down due process norms for rational trials to replace the "irrational" ordeals. The Council's decisions swiftly brought about procedural consequences across Europe. On the Continent, inquisitorial procedure spread. In England, the crown built upon the already existing accusing jury. The resultant petty jury became the principal instrument, then and ever since, for final determinations of guilt or innocence in Anglo-American jurisdictions.

Without the long chain of religio-historical events that convulsed seventeenth-century England, one can only wonder if a right against self-incrimination would ever have emerged in English and American law in anything like the form it has. Theological convictions, ecclesiastical strife, and jurisdictional politics directly affected how the privilege formed and how it functioned in different environments. Indeed, religion was present at the inception of the privilege. Well over a thousand years before England struggled with the question of self-incrimination, John Chrysostom, Archbishop of Constantinople, had preached to his people that "no one is obliged to betray himself in public." When, in the twelfth century, Gratian sought to bring order to the many church canons of his day, he looked back to Chrysostom's phrase, now captured in the Latin *non tibi dico ut te prodas in public* (I do not say that you should betray yourself in public). Bernard of Parma, referencing both Chrysostom and Gratian, added the gloss *nemo tenetur prodere se* (no one is held to betray himself). The phrase was meant, he hastened to say, to protect secret matters of the heart in a sacramental context. Some four hundred years later, in the religious controversies of Reformation and post-Reformation England, the maxim became a useful tool in the hands of religious dissenters. They resisted being compelled under oath to uncover private religious beliefs and convictions of conscience. Then, the original limitation of the non-incrimination principle to "secret" crimes fell away altogether in the hands of later seventeenth-century defense lawyers. The common good was no longer thought sufficient to justify compelling suspects to imperil themselves in answering questions from judicial authority. Now, having been schooled by new experiences, a new calculus was at work. A greater stress on the integrity of the person took priority over the discovery of truth. If the truth was to appear, the prosecution would have to carry the burden alone. Aquinas would not have agreed. But the "artificial reason" of the late seventeenth century had arrived at conclusions different from those of the thirteenth.

ii.

As in the creation of procedural safeguards, so, too, in the course of their denial, we can recognize the role of historical context and cultural attitudes, and how they shift about.

English judges in state trials sometimes rebuffed the demands of criminal defendants. Walter Raleigh called in vain to see his accuser. Defendants complained that they did not know the charges against them; that they were denied a copy of the indictment; that they had grossly inadequate time to prepare their defenses; that they had no counsel; that their witnesses could not appear or testify under oath. Modern readers will likely find themselves in sympathy with those disadvantaged accused. But, in rejecting defendants' procedural claims, the judges did not think themselves unjust or unreasonable. Common-law criminal trial procedure relied on spontaneity as a guide to truth. For that reason, English judges of the sixteenth and seventeenth centuries regularly denied the assistance of defense counsel in matters of fact in felony cases brought by indictment. In doing so, the bench did not think itself biased or hostile to justice. Counsel, it was feared, might obfuscate truth rather than illuminate it, thereby frustrating the jury's task of deciding rightly according to its conscience.[7] It was the same reasoning that deprived the accused of adequate notice of charges and the provision of copies of indictments. Allowing such claims would have enabled defendants to prepare possibly false stories or to sponsor perjurious witnesses for the defense. The customary unrehearsed exchanges between parties at trial aided juries in determining the truth. Or, so good judges commonly thought.

But experience offered still further, and different, lessons in the late seventeenth century, when, once again, politics motivated procedural change. Opponents in parliament were imperiling one another's lives through partisan accusations of treason. Vengeful trials increased the urgency for defensive protections. Jurors had to be concerned, too, that they might fail in fulfilling their solemn duty to render reliable verdicts. In a time of such political rivalry, limits on the assistance of defense counsel and restrictions on notice of charges and sworn testimony from defense witnesses seemed to imperil rather than promote reliable verdicts. Measures in support of spontaneity could now be seen as contributing to untrustworthy verdicts. Spontaneity for the sake of truth came at the cost of preparing a defense. Now, under the pressure of new events, a "grave and learned" parliament adopted a fresh view of what was fair and reliable. It appreciated more acutely that defendants should not be "debarred of all just and equal means for Defence of their Innocencies."[8] Accordingly, the new 1696 treason act mandated a set of defensive safeguards that in effect curtailed the free

---

[7] William Hawkins lauded the restriction on counsel on the ground that an accused person needs "no manner of skill to make a plain and honest defence . . . the simplicity and innocence, artless ingenuous behaviour of one whose conscience acquits him having something in it more moving and convincing than the highest eloquence of persons speaking in a cause not their own." In contrast, "the very speech, gesture and countenance, and manner of defence of those who are guilty, when they speak for themselves, may often help to disclose the truth." William Hawkins, 2 *A Treatise of the Pleas of the Crown* (E and R Nutt 1739) (2 vols) 400.

[8] 7 & 8 Will III, c 3, s 1 (1696).

reign of spontaneity at trial. The 1696 statute radically altered what was previously held to be a proper trial procedure.

In considering the formation of procedural principles, an additional "experience" of the past, and perhaps of the present, deserves consideration, as well. Social class can play a powerful role, for weal or woe, in the process of creating just procedures and determining for whom they should be provided. Rome made distinctions for trial and for the use of torture between the *honestiores* and the common criminal; between the treatment of free persons and slaves. The pseudo-Isidorian clerics forged their documents in order to protect bishops and higher clerics. When, at Runnymede, the barons pressed King John for Magna Carta and when later English parliamentarians enacted safeguards at treason trials, those powerful actors were in large measure motivated by self-interest. It was not the common people who were the first to fashion protective procedures for themselves. But, though originally made in the context of a particular class, principles of fairness seem to have embedded within themselves a latent potential to break out of their original bounds. When Roman and ecclesiastical principles melded into the due process doctrines of the *ius commune*, they were not limited in principle to a high class. Magna Carta's assurances of due process for the "free man" came to protect all the people of England and of the colonies, not just noble peers, but villeins and women, as well. In America, the procedural principles of the 6th Amendment originally applied weakly, at best, and mostly not at all, to enslaved persons; but in a society that purported to be conceived on the basis of equality, principles of fairness would not remain confined.[9] When a government—imperial, ecclesiastical, monarchical, or democratic—violates or restricts to only some kinds of persons its principles of fairness, voices inevitably arise to tear down the barriers.

Generations have found "by long study, observation, and experience" that there is a core of procedural rights that repeatedly reassert themselves, if denied. Essential to a sense of fairness are the right of the one accused to a trial before being stigmatized or punished; to be present at that trial; before an impartial fact-finder; without having to be the source of evidence against oneself; to know what the accusations are and who the accusers are; to be provided a meaningful opportunity to present one's defense; to be treated as innocent unless proven guilty; according to a high standard of proof and a regular judicial order; with the aid of some kind of counsel, and generally without subjection twice for trial on the same charges. Asserted in varying and often imperfect forms in ancient Rome, in the Middle Ages, on the Continent, as well as in England, and in America, these principles have been variously called "natural," "fundamental," "immemorial," and undeniable.

How can a society, agreeing on the essential principles of procedural justice in criminal trials, protect against the shifting currents of historical, religious, political, and cultural flux that may threaten its rights?[10] The seventeenth-century Levellers sought stability through agreements of the people. Parliament rejected their attempts. Post-Revolutionary Americans, having freed themselves from the threats of crown

[9] Thompson (n 6) 262–269.
[10] See William S Holdsworth, 5 *A History of English Law* (Little, Brown and Co 1924) (17 vols) 196 (cautioning that hard-earned procedures for fair trials can be undone, if government and respect for law weaken).

authority, thought a written bill of rights would safeguard against encroachments by a newly established federal power. After some reluctance, Madison had come to believe that, "so far as a declaration of rights can tend to prevent the exercise of undue power, it cannot be doubted but such declaration is proper."[11] The Bill of Rights would "limit and qualify the powers of government."[12] Madison recognized, however, that "the greatest danger" to rights lay not in the executive or the legislative branches but "in the body of the people." It is they, he said, who hold "the highest prerogative of power." If that power is unrestrained, an abusive majority might "seek to oppress the rights of a minority."[13] To protect against that, Madison told the Congress, they could place their hope in the judiciary. The courts, he said, would stand as "the guardians of those rights . . . an impenetrable bulwark against every assumption of power in the legislative or executive."[14]

Yet, Madison recognized that "all power is originally vested in, and consequently derived from the people." He must have known, as well, that the responsibility for the preservation of the people's rights would rest not on the branches of their government, but on the people themselves. It is they who ratified their rights. If they wish to protect them in the "many successions of ages" to come, they might bear in mind John Sadler's and John Lilburne's salutary caution:

Indeed the very form, and life and power, or substance of the justest Lawes, doth much consist in processe, which by some may now be thought a shadow, or a ceremony left at pleasure, for a blustring wind, or any furious hand to shake as much, as long as it shall please, and then to salve it up, by saying to the Root, We mean you good, and do but lay you bare, that so you may the more behold, and more admire our justice in the end, when all the boughs and branches shall be gone, that do but hinder all your prospect.[15]

[11] Charles F Hobson and others (eds) 12 *The Papers of James Madison* (University Press of Virginia 1979) 204.
[12] Ibid.
[13] Ibid.
[14] Ibid 207.
[15] John Lilburn, *The Afflicted Man's Outcry against the Injustice and Oppression Exercised . . .* (London [s.n.] 1653) 6, quoting John Sadler, *Rights of the Kingdom or, Customs of Our Ancestours* (London, printed by Richard Bishop 1649) 161.

Bibliography

Primary Roman Sources in Print

Ammianus Marcellinus, *Ammianus Marcellinus* (John Carew Rolfe tr, Harvard University Press; W Heinemann ltd 1935)

Apuleius, *The Apologia and Florida of Apuleius of Madaura* (HE Butler tr and ed), Greenwood Press 1909)

———, "Apuleius of Madauros Metamorphoses: Book X: Chapter 6" (JA Hanson tr and ed, Harvard University Press 1989)

Cicero MT, *The Verrine Orations: In Two Volumes* (LHG Greenwood tr, Harvard University Press 1966)

Gaudemet J, "Le Bréviare d'Alaric et les Epitome" in Société d'histoire des droits de l'antiq- uité (ed), *Ius Romanum Medii Aevi* (Giuffrè 1965) (pt 1) 1

Haenel GF (ed), *Lex romana Visigothorum ad LXXVI* (Apud Guilelmum Besserum 1849)

Harries J and Wood IN (eds), *The Theodosian Code* (Cornell University Press 1993)

Ioulianos S, *Iuliani epitome latina Novellarum Iustiniani* (Gustav Hänel ed, prostat apud Hinrichsium 1873)

Justinian, *The Digest of Justinian* (Latin text edited by Theodor Mommsen, Paul Krueger; English translation editor Alan Watson) (4 vols) (University of Pennsylvania Press 1985)

———, *The Institutes of Justinian: Text, Translation, and Commentary* (North-Holland Pub Co 1975)

———, *Corpus Juris Civilis, Pandectis Ad Florentinum Archetypum Expressis* (Amstelodami, Apud Johannem Blaeu. Ludovicum, & Danielem Elzevirios 1663)

———, *Novellae, Constitutiones Divi Caesaris Iustiniani* (Nicolo Bevilaqua 1569)

Lex acilia in S Riccobono and others (eds), 1 *Fontes iuris romani antejustiniani* (2nd edn, apud S a G Barbèra Florence 1941) 84. An English translation appears in AC Johnson (ed), *Ancient Roman Statutes: A Translation* (Allan Chester Johnson tr, University of Texas Press 1961) 38

Paulus J and others, *Collectio librorum juris antejustiniani in usum scholarum* (Paul Krueger ed, Weidmann 1878)

Quintilian, *The Institutio Oratoria of Quintilian* (HB Butler ed and tr, Harvard University Press; W Heinemann 1920)

Riccobono S and others (eds), *Fontes iuris romani antejustiniani* (2nd edn, apud S a G Barbèra 1941)

Rotondi G (ed), *Leges Publicae Populi Romani* (Societa Editrice Libraria 1912)

Zeumer K and Werminghoff A (eds), *Leges Visigothorum* (Impensis Bibiopolii Hahniani 1902)

Primary Ecclesiastical Sources in Print

Anselm of Lucca, Friedrich Thaner (ed), *Anselmi episcopi Lucensis Collectio canonum una cum collectione minore* (Innsbruck 1906)

Aquinas T, *Divi Thomae Aquinatis ordinis praedicatorum doctoris angelici a Leone XIII P.M. gloriose regnante catholicarum scholarum patroni coelestis renunciati Summa theologica* (Editio altera romana ad emendatiores editiones impressa et noviter accuratissime recognita. Ex typographia Forzani et S 1894)

Augustine, *De utilitate agendae poenitentiae* (Sermo 351) 39 PL 1535

———, *Sancti Aurelli Augustini: de civitate Dei*, 47 Corpus Christianorum Series Latina (Turnholt 1955) 670

———, *Confessions*, 27 Corpus Christianorum Series Latina (Turnholt 1983)

Besse J-C, *Histoire des Textes de Droit de l'Église au Moyen-Âge de Denys à Gratien: Collectio Anselmo Dedicata Étude et Textes* (Extraits) (Libraires techniques 1960)

Bullarum, Diplomatum, et Privilegiorum Sanctorum Romanorum Pontificum Taurensis editio (Tomus III) (A Tomassetti and others eds, Seb Franco, H Fory et H Dalmazzo 1858) 552

Burchard of Worms, *Decretum*, 140 PL 537

Chrysostom J, *Epistle on Paul's Letter to the Hebrews* 63 PG 216

Constitutions of the Fourth Lateran Council in Antonio García y García, *Constitutiones Concilii quarti Lateranensis una cum Commentariis glossatorum* (MIC Series A: Corpus Glossatorum 2; Biblioteca Apostolica Vaticano 1981)

Deusdedit, *Liber canonum* (1087) in von Glanvell VW (ed), *Die Kanonessammlung des Kardinals Deusdedit* (Paderborn 1905)

Diuersorum patrum sententiae sive Collectio in LXXIV titulus digesta (John T Gilchrist tr, Pontifical Institute of Medieval Studies 1980)

Durandus, Gullielmus, Gvl. Durandi Episcopi, *Speculum iudiciale* (2 vols) (Basel 1574, reprint Scientia Verlag Aalen 1975)

Evald P and Hartmann LM (eds), *2 Gregorii papae Registrum epistolarum* (MGH epistolae 1889, 2nd edn, apud Weimannos 1957)

Gratia Arentinus, *Summa de iudiciario ordine* in Bergmann FC (ed), *Pillii, Tancredi, Gratiae Libri de iudiciorum ordine* (Göttingen 1852; photo reprint Scientia Verlag 1965)

Gratian, *Decretum Magistri Gratiani* in 1 Friedberg E and Richter E (eds), *Decretum Magistri Gratiani* (B Tauchnitz 1879, reprint Akademische Druck- u Verlagsanstalt 1959)

Gregory I, *Gregorii I papae Registrum epistolarum* (Editio secunda, apud Weidmannos 1957)

Gregory IX, *Decretales* in 2 Friedberg E and Richter E (eds), *Decretum Magistri Gratiani* (B Tauchnitz 1879, reprint Akademische Druck- u Verlagsanstalt 1959)

———, *Decretales D. Gregorii Papae IX. Svae Integritati, Vna Cvm Glossis Restitvtae; ad Exemplar Romanum Diligenter Recognitae* (Bernardo Bottoni ed, Apud Iuntas 1615)

Hincmar, *De presbiteris criminosis: ein Memorandum Erzbischof Hinkmars von Reims über straffällige Kleriker* (Gerhard Schmitz ed, Hahnsche Buchhandlung 2004)

Innocent IV, *Apparatus in quinque libros Decretalium* (Frankfurti ad Mainum 1570, reprint Frankfurt am Main 1968)

Isidore of Seville, *Synonyma*, 83 PL 825

Ivo of Chartres, *Divi Ivonis Decretum*, 161 PL 59

———, *Panormia*, 161 PL 1042

John VIII, *Lupenandum presbyterum* in Caspar E (ed), *Monumenta Germaniae Historica*, 7 Epistolarum 292 (Berlin 1928)

———, *Audquarius venerabilis* in Caspar E (ed), *Monumenta Germaniae Historica*, 7 Epistolarum, 298, 299 (Berlin 1928)

Leo I, *Sancti Leonis Magni Romani Pontificis Opera Omnia*, in 55 PL 1211

Mansi GD and others (eds), *Sacrorum Conciliorum Nova et Amplissima Collectio: In qua Praeter Ea Quae Phil. Labbeus et Gabr. Cossartius et Novissime Nicolaus Coleti in Lucem Edidere Ea Omnia Insuper Suis in Locis Optime Disposita Exhibentur* (H Welter 1901)

Nicolas I, *Ad consulta vestra* c 71 in Perels E (ed), *Monumenta Germaniae Historica*, 6 Epistolarum 568, 595 (Berlin 1912)

——, *Responsa to the Bulgarians* in Perels E (ed), *Monumenta Germaniae Historica*, 6 Epistolarum 568, 595 (Berlin 1912)

——, *Audito, revertente* in Perels E (ed), *Monumenta Germaniae Historica*, 6 Epistolarum 322, 323 (Berlin 1912)

Nouum Testamentum Domini Nostri Jesu Christi latine secundum editionem Sancti Hieronymi (2 vols) (John Wordworth and Henry J White eds, OUP 1905)

Paucapalea, "Preface to the *Summa* of Paucapalea on Gratian's Decretum, c. 1150" in Somerille R and Brasington BC (eds and trs), *Prefaces to Canon Law Books in Latin Christianity* (Yale University Press 1998)

Prosper of Aquitaine, *S. Prosperi Aquitani Sententiarum ex Operibus S. Augustini Delibatarum Liber Unus* in 51 PL 427

Ps-Isidore, *Decretales pseudo-Isidorianae et capitula Angilramni ad fidem librorum manuscriptorum recensuit, fontes indicavit, commentationem de collectione pseudo-Isidori* (Paul Hinschius ed, B Tauchnitz 1863)

Ps-Isidore, *Capitula Angilramni* in Schon K-G, *Die Capitula Angilramni: eine prozessrechtliche Falschung Pseudoisidors* (Hahnsche Buchhandlung 2006)

Regino, *Reginonis abbatis Prumiensis Libri duo de synodalibus causis et disciplinis ecclesiasticis, ex diversis sanctorum patrum conciliis atque decretis collecti* (Sumtibus G Engelmann 1840)

Stephen of Tournai, *Die Summa des Stephanus Tornacensis über das Decretum Gratiani* (Joh Friedrich von Schulte ed, Emil Roth 1891)

Stephen of Tournai, "Preface to the *Summa* of Stephen of Tournai on Gratian's *Decretum*" in Somerville R and Brasington BC (eds and trs), *Prefaces to Canon Law Books in Latin Christianity* (Yale University Press 1998)

Stephen V, *Consuluisti etiam* in Caspar E (ed), *Monumenta Germaniae Historica*, 7 Epistolarum 347, 348 (Berlin 1928)

Tancred (Tancredus Bononiensis), *Ordo iudiciarius* in Bergmann FC (ed), *Pillii, Tancredi, Gratiae Libri de iudiciorum ordine* (Göttingen 1852, photo reprint Scientia Verlag 1965)

——, *Summula de Criminibus* in Fraher RM, "Tancred's Summula de Criminibus: A New Text and a Key to the Ordo Iudiciarius" (1979) 9 Bulletin of Medieval Canon Law 23

von Schwerin C, "Rituale für Gottesurteile" (Sitzungsberichte der Heidelberger Akademie der Wissenschaften, Philosophisch-historische Klasse, Abhandlung 3, Heidelberg 1933)

Zosimus, "Epistle to the bishops of Africa" in 20 PL 654 (417)

Primary *Ius Commune* Sources in Print

Accursius, Glossa ordinaria, in Novellae Constitutiones Divi Caesaris Iustiniani (Venice, Nicolo Bevilacqua 1569) 250

Azo, *Lectvra Azonis et Magni Apparatvs ad Singvlas Leges Dvodecim Librorvm Codicis Ivstiniani* (Apud Sebastianum Niuellium sub Ciconiis, Via Iacobaea 1581)

———, *Summa Azonis* (sub signo Angeli Raphaelis Gaspare Bindoni 1581)

da Fano M, "*De Positionibus*" in Nicolini U (ed), *Tratatti "De Positionibus" Attribuiti a Martino Da Fano in Un Codice Sconosciuto Dell' Archiginnasio Di Bologna (B 2794, 2795)* (Vita e Pensiero 1935) 67

Damhouder JD, *Praxis rerum criminalium* (Antwerp 1556)

de Pasageriis R, *Summa Totius Artis Notariae* (Venice 1546, reprint A Forni 1977)

de Saxoferrato B, Consilium 194, Bartolus, *Consilia, quaestiones et tractatus Bartoli à Saxoferrato* (Compania della Stampa 1589)

———, Commentary on Secundam Digesti Novi Partem on Dig 48.18.22 (21) no 9, in Bartoli à Saxaferrato, 6 *Omnium Iuris Interpretum Antesignani Commentaria* (Giunta Lucantonio 1602)

———, *Omnia, quæ extant, opera ... Tomus primus [vndecimus] ..: 6 Bartoli à Saxoferrato, ... Commentaria, In secundam Digesti noui partem* (Giunta Lucantonio 1602)

degli Ubaldi B and Polo G, *Baldi Vbaldi de Perusini, Consiliorum, sive responsorum* (apud Hieronymum Polum 1575)

Durand G, *Speculum judicale* (Scientia Verlag 1975)

Gambiglioni, A (Angelus Aretinus), *Angeli Aretini De Maleficiis Tractatus* (Venetiis, apud Cominum de Tridino Montisferrati 1573)

Gandinus, A, "Tractatus de maleficiis, De falsariis et falsitatibus" in Kantorowicz H (ed), 2 *Albertus Gandinus und das Strafrecht der Scholastik* (2 vols; vol 1, J Guttentag 1907; vol 2, Walter De Gruyter & Co 1926) (2 vols) 1

Gaudemet J, "Le Bréviare d'Alaric et Les Epitome 5" in *Jus Romanum Medii Aevi* (Milan 1965)

Hippolytus de Marsiliis, *Practica Hipp. de Mar. Practica causarum criminalium domini Hippolyti de Marsilijs I.V.* (apud Iacobum Giuncti in vico Mercuriali 1538)

Mancini V, *Vincentii Mancini ... De confessionibus tam iudicialibus quam extraiudicial-ibus: in causis ciuilibus, criminalibus, & mixtis, in quocunque foro procuratoribus, aduocatis, & alijs quibuscunque causidicis vtilis, & necessarius tractatus* (apud Iacobum Mascardum 1611)

Menochius J, *Iacobi Menochii Tractatus de Praesumtionibus, Coniecturis, Signis, & Indiciis, Commentaria in Sex Distincta Libros* (apud Samvelem Crispinvm 1609)

Wielant P, *Practijcke Criminele* (c 1510) (first published Gent 1872, Scientia Verlag Aalen 1978)

Primary English Sources in Print

"Observations upon certain Proceedings in the Star Chamber against Lord Vaux, Sir Thomas Tresham, Sir William Catesby, and others for refusing to swear that they had not harbored Campion the Jesuit" in 30 *Archaeologia, Or, Miscellaneous Tracts Relating to Antiquity* (The Society of Antiquaries 1844)

Atkyns R, *A Defence of the Late Lord Russel's Innocency by Way of Answer or Confutation of a Libellous Pamphlet Intituled, An Antidote against Poyson : With Two Letters of the Author of This Book, upon the Subject of His Lordship's Tryal ...* (printed for Timothy Goodwin 1689)

Baker JH (ed), *Reports from the Lost Notebooks of Sir James Dyer* (Selden Society 1993)

Baker P and Vernon E, *The Agreements of the People, the Levellers, and the Constitutional Crisis of the English Revolution* (Palgrave Macmillan 2012)

Blackstone W, *Commentaries on the Laws of England* (Clarendon Press 1765)

Bolland CW and others (eds and trs), *5 Year Books of Edward II: The Eyre of Kent, 6 & 7 Edward II (1313–1314)*, 24 SS (Bernard Quatrich 1910)

Booth A, *Examen Legum Angliæ, or, the Laws of England Examined, by Scripture, Antiquity and Reason* (James Cottrel 1756)

Bowyer R, *The Parliamentary Diary of Robert Bowyer, 1606–1607* (The University of Minnesota Press; H Milford, OUP 1931)

Bracton H, *Bracton on the Laws and Customs of England* (George E Woodbine ed, Samuel E Thorne tr, William S Hein & Co 1997)

Brook, Report of the Conference at Serjeants Inn, 109 SS (1993)

Bruce J, "Observations upon Certain Proceedings in the Star-Chamber against Lord Vaux, Sir Thomas Tresham, Sir William Catesby, and Others, for Refusing to Swear That They Had Not Harboured Campion the Jesuit" 30 *Archaeologia, or, Miscellaneous Tracts Relating to Antiquity* (The Society of Antiquaries of London 1844)

Brydell J, *Enchiridion legum* (printed by Elizabeth Flesher 1673)

Burn, R and Parker J, *Conductor Generalis: Or, the Office, Duty and Authority of Justices of the Peace* (printed by John Patterson 1788)

Care H, *English Liberties, or the Free-Born Subject's Inheritance ... of Trials by Juries, and of the Qualifications of Juries* (4th edn, In the Savoy: printed by Eliz Nutt and R Gosling, assigns of Edward Sayer, Esquire)

Clerke F, *Praxis Francisci Clarke in Curiis Ecclesiasticis* (printed per Nathaniel Thompson 1666)

Cobbett W, Howell TB, and Howell TJ (eds), *A Complete Collection of State Trials and Proceedings for High Treason and Other Crimes and Misdemeanors from the Earliest Period to the Year 1783 (1809–28)* (21 vols) (1st edn 1719; TC Hansard 1816)

Coke E, *The First Part of the Institutes of the Laws of England. Or, a Commentary upon Littleton* (Francis Hargrave and Charles Butler eds, printed for James Moore 1791)

———, *The Second Part of the Institutes of the Laws of England. Containing the Exposition of Many Ancient and Other Statutes* (printed for E and R Brooke 1797)

———, *The Third Part of the Institutes of the Laws of England: Concerning High Treason, and Other Pleas of the Crown. And Criminal Causes* (printed for E and R Brooke 1797)

———, "Memorandum on Chapter 29 (1604)" in John H Baker, *Selected Readings and Commentaries on Magna Carta 1400–1604* (Selden Society 2015) 394

Conset H, *The Practice of the Spiritual or Ecclesiastical Courts: Wherein is Contained, Their Original Stile and Causes Usually Tryed in Them* (2nd edn, W Battersby 1700)

Cosin R, *An Answer to the Two First and Principall Treatises of a Certeine Factious Libell, Put Foorth Latelie, without Name of Author or Printer* (by Henrie Denham for Thomas Chard 1584)

———, *An Apologie for Sundrie Proceedings by Iurisdiction Ecclesiasticall* (by the deputies of Christopher Barker 1593)

Dalton M, *The Country Justice: Containing the Practice of the Justices of the Peace, as Well in, as Out of the Sessions. Gathered for the Better Help of Such Justices of Peace, as Have Not Been Much Conversant in the Study of the Laws of This Realm* (printed for John Walthoe 1715)

Dasent JR (ed), *2 Acts of the Privy Council of England* (Eyre and Spottiswoode 1890)

Duncombe G, *Trials per Pais. Or the Law of England Concerning Juries by Nisi Prius, &c. With a Compleat Treatise of the Law of Evidence, ...* (5th edn, printed by Eliz Nutt, and R Gosling 1718)

Dyer J, 1 *Reports of Cases in the Reigns of Hen. Viii. Edw. VI. Q. Mary, and Q. Eliz. Taken and Collected by Sir James Dyer* (sold by J Butterworth, Fleet-Street 1794)

Edward VI, *Chronicle and Political Papers* (published for the Folger Shakespeare Library by Cornell University Press 1966)

Fitzherbert A, *L'Office et Aucthoritie de Justices de Peace* (Richard Tottell, R Crompton rev. 1584, photo reprint 1972)

Fortescue J, *De laudibus legum Angliae* (In Praise of the Laws of England) in Shelley Lockwood (ed), *On the Laws and Governance of England* (CUP 1997)

Foxe J, Stoughton J, and Pratt J, *The Acts and Monuments of John Foxe* (The Religious Tract Society 1877)

Fuller N, *The Argument of Master Nicholas Fuller, in the Case of Thomas Lad and Richard Maunsell* (imprinted at William Jones's secret press 1607)

Hale Commission, Somers Tracts, "Several Draughts of Acts," in Walter Scott, Esq (ed), 2 *A Collection of Scarce and Valuable Tracts* (2d edn printed for T Caldwell 1809) (13 vols)177–245

Hale M, *The History of the Common Law of England. Divided into Twelve Chapters. By Sir Matthew Hale, Kt. Late Lord Chief Justice of the Court of King's Bench* (2nd edn, printed by E and R Nutt and others 1716)

———, *Historia Placitorum Coronæ. The History of the Pleas of the Crown in Two Volumes* (In the Savoy: printed by E and R Nutt, and R Gosling, assigns of Edward Sayer, Esquire 1736)

——— and Giles Jacob, *Pleas of the Crown* (J N Assignee of Edw Sawyer 1716)

Hawkins W, *Treatise of the Pleas of the Crown* (E and R Nutt, and R Gosling 1739)

Hawles J, *Remarks upon the Tryals of Edward Fitzharris, Stephen Colledge, Count Coningsmark, the Lord Russel, Collonel Sidney, Henry Cornish, and Charles Bateman* (printed for Jacob Tonson 1689)

Helmholz RH and Selden Society, *Three Civilian Notebooks, 1580–1640* (Selden Society 2011)

"Henry VIII: August 1540," 1–10, Gairdner J and Brodie RH (eds), 15 *Letters and Papers, Foreign and Domestic, of the Reign of Henry VIII, British History Online* <https://www.british-history.ac.uk/letters-papers-hen8/vol15> (accessed October 28, 2024)

Horwood AJ (ed), 3 *Year Books of the Reign of Edward the First: Years XXX and XXXI* (1302–1303) (Longmans, Green 1963)

Hudson W, *A Treatise of the Court of Star Chamber* in Hargrave F (ed), *A Treatise of the Court of Star Chamber by William Hudson* (first published London 1792, reprint The Legal Classics Library 1986)

Lambarde W, *Eirenarcha of the Office of Justices of Peace* (1581/82, photo reprint Professional Books Ltd 1972)

———, *Eirenarcha: Or of the Office of the Iustices of Peace in Foure Bookes: Gathered 1579: First Published 1581: And Now Reuised, Corrected, and Enlarged* (printed by Ralph Newbery 1588)

Letter patent of 26th January, 1219, printed in Rymer T and Sanderson R (eds), 1 *Foedera, conventiones, litterae...* (3 vols) (London 1816) 154

Lilburne J and Walker C, *The Tryal of Lieutenant Colonel John Lilburn...October 1649 by Theodorus Varax* (2nd edn, printed for H Hills 1710).

The Manuscripts of the House of Lords, 1689–1690: Presented to Both Houses of Parliament by Command of Her Majesty (HM Stationery Office 1889)

Marsden RG (ed), 1 *Select Pleas in the Court of Admiralty* (Bernard Quatrich 1894)

Morice J, *A Briefe Treatise of Oathes exacted by the ordinaries and ecclesiasticall iudges, to answere generallie to all such articles or interrogatories, as pleaseth them to propound And of their forced and constrained oaths ex officio, wherein is proued the same are vnlawful* (printed for Richard Schilders 1590)

Nine Commissioners, "Oaths in Ecclesiastical Courts," State Papers, Domestic, Elizabeth, PRO P.12/238, no 47

Pratt J (ed), 5 *The Acts and Monuments of John Foxe* (4th edn, The Religious Tract Society 1877)

Pritchard MJ and Yale DEC (eds), *Hale and Fleetwood on Admiralty Jurisdiction* (SS 1993)

Pulton F, *De Pace Regis et Regni Viz. A Treatise...* (Companie of Stationers 1609)

Robertson JC and others, *Materials for the History of Thomas Becket: Archbishop of Canterbury (Canonized by Pope Alexander III., A. D. 1173)* (Bosham Herbert and others eds, Longman 1875)

Robinson H, *Certain Considerations in Order to a More Speedy, Cheap, and Equall Distribution of Justice throughout the Nation* (Matthew Simmons 1651)

Rotuli Parliamentorum; ut et Petitiones, et Placita in Parliamento (vol 4) (London s.n. 1767–1777) (6 vols)

Rymer T and Sanderson R (eds), 1 *Foedera, conventiones, litterae, et cujuscunque generis acta publica, inter Reges Angliae et alios quosvis imperatores, reges, pontifices, principes, bel communitates; ab ingressu Gulielmi I. in Angliam, A.D. 1066. Ad nostra usque tempora habita aut tract* (n.p. 1816)

Sadler J, *Rights of the Kingdom; or, Customs of Our Ancestours: Touching the Duty, Power, Election, or Succession, of Our Kings and Parliaments; Our True Liberty, . . . Discussed through the Brittish, Saxon, Norman, Lawes and Histories . . .* (printed by Richard Bishop 1649)

Saint German C, *The Dialogue in English, Betweene a Doctor of Divinitie, and a Student in the Lawes of England* (printed by the assignes of Iohn More, Esquire 1638)

Seipp D (ed), *The Year Book Reports (1268–1535)* <http://www.bu.edu/law/seipp>

Smith T, *De Republica Anglorum. The Maner of Gouernement or Policie of the Realme of England* (Henrie Midleton 1583)

Spelman J and Baker JH, *The Reports of Sir John Spelman* (Selden Society 1977)

Starke R, *Office and Authority of a Justice of Peace: Explained and Digested, under Proper Titles* (printed by Alexander Purdie and John Dixon 1774)

Staunford, W, *Les Plees Del Coron* (n.p., Richard Tottell 1557) in Glazebrook PR (ed), *Les Plees del Coron* (photo reprint, Professional Books Ltd 1971)

Stephenson C, *Sources of English Constitutional History: A Selection of Documents from A.D. 600 to the Present* (2 vols) (Harper & Brothers 1972)

Strype J, 2 *Ecclesiastical Memorials Relating Chiefly to Religion and the Reformation of it* (Clarendon Press 1822)

——, *A Short Discourse, Being the Judgment of Several of the Most Learned Doctors of the Civil Law, Concerning the Practice of Their Courts, and the Oath Ex Officio*, printed in Appendix, bk III, no II in John Strype, *The Life and Acts of...John Whitgift* (London 1718)

Stubbs W and Carless Davis HW, *Select Charters and Other Illustrations of English Constitutional History from the Earliest Times to the Reign of Edward the First* (9th edn, FB Rothman 1985)

Style W, *Regestum Practicale, or, the Practical Register Consisting of Rules, Orders, and Observations Concerning the Common-Laws, and the Practice Thereof* (printed by AM for Charles Adams 1657)

Tanner JR, *Tudor Constitutional Documents: A.D. 1485–1603* (CambridgeUniversity Press 1951)

The Great Roll of the Pipe for the Fifteenth Year of the Reign of King Henry the Second: A.D. 1168–1169 (printed by Wyman & Sons 1890)

"Trial of the Peers Bill" in *Manuscripts of the House of Lords 1689–1690* (Twelfth Report, Appendix pt VI, Historical Manuscripts Commission, Eyre & Spottiswoode 1889) 31

Twiss T (ed), 2 *Monumenta Juridica. The Black Book of the Admiralty, with an Appendix* (4 vols) (Longman & Co; Trubner & Co 1871–1876)

Webb G, 1 *Office and Authority of a Justice of Peace* (William Parks 1736)

Yonge W, *A Vademecum...together with an Epitome of Master Staniford's Plees of the Crowne* (London, printed for R.B. 1643)

Seventeenth-Century Tracts

Modern editions of many Leveller tracts are available

Haller W and Davies G (eds), *The Leveller Tracts 1647–1653* (Columbia University Press 1944)

Hart DM and Kenyon R (eds), *Tracts on Liberty by the Levellers and Their Critics (1638–1660)* (7 vols) (Liberty Fund 2014–2018)

Sharp A (ed), *The English Levellers* (CUP 1998)

Wolfe DM (ed), *Leveller Manifestoes of the Puritan Revolution* (T Nelson 1944)

The original printing of the following tracts are accessible online

An Agreement of the People for a Firme and Present Peace, upon Grounds of Common-Right and Freedome; as It Was Proposed by the Agents of the Five Regiments of Horse; and since by the Generall Approbation of the Army, Offered to the Joynt Concurrence of All the Free Commons of England (s.n. 1647)

An Agreement of the People of England and the Places Therewith Incorporated, for a Secure and Present Peace, upon Grounds of Common Right, Freedom and Safety (s.n., printed for John Partridge and others 1649)

Anonymous, *The Case of the Armie Truly Stated Together with the Mischiefes and Dangers That Are Imminent, and Some Sutable Remedies, Humbly Proposed by the Agents of Five Regiments of Horse, to Their Respective Regiments, and the Whole Army* (s.n. 1647)

———, *The Lavvs Discovery: Or a Brief Detection of Sundry Notorious Errors and Abuses Contained in Our English Laws, Whereby Thousands Are Annually Stript of Their Estates, and Some of Their Lives. By a Well-Wisher to His Countrey* (printed by R I 1653)

———, *The Humble Petition of Divers Constant Adherers to This Parliament, and Faithfull Assertors of the Fundamentall Lawes and Liberties of the Commonwealth* (s.n. 1652)

———, *The Onely Right Rule for Regulating the Lawes and Liberties of the People of England Presented in Way of Advise to His Excellency the L. Generall Cromwell, and the Rest of the Officers of the Army, January 28. 1652. By Divers Affectionate Persons to Parliament, Army, and Commonwealth, Inhabiting the Cities of London, Westminster, Borough of Southwark, and Places Adjacent* (printed for the subscribers 1652)

———, *To the Right Honourable, and Supreame Authority of This Nation, the Commons in Parliament Assembled. The Humble Petition of Many Thousands, Earnestly Desiring the Glory of God, the Freedom of the Common-Wealth, & the Peace of All Men* (s.n. 1647)

———, *To the Right Honourable the Commons of England in Parliament Assembled. The Humble Petition of Divers Wel Affected Persons Inhabiting the City of London, Westminster, the Borough of Southwark, Hamlets and Places Adjacent. With the Parliaments Answer There Unto* (s.n. 1648)

———, *The Remonstrance of Many Thousands of the Free-People of England .... Also Their Petition of January 19. 1647. and of September 11. 1648. Together with the Agreement of the Free People of England May. 1. 1649. With Their Solemn Engagement for Redeeming, Setling, and Securing the Peoples Rational, and Just Rights, and Liberties, against All Tyrants Whatsoever, Whether in Parliament, Army, or Councel of State* (s.n. 1649)

———, *To the Supreme Authority, the Parliament of the Common-Vvealth of England. The Humble Petition of Divers Constant Adherers to This Parliament, and Faithfull Assertors of the Fundamentall Lawes and Liberties of the Commonwealth* (s.n. 1652)

———, *The Fundamental Lawes and Liberties of England Claimed, Asserted, and Agreed unto, by Severall Peaceable Persons of the City of London, Westminster, Southwark, Hamblets, and Places Adjacent* (s.n. 1653)

Bradford W, *The Excellent Priviledge of Liberty & Property Being the Birth-Right of the Free-Born Subjects of England. Containing I. Magna Carta, . . . And Lastly, the Charter of Liberties Granted by the Said VVilliam Penn to the Free-Men and Inhabitants of the Province of Pennsilvania and Territories Thereunto Annexed, in America* (printed by William Bradford 1687)

Cook J, *The Vindication of the Professors & Profession of the Law: So Farre Forth as Scripture and Right Reason May Be Judge, and Speedy Justice* (for Matthew Walbancke 1646)

Jones J, *Jurors Judges of Law and Fact or, Certain Observations of Certain Differences in Points of Law* (printed by W D 1649)

Lilburne, J, *Foundations of Freedom; or an Agreement of the People* (published for the satisfaction of all honest interests 1648)

———, *The Just Defence of John Lilburn, against Such as Charge Him with Turbulency of Spirit* (s.n. 1653)

———, *Liberty Vindicated against Slavery / by a Lover of His Country, and Sufferer for the Common Liberty* (s.n. 1646)

———, *The Humble Petition of Many Thousands, Earnestly Desiring the Glory of God, the Freedom of the Common-Wealth, & the Peace of All Men* (s.n. 1647)

———, *Tvvo Letters Vvrit by Lievt. Col. John Lilburne, Prerogative Prisoner in the Tower of London, to Col Henry Martin, a Member of the House of Commons* (s.n. 1647)

———, *England's New Chains Discovered* (s.n. 1648)

———, *The Legal Fundamental Liberties of the People of England, Revived, Asserted and Vindicated. Or an Epistle, Written the 8. of Iune, 1649. by Lieutenant Colonel John Lilburn (Arbitrary and Aristocratical Prisoner in the Tower of London) to Mr. William Lenthal...* (s.n. 1649)

———, *The Afflicted Man's Outcry, against the Injustice and Oppression Exercised upon; or, An Epistle of John Lilburn, Gent. Prisoner in Newgate, August 19. 1653. to Mr. Feak, Minister at Christ Church in London* (s.n. 1653)

———, *An Agreement of the Free People of England. Tendered as a Peace-Offering to This Distressed Nation. By Lieutenant Colonel Iohn Lilburne, Master William Walwyn, Master Thomas Prince, and Master Richard Overton, Prisoners in the Tower of London, May the 1. 1649* (1649)

———, *England's Birthright Justified* (s.n. 1645)

Overton R, *An Appeale from the Degenerate Representative Body the Commons of England Assembled at Westminster: To the Body Represented, the Free People in General of the Several Counties, Cities, Townes, Burroughs, and Places within This Kingdome of England, and Dominion of Wales* (s.n. 1647)

Penn W, *Excellent Privilege of Liberty and Property Being a Reprint and Fac-Simile of the First American Edition of Magna Charta Printed in 1687* (The Philobiblon Club 1687)

Persons R, *The Jesuit's Memorial for the Intended Reformation of England under Their First Popish Prince Published from the Copy That Was Presented to the Late King James II : With an Introduction, and Some Animadversions by Edward Gee ...* (Richard Chiswell 1690)

Robinson H, *Certain Considerations in Order to a More Speedy, Cheap, and Equall Distribution of Justice throughout the Nation* (Matthew Simmons 1651)

Thompson W, "An Agreement of the People of England," *Englands Standard Advanced in Oxfordshire, or, a declaration from Mr. Wil. Thompson and the Oppressed People of This Nation, Dated at Their Randezvouz, May 6, 1649* (s.n. 1649)

To the Supreme Authority, the Parliament of the Common-Wealth of England the Humble Petition of Divers Constant Adherers to This Parliament, and Faithfull Assertors of the Fundamentall Lawes and Liberties of the Commonwealth (printed for Thomas Brewster 1659)

Walwyn W, *Englands Lamentable Slaverie, Proceeding from the Arbitrarie Will, Severitie, and Injustnes of Kings, Negligence, Corruption, and Unfaithfulnesse of Parliaments, Coveteousnesse, Ambition, and Variablenesse of Priests, and Simplicitie, Carelesnesse, and Cowardlinesse of People* (s.n. 1645)

———, 1 *Juries Justified, or, a Word of Correction to Mr. Henry Robinson for His Seven Objections against the Trial of Causes, by Juries of Twelve Men* (1651)

Primary Colonial Sources in Print

"First Continental Congress: Declaration and Resolves (October 14, 1774)" in Rakove JN (ed), *Founding America: Documents from the Revolution to the Bill of Rights* (Barnes & Noble Classics 2006) 39

"Instructions for the Deputies Appointed to Meet in General Congress on the Part of This Colony" [Virginia] (1774) (Early American Imprints, Series I: Evans, 1639–1800)

"The Examination of Doctor Benjamin Franklin, before an August Assembly, Relating to the Repeal of the Stamp Act" in Wood GS (ed), *The American Revolution: Writings from the Pamphlet Debate I: 1764–1772* (The Library of America 2015) 335

"The Votes and Proceedings of the Freeholders and Other Inhabitants of the Town of Boston" in Wood GS (ed), *The American Revolution: Writings from the Pamphlet Debate I: 1764–1772* (The Library of America 2015) 763

45 *1776 Journals of the Continental Congress* (Massachusetts Historical Society 1919)

A Declaration by the Representatives of the United Colonies of North-America, Now Met in General Congress at Philadelphia, Setting Forth the Causes and Necessity of Their Taking up Arms (Benjamin Edes 1775)

Acts and Laws of the Province of Massachusetts Bay in New England, *Charters and General Laws of the Colony and Province of Massachusetts Bay* (Boston, T B Wait and Co 1811)

Adam J, Wroth LK, and Zobel HB (eds), 2 *Legal Papers of John Adams* (The Belkap Press 1965)

Bailyn B (ed), *The Debate on the Constitution* (The Library of America 1993)

Baldwin E, "An Appendix, Stating the Heavy Grievances the Colonies Labour under from Several Late Act of the British Parliament..." in Gordon S Wood (ed), *The American Revolution: Writings from the Pamphlet Debate II: 1773–1776* (The Library of America 2015) 343

Dulany D, "Considerations on the Propriety of Imposing Taxes in the British Colonies, for the Purpose of raising a Revenue, by an Act of Parliament" in Gordon S Wood (ed), *The American Revolution: Writings from the Pamphlet Debate II: 1773–1776* (The Library of America 2015) 270

Grimké, JF, *Public Laws of South Carolina, 1682–1790* (R Aitkin and Son 1790)

Hening WW and Campbell J, 1 *The Statutes at Large: Being a Collection of All the Laws of Virginia, from the First Session of the Legislature, in the Year 1619. Published Pursuant to an Act of the General Assembly of Virginia, Passed on the Fifth Day of February One Thousand Eight Hundred and Eight* (printed for the editor by R & W & G Bartow 1823)

Hobson C and others (eds), 12 *The Papers of James Madison* (University of Virginia Press 1979)

Jefferson T, 12 *Works of Thomas Jefferson* (Paul Leicester Ford ed, G.P. Putnam's Sons 1904–1905)

Johnson S, *Taxation No Tyranny; an Answer to the Resolutions and Address of the American Congress* (4th edn, T Cadell 1775)

4 *Journals of the Continental Congress, 1774–1789. Edited from the Original Records in the Library of Congress...* (GPO 1906)

45 *Journals of the House of Representatives of Massachusetts:1768–1769* (Massachusetts Historical Society 1919)

Madison J, "Speech Introducing Amendments in the House of Representatives" (June 8, 1789) in Rakove JN (ed), *Founding America: Documents from the Revolution to the Bill of Rights* (Barnes & Noble Classics 2006) 614

———, "Speech of August 17, 1789" in Congressional Register, II, 227

Mason G, 1 *The Papers of George Mason* (Robert A Rutland ed, University of North Carolina Press 1970)

Mather M, *America's Appeal to the Impartial World* (Ebenezer Watson 1775) reprinted in Wood GS (ed), *The American Revolution: Writings from the Pamphlet Debate: II: 1773–1776* (The Library of America 2015) 595

Potter HD and others (eds), *North Carolina Revised Laws, 1715–1796* (J Gales 1821)

The Proceedings of the Convention of Delegates, Held at the Capitol in the City of Williamsburg in the Colony of Virginia, on Monday the 6th of May, 1776 (Ritchie, Trueheart, Du-Val 1816)

Proceedings of the Congress at New York (Jonas Green 1766, photo facsimile Boston 1938) 15, para VII

Reed HC and Miller GJ (eds), *Burlington Court Book: A Record of Quaker Jurisprudence in West New Jersey, 1680–1709* (The American Historical Association 1944)

Stagg JCA (ed), *The Papers of James Madison Digital Edition* (University of Virginia Press 2010)

Thorpe FN and William S Hein & Company, *The Federal and State Constitutions, Colonial Charters, and Other Organic Laws of the States, Territories, and Colonies Now or Heretofore Forming the United States of America* (WS Hein 1993)

Webb G, *The Office and Authority of a Justice of the Peace...Collected from the Common Statute Law of England...Adapted to the Constitution and Practice of Virginia* (Williamsburg, printed by William Parks 1736)

Whitmore WH, *Colonial Laws of Massachusetts. Reprinted from the Edition of 1660, with the Supplements to 1672. Containing also, the Body of Liberties of 1641* (Rockwell and Churchill 1889)

Wood GS, *The American Revolution: Writings from the Pamphlet Debate* (The Library of America 2015)

Secondary Sources

Acevedo JF, "The Ideological Origins of the Right to Counsel" (2016) 68 S C L Rev 87

Albertario E, "L'uso Classico e l'uso Giustinianeo Di 'Extorquere'" (1911) 32 ZSS (Rom Abt) 307

Alschuler AW and Deiss AG, "Brief History of the Criminal Jury in the United States, A" (1994) 61 U Chi L Rev 867

Alschuler AW, "A Peculiar Privilege in Historical Perspective" in Helmholz RH and others (eds), *The Privilege against Self-Incrimination: Its Origins and Development* of Chicago Press 1997) 181

Anföldi A, *The Conversion of Constantine and Pagan Rome* (Clarendon Press 1948)

Anonymous, "A Morning at the Star-Chamber" (1857) 7 Rambler (n.s.) 15

Arnold MS and others (eds), *On the Laws and Customs of England: Essays in Honor of Samuel E. Thorne* (The University of North Carolina Press 2017)

Austin RG, s.v. "Quintilianus" in Hammond NGL and Scullard HH (eds), *The Oxford Classical Dictionary* (2nd edn, Clarendon Press 1970) 907

Bablitz LE, *Actors and Audience in the Roman Courtroom* (Routledge 2007)

Bailyn B, *The Ideological Origins of the American Revolution* (reprint of 1967 edn, The Belknap Press of Harvard University 2017)

Baix F, "Benoit le Lévite" in Baudrillart A and others (eds), 8 *Dictionnaire d'histoire et de géographie ecclésiastiques* (Letourzey et Ané 1935) 213

Baker JH, *The Reinvention of Magna Carta 1216–1616* (CUP 2017)

———, *Selected Readings and Commentaries on Magna Carta 1400–1604* (Selden Society 2015)

———, "The Legal Force and Effect of Magna Carta" in Holland RJ (ed), *Magna Carta: Muse and Mentor* (Reuters 2014) 65

———, "Criminal Courts and Procedure 1550–1800" in Baker J, 2 *Collected Papers on English Legal History* (CUP 2013) (3 vols) 1015

———, 1 *The Oxford History of the Laws of England* (OUP 2004)

———, "Some Early Newgate Reports 1315–1328" in Baker J, 2 *Collected Papers on English Legal History* (CUP 2013) 967

———, 6 *Oxford History of the Laws of England* (OUP 2003)

———, "The Pleas of the Crown:Criminal Procedure" in Baker JH, *An Introduction to English Legal History* (4th edn, Butterworths LexisNexis 2002) 500

———, "Personal Liberty under the Common Law, 1200–1600" in Baker JH, 1 *Collected Papers of Sir John Baker* (CUP) (3 vols) 871

———, "Introduction" to Baker JH (ed), *Reports of the Lost Notebooks of Sir James Dyer* (109 SS 1994) xxi

———, "Criminal Courts and Procedure at Common Law, 1500–1800" in Baker JH, *The Legal Profession and the Common Law: Historical Essays* (Hambledon Press 1986)

———, "Introduction" in Baker JH (ed), *The Reports of Sir John Spelman Part II* (94 SS 1977) 5

Baker P and Vernon E (eds), *The Agreements of the People, the Levellers, and the Constitutional Crisis of the English Revolution* (Palgrave 2012)

Baker TR, *Law and Society in Later Medieval England and Ireland: Essays in Honour of Paul Brand* (Taylor & Francis Group 2017)

Baldwin JW, "The Intellectual Preparation for the Canon of 1215 against Ordeals" (1961) 36 Speculum 613

Barnes, TG, *Shaping the Common Law: From Glanvill to Hale, 1188–1688* (Stanford Law Books 2008)

———, "Mr. Hudson's Chamber" in William Hudson, *A Treatise of the Court of Star Chamber As Taken from Collectanea Juridica* (Francis Hargrave ed, printed for E. and R. Brooke 1792, reprint The Legal Classics Library 1986) i

———, "Star Chamber Mythology" (1961) 5 Am J Legal Hist 1

Barthélemy D, "Presence de l'aveu dans le déroulement des ordalies (IXe–XIIIe siècle)" in *L'Aveu. Antiquité et moyen-âge* (L'École française de Rome 1986) 191

Bartlett R, *Trial by Fire and Water: The Medieval Judicial Ordeal* (Clarendon Press; OUP 1986)

Baudrillart A, Aubert R, and Meyer A de, *Dictionnaire d'histoire et de Géographie Ecclésiastiques* (Letouzey et Ané 1912)

Bauman RA, *Crime and Punishment in Ancient Rome* (Routledge 1996)

Bautz FW, *Biographisch-bibliographisches Kirchenlexikon* (Bautz 1970)

Bayne C and Dunham W (eds), "Council in the Star Chamber, The Introduction" (1956) 75 Select Cases in the Council of Henry VII xi

Baynes NH, *Constantine the Great and the Christian Church* (2nd edn, OUP for the British Academy 1972)

Beaney WM, *Right to Counsel in American Courts* (University of Michigan Press 1955)

Beattie JM, *Crime and the Courts in England, 1660–1800* (OUP 1986)

———, "Scales of Justice: Defense Counsel and the English Criminal Trial in the Eighteenth and Nineteenth Centuries" (1991) 9 Law and History Review 221

Beaudoin É, "Remarques sur la preuve par le serment du défendeur dan le Droit franc" (1896) 8 Annales de l'Université de Grenoble 407

Beck HGJ, "Hincmar of Reims" in Marthaler BL and others (eds) 6 *New Catholic Encyclopedia* (2nd edn, Gale 2003) (15 vols) 837

Bellamy JG, *The Criminal Trial in Later Medieval England: Felony before the Courts from Edward I to the Sixteenth Century* (University of Toronto Press 1998)

———, *The Tudor Law of Treason: An Introduction* (Routledge & Kegan Paul, University of Toronto Press 1979)

Bellany A, "The Torture of John Felton, 1628" in Lorna Hutson (ed), *The Oxford Handbook of English Law and Literature: 1500–1700* (OUP 2017) 548

Berger A, *Encyclopedic Dictionary of Roman Law* (American Philosophical 1953, reprint 1991)

Berman HJ, *Law and Revolution: The Formation of the Western Legal Tradition* (Harvard University Press 1983)

Berry MF, "Slavery, the Constitution, and the Founding Fathers" (1988) 1 Afro-Americans and the Evolution of a Living Constitution: A Symposium of the Smithsonian Institution and the Joint Center for Political Studies 3

Besse J-C, *Histoire des Textes de Droit de l'Église Au Moyen-Age de Denys à Gratien: Collectio Anselmo Dedicata, Étude et Textes (Extraits)* (Librairies techniques 1960)

Bickerman EJ, *Chronology of the Ancient World* (2nd edn, Cornell University Press 1980)

Biener FA, *Geschichte der Novellen Justinian's* (F Dümmler 1824)

Bilder MS, "Charter Constitutionalism: The Myth of Edward Coke and the Virginia Charter" (2016) 94 North Carolina Law Review 1545

———, "English Settlement and Local Governance" in Christopher Tomlins and Michael Grossberg (eds), 1 *The Cambridge History of Law in America: Volume 1: Early America (1580–1815)* (CUP 2008) (3 vols) 63

———, *The Transatlantic Constitution: Colonial Legal Culture and Empire* (Harvard University Press 2004)

———, "The Lost Lawyers: Early American Legal Literates and Transatlantic Legal Culture" (1999) 11 Yale JL & Human 47

Billings WM, "Pleading, Procedure, and Practice: The Meaning of Due Process of Law in Seventeenth-Century Virginia" (1981) 47 The Journal of Southern History 569

Bodet GP, "Coke's Third Institutes: A Primer for Treason Defendants" (1970) 20 U Toronto LJ 469

Bolland WC, "Introduction" in Bolland WC (ed), 24 *The Year Books of Edward II: The Eyre of Kent, 6 & 7 Edward II (1313–1314)* (Quatrich; Selden Society 1909) xvii

Boyer AD, "The Trial of Sir Walter Ralegh, the Trial of Treason and the Origins of the Confrontation Clause" (2005) 74 Miss LJ 869

———, *Sir Edward Coke and the Elizabethan Age* (Stanford University Press 2003)

Braddick M, *The Common Freedom of the People: John Lilburne and the English Revolution* (OUP 2018)

Brailsford HN, *The Levellers and the English Revolution* (Stanford University Press 1961)

Brasington BC, *Order in the Court: Medieval Procedural Treatises in Translation* (Brill 2016)

Braz I, "The Privilege Against Self-Incrimination in Anglo-american Law: The Influence of Jewish Law" in Rakover N (ed), *Jewish Law and Current Legal Problems* (Jerusalem 1984) 161

Broadwater J, *George Mason, Forgotten Founder* (University of North Carolina Press 2006)

Brooke CNL, "Approaches to Medieval Forgery" (1968) 3 Journal of the Society of Archivists 377

Brooke ZN, *The English Church and the Papacy* (CUP 1952)

Brooks CW, "Morice, James" in David Cannadine (ed), *Oxford Dictionary of National Biography* (OUP 2004) <https://doi.org/10.1093/ref:odnb/37783> (accessed October 29, 2024)

Browe P, *De ordaliis* (apud aedes Pont Universitatis Gregorianae 1932)

Brown B, "John Mercer: Merchant, Lawyer, Author, Book Collector" in Warren M Billings and Brent Tarter (eds), *"Esteemed Bookes of Lawe" and the Legal Culture of Early Virginia* (University of Virginia Press 2017) 109

Brown P, *Augustine of Hippo: A Biography* (University of California Press 2000)

Brundage JA, "Full and Partial Proof in Classical Canonical Procedure" (2007) 67 Jurist 58

———, *The Medieval Origins of the Legal Profession: Canonists, Civilians, and Courts* (University of Chicago Press 2008)

Brunt PA, "Evidence given under Torture in the Principate" (1980) 97 ZRG (RA) 256

Bruyning L, "Il Processo Longobardo Prima e Dopo l'invasione Franca" (1984) 57 Rivista di storia del diritto italiano 121

Bryson WH (ed), *Virginia Law Books: Essays and Bibliographies* (American Philosophical Society 2000)

———, *Census of Law Books in Colonial Virginia* (University Press of Virginia 1978)

Bušek V, "Episcopalis Audientia, Eine Friedens- Und Schiedsgerichtsbarkeit" (1939) 28 ZRG (KA) 453

Bush ML, *The Government Policy of Protector Somerset* (E Arnold 1975)

Buti I, "La 'cognitio extra ordinem': da Augosto a Diocleziano" in Hildegard Temporini and W Haase (eds), *Aufstieg und Niedergang der römischen Welt: Geschichte und Kultur Roms im Spiegel der neueren Forschung* (W de Gruyter 1972) 29

Butler SM, *Pain, Penance, and Protest: Peine Forte et Dure in Medieval England* (CUP 2022)

Caillemer E, *Le Droit Civil Dans Les Provinces Anglo-Normandes Au XIIe Siècle* (F Le Blanc-Hardel 1883, reprint Wentworth Press 2018)

Cairns DJA, *Advocacy and the Making of the Adversarial Criminal Trial, 1800–1865* (Clarendon Press 1998)

Cairns J and Macleod G, *The Dearest Birth Right of the People of England: The Jury in the History of the Common Law* (Hart 2002)

Calasso F, "Bartolo da Sassaferrato" in Ghilaberti AM (ed), 6 *Dizionario Biografico degli Italiani* (Istituto della Enciclopedia italiana 1966) (100 vols) 642

Chapin B, "The American Revolution as *Lese Majesty*" (1955) 79 The Pennsylvania Magazine of History and Biography 310

———, "Colonial and Revolutionary Origins of the American Law of Treason" (1960) 17 William & Mary Law Quarterly 3

Checchini A, "L'ordinamento processuale romano nell' alto medioevo" (1933) 6 Rivista di storia del diritto italiano 265

———, *Studi sull' ordinamento processuale romano e germanico. Pt I. II processo romano* (Padua Tipografia Seminario (1925)

———, "Studi storico-critici sulla 'Interpretatio' al Codice Teodosiano" in *Scritti giuridici e storico giuridici* (Facoltà di Giurisprudenza dell' Università di Padova 1958) 141

Chroust A-H and Murphy JR, "Lex Acilia and the Rise of Trial by Jury in the Roman World" (1948) 24 Notre Dame Lawyer 1

Cohen B, "Evidence in Jewish Law" in 1 *La Preuve* (16 Receuils de la Societé Jean Bodin 1964) 103

Cohn MC, *Geschichte der Quellen und Literatur des Römischen Rechts im frühen Mittelalter* (Scientia Verlag 1963)

Coke E, *A Catalogue of the Library of Sir Edward Coke* (Yale University Press; G Cumberlege, OUP 1950)

Colbourn HT, "Thomas Jefferson's Use of the Past" (1958) 15 The William and Mary Quarterly 56

Condorelli O, Schmoeckel M, and Roumy F, *Der Einfluss der Kanonistik auf die europäische Rechtskultur* (Böhlau 2012)

Connolly S, *Lives behind the Laws: The World of the Codex Hermogenianus* (Indiana University Press 2010)

Copeland PC and MacMaster RK, *The Five George Masons* (University of Virginia Press 2016)

Coquillette DR, *The Anglo-American Legal Heritage* (2nd edn, North Carolina Academic Press 2004)

———, *The Civilian Writers of Doctors' Commons, London: Three Centuries of Juristic Innovation in Comparative, Commercial, and International Law* (Duncker & Humblot 1988)

———, *Justinian in Braintree: John Adams, Civilian Learning, and Legal Elitism, 1758–1775* (Colonial Society of Massachusetts 1984)

Corcoran S, "Hincmar and His Roman Legal Sources" in Stone R and West C, *Hincmar of Rheims: Life and Work* (Manchester University Press 2015) 129

Coss PR, *The Moral World of the Law* (CUP 2000)

Costa E, 2 *Cicerone Giureconsulto* (2 vols) (2nd edn, Nicola Zanichelli 1927)

Cowan B and Sowerby S (eds), *The State Trials and the Politics of Justice in Later Stuart England* (The Boydell Press 2021)

Crook JA, *Legal Advocacy in the Roman World* (Cornell University Press 1995)

Cross C, "Udall, John" in David Cannadine (ed) *Oxford Dictionary of National Biography* <https://doi.org/10.1093/ref:odnb/27973> (accessed November 1, 2024)

d'Ors A, "El Codigo de Eurico" in 2 *Estudios Visigoticos* (Consejo Superior Investigaciones Cientificas 1960) 62

Dahyot-Dolivet J, "La Procédure Pénale d'office En Droit Romain" (1968) 41 Apollinaris 89

Damaška M, *Evaluation of Evidence: Pre-Modern and Modern Approaches* (CUP 2019)

———, "The Quest for Due Process in the Age of Inquisition" (2012) 60 Am J Comp L 919

———, "Of Hearsay and Its Analogs the Hearsay Reform Conference" (1991) 76 Minnesota Law Review 425

———, "Hearsay in Cinquecento Italy" in Michele Taruffo (ed), *Studi di Onore di Vittorio Denti* (CEDAM 1994) 59

Davenport EH, *The False Decretals* (BH Blackwell 1916)

Davies RR, "Mortimer, Roger, First Earl of March (1287–1330)" in David Cannadine (ed), *Oxford Dictionary of National Biography* <https://doi.org/10.1093/ref:odnb/19354> (accessed October 29, 2024)

Davies TA, *The Quakers in English Society, 1655–1725* (Clarendon Press 2000)

Dawson JP, *A History of Lay Judges* (Harvard University Press; OUP 1960)

De Krey GS, *Following the Levellers: Political and Religious Radicals in the English Civil War and Revolution, 1645–1649* (Palgrave Macmillan UK 2017)

———, *Following the Levellers: Political and Religious Radicals from the Commonwealth to the Glorious Revolution, 1649–1688* (Palgrave Macmillan 2018)

de La Hera A, "Études d'Histoire Du Droit Canonique (2 vols; Sirey 1965)" (2018) 5 Ius canonicum 582

de Smedt C, "Les Origines Du Duel Judiciare" (1894) 63 Études religieuses pholosophiques, historiques et littéraires 337

———, "Le Duel Judiciare et l'Église" (1895) 64 Études religieuses pholosophiques, historiques et littéraires 35

de Wretschko A, "De usu Breviarii Alariciani forensico et scholastico per Hispaniam, Galliam, Italiam, regionesque vicinas" in Mommsen T and others (eds), 1/1 *Theodosiani Libri XVI cum constitutionibus Sirmondianis* (apud Weimannos 1905) cccvii

Declareuil J, "Les Preuves Judiciares Dans Le Droit Franc, du Vᵉ Au VIIIᵉ Siécle" (1899) 23 Nouvelle Revue Historique de droit français et étranger 313

Deimling B, "The Court: From Church Portal to Town Hall" in Hartmann W and Pennington K (eds), *The History of Courts and Procedure in Medieval Canon Law* (The Catholic University of America Press 2016) 30

Devisse J, *Hincmar et la loi* (s.n. 1962)

———, *Hincmar, archevêque de Reims, 845–882* (Droz 1975)

Di Berardino A, "Christian Liturgical Time and Torture (Cod. Theod. 9, 35, 4 and 5)" (2011) 51 Augustinianum 191

Díez GM, "La Tortura Judicial En La Legislaciòn Històrica Española" (1962) 32 Anuario de Historia del Derecho Español 223

Dobson A, *William Hogarth* (McClure, Phillips & Co; William Heineman 1902)

Donahue, Jr C, "Proof by Witnesses in the Church Courts of Medieval England: An Imperfect Reception of Learned Law" in Arnold MS and others (eds), *On the Laws and Customs of England: Essays in Honor of Samuel E. Thorne* (University of North Carolina Press 2017) 127

———, "Order in the Court: Medieval Procedural Treatises in Translation" (2017) 34 Bull Medieval Canon L (n.s.) 281

———, "Procedure in the Courts of the Ius commune" in Hartmann W and Pennington K (eds), *The History of Courts and Procedure in Medieval Canon Law* (Catholic University Press of America 2016) 83

———, "The Ecclesiastical Courts: Introduction" in Hartmann W and Pennington K (eds), *The History of Courts and Procedure in Medieval Canon Law* (Catholic University Press of America 2016) 247

———, "Biology and the Origins of the English Jury Forum: The Origins of the Jury: Comment" (1999) 17 LHR 591

———, "Ius Commune, Canon Law, and Common Law in England Symposium: Relationships Among Roman Law, Common Law, and Civil Law" (1991) 66 Tulane Law Review 1745

Dossey L, "Judicial Violence and the Ecclesiastical Courts in Late Antique North Africa" in Mathisen RW (ed), *Law, Society, and Authority in Late Antiquity* (OUP 2001) 98

Douglas DC and Greenway GW (eds), 2 *English Historical Documents 1042–1189* (2 vols) (2nd edn E Methuen, OUP 1979)

Downer LJ (ed and tr), *Leges Henrici Primi* (Clarendon Press 1972)

Dudden FH, *Gregory the Great, His Place in History and Thought* (2 vols) (Longmans, Green & Co 1905)

Dupont J, " 'Aequitas Romana. Note Sur Actes 25:16' " (1961) 49 Recherches de science religieuse 354

Duval Y, *Les chrétientés d'occident et leur évêque au IIIe siècle: 'Plebs in ecclesia constituta (Cyprien, Ep. 63)* (Institut d'études augustiniennes 2005)

Elliot MD, "New Evidence for the Influence of Gallic Canon Law in Anglo-Saxon England" (2013) 64 The Journal of Ecclesiastical History 700

Elton GR, *The Tudor Constitution: Documents and Commentary* (2nd edn, CUP 1982)

———, *England under the Tudors* (2nd edn, Barnes and Noble Import Division 1977)

———, *Star Chamber Stories* (Methuen Library; Barnes and Noble 1974)

———, *Policy and Police: The Enforcement of the Reformation in the Age of Thomas Cromwell* (CUP 1972)

———, "Review: The Good Duke" (1969) 12 Historical Journal 702

Emlyn S, "Introduction to State Trials" in Emlyn S (ed), 1 *St Tr* (1730) xxii

Ermann J, "Die Folterung Freier im Römischen Strafprozess der Kaierzeit bis Antonius Pius" (2000) 117 ZRG (RA) 424

Esmein A, "Delit d'Adultere a Rome, Le" (1878) 2 Nouvelle Revue Historique de Droit Français et Etranger 397

———, "Jugement de Daniel, Le" (1907) 31 Nouvelle Revue Historique de Droit Français et Etranger 729

Esmein A, Mittermaier CJA, and Garraud R, *A History of Continental Criminal Procedure, with Special Reference to France* (Little, Brown and Co 1913)

Evans G, "Lanfranc, Anselm and a New Consciousness of Canon Law in England" in Norman Doe and others (eds), *English Canon Law* (Cardiff 1998) 1

Fanning W, s.v. "synod" in Herbermann C and others (eds), 14 *The Catholic Encyclopedia* (Robert Appleton Co 1912) 388

Feldman N, *The Three Lives of James Madison: Genius, Partisan, President* (Random House 2017)

Findlay SW, *Canonical Norms Governing the Deposition and Degradation of Clerics; a Historical Synopsis and Commentary* (The Catholic University of America Press 1941)

Fiorelli P, 1 *La tortura giudiziaria nel diritto commune* (2 vols) (Milan 1953)

Fiorelli P and Giuffré A, "Confessione a) Diritto Romano e Intermedio" in Giuffrè A (ed), 8 *Enciclopedia del diritto* (Varese 1961) 864

Fiori A, "Roman Law Sources and Canonical Collections in the Early Middle Ages" (2017) 34 Bull Medieval Canon L (n.s.) 1

Firey A, "Codices and Contexts: The Many Destinies of the Capitula Angilramni and the Challenges of Editing Small Canon Law Collections" (2008) 94 Zeitschrift der Savigny-Stiftung für Rechtsgeschichte. Kanonistische Abteilung 288

———, *A Contrite Heart: Prosecution and Redemption in the Carolingian Empire* (Brill 2009)

Fisher G, "The Jury's Rise as Lie Detector" (1997) 107 Yale LJ 575

Fitting H, *Alter und Folge der Schriften römischer Juristen von Hadrian bis Alexander* (2nd edn, Verlag von Max Niemeyer 1908)

Fournier P, *Histoire des collections canoniques en Occident depuis les Fausses décrétales jusqu'au Décret de Gratien* (Recueil Sirey 1931)

Fowler-Magerl L, *Ordo iudiciorum vel ordo iudiciarius* (Klosterman 1984)

———, *Ordines Iudiciarii and Libelli de Ordine Indiciorum (From the Middle of the Twelfth to the End of the Fifteenth Century)* (Turnhout Brepols 1994)

Foxley R, "John Lilburne and the Citizenship of 'Free-Born Englishmen'" (2004) 47 The Historical Journal 849

———, *The Levellers: Radical Political Thought in the English Revolution* (Manchester University Press 2013)

Fraher RM, "Preventing Crime in the High Middle Ages: The Medieval Lawyers' Search for Deterrence" in Sweeney JR and Chodorow S (eds), *Popes, Teachers, and Canon Law in the Middle Ages* (Cornell University Press 1989) 224

———, "The Theoretical Justification for the New Criminal Law of the High Middle Ages: 'Rei Publicae Interest, Ne Crimina Remaneant Impunita'" (1984) 1984 University of Illinois Law Review 577

———, "Tancred's Summula de Criminibus: A New Text and a Key to the Ordo Iudiciarius" (1979) 9 Bull Medieval Canon L (n.s.) 23

———, " 'Ut nullus describatur reus prius quam convincatur': Presumption of innocence in medieval canon law?" in Kuttner S and Pennington K (eds), *Proceedings of Sixth International Congress Medieval Canon Law* (Città del Vaticano 1985) 493

Friedland ML, *Double Jeopardy* (Clarendon Press 1969)

Friedman D, "Torture and the Common Law" (2006) 2 European Human Rights Law Review 180

Froude JA and William Thomas (eds), *The Pilgrim: A Dialogue on the Life and Actions of King Henry VIII by William Thomas, Clerk of the Council to Edward VI (1554)* (Parker, Son, and Bourn 1861)

Froude JA, *History of England from the Fall of Wolsey to the Death of Elizabeth* (Scribner, Armstrong, and Co 1872)

Fuhrmann H, *Einfluss und Verbreitung der pseudoisidorischen Fälschungen: von ihrem Auftauchen bis in d. neuere Zeit* (Hiersemann 1972)

———, "Pseudo-Isidorian Forgeries" in Jasper D and Fuhrmann H (eds), *Papal Letters in the Early Middle Ages* (Catholic University of America Press 2001) 135

Fux P-Y and others, *Augustinus Afer: Saint Augustin, africanité et universalité : actes du colloque international, Alger-Annaba, 1–7 avril 2001* (Editions Universitaires 2003)

Gairdner J and Brodie RH (eds), 15 *Letters and Papers, Foreign and Domestic, Henry VIII* (21 vols) (PRO 1896)

Ganshof FL, *Recherches sur les capitulaires* (Sirey 1958)

Garcìa y Garcìa A, "Ecclesiastical Procedure in Medieval Spain" in Hartmann W and Pennington K (eds), *The History of Courts and Procedure in Medieval Canon Law* (The Catholic University of America Press 2016) 392

Gardiner SR, *History of England from the Accession of James I. to the Outbreak of the Civil War, 1603–1642* (Longmans, Green, and Co 1887)

Garner BA, "A Lexigographic Look at Magna Carta" in Holland RJ (ed), *Magna Carta: Muse and Mentor* (Reuters 2014) 85

Garnsey P, *Social Status and Legal Privilege in the Roman Empire* (OUP 1970)

Gaudemet J, "La législation religieuse de Constantin" (1947) 33 Revue d'histoire de l'Église de France 25

———, "Le Bréviare d'Alaric et les Epitome" in *Société d'histoire des droits de l'antiquité* (ed), *Ius romanum Medii Aevi* (Giuffrè 1965)

———, "Les Ordalies Au Moyen Âge: doctrine, legislation et pratique canoniques" in 17 La Preuve (Recueils de la Socièҭe Jean Bodin 1965) 99

———, *La formation du droit séculier et du droit de l'Église aux IVe et Ve siècles* (2nd edn, Sirey 1979)

Gauthier A, "L'utilisation Du Droit Romain dans la Lettre de Grégoire le Grand à Jean le Défenseur" (1977) 54 Angelicum 417

Genestal R, "Les Origines du Privilège Clérical" (1908) 32 Nouvelle revue historique de droit français et étranger 161

Genzmer E, "Eine Anonyme Kleinschrift de testibus aus der Zeit um 1200" in 3 *Festschrift Paul Koschaker zum 60. Geburtstag* (3 vols) (Hermann Böhlaus 1939) 376

Gibb MA, *John Lilburne, the Leveller: A Christian Democrat* (Lindsay Drummond 1947)

Gilchrist J, *The Collection in Seventy-Four Titles: A Canon Law Manual of the Gregorian Reform* (Pontifical Institute of Medieval Studies 1980)

Gleissner, Richard A, "The Levellers and Natural Law: The Putney Debates 1647" (1980) 20 Journal of British Studies 74

Goering J, "The Internal Forum and the Literature of Confession" in Hartmann W and Pennington K (eds), *The History of Medieval Canon Law in the Classical Period, 1140–1234: From Gratian to the Decretals of Gregory IX* (The Catholic University of America Press 2008) 379

Golinkin D and others, "Susanna and the Singular History of Singular Witnesses" in Golinkin D and others (eds), *Essays on Halakhah in the New Testament* (Brill 2008) 89

———, "Chapter Three. The Trials of Jesus and Jeremiah" in Golinkin D and others (eds), *Essays on Halakhah in the New Testament* (Brill 2008) 33

Gray CM, "Self-Incrimination in Interjurisdictional Law: The Sixteenth and Seventeenth Centuries" in Helmholz RH and others (eds), *The Privilege against Self-Incrimination: Its Origins and Development* (University of Chicago Press 1997) 47

———, "Prohibitions and the privilege against self-incrimination" in Guth DJ and McKenna J (eds), *Tudor Rule and Revolution: Essays for G R Elton from His American Friends* (CUP 1982) 345

"Graziano" in Birocchi I and others (eds), 59 *Dizionario biografico dei giuristi italiani (XII-XX Secolo)* (Il Mulino 2013) 1058

Greaves RL, "Sadler, John" in Cannadine D (ed) 48 *Oxford Dictionary of National Biography* (OUP 2004) 560

Green C, "United States: A Revolutionary History of American Statehood" (2020) 119 Mich L Rev 1

Green TA, "Light Hidden under *Bushel's Case*" in Witte Jr J and others, *Texts and Contexts in Legal History: Essays in Honor of Charles Donahue* (The Robbins Collection 2016) 397

———, *Verdict According to Conscience: Perspectives on the English Criminal Trial, 1200–1800* (University of Chicago Press 1985)

Greenberg J, *The Radical Face of the Ancient Constitution* (CUP 2001)

Greenidge AHJ, *The Legal Procedure of Cicero's Time* (Lawbook Exchange 1999)

Gregg P, *Free-Born John: A Biography of John Lilburne* (MW Books Ltd 1961)

Grelweski S, "La Réaction Contre Les Ordalies en France depuis le IXe Siècle jusqu'au Decret de Gratien" (Thesis, University of Strasbourg 1924)

Grigsby HB, *The Virginia Convention of 1776* (JW Randolph1855)

Groot R, "The Early Thirteenth-Century Criminal Jury" in Cockburn JS and Green TA (eds), *Twelve Good Men and True: The Criminal Trial Jury in England, 1200–1800* (Princeton University Press 2014) 3

———, "The Jury in Private Criminal Prosecutions before 1215" (1983) 27 Am J Legal Hist 113

———, "The Jury of Presentment before 1215" (1982) 26 Am J Legal Hist 1

Hall K, *The Magic Mirror: Law in American History* (2nd edn, OUP 2009)

Hallam H, 1 *The Constitutional History of England* (W J Widdleton 1871)

Haller J, "Gregor VII. und Innozenz III" in Marcks E and von Müller KA (eds), 1 *Meister der Politik* (2 vols) (Deutsche Verlags-Anstalt 1922) 323

Haller W, *The Leveller Tracts, 1647–1653* (Columbia University Press in cooperation with Henry E Huntington Library and Art Gallery 1944)

Harries J, *Law and Crime in the Roman World* (CUP 2007)

———, *Law and Empire in Late Antiquity* (CUP 1999)

Hart Jr JS, *The Rule of Law, 1603–1660* (Pearson Education Ltd 2003)

Hartmann W and Pennington K (eds), *The History of Courts and Procedure in Medieval Canon Law* (The Catholic University of America Press 2016)

Hartmann W and Schmitz G, *Fortschritt durch Fälschungen?: Ursprung, Gestalt und Wirkungen der pseudoisidorischen Fälschungen: Beiträge zum gleichnamigen Symposium an der Universität Tübingen vom 27. und 28. Juli 2001* (Hahn 2002)

Hassall WO (ed), *A Catalogue of the Library of Sir Edward Coke* (Yale University Press 1950)

Havet J, *Lettres de Gerbert (983–997)* (Alphonse Picard ed, Librarie des Archives nationales et de la Société de l' École des Chartres 1899, reprint Kessinger Publishing LLC 2010)

Hay D, *Albion's Fatal Tree: Crime and Society in Eighteenth-Century England* (Allen Lane 1975)

Heath J, *Torture and English Law: Administrative and Legal History from the Plantagenets to the Stuarts* (Greenwood Press 1982)

Heiser L, "Die Responsa ad consulta Bulgarorum des Papstes Nikolaus I (858–867): ein Zeugnis päpstlicher Hirtensorge und ein Dokument unterschiedlicher Entwicklungen in den Kirchen von Rom und Konstantinopel" (Inaugural-Dissertation der Westfälischen Wilhelms-Universität Münster 1978)

Helfferich A, *Entstehung und Geschichte des Westgothen-Rechts* (Georg Reimer 1858)

Heller FH, *The Sixth Amendment to the Constitution of the United States: A Study in Constitutional Development* (University of Kansas Press 1951)

Helmholz RH, *Natural Law in Court: A History of Legal Theory in Practice* (Harvard University Press 2015)

———, "Introduction" in Helmholz RH (ed), 127 *Three Civilian Notebooks (1580–1640)* (Selden Society 2011) vii

———, "Citations and the Construction of Procedural Law in the Ius Commune" in Cairns JW and du Plessis PJ (eds), *The Creation of the Ius Commune: From Casus to Regula* (Edinburgh University Press 2010) 257

———, "Natural Law and Human Rights in English Law: From Bracton to Blackstone Symposium: Rethinking Rights: Historical, Political, and Theological Perspectives: Keynote Addresses" (2005) 3 Ave Maria Law Review 1

———, 1 *The Oxford History of the Laws of England: The Canon Law and Ecclesiastical Jurisdiction from 597 to the 1640s* (OUP 2004)

———, "Natural Human Rights: The Perspective of the Ius Commune" (2002) 52 Catholic University Law Review 301

———, "The Law of Compurgation" in Helmholz RH, *The Ius Commune in England: Four Studies* (OUP 2001) 90

———, "Crime, Compurgation and the Courts of the Medieval Church" in Helmholz RH, *Canon Law and the Law of England* (Hambledon Press 1988) 119

———, "Introduction" in Helmholz RH and others, *The Privilege against Self-Incrimination: Its Origins and Development* (The University of Chicago Press 1997) 13

———, *Roman Canon Law in Reformation England* (CUP 1990)

———, "The Early History of the Grand Jury and the Canon Law" (1983) 50 U Chi L Rev 613

———, "Magna Carta and the Ius Commune" (1999) 66 The University of Chicago Law Review 297

———, "The Privilege and the Ius Commune: The Middle Ages to the Seventeenth Century" in RH Helmholz and others (eds), *The Privilege against Self-Incrimination: Its Origins and Development* (University of Chicago Press 1997) 17

———, "The Law of Double Jeopardy" in RH Helmholz, *The Spirit of Classical Canon Law* (University of Georgia Press 1996) 284

———, "Continental Law and Common Law: Historical Strangers or Companions" (1990) 1990 Duke Law Journal 1207

———, *Roman Canon Law and the Law of England* (CUP 1990)

Herman L, "The Unexplored Relationship between the Privilege against Compulsory Self-Incrimination and the Involuntary Confession Rule (Part I)" (1992) 53 Ohio St LJ 101

Herrmann F and Speer B, "Facing the Accuser: Ancient and Medieval Precursors of the Confrontation Clause" (1994) 34 Va J Intl L 516

———, "The Establishment of a Rule against Hearsay in Romano-Canonical Procedure" (1995) 36 Va J Intl L 1

Herrmann J, "Ein Streitgespräch Mit Verfahrensrechtlichen Argumenten Zwischen Kaiser Konstantius Und Bischof Liberius" in Herrmann J (ed), *Kleine Schriften zur Rechtsgeschichte* (Beck 1990) 321

———, "Tertullians Verfahrensrügen Und Die Frühen Märtyrerakten" in Herrmann J (ed), *Kleine Schriften zur Rechtsgeschichte* (Beck 1990) 331

Hildenbrand KH, *Die Purgatio Canonica und Vulgaris* (Literarisch-artistiche Anstalt 1841)

Hill LM, "The Two-Witness Rule in English Treason Trials: Some Comments on the Emergence of Procedural Law" (1968) 12 Am J Legal Hist 95

Himstedt H, *Die Neuen Rechtsgedanken im Zeugenbeweis des Oberitalienischen Stadtrechtsprozesses des 13. Und 14. Jahrhunderts* (Rothschild 1909)

"Hincmar of Reims" in D Hoiber and others (eds), 1 *The New Encyclopedia Britannica* (15th edn, Encyclopedia Britannica 2007) (n.a.) (32 vols) 932

Hinschius P (ed), *Decretales Pseudo-Isidorianae et Capitula Angliramni* (B Tauchnitz 1863)

———, *Das Kirchenrecht der Katholiken und Protestanten in Deutschland* (Akademische Druck- u Verlagsanstalt 1959)

Höflich M and Grabher J, "The Establishment of Normative Legal Texts: The Beginnings of the Ius commune" in Hartmann W and Pennington K (eds), *The History of Medieval Canon Law in the Classical Period, 1140–1234 from Gratian to the decretals of Pope Gregory IX* (Catholic University of America 2008) 1

Holdsworth WS, 9 *A History of English Law* (17 vols) (Little, Brown and Co 1922–1972)

Holtappels P, *Die Entwicklungsgeschichte des Grundsatzes "in dubio pro reo"* (Hamburg Cram, de Gruyter & Co 1965)

Honoré T, "The Making of the Theodosian Code" (1986) 103 ZRG (RA) 133

———, *Emperors and Lawyers* (2nd edn, OUP 1994)

———, "Roman Law AD 200–400: From Cosmopolis to Rechtsstaat?" in Swain S and Edwards M (eds), *Approaching Late Antiquity: The Transformation from Early to Late Empire* (OUP 2004) 109

———, *Ulpian, Pioneer of Human Rights* (2nd edn, OUP 2002)

Houliston V, *Catholic Resistance in Elizabethan England: Robert Persons's Jesuit Polemic, 1580–1610* (Ashgate; Institutum Historicum Societatis Iesu 2007)

———, "Persons [Parsons], Robert" in David Cannadine (ed), *Oxford Dictionary of National Biography* (OUP 2004) <https://doi.org/10.1093/ref:odnb/21474>.

Hudson J, "Magna Carta, the Ius Commune, and English Common Law" in Loengard JS (ed), *Magna Carta and the England of King John* (Boydell & Brewer 2010) 99

Hughes JA, *Witnesses in Criminal Trials of Clerics: An Historical Synopsis and Commentary* ... (The Catholic University of America 1937)

Humfress C, *Orthodoxy and the Courts in Late Antiquity* (OUP 2007)

———, "A New Legal Cosmos: Late Roman Lawyers and the Early Medieval Church" in Linehan P and Nelson JL (eds), *The Medieval World* (Routledge 2001) 557

Hunard ND, "The Jury of Presentment and the Assize of Clarendon" (1941) 56 English Historical Review 374

Hunter J, "The Development of the Rule Against Double Jeopardy" (1984) 5 J Legal Hist 3

Hyams P, "Due Process versus the Maintenance of Order in European Law: The Contribution of the Ius Commune" in Coss P (ed), *The Moral World of the Law* (CUP 2000) 62

———, "Trial by Ordeal: The Key to Proof in the Early Common Law" in Arnold MS and others (eds), *On the Laws and Customs of England: Essays in Honor of Samuel E. Thorne* (University of North Carolina Press 1981) 90

Ingram M, "Cosin, Richard" in David Cannadine (ed), *Oxford Dictionary of National Biography* (OUP 2004) <https;//doi.org/10.1093/ref:odnb/6373> (accessed October 29, 2024)

Jackson BS, "Susanna and the Singular History of Singular Witnesses" (1977) 2 Acta Juridica 37

Jacobi E, "Der Prozeß Im Decretum Graziani Und Bei Den Ältesten Dekretisten" (1913) 3 ZSS (KA) 223

Jaeger H, "La Preuve judiciare d'apres la tradition rabbinique et patristique" in *La Preuve* (16 Recueils de la Societé Jean Bodin 1964) 415

James ER, "A List of Legal Treatises Printed in the British Colonies and the American States before 1801" (1934) 1 Harvard Legal Essays: Written in Honor of and Presented to Joseph Henry Beale and Samuel Williston 159

Jardine D, "A Reading on the Use of Torture in the Criminal Law of England, Previously to the Commonwealth: Delivered at New Inn Hall in Michaelmas Term, 1836" (1838) 67 The Edinburgh Review 103

Jenks S, "The Writ and the Exception *de odio et atia*" (2002) 23 J Legal Hist 1

Johnson HA, *Imported Eighteenth-Century Law Treatises in American Libraries, 1700–1799* (University of Tennessee Press 1978)

Jolowicz HF, *Historical Introduction to the Study of Roman Law* (3rd edn, CUP 1972)

Jonakait RN, "Finding the Original Meaning of American Criminal Procedure Rights: Lessons from Reasonable Doubt's Development" (2012) 10 The University of New Hampshire Law Review 97

———, "The Rise of the American Adversary System: America before England" (2009) 14 Widener L Rev 323

———, "The Origins of the Confrontation Clause: An Alternative History" (1995) 27 Rutgers LJ 77

———, "Notes for a Consistent and Meaningful Sixth Amendment Supreme Court Review—Foreword" (1991) 82 Journal of Criminal Law and Criminology 713

Jones AHM, *The Criminal Courts of the Roman Republic and Principate* (Blackwell 1972)

———, *Constantine and the Conversion of Europe* (Hodder & Stoughton for The English Universities Press 1948)

Jones AHM and others (eds), 1 *Prosopography of the Later Roman Empire* (3 vols) (CUP 1971)

Jones WJ, "Due Process and Slow Process in the Elizabethan Chancery" (1962) 6 American Journal of Legal History 123

Jordan WK, *Edward VI: The Young King* (Belknap Press of Harvard University Press 1968)

———, *Edward VI: The Threshold of Power: The Dominance of the Duke of Northumberland* (Allen & Unwin, Belknap Press of Harvard University Press 1970)

———, *The Chronicle and Political Papers of King Edward VI* (Cornell University Press 1966)

Jurow K, "Untimely Thoughts: A Reconsideration of the Origins of Due Process of Law" (1975) 19 Am J Legal Hist 265

Kaiser W, *Die Epitome Iuliani* (Max-Planck-Institut 2004)

Kalb H, *Studien zur Summa Stephans von Tournai, Ein Beitrag zur kanonistischen Wissenschaftsgeschichte des späten 12. Jahrhunderts* (Universitätsverlag Wagner, Innsbruck 1983)

Kamali EP, "Trial by Ordeal by Jury in Medieval England, or Saints and Sinners in Literature and Law" in Gilbert K and White SD (eds), *Emotion, Violence, Vengeance and Law in the Middle Ages: Essays Presented in Honour of William Ian Miller* (Brill 2018) 49

———, "Confession and Circumstantial Inquiry" in Kamali EP, *Felony and the Guilty Mind in Medieval England* (CUP 2019) 165

Kamali EP and Green TA, "A Crossroads in Criminal Procedure: Assumptions Underlying England's Adoption of Trial by Jury" in Baker TR (ed), *Law and Society in*

Later Medieval England and Ireland: Essays in Honour of Paul Brand (Taylor & Francis Group 2017) 51

Kantorowicz H, *Albertus Gandinus und das Strafrecht der Scholastik* (vol 1, J Guttentag 1907; vol 2, W Degruyter 1926)) (2 vols)

Kaye JM, "The Making of English Criminal Law" (1977) The Criminal Law Review 4

Kelly HA, "The Fourth Lateran *Ordo* of Inquisition Adapted to the Prosecution of Heresy" in Prudlo DS (ed), *A Companion to Heresy Inquisitions* (Brill 2019) 73

———, "Oath-Taking in Inquisitions" (2018) 35 Bulletin of Medieval Canon Law 215

———, "Judicial Torture in Canon Law and Church Tribunals: From Gratian to Galileo" (2015) 101 The Catholic Historical Review 754

———, "Mixing Canon and Common Law in Religious Prosecutions under Henry VIII and Edward VI: Bishop Bonner, Anne Askew, and Beyond" (2015) 46 The Sixteenth Century Journal 927

———, "Inquisition and the Prosecution of Heresy: Misconceptions and Abuses" (1989) 58 Church History 439

Kelly JM, "Audi Alteram Partem Note" (1964) 9 Natural Law Forum 103

———, *A Short History of Western Legal Theory* (OUP 1992)

Kerly DM, *An Historical Sketch of the Equitable Jurisdiction of the Court of Chancery: Being the Yorke Prize Essay of the University of Cambridge for 1889* (CUP 1890)

King PD, *Law and Society in the Visigothic Kingdom* (CUP 1972)

Kirschenbaum A, *Self-Incrimination in Jewish Law* (Burning Bush Press 1970)

Klerman D, "Was the Jury Ever Self-Informing" (2003) 77 Southern California Law Review 123

Knollenberg B, *Growth of the American Revolution, 1766–1775* (Liberty Fund 2003)

Koch WC, "Magna Carta's Enactment" in Holland RJ (ed), *Magna Carta: Muse and Mentor* (Reuters in association with the Library of Congress 2014) 39

Köster R-J, *Die Rechtsvermutung der Unschuld: historische und dogmatische Grundlagen* (Rheinische Friedrich-Wilhelms-Universität Bonn 1979)

Krampe C, "Qui tacet, consentire videtur: Über die Herkunft einer Rechtsregel" in Schwab D and others (eds), *Staat, Kirche, Wissenschaft in einer pluralistischen Gesellschaft: Festschrift zum 65. Geburtstag von Paul Mikat* (Duncker & Humblot 1989) 367

Kraus JW, "Private Libraries in Colonial America" (1974) 9 The Journal of Library History 31

Kunkel W, *Kleine Schriften: Zum römischen Strafverfahren und zur römischen Verfassungsgeschichte* (H Böhlaus Nachfolger 1974)

Kuttner S and Rathbone E, "Anglo-Norman Canonists of the Twelfth Century: An Introductory Study" (1951) 7 Traditio 279

Kuttner S, *Gratian and the Schools of Law, 1140–1234* (Variorum Reprints 1983)

Landau P, "Ursprünge und Entwicklung des Verbotes Doppelter Strafverfolgung wegen desselbens Verbrechen in der Geschichte des Kanonischen Rechts" (1970) 56 ZRG (KA) 124

———, "Gratian and the Decretum Gratiani" in Hartmann W and Pennington K (eds), *The History of Medieval Canon Law in the Classical Period, 1140–1234 from Gratian to the Decretals of Pope Gregory IX* (Catholic University of America 2008) 22

Landsman S, *Rise of the Contentious Spirit: Adversary Procedure in Eighteenth Century England* (1990) 75 Cornell L Rev 496

Langbein JH, *History of the Common Law: The Development of Anglo-American Legal Institutions* (Aspen Publishers/Wolters Kluwer Law & Business 2009)

———, *Torture and the Law of Proof: Europe and England in the Ancien Regime* (University of Chicago, paperback 2006)

———, *The Origins of the Adversary Criminal Trial* (OUP 2003)

———, "Trinity Hall and the Relations of European and English Law from the Fourteenth to the Twenty-First Centuries" in *The Milestones Lectures* 75 (Trinity Hall Cambridge 2001) 75

———, "The Privilege and Common Law Criminal Procedure: The Sixteenth Century to the Eighteenth Centuries" in Helmholz RH and others (eds), *The Privilege against Self-Incrimination: Its Origins and Development* (University of Chicago Press 1997) 82

———, "Historical Foundations of the Law of Evidence: A View from the Ryder Sources" (1996) 96 Columbia Law Review 1168

———, "Shaping the Eighteenth-Century Criminal Trial: A View from the Ryder Sources" (1983) 50 University of Chicago Law Review 1

———, "The Criminal Trial before the Lawyers" (1978) 45 Chi L Rev 263

———, *Prosecuting Crime in the Renaissance: England, Germany, France* (Harvard University Press 1974)

———, "The Origins of Public Prosecution at Common Law" (1973) 17 AJLH 313

Lauria M, "Accusatio-Inquisitio" (1933) 56 Atti della Reale Academica di scienze morali e politiche 303

Lavender P and Bergström MA (eds), *Faking It!: The Performance of Forgery in Late Medieval and Early Modern Culture* (Brill 2023)

Leeson PT, "Ordeals" (2012) 55 Journal of Law & Economics 691

Lenski NE, "Evidence for the Audientia Episcopalis in the New Letters of Augustine" in Mathison RH (ed), *Law, Society, and Authority in Late Antiquity* (OUP 2001) 83

Levy E, *Pauli Sententiae: A Palingenesia of the Opening Titles as a Specimen of Research in West Roman Vulgar Law* (Cornell University Press 1945, Rothman Reprints 1969)

Lévy J-P, *La Hierarchie des preuves dans le droit savant du Moyen-Âge depuis la renaissance du droit romain jusqu'à la fin du XIVe siècle* (Librarie du Recueil Sirey 1939)

Levy LW, *Constitutional Opinions: Aspects of the Bill of Rights* (OUP 1986)

———, *Origins of the Fifth Amendment* (Macmillan Publishing Co 1986)

———, "Appendix: Talmudic Law" in *Origins of the Fifth Amendment* (2nd edn, Macmillan Publishing Co 1986) 433

Lewis CT and Short C (eds), *A Latin Dictionary* (OUP 1879)

Lewis JU, "Sir Edward Coke (1552–1688): His Theory of Artificial Reason as a Context for Modern Basic Legal Theory" (1968) 84 LQR 330

Liebs D, "Die Herkunft der 'Regel *bis de eadem re ne sit actio*'" (1967) 84 ZRG (RA) 104

———, *Vor den Richtern Roms: berühmte Prozesse der Antike* (Verlag CH Beck 2007)

———, *Summoned to the Roman Courts: Famous Trials from Antiquity* (Rebecca L R Garber and Carol Curtin trs, University of California Press 2012)

Litewski W, "Mündliche Klage und Klageschrift in den ältesten ordines iudiciarii" in Köbler G and Nehlsen H (eds), *Wirkungen europäischer Rechtskultur: Festschrift für Karl Kroeschell zum 70. Geburtstag* (CH Beck 1977) 666

Loening R, *Der Reinigungseid bei Ungerichtsklagen im deutschen Mittelalter* (Ulan Press 2012)

Macnair MRT, *The Law of Proof in Early Modern Equity* (Comparative Studies in Continental and Anglo-American Legal History, Duncker & Humblot 1999)

——, "Vicinage and the Antecedents of the Jury" (1999) 17 LHR 537

——, "The Early Development of the Privilege against Self-Incrimination" (1990) 10 Oxford Journal of Legal Studies 66

Maier P, *From Resistance to Revolution; Colonial Radicals and the Development of American Opposition to Britain, 1765–1776* (Knopf 1972)

——, *American Scripture: Making the Declaration of Independence* (distributed by Random House, Inc 1997)

Marsden RG (ed), *Documents Relating to Law and Custom of the Sea* (printed for the Navy Records Society 1915)

—— (ed), 1 *Select Pleas in the Court of Admiralty* (Bernard Quatrich 1894) (vol 1)

Martroye F, "Les 'defensores ecclesiae' aux Ve et VIe Siecles" (1923) 2 Revue historique de droit français et étranger (4th ser) 597

Masschaele J, *Jury, State, and Society in Medieval England* (Palgrave Macmillan 2008)

Mathisen RW, *Law, Society, and Authority in Late Antiquity* (OUP 2001)

Matthews JF, "Interpreting the Interpretationes of the Breviarium" in Mathisen RW (ed), *Law, Society, and Authority in Late Antquity* (OUP 2001) 11

——, "The Making of the Text" in Harries J and Wood IN (eds), *The Theodosian Code* (Cornell University Press 1993) 19

Mausen Y and others (eds), *Der Einfluss der Kanonistik auf die europäische Rechtskultur. 4. Prozessrecht* (Böhlau 2014)

May G, "Anklage- Und Zeugnisfähigkeit nach der Zweiten Sitzung des Konzils zu Karthago Vom Jahre 419" (1960) 140 Theologische Quartalschrift 163

McAuley F, "Canon Law and the End of the Ordeal" (2006) 26 Oxford Journal of Legal Studies 473

McIlwain CH, "Due Process of Law in Magna Carta" (1914) 14 Col L Rev 27

McKechnie WS, *Magna Carta: A Commentary on the Great Charter of King John* (2nd edn, J Maclehose & Sons 1914)

McPherson BH, *The Reception of English Law Abroad* (Supreme Court of Queensland Library 2007)

McSweeney TJ, "Magna Carta and the Right to Trial by Jury" in Holland RJ (ed), *Magna Carta, Muse and Mentor* (Thomson Reuters in association with the Library of Congress 2014) 139

Meranze M, "Penalty and the Colonial Project: Crime, Punishment, and the Regulation of Morals in Early America" in Grossberg M and Tomlins C (eds), 1 *Cambridge History of Law in America* (CUP 2008) (3 vols) 178

Miller HH, *George Mason, Gentleman Revolutionary* (University of North Carolina Press 1975)

——, *The Case for Liberty* (University of North Carolina Press 1965)

Milsom SFC, *Historical Foundations of the Common Law* (2nd edn, Butterworths 1981)

Moglen E, "The Privilege in British North America: The Colonial Period to the Fifth Amendment" in Helmholz RH and others (eds), *The Privilege against Self-Incrimination: Its Origins and Development* (The University of Chicago Press 1997) 109

Mommsen T, *Römisches Strafrecht* (Duncker & Humblot 1899)

Morgan ES and Morgan HM, *The Stamp Act Crisis: Prologue to Revolution* (3rd edn, Chapel Hill 1995)

Morgan G and Rushton P, "Arson, Treason and Plot: Britain, America and the Law, 1770–1777" (2015) 100 History 374

Moriarty EJ, "Oaths in Ecclesiastical Courts, an Historical Synopsis and Commentary" (Thesis, The Catholic University of America 1937)

Morris TD, "Slaves and the Rules of Evidence in Criminal Trials-Symposium on the Law of Slavery: Criminal and Civil Law of Slavery" (1992) 68 Chi-Kent L Rev 1209

Morrison CA, "Some Features of the Roman and English Law of Evidence" (1958–1959) 33 Tul L Rev 577

Mossakowski W, "The Introduction of an Interdiction of Oral Accusation in the Roman Empire" (1996) 43 Revue international des droits de l'antiquité (3rd ser) 269

Mousourakis G, *The Historical and Institutional Context of Roman Law* (Ashgate 2003)

Müller AV, "Zum Verhältnisse Nicolaus I Und Pseudo-Isidors" (1900) 25 Neues Archiv 652

Muller WP, "The recovery of Justinian's Digest in the Middle Ages" (1990) 20 Bull Medieval Canon Law (n.s.) 1

München N, *Das kanonische Gerichtsverfahren und Strafrecht* (Cologne & Neuss 1865)

München N, *Das kanonische Gerichtsverfahren und Strafrecht* (Cologne & Neuss 1865)

Musson, Anthony, " 'The Influence of Canon Law in the Administration of Justice'" in Mausen Y and others (eds), 4 *Der Einfluß der Kanonistik auf die europäische Rechtskultur (Prozeßrecht)* (Böhlau 2014) 325

———, "Twelve Good Men and True? The Character of Early Fourteenth-Century Juries" (1997) 15 LHR 115

———, *Public Order and Law Enforcement: The Local Administration of Criminal Justice, 1294–1350* (Boydell Press 1996)

Nann JB and Cohen ML, "Colonial Law, 1600s–1770s" in *The Yale Law School Guide to Research in American Legal History* (Yale University Press 2018) 75

Nemeth CP, *Aquinas in the Courtroom: Lawyers, Judges, and Judicial Conduct* (Greenwood Press 2001)

Nicholas B, "Jurisprudence" in Hammond NGL and Scullard HH (eds), *The Oxford Classical Dictionary* (2nd edn, Clarendon Press 1970) 569

Niermeyer JF, *Mediae Latinitatis lexicon Mittellateinisches Wörterbuch* (2nd rev edn, Brill 2002)

Noonan JT, *Bribes* (Macmillan 1984)

Nörr K, "Bologna and the Court of Admiralty, a Latin Text in the Black Book" in Linehan P (ed), 8 *Proceedings of the Seventh International Congress of Medieval Canon Law* (Monumenta iuris canonici Series C, Subsidia 1988) 475

———, "Ordo Iudiciorum und Ordo Iudiciarius" (1967) 11 Studia Gratiana 327

Nottarp H, *Gottesurteilstudien* (Kösel Verlag 1956)

Nourse GB, "Law Reform under the Commonwealth and Protectorate" (1959) 75 LQR 512

Ogle A, *The Tragedy of the Lollards' Tower* (Pen-in-Hand 1949)

Parkin-Speer D, "John Lilburne: A Revolutionary Interprets Statutes and Common Law Due Process" (1983) 1 Law and History Review 276

Patetta F, *Le Ordalie* (Fratelli Bocca 1890)

Pennington K, *The Prince and the Law, 1200–1600: Sovereignty and Rights in the Western Legal Tradition* (University of California Press 1993)

———, "Canonical Jurisprudence and Other Legal Systems in the Medieval and Early Modern" in Miñambres J (ed), *Diritto Canonico e Culture Giuridiche nel Centenario del Codex Iuris Canonici del 1917* (Edizione Santa Croce 2019) 109

———, "The Fourth Lateran Council, Its Legislation, and the Development of Legal Procedure" in Witte Jr J and others (eds), *Texts and Contexts in Legal History: Essays in Honor of Charles Donahue* (Robbins Collections Publications 2016) 179

———, "Introduction to the Courts" in Hartmann W and Pennington K (eds), *The History of Courts and Procedure in Medieval Canon Law* (The Catholic University of America Press 2016) 3

———, "The Jurisprudence of Procedure" in Hartmann W and Pennington K (eds), *The History of Courts and Procedure in Medieval Canon Law* (Catholic University of America Press 2016) 133

———, "Reform in 1215: *Magna Carta* and the Fourth Lateran Council" (2015) 32 BMCL 97

———, "The Biography of Gratian, the Father of Canon Law" (2014) 59 Villanova Law Review 679

———, "Torture and Fear: Enemies of Justice" (2008) 19 Revista internazionale di diritto commune 203

———, "The Development of Criminal Procedure in England" in *DMA: Supplement I* (Charles Scribner's Sons 2004) 309

———, "Innocent until Proven Guilty: The Origins of a Legal Maxim" (2003) 63 Jurist 106

———, "Innocent III and the Ius commune" in Helmholz R and others (eds), *Grundlagen des Rechts: Festschrift für Peter Landau zum 65. Geburtstag* (Ferdinand Schöningh 2000) 352

Perry RL (ed), *Sources of Our Liberties: Documentary Origins of Individual Liberties in the United States Constitution and Bill of Rights* (revised edn, American Bar Foundation 1978)

Pertin J-Y, *Justice et gouvernement dans l'Église d'après les Lettres de saint Grégoire le Grand* (L'Harmattan 2015)

Pertz GH (ed), *Benedicti diaconi capitularia spuria* in Monumenta Germaniae Historica, 2 Legum, pt 2 (Hannover 1887) 45

Phifer JR, "Law, Politics, and Violence: The Treason Trials Act of 1696" (1980) 12 Albion (Boone) 235

Plucknett FT, *Concise History of the Common Law* (Little, Brown and Co 1956)

Pocock JGA, *The Ancient Constitution and the Feudal Law: A Study of English Historical Thought in the Seventeenth Century* (CUP 1957, reprint 1987)

Pollard AF, *England Under Protector Somerset: An Essay* (Russell and Russell 1966)

Poschmann B, "Die Echtheit des Augustinischen Sermo 351" (1934) 46 Revue Bénédictine 18

Post JB, "The Admissibility of Defence Counsel in English Criminal Procedure" (1984) 5 Journal of Legal History 23

Prall E, *The Agitation for Law Reform During the Puritan Revolution, 1640 to 1660* (Martinus Nijhoff 1966)

Preyer K, "Crime, the Criminal Law and Reform in Post-Revolutionary Virginia" (1983) 1 LHR 53

Prichard MJ and others, *Hale and Fleetwood on Admiralty Jurisdiction* (Selden Society 1993)

Pugh RB, "The Duration of Criminal Trials in Medieval England" in Ives EW and Manchester AH (eds), *Law, Litigants and the Legal Profession* (Royal Historical Society; Humanities Press Inc 1983) 104

Putnam BH (ed), "A Commentary on the Indictments" in *Proceedings Before the Justices of the Peace in the Fourteenth and Fifteenth Centuries* (Spottiswoode & Ballantyne 1938) cxxxii

Quintard-Morénas F, "The Presumption of Innocence in the French and Anglo-American Legal Traditions" (2010) 58 The American Journal of Comparative Law 107

Rackow F, "The Right to Counsel: English and American Precedents" (1954) 11 William & Mary Quarterly 3

Rakove JN, *Declaring Rights: A Brief History with Documents* (Bedford Books 1998)

Rathbone E, "Roman Law in the Anglo-Norman Realm" (1967) 11 Studia Gratiana 255

Reeves J, *Reeves' History of the English Law from the Time of the Romans to the End of the Reign of Elizabeth ...* (M Murphy 1880)

Reid JP, *Constitutional History of the American Revolution, Vol. 1* (The University of Wisconsin Press 1986)

Reno III EA, *The Authoritative Text: Raymond of Penyafort's Editing of the Decretals of Gregory IX* (Columbia University 2011)

Reynolds RE, s.v. "Law, Canon: to Gratian" in Shrayer JR (ed), 7 *Dictionary of the Middle Ages* (Scribner 1986) 395

———, "The Pseudo-Hieronymian *De septem ordinibus Ecclesiae*: Notes on Its Origins, Abridgements and Use in the Early Medieval Canonical Collections" (1970) 80 Revue Bénédictine 238

Rezneck S, "The Statute of 1696: A Pioneer Measure in the Reform of Judicial Procedure in England" (1930) 2 The Journal of Modern History 5

Rice JD, "The Criminal Trial before and after the Lawyers: Authority, Law, and Culture in Maryland Jury Trials, 1681–1837" (1996) 40 The American Journal of Legal History 455

Richards J, *Consul of God: The Life and Times of Gregory the Great* (Routledge & Kegan Paul 1980)

Robertson JC and others, *Materials for the History of Thomas Becket: Archbishop of Canterbury (Canonized by Pope Alexander III., A. D. 1173)* (of Bosham Herbert and others eds, Longman 1875)

Robinson OF, *Penal Practice and Penal Policy in Ancient Rome* (Routledge 2007)

———, *The Criminal Law of Ancient Rome* (Johns Hopkins University Press 1995)

———, "Slaves and the Criminal Law" (1981) 98 ZRG (RA) 213

Roby HJ, *An Introduction to the Study of Justinian's Digest: Containing an Account of Its Composition and of the Jurists Used or Referred to Therein* (CUP 1884)

Rolker C, *Canon Law and the Letters of Ivo of Chartres* (CUP 2010)

———, "Ivo of Chartres (Yves de Chartres) (c 1040–1115)" in Descamps O and Domingo R (eds), *Great Christian Jurists in French History* (CUP 2019) 19

Rosenberg IM and Rosenberg YL, "In the Beginning: The Talmudic Rule against Self-Incrimination" (1988) 63 New York University Law Review 955

Rosmini G, "Le Quaestiones Perpetuae nella Storia del Diritto Penale e Giudiziario Romano, Pt 2" (1895) 55 Archivio Giuridico 63

Rowland K, *The Life of George Mason, 1725–1792: Including His Speeches, Public Papers, and Correspondence* (2 vols) (G P Putnam's Sons 1892)

Rudstein DS, "A Brief History of the Fifth Amendment Guarantee against Double Jeopardy" (2005) 14 Wm & Mary Bill Rts J 193

Ruth R, *Zeugen und Eideshelfer in den deutschen rechtsquellen des Mittelalters* (pt 1) (M & H Markus 1922)

Rutland RA, "Note" in Rutland RA (ed), 1 *The Papers of George Mason, 1749–1778* (University of North Carolina Press 1970) (3 vols) 274

Salvioli G, "Storia della procedura civile e criminale" in Del Giudice P (ed), 3 *Storia del Diritto Italiano* (pt 2) (U Hoepli 1927) 284

Schmoeckel M, *Die Jugend Der Justicia. Archäologie Der Gerechtigkeit Im Prozessrecht Der Patristik* (Mohr Siebeck 2013)

Schnapper B, "Testes inhabiles, Les témoins reprochables dans l'ancien droit pénal" (1965) 33 Tijdschrift voor Rechtsgeschiedenis 575

Schrörs H, *Hinkmar, Erzbischof von Reims; sein Leben und seine Schriften* (G Olms 1967)

Schwartz B, *The Great Rights of Mankind: A History of the American Bill of Rights* (OUP 1977)

Schwartz E, "Der Prozess des Eutyches" (1929) 5 Sitzungsberichte der Bayerischen Akademie der Wissenschaften, Philosophisch-historische Abteilung 66

Schwentner B, "Die Stellung Der Kirche zum Zweikampfe bis zu den Dekretalen Gregors IX" (1930) 111 Theologische Quartalschrift 190

Seckel E, "Pseudoisidor" in Hauck A (ed), 16 *Realencyclopädie der protestantischen Theologie und Kirche* (24 vols) (JC Hinrich'sche Buchhandlung 1905) 265

Seipp DJ, "Crime in the Year Books" in Stebbings C (ed), *Law Reporting in England* (Hambledon Press 1995) 15

———, "The Reception of Canon Law and Civil Law in the Common Law Courts before 1600" (1993) 13 Oxford Journal of Legal Studies 388

———, "Magna Carta in the Late Middle Ages: Over-Mighty Subjects, Under-Mighty Kings, and a Turn Away from Trial by Jury" (2016) 25 The William and Mary Bill of Rights Journal 665

———, "Bracton, the Year Books and the 'Transformation of Elementary Legal Ideas' in the Early Common Law" (1989) 7 LHR 175

Senior W, *Doctors' Commons and the Old Court of Admiralty: A Short History of Civilians in England* (Longmans, Green & Co 1922)

Shagan EH, "The English Inquisition: Constitutional Conflict and Ecclesiastical Law in the 1590s" (2004) 47 The Historical Journal 541

Shapiro AH, "Political Theory and the Growth of Defensive Safeguards in Criminal Procedure: The Origins of the Treason Trials Act of 1696" (1993) 11 Law & Hist Rev 215

Shapiro BJ, *"Beyond Reasonable Doubt" and "Probable Cause": Historical Perspectives on the Anglo-American Law of Evidence* (University of California Press 1991)

———, *A Culture of Fact: England, 1550–1720* (Cornell University Press 2000)

———, *Political Communication and Political Culture in England, 1558–1688* (Stanford University Press 2012)

Sharp A (ed), *The English Levellers* (CUP 1998)

———, "Lilburne, John (1615?–1657)" in Cannadine D (ed) *Oxford Dictionary of National Biography* (OUP 2004) <https://doi.org/10.1093/ref:odnb/16654> (accessed October 29, 2024)

Sherwin-White AN, "The Lex Repetundarum and the Political Ideas of Gaius Gracchus" (1982) 72 The Journal of Roman Studies 18

Shoemaker KB, "Criminal Procedure in Medieval European Law: A Comparison Between English and Roman-Canonical Developments After the IV Lateran Council" (1999) 85 ZRG (KA) 174

Sigler JA, "A History of Double Jeopardy" (1963) 7 American Journal of Legal History 285

Sinatti D'Amico F, *Le Prove Giudiziarie nel Diritto Longobardo* (Giuffre 1968)

Smith LB, "English Treason Trials and Confessions in the Sixteenth Century" (1954) 15 Journal of the History of Ideas 471

Spilsbury WH, *Lincoln's Inn: Its Ancient and Modern Buildings* (2nd edn, Reeves and Turner 1873)

Sprandel R, *Ivo von Chartres und seine Stellung in der Kirchengeschichte* (A Hiersemann 1962)

Stein P, *Regulae Iuris* (Edinbrugh University Press 1966)

Steinventer A, "Der antike kirchliche Rechtsgang und seine Quellen" (1934) 23 ZRG (KA) 1

Stenton DMP, *Pleas before the King or His Justices, 1198–1202* (Quaritch 1952)

Stephen JF, *A History of the Criminal Law of England* (3 vols) (Macmillan & Co 1883)

Stickler A-M, "Ordines judiciarii" in Naz R (ed), 6 *Dictionnaire de droit canonique* (Librairie Letouzey et Ané 1957) 1134

Stone R and West C, *Hincmar of Rheims: Life and Work* (Manchester University Press 2015)

Stone R, "Canon Law before Canon Law: Using Church Canons, 400–900 AD," paper presented to Cambridge Late Antiquity Network Seminar (February 11, 2014) 1

Strachan-Davidson JL, 2 *Problems of the Roman Criminal Law* (OUP 1912) (2 vols)

Stuckenberg CF, *Untersuchungen zur Unschuldsvermutung* (Walter de Gruyter 1998)

Stuckey M, *The High Court of Star Chamber* (Gaunt 1998)

Sullivan WP, "Admissibility in Roman-Canon Procedure: The Emergence of the Law of Positions" (Dissertation submitted to the Faculty of the Division of the Humanities Department of Classics and the Faculty of the Division of the Social Sciences Department of History, University of Chicago, ProQuest LLC 2020)

Summerson HRT, "The Early Development of the Peine Forte et Dure" in Ives EW and Manchester AH (eds), *Law, Litigants, and the Legal Profession* (Royal Historical Society 1983) 116

Swain S and Edwards MJ, *Approaching Late Antiquity: The Transformation from Early to Late Empire* (OUP 2004)

Tajra H, *The Trial of St. Paul* (Mohr 1989)

Tarter B, "Mason, George (1725–1792), Planter and Revolutionary Statesman" in Chávez-García M (ed), *American National Biography* (OUP 1999) https://doi.org/10.1093/anb/9780198606697.article.0100577 (accessed October 29, 2024)

Tate JC, "Roman and Visigothic Procedural Law in the False Decretals of Pseudo-Isidore" (2004) 90 ZRG (KA) 510

Thomas Y, *"Confessus pro iudicato,* l'aveu civil et l'averu penal à Rome" in *L'aveu. Antiquité et moyen-age* (L'École française de Rome 1986) 89

Thompson F, *Magna Carta: Its Role in the Making of the English Constitution, 1300–1629* (University of Minnesota Press 1948)

———, "Magna Carta and the Printers and Chroniclers" in *Magna Carta: Its Role in the Making of the English Constitution, 1300–1629* (University of Minnesota Press 1948) 139

Toulson, Lord, "Fundamental Rights and the Common Law: Keynote Address given at the Fundamental Rights Conference: A Public Law Perspective, LSE" (October 10, 2015) <supremecourt.uk/docs/speech-151010.pdf> (accessed October 29, 2024)

Tout TF, *Medieval Forgers and Forgeries* (Longmans, Green & Co 1920)

Towne SC, "The Historical Origins of Bench Trial for Serious Crimes" (1982) 26 Am J Legal Hist 123

Trumble WR and Stevenson A, s. v. "Barbarian" in *Shorter Oxford English Dictionary on Historical Principles* (5th edn OUP 2002) 156

Tubbs JW, *The Common Law Mind: Medieval and Early Modern Conceptions* (Johns Hopkins University Press 2000)

Turner RV, "The Origins of the Medieval English Jury: Frankish, English, or Scandinavian?" (1968) 7 Journal of British Studies 1

Ubbelohde C, *The Vice-Admiralty Courts and the American Revolution* (Chapel Hill 1960)

Uhalde K, *Expectations of Justice in the Age of Augustine* (University of Pennsylvania Press 2007)

Ullmann W, "Some Medieval Principles of Criminal Procedure" (1947) 59 Juridical Review 1

———, "The Defense of the Accused in the Medieval Inquisition" in Garnett G (ed), *Law and Jurisdiction in the Middle Ages* (Variorum Reprints 1988) 481

Vacandard E, "L'Église et Les Ordalies" in (J Gabalda (ed), 1 *Étude de critique et d'histoire religieuse* (5th edn, Lecoffre 1913) 189

van Caenegem RC, *The Birth of the English Common Law* (2nd edn, CUP 2012)

———, "The Modernity of Medieval Law" (2000) 68 Tijdschrift voor Rechtsgeschiedenis/ Legal History Review 313

———, "Reflexions on Rational and Irrational Modes of Proof in Medieval Europe" (1990) 58 Tijdschrift voor Rechtsgeschiedenis/Legal History Review 263

———, "Public Prosecution of Crime in Twelfth-Century England" in Brooke CNL and others (eds), *Church and Government in the Middle Ages: Essays Presented to C. R. Cheney* (CUP 1976) 41

———, "L'histoire du droit et la chronologie: Réflexions sur la formation du 'Common Law' et la procédure romano-canonique" in 2 *Études d'histoire du droit canonique dédiées à Gabriel Le Bras* (2 vols) (Paris 1965) 1459

van der Wal N, *Manuale Novellarum Justiniani: aperçu systématique du contenu des Novelles de Justinien* (Wolters 1964)

van Vliet H, *No Single Testimony: A Study on the Adoption of the Law of Deut.19.15* (Kemink & Zoon 1958)

Veall D, *The Popular Movement for Law Reform, 1640–1660* (Clarendon Press 1970)

Verbraken P-P, *Études critiques sur les sermons authentiques de Saint Augustin* (In abbatia S Petri 1976)

Vismara G, *Episcopalis Audientia* (Società editrice Vita e Pensiero 1937)

Vogt J, "Zur Frage des christlichen Einflusses auf die Gestezgebung Konstantins des Grossen" in 2 *Festschrift für Leopold Wenger* (2 vols) (CH Beck 1945) 118

Volokh A, "N Guilty Men Aside" (1997) 146 University of Pennsylvania Law Review 173

von Döllinger JJI and Huber J, *Der Papst und das Konzil* (EF Steinacker 1869)

von Funk FX, *Die apostolischen Konstitutionen; eine litterar-historische Untersuchung* (Minerva 1970)

von Schwerin C, "Rituale für Gottesurteile" (Sitzungsberichte der Heidleberger Akademie der Wissenschaften, Philosophisch-historische Klasse, Abhandlung 3, Heidelberg 1933)

Walker DM, *The Oxford Companion to Law* (OUP 1980)

Warnicke RM, *William Lambarde: Elizabethan Antiquary, 1536–1601* (Pillimore 1973)

Watson A, "Prolegomena to Establishing Pre-Justianianic Texts" (1994) 62 Tijdschrift voor Rechtsgeschiedenis 113

Weigand R, *Die Naturrechtslehre der Legisten und Dekretisten* (München 1967)

Weintraub M, "*Ain Adam Atsmo Rasha*: The Bar against Self-Incrimination as a Protection against Torture in Jewish and American Law" in *Rabbis for Human Rights—North America* (2005) <www.truah.org> (accessed October 29, 2024)

Wenger E, *Die Quellen des römischen Rechts* (Adolf Holzhausen NFG 1953)

Weslager CA, *The Stamp Act Congress* (University of Delaware Press 1976)

Westen P, "The Compulsory Process Clause" (1974) 73 Mich L Rev 73

White AB, "The Name Magna Carta" (1915) 30 EHR 472

Whitman JQ, *The Origins of Reasonable Doubt: Theological Roots of the Criminal Trial* (Yale University Press 2008)

Wieacker F, "Lateinische Kommentare Zum Codex Theodosianus" in *Symbolae Friburgenses in honorem Ottonis Lenel* (Tauchnitz 1935) 259

Wigmore JH, 5 *Evidence in Trials at Common Law* (Little, Brown and Co 1974)

———, "Required Numbers of Witnesses; A Brief History of the Numerical System" (1901) 15 HLR 12

———, "*Nemo Tenetur Seipsum Prodere*" (1891) 5 Harvard Law Review 71

———, "Confessions: A Brief History and a Criticism" (1899) 33 American Law Review 376

Williams N, *Captains Outrageous* (Barrie & Rockcliff 1961)

Wiltshire SF, *Greece, Rome, and the Bill of Rights* (1st edn, University of Oklahoma Press 1992)

Winroth A, *The Making of Gratian's Decretum* (CUP 2004)

Witte Jr, "A New Magna Carta for the Early Modern Common Law: An 800th Anniversary Essay Symposium: Christianity and Human Rights" (2015) 30 Journal of Law and Religion 428

———, *The Reformation of Rights: Law, Religion, and Human Rights in Early Modern Calvinism* (CUP 2007)

Wlassak M, "Anklage Und Streitbefestigung im Kriminalrecht der Römer" in 184 (bd 1) *Sitzungsberichte, kaiserliche Akademie der Wissenschaften* (Alfred Hölder 1917) 6

Wolfe DM (ed), *Leveller Manifestoes of the Puritan Revolution* (T Nelson 1944)

Wood GS (ed), *The American Revolution: Writings from the Pamphlet Debate I: 1764–1772* (The Library of America 2015)

———, *The American Revolution: Writings from the Pamphlet Debate II: 1773–1776* (The Library of America 2015)

Wormald P, "Neighbors, Courts, and Kings: Reflections on Michael Macnair's Vicini Forum: The Origins of the Jury: Comment" (1999) 17 Law and History Review 597

———, *The Making of English Law: King Alfred to the Twelfth Century* (Blackwell Publishers 1999)

Wright S, "Fuller, Nicholas (1543–1620), Lawyer and Politician" in Cannadine D (ed), *Oxford Dictionary of National Biography* (2004) <https://doi.org/10.1093/ref:odnb/62362> (accessed October 29, 2024)

Wurman I, "Law Historians' Fallacies" (2015) 91 North Dakota Law Review 161

York NL, "Imperial Impotence: Treason in 1774 Massachusetts" (2011) 29 Law and History Review 657

Zechiel-Eckes K, "Auf Pseudoisidors Spur. Oder: Versuch, einen dichten Schleier zu lüften" in Hartmann W and Schmitz G (eds), *Fortschritt durch Fälschungen? Ursprung, Gestalt und Wirkungen der pseudoisidorischen Fälschungen* (Hahn 2002) 1

Zeumer K (ed), *Leges Visigothorum* (MGH, I Legum Sectio I, Bibiolpolii Hahniani 1902)

Zilletti U, "Sul Valore Probatorio della Testimonianza nella 'Cognitio Extraordinem'" (1963) 29 Studia et documenta historiae et iuris 150

Zordan G, *Il diritto e la procedura criminale nel Tractatus de maleficiis de Angelo Gambiglioni* (CEDAM 1976)

Zweigert K, *An Introduction to Comparative Law* (2nd rev edn, OUP 1987)

Index

For the benefit of digital users, indexed terms that span two pages (e.g., 52–53) may, on occasion, appear on only one of those pages.

Figures are indicated by an italic *f* following the page number.